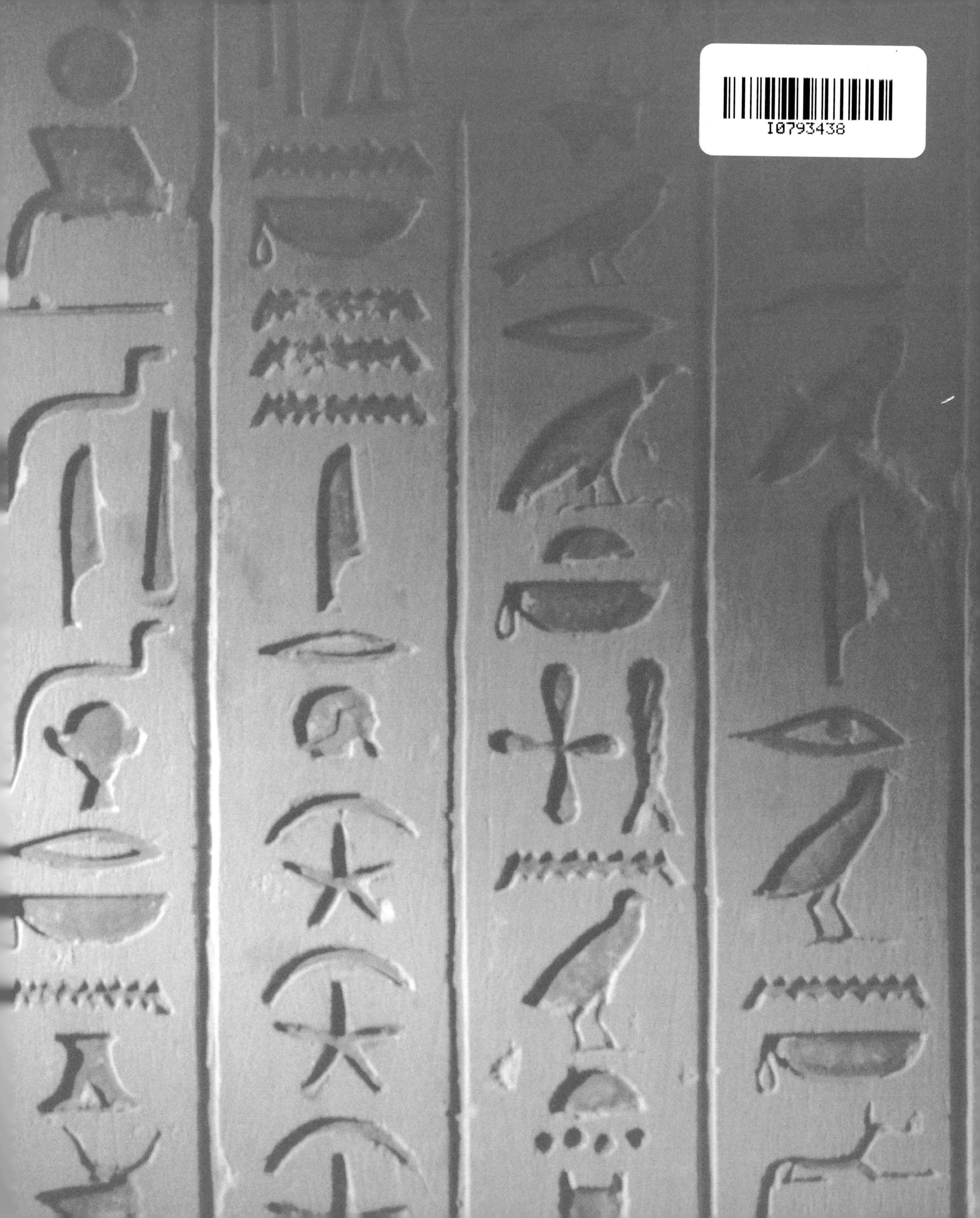

TREASURES *of* EGYPT

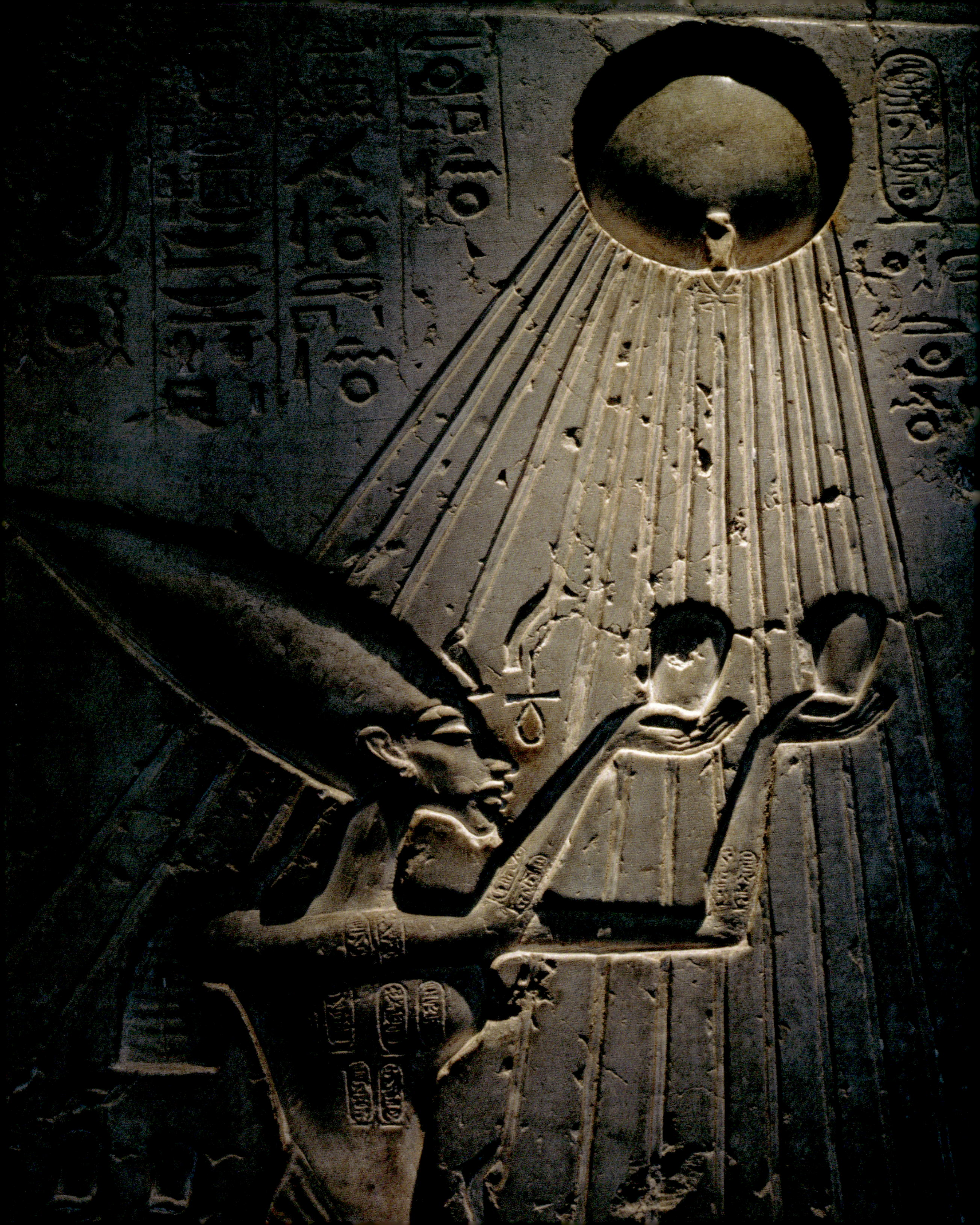

TREASURES *of* EGYPT

A LEGACY IN PHOTOGRAPHS FROM THE PYRAMIDS TO CLEOPATRA

GENERAL EDITOR ANN R. WILLIAMS

NATIONAL GEOGRAPHIC
WASHINGTON, D.C.

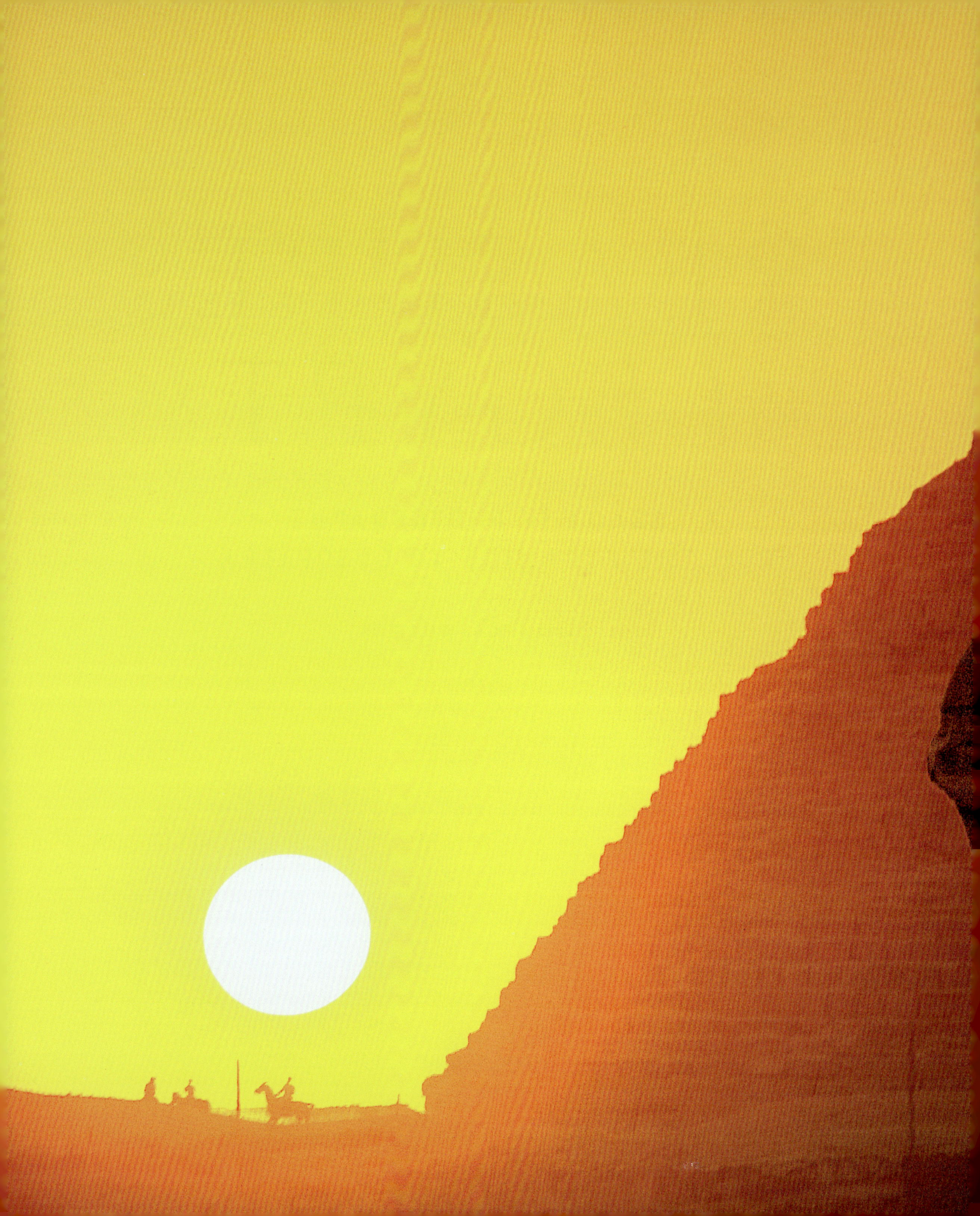

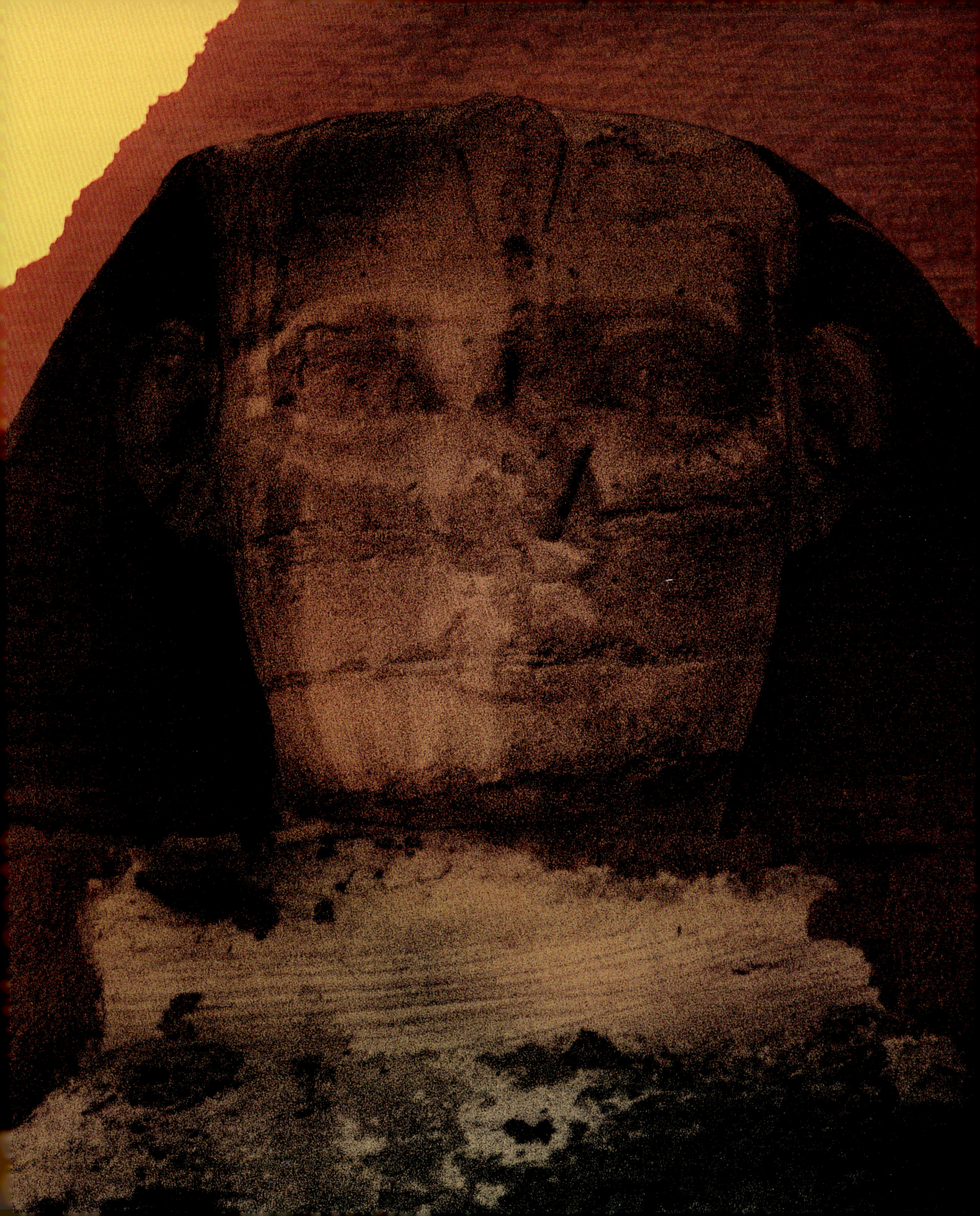

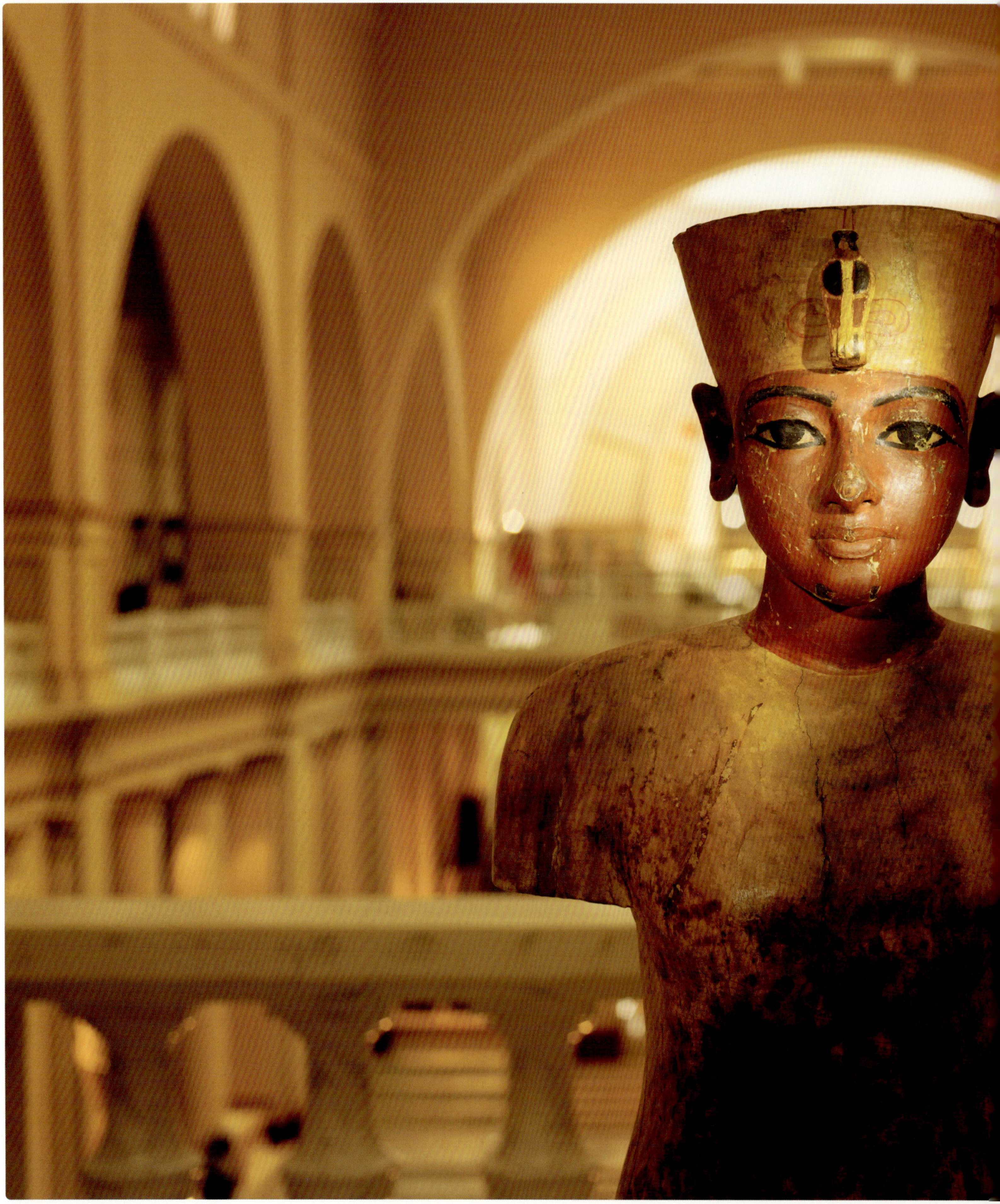

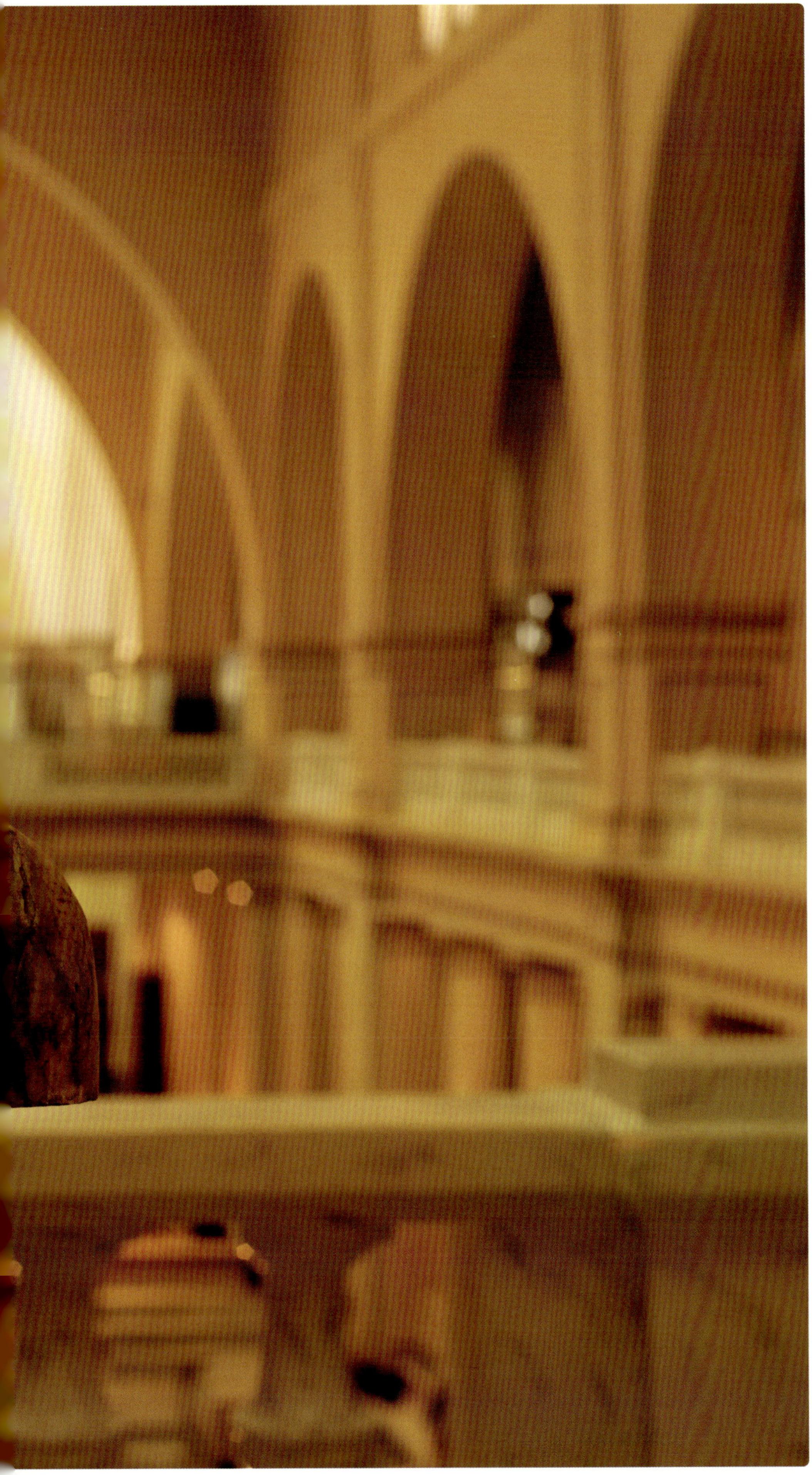

On the second-floor balcony of the Egyptian Museum in Cairo (left), which opened in 1902, a sculpted portrait of King Tutankhamun (about 1332–1322 B.C.) awaits transfer to the Grand Egyptian Museum (GEM), a newly constructed, state-of-the-art facility on the Giza plateau.

PREVIOUS PAGES: At the world-renowned site of the Giza Pyramids, the iconic silhouettes of the Sphinx and a soaring royal tomb evoke the grandeur of Egypt's early kings —and their continuing power to impress all who gaze upon the monuments they created.

FRONTISPIECE: In a relief from the 14th century B.C., King Akhenaten makes offerings to the Aten, his chosen god, and receives divine blessings and eternal life in return.

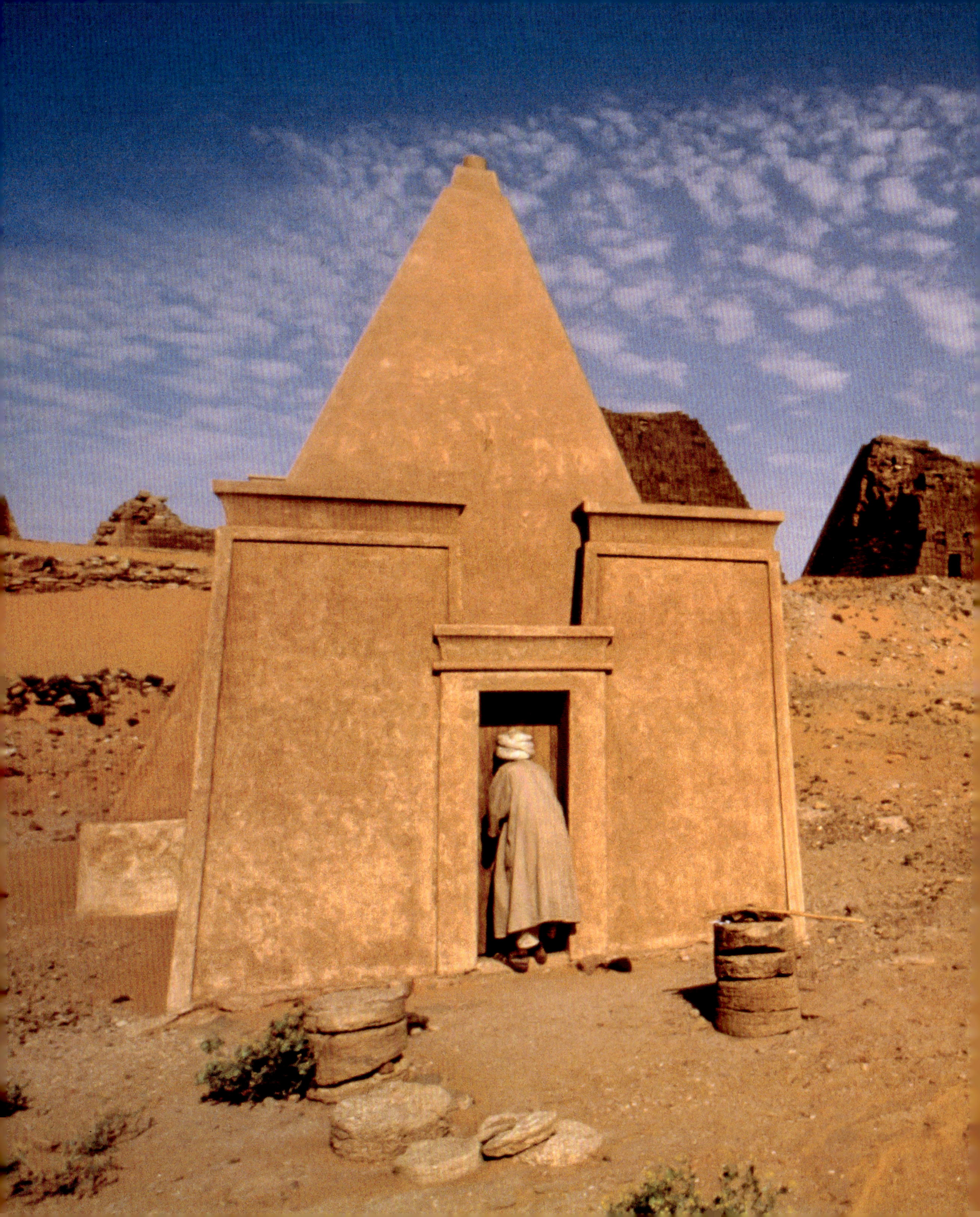

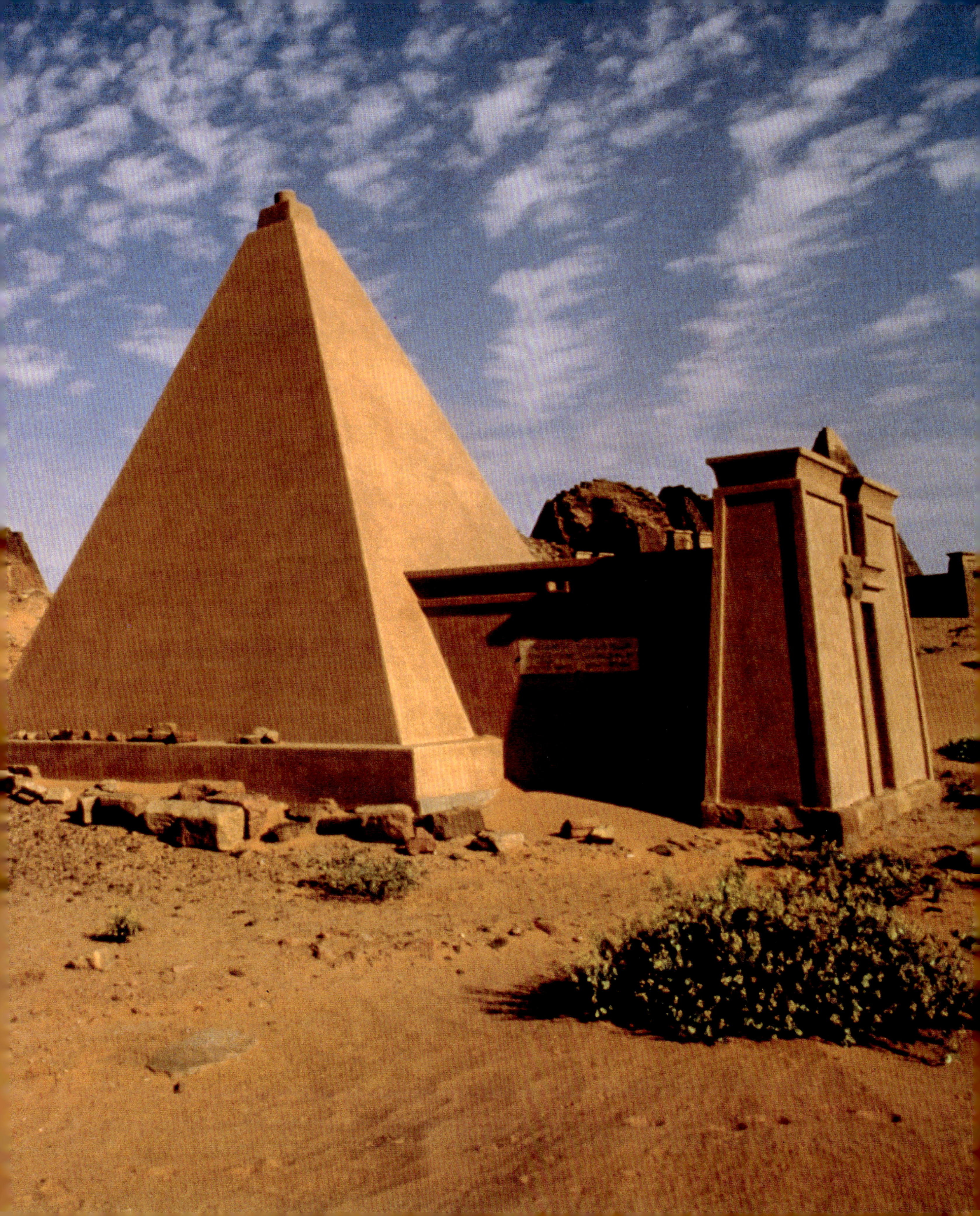

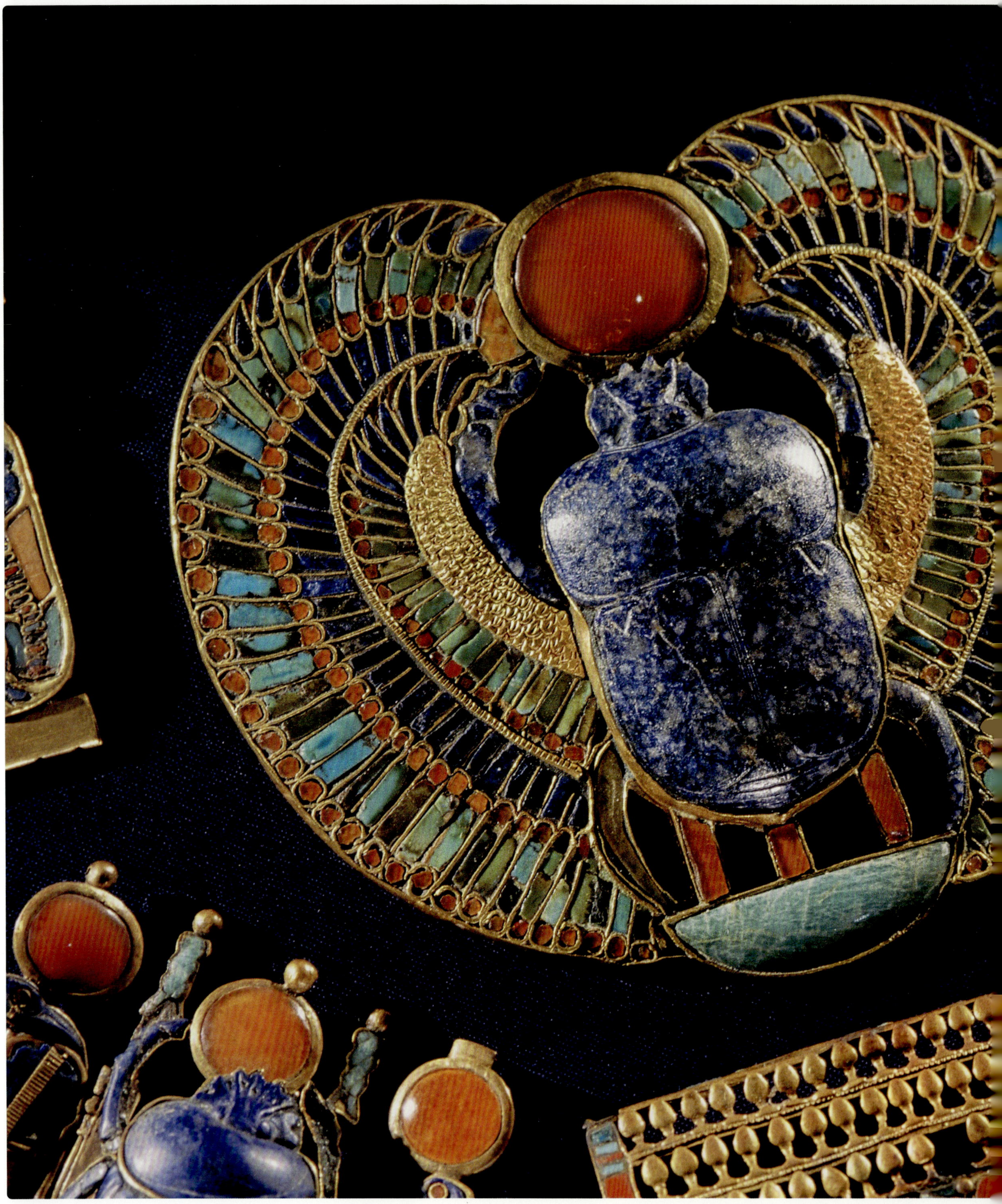

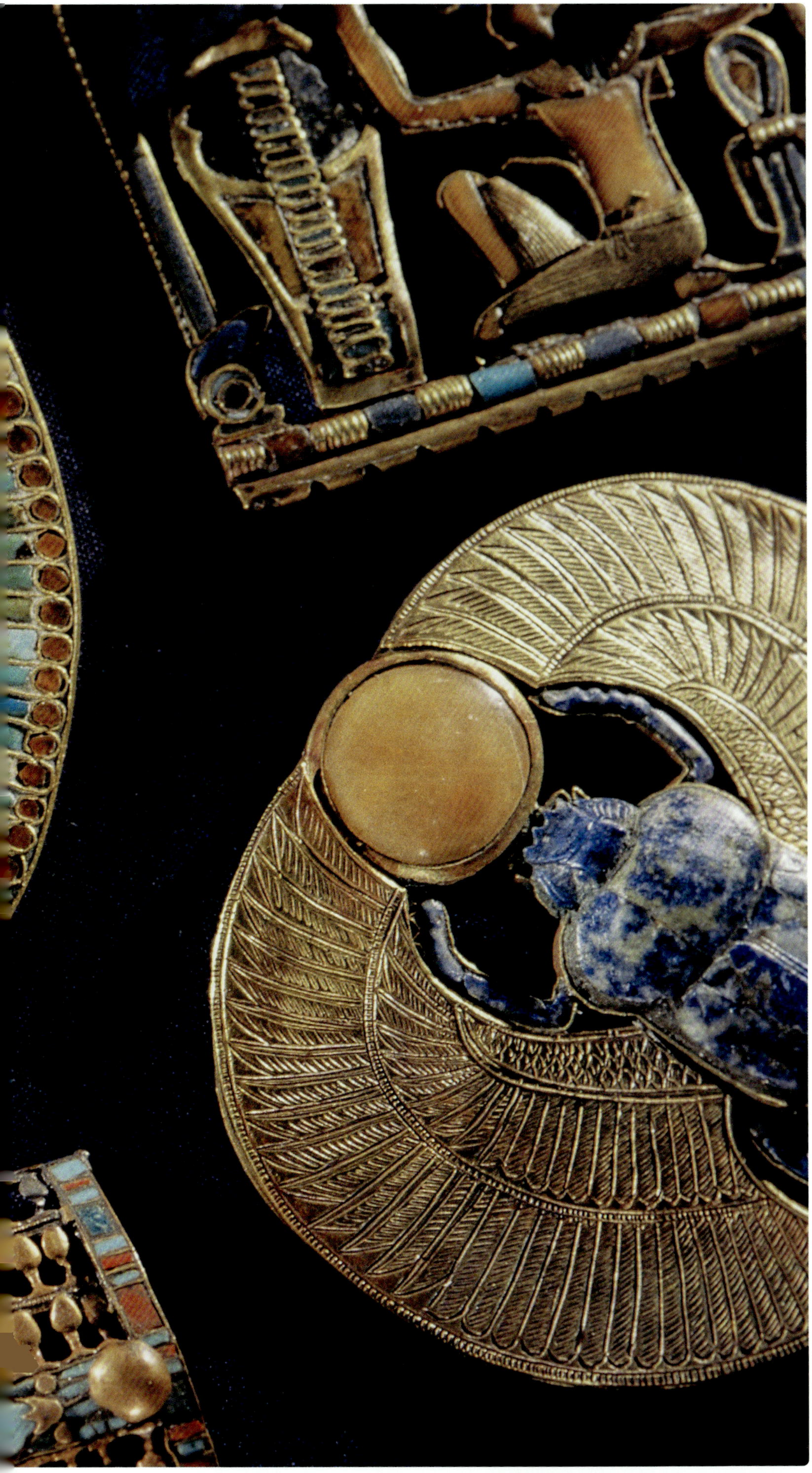

More than 200 pieces of jewelry were found in the tomb of King Tutankhamun (about 1332–1322 B.C.), including these treasures (left). The scarab beetle of lapis lazuli represents Khepri, a god associated with the sun at dawn and thus rebirth.

PREVIOUS PAGES: Royal tombs at the site of Meroë in Sudan (about 720–300 B.C.) combine a local interpretation of the Egyptian pyramid with borrowed elements from Greece and Rome.

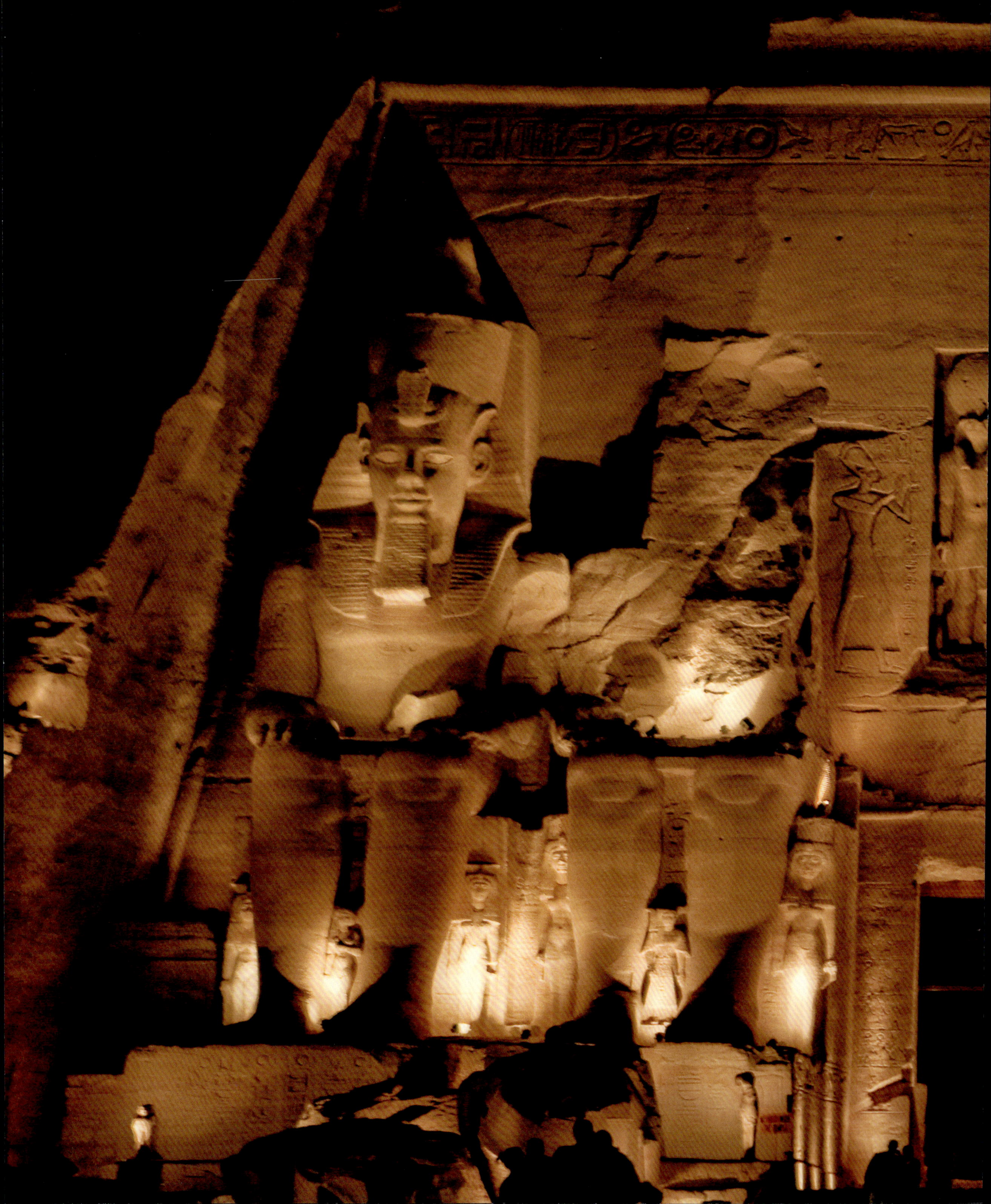

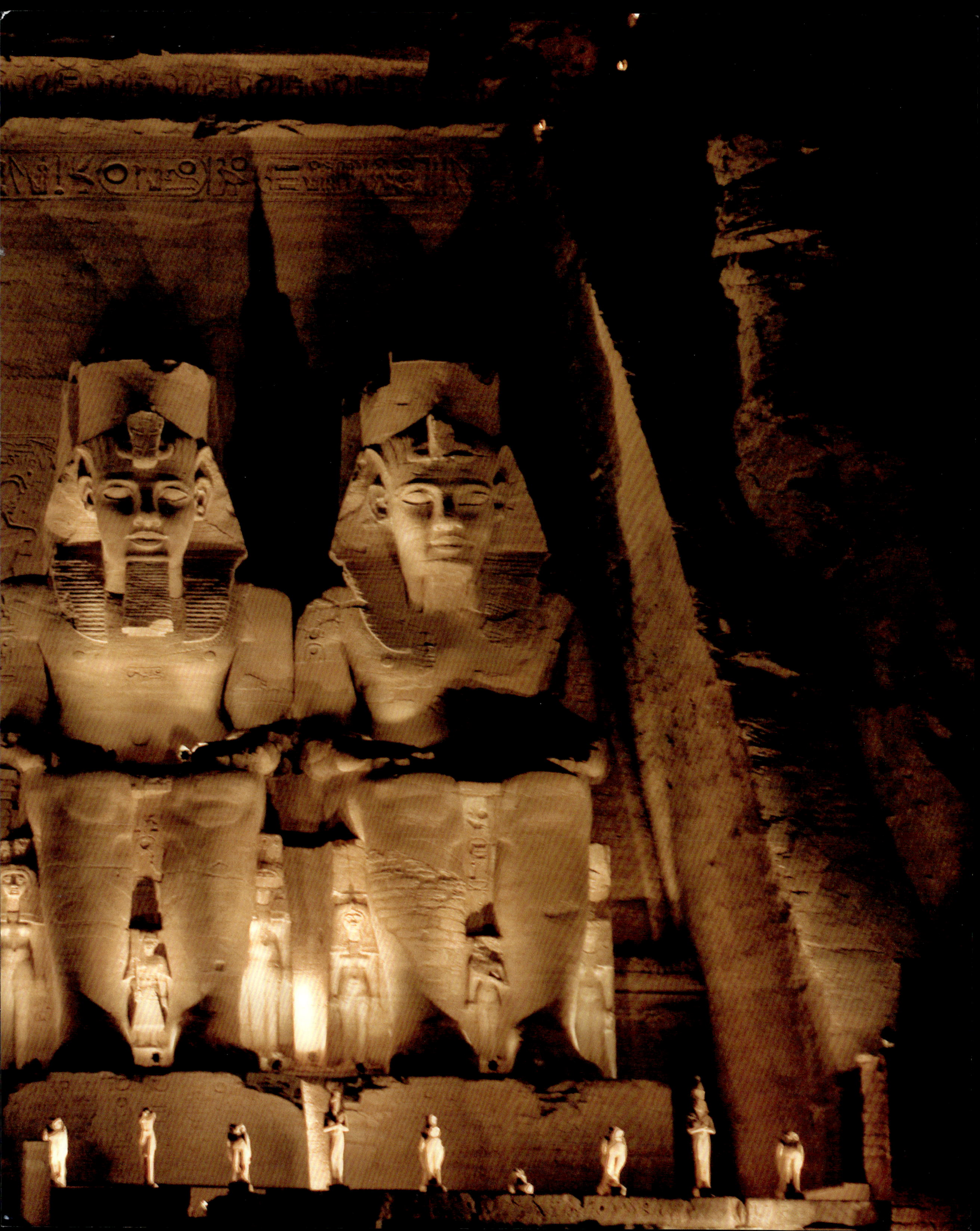

Now a legend, the teenage King Tutankhamun was laid to rest in about 1322 B.C. with unimaginable wealth, including this masterpiece of goldsmithing (right): a mask of gold, carnelian, quartz, obsidian, turquoise, and glass weighing more than 24 pounds (11 kg).

PREVIOUS PAGES: The glory of King Ramses II endures in stone at his Abu Simbel temple. By the time of his death in about 1213 B.C., he had come to embody imperial Egypt so strongly that nine later kings adopted his name.

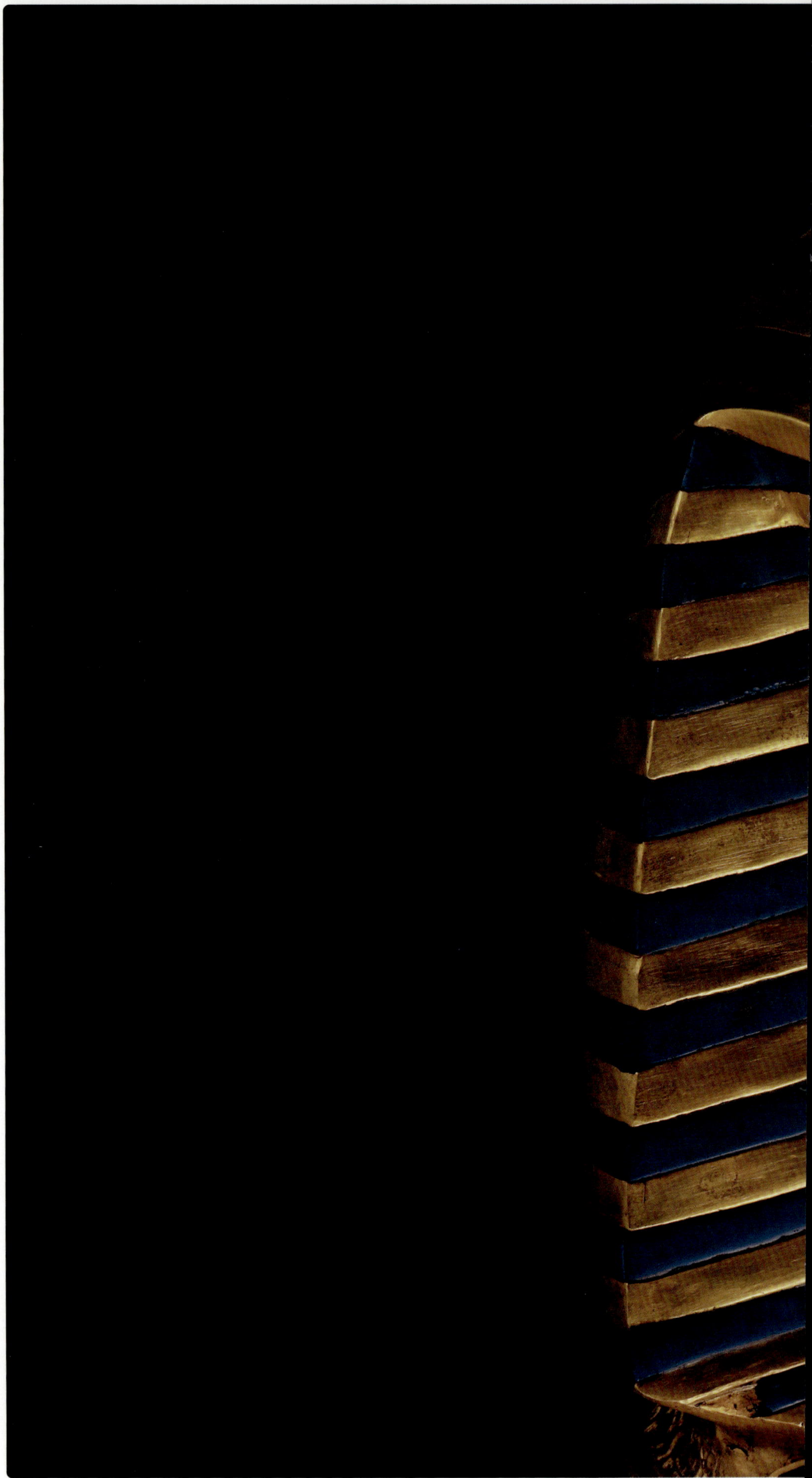

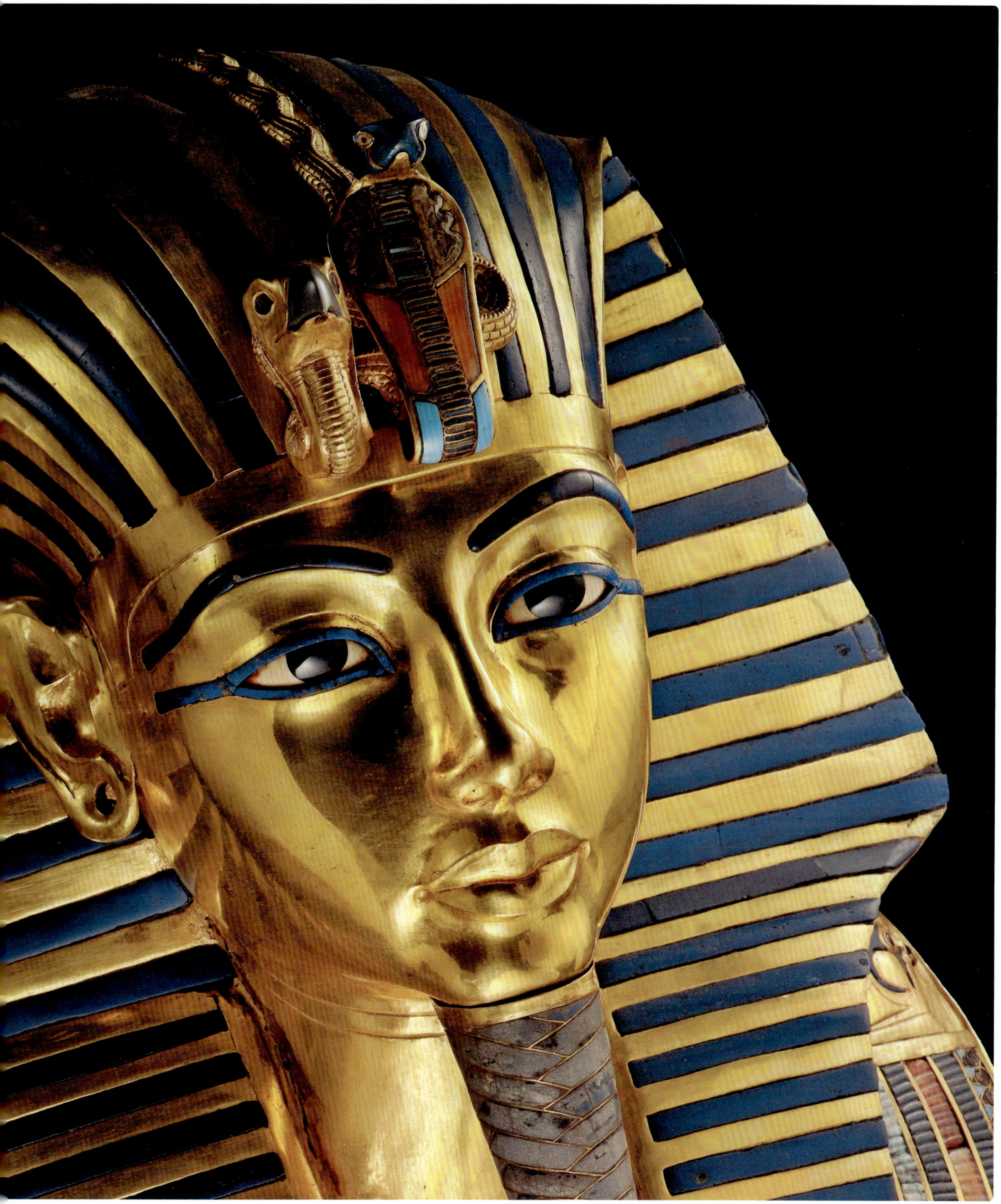

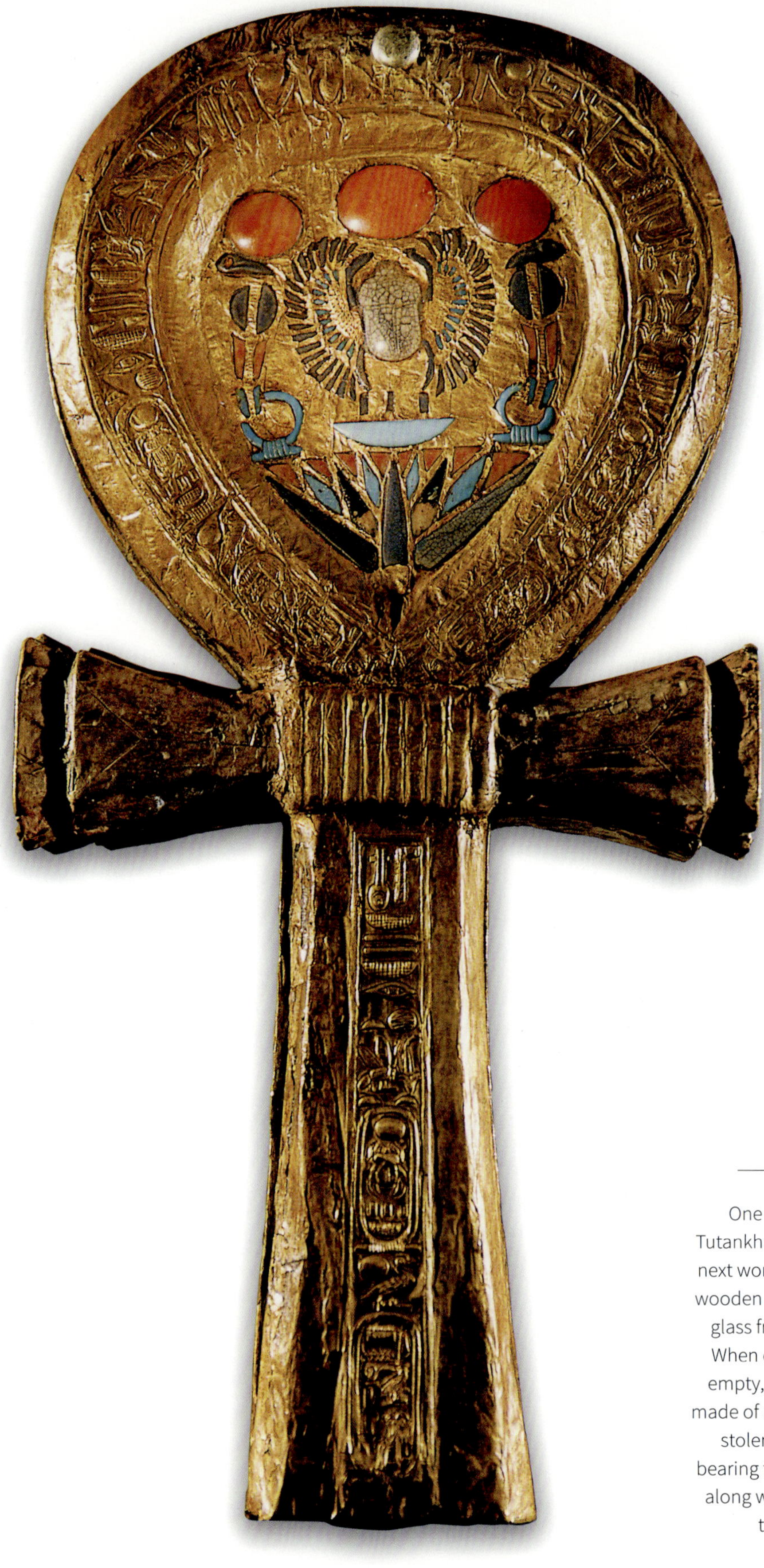

One of the personal effects Tutankhamun took with him to the next world was a mirror in a gilded wooden case inset with stones and glass from the 14th century B.C. When discovered, the case was empty, though; the mirror, likely made of a precious metal, had been stolen. But the case survives, bearing the king's names and titles along with iconography invoking the idea of renewal.

CONTENTS

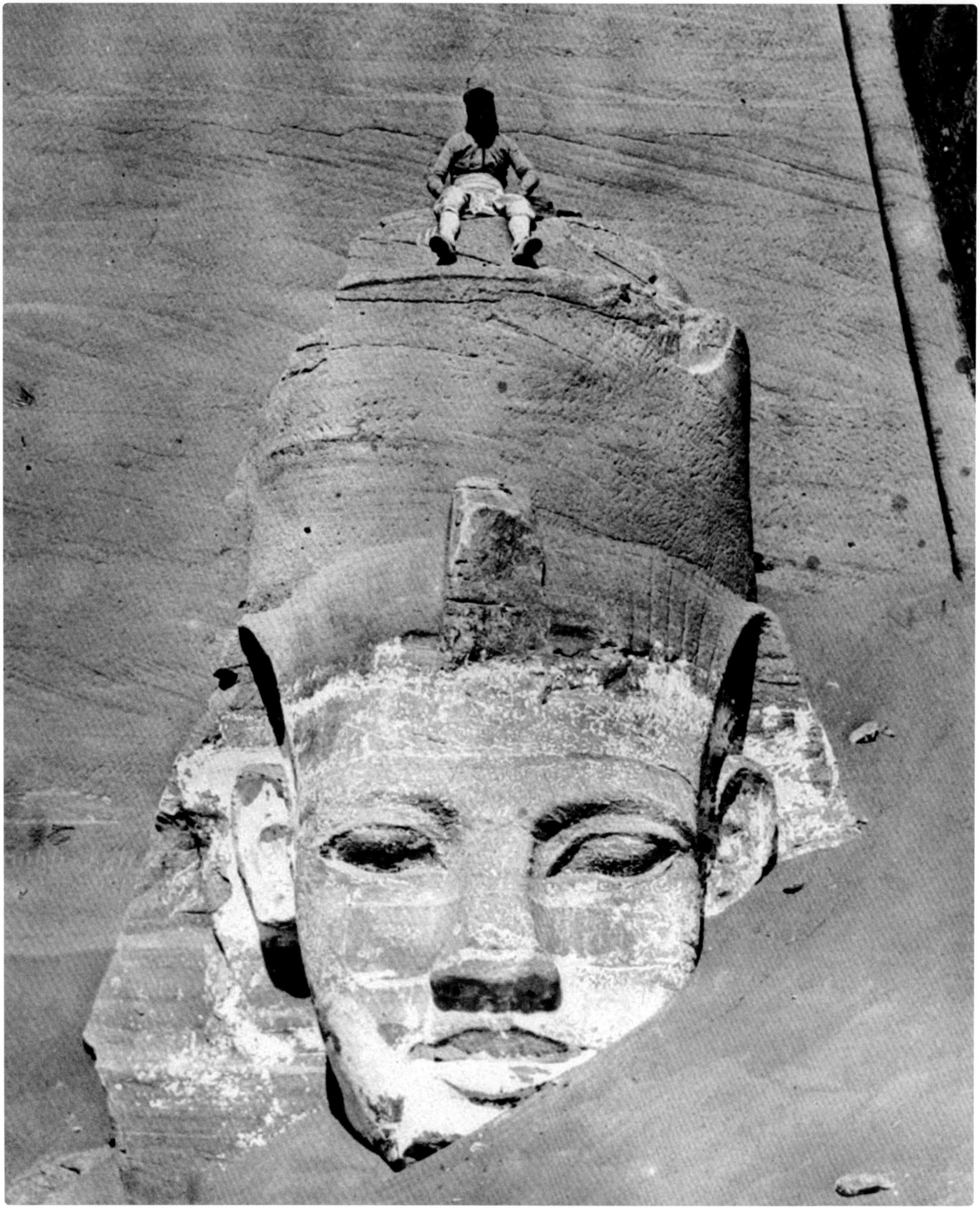

FOREWORD

FREDRIK HIEBERT, PH.D.

SOME EXPERTS ESTIMATE that only 30 percent of Egypt's history has been excavated; others say the figure is even lower and many more wonders await. But for me, one thing is certain: As Archaeologist-in-Residence at the National Geographic Society, I know that Egypt holds a magical place in my heart.

It turns out I share a similar history with Howard Carter, the man who after years of persistence unearthed the largely intact tomb of the boy-king Tutankhamun in November 1922. Like Carter, I was first trained as an artist. We both came to work in Egypt as teenagers, carefully drawing its artifacts and architecture on excavations. We fell in love with the country's splendor—and we both became archaeologists.

The comparison stops there, I suppose, since Carter's find in the Valley of the Kings was arguably the country's most spectacular archaeological revelation—one you will read about in these pages. By contrast, I arrived to excavate a mud-brick warehouse on Egypt's arid Red Sea coast. On our last day at the site, I lifted out a still intact reed mat. Staring up at me in the sand was the key of the merchant who had hidden it 1,500 years ago, surely expecting to return. In that moment, I felt an overwhelming sense of connection with the past—along the lines of what Carter must have felt when he first peered into Tutankhamun's burial chamber.

As you peruse this special book, you'll see that moments like this happen often in the archaeology of ancient Egypt—and many such moments yet await the archaeologists of the future. The tantalizing prospect of new finds reconnects us in the closest possible way to the past. But always, the beauty and mystery of ancient Egypt attracts us in a unique way. Fascinating new finds in this sphere not only take us back in time, but also unleash the prospect of more puzzles to be solved.

As Egypt opens the doors of its new state-of-the-art museums and attention is focused on the centennial anniversary of the discovery of Tutankhamun's final resting place, the world will once again dream of the potentially dazzling array of art, untold stories, and new secrets still to be revealed in this alluring country.

For now, I sincerely hope that you will enjoy National Geographic's fascinating new window on the treasures of Egypt. ▲

In 1850, French writer and photographer Maxime Du Camp shot this photograph of one of Ramses II's colossal statues at Abu Simbel—after shifting away sand and posing his assistant atop the sculpture for scale. Du Camp's traveling companion, Gustave Flaubert, wrote of their tour, "The Egyptian temples bore me profoundly."

INTRODUCTION

ANN R. WILLIAMS

A CENTURY AGO, as news of the discovery of King Tutankhamun's tomb rocketed around the world in late 1922, *National Geographic* reported firsthand on archaeologist Howard Carter's initial work on the treasure-filled burial. "On February 17 I arrived in Luxor, crossed the river and started on foot for the Tombs of the Kings," staff correspondent Maynard Owen Williams wrote in the May 1923 issue of the magazine. "I did not hasten toward my goal. I wanted to plod along on foot . . . to feel the African sun on my back, and to watch the camels stalk by on their way to the cane fields."

Williams was there for the spectacular archaeology, certainly. But in his classic geographical survey, he also put the emerging science of methodically investigating the long-dead past into the context of the living country where the archaeology was being carried out.

In the Valley of the Kings, Williams chronicled the scrum of reporters and photographers, the visits by wealthy tourists, and the arrival of dignitaries—from Queen Elizabeth of Belgium to Lord Allenby, the British high commissioner for Egypt and the Sudan. Everyone hoped to get a glimpse of the fabulous riches that surrounded the teenage pharaoh when he was laid to rest in about 1322 B.C.

Illustrated with photographs taken by Williams himself and gleaned from the *New York Times* and other sources, the 31-page story took readers into the burial's artifact-packed antechamber. It also gave them a front-row seat as one stunning item after another was carried from the tomb and transported to Carter's nearby workshop in the already cleared tomb of King Seti II.

For National Geographic, the story was a coup—one of the best published snapshots of the discovery's early days. And for countless readers, it was the beginning of a love affair with ancient Egypt. The jewelry, the gilded statues, the funerary furniture decorated with strange beasts were all mesmerizing, and people wanted to see more. The news kept coming as Carter delved deeper into the tomb to reveal an intact burial and then spent the next decade cataloging all the king's more than 5,000 personal effects.

Inside Ramses II's temple at Abu Simbel, statues of the pharaoh stand at the pillars that support the roof. The walls of the chamber display reliefs that show the king in the many battles he fought during his long reign (about 1279–1213 B.C.).

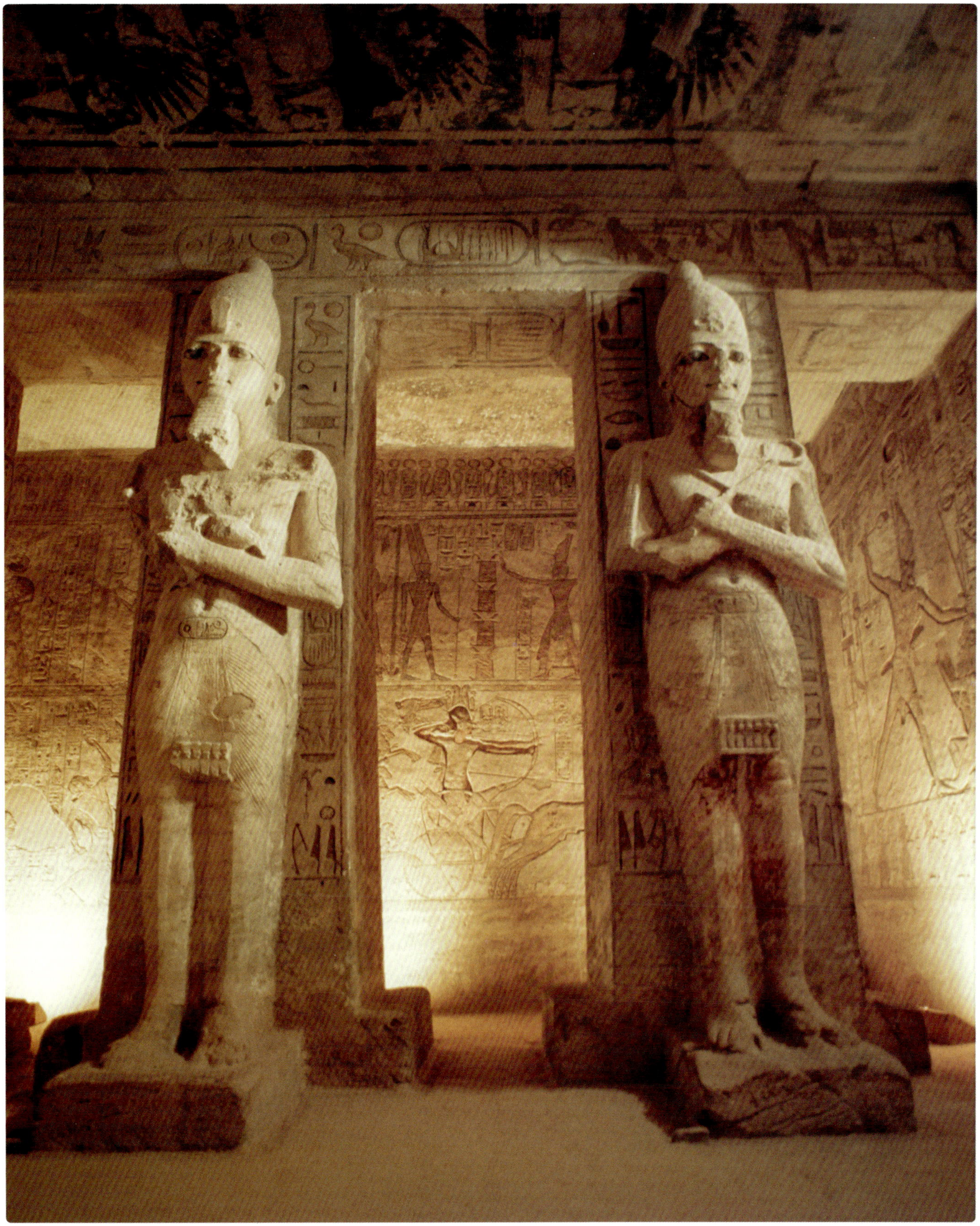

The March of Time

Spanning several millennia, the glories of ancient Egypt represent one of the world's most enduring civilizations. Terms like "Old Kingdom" didn't exist in antiquity, though. The labels on this time line are modern ideas, created for ease of reference.

3000 B.C.

2000 B.C.

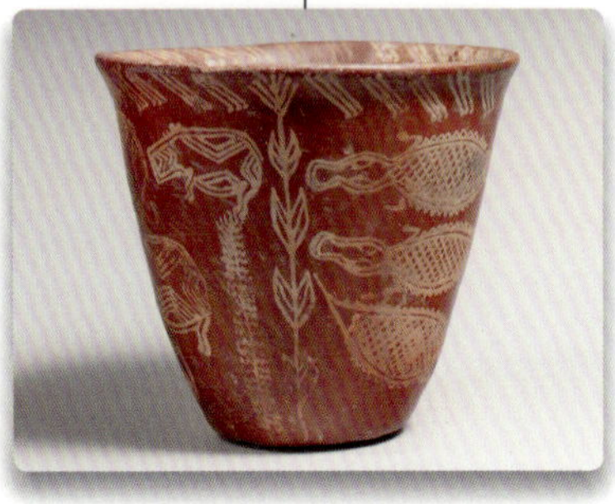

about 5900–3100 B.C.

PREDYNASTIC PERIOD

Communities develop painted pottery, mummification, and trade.

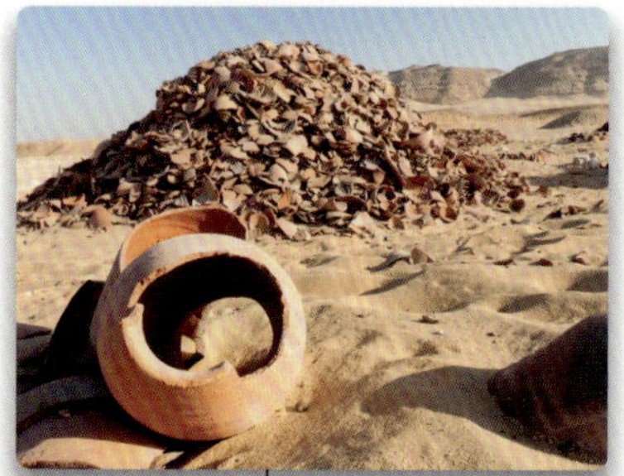

about 3100–2575 B.C.

EARLY DYNASTIC PERIOD

Early kings based near Abydos unify Egypt's north and south.

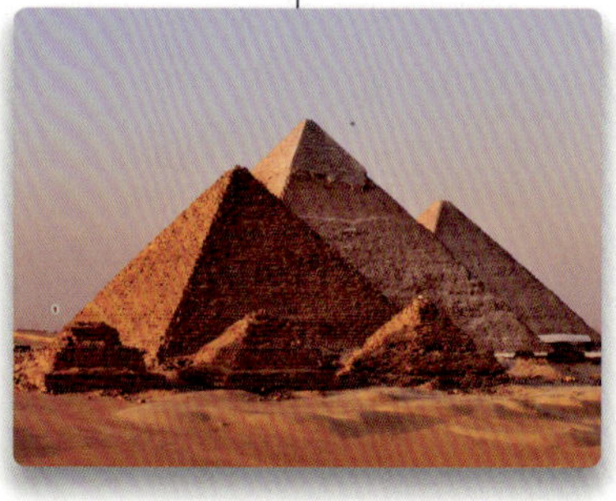

about 2575–2125 B.C.

OLD KINGDOM

Kings build pyramid tombs in the desert near Memphis, the capital.

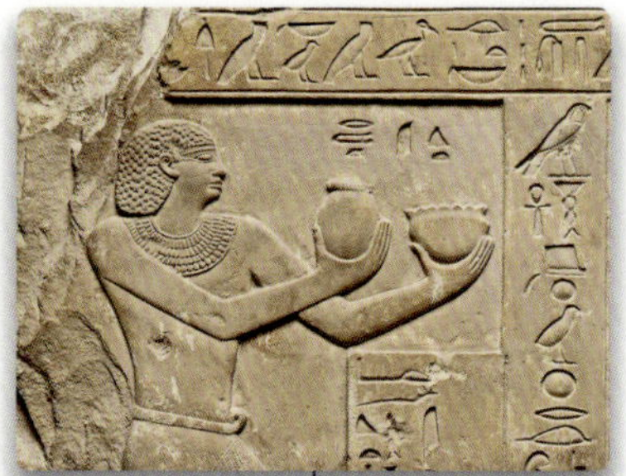

about 2125–1975 B.C.

FIRST INTERMEDIATE PERIOD

The central government collapses, and provinces compete for power.

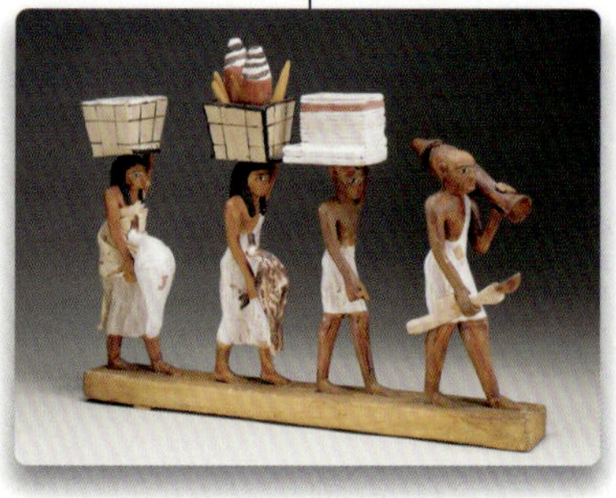

about 1975–1630 B.C.

MIDDLE KINGDOM

The reunification of the country brings peace and prosperity.

In recent decades, Tutankhamun has continued to serve as a gateway for millions to the wonders of ancient Egypt. As selected pieces from his tomb toured the globe on several occasions, crowds stood in long lines outside museums to get a look. People still speak with awe about seeing the magnificent gold mask in the "Treasures of Tutankhamun" exhibit from the 1970s. That and other iconic artifacts will likely never leave Egypt again; no amount of insurance could cover masterpieces that have come to symbolize the ancient realm's almost unimaginable wealth and power.

The year 2022 marks another key anniversary for Egyptologists and Egyptophiles: French linguist Jean-François Champollion's breakthrough in deciphering ancient Egyptian hieroglyphic texts, announced in September 1822. The rules that governed the script had been lost for many centuries; until Champollion, explorers and scholars had been unable to make much sense of the signs that covered temples and tombs, soaring stone obelisks, and delicate sheets of papyrus.

"Hieroglyphic writing is a complex system, a script all at once figurative, symbolic, and phonetic, in one and the same text, in one and the same sentence—and, I might even venture, in one and the same word," Champollion later explained. For starters, a hieroglyphic sign can represent exactly what it looks like. A bull is a bull, for example. But that same sign can also represent the idea of a herd of cattle. And it can stand for the sound "ka" in a compound word, in the same way bull is used

about 1630–1539 B.C.

SECOND INTERMEDIATE PERIOD

Foreigners known as Hyksos establish their own capital in the delta.

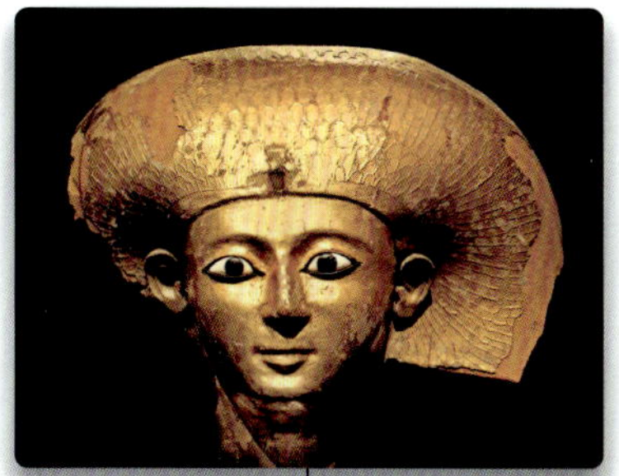

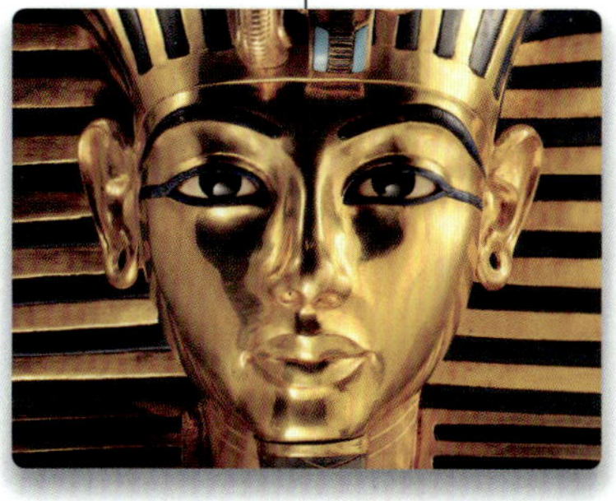

about 1539–1075 B.C.

NEW KINGDOM

Great warrior kings rule a wealthy, powerful country, united again.

about 1075–715 B.C.

THIRD INTERMEDIATE PERIOD

Libyans conquer the country's north, while Egyptians rule in the south.

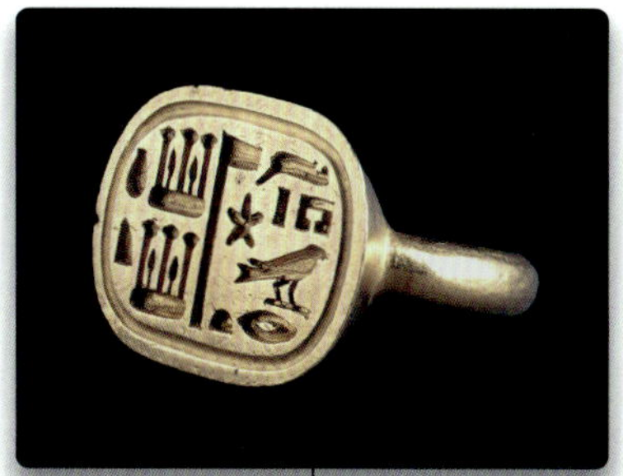

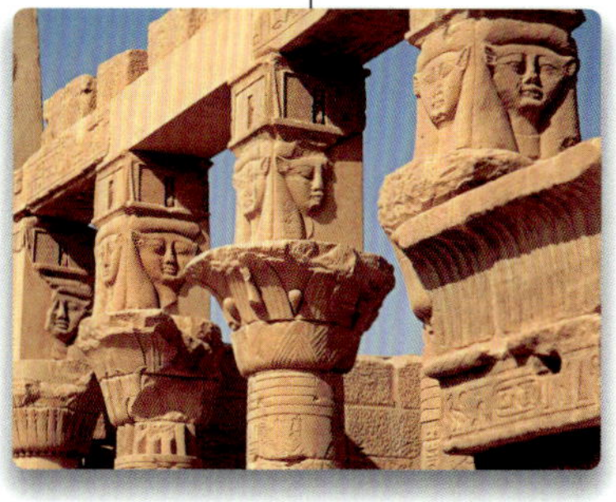

about 715–332 B.C.

LATE PERIOD

Invaders from Kush take the throne, then Persians do the same.

332–30 B.C.

PTOLEMAIC PERIOD

Alexander the Great and his successors usher in a Hellenistic era.

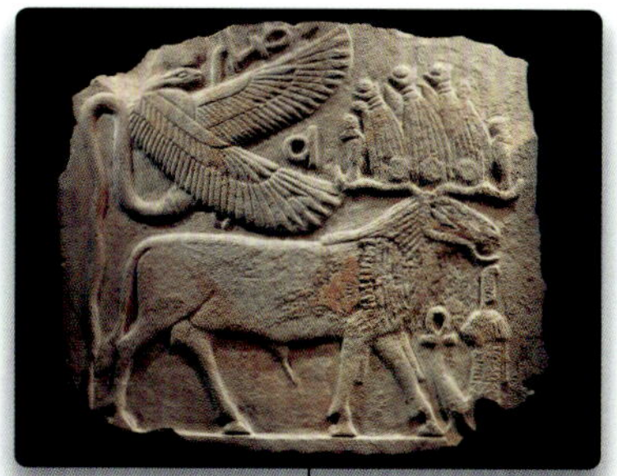

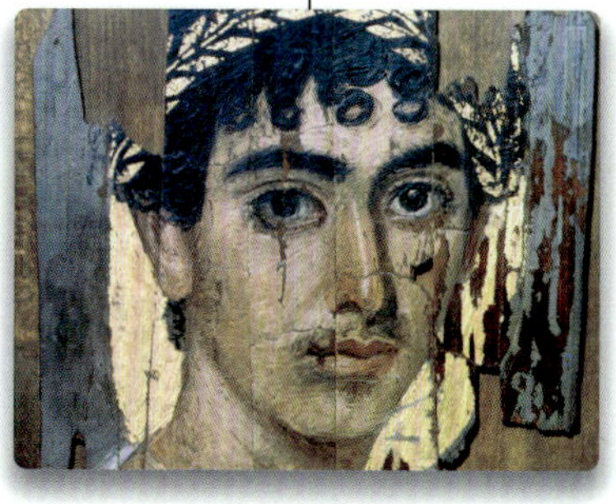

30 B.C.–A.D. 395

ROMAN PERIOD

Rome conquers Egypt, which becomes a province in a vast empire.

to form the word bullfinch. Context is everything in figuring out exactly what an ancient scribe meant to say.

Cracking the code opened a wide new window into ancient Egyptian lives. Suddenly, people from the past were communicating in their own words to modern readers. Kings bragged of conquests and made their commands known. Well-connected officials were buried with detailed instructions for how to get to the afterworld. A farmer named Khun-Anup, nicknamed the Eloquent Peasant, pleaded for justice after a landowner stole his donkey and the goods it was carrying.

As experts have pieced together the details of Egypt's 3,000-year pharaonic history—the dynasties that rose and fell, the battles won and lost—a fascinating picture of this ancient civilization has come into view. We now know the names of kings, their queens, and their children. Of courtiers and priests. Of cities and towns. Of the many gods and goddesses who oversaw every aspect of Egyptian life. We see the clever inventions—the plow, a calendar, majestic pyramids, and stationery made from the fibers of papyrus plants, the origin of the English word paper. Stretching across time and space, the story grows with every new discovery. Those of us hooked on this great, sweeping saga eagerly await the start of the dig season around October every year—and the news of what artifacts archaeologists are turning up.

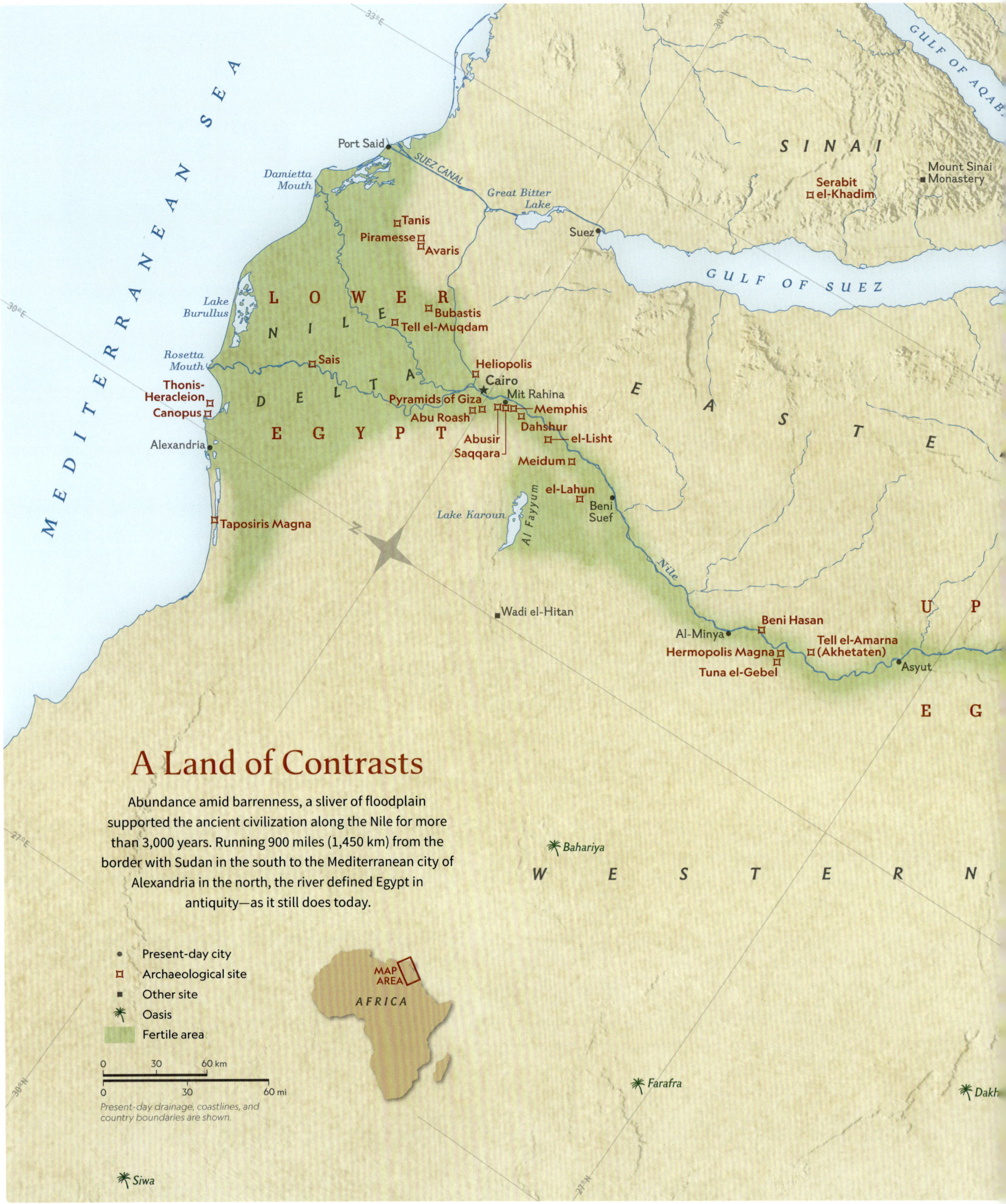

A Land of Contrasts

Abundance amid barrenness, a sliver of floodplain supported the ancient civilization along the Nile for more than 3,000 years. Running 900 miles (1,450 km) from the border with Sudan in the south to the Mediterranean city of Alexandria in the north, the river defined Egypt in antiquity—as it still does today.

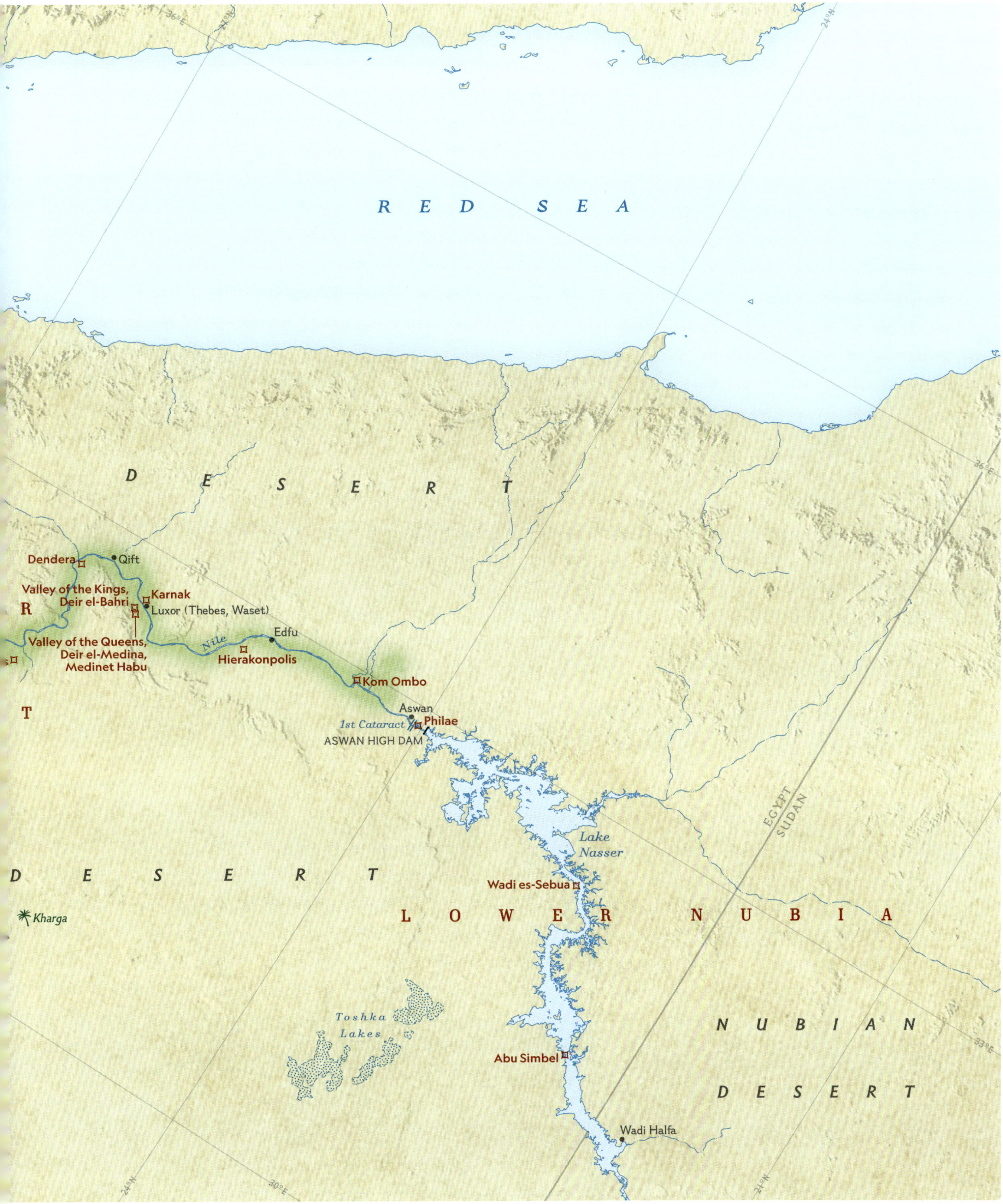

RED SEA
DESERT
Dendera
Qift
Valley of the Kings,
Deir el-Bahri
Karnak
Luxor (Thebes, Waset)
Edfu
Nile
Valley of the Queens,
Deir el-Medina,
Medinet Habu
Hierakonpolis
Kom Ombo
Aswan
1st Cataract
Philae
ASWAN HIGH DAM
Lake
Nasser
EGYPT
SUDAN
DESERT
Wadi es-Sebua
Kharga
LOWER NUBIA
Toshka
Lakes
NUBIAN
DESERT
Abu Simbel
Wadi Halfa
36°E
27°N
24°N
33°E
30°E
21°N

Since its founding in 1888, National Geographic has covered the great moments of discovery and archaeological research in Egypt. Examples include William Matthew Flinders Petrie's work at Abydos, the first kings' burial site, in the early 1900s; the discovery in the 1950s of a 4,500-year-old funerary boat of imported Lebanese cedar buried at Giza; the complex engineering involved in moving King Ramses II's temple to higher ground at Abu Simbel during the construction of the Aswan High Dam in the 1960s; the excavation of the pyramid builders' living quarters at Giza in the late 1990s; and the CT scan of Tutankhamun's mummy in the Valley of the Kings one stormy night in 2005.

The book you hold distills this recovered history into a vivid visual odyssey that documents the remarkable history of this ancient empire in a series of powerful images. These include rare early photographs taken before sites were excavated and restored, along with little-known images of such treasures as the gold and silver artifacts buried with King Psusennes I in Tanis in about 995 B.C., whose discovery was overshadowed by the outbreak of World War II.

As you turn these pages, we hope you will be inspired by the unique flavor and history of ancient Egypt's diverse regions and foreign territories. You'll also meet some of the most prominent figures in Egyptology, whose stories evoke the adventure of exploration and track the evolution of archaeology into a disciplined, modern science. And finally, you'll discover some of the mysteries of the ancient Egyptian culture, from the cartouches that encircle kings' names to the way bread was baked to feed the builders of the great pyramids.

As time moves on, our knowledge of ancient Egypt changes—as does the way in which we gain it. Gone are wealthy patrons like Lord Carnarvon, who sponsored the search for King Tut's tomb over a period of six years. Today, far fewer Egyptian digs are run by foreigners, who once had a virtual monopoly on the thrill of discovery. Today, Egypt is training its own specialists, who increasingly are the ones making the newsworthy finds.

Change is afoot in museums, too. One artifact after another has been leaving the antiquated galleries of the beloved Egyptian Museum, near Tahrir Square in downtown Cairo, for state-of-the-art venues elsewhere. Earlier this year, the museum's royal mummies were the center of a televised extravaganza as they were paraded in specially designed trucks to their new home: the National Museum of Egyptian Civilization.

Artifacts have also been moving to the Grand Egyptian Museum (GEM), a spacious, billion-dollar facility of galleries, conservation labs, and conference halls on a grand plaza full of palm trees in sight of the Giza pyramids. A colossal statue of King Ramses II, which stood outside Cairo's main train station for half a century, was relocated to the GEM in 2018 and now towers over an atrium of sun-dappled stone.

King Tut's artifacts have gone to the GEM too, crated up one by one and transported over the course of the last several years. The opening of the museum is set for this centennial year. Among the 50,000 priceless objects visitors will see are all the teenage pharaoh's possessions—including his gold mask—in a special suite of rooms inspired by the arrangement of the tomb. In a curatorial tour de force, the artifacts will be displayed in this one place, brought together for the first time since Howard Carter laid eyes on them in a long-forgotten grave that has since become legendary.

However much change rocks our world, for better or for worse, there are always some steadying certainties. With almost every shovel of sand shifted in Egypt, another artifact comes to light. These precious traces of the past are reminders of the creativity, inventiveness, and resilience that carried the ancient Egyptians through good times and bad for millennia. These same qualities will continue to serve us all for as long as the human mind produces new ideas in flashes of brilliance. ▲

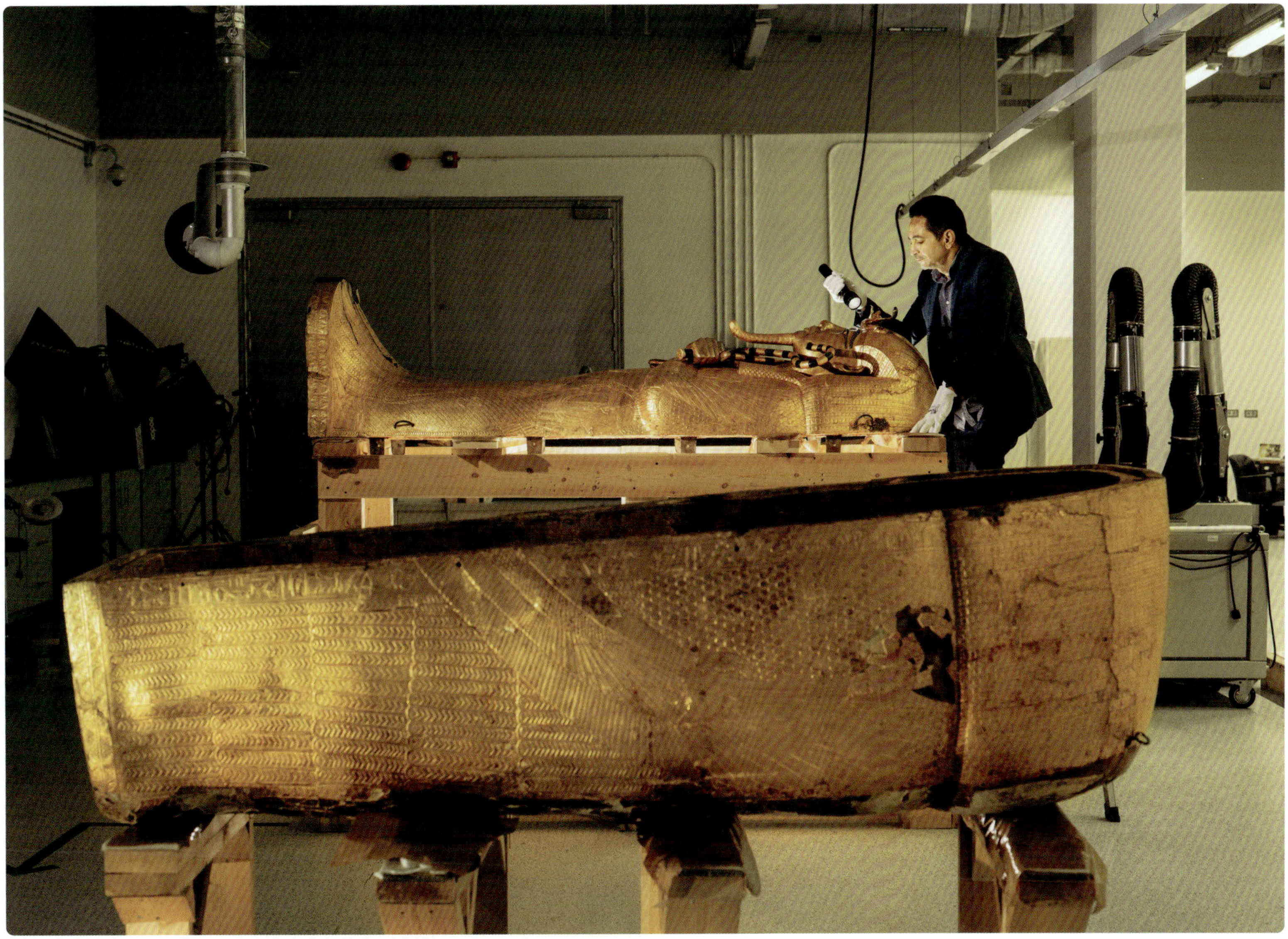

In one of the Grand Egyptian Museum's several high-tech conservation labs, technical affairs director Hussein Kamal inspects Tutankhamun's outer coffin after its careful transfer from the Egyptian Museum in downtown Cairo. The first of three nested coffins that held the king's mummy, this royal artifact was crafted of plastered and gilded wood in about 1322 B.C.

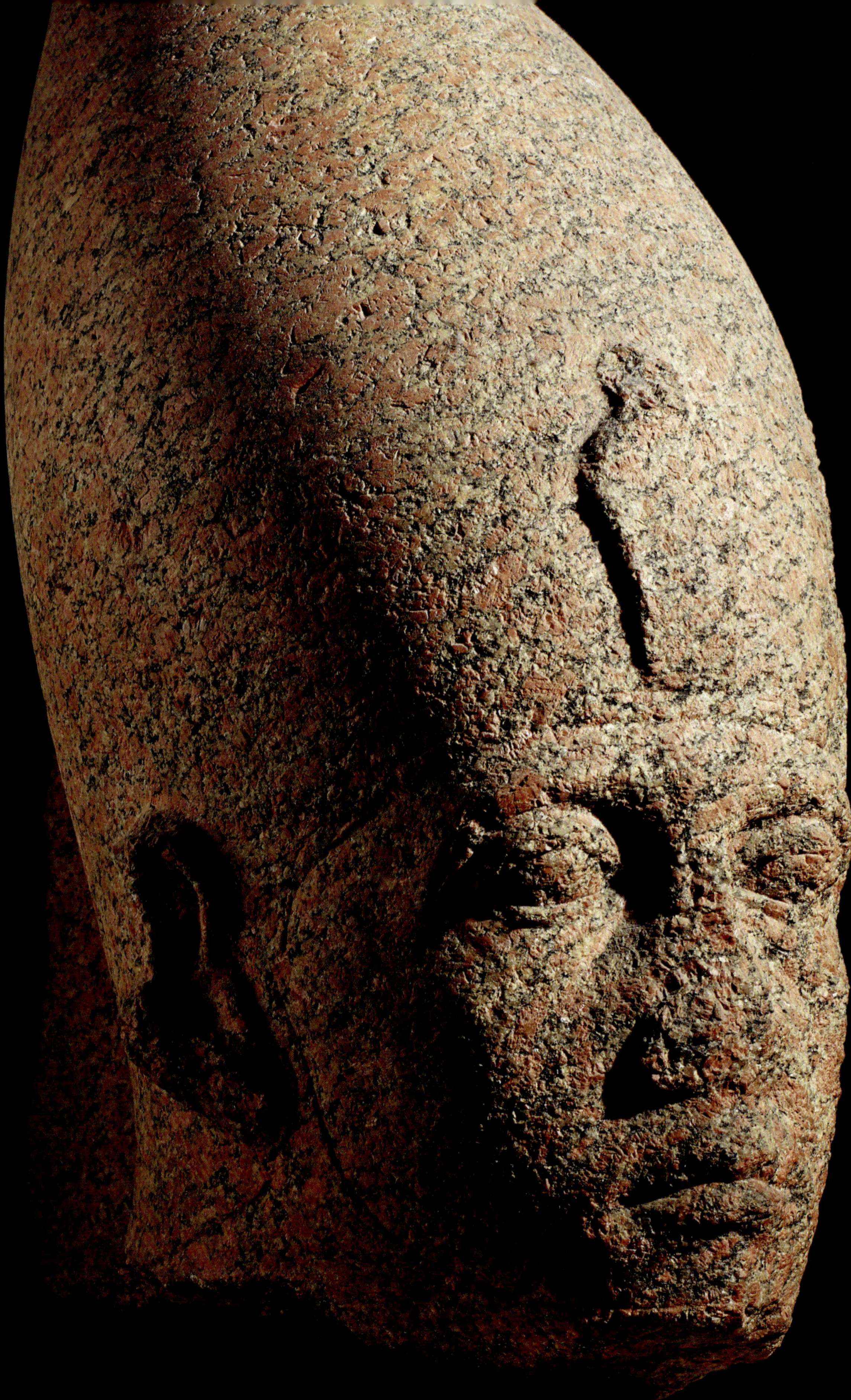

CHAPTER ONE

ABYDOS AND HIERAKONPOLIS

The Cradle of Kingship

AT THE END of the last ice age, around 10,000 B.C., the land we now call Egypt was a vast savannah. Summer rains fed lakes and allowed grasses to flourish, creating an ecosystem that supported herds of giraffes, rhinos, and elephants, as well as nomadic pastoralists and their cattle. But sometime around 5000 B.C., the climate began to change. The land became increasingly arid, driving the peoples of the Sahara toward spring-fed oases such as Dakhla and Kharga—and to the Nile River, the one great source of water whose constant flow could sustain life.

As villages and towns arose, so did local rulers who managed the communal labor that harnessed the river's annual floods so crops could be irrigated. By about 3500 B.C., small kingdoms had emerged along the length of the river (see map, pages 24–25). Cities in the south soon gained the political upper hand. Some 50 miles (80 km) south of modern Luxor, ancient Nekhen was one of those. In its day, it may have been the largest city in ancient Egypt, spreading some three miles (5 km) along the edge of the Nile's western floodplain. Its association with the god Horus would inspire a later Greek name, Hierakonpolis, "city of the falcon."

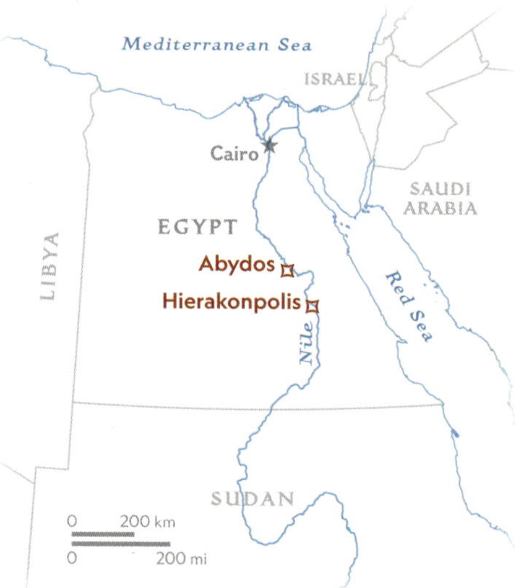

The community was large enough to support industries, archaeologists have learned. Several breweries filled with huge vats were found on the outskirts of town, even the smallest of which could have produced 300 gallons (1,135 L) of wheat beer a day. In another neighborhood where more than a dozen artisans created pottery, one somehow mismanaged the kiln and burned down his house, thus preserving charred roof beams that were uncovered 5,500 years later.

Excavations have also uncovered traces of a large walled courtyard, entered by a monumental gate, where wild animals were sacrificed. Crocodiles, hippopotamuses, gazelles, and Barbary sheep met their end there—likely in ceremonies that represented the ruler imposing the order of civilization over the chaos of nature, one of the fundamental concepts of ancient Egyptian kingship.

Burials have revealed another cultural touchstone that would continue through time: early attempts at mummification. In a few graves of the working class, the internal organs of the deceased had been removed, wrapped in resin-infused fabric, and replaced in the body.

Prompted by artifacts flooding onto the antiquities market in the area, formal excavations at the site began in 1897. Two objects found during the first dig season seem to suggest Nekhen played a key role in the birth of ancient Egyptian kingship. The first, a ceremonial stone mace head, bears the name of King Scorpion, as well as carved scenes that may indicate he was one of the early rulers who began to conquer other cities and consolidate power. The second is a commemorative stone palette depicting a ruler named Narmer (also known as Menes), who wears a crown associated with northern Egypt on one side and another associated

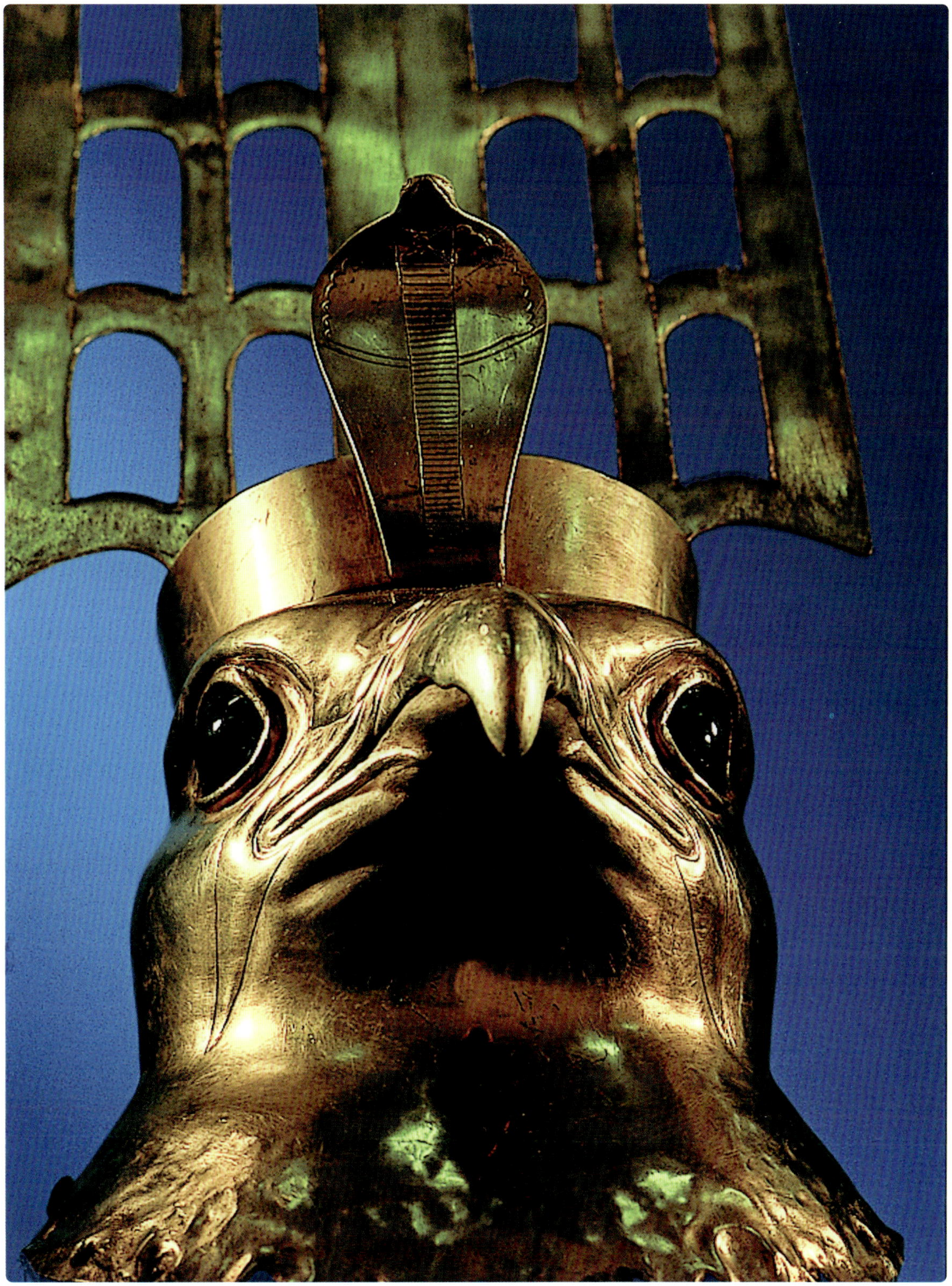

A ferocious falcon's head crafted from gold and obsidian (above) represents the god Horus, protector of the king. Dating to the sixth dynasty (about 2325 B.C.), it was uncovered at Hierakonpolis.

PREVIOUS PAGES: Following tradition, the 12th dynasty's Senwosret III (about 1836–1818 B.C.) had his image immortalized in granite. Such enduring monuments testify to the ancient kings' desire to leave an eternal legacy.

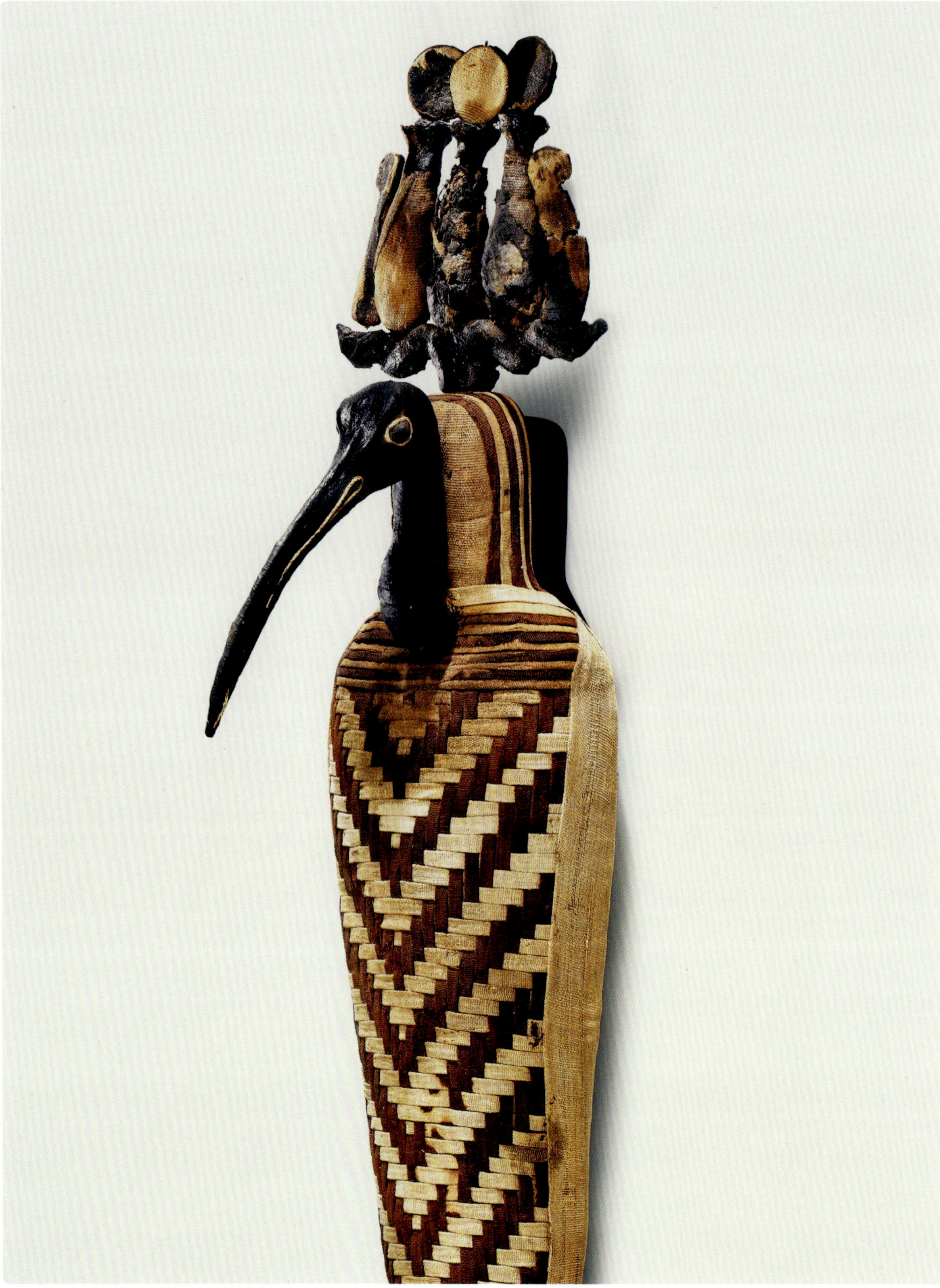

Two millennia ago, this elaborate votive offering was deposited at Abydos. The appearance is deceiving; the exterior indicates that it should contain a mummified ibis, but there are only feathers inside.

“Abydos . . . became a cult center, the location of an annual festival honoring Osiris, a pilgrimage destination, and a place where ordinary Egyptians aspired to be buried.”

with southern Egypt on the other. Reliefs show the king smiting an enemy and taking part in a victory parade past the beheaded bodies of enemies, implying that he was the triumphant warrior king who finally managed to unite Egypt into one country.

SOME 60 MILES (95 KM) NORTHWEST of Luxor, the site of Abydos holds the graves of the early kings who laid political and cultural foundations that would last for the next three millennia. These men created burial complexes with two separate elements: a large enclosure of mud brick, located near the floodplain to the west of the Nile, where funerary rituals took place, and more than a mile (1.6 km) away, an underground tomb at the edge of the desert, which ancient Egyptians viewed as the realm of the dead. But before building could begin, the construction crew had to tear down the ritual enclosure of a king’s deceased predecessor. The structure of Khasekhemwy, the second dynasty’s last king, was the only one to survive. Its massive walls, 4,600 years old and three stories tall, still surround almost two acres (0.8 ha) of sand.

Near this enclosure, and the traces of the demolished ones of earlier kings, archaeologists have made surprising discoveries. In one place, a fleet of 14 boats had been buried for a first-dynasty king’s use in the afterlife; each planked vessel was about 75 feet long (23 m) and would have required up to 30 rowers. This tradition would continue with the much larger boats that fourth-dynasty king Khufu buried at Giza, and the much smaller model boats found in King Tutankhamun’s tomb.

An early practice that did not continue was sacrificing servants to serve the king in the next life. The first king of the first dynasty, Hor-Aha, had six people buried at his enclosure and 35 more at his tomb. The next king, Djer, had 269 buried by his enclosure and more than 300 at his tomb. Royal staff probably rebelled at this, though, and by the second dynasty the mass burials had ended.

Third-dynasty king Djoser would shift the center of royal burials to the north, near the city of Memphis, where he launched the age of pyramids with the construction of his revolutionary stone tomb stepping toward the sky in tiers.

In time, though, people came to believe that the god Osiris was buried at Abydos. The site became a cult center, the location of an annual festival honoring Osiris, a pilgrimage destination, and a place where ordinary Egyptians aspired to be buried. Several kings built temples there, and the site was considered sacred until the start of the Christian era in the seventh century A.D.

Although the original purpose of Khasekhemwy’s funerary enclosure was long forgotten, people in the first millennium B.C. used it for their own religious expression. Archaeologists discovered scores of ceramic vessels containing ibises and their eggs buried in the sand there. In fact, cemeteries of votive animal offerings dating from the same period dot the rest of Abydos. Each mummified dog, hawk, cat, mongoose, shrew, and ibis was meant to intercede with the gods on behalf of the donor for eternity. ▲

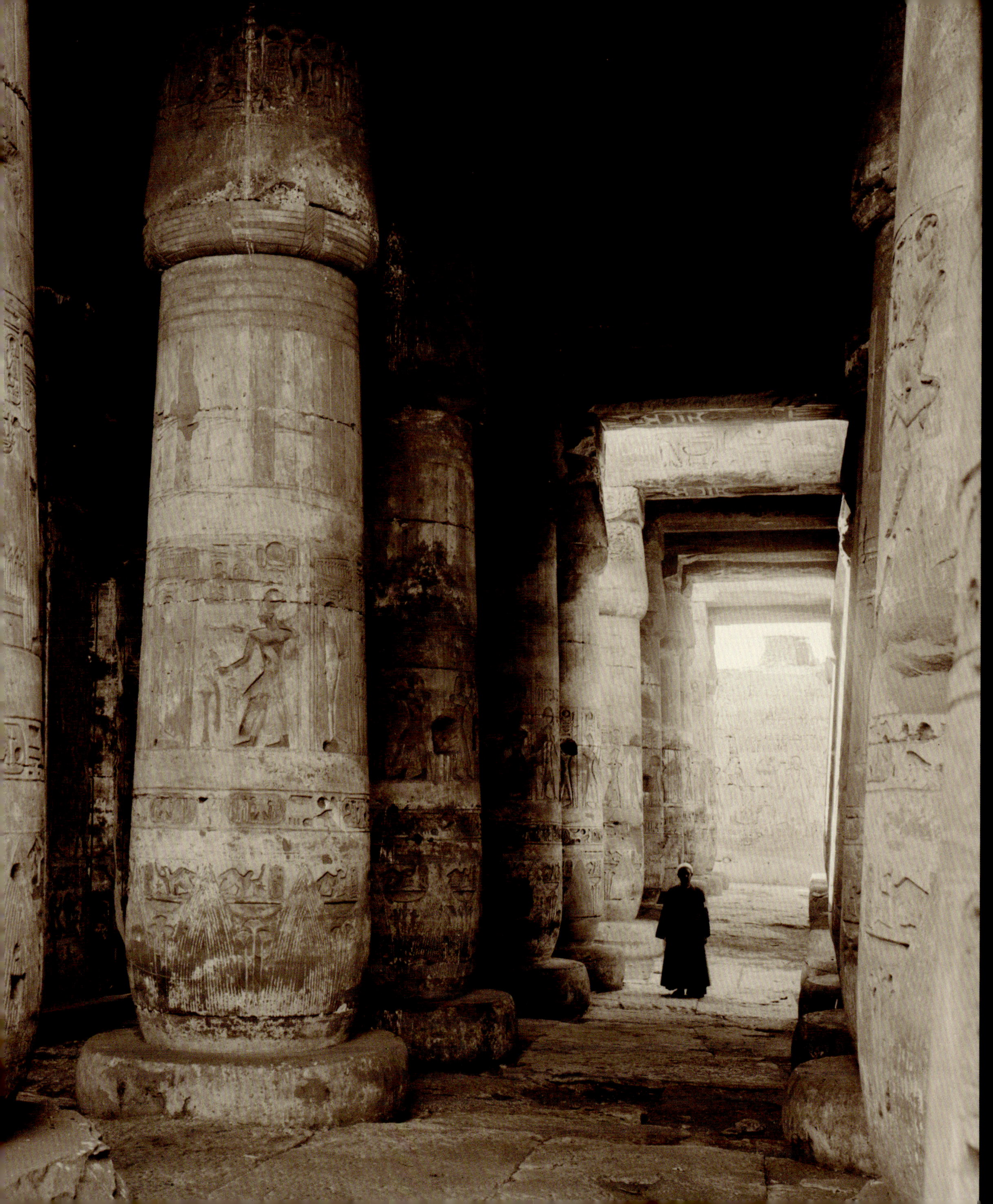

FIRST PHOTOS

Inside, the temple of Seti I at Abydos doesn't look much different today (below) than it did in the early 1900s (opposite). Ritual processions in the 13th century B.C. would pass by these soaring lotus bud columns to reach a row of seven chapels, each dedicated to a different god: Seti himself, Ptah, Re-Horakhty, Amun, Osiris, Isis, and Horus.

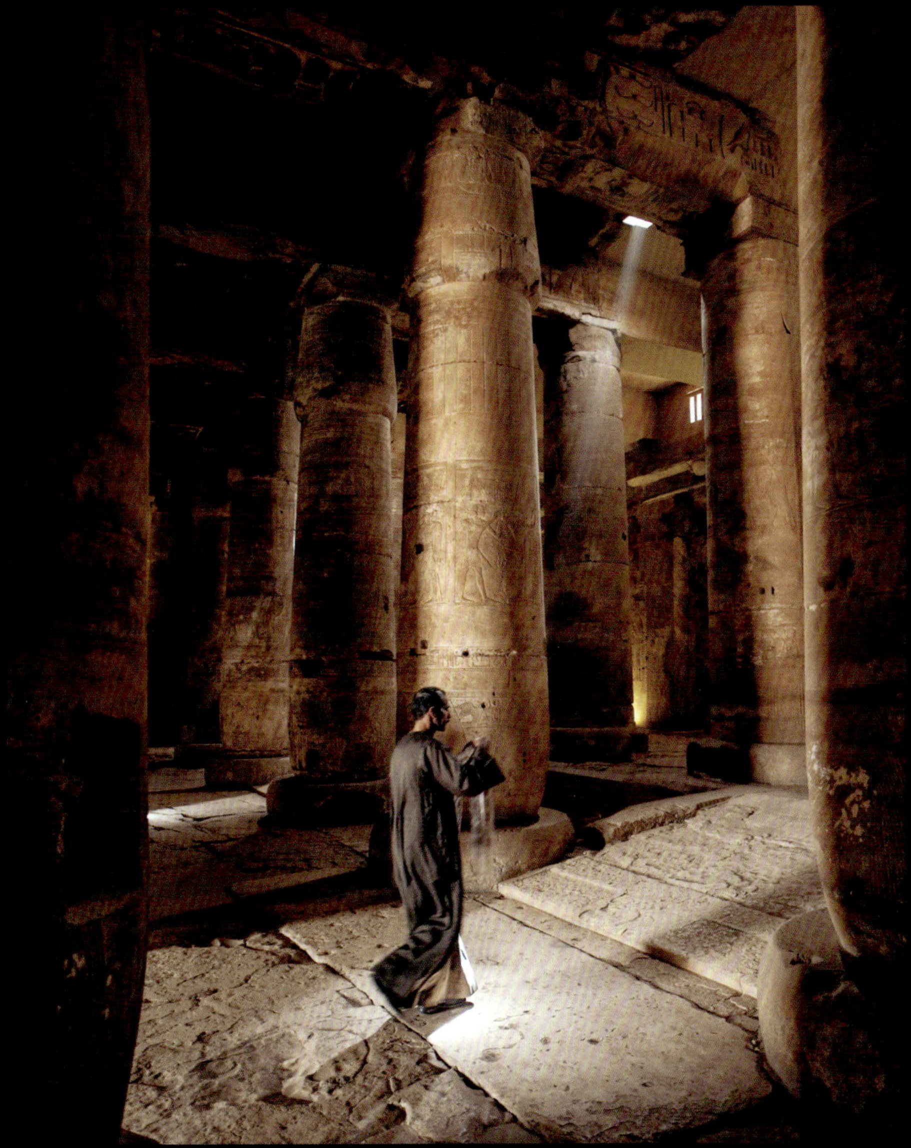

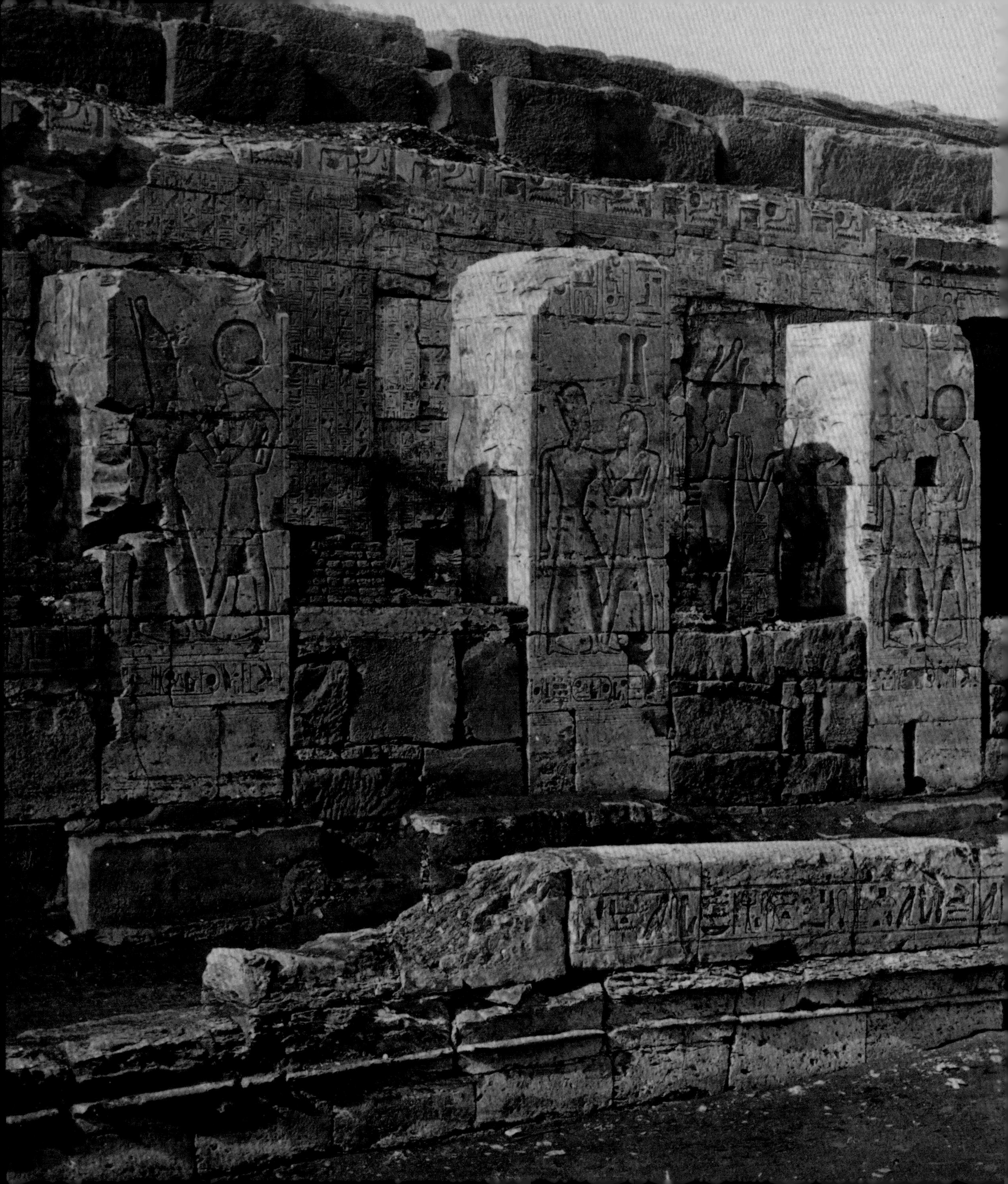

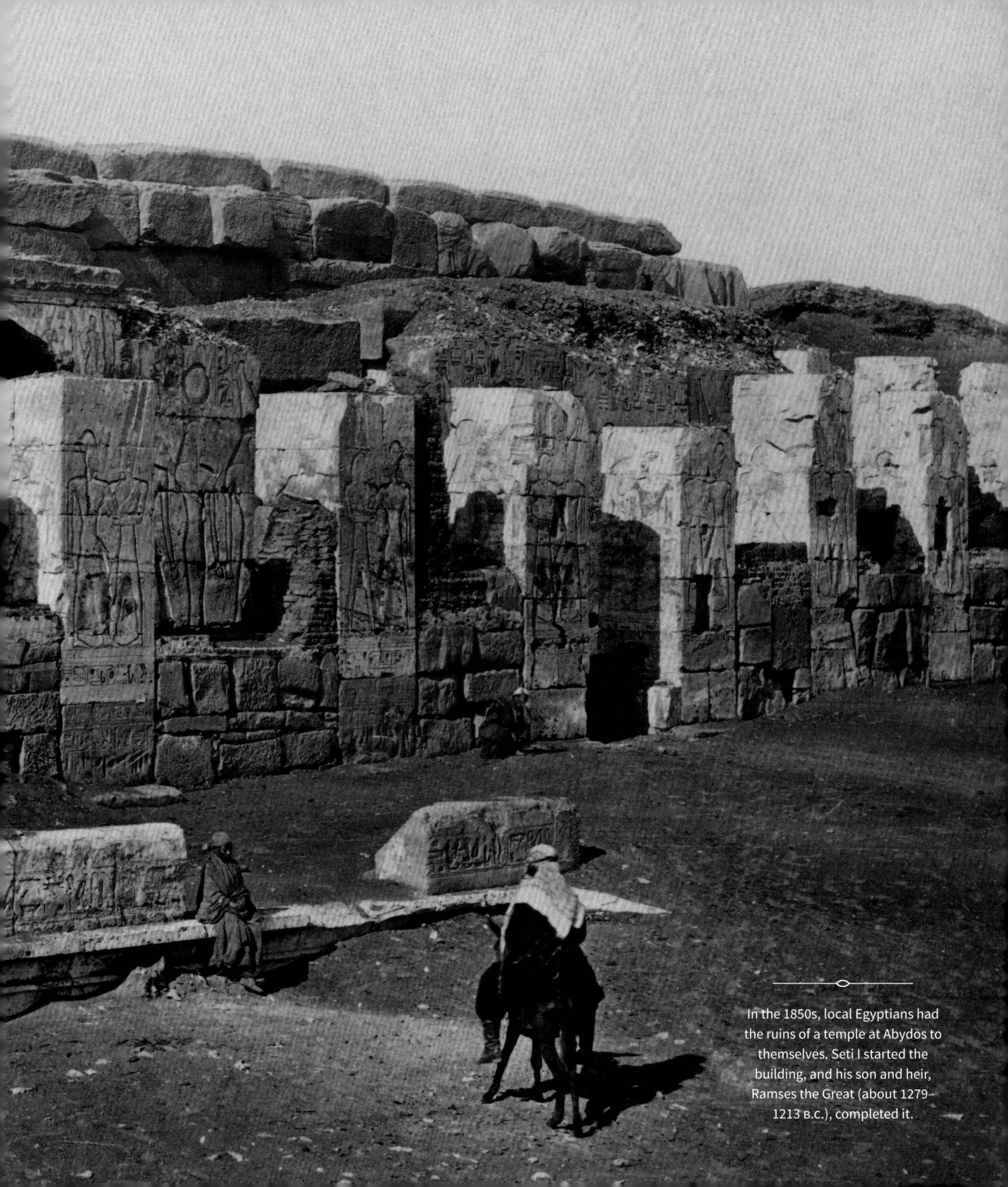

In the 1850s, local Egyptians had the ruins of a temple at Abydos to themselves. Seti I started the building, and his son and heir, Ramses the Great (about 1279–1213 B.C.), completed it.

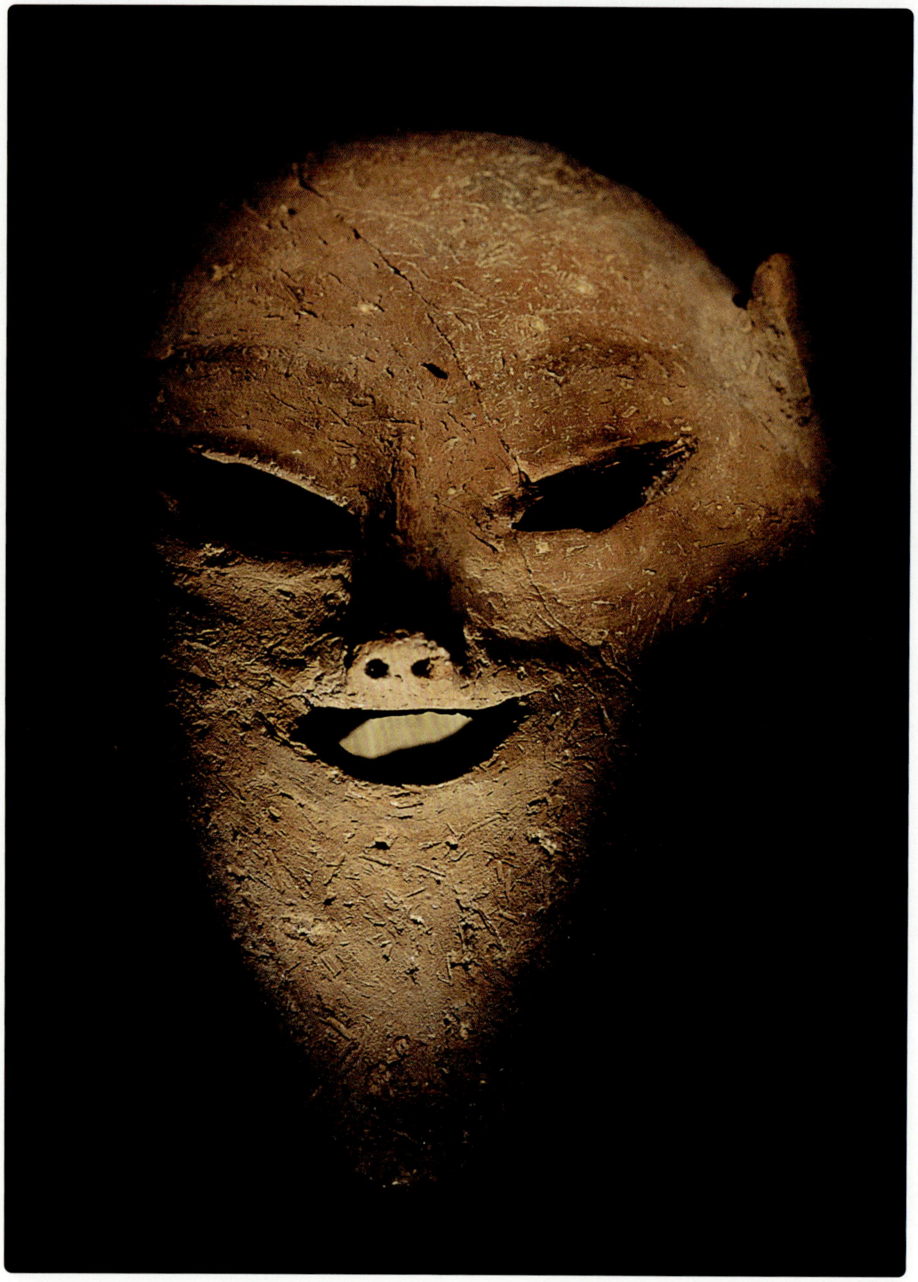

Predynastic graves at Hierakonpolis yielded this ceramic mask (above) and parts of three others. Dated to about 3700 B.C., they're the earliest such funerary artifacts uncovered in Egypt.

Flashing eyes of stone (opposite) enliven the copper face of Pepi I (about 2300 B.C.). Found under a temple at Hierakonpolis, the life-size statue, now hollow, likely once had a wooden core.

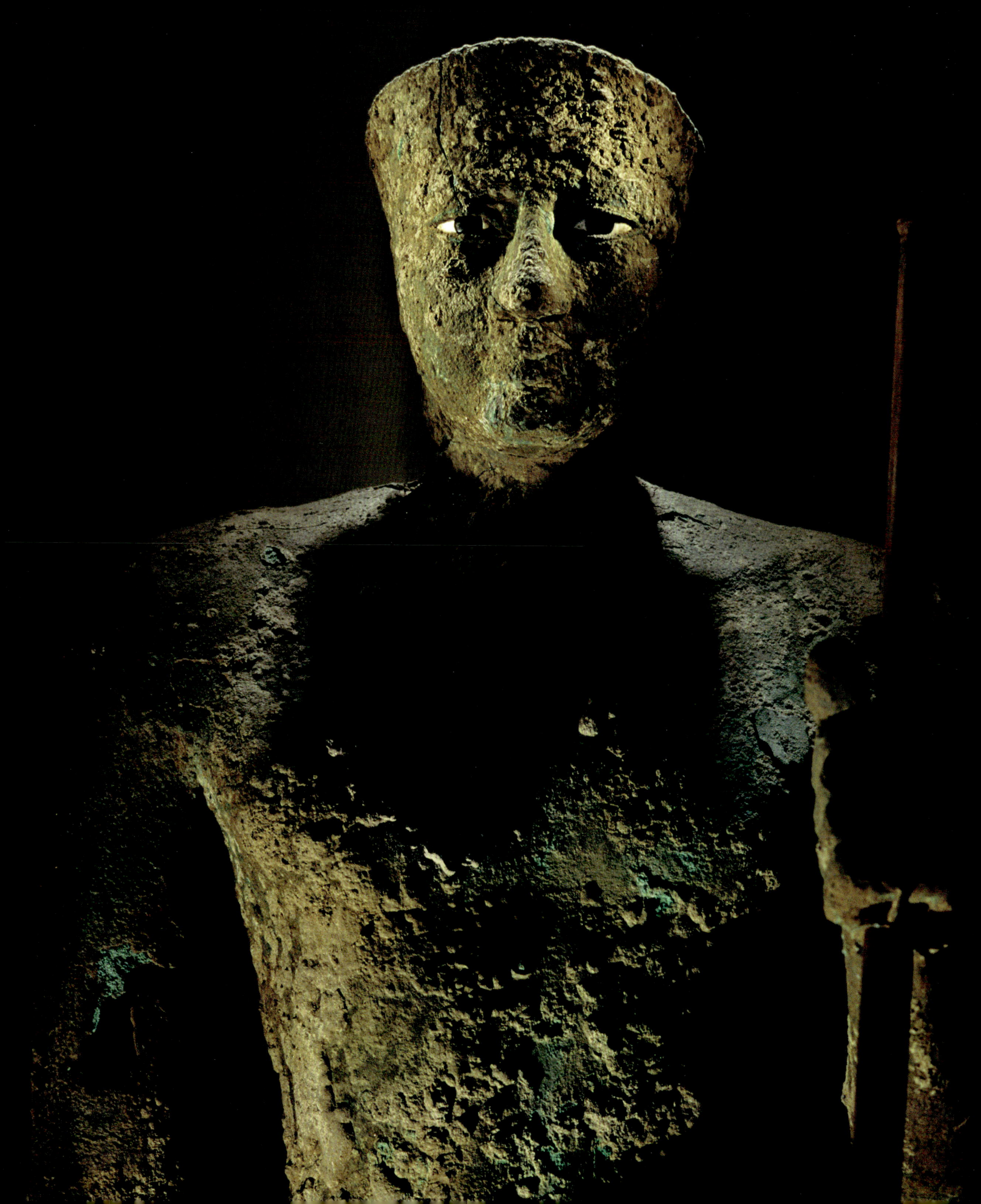

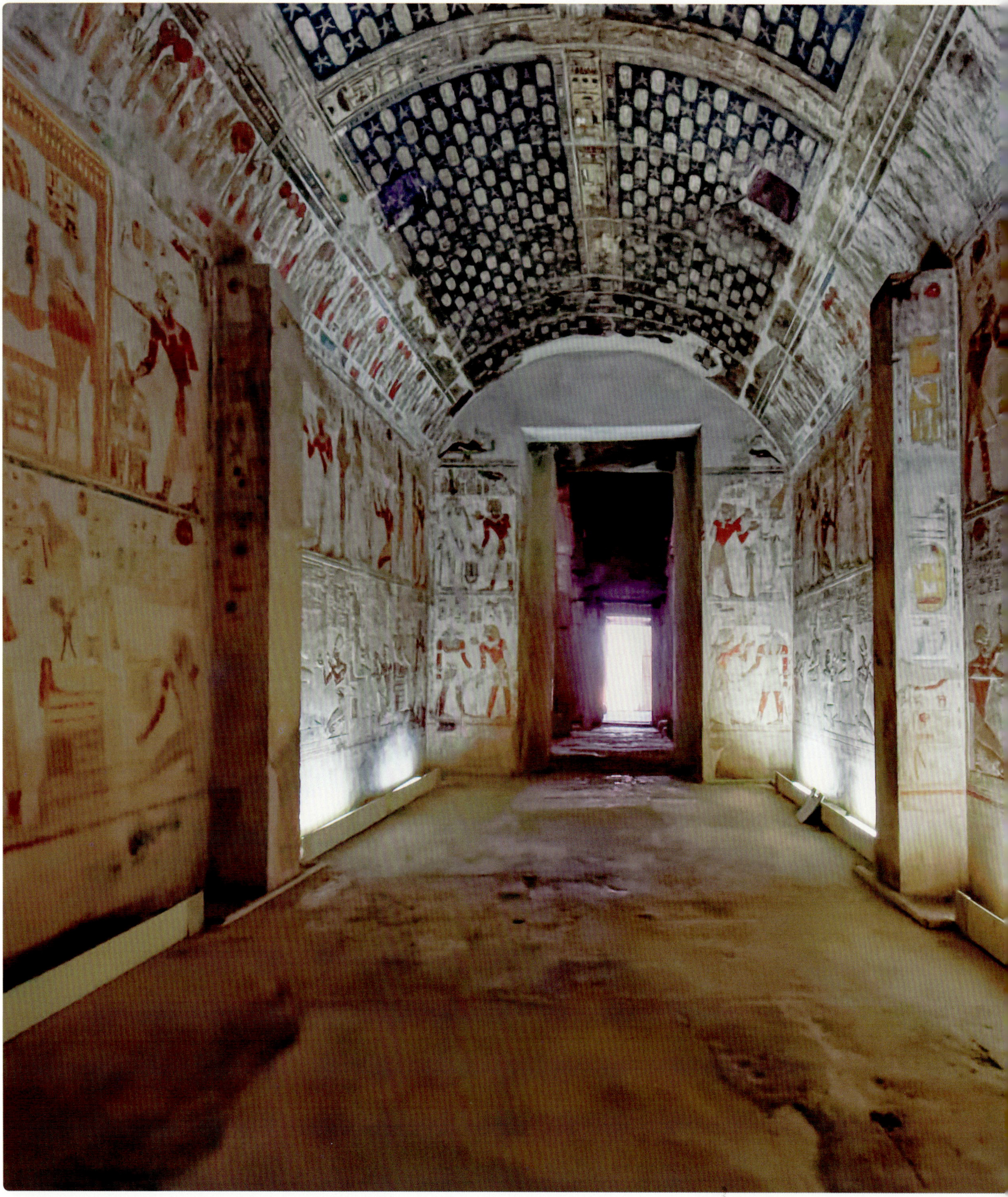

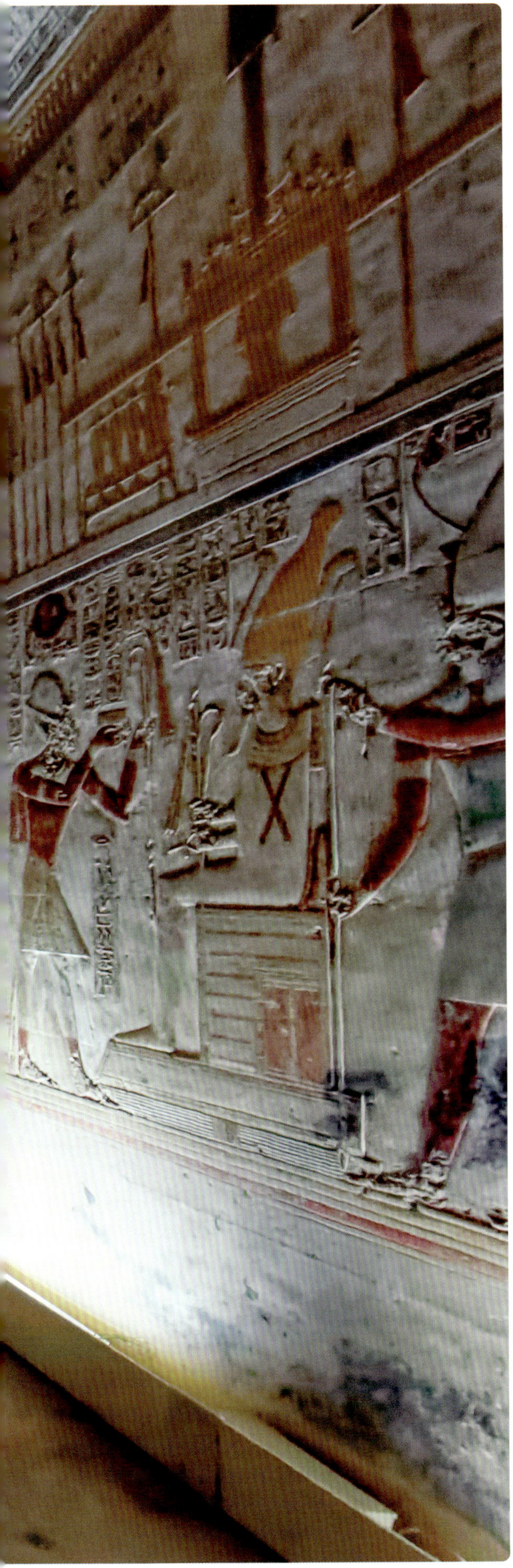

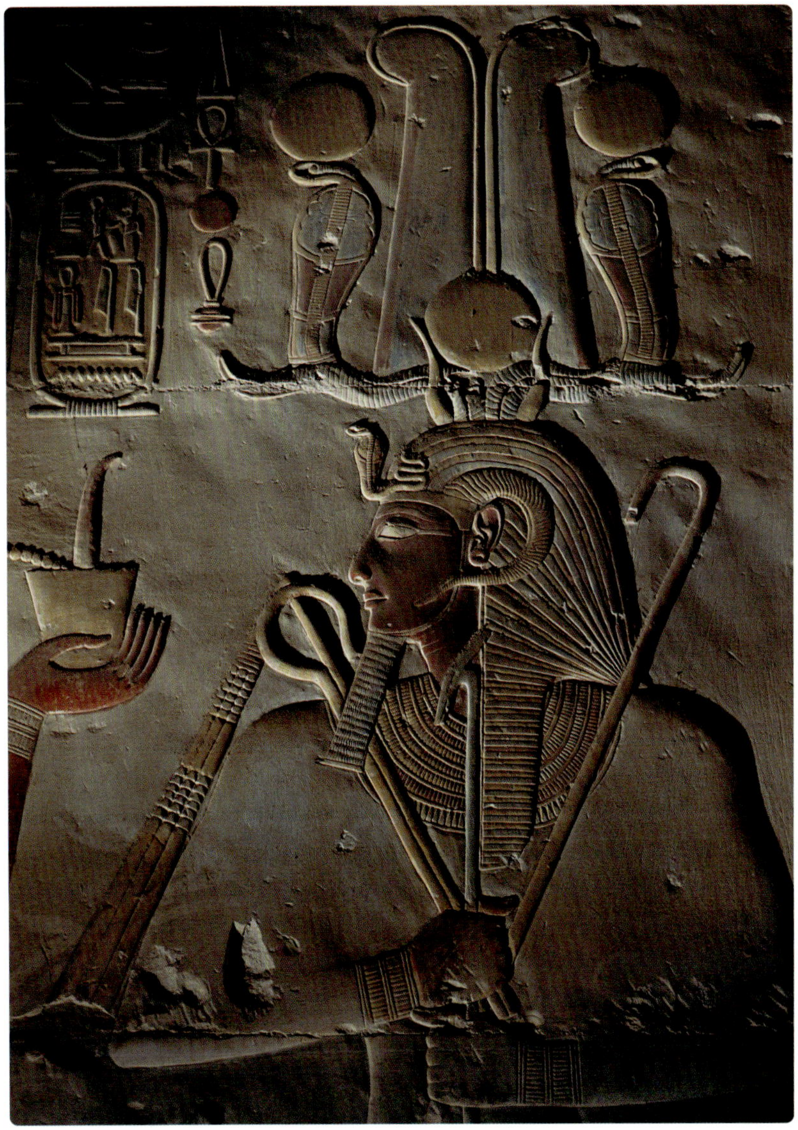

In a chapel of Seti I's temple at Abydos (left), reliefs celebrate the many forms of the god Osiris. Recent conservation removed centuries of soot, restoring the brilliance of the paint.

Symbolizing royal and divine powers, Seti I's complex regalia (above) includes a regal striped cloth headdress, called a *nemes,* as well as protective cobras, a ram's horns, and two tall bird plumes.

The Father of Egyptology

THERE WAS NOTHING scientific about early excavations in Egypt; locals and foreigners alike dug willy-nilly in their search for treasure to sell or to ship back home to fill museums and mansions. But British archaeologist William Matthew Flinders Petrie changed the game. Beginning in 1880, he brought a controlled methodology to dozens of iconic sites in Egypt, from Abydos and Tell el-Amarna to Luxor and Memphis (below), turning Egyptology into a discipline of documenting artifact types and dates.

A stickler for detail, Petrie produced the first stratified excavation wall in Egypt, exposing the slow accumulation of debris that modern archaeologists read as a map to every site. Instead of dazzling art, he focused on the bowls, flint blades, and fragments of reliefs that represent daily life. Today, Petrie's personal collection—tens of thousands of ordinary objects—forms the core of a London museum named after him.

Petrie was also a prolific author, publishing many hundreds of accounts of his work. One inspired the first article about archaeology in *National Geographic* magazine: a report about royal burials uncovered at Abydos, published in November 1901.

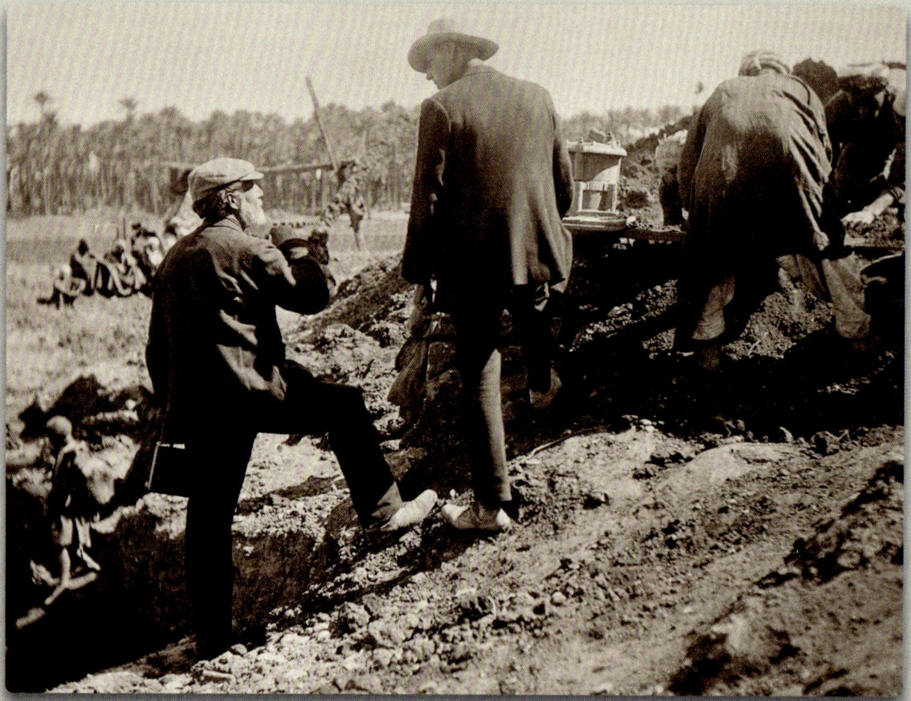

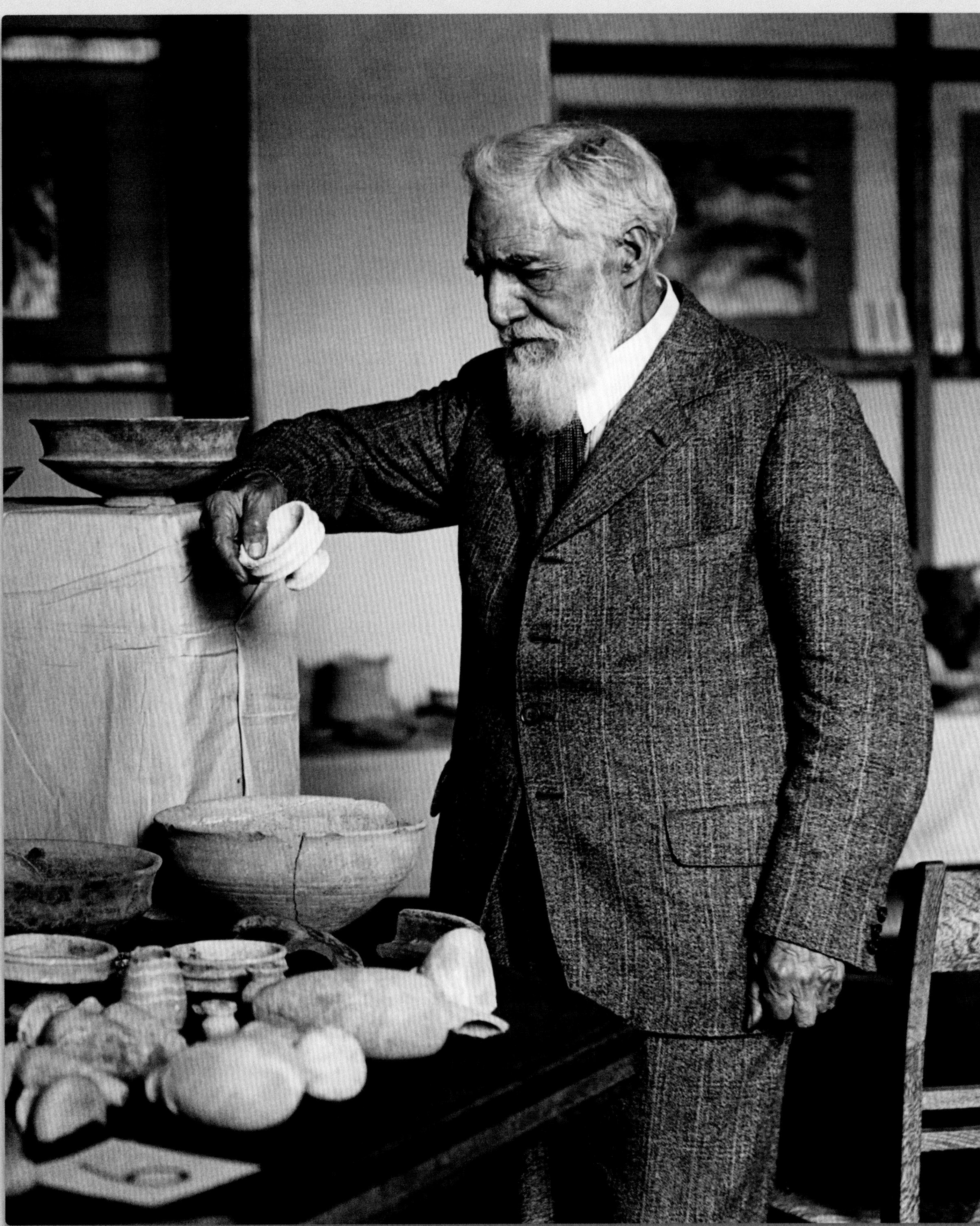

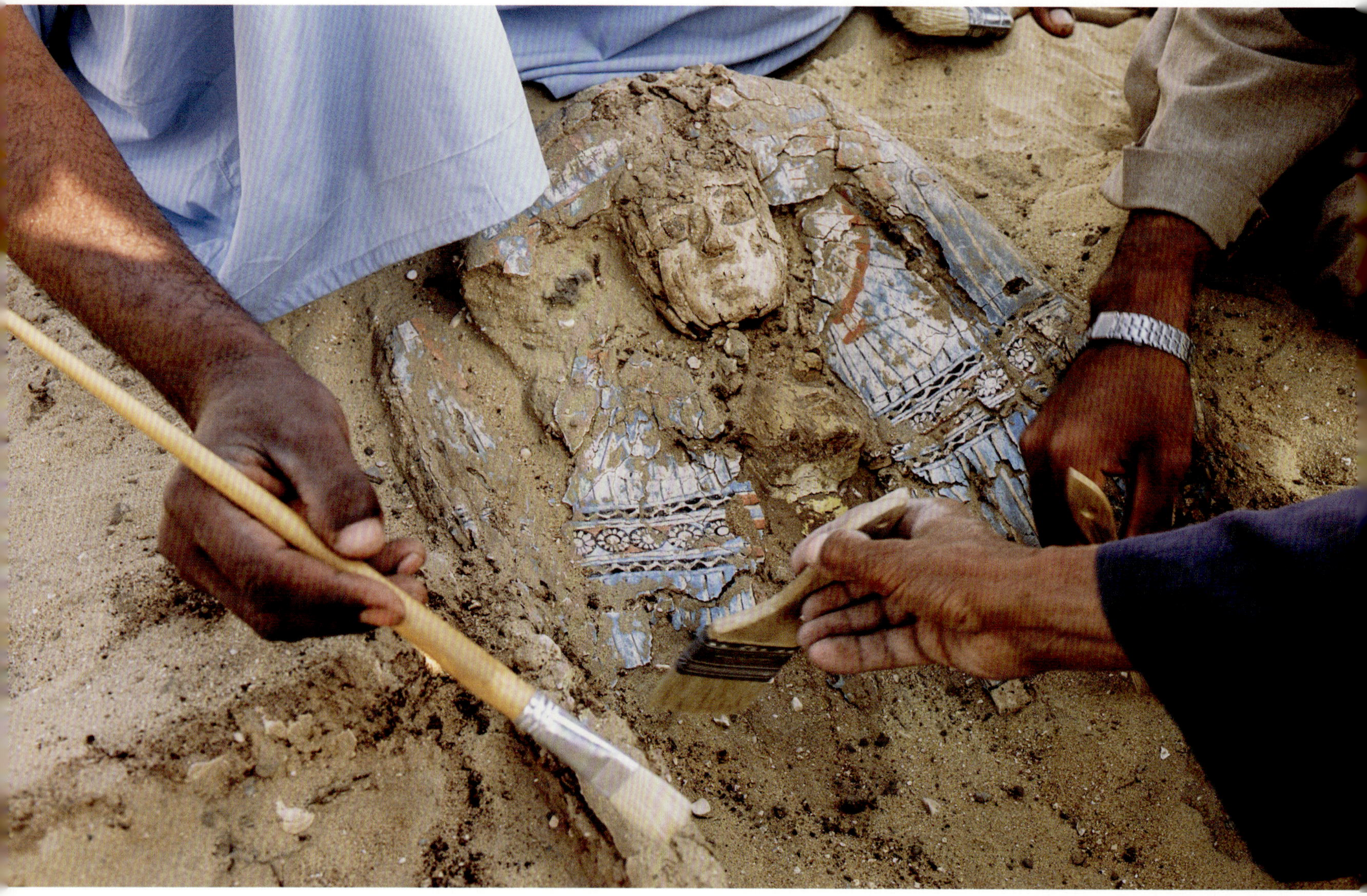

Countless graves lie beneath the sand of Abydos, center of the cult of Osiris. Some, like this one just coming to light, hold a wooden coffin damaged by insects and time.

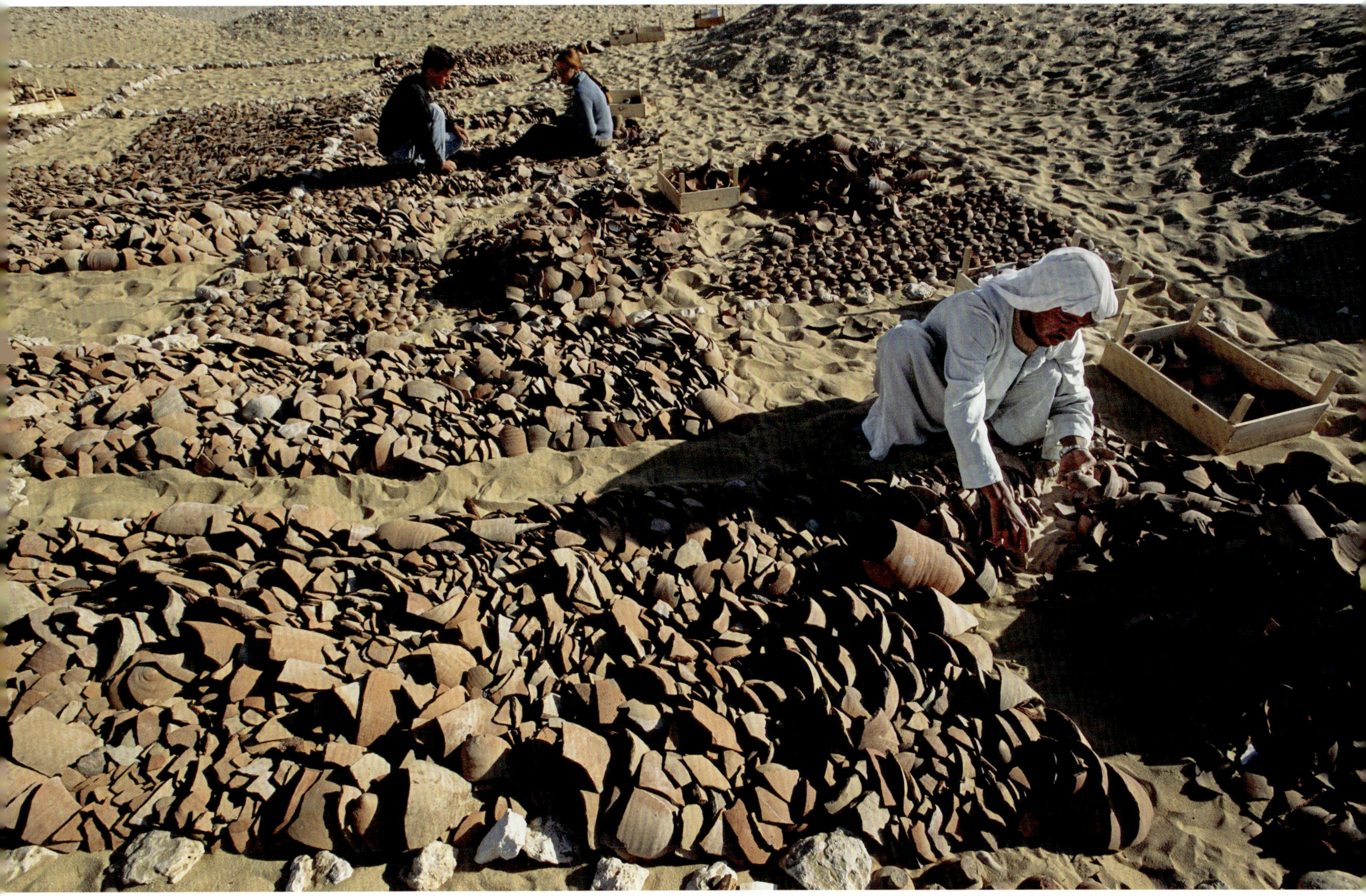

Over many centuries, ancient pilgrims left offerings in ceramic vessels at Abydos. Sherds now litter the ground, inspiring an Arabic name for a section of the site, Umm el-Qaab—mother of pots.

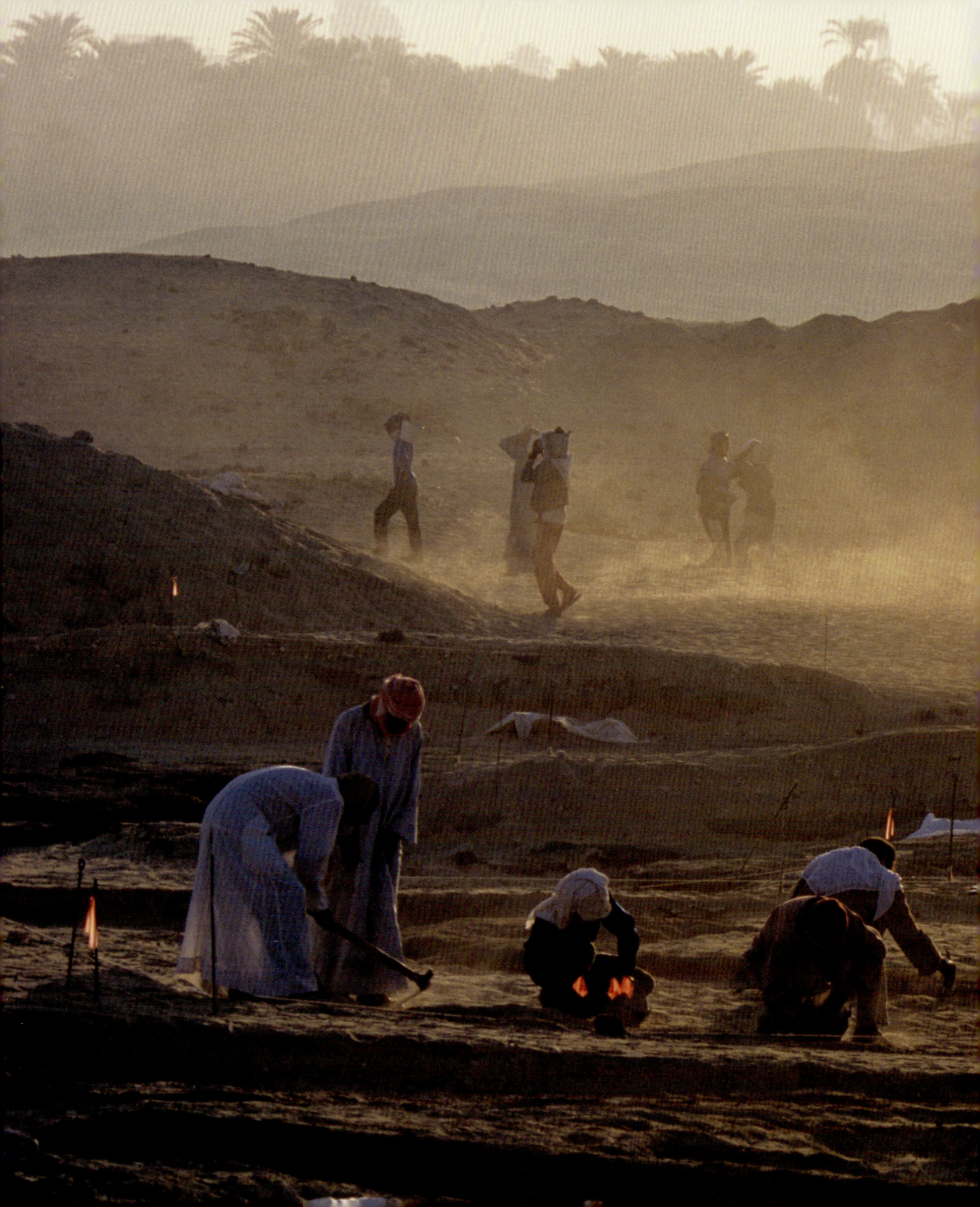

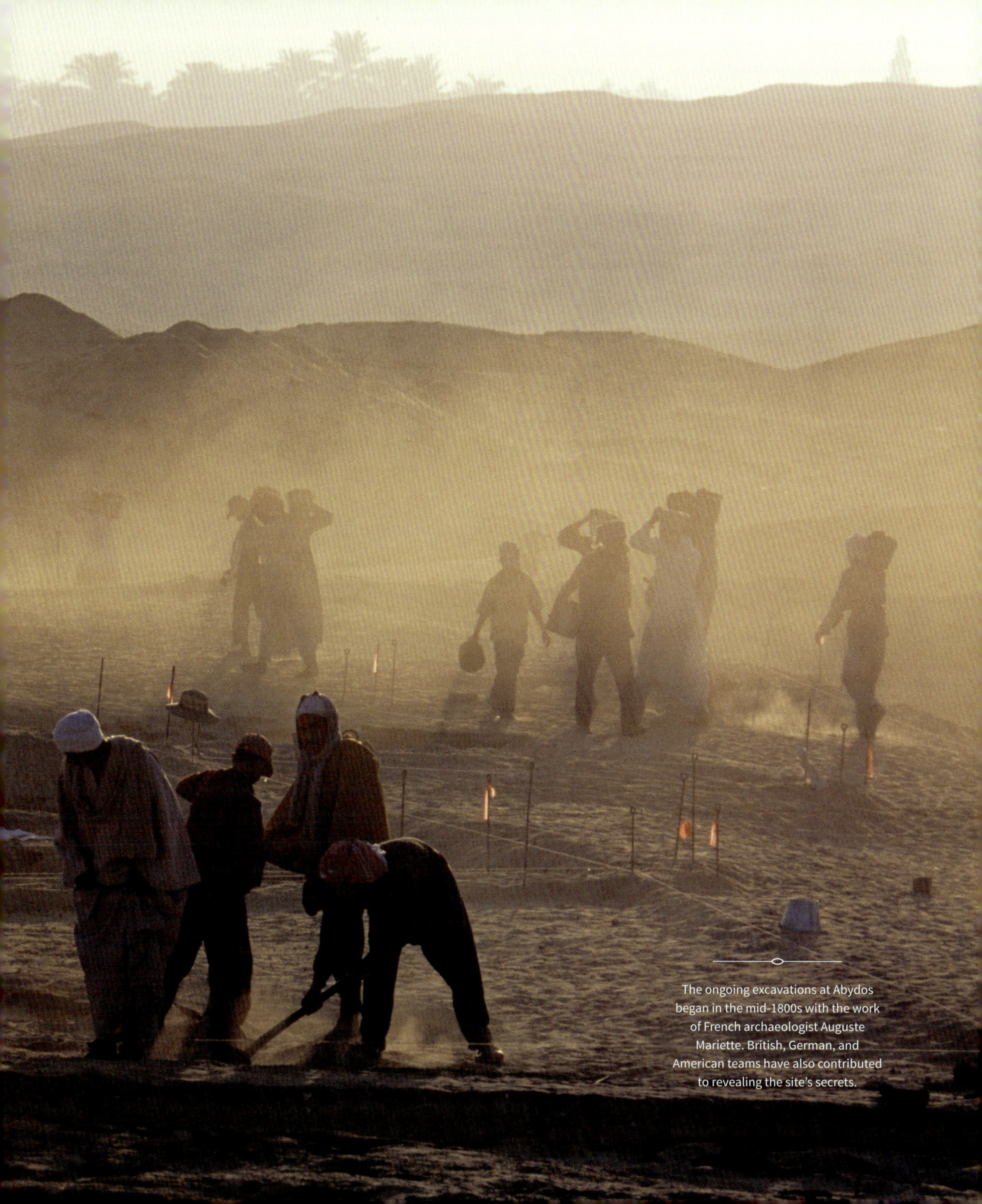

The ongoing excavations at Abydos began in the mid-1800s with the work of French archaeologist Auguste Mariette. British, German, and American teams have also contributed to revealing the site's secrets.

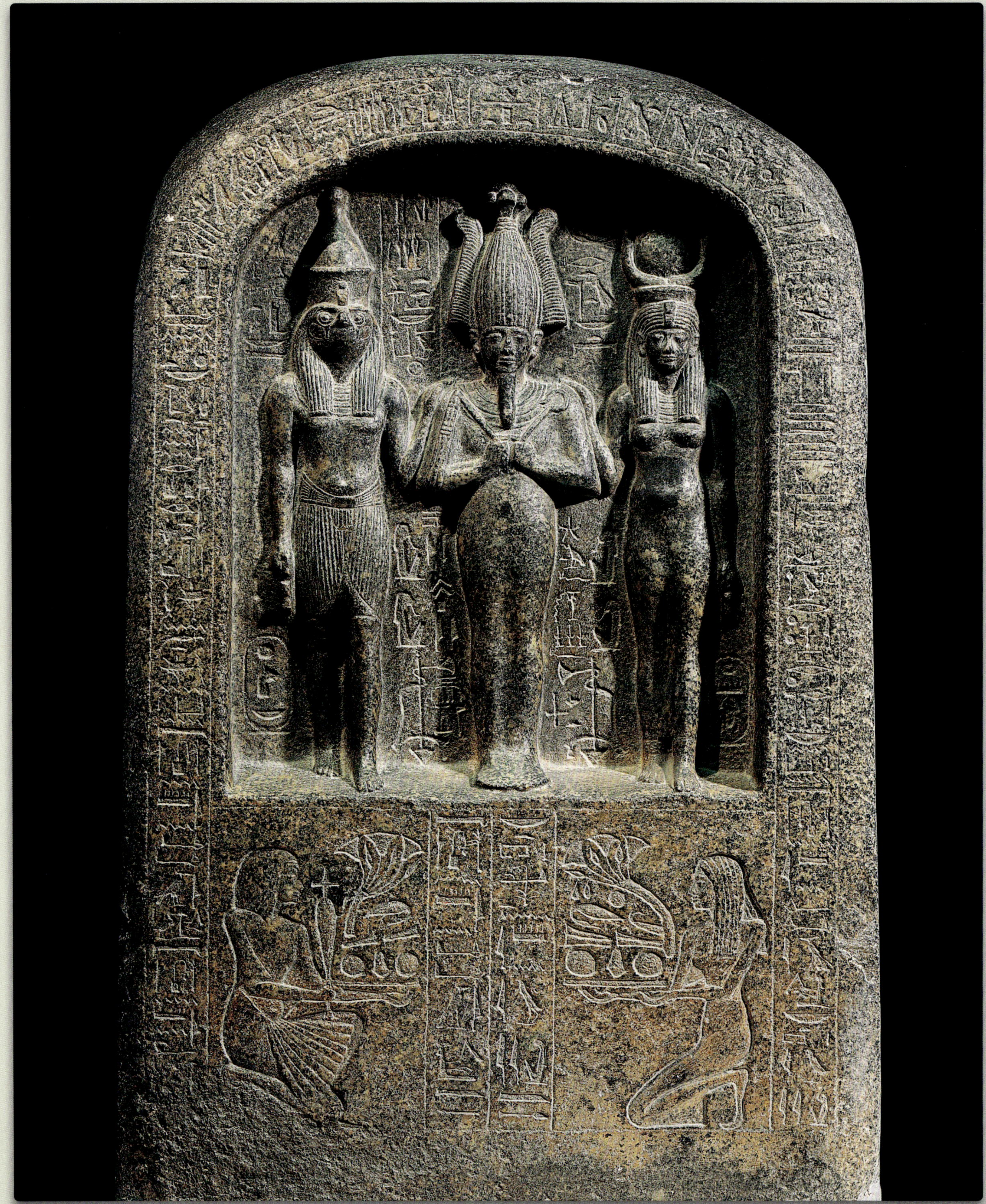

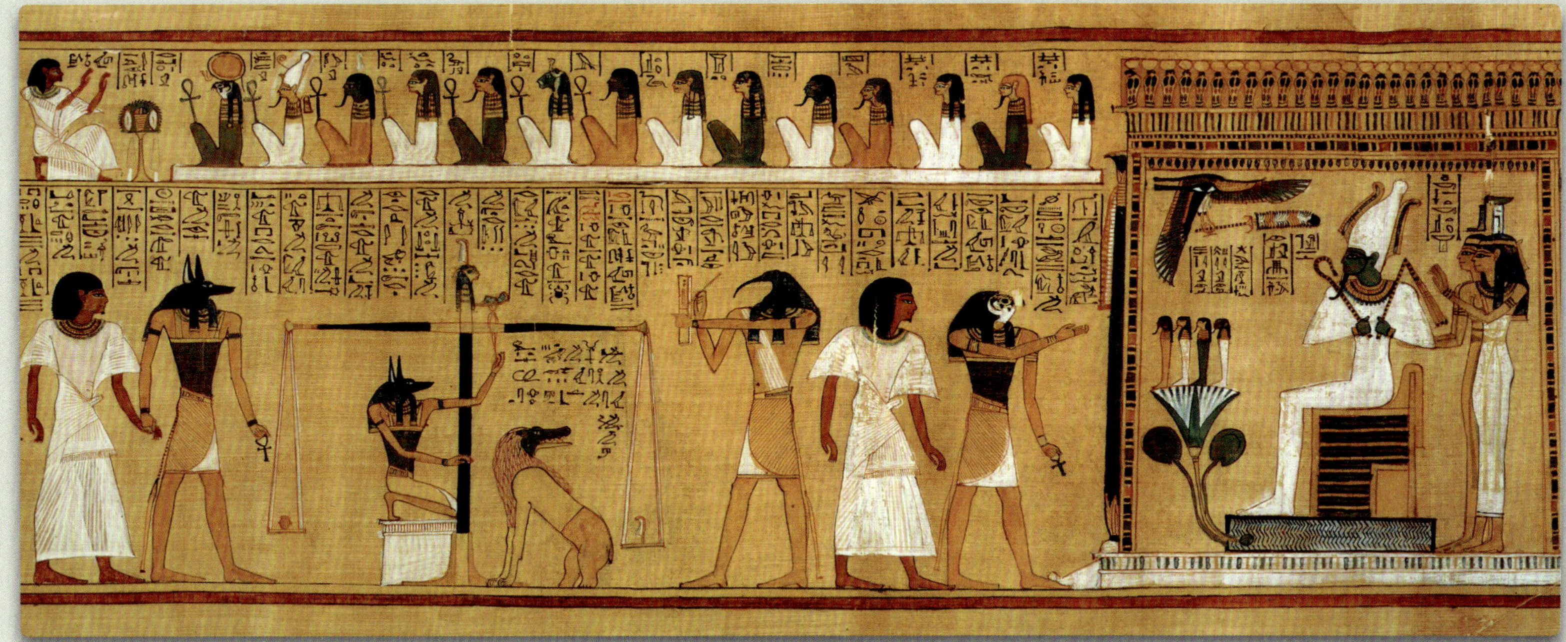

A Holy Trinity

ONE OF THE FOUNDATIONAL MYTHS of ancient Egyptian religion begins with the age-old drama of sibling rivalry. Osiris was an earthly king who ruled so wisely that his brother Seth became wildly jealous. Seth killed Osiris, dismembered his body, and scattered the pieces throughout Egypt.

Isis, Osiris's sister-wife, recovered those body parts, and Osiris was reassembled—but in the shape of a mummy. Osiris is often depicted in that form in Egyptian art, symbolizing rebirth and regeneration.

With her resurrected husband, Isis conceived a son, Horus—the trio depicted on this 19th-dynasty stela (opposite). In an epic struggle, Horus avenged his father. Osiris became king of the underworld—as depicted in this judgment scene on a 19th-dynasty papyrus (above)—Horus the divine ruler of this world, and Isis the model wife and mother.

Seth, relegated to the deserts, was the god of evil and chaos.

In time, folklore held that the tomb of a real king at Abydos was actually where Osiris was buried. People began to make pilgrimages to the site, leaving offerings in ceramic pots whose sherds now litter the sand. Some commoners even managed to be buried among the royalty at Abydos: an ultimate act of devotion and faith.

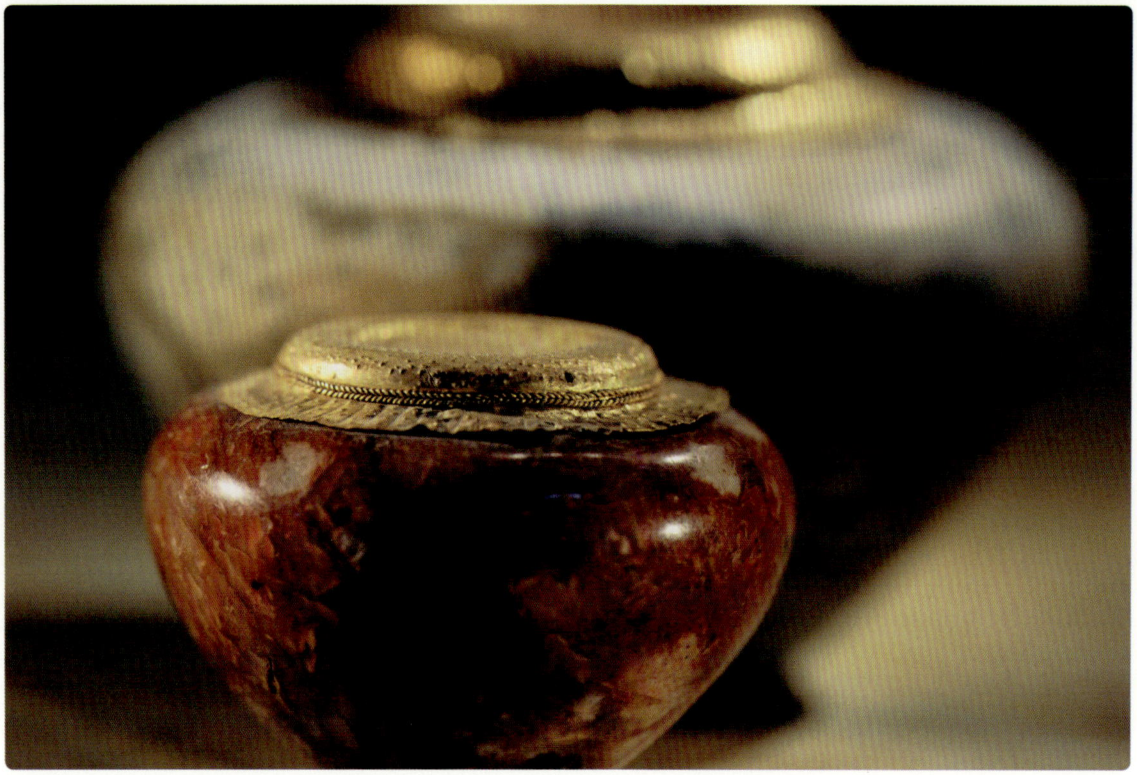

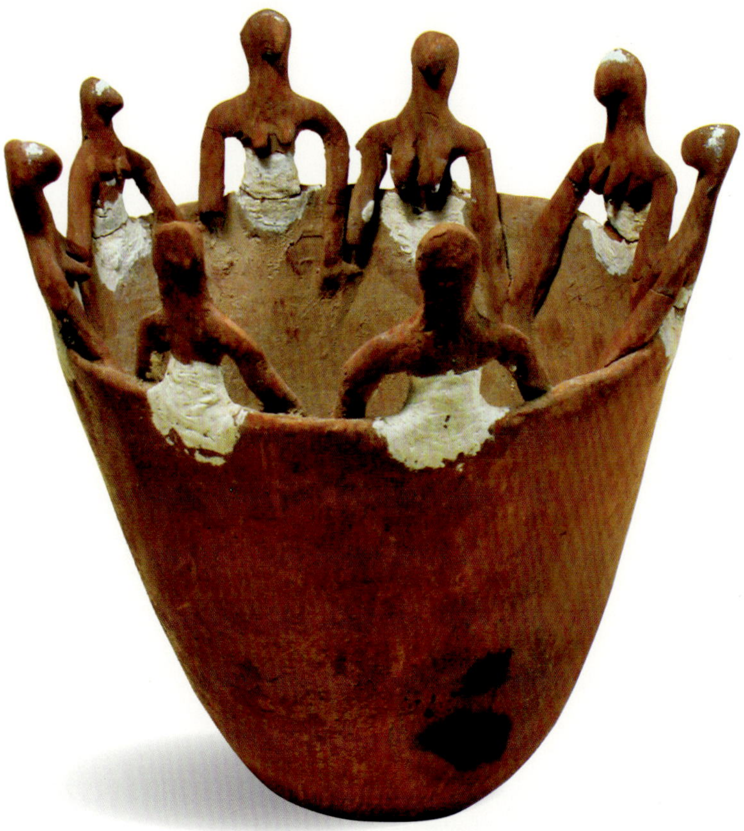

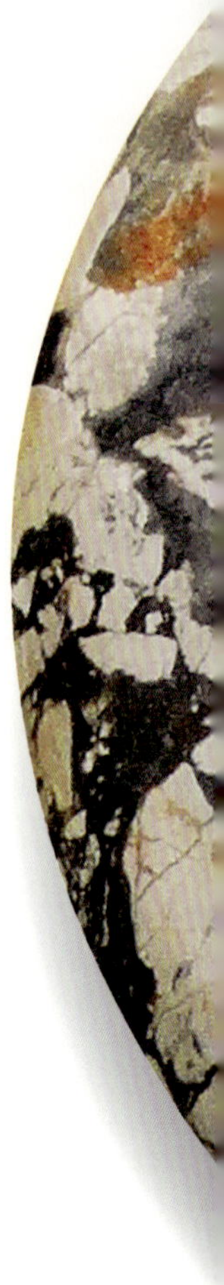

Funerary goods from the tomb of Khasekhemwy, the last king of the second dynasty (about 2650 B.C.), include more than 200 stone vases. Six of dolomite and one of carnelian (above) had gold caps.

The caps, as seen on this dolomite vessel (right), were meant to imitate the cloth covers of unguent containers tied on with a string. A clay seal bore the name of the owner.

A unique predynastic vase (left) from about 3700 B.C. was found in the grave of a premature baby at Abydos. The eight female figures retain traces of the bitumen wigs they originally wore.

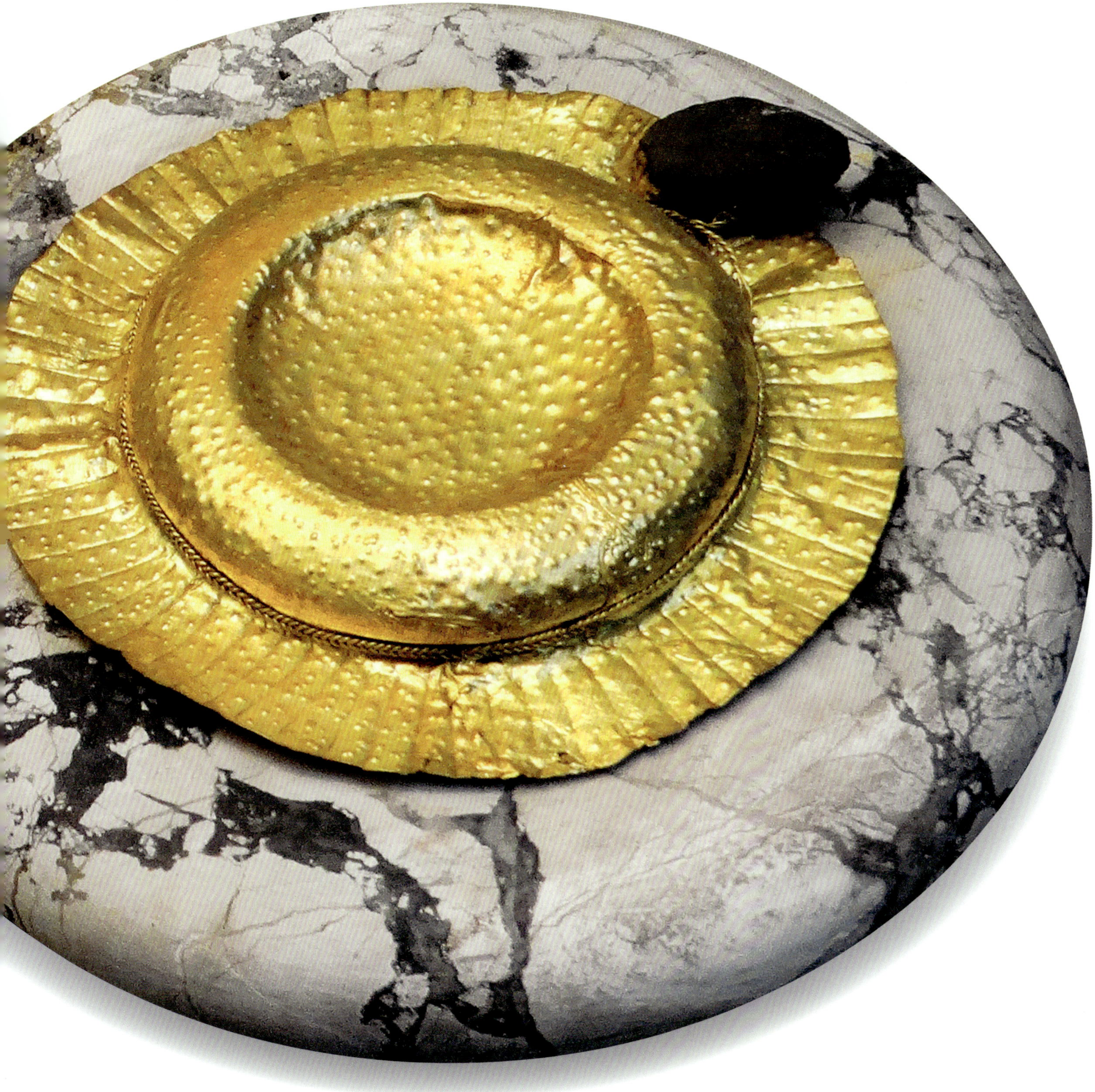

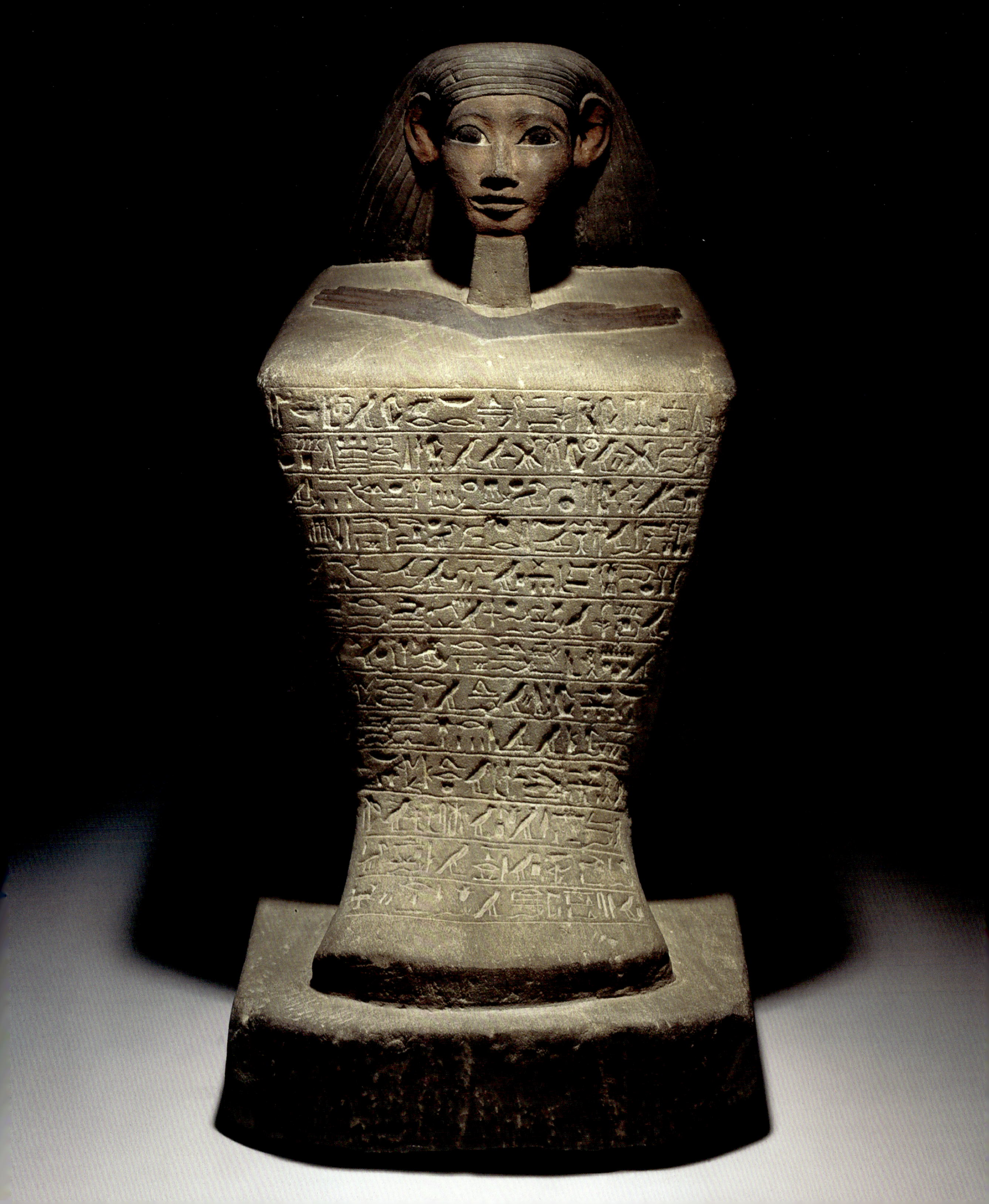

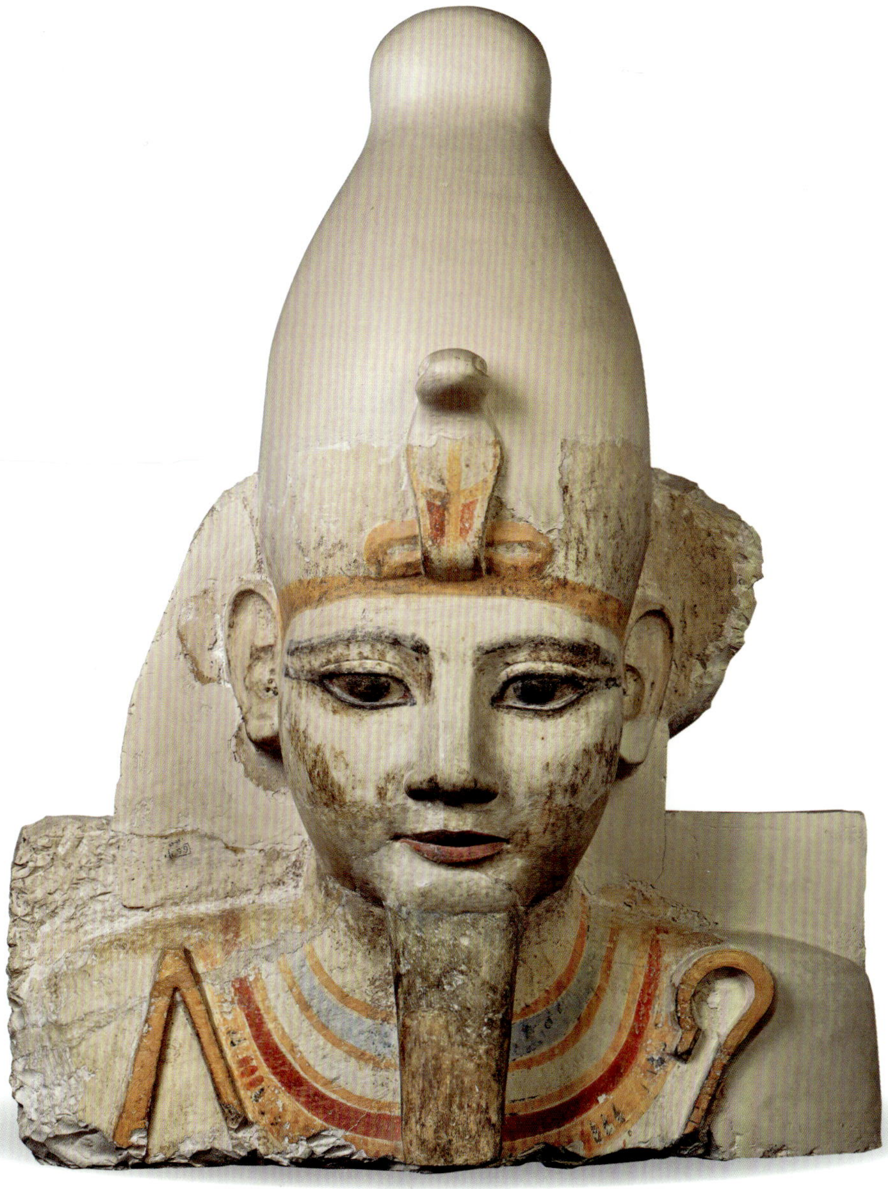

This statue of Sitepehu (opposite), an overseer of priests who is seated and wears a long cloak, was found in his tomb at Abydos. He served during the reign of Queen Hatshepsut (about 1470 B.C.).

More than five feet (1.5 m) tall, a limestone portrait (above) of Ramses II (about 1279–1213 B.C.) once belonged to a colossal statue decorating a rectangular pillar in a temple courtyard at Abydos.

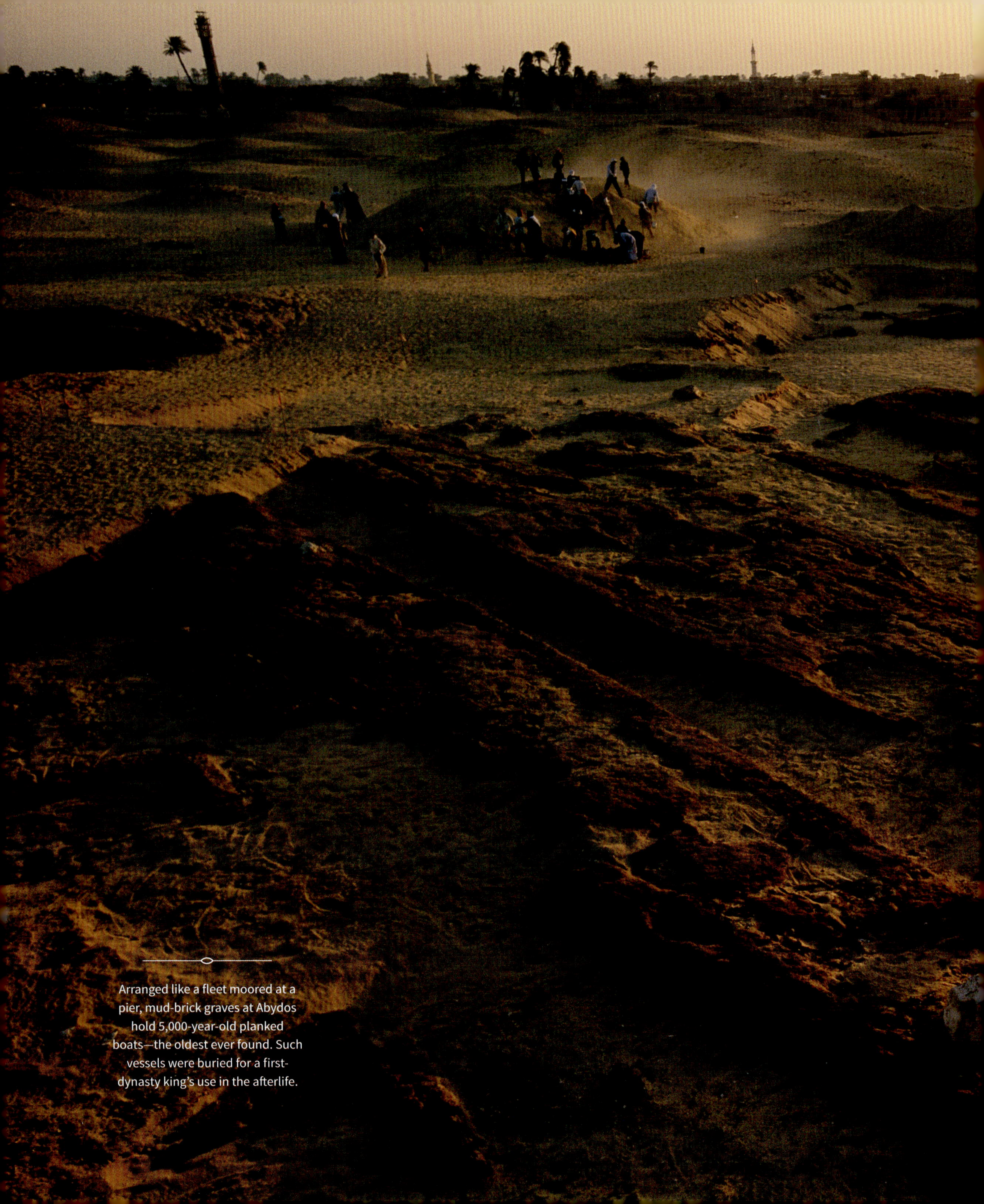

Arranged like a fleet moored at a pier, mud-brick graves at Abydos hold 5,000-year-old planked boats—the oldest ever found. Such vessels were buried for a first-dynasty king's use in the afterlife.

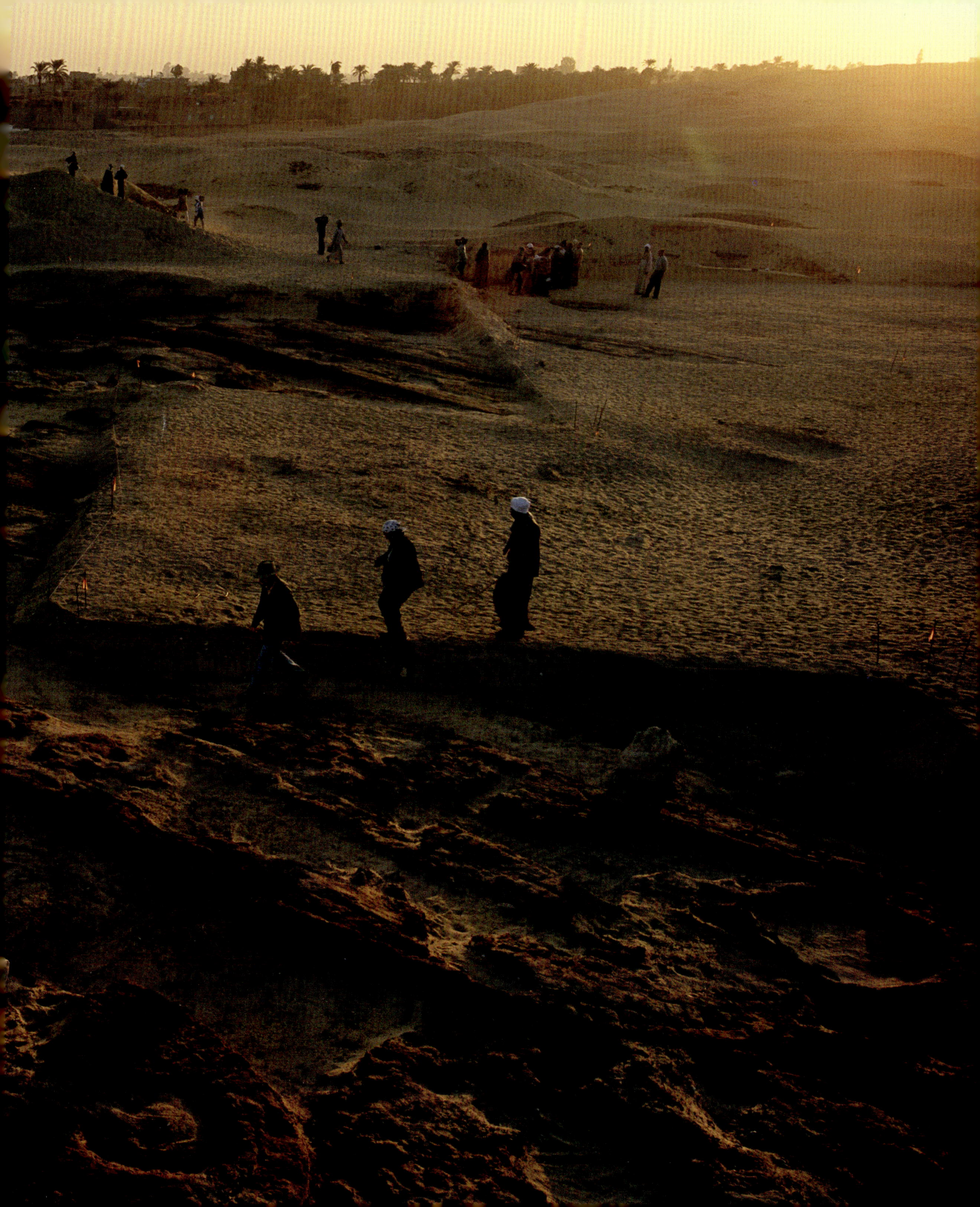

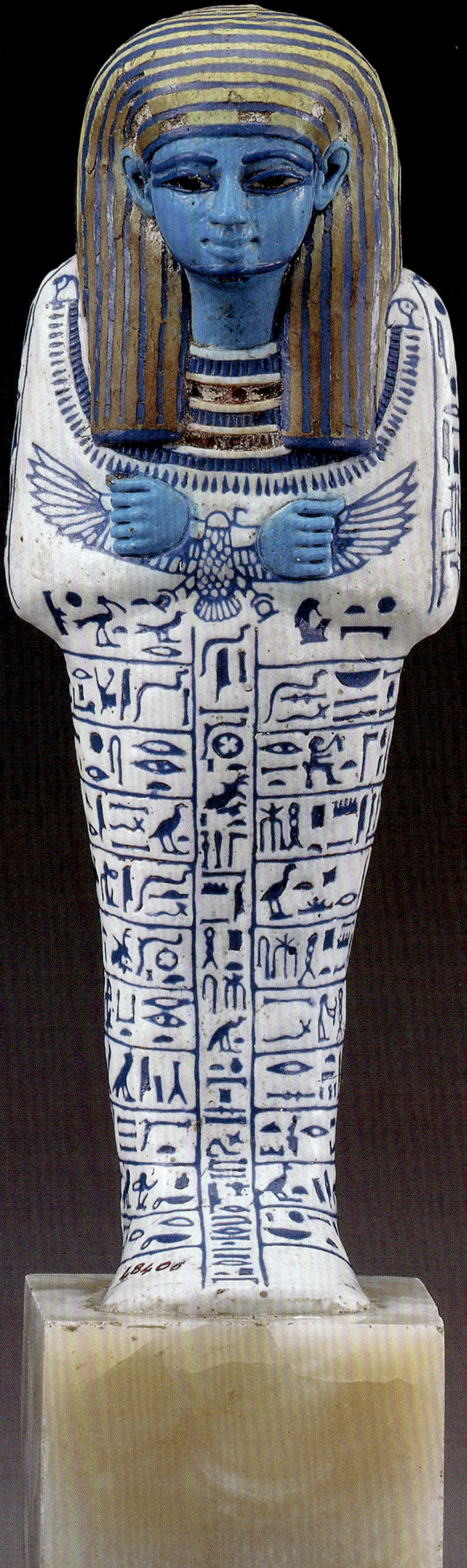

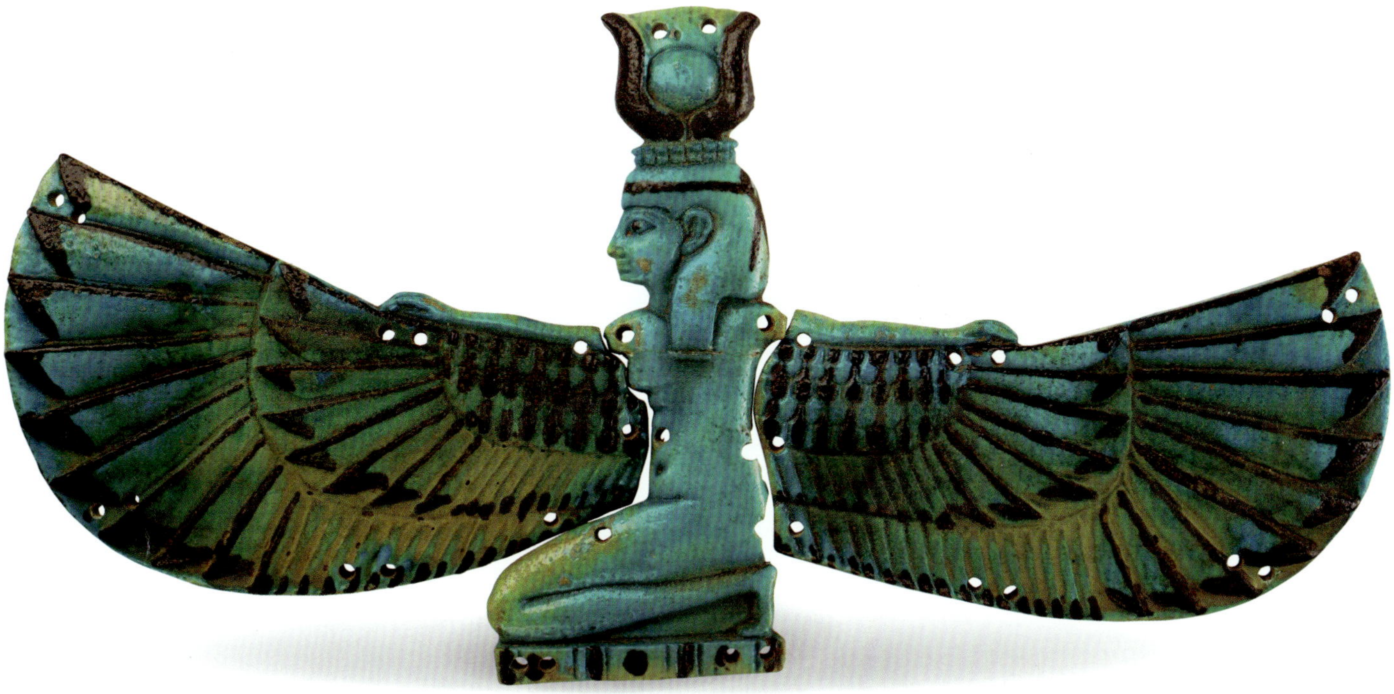

Likely from Abydos, this winged goddess (above) dates to sometime between 1295 and 712 B.C. Holes would have allowed the figure to be attached to a mummy's wrappings or to a net laid atop those wrappings.

A *senet* game set (below) from about 1450 B.C., now restored, was found in an Abydos tomb. The game was sometimes included in funerary goods because of its association with the journey to the afterlife.

This shabti, or servant figurine (opposite), was created to work in the afterlife of a man named Ptahmose, a vizier, mayor, and high priest of Amun during the reign of Amenhotep III (about 1390–1353 B.C.).

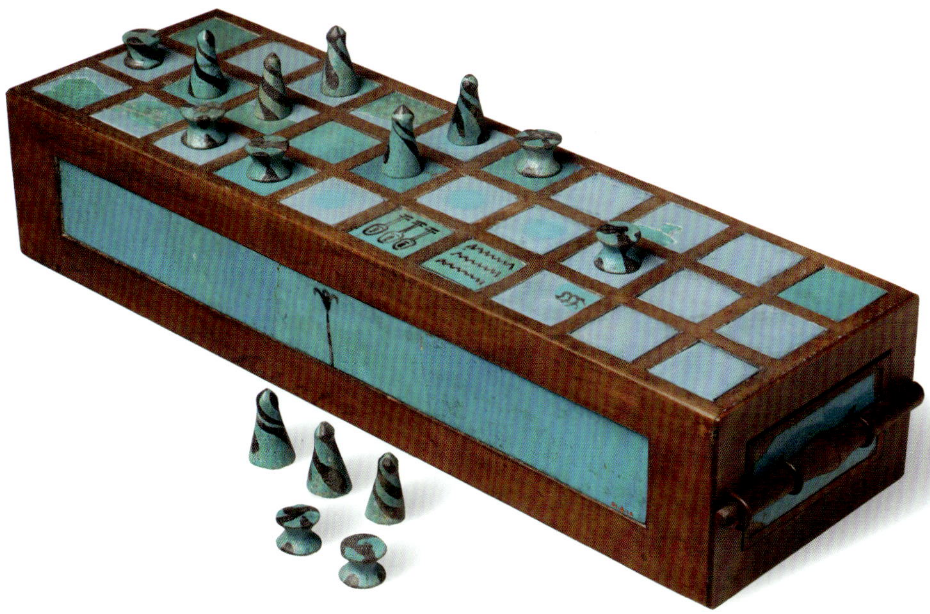

From the start of the pharaonic era, artisans produced jewelry with striking colors and compositions. These bracelets were found on a mummified forearm in the tomb of first-dynasty king Djer (about 2950 B.C.). They may have belonged to a royal female whose remains were torn apart by looters centuries after her burial. In the top bracelet, alternating gold and turquoise beads take the shape of a serekh: a palace façade, topped by a falcon, that was used to frame a king's name. The turquoise was likely mined in the Sinai Peninsula, the gold in Nubia. Other bracelets include lapis lazuli, likely from Afghanistan, and amethyst, probably from the Eastern Desert.

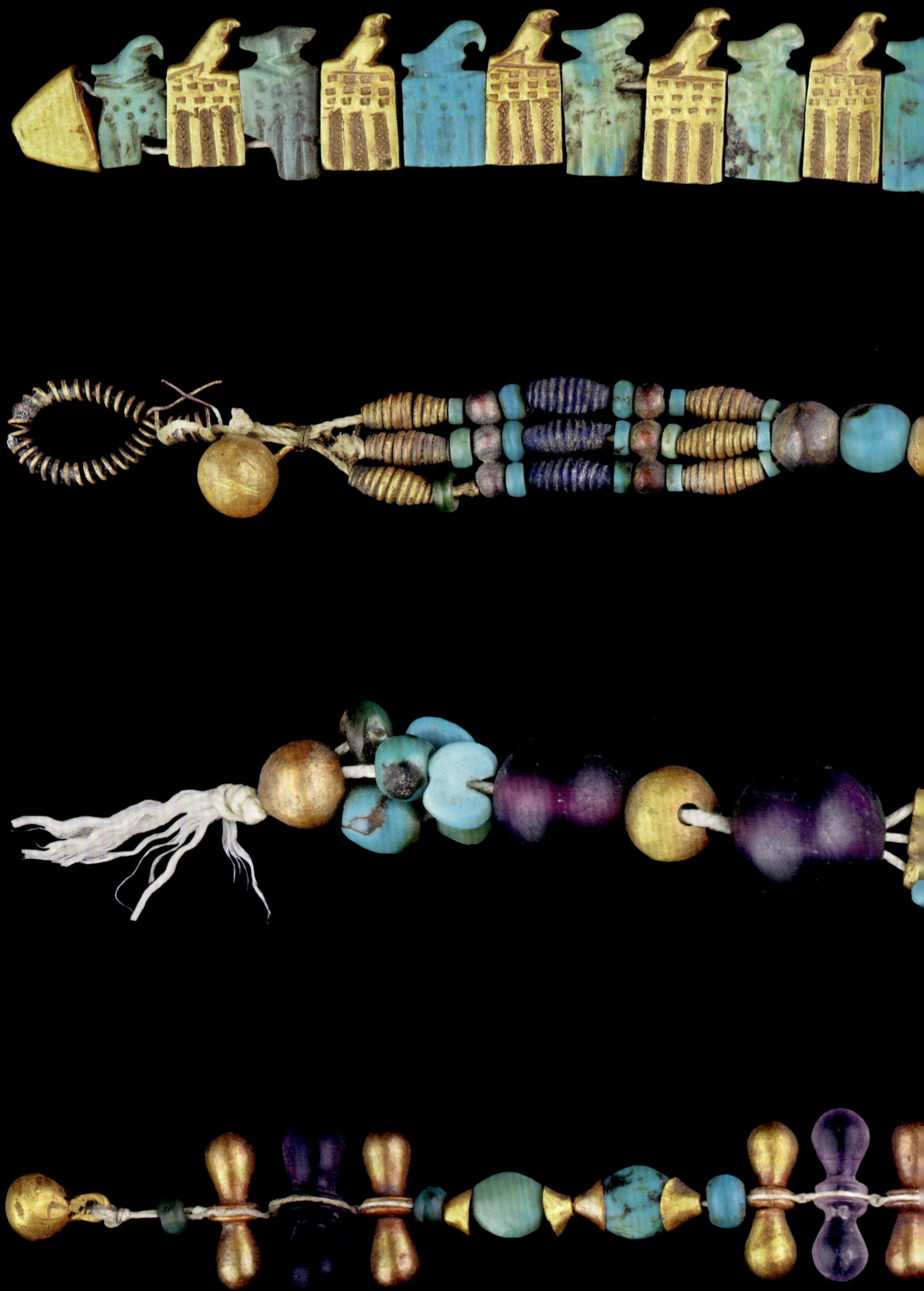

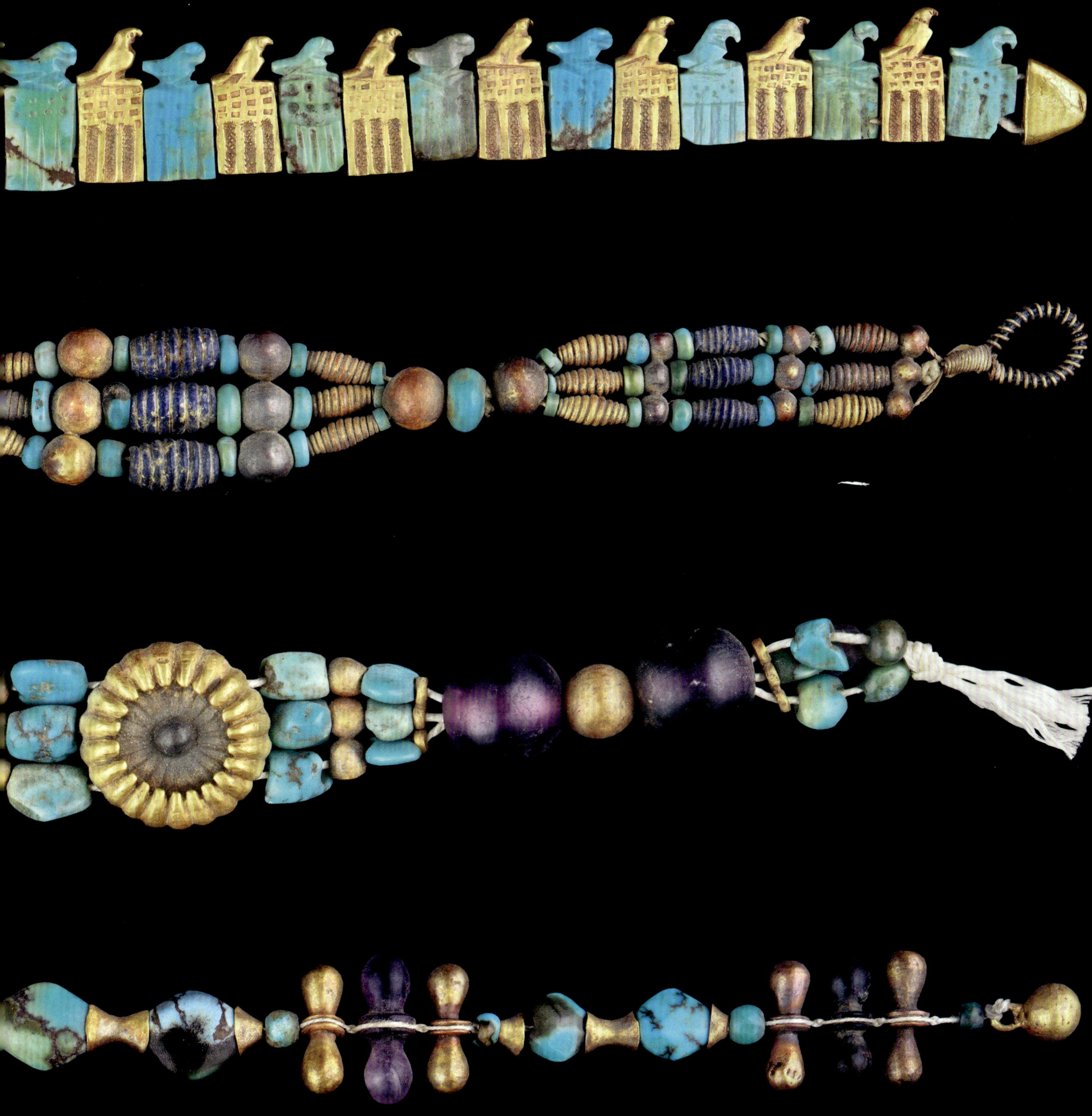

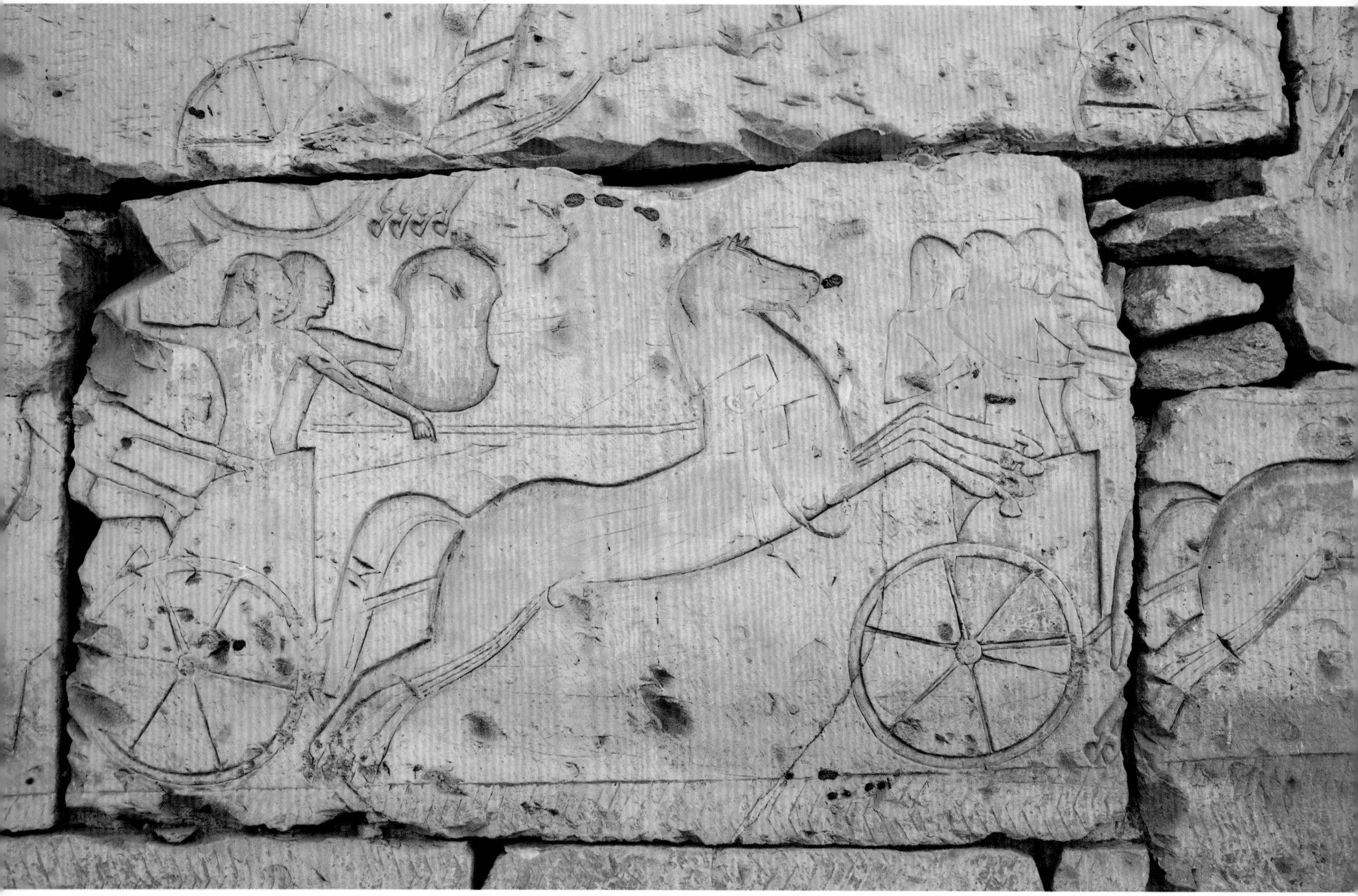

On a temple wall at Abydos, Ramses II appears in his famous battle against the Hittites at Kadesh in 1275 B.C. Horses and light chariots had been introduced to Egypt several centuries earlier.

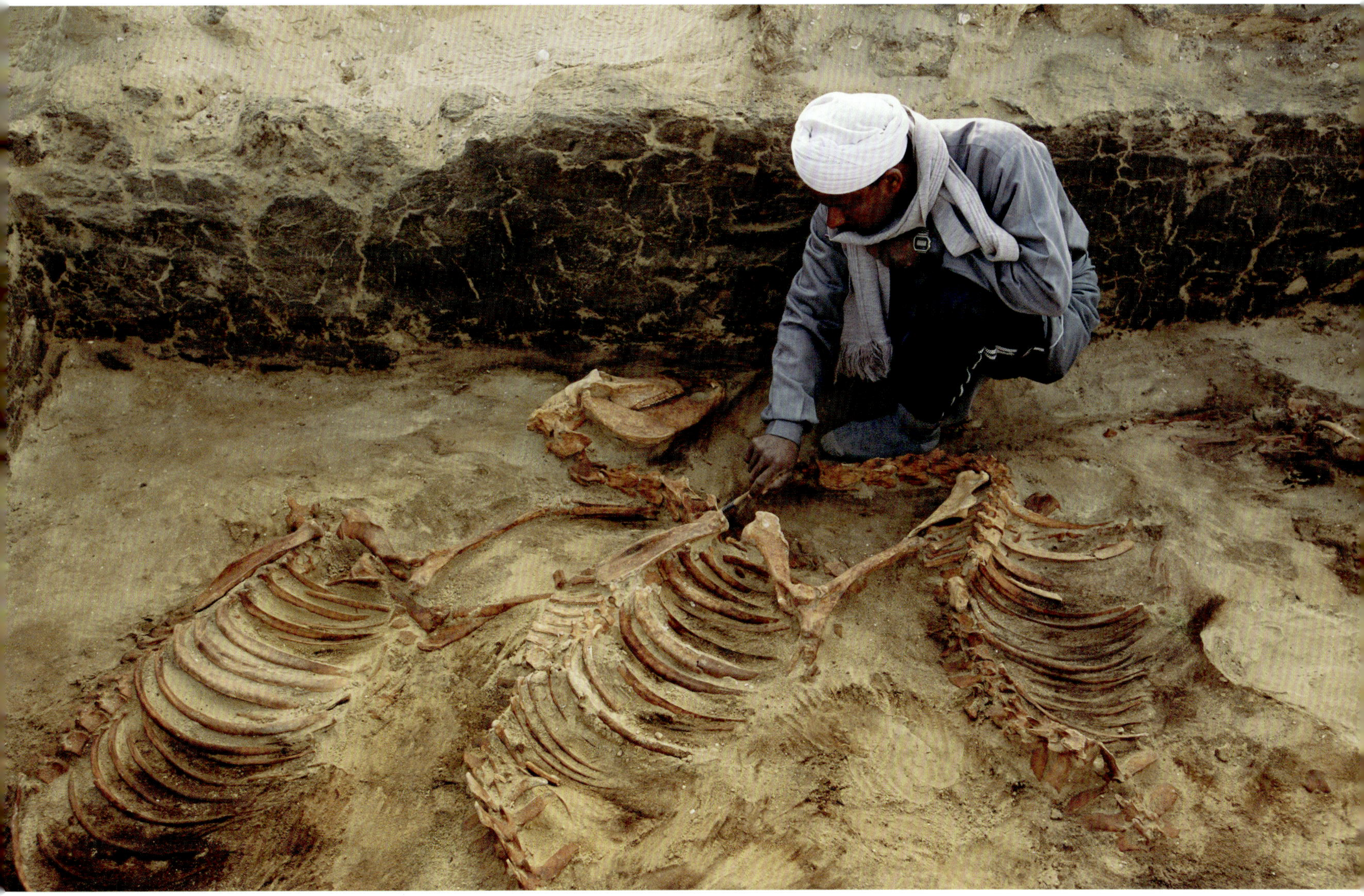

Donkeys that had worked as pack animals were sacrificed and reverently laid to rest at Abydos in about 3000 B.C. They were meant to serve in the afterlife of an early king whose name is currently unknown.

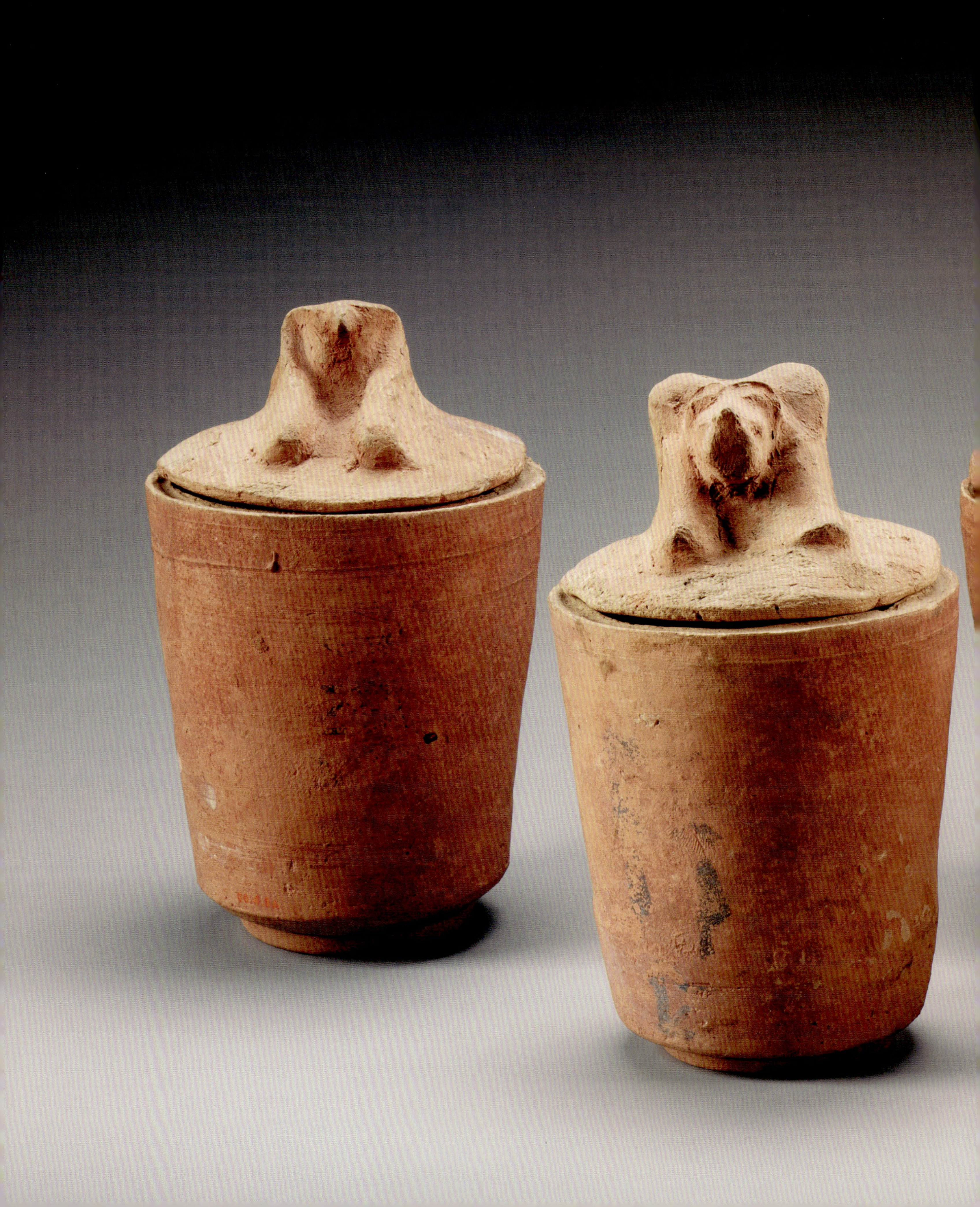

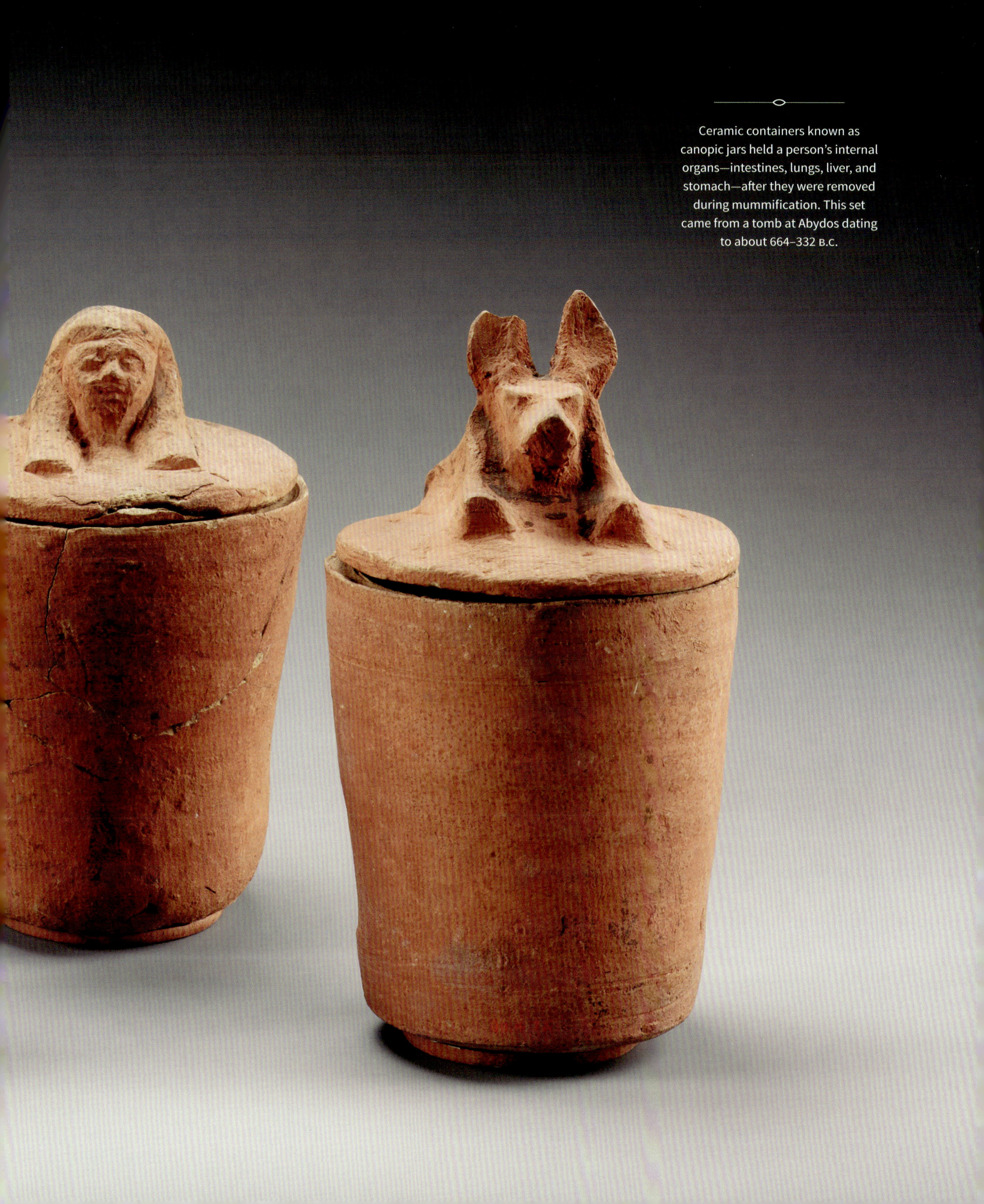

Ceramic containers known as canopic jars held a person's internal organs—intestines, lungs, liver, and stomach—after they were removed during mummification. This set came from a tomb at Abydos dating to about 664–332 B.C.

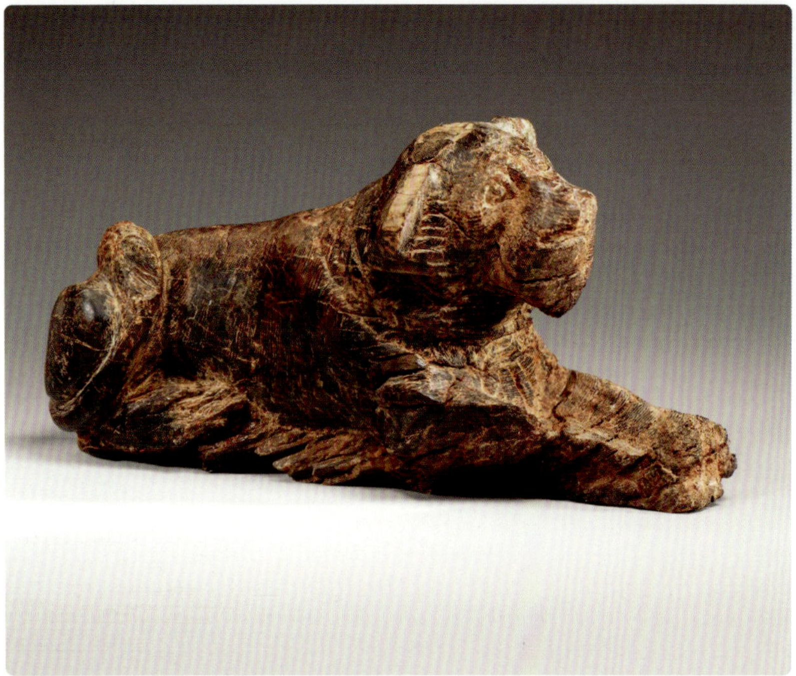

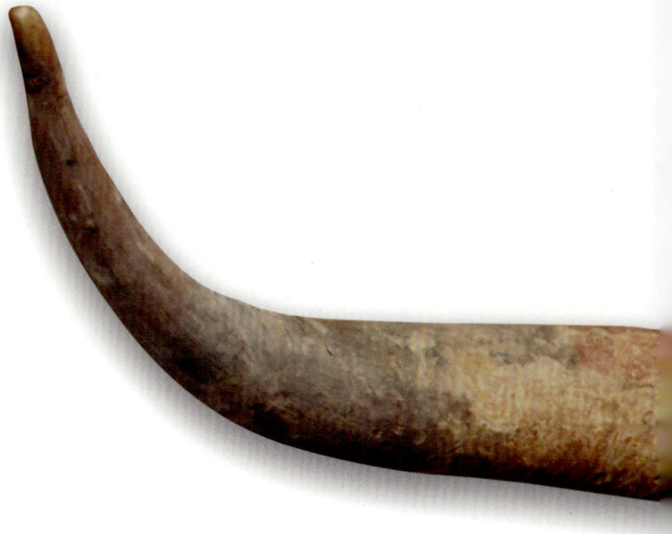

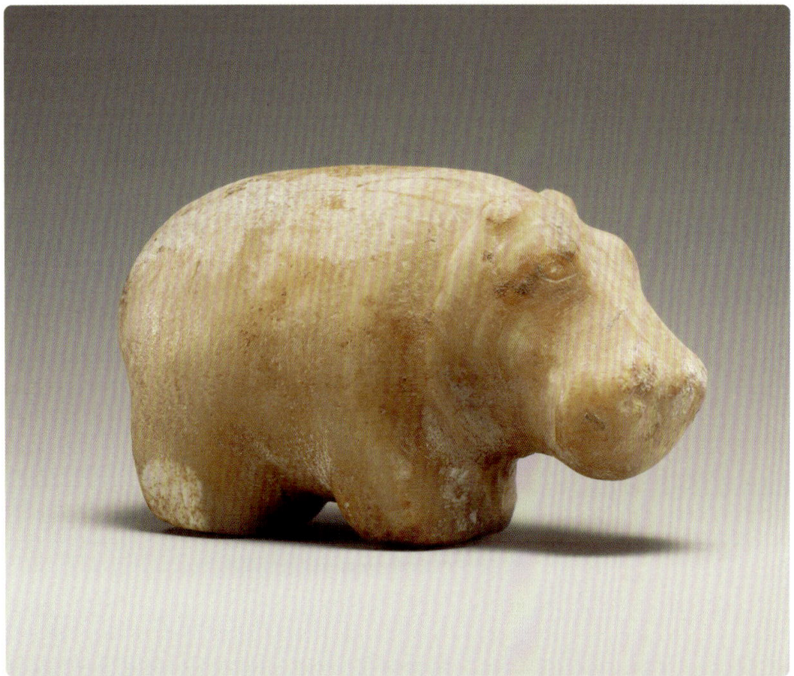

A lion carved from ivory (top left) was found in the Osiris temple at Abydos. Dated to about 3100–2649 B.C., it was likely a piece from a game called *mehen,* played on a board shaped like a coiled snake.

A steatite hippopotamus (bottom left) from about 3100–2649 B.C. came from a deposit near a shrine at Abydos. It was likely a gift to Khentiamentiu, an ancient deity associated with the necropolis there.

A painted bull's cranium (right) from about 1640–1550 B.C. likely marked a grave at Abydos. The deceased would have been one of the Medjay, nomads who often worked as warriors and desert police.

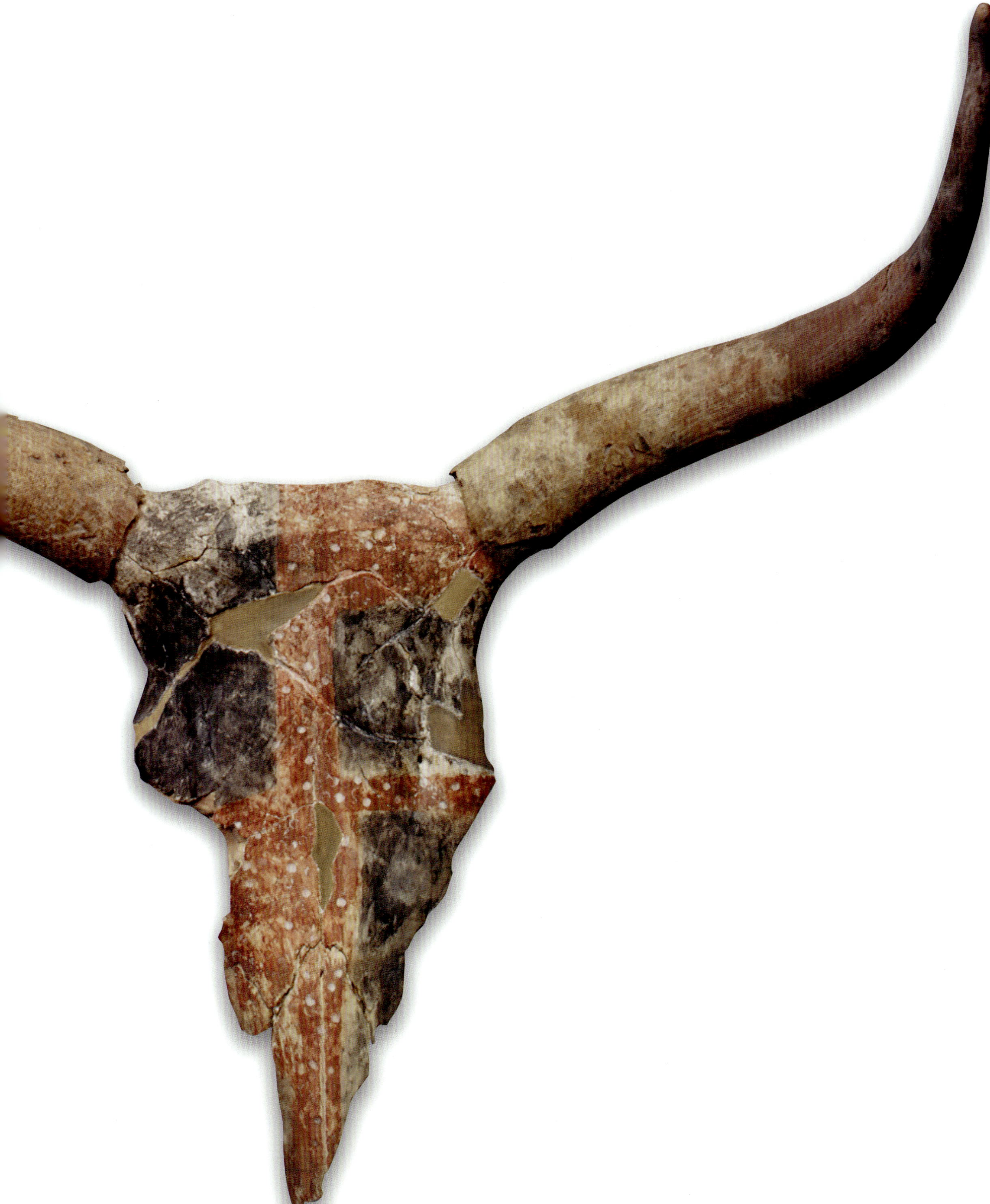

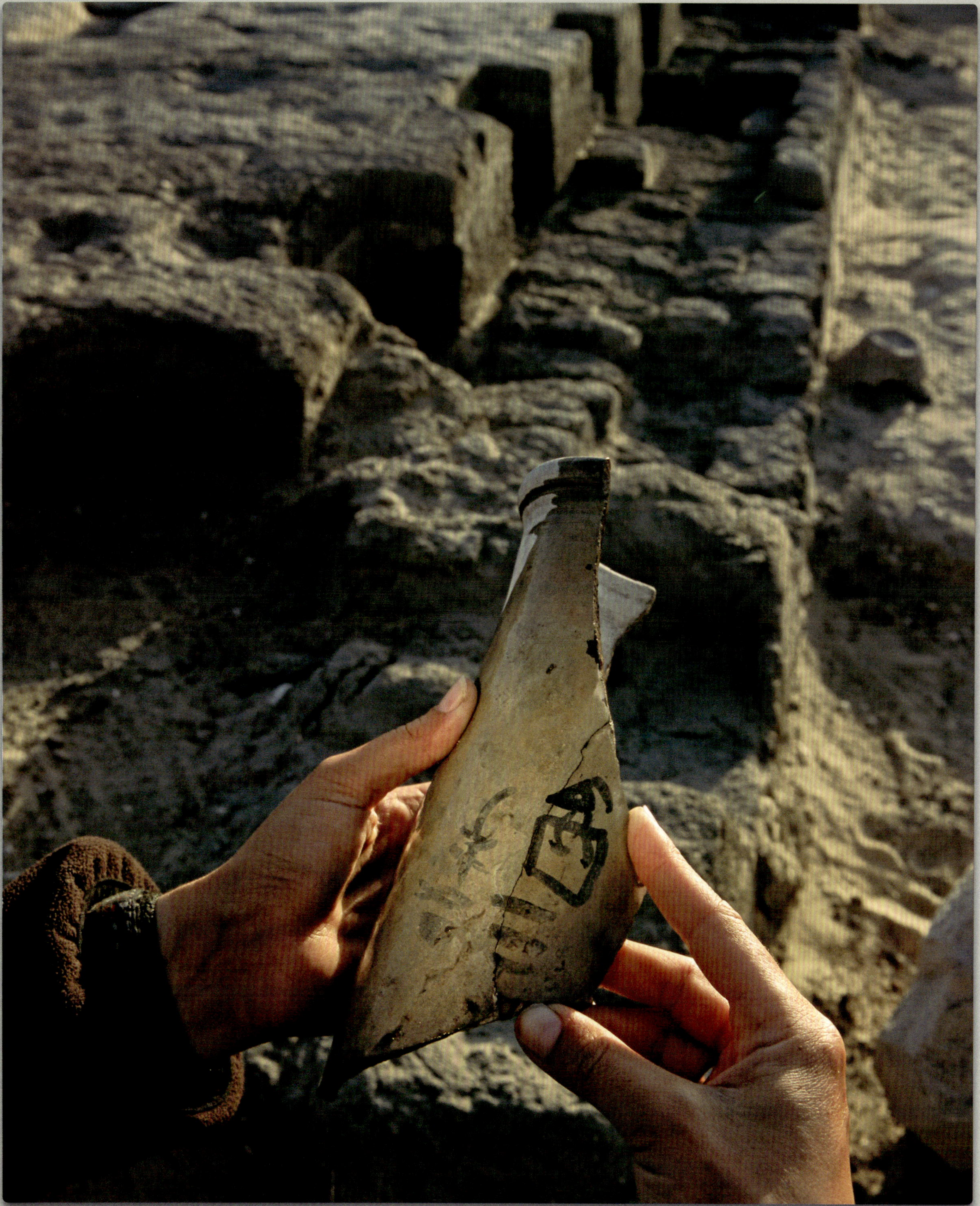

DIGGING DEEPER

What's in a Name?

AS KINGSHIP EMERGED in southern Egypt, artists began to write royal names on all sorts of objects. A jar fragment found at Abydos (opposite) bears the hastily rendered name of early ruler Hor-Aha. The same name appears more clearly on this vase fragment (below): In a symbol called a *serekh,* hieroglyphs spelling the royal moniker appear above a stylized early dynastic palace façade, with a rectangular wall enclosing everything. A falcon representing Horus, the god who protected the king throughout Egyptian history, stands above the serekh. Narmer's Palette, a carved stone from Hierakonpolis that commemorated the country's unification, also bears this symbol. The name Narmer is expressed as a catfish *(nar)* and a chisel *(mer)*.

Beginning in the fourth dynasty, the king's name was written inside an oval. When Napoleon Bonaparte's army invaded Egypt in 1798, soldiers called the oval forms *cartouches*—their word for gun cartridges—because of the similar shape. The oval, representing the loop of a knotted rope, symbolized protection—and perhaps even the sun encircling the universe.

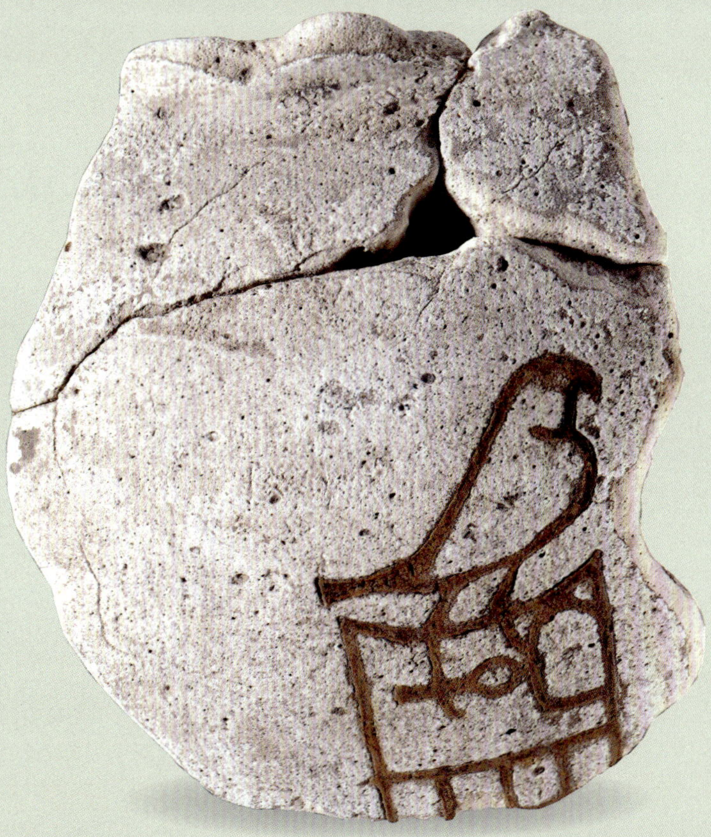

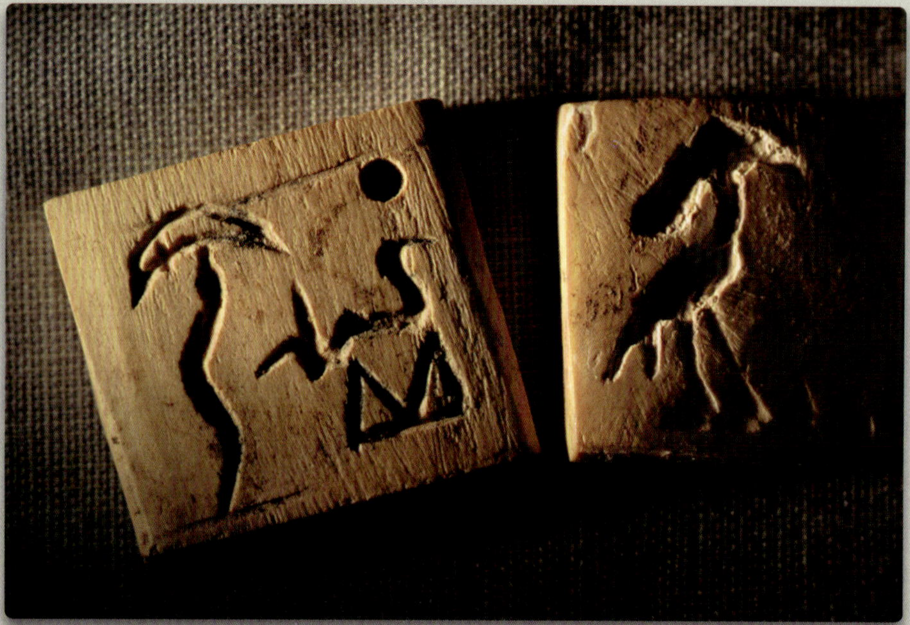

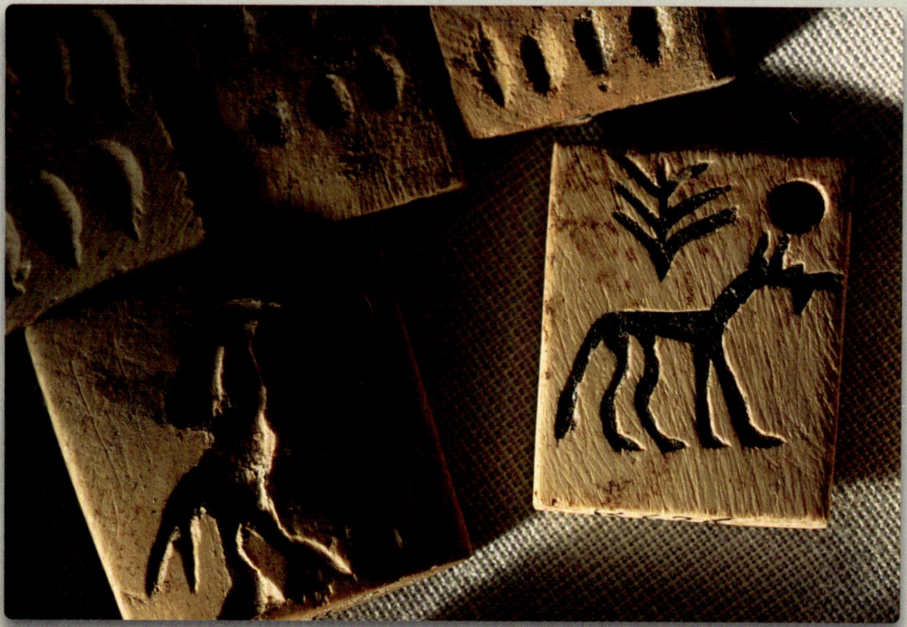

EARLY WORDS

Less than an inch (2.5 cm) wide, these inscribed bone tags (top and bottom left) were buried with a predynastic king at Abydos. Dated to about 3200 B.C., they are Egypt's oldest known artifacts with writing. The tags were once attached to containers—likely cedar chests—and recorded quantities of goods such as grain and textiles, as well as the places the products came from.

The name of Queen Merneith appears on a limestone stela found at Abydos (opposite). The consort of Djer, an early king (about 2950 B.C.), Merneith likely acted as regent for her underage son Den when he took the throne.

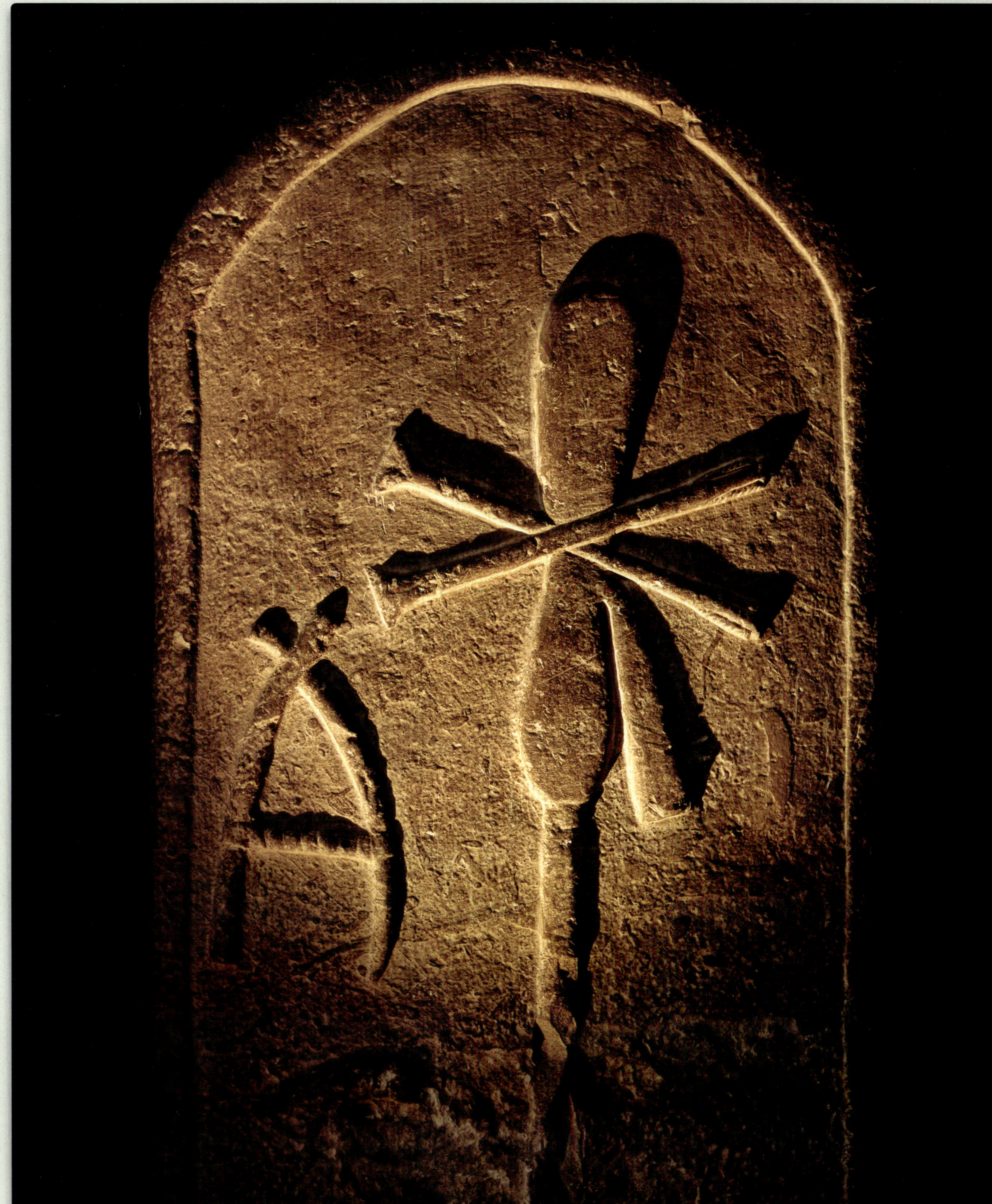

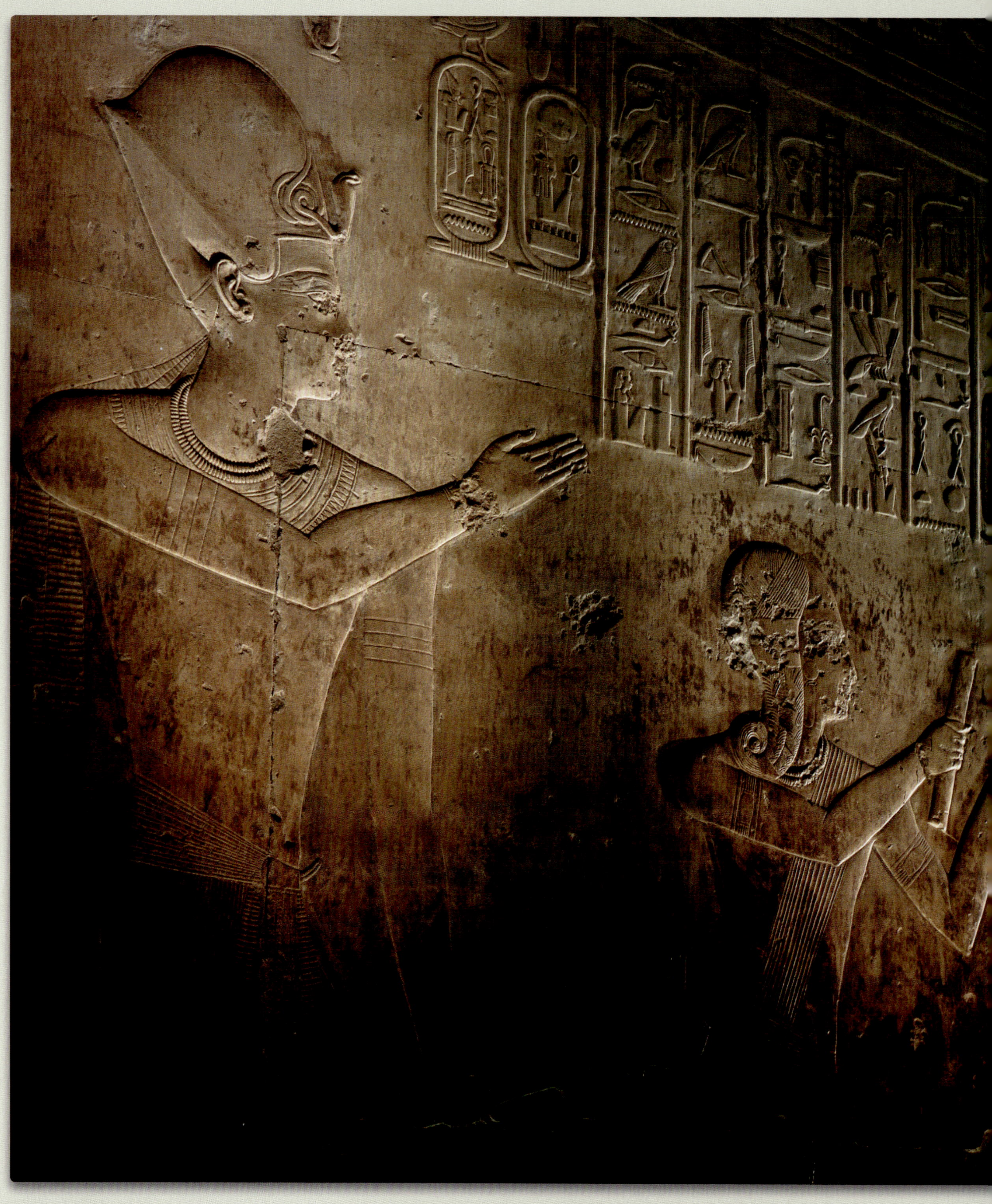

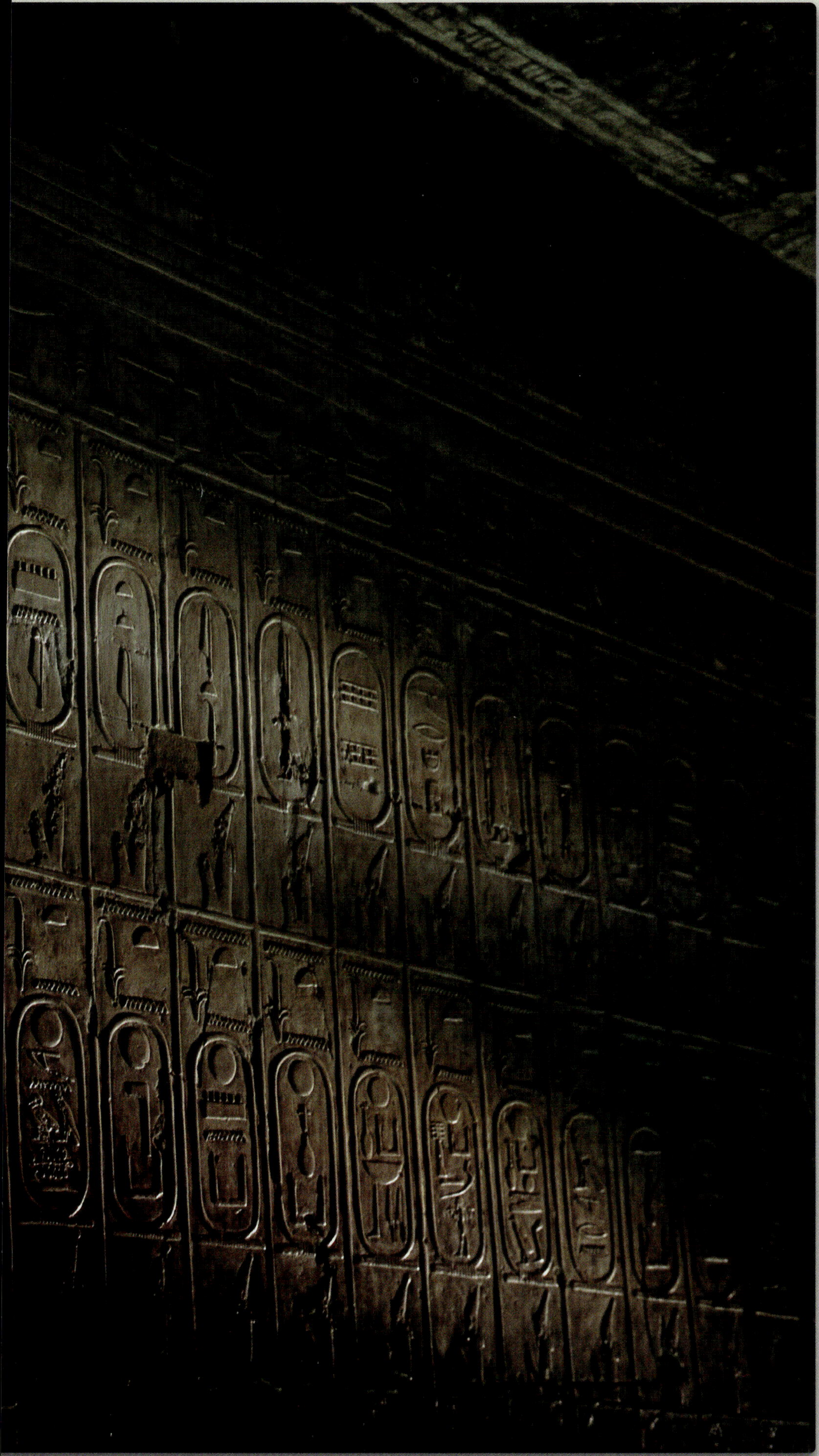

LINES OF SUCCESSION

Inscribed on a wall of Seti I's temple at Abydos, one of the most complete surviving chronological king lists includes the names of 76 rulers. Accompanied by his son Ramses, at far left, Seti gestures toward cartouches that begin with Menes, the traditional first king of a unified Egypt (about 2950 B.C.), and end with Seti himself (about 1290–1279 B.C.). However, some rulers, such as the heretic Akhenaten, are omitted.

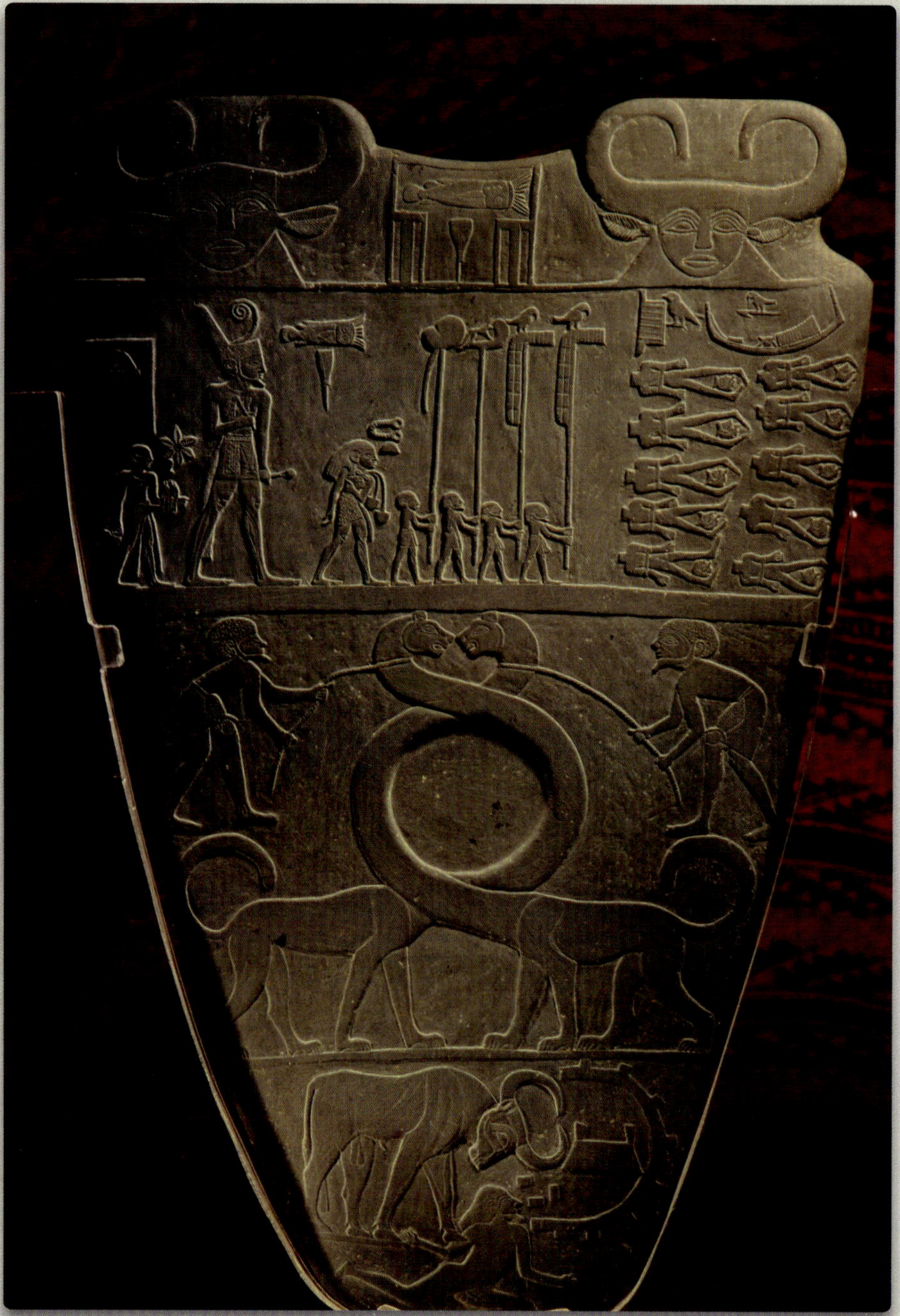

MOMENTS OF TRIUMPH

Imitating a palette normally used to mix mineral cosmetics, a monumental carved stone commemorates the unification of Egypt by King Menes, also known as Narmer. Dating to about 2950 B.C., it was ritually buried with other objects in a cache at Hierakonpolis.

On one side (opposite), the king is shown smiting an enemy. In an upper register on the other side (above), he parades before his defeated and decapitated foes.

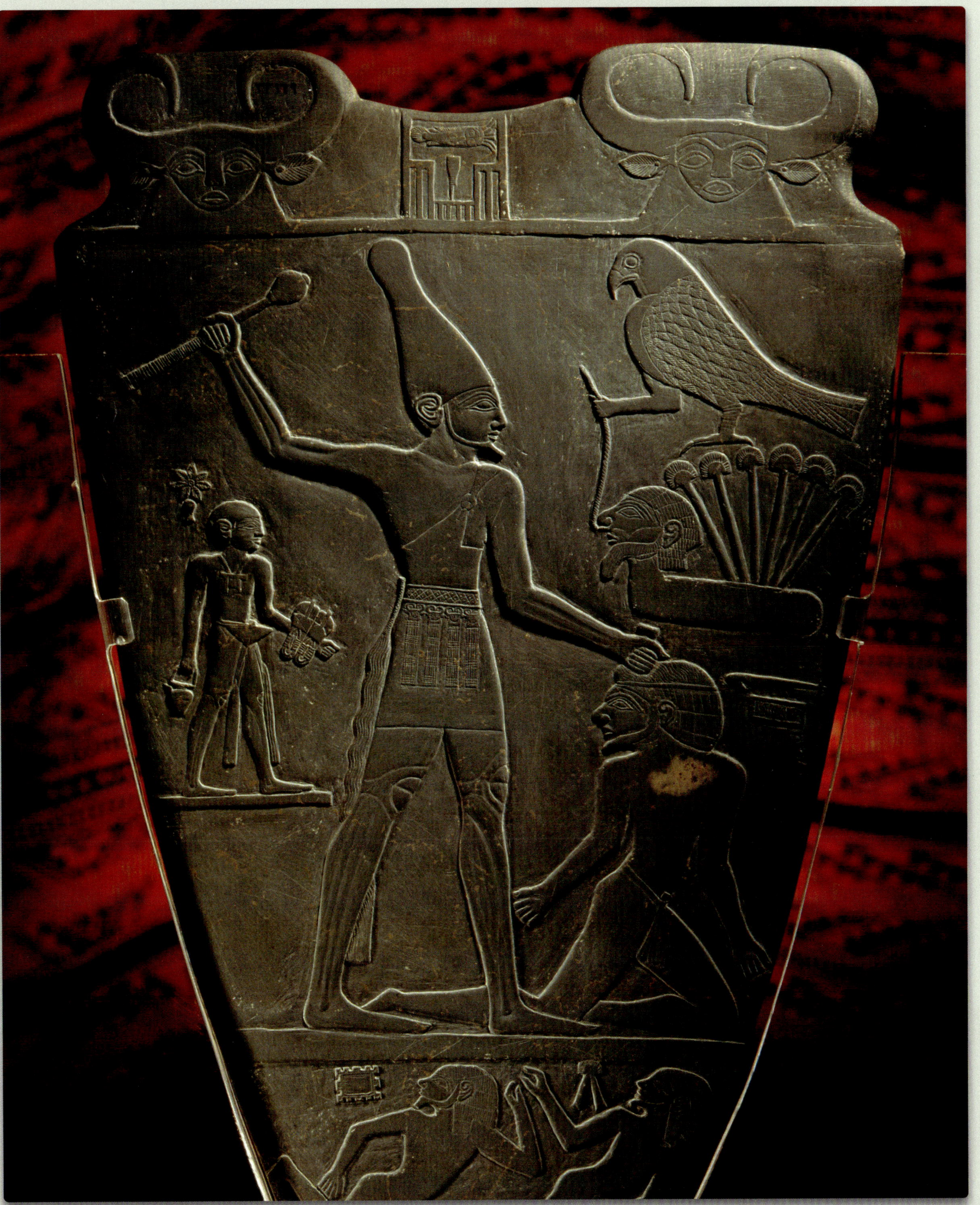

CHAPTER TWO

THE NILE

Timeless Waters

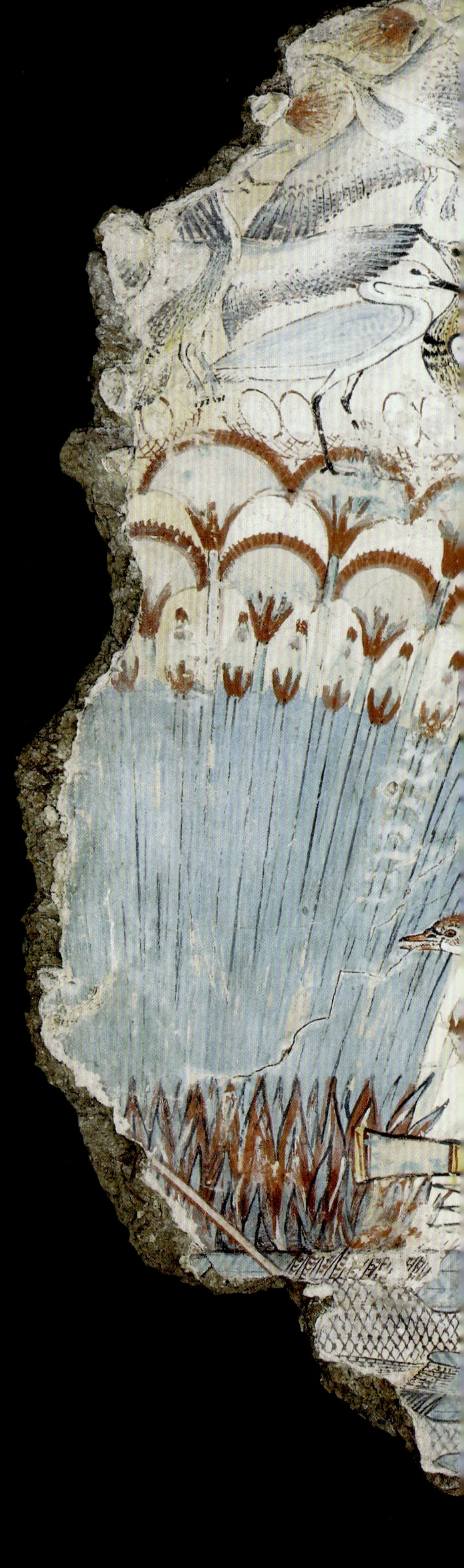

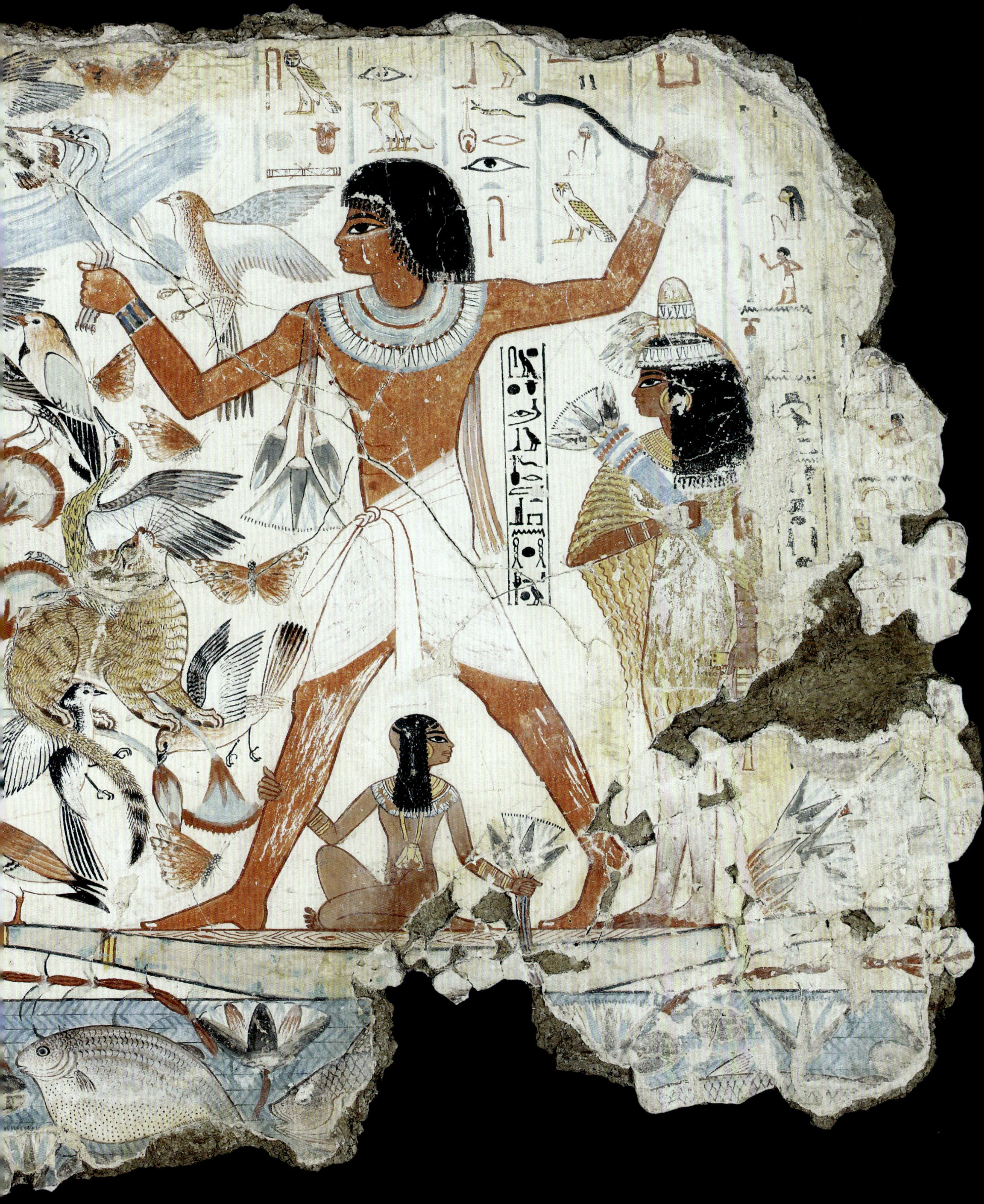

AMID THE CITIES and towns of modern Egypt that increasingly sprawl along the country's storied waterway, there are still places between Aswan in the far south and Alexandria in the north that offer glimpses of what the riverscape was like in the days of the pharaohs. There are stretches where clear water ripples over rocks and sand, where palm trees line the river's banks, and where the currents swirl past rocky desert cliffs gilded by the sun. The Nile still dominates the geography of Egypt, as it did in antiquity. But millennia ago, it was untamed and imposed its own rhythm on the land.

Those many centuries ago, Egypt was a country of mostly farmers. Every year between June and September, the river swelled from the monsoon rains that fell far to the south. The Egyptians called this season *akhet,* the time when the Nile overran its banks and spread across the floodplain. As the water receded, it left behind the fertile soil it had carried from the volcanic highlands of Ethiopia. These deposits inspired the ancient name for the country, Kemet, or "the black land." After this period of natural fertilization, the time of tilling and planting, known as *peret,* began. And then, between March and May, came *shemu,* the time of harvest.

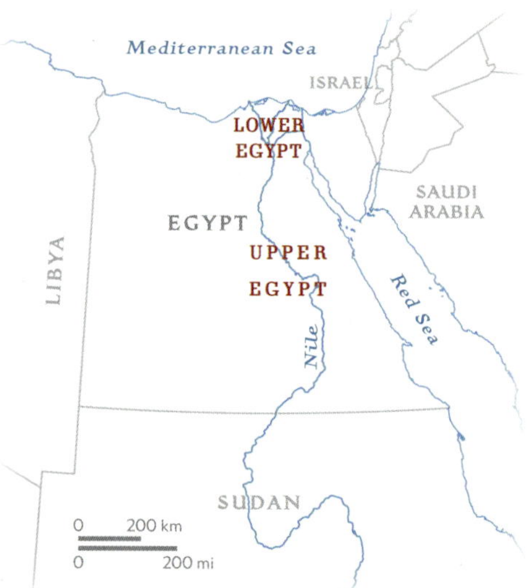

Images of the land's bounty appear on the walls of many tombs, placed there by people who wanted to make sure they had an ample supply of food in the great beyond. Offering tables are stacked high with figs, pomegranates, and grapes; leeks, onions, and lettuce; rounds of bread, roasted fowl, and choice cuts of meat. Rows of jars hold wine and beer. There are herds of fat cattle, sheep, and goats. Even hives of bees and pots of honey make occasional appearances.

Also depicted on tomb walls are scenes of ancient Egyptians fishing in the Nile, floating in their skiffs while setting traps, casting nets, and dangling lines with hooks. People hunted geese and ducks, too, in the thickets of reeds and papyrus plants that grew at the marshy edges of the river.

These activities could be dangerous, though. The water teemed with crocodiles, sometimes 20 feet (6 m) long, whose toothy jaws could snap up prey in a flash. Hippopotamuses were equally feared. Powerful and unpredictable, they could inflict fatal wounds with their sharp tusks. Despite this, Egyptian hunters brought down hippos with harpoons to get the meat, fat, and hide. Royal imagery began to include hippos in about 3000 B.C., depicting the king as he hunted the beasts, thus symbolically defeating chaos and fulfilling his duty to maintain order for his people.

The Nile played a key role in unifying the country, serving as the main means of travel between the south, known as Upper Egypt, and the north, Lower Egypt. Gliding along the water in a boat, despite the perils, was surely faster and more pleasant than trotting overland on a dusty donkey, or later by horse (and chariot, if you were the king).

The country's riverine geography also helped protect it. A series of rocky outcroppings below Aswan, known as cataracts, prevented boats from sailing into Egypt from farther south in Africa. In the north, the tangled branches of

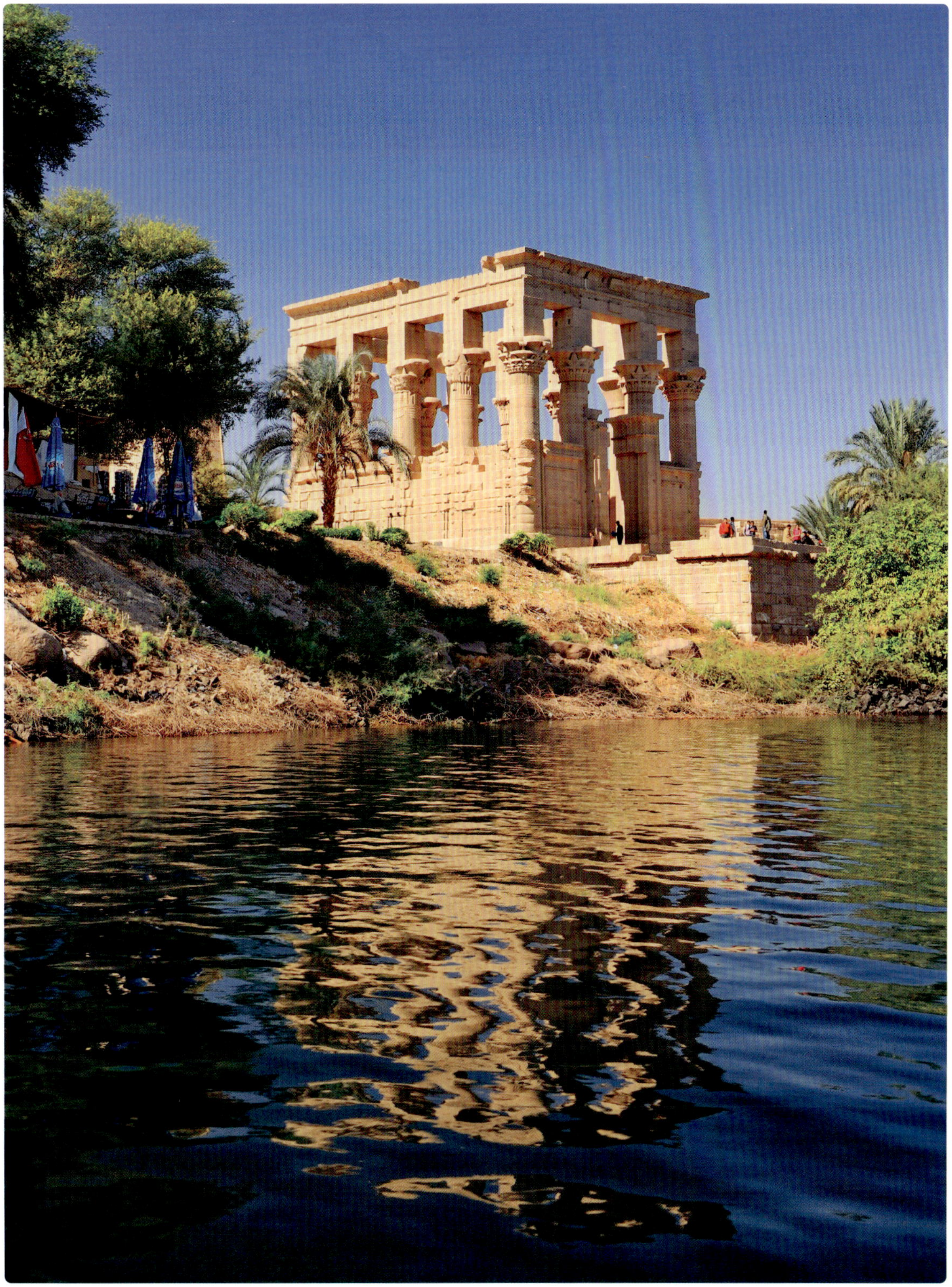

Once located on the island of Philae, a temple known as Trajan's Kiosk (above) was among the buildings moved to higher ground before the Aswan High Dam blocked the Nile to create Lake Nasser. The sacred Philae complex dates to about 380 B.C.–A.D. 300.

PREVIOUS PAGES: A man named Nebamun is shown in his tomb hunting birds along the Nile with his wife and daughter in about 1350 B.C.—an activity he hoped to enjoy in the afterlife.

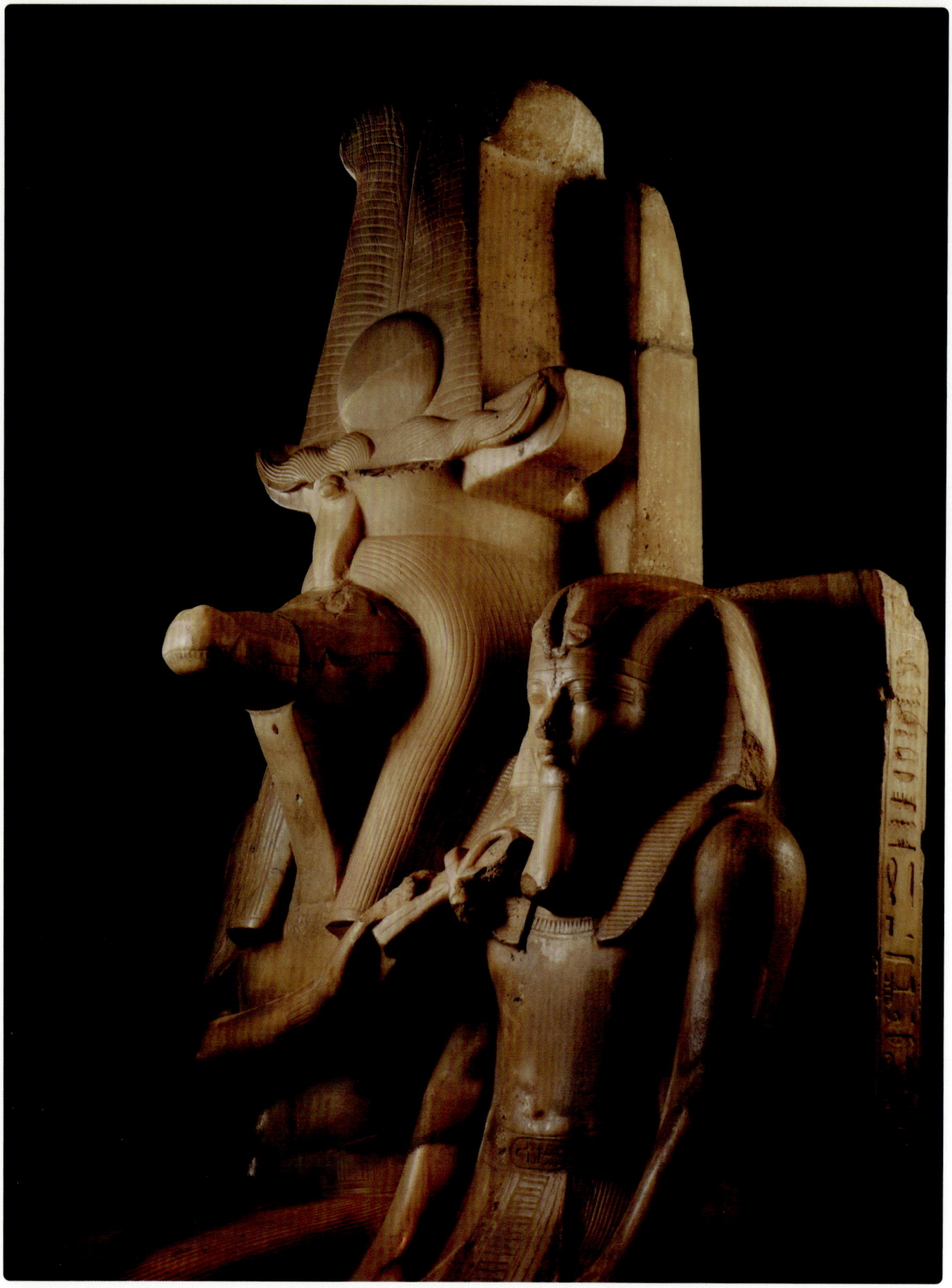

A god of fertility and creation, the crocodile-headed Sobek offers an ankh, the symbol of life, to King Amenhotep III (about 1390–1353 B.C.). This calcite statue once stood in a temple dedicated to the deity.

the river in the delta were complicated to navigate; where they came together, the waterway could be guarded to keep unwanted outsiders from cruising in. The deserts flanking the river provided their own protection, since trips—most especially for trade—had to be carefully planned, with caches of water to keep people and animals alive as they crossed the arid sands.

The Nile was both a blessing and a curse. When all went well, the level of annual flooding could be predicted within a few feet. Farmers could till their fields, create catchment basins and canals for irrigation, and still have time left over to work on large-scale royal projects like pyramid building. But when the flood was too high, the rampaging waters could destroy mud-brick homes and drown people and animals in the communities perched at the edge of the normal floodplain. And when drought struck, as it did at the end of the Old Kingdom around 2200 B.C., it likely caused power to shift from the detached king in his palace to local leaders, who could guide their communities in adapting to the resulting agricultural crisis.

In antiquity, people could only pray to the gods for a good year, and hope. In the modern era, several dams designed to help regulate the flooding were built between 1861 and 1930. The first dam at Aswan was completed in 1902 and subsequently enlarged twice.

But the river wasn't entirely tamed until the construction of the Aswan High Dam, which began in 1959. As the project moved forward, archaeologists and engineers worked to save as many antiquities as they could from sites that would soon be flooded. (As one scientist observed, they had "temples to save, thousands of inscriptions and graffiti to record, untold numbers of cemeteries [and] town mounds . . . to excavate, acres to map archaeologically.") Most famously, teams of experts moved the temples at Abu Simbel and Philae to ground that was high and dry. The dam's completion, in 1970, created Lake Nasser, whose waters now churn through turbines to create a steady supply of hydroelectric power.

> "The Nile played a key role in unifying the country, serving as the main means of travel between the south, known as Upper Egypt, and the north, Lower Egypt. Gliding along the water in a boat . . . was surely faster and more pleasant than trotting overland on a dusty donkey, or later by horse (and chariot, if you were the king)."

But Egypt's position could change significantly in the future. In 2011, Ethiopia started to build a barrier on its own branch of the Nile. Called the Grand Ethiopian Renaissance Dam, the project promises to bring electricity to millions with the largest hydroelectric plant in Africa. The country has now begun to fill the reservoir behind the dam, already creating disruptions in the water available to neighboring Sudan downriver.

Egypt can offset the diminished flow by releasing water from Lake Nasser—for a while. But during potential years of prolonged drought, the nature of the river as it flows through the country could shift dramatically, bringing political, cultural, and even existential changes to a nation that has relied on the gifts of the Nile for millennia. ▲

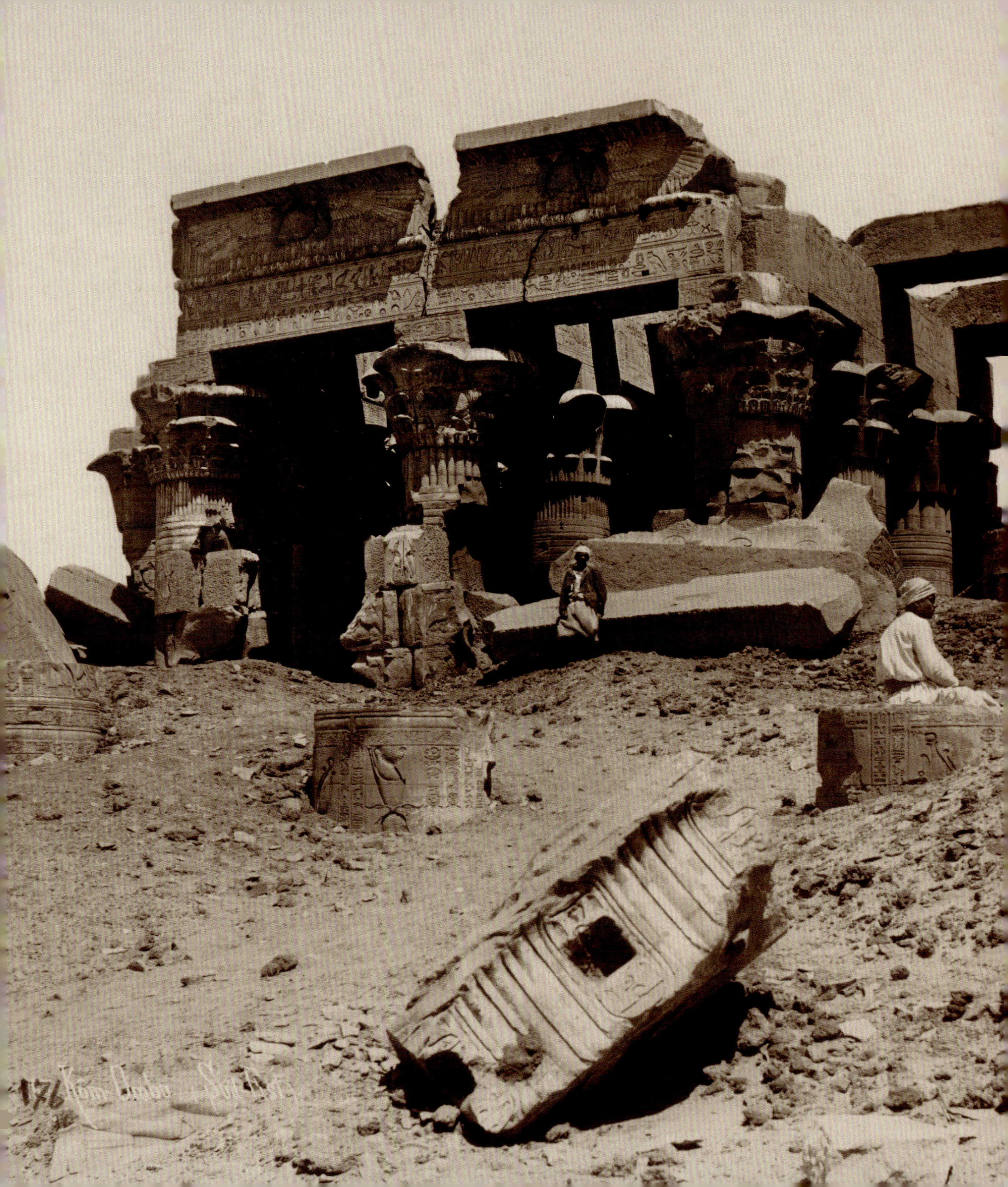
176 Kom Ombo

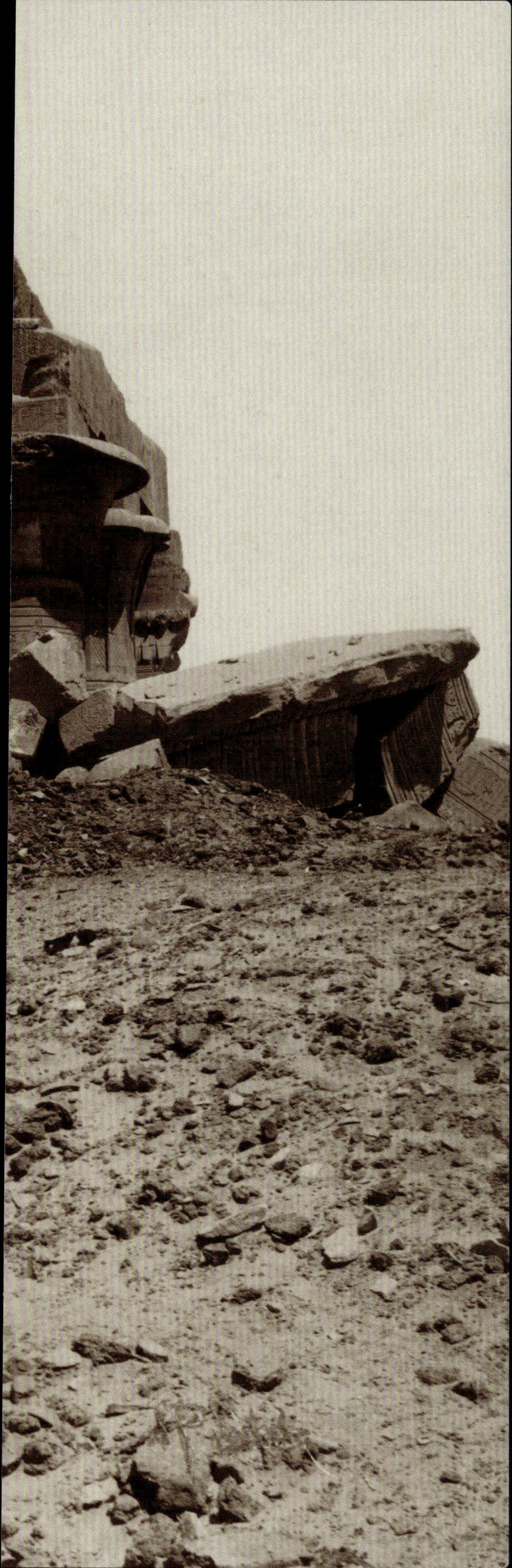

FIRST PHOTOS

In the 1860s, windblown debris buried the lower part of the temple dedicated to Sobek and Horus at Kom Ombo (left). Excavation of the Greco-Roman ruins (332 B.C.–A.D. 395) began in 1893.

Steps away from the now cleared temple at Kom Ombo (below) is a nilometer—a well with a descending staircase that allowed the ancient Egyptians to monitor the progress of the Nile's annual flood.

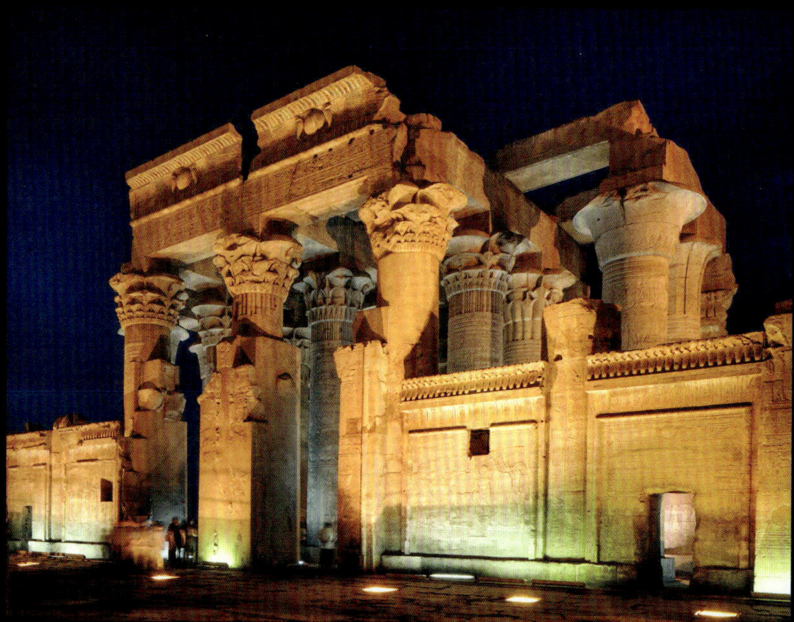

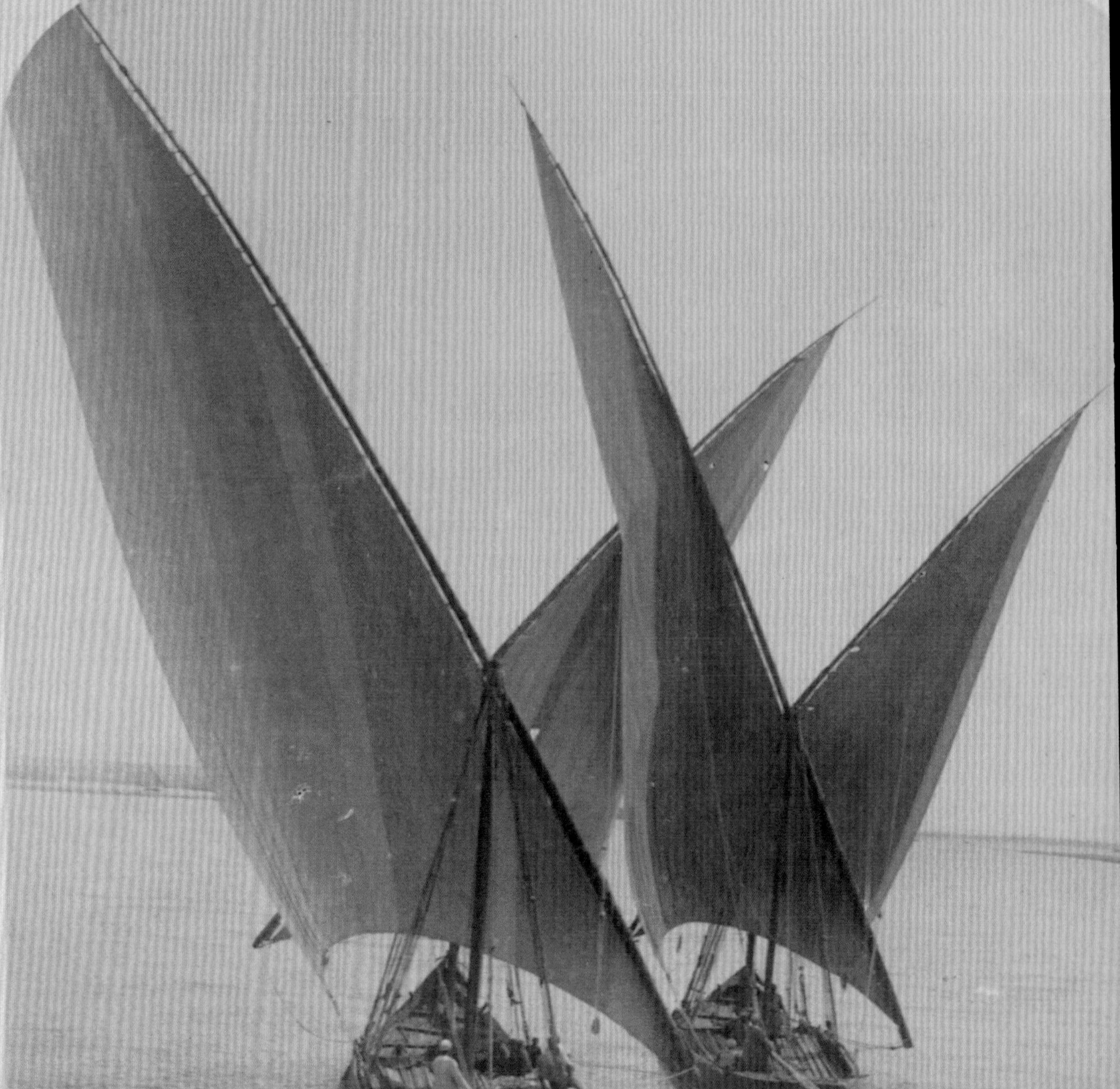

Strohmeyer & Wyman, Publishers,
New York, N.Y.

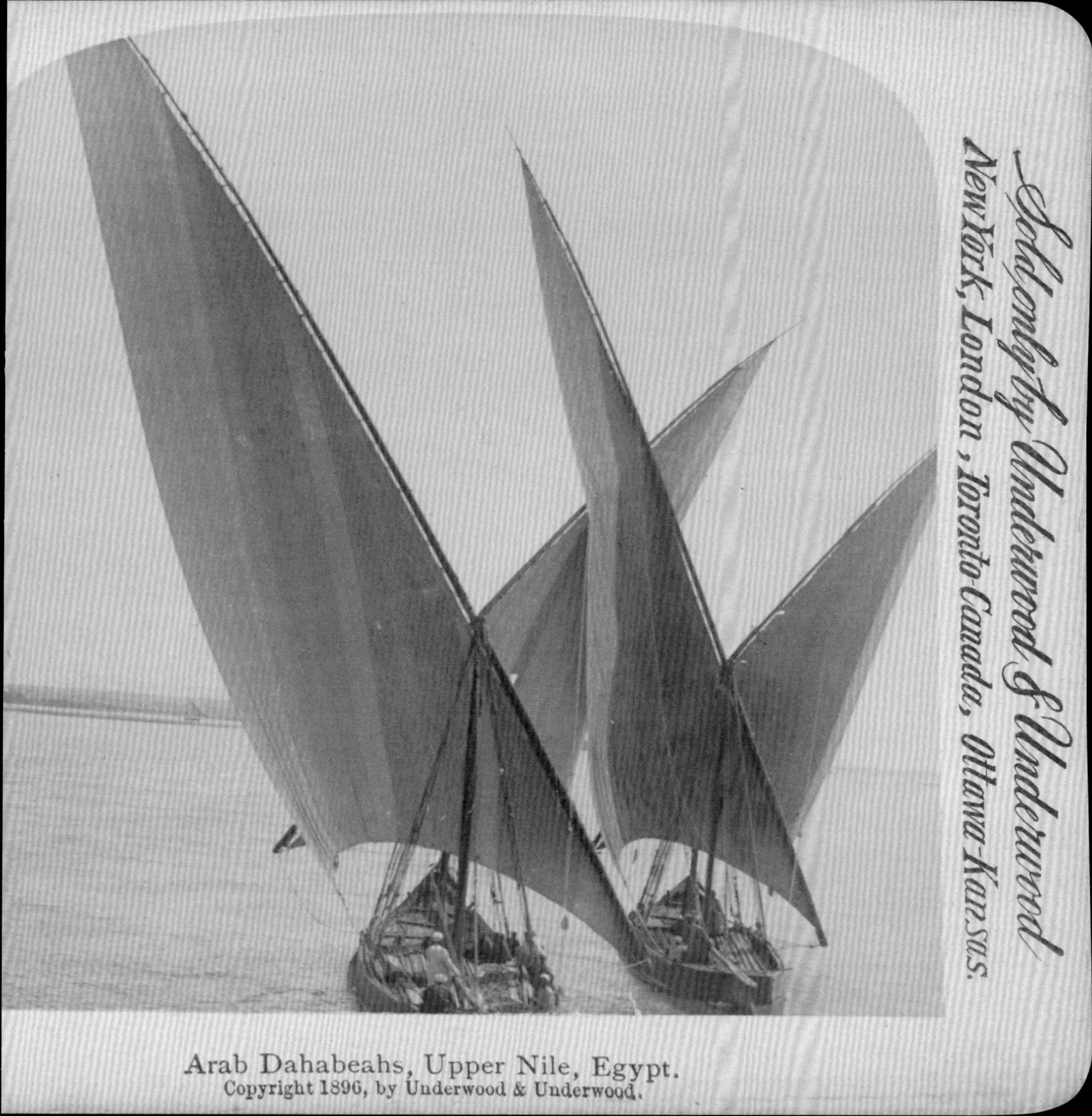

Graceful boats on the Nile, appearing in almost identical side-by-side images from 1896, would have come to life in three dimensions when viewed through a device called a stereoscope.

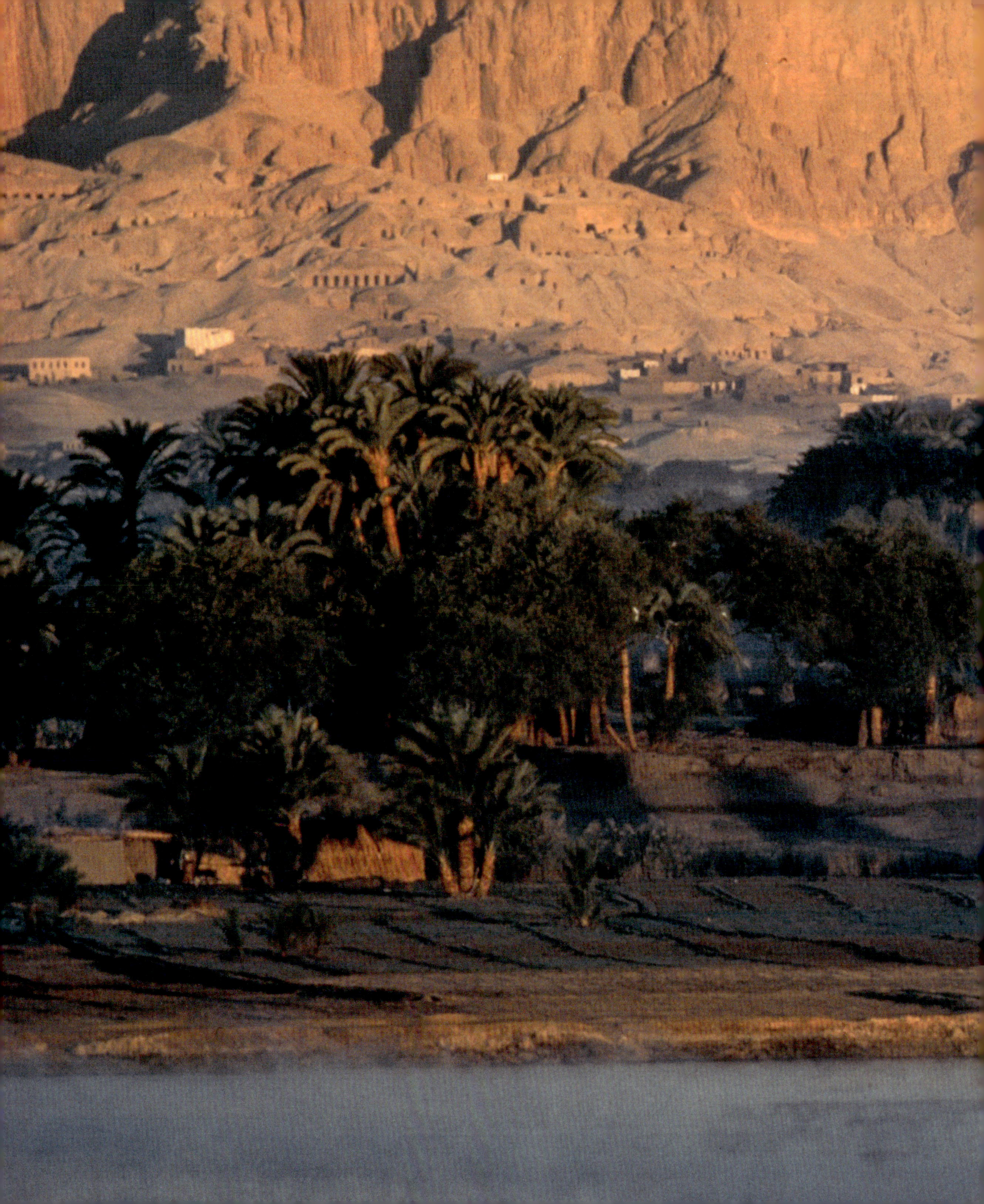

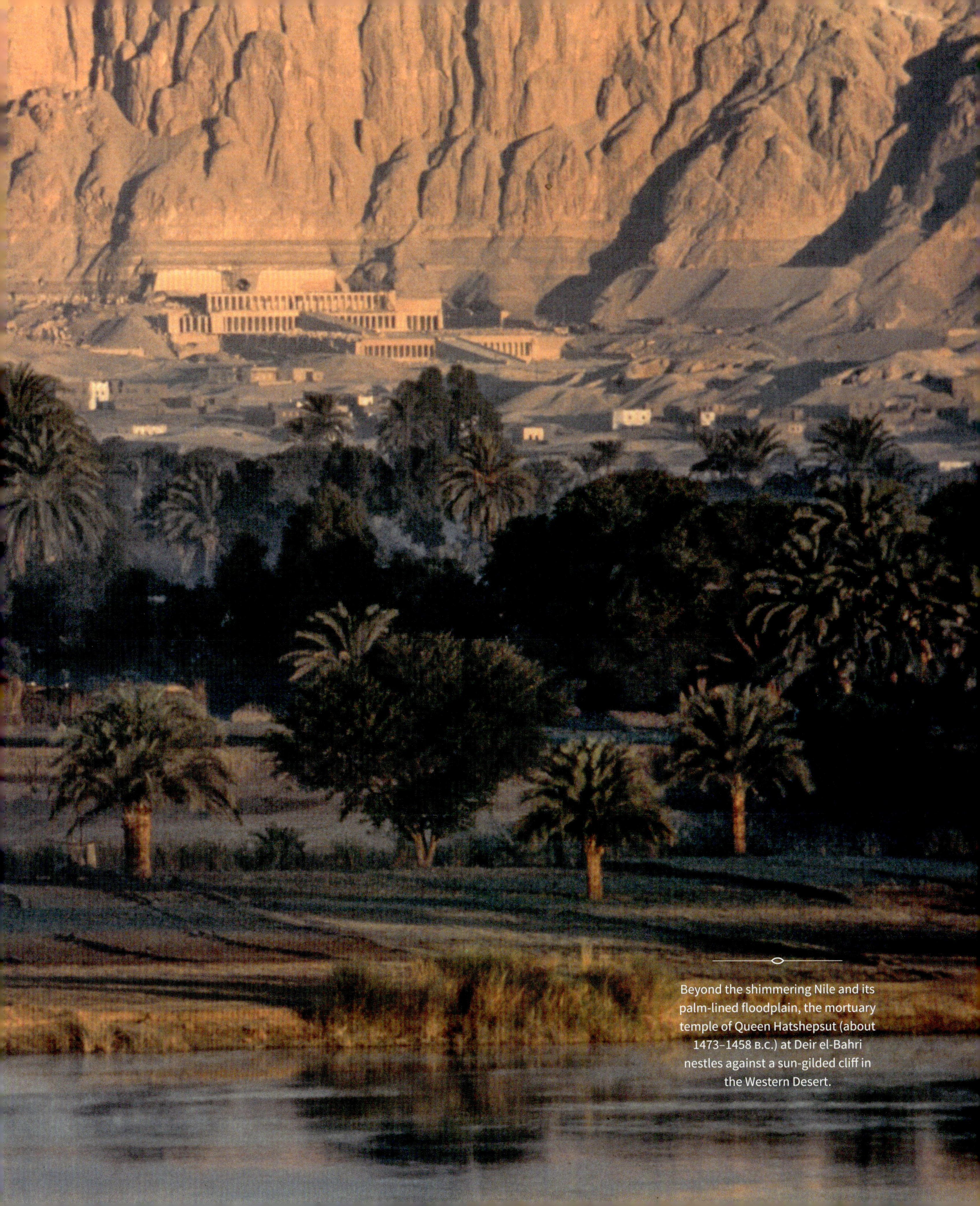

Beyond the shimmering Nile and its palm-lined floodplain, the mortuary temple of Queen Hatshepsut (about 1473–1458 B.C.) at Deir el-Bahri nestles against a sun-gilded cliff in the Western Desert.

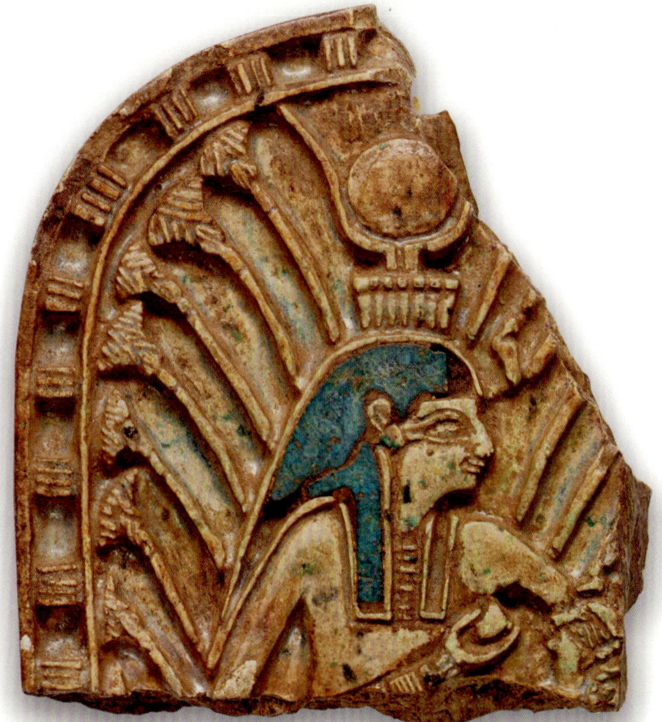

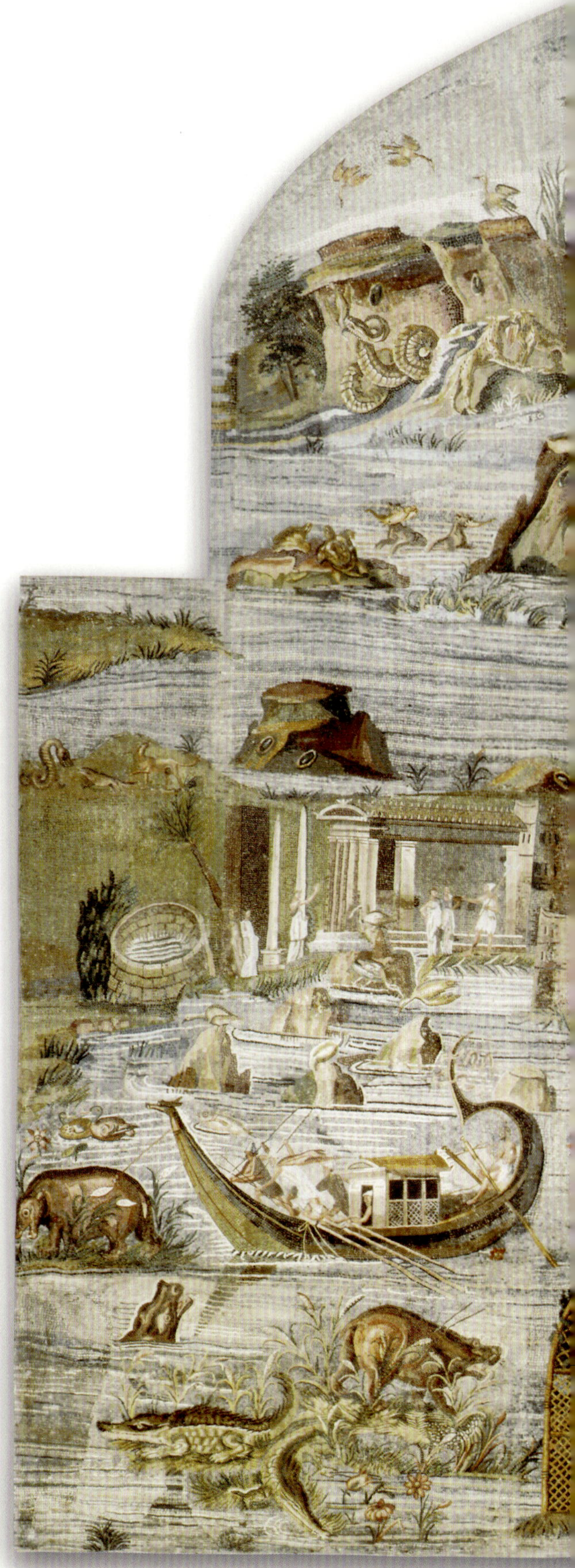

Surrounded by tall papyrus plants growing along the Nile, the goddess Isis nurses her son, Horus (above), on a piece of glazed steatite from a box lid or necklace dating to about 1075–664 B.C.

A monumental floor mosaic created in central Italy in the first century B.C. shows exotic scenes along the Nile (right). From Ethiopia at the top, the river winds past animals, people, and temples, ending up in what is likely Alexandria's busy harbor.

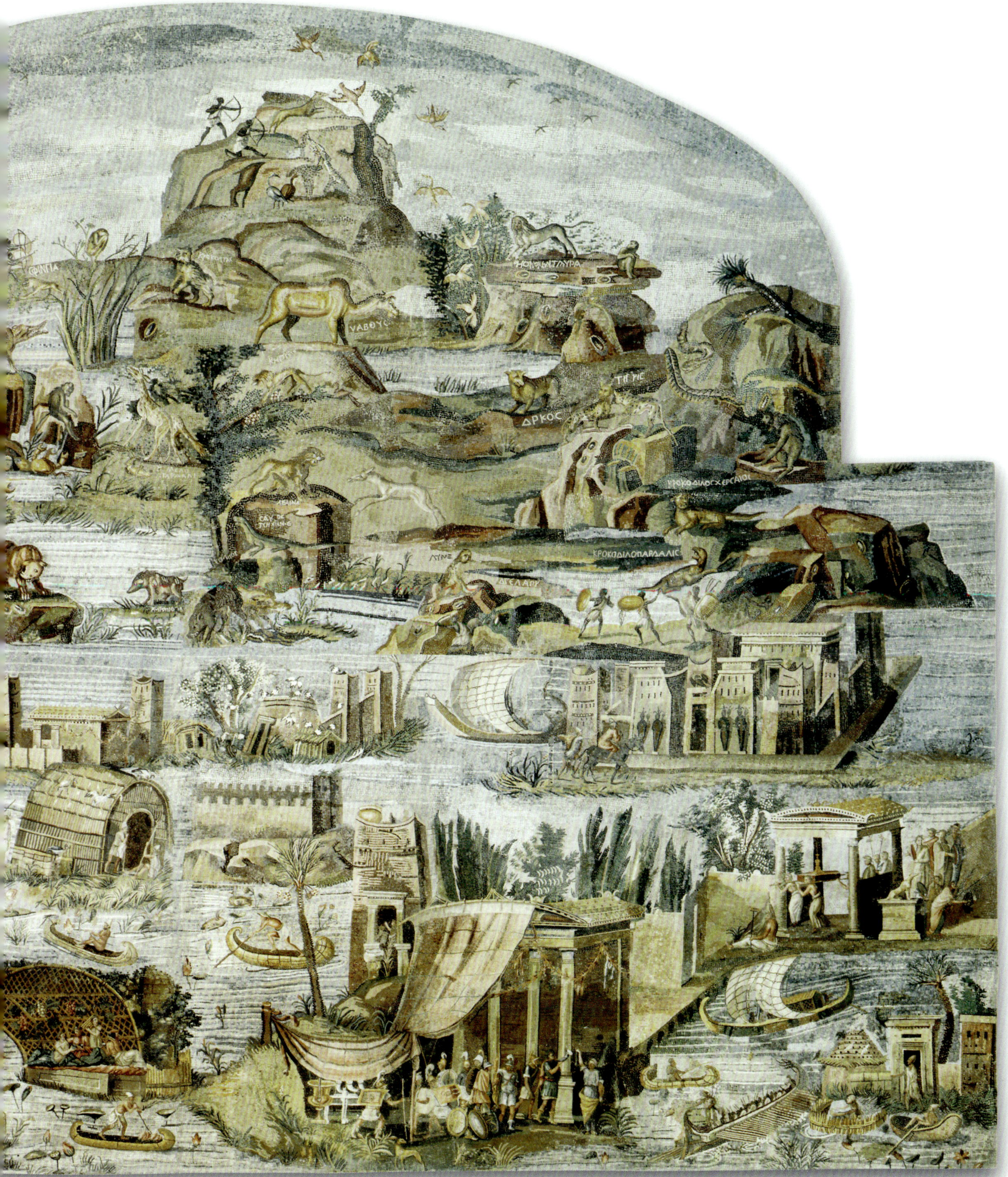

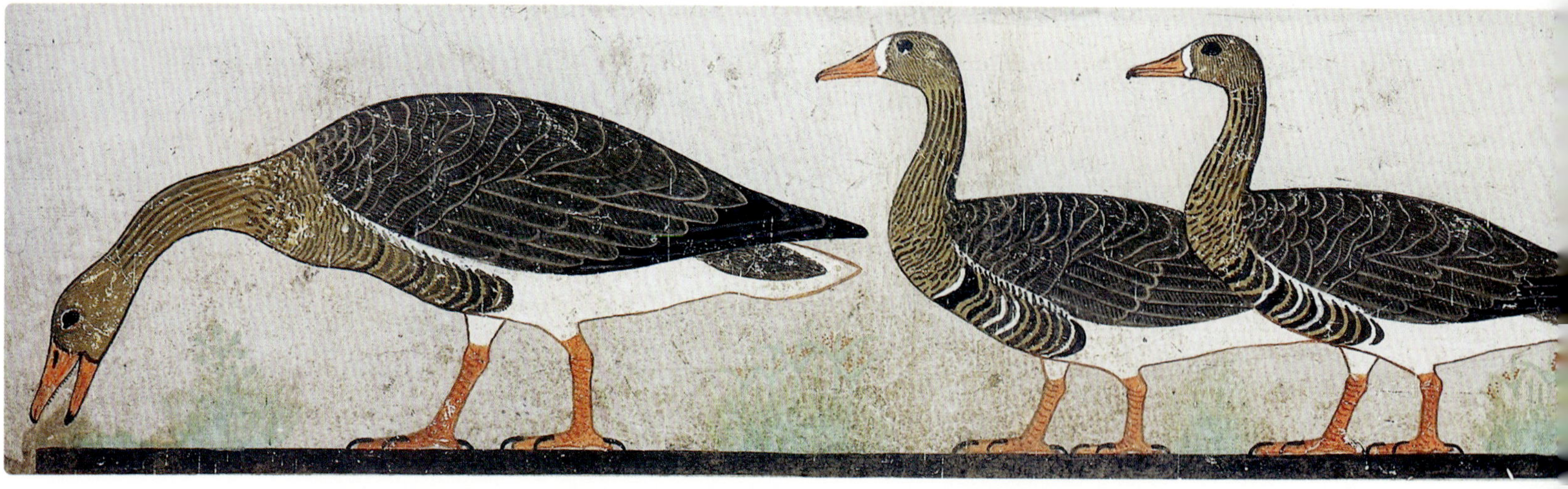

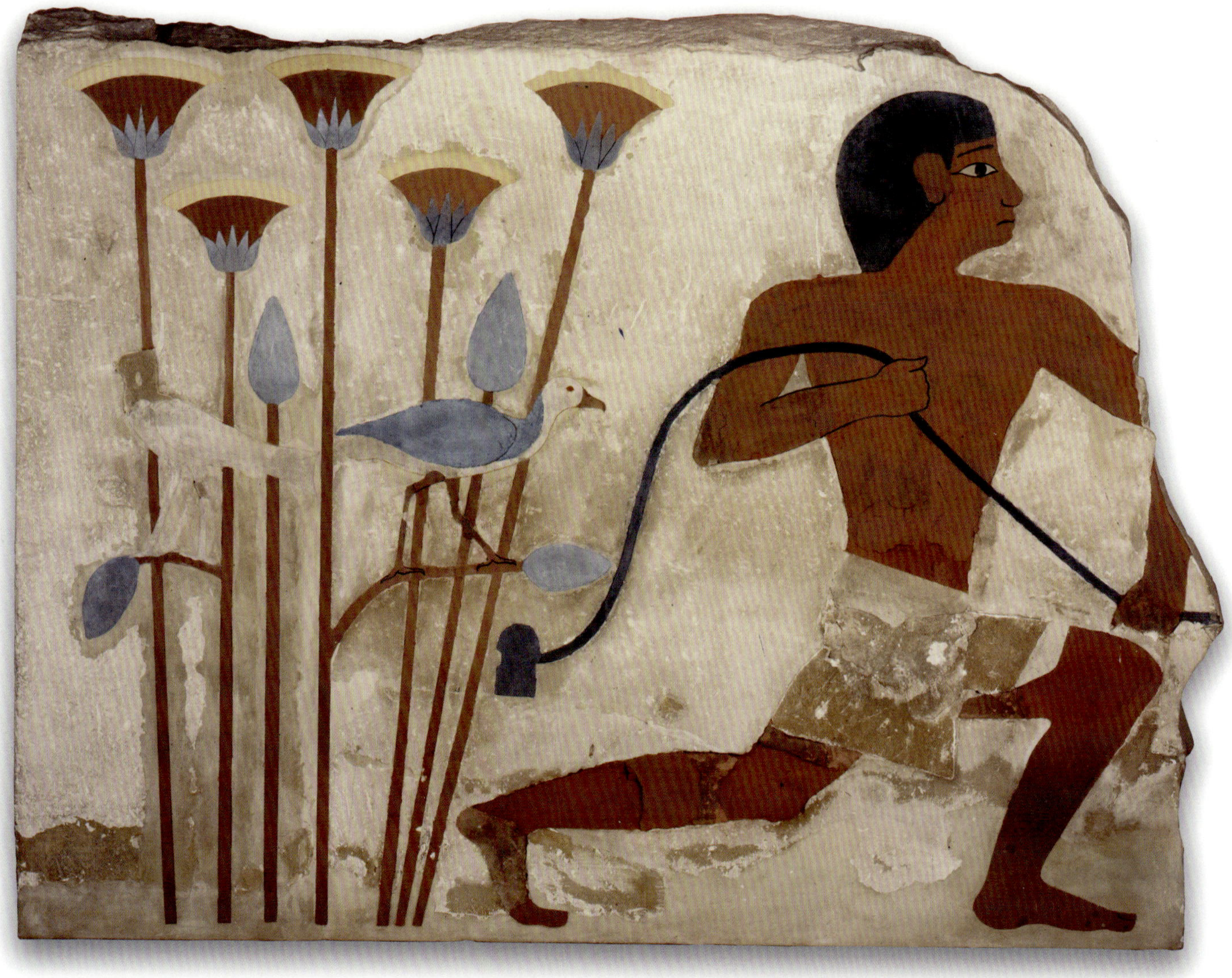

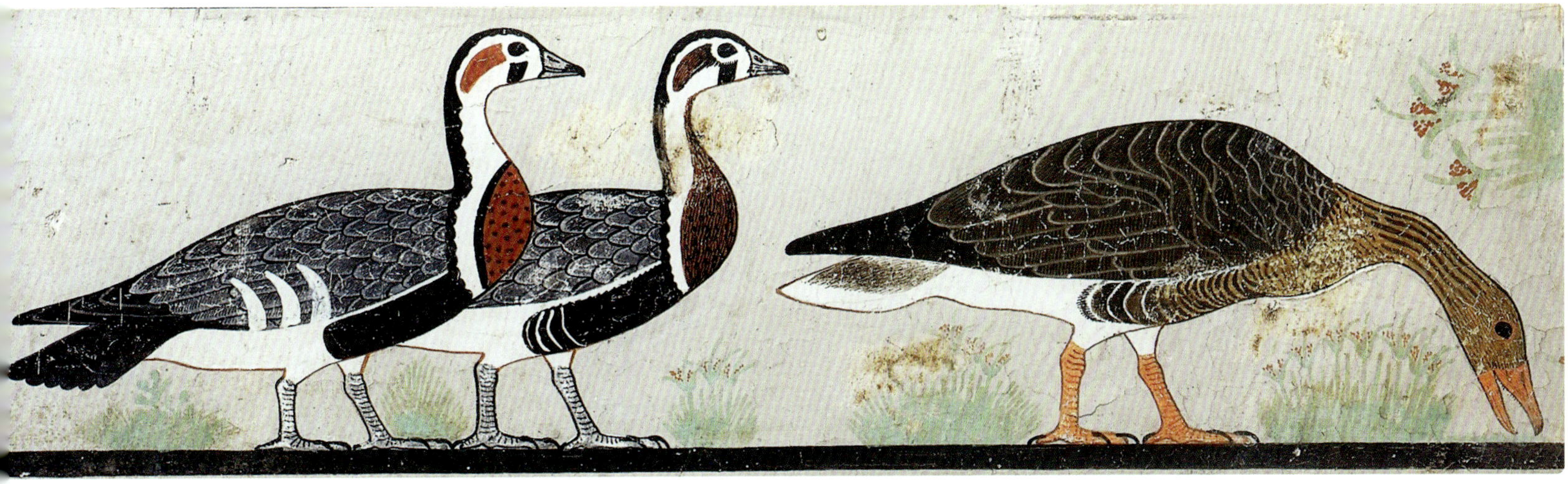

At Meidum, the tomb of Nefermaat and Itet, a fourth-dynasty prince and his wife (about 2575 B.C.), was decorated with many scenes of activities that occurred on their estate. A now restored painting on a lintel (opposite) shows a fowler springing a net to catch a bird in a papyrus marsh.

This gaggle of wild geese (above) came from that same tomb. A modern researcher has identified the red-breasted bird as an extinct species.

Birds caught in a net (right) appear in a relief from an 11th-dynasty temple (about 1960–1948 B.C.). The net's mesh appears in crisscrossed dashes of light paint against the darker bodies of the birds.

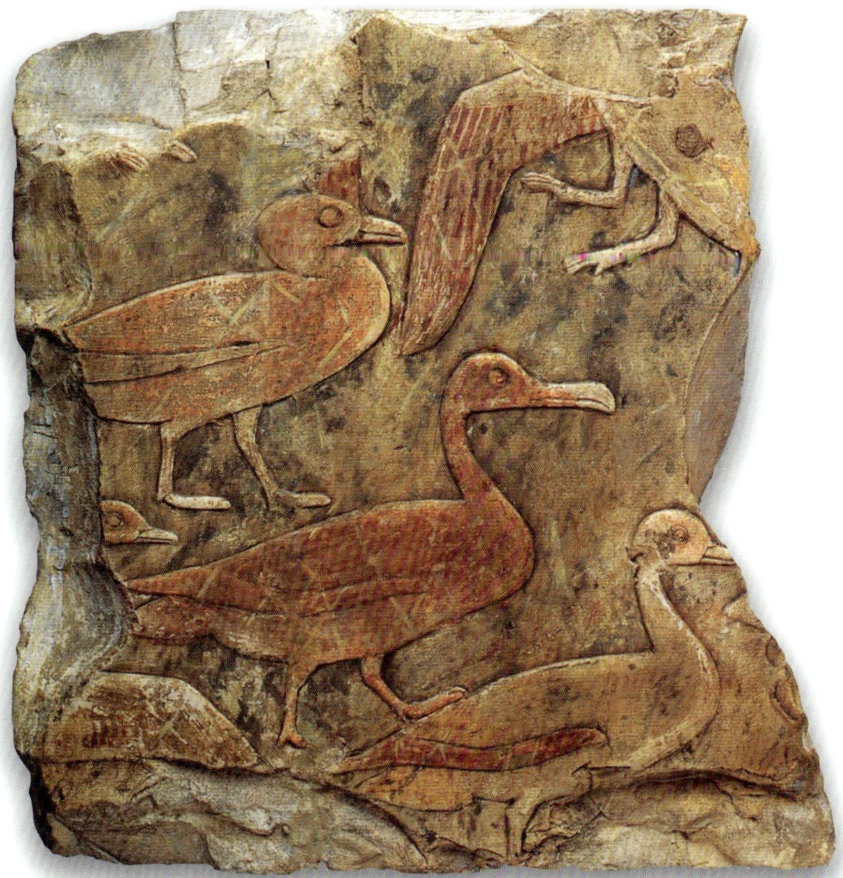

In a finely decorated tomb at Saqqara, a fisherman on a papyrus-reed raft sets a trap to catch some of the Nile's plentiful fish. Mereruka, a son-in-law of King Teti (about 2325 B.C.), was buried here.

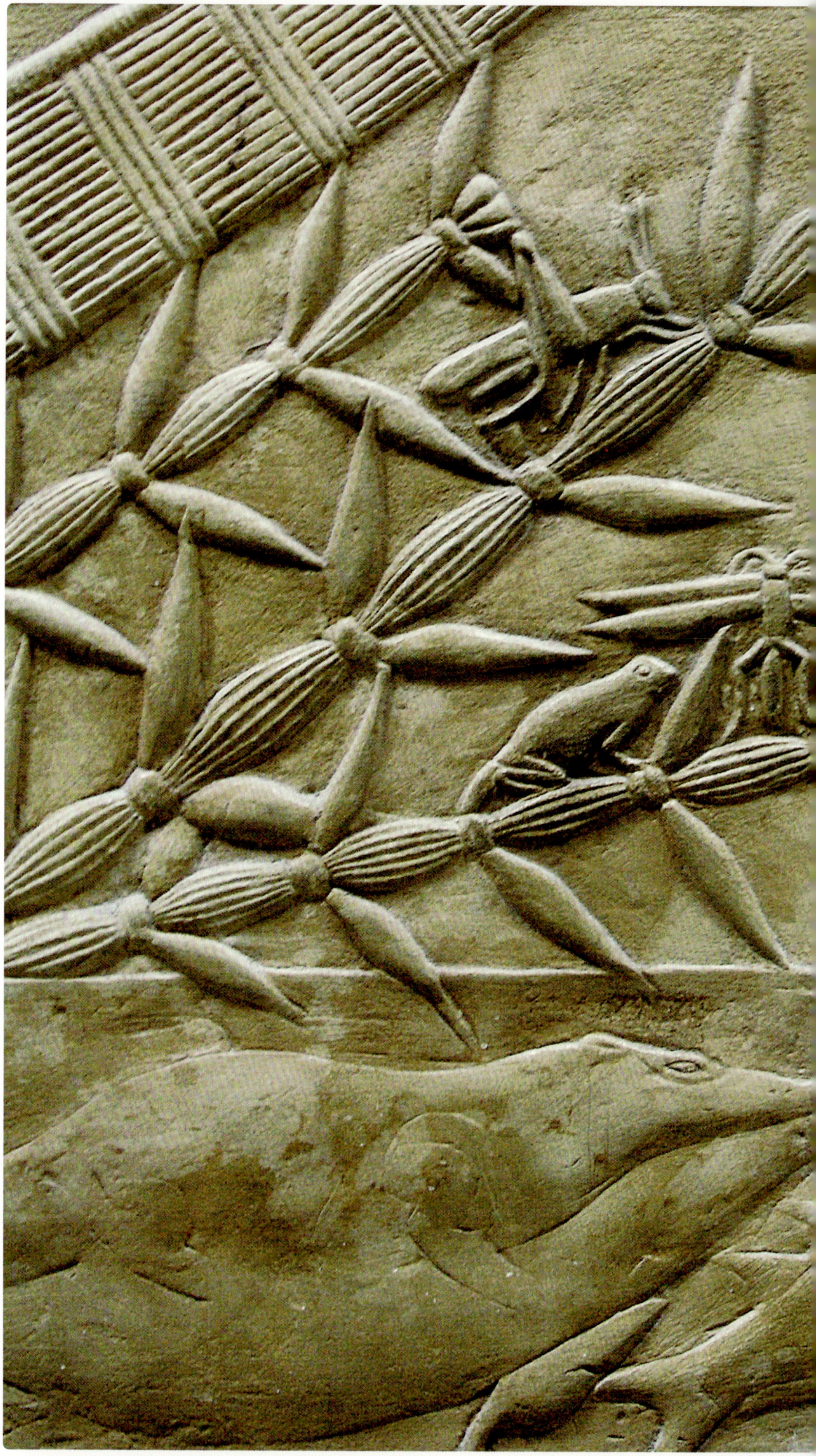

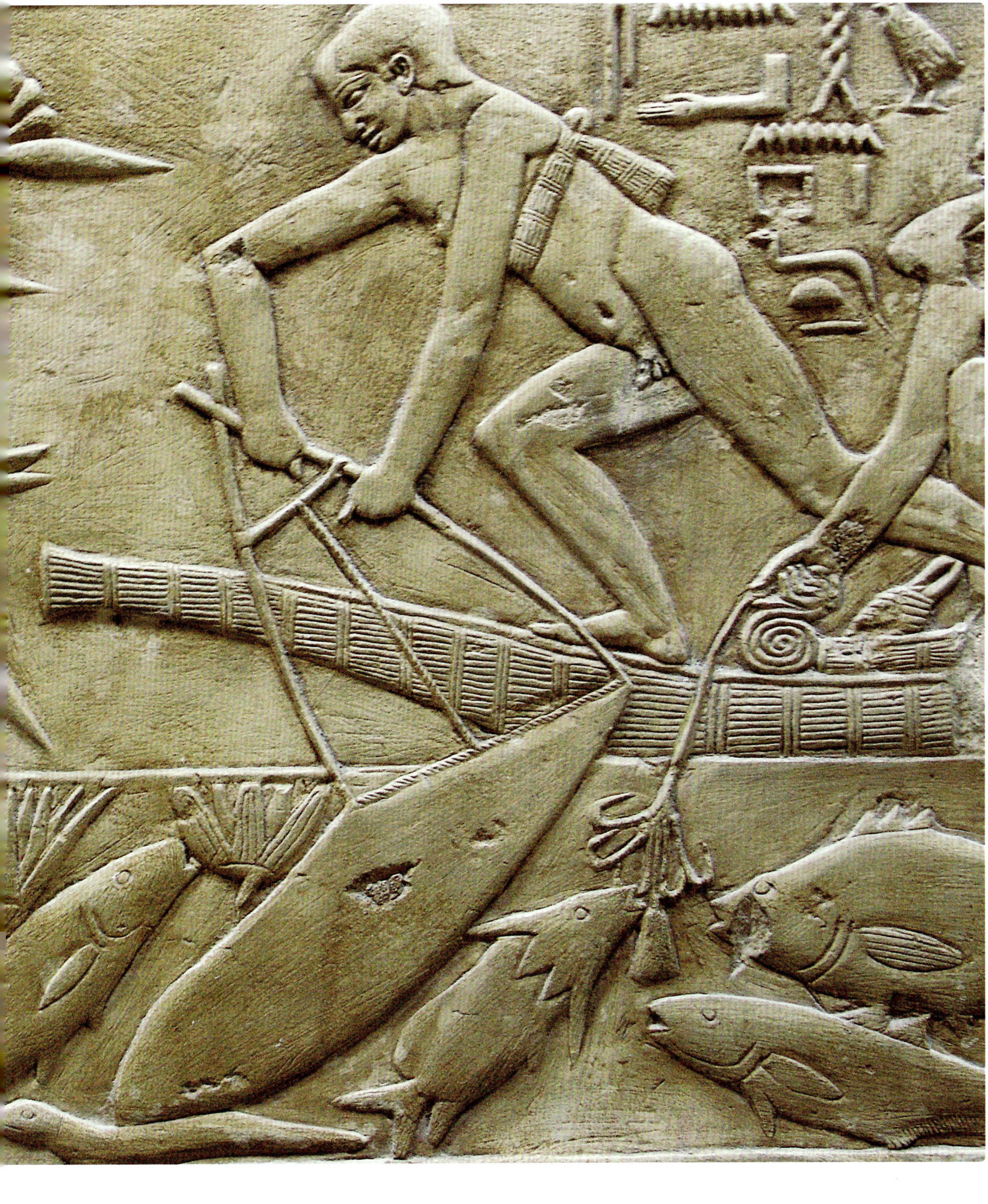

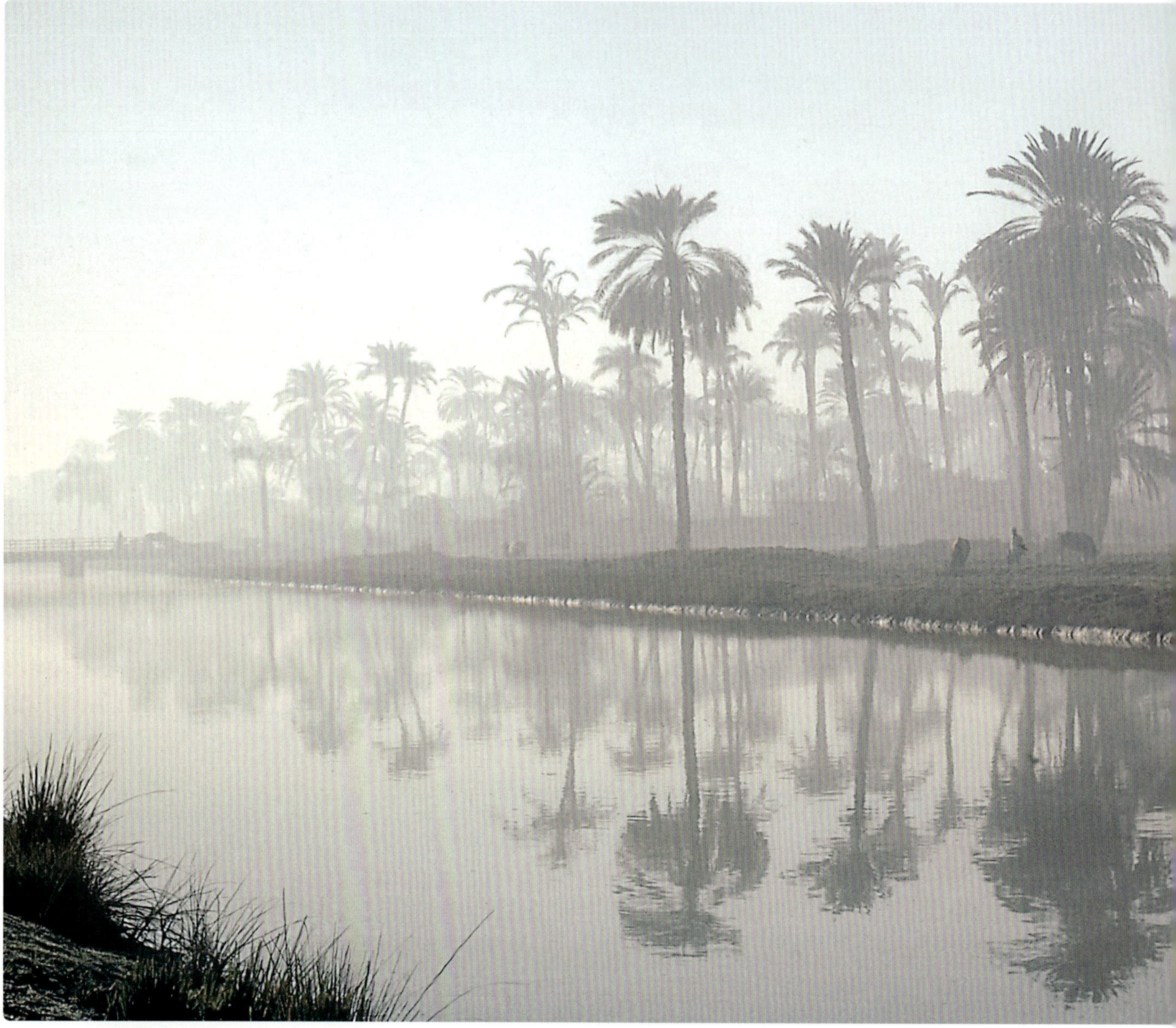

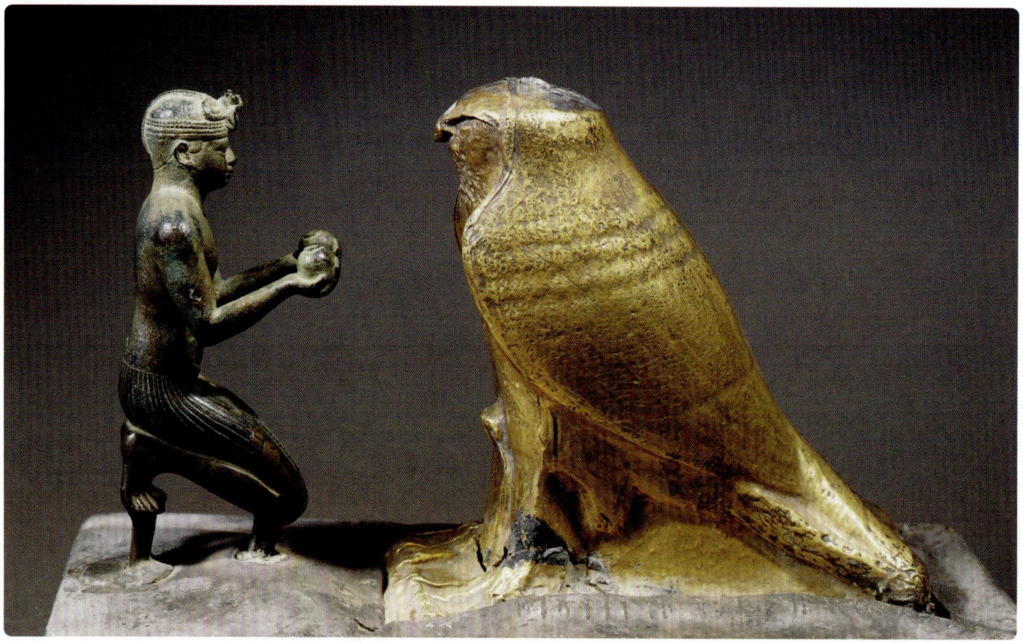

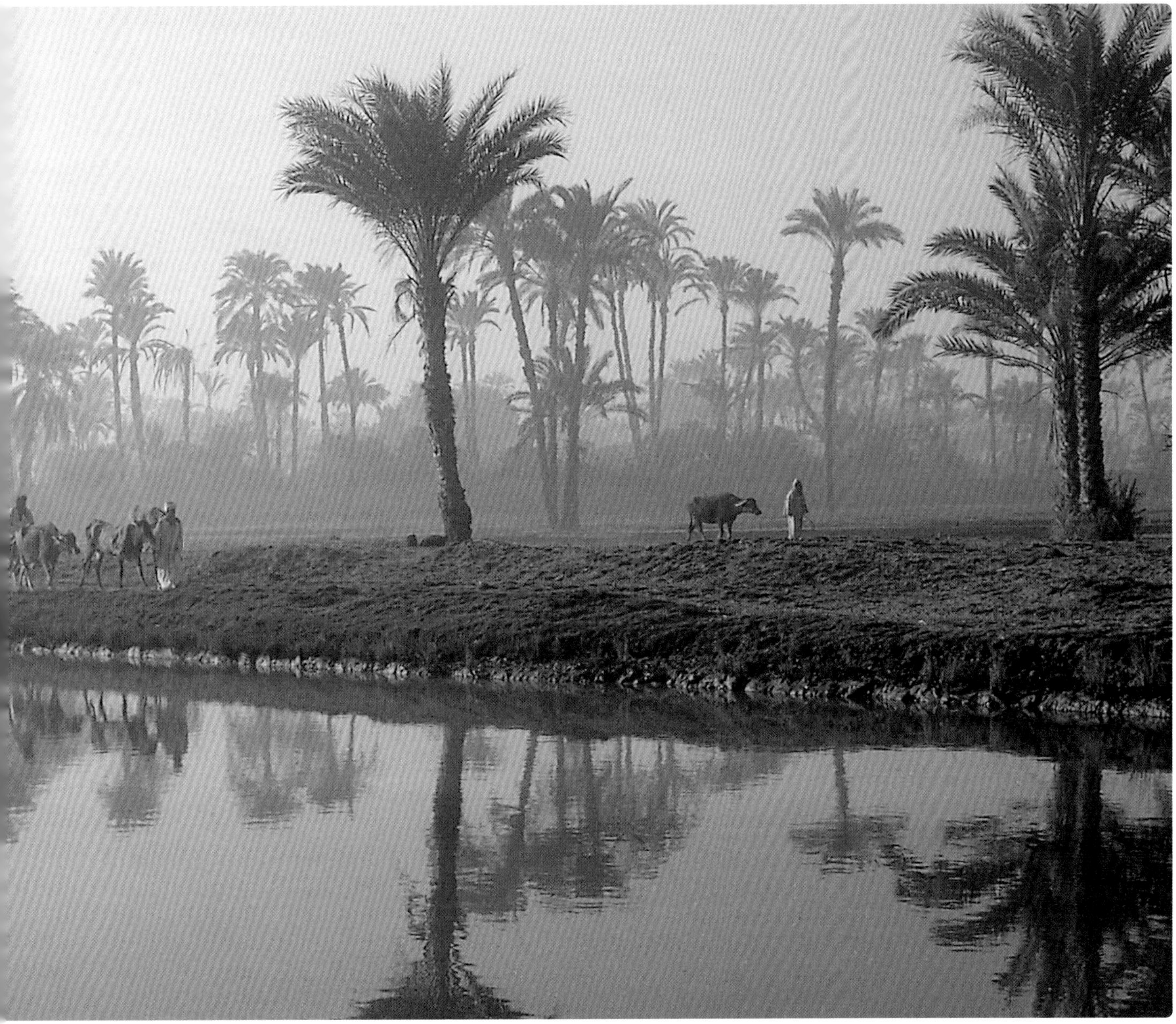

Before the early morning mist burns off, farmers head to their fields (above). Many Egyptians still earn a living through agriculture as their ancestors did, following the rhythms of the natural world.

Ancient Egyptians saw a multitude of wild creatures as they tilled the land, fished in the Nile, and hunted in the river's marshes. Many of their gods took the form of animals. This statuette (opposite) shows Hemen, an avian deity, receiving an offering of wine from King Taharqa (about 690–664 B.C.).

FOLLOWING PAGES: In his tomb near the Valley of the Kings, a scribe named Nakht from about 1400 B.C. appears with his wife and children as he hunts in a papyrus thicket, a fertile place symbolizing renewed life.

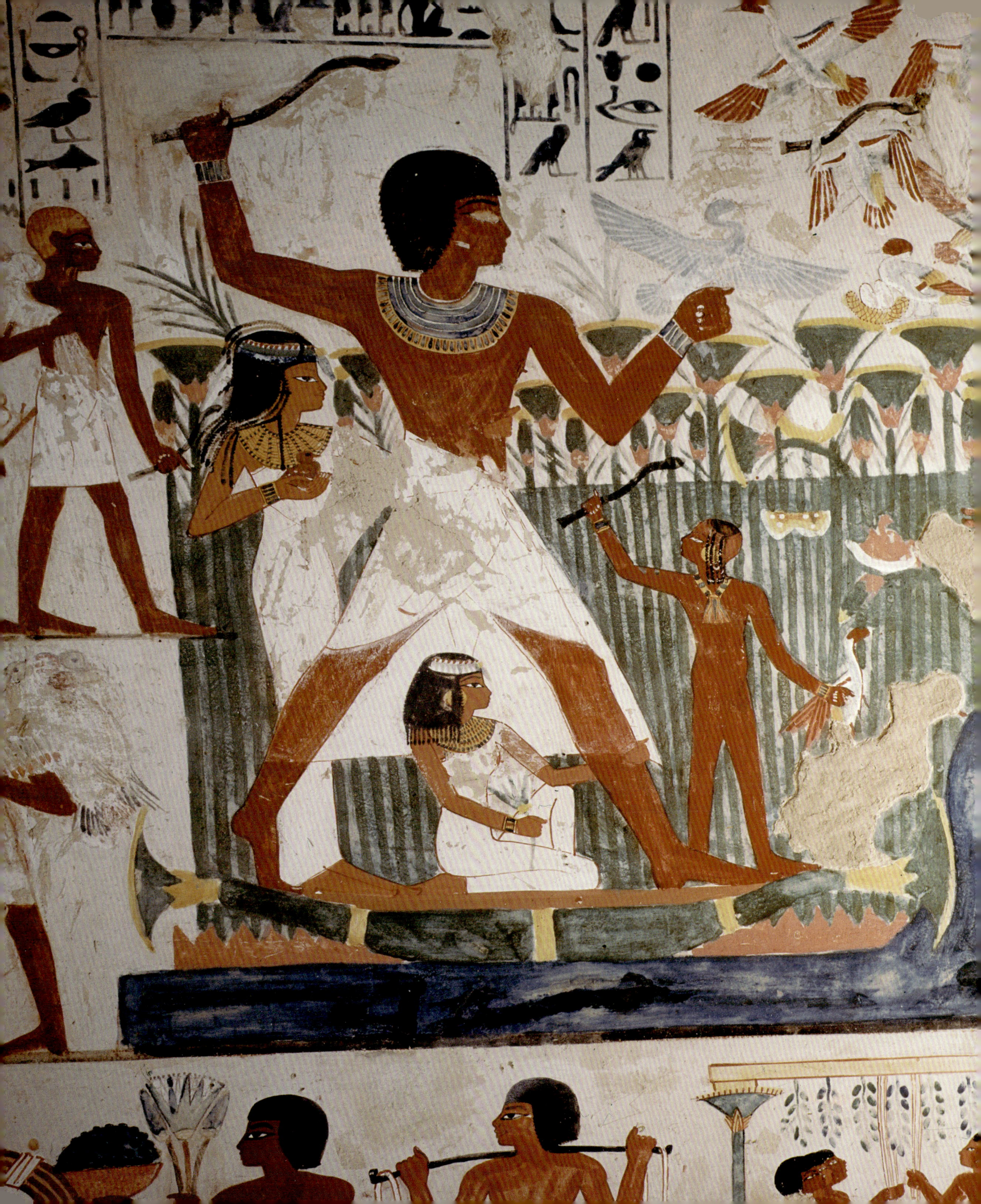

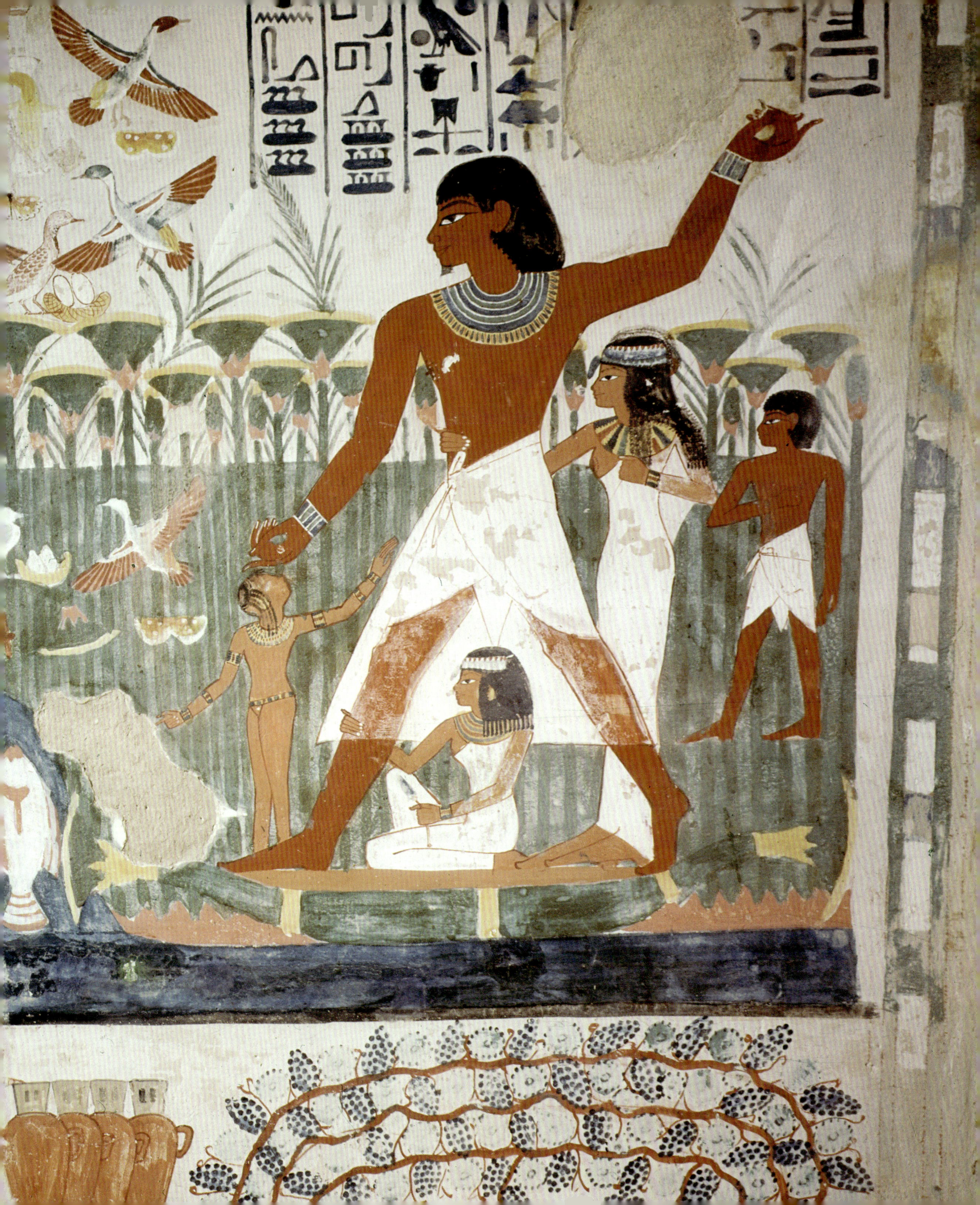

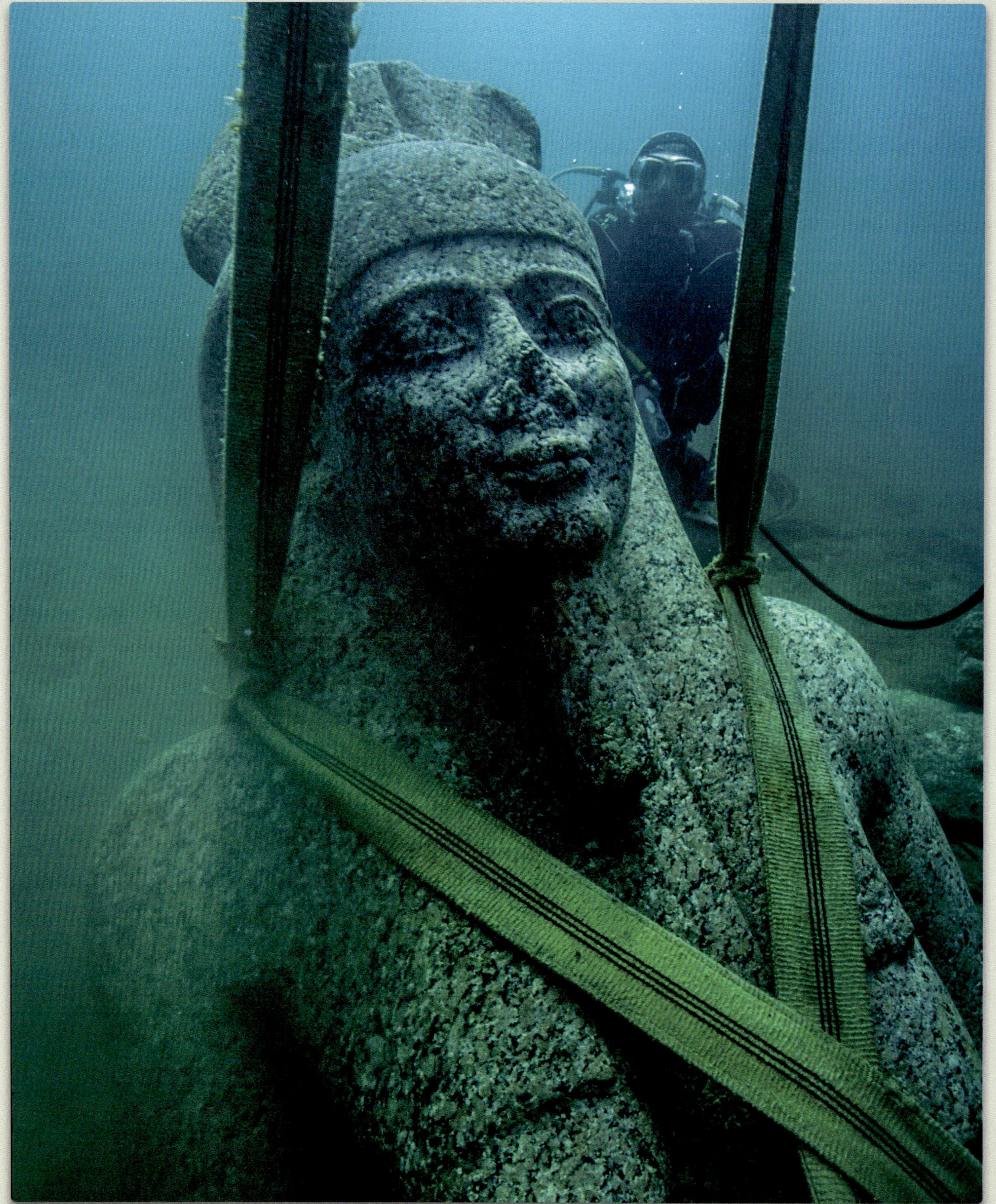

Lord of the Fishes and Birds

THE NILE'S ANNUAL FLOOD was so important to the ancient Egyptians' survival that they worshipped a god, Hapy, who personified it. When the high water started to sweep past villages in June, people spoke of "the arrival of Hapy." It was a joyous time, expressed in this hymn: "When he floods, earth rejoices! / Every belly jubilates, / Every jawbone takes on laughter."

Because the flooding brought fertility to the land by enriching fields and delivering water for irrigation, Hapy usually appears with a plump stomach and pendulous breasts. In 2001, a French team led by Franck Goddio retrieved this colossal statue of the god (opposite) from Abu Qir Bay, off the north coast of Egypt. The stalks of papyrus that spring from his head—as seen in this relief from the Hathor Temple at Dendera (right)—symbolize the lush vegetation that flourished along the Nile.

As the deity who determined the health of the river's ecosystem, Hapy was called "lord of the fishes and birds." As the source of life as the ancient Egyptians knew it, he was considered a creator god. And as a phenomenon with a usually predictable rhythm, he was a symbol of the order of the cosmos.

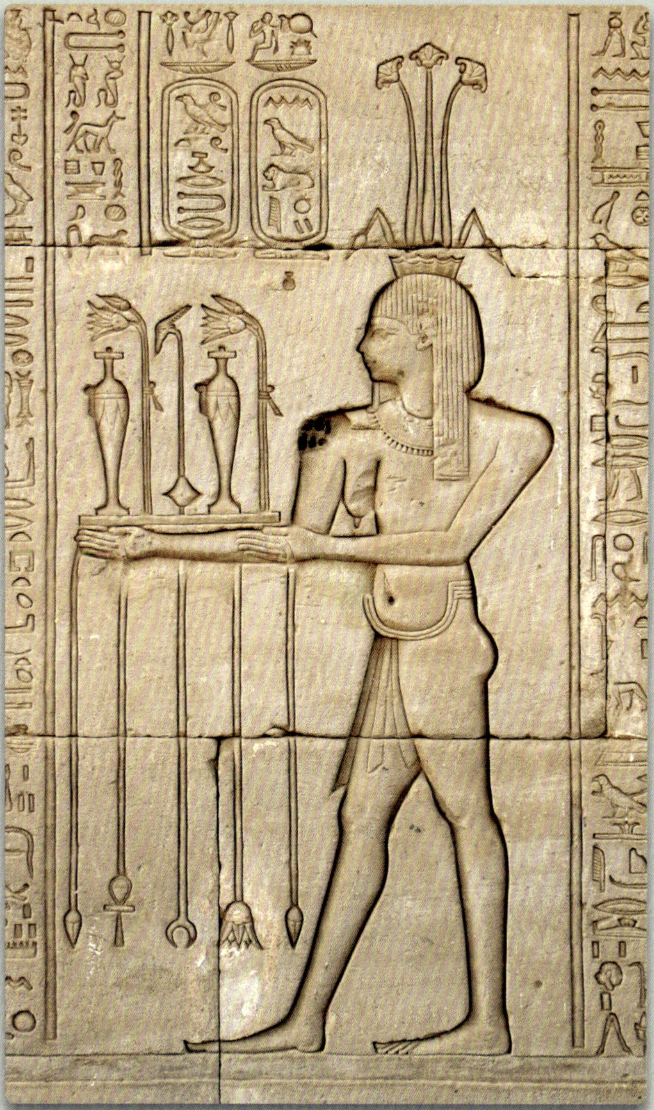

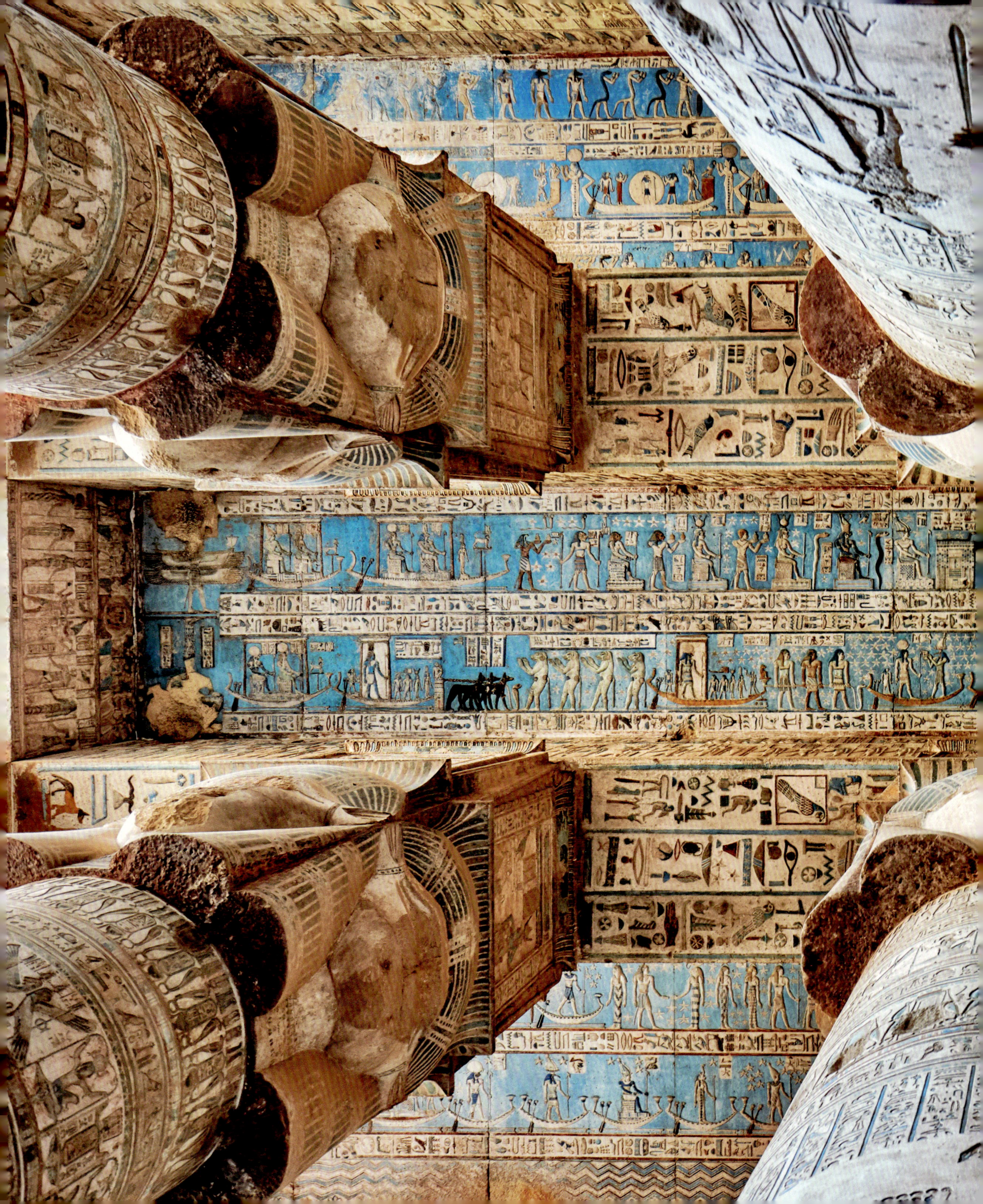

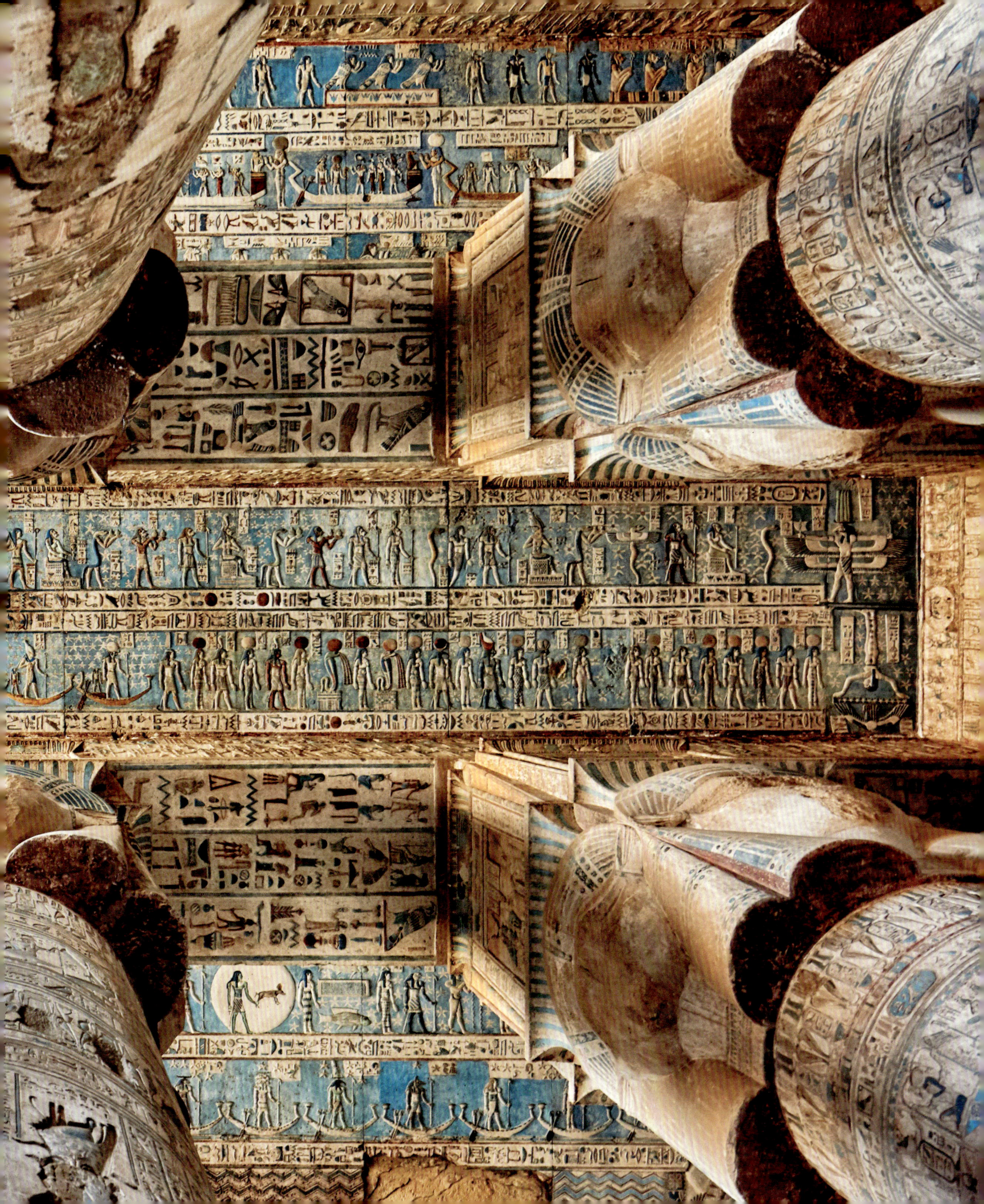

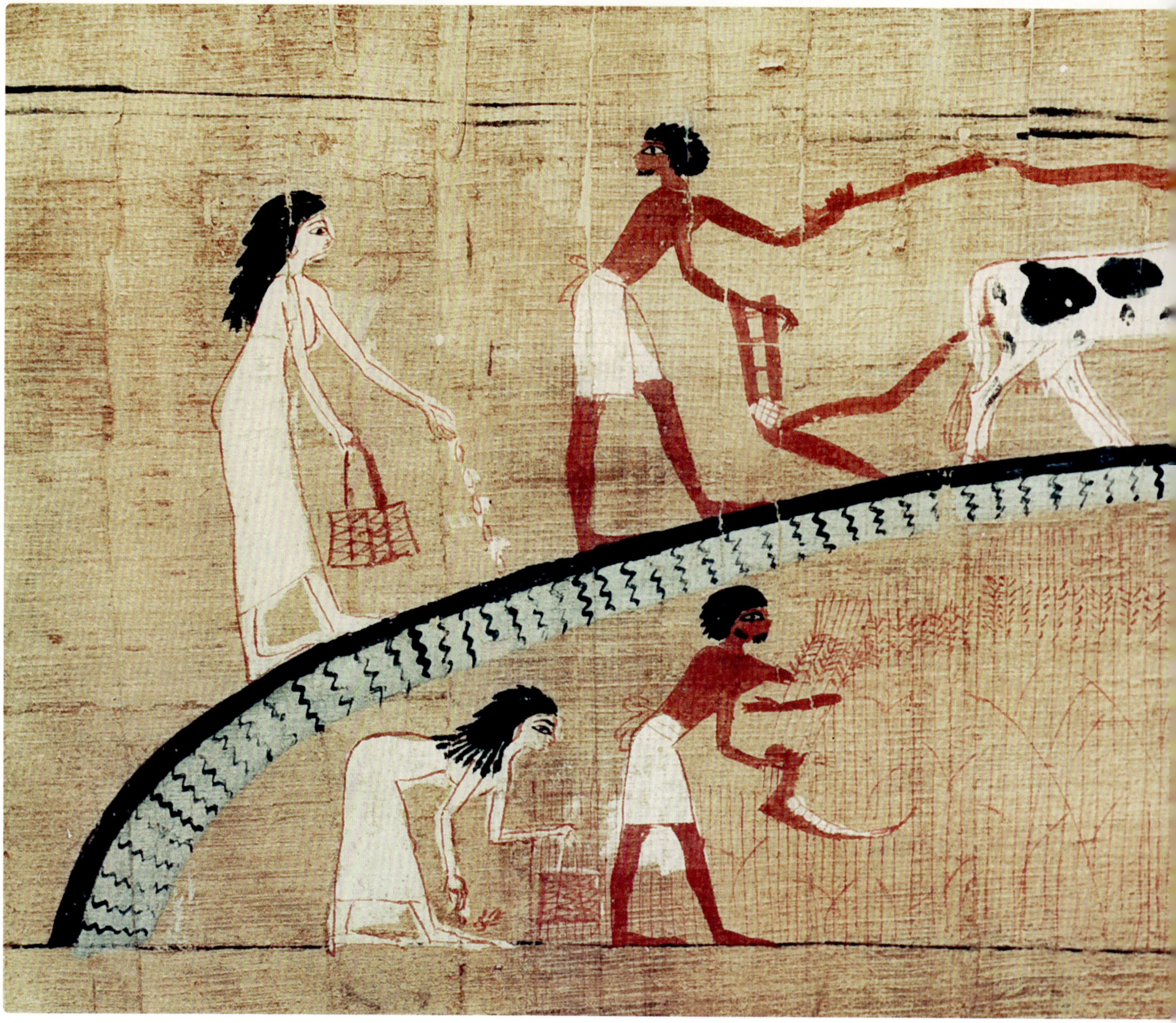

The Book of the Dead contains spells to help the deceased travel to the afterlife. This copy (above), belonging to Lady Cheritwebeshet (about 1069–945 B.C.), depicts agriculture in the fields of eternal paradise, which lie along the cool waters of a river.

Crocodiles in real life would have sunned themselves in rows on the sandbanks of the Nile, inspiring this arrangement of mummified creatures (opposite) in a museum in Kom Ombo.

PREVIOUS PAGES: The intricately painted ceiling of the Greco-Roman temple at Dendera (332 B.C.–A.D. 395) dedicated to the goddess Hathor presents complex imagery of deities, astronomical bodies, and signs of the zodiac, some sailing across the sky on boats.

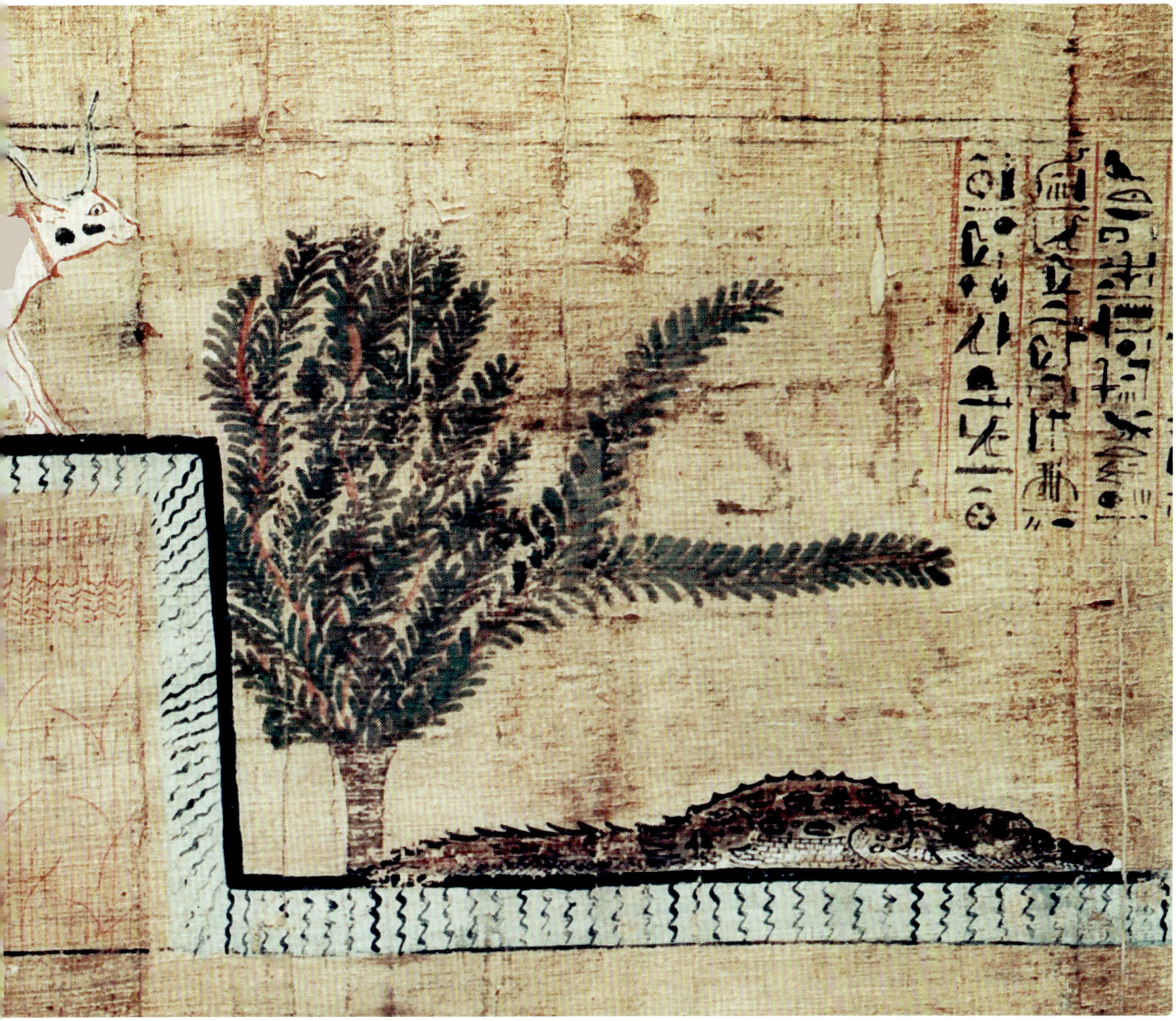

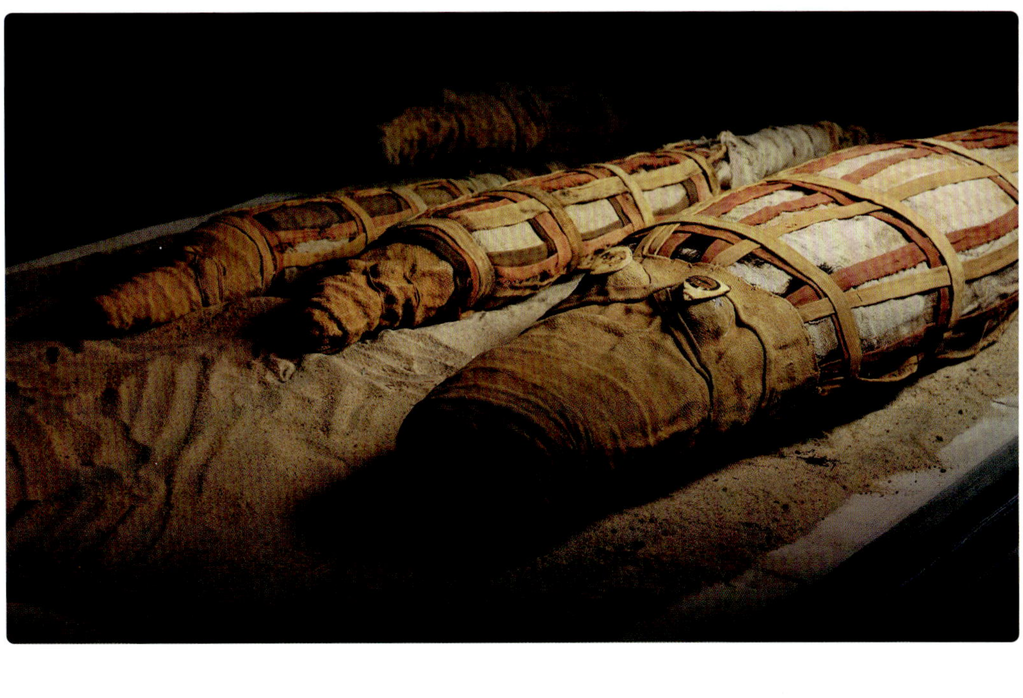

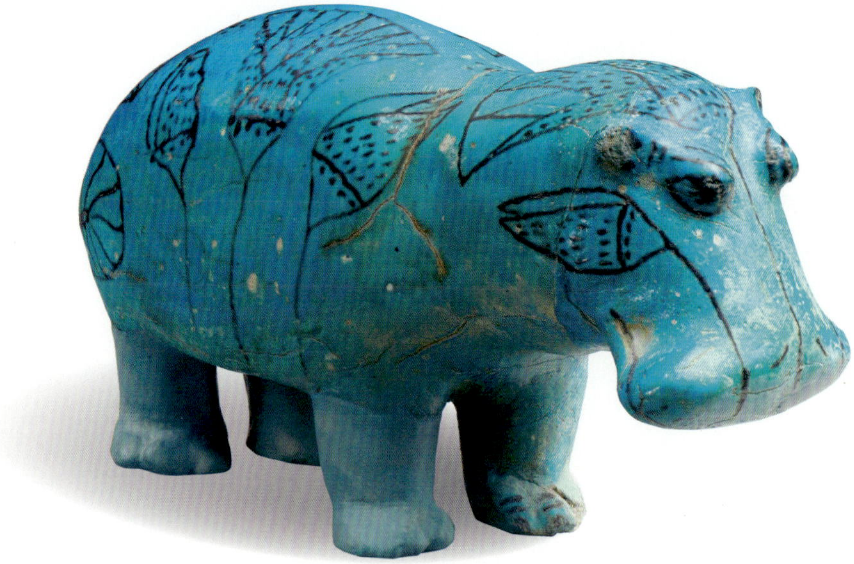

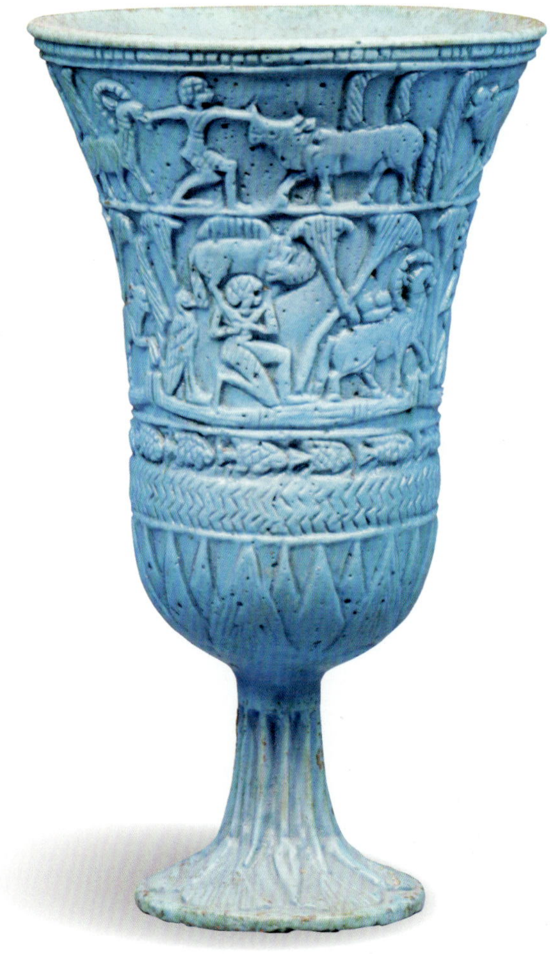

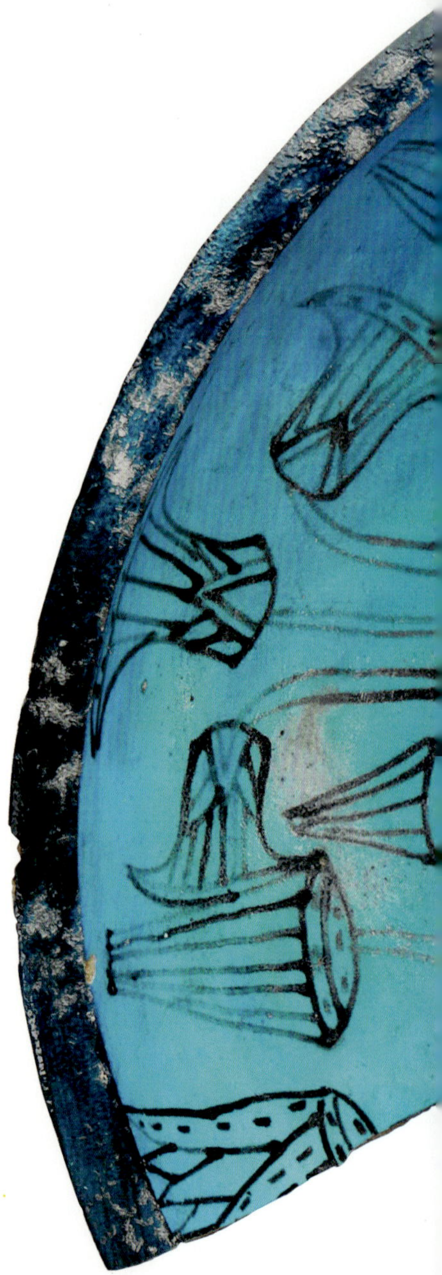

Adorned with marsh plants, a ceramic hippopotamus—now restored (above)—was buried with its legs broken, likely to prevent it from harming the deceased official in whose tomb it was found (1961–1878 B.C.).

Made of the same blue-glazed ceramic, called faience, a chalice (left) dated to about 945–715 B.C. takes the form of a sacred blue lily, a waterborne flower that was associated with rebirth.

A faience bowl (right), found near an 18th-dynasty shrine (1479–1458 B.C.), represents a pool filled with blue lilies.

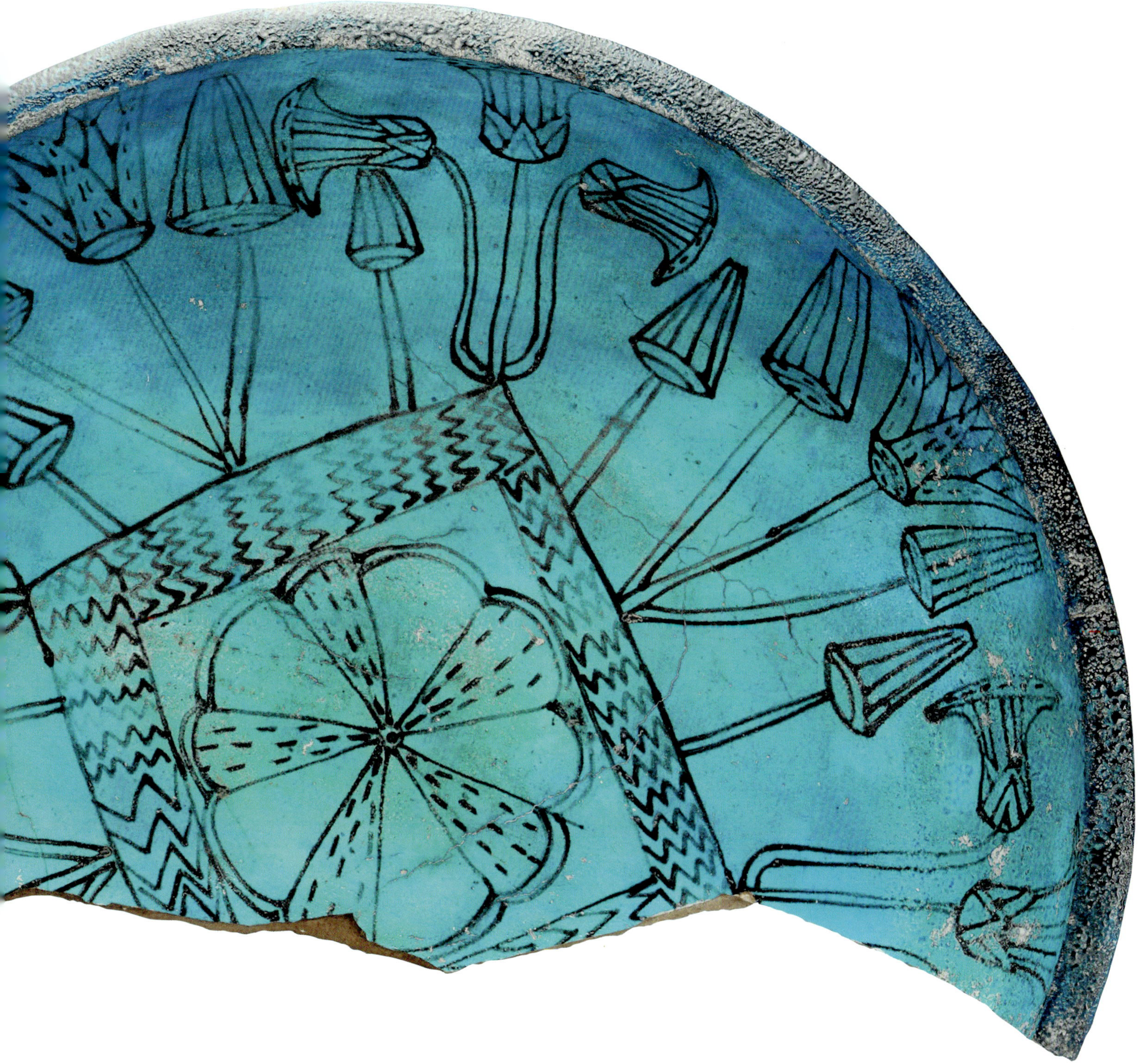

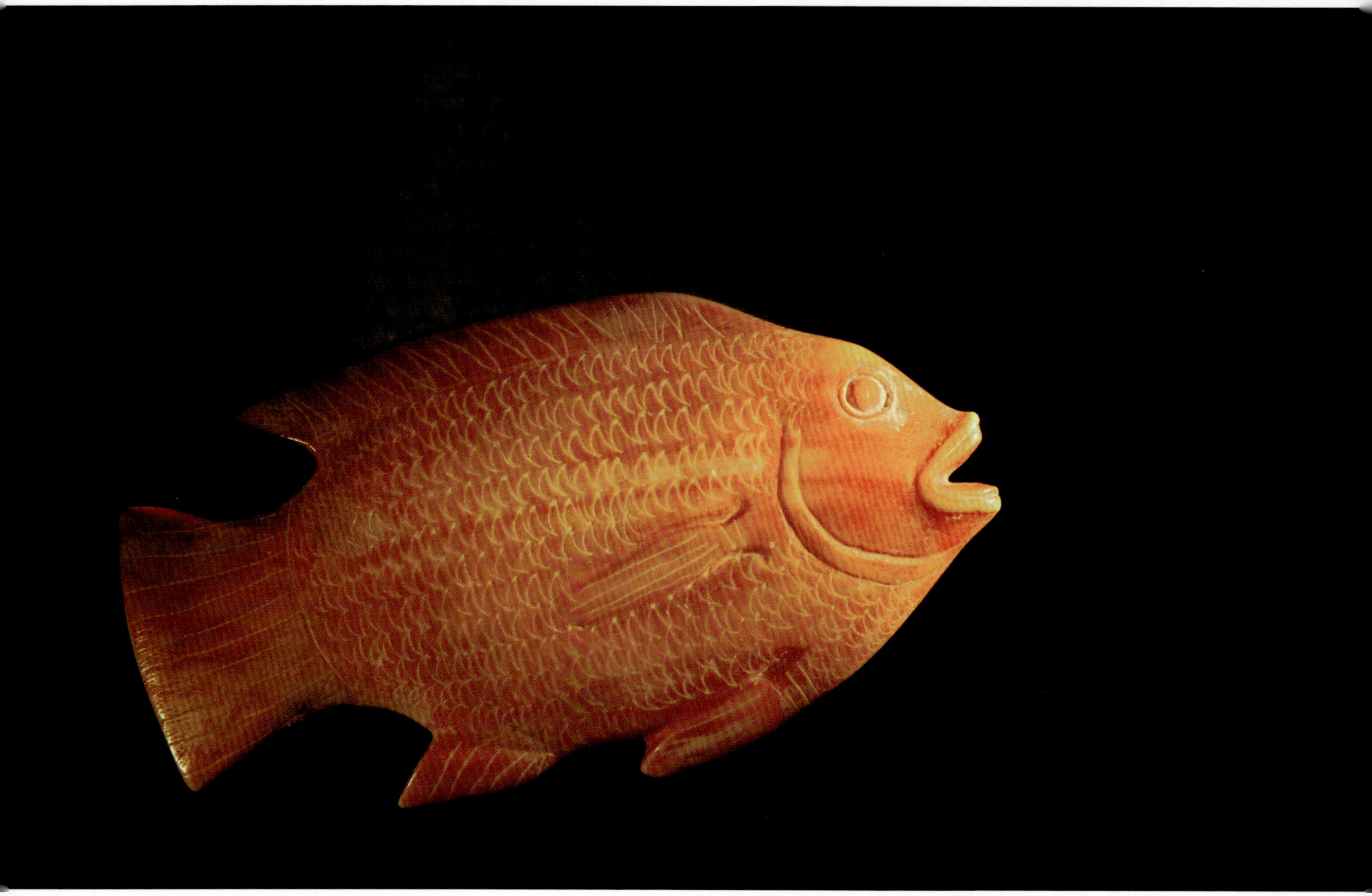

An exquisitely carved ivory fish was found at Saqqara in the 18th-dynasty tomb of a vizier named Aper-El (about 1350 B.C.). The reverse side contains a well that once held a cosmetic ointment.

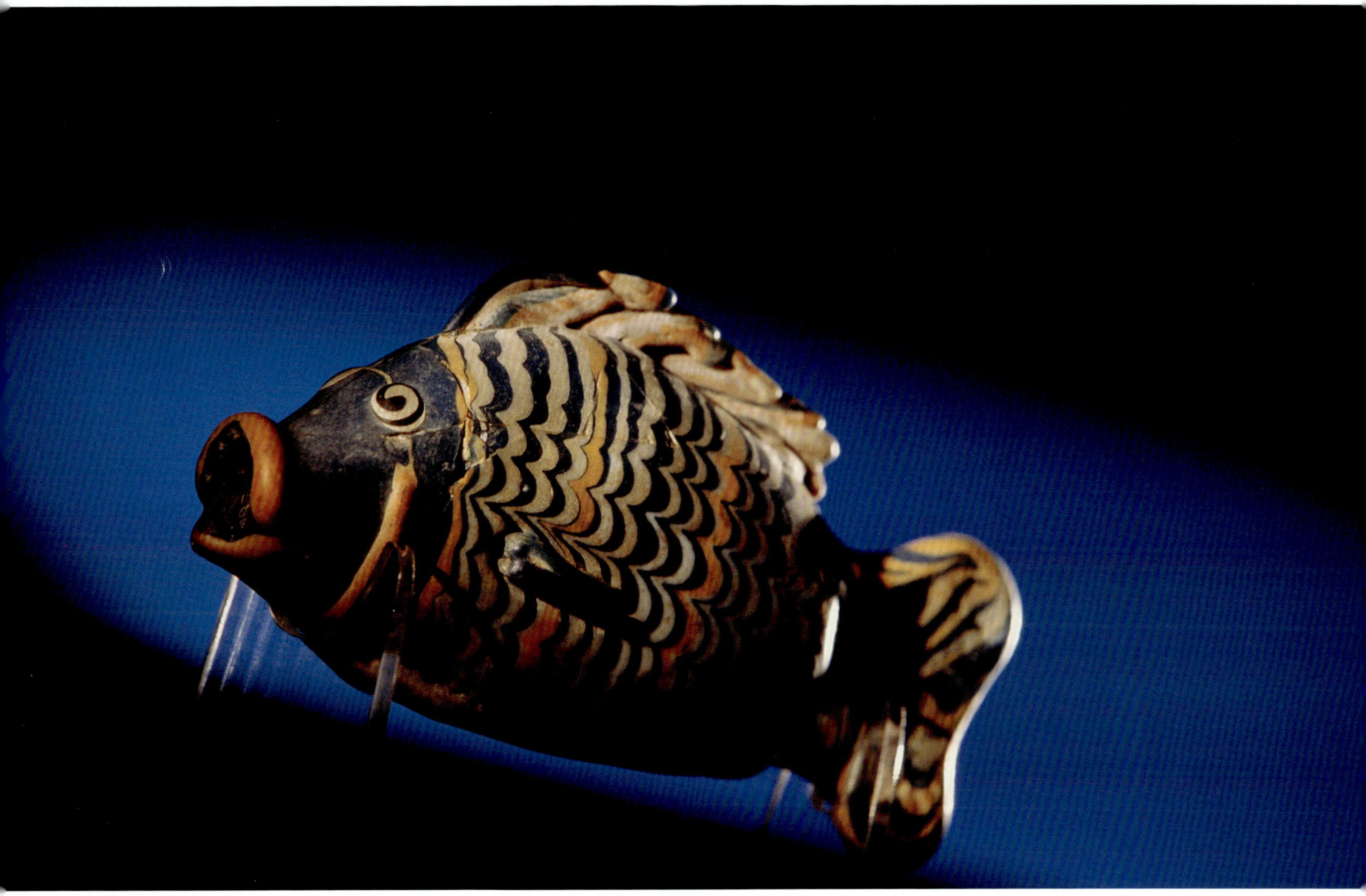

A fragile glass fish was discovered under a plaster floor of a house at Tell el-Amarna, the site of King Akhenaten's capital (about 1353–1336 B.C.). It likely had a stand to hold it up.

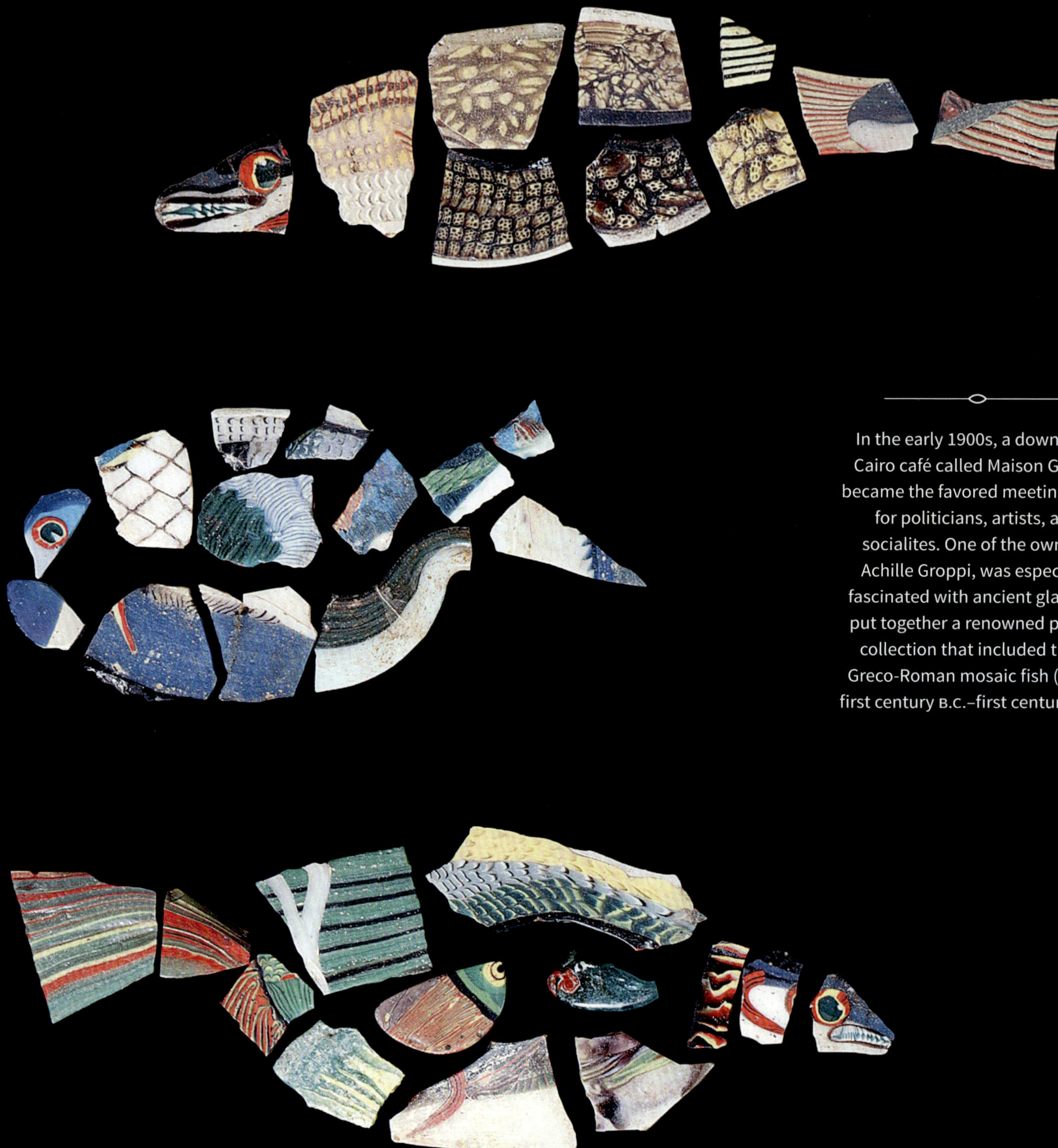

In the early 1900s, a downtown Cairo café called Maison Groppi became the favored meeting place for politicians, artists, and socialites. One of the owners, Achille Groppi, was especially fascinated with ancient glass. He put together a renowned private collection that included these Greco-Roman mosaic fish (about first century B.C.–first century A.D.).

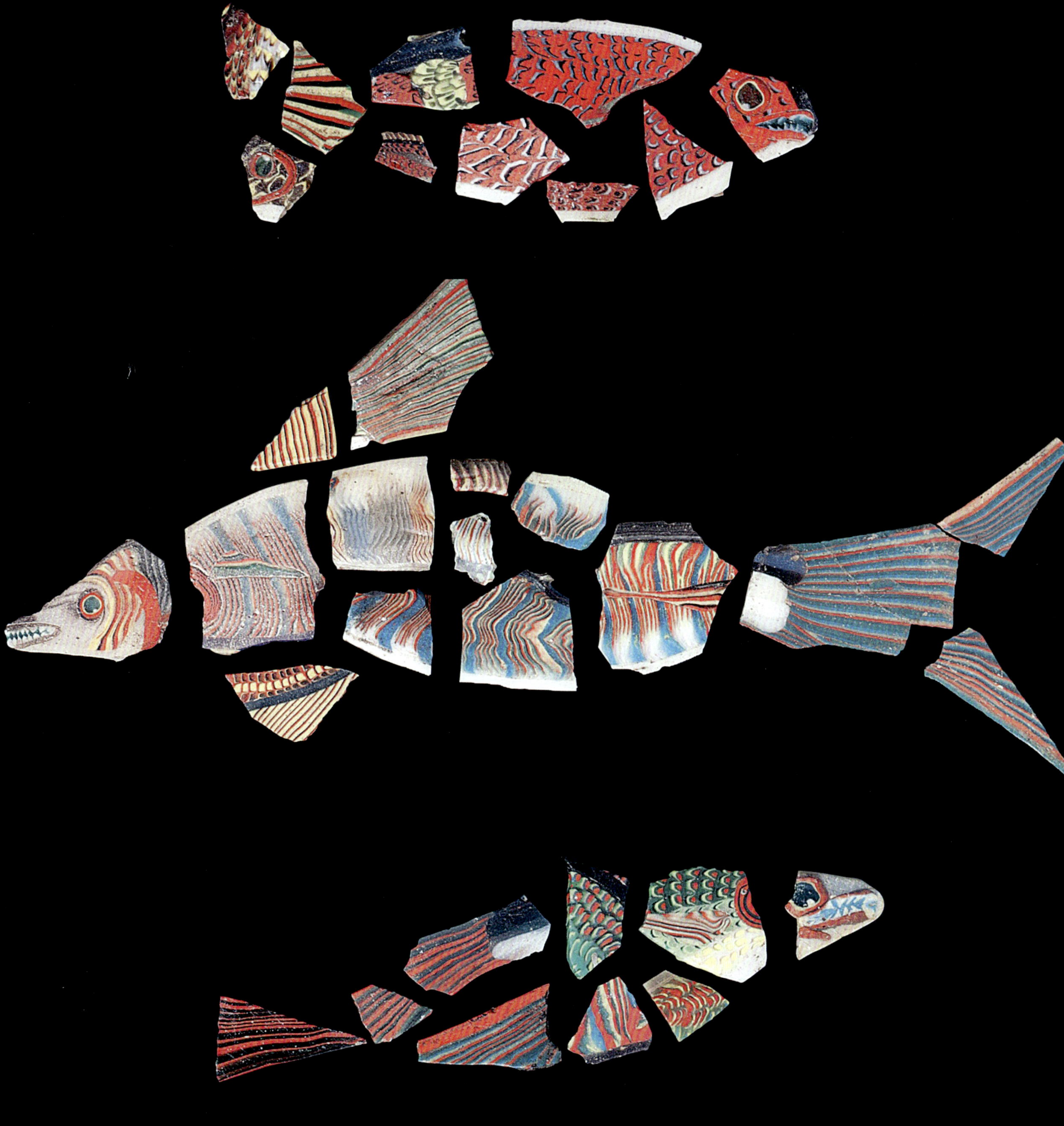

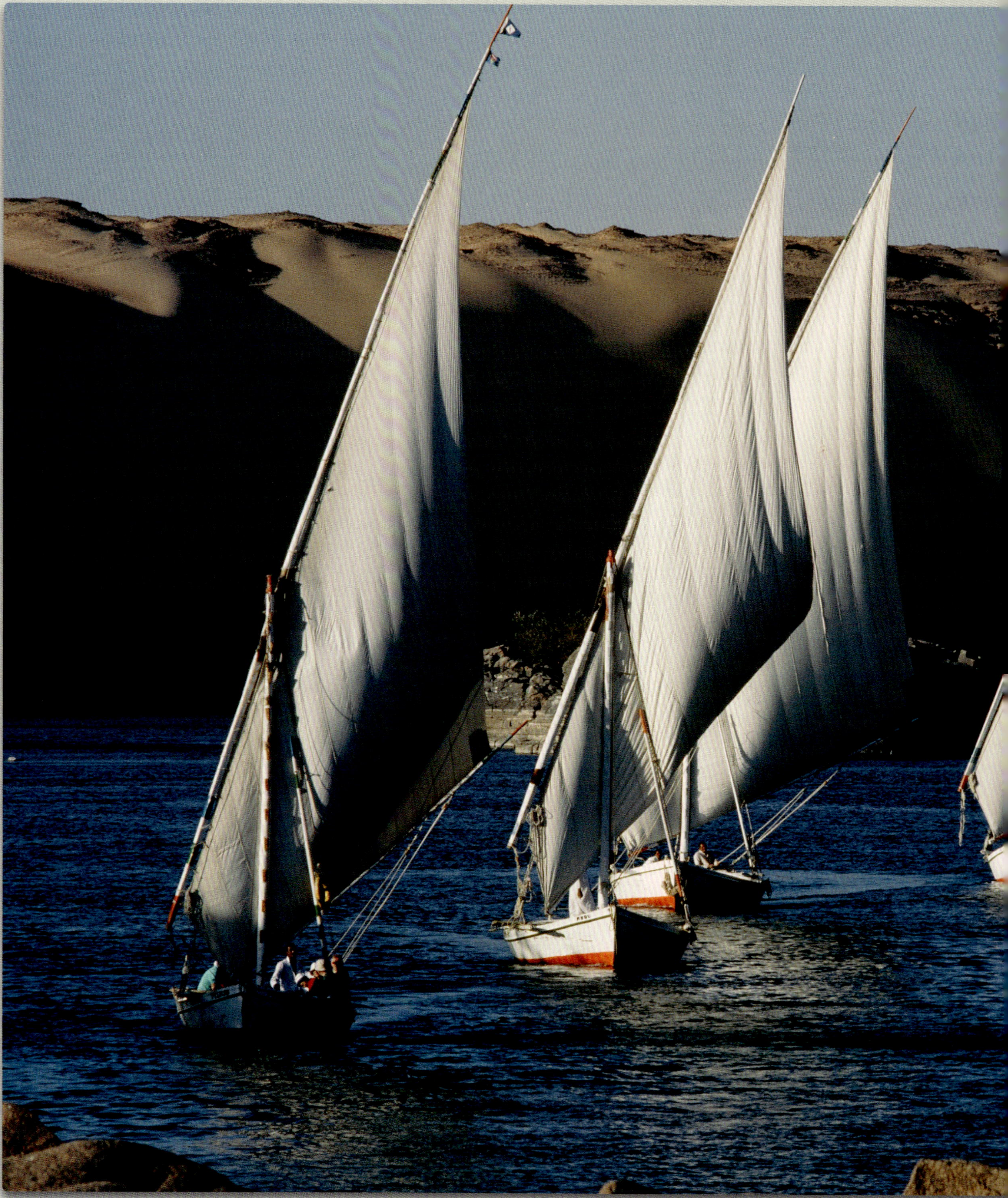

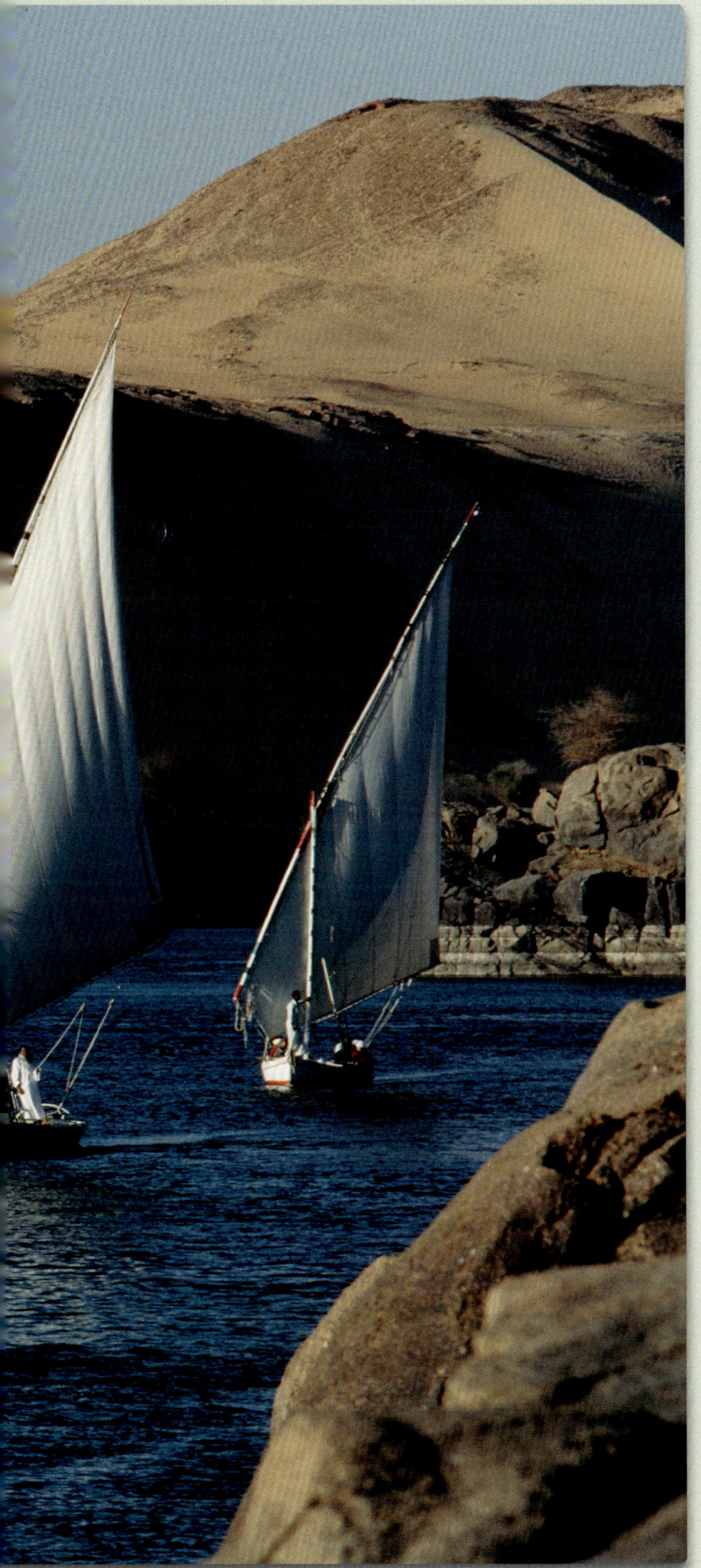

DIGGING DEEPER

Cruising the River

THE NILE WAS Egypt's great highway, linking all the communities along its length. Boats for traveling on it ranged from simple skiffs of bound papyrus reeds (which ordinary people often used for hunting in the marshes), large barges constructed of acacia wood planks (used for transporting goods such as building stones), and grand royal vessels crafted of Lebanese cedar (like the ones buried at Giza near the pyramids).

Modern feluccas (left) give a sense of what the river must have looked like in antiquity. The prevailing wind blew to the south, so traveling in that direction—expressed by the word *khent,* meaning "to go upstream"—could be done under sail. Traveling north—*khed,* or "to go downstream" —might rely on the current, with some rowing.

In the afterlife, Egyptians hoped to be able to participate in all the activities they enjoyed in their current incarnation, including performing their jobs. As a result, many boats appear on tomb walls to make them magically available for the deceased. The king needed to oversee his realm eternally, so he took with him the finest boats that carpenters could build.

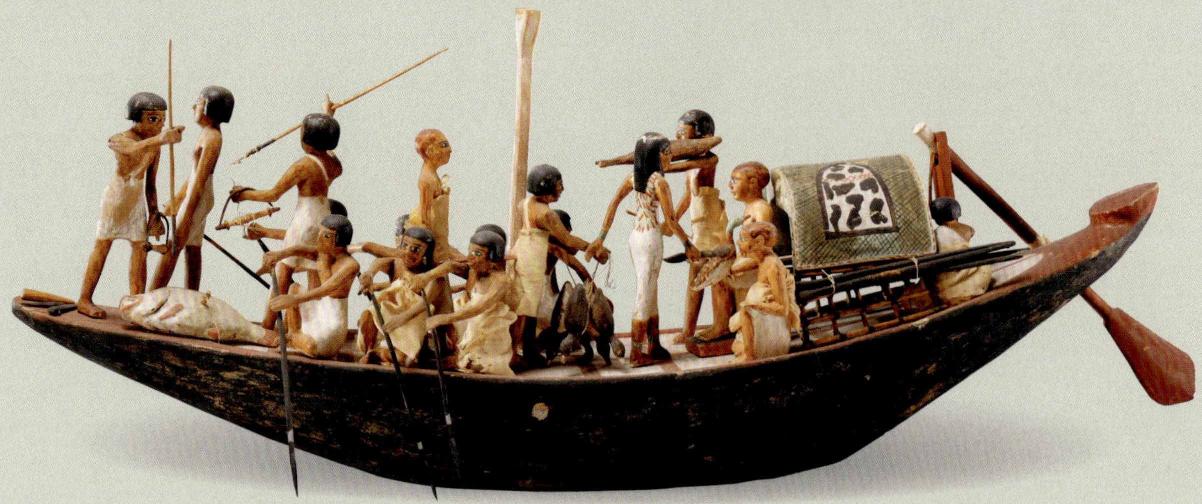

RIVER TRANSPORT

A wooden boat almost four feet (1.2 m) long (above) evokes one of the pleasures of elite life—fishing on the Nile, with servants to do the work. The model was buried with Meketre, an 11th-dynasty official (about 2000 B.C.).

Meketre's tomb also included this paddled boat (below) among the models meant for his use in the afterlife. Ritual journeys were taken on this kind of vessel.

Paddles also propelled the boat of King Khufu (about 2550 B.C.). Buried in his funerary complex at Giza and displayed there after discovery (opposite), it is now at the Grand Egyptian Museum.

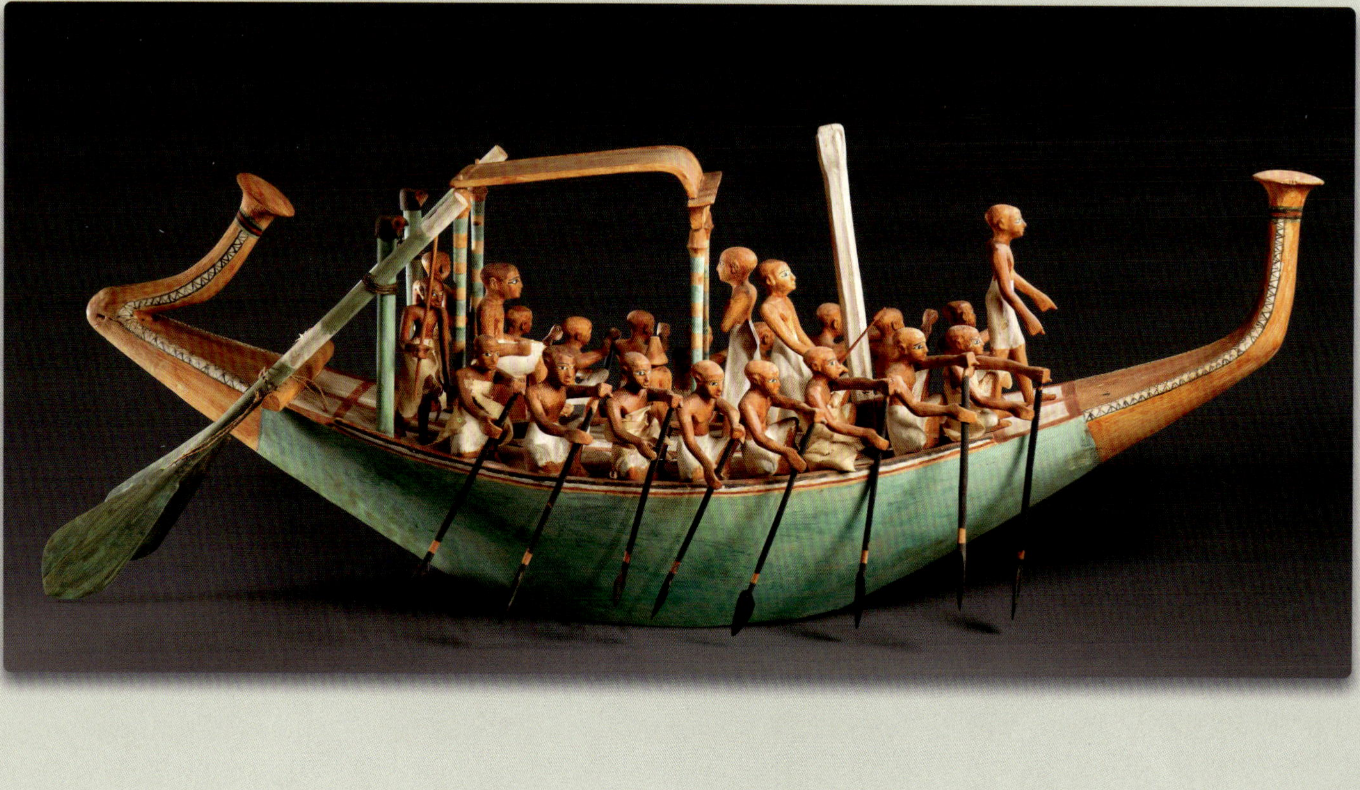

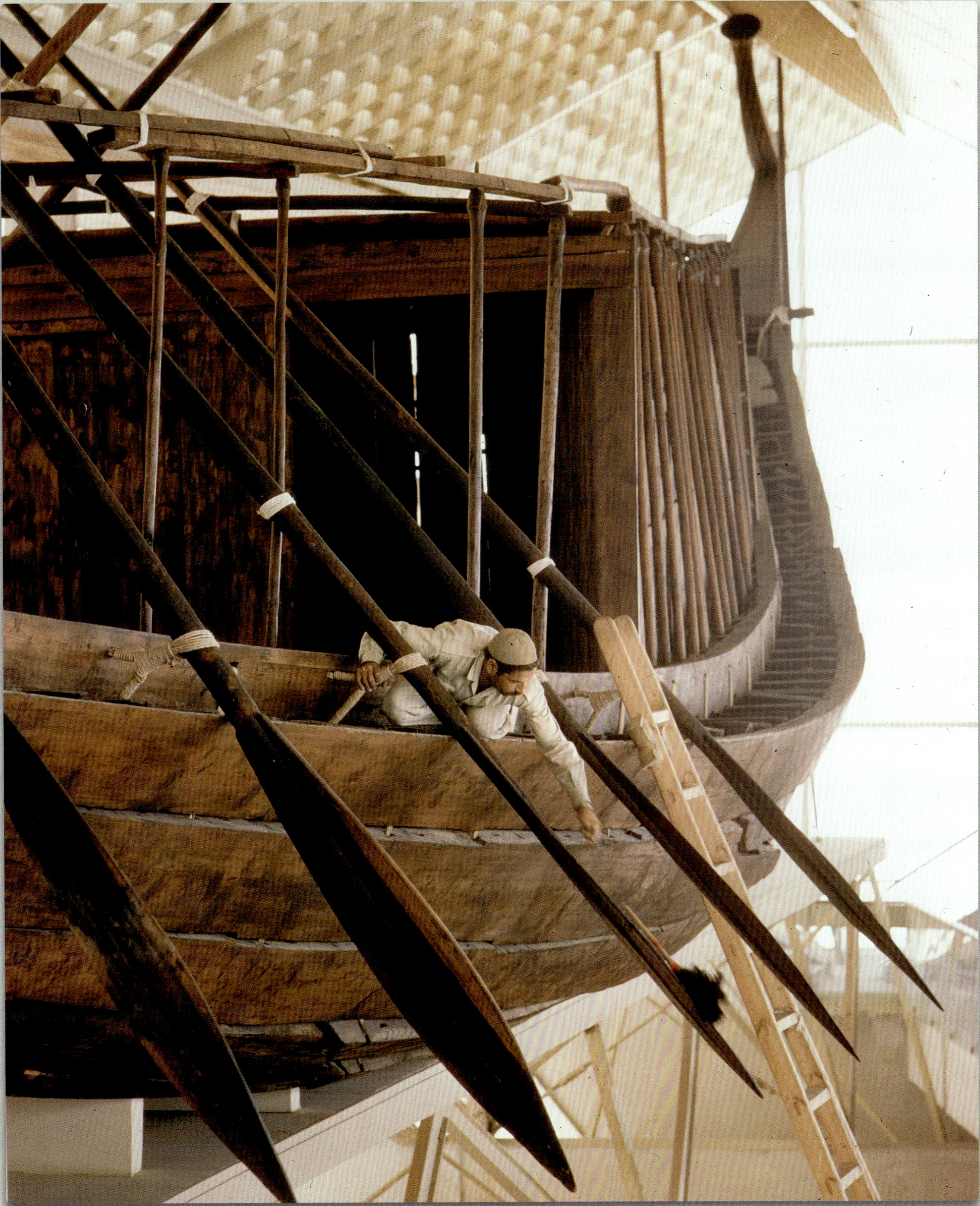

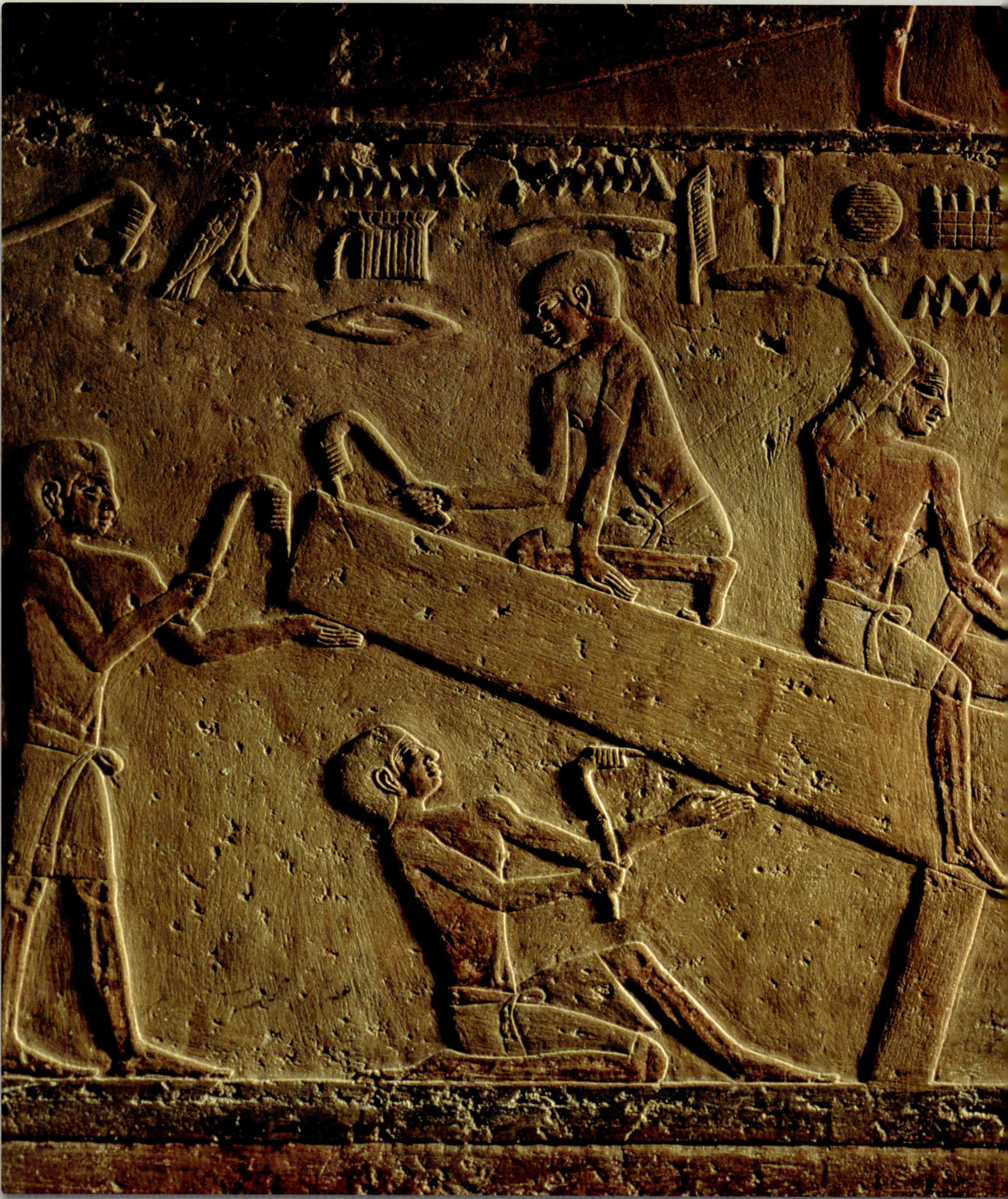

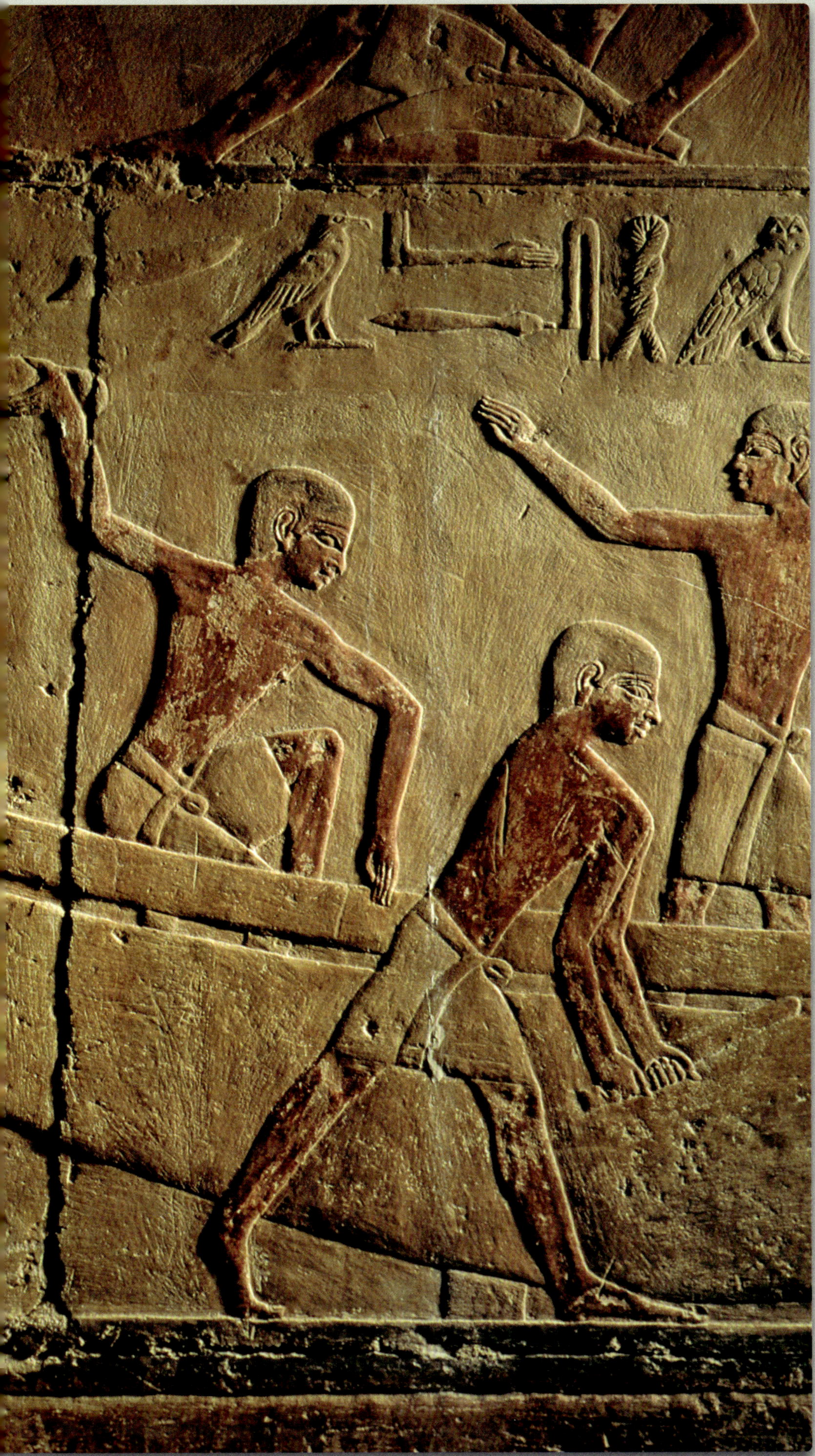

LAUNCHING INTO THE AFTERLIFE

Boat building was an important job on the estate of fifth-dynasty official Ti (about 2460 B.C.). His tomb at Saqqara depicted that in detail, along with tasks such as raising ducks and geese, butchering oxen, tanning hides, harvesting flax and grain, threshing grain, baking bread, and brewing beer.

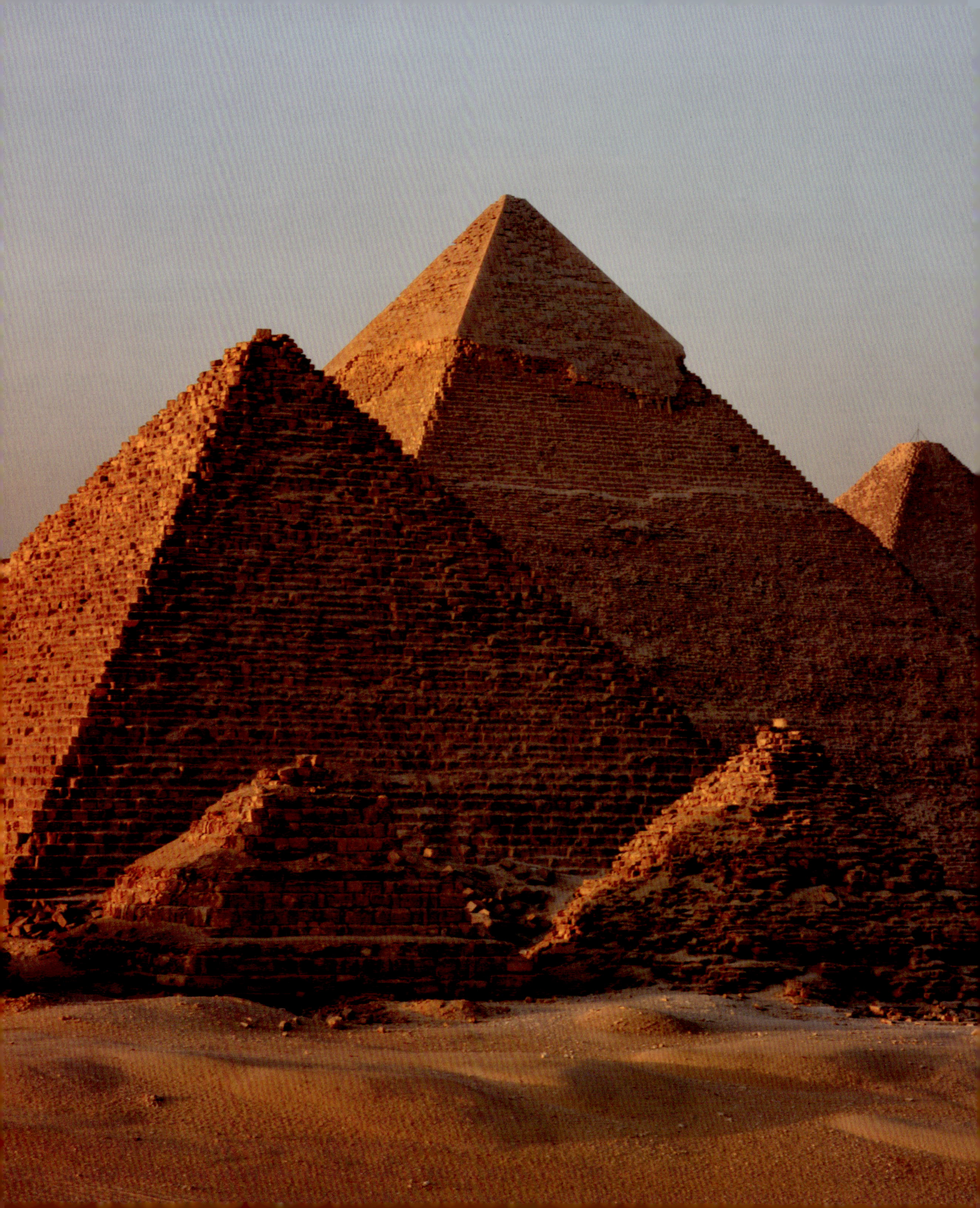

CHAPTER THREE

MEMPHIS

A Royal City and Its Pyramids

The pyramids at Giza, which mark the tombs of early kings, have always been mesmerizing. When they were new, some 4,500 years ago, they were by far the biggest structures that anyone had ever seen. The largest, Khufu's Great Pyramid, rose more than 470 feet (140 m) above the desert sand.

All three structures were covered in polished white limestone, which must have been blinding in full sunlight. Though that brilliant casing is now gone, recycled for later construction projects, the ancient tombs have lost none of their grandeur. They dwarf buildings, people, cars, and camels and are visible from downtown Cairo, about three and a half miles (5.5 km) away.

These pyramids are part of an ancient cemetery extending about 50 miles (80 km) from north to south, whose sections are now known by modern names: Giza, Abusir, Saqqara, Dahshur, Abu Roash, and Meidum. The earliest burials along that stretch date to the very first dynasty and were associated with Egypt's first capital, known today by its Greek name, Memphis.

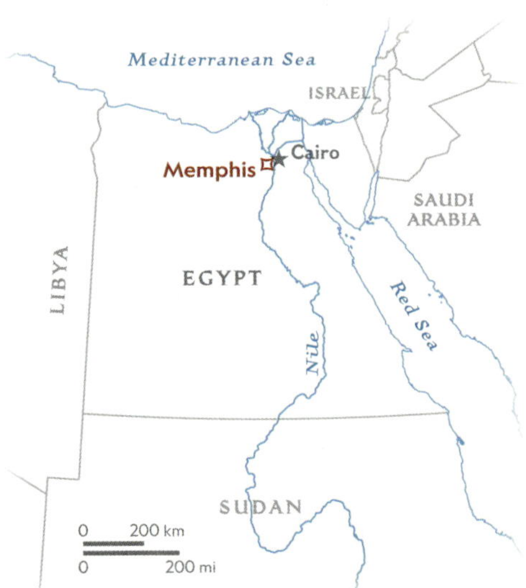

Though the first kings of a unified Egypt came from the area around Abydos in the south, they established their great administrative city here, where the Nile split into meandering courses that created a delta as they deposited silt on the way to the Mediterranean Sea. The city was called Ineb-Hedj, or the "white wall," suggesting that it was a fortress from which the king controlled traffic on the river and trade routes over the land.

In time, Ineb-Hedj became a large, cosmopolitan political and religious center that would survive as a seat of power for the rest of pharaonic history. Much of the city has been lost beneath silt, sand, and urban development, but a few traces are still visible near the modern town of Mit Rahina, including the ruins of a temple to Ptah (the city's patron god), a colossal statue of Ramses II, and part of the dazzling wall, which Russian archaeologists uncovered in 2015.

High officials were already being buried at Saqqara when third-dynasty king Djoser decided to upend tradition by building his own tomb there, instead of at Abydos as his predecessors had done. In fact, Djoser and his architect, Imhotep, would spark a further revolution by reimagining the shape of a king's final resting place.

Previous tombs had been shaped like a low bench, called a *mastaba* in Arabic. But for this new tomb at Saqqara, begun in about 2660 B.C., six mastaba-like stone tiers were stacked atop each other. Rising to a height of 197 feet (60 m), it was the world's first monumental stone construction and is today called the Step Pyramid.

Its symbolism is complex, and not entirely understood. The steps likely represent a stairway to the heavens. But the structure may also have been built to embody the primordial mound rising from the watery chaos of creation, in the same way that the first hillock of land reappeared every year as the Nile flood receded.

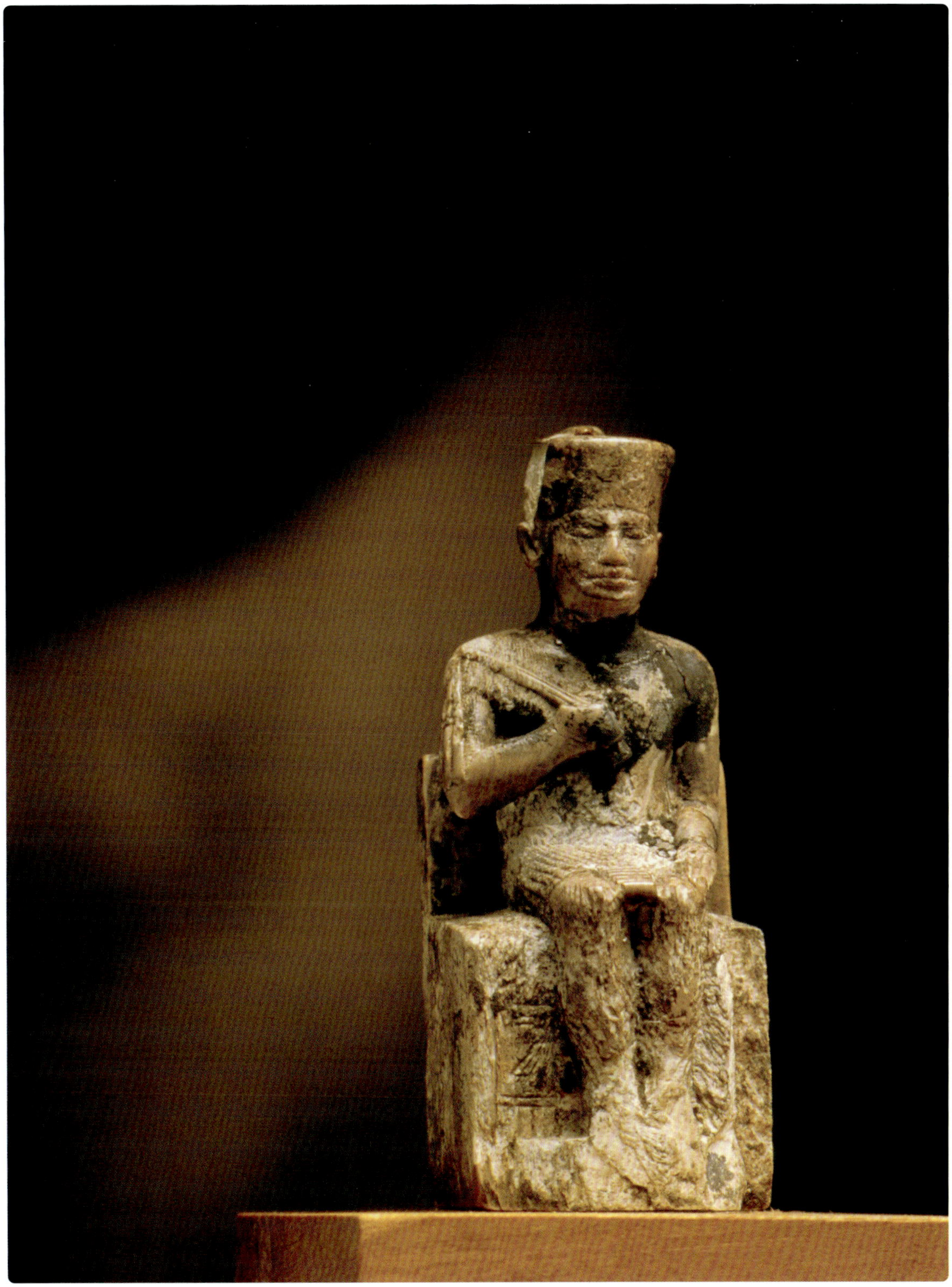

A tiny figurine carved in ivory (above) is the only complete existing portrait of King Khufu, who was laid to rest in the grandest of the pyramids at Giza.

PREVIOUS PAGES: The monumental tombs of Kings Khufu, Khafre, and Menkaure (about 2550–2450 B.C.)—father, son, and grandson—dominate the horizon at the Giza royal cemetery.

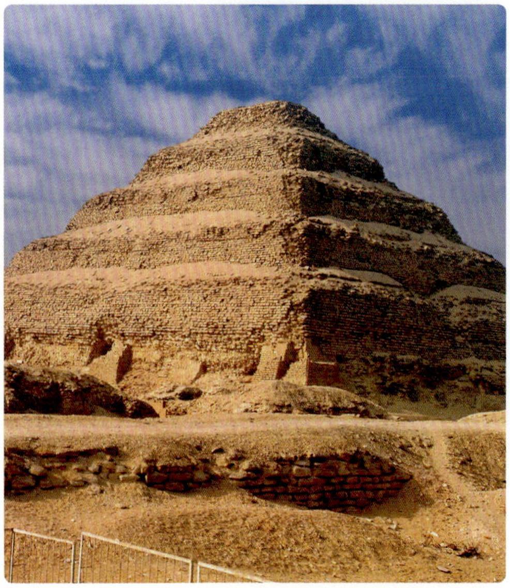 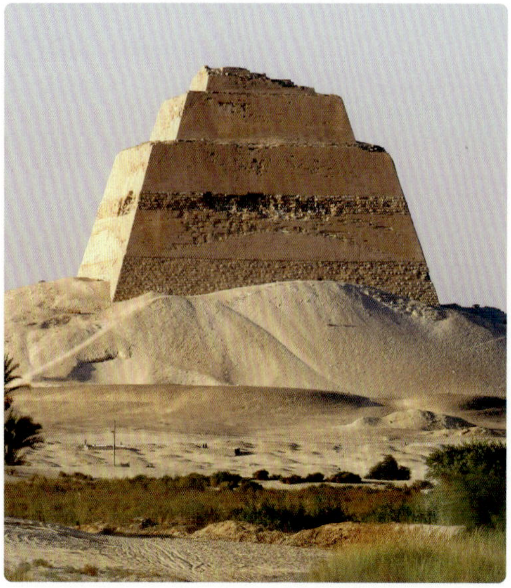 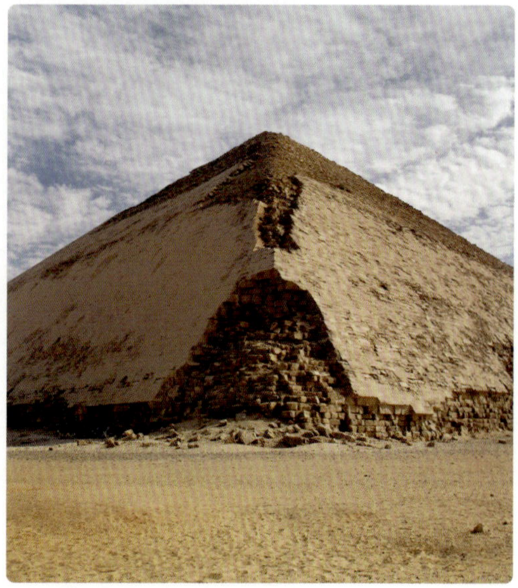

LEFT TO RIGHT: Old Kingdom rulers experimented with pyramid tomb construction until they got the profile just right. Djoser's Step Pyramid is the oldest monumental stone building in the world (about 2650 B.C.). Snefru built his first tomb, a strange three-tiered tower, at Meidum (about 2575 B.C.). He then went on to a new project, the Bent Pyramid at Dahshur.

At the start of the fourth dynasty, in about 2600 B.C., a king named Snefru would continue to experiment with the pyramid shape. At Meidum, he began to erect a burial monument with steep-sided tiers. But for unknown reasons he abandoned this project and started on another, with smooth sides, at Dahshur. The initial angle of the second attempt must have been too steep, though. Near the top, the angle was reduced, creating a kink that gives the structure its modern name, the Bent Pyramid. Still not satisfied, Snefru tried one more time, also at Dahshur, with a gently sloped structure called the Red Pyramid. Egyptologists believe the king was probably interred there, though looters in antiquity most likely removed the king's body while carrying off his funerary goods.

Snefru's successor, Khufu, chose the northern part of the cemetery, now known as Giza, for his tomb. There he brought the pyramid to its fullest expression, with long, smooth sides slanting downward like the rays of the sun. The burial chamber is hidden inside, along with other voids and passages with purposes that remain mysterious. Outside lay the king's mortuary temple, two buried boats, pyramids for his queens, mastabas for his courtiers, and a deep shaft that held some of the funerary goods of his mother, Hetepheres.

Khufu's son Khafre also built his pyramid at Giza, and it's likely he had the iconic Sphinx carved from bedrock along the causeway leading to his tomb. His son, Menkaure, followed with his own pyramid, completing the monumental architectural trio.

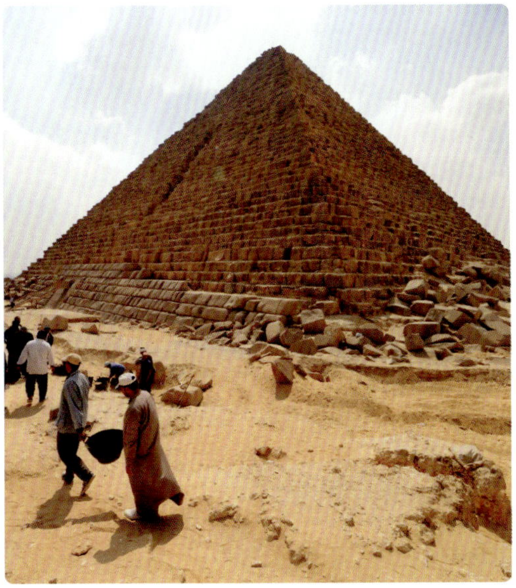

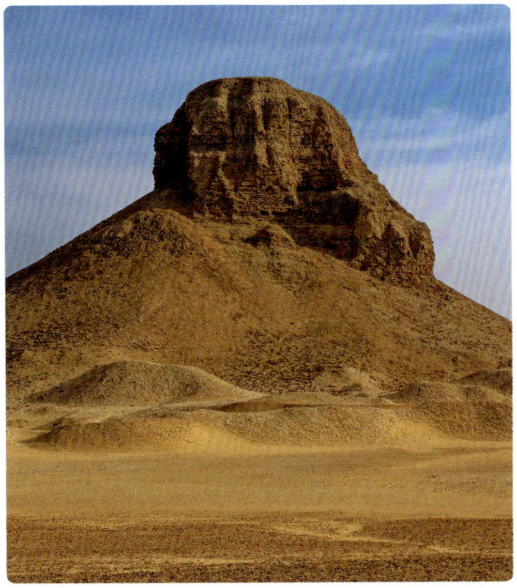

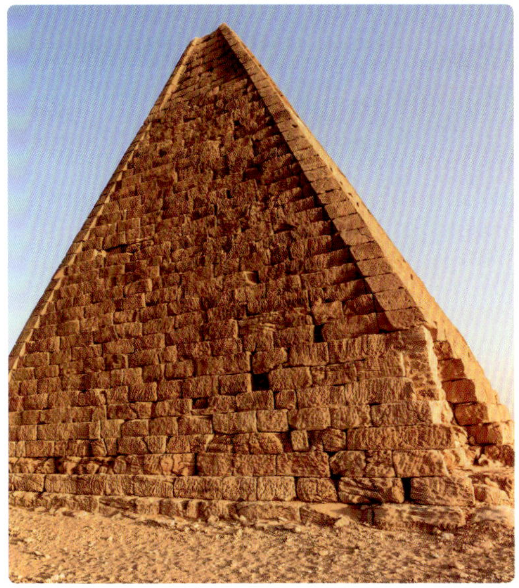

LEFT TO RIGHT: By the time of Menkaure's tomb at Giza (about 2475 B.C.), the pyramid had been perfected. Amenemhet III's tomb at Dahshur (about 1818–1770 B.C.) was robbed of its limestone casing and is now just crumbling mud brick. Influenced by Egypt, Kushite royalty created steep-sided pyramids at Gebel Barkal (third to first centuries B.C.) and other sites now in Sudan.

All this construction, which occurred over the course of three generations, must have required a workforce of thousands that was apparently divided into teams. Graffiti in Khufu's pyramid include the name of one of these, "Friends of Khufu Gang." At Menkaure's mortuary temple, the name "Friends of Menkaure Gang" appears on one side, while the other side is inscribed with "Drunkards of Menkaure Gang," possibly signaling a rivalry.

The ruins of other pyramids dot the vast cemetery; they've been stripped of their casings and are now crumbling mounds. But not just royals built their tombs here. Throughout the centuries, countless officials also chose to be buried at the Memphis necropolis. Even as kings, queens, and courtiers were interred in and around the Valley of the Kings near Luxor, notables like 18th-dynasty vizier Aper-El, treasurer Maya, and King Tut's wet nurse Maia chose this spot as their final resting place.

Egyptian kings would continue to build pyramids into the Middle Kingdom, until about 1800 B.C., but many of the later structures had a core of mud brick that eroded once the outer stones were removed for reuse. During the 25th dynasty, the Nubian kings who conquered Egypt around 770 B.C. would begin to build steep-sided pyramid tombs in their own homeland. But the age of the grand pyramids at Memphis would never again be equaled. Every visitor today stands in awe, just as Napoleon did as he led his invading army onto the Giza plateau in July 1798 and declared, "Soldiers, from the height of these pyramids, forty centuries look down upon you." ▲

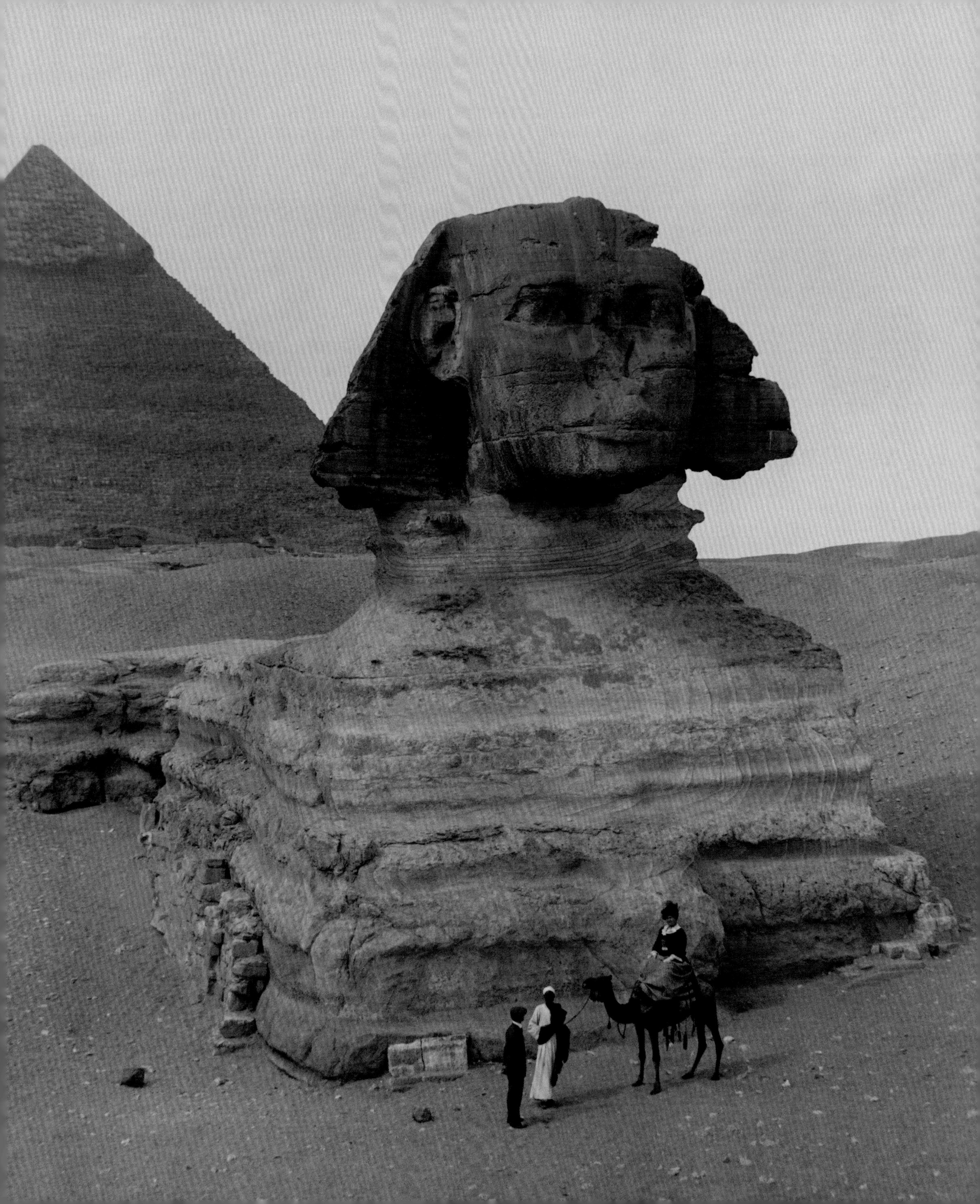

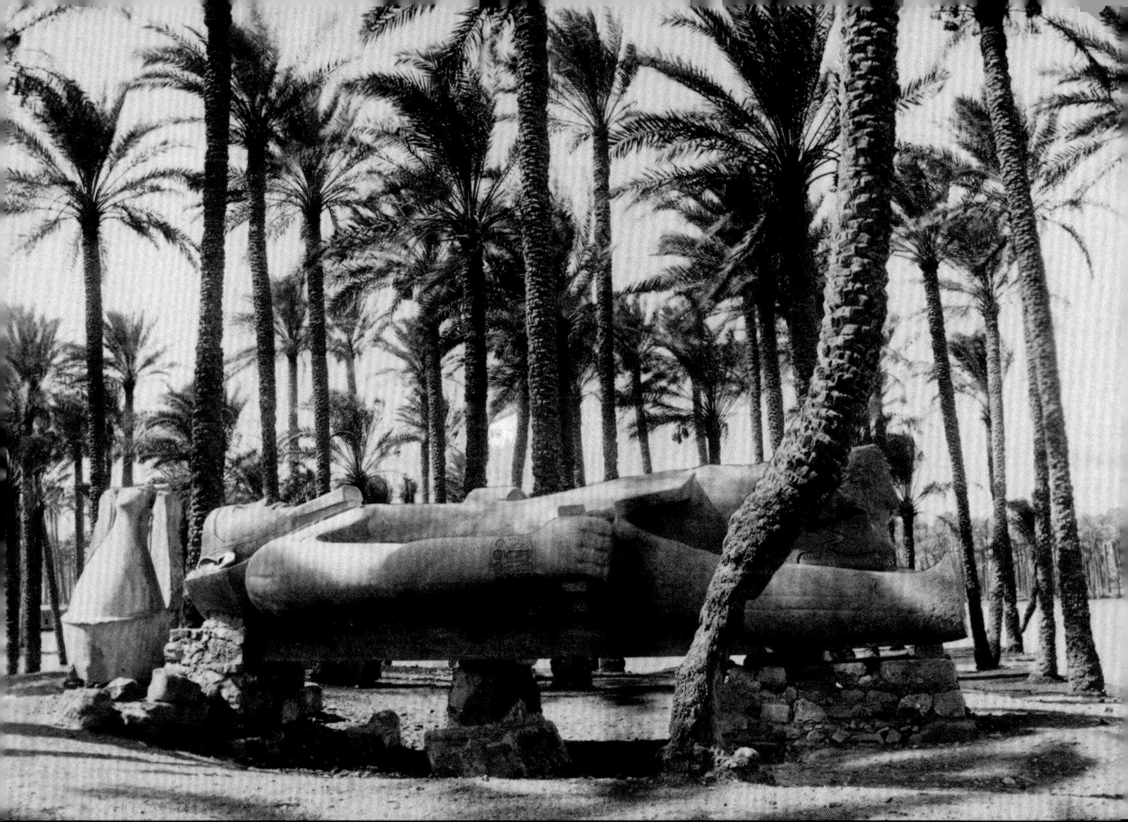

In 1913, *National Geographic* published this photo (above) of a Ramses II statue at the site of Memphis. More than 42 feet (12.5 m) tall from head to knees, it stood outside a temple in the 13th century B.C.

A 1922 issue of the magazine showed visitors at the Sphinx and Pyramids at Giza (opposite), then as now at the top of the list of must-see ancient sites for many international travelers.

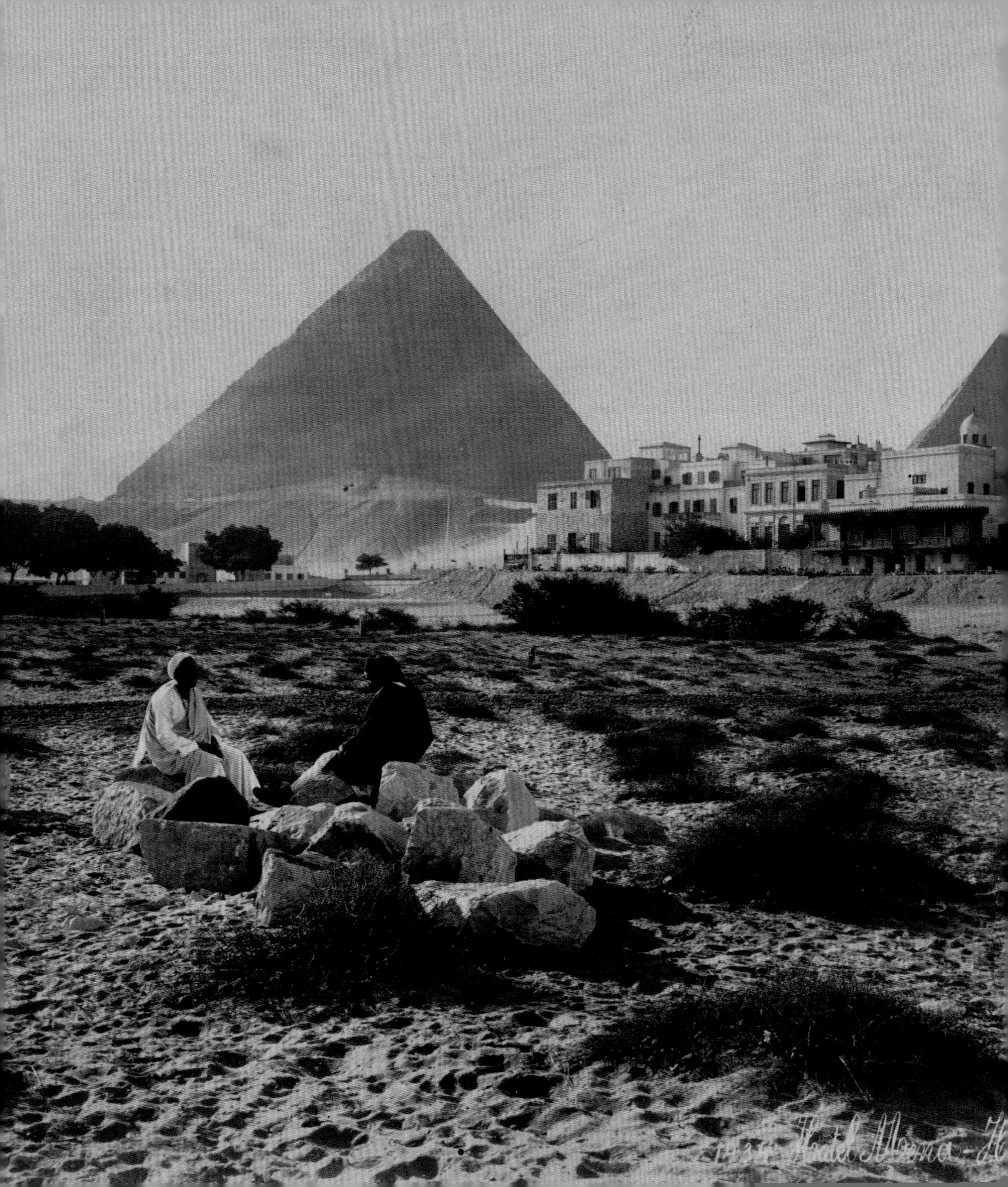
Hotel Mena -

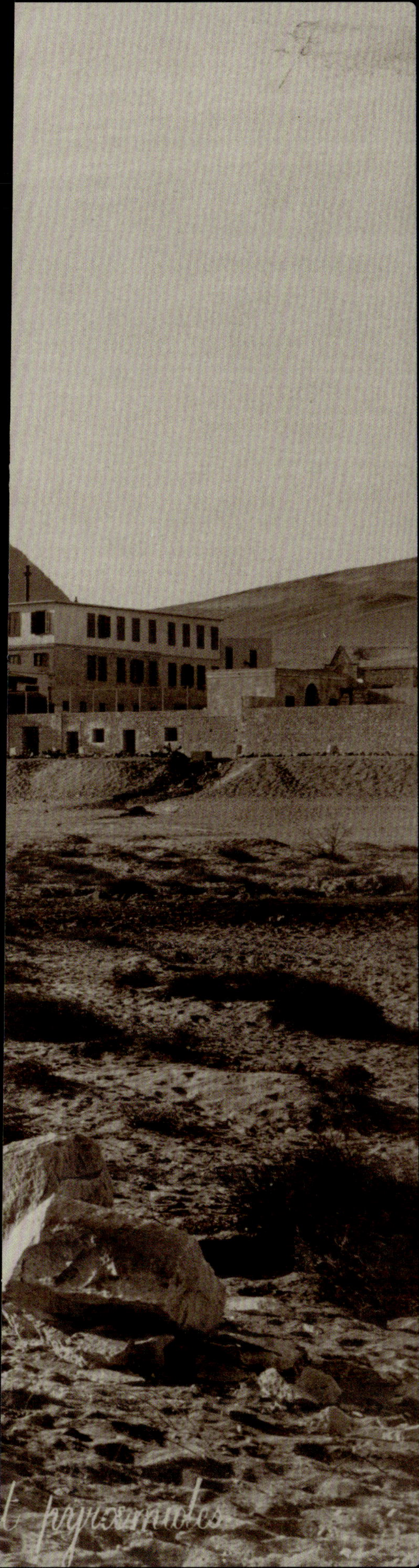

A photo from the late 1800s shows the Mena House Hotel and the Giza Pyramids (left). Archaeologists of the period decided who was going to excavate where while gazing out from a hotel balcony.

Built as an elite hunting lodge, the Mena House was expanded to host guests attending the Suez Canal opening in 1869. Today, it's an oasis for travelers (below), offering rooms with pyramid views.

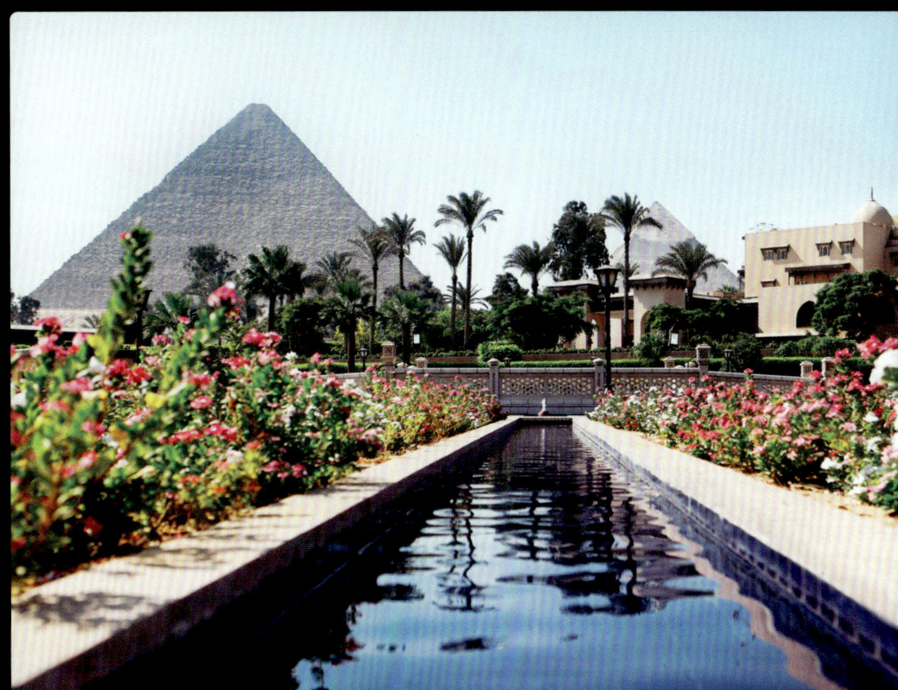

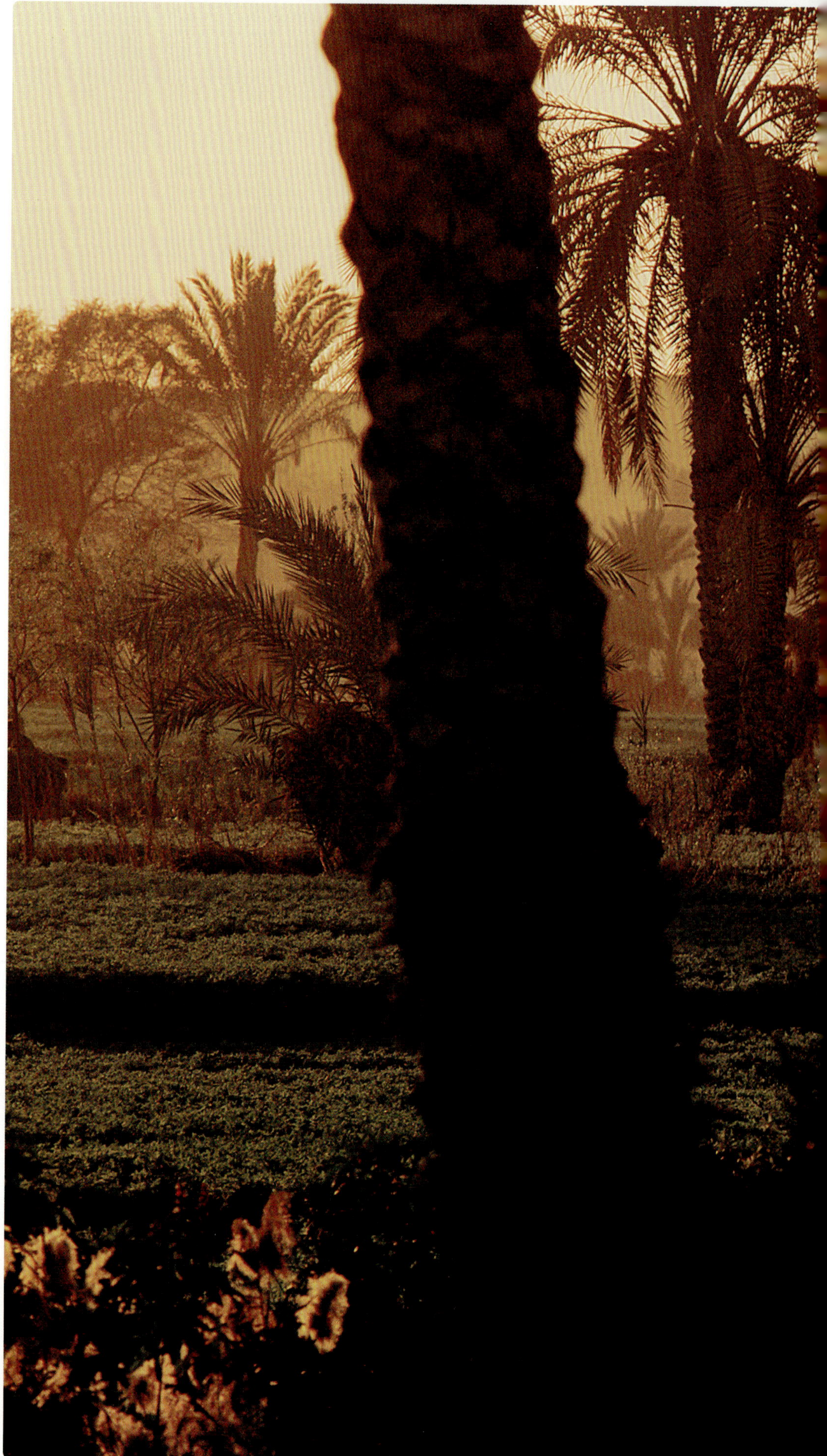

As the setting sun gilds the Step Pyramid at Saqqara, a farmer's children ride their donkey home, passing palm trees and cultivated plots of alfalfa on the Nile's fertile floodplain.

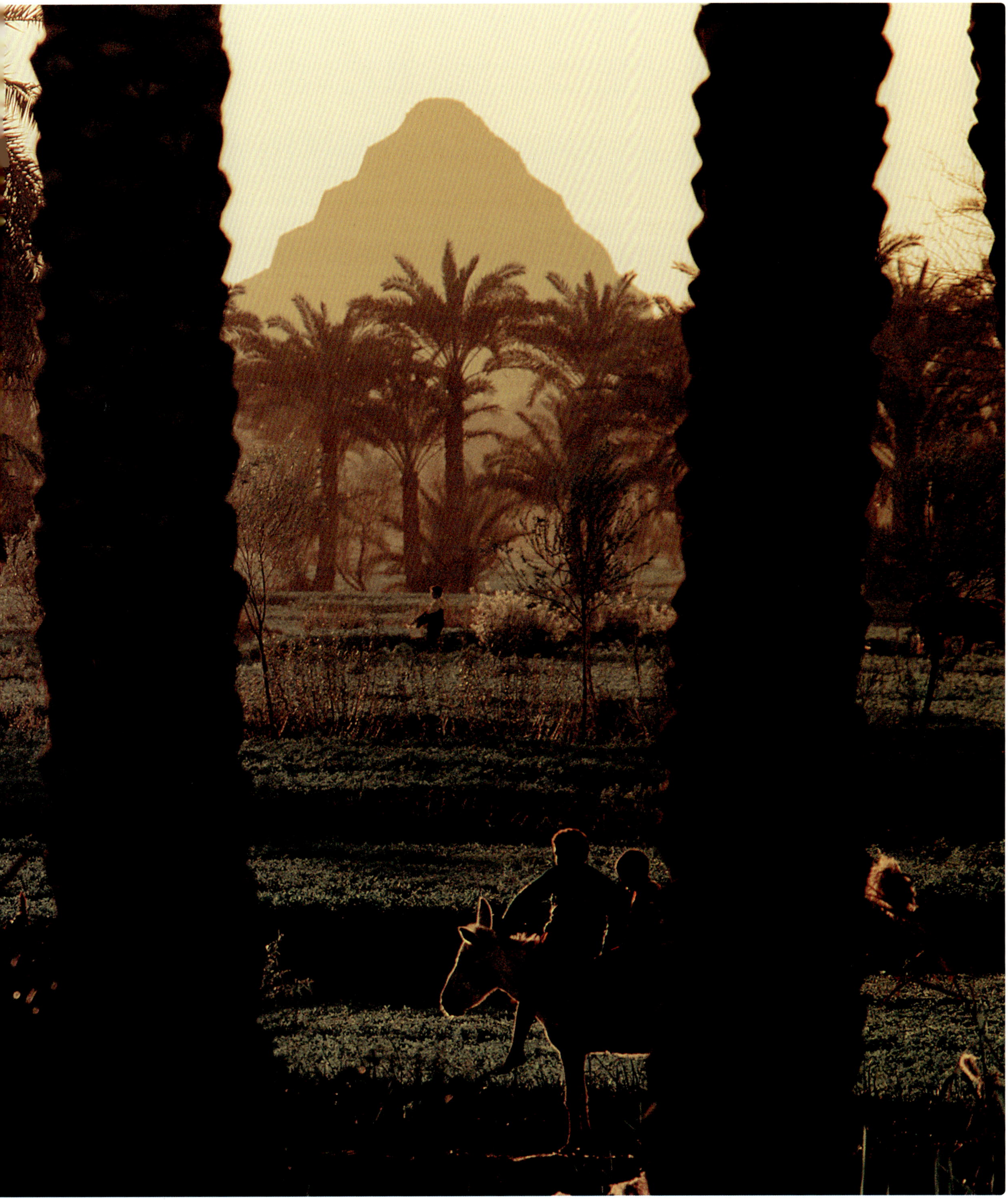

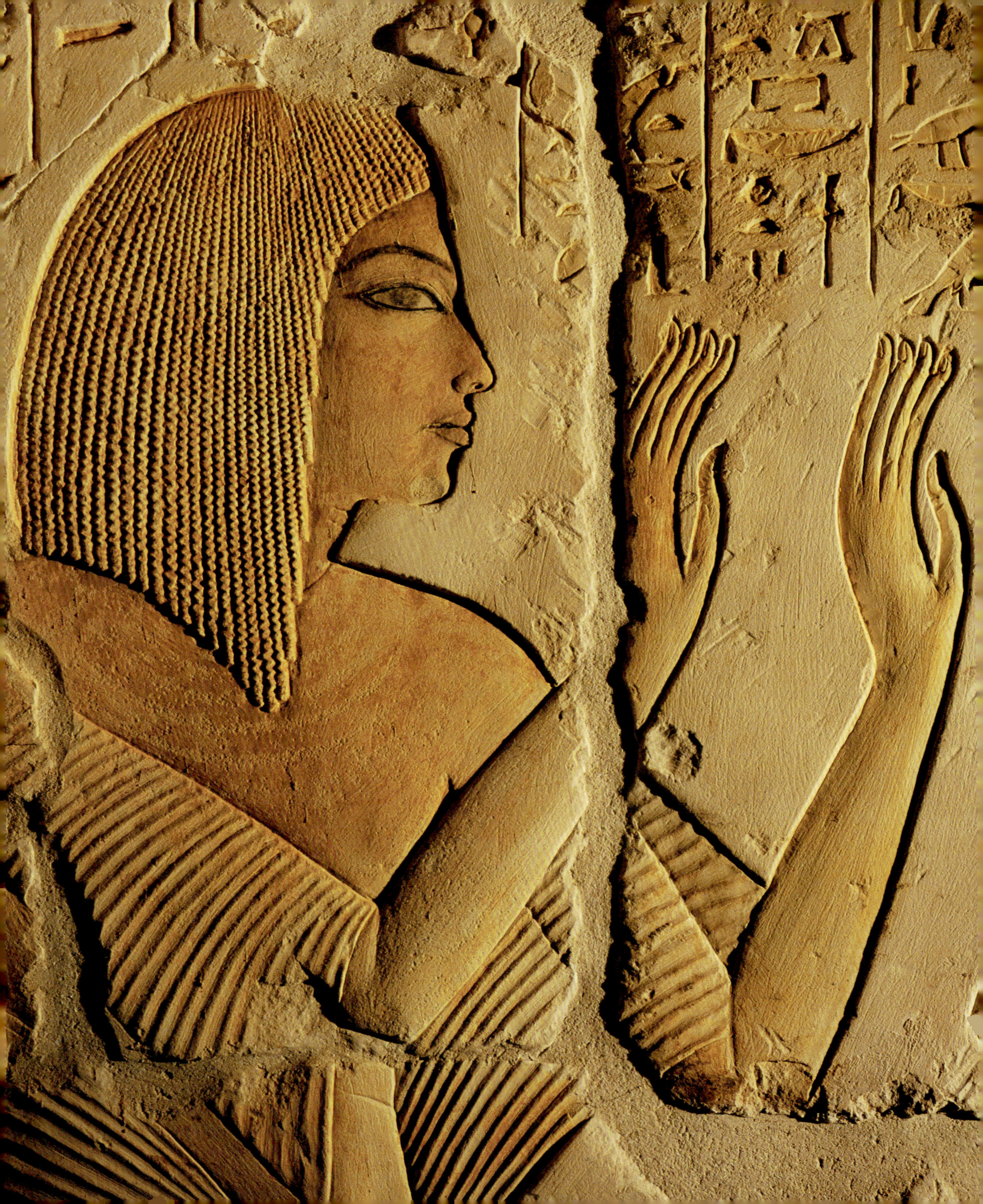

On a wall of his tomb at Saqqara, a man named Maya (opposite) is shown praying to the gods. During the reign of King Tutankhamun (about 1332–1322 B.C.), Maya served as overseer of the treasury.

A vizier and architect, Imhotep designed the Step Pyramid of King Djoser (about 2650–2630 B.C.). This bronze statuette of him (below), from Saqqara, dates to the first century B.C., when Imhotep was worshipped as a god.

Also from the first century B.C., a leaded bronze statuette of Harpokrates (right)—the god Horus as a child—was found in the sacred animal catacombs at Saqqara.

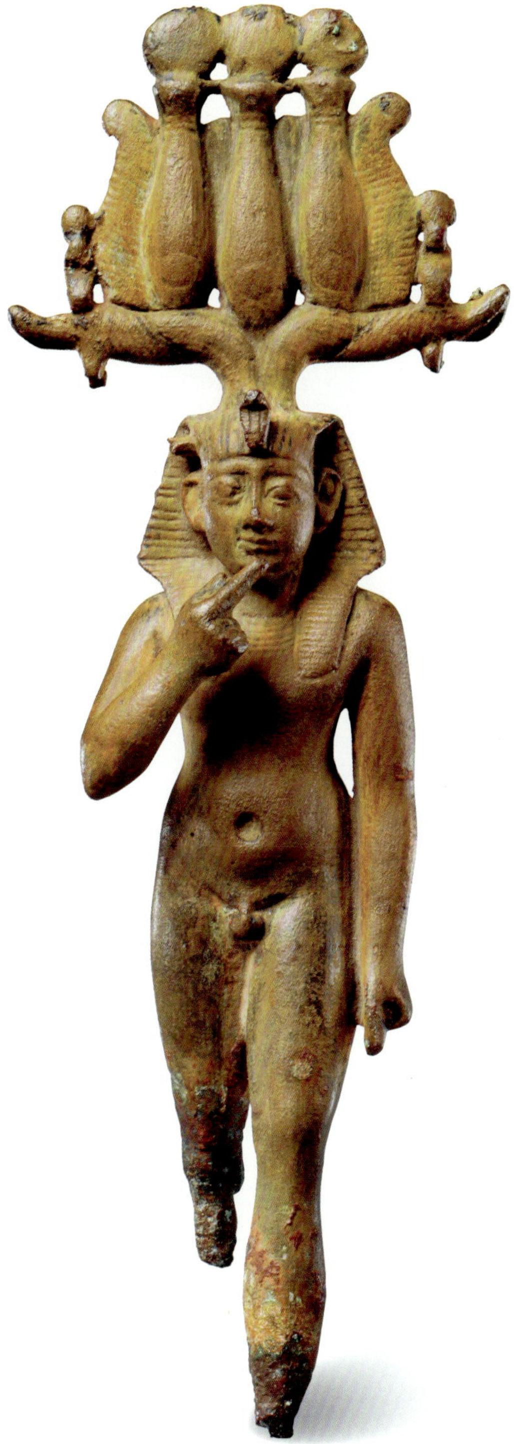

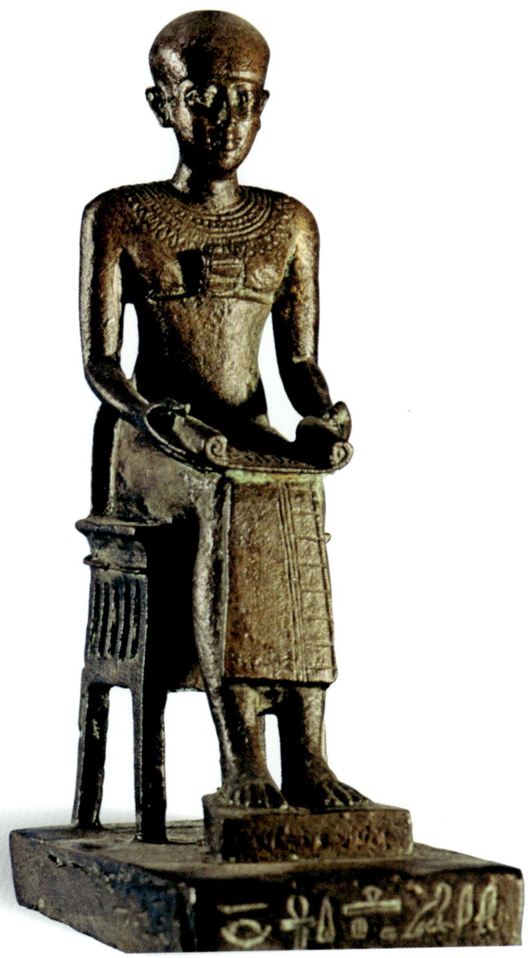

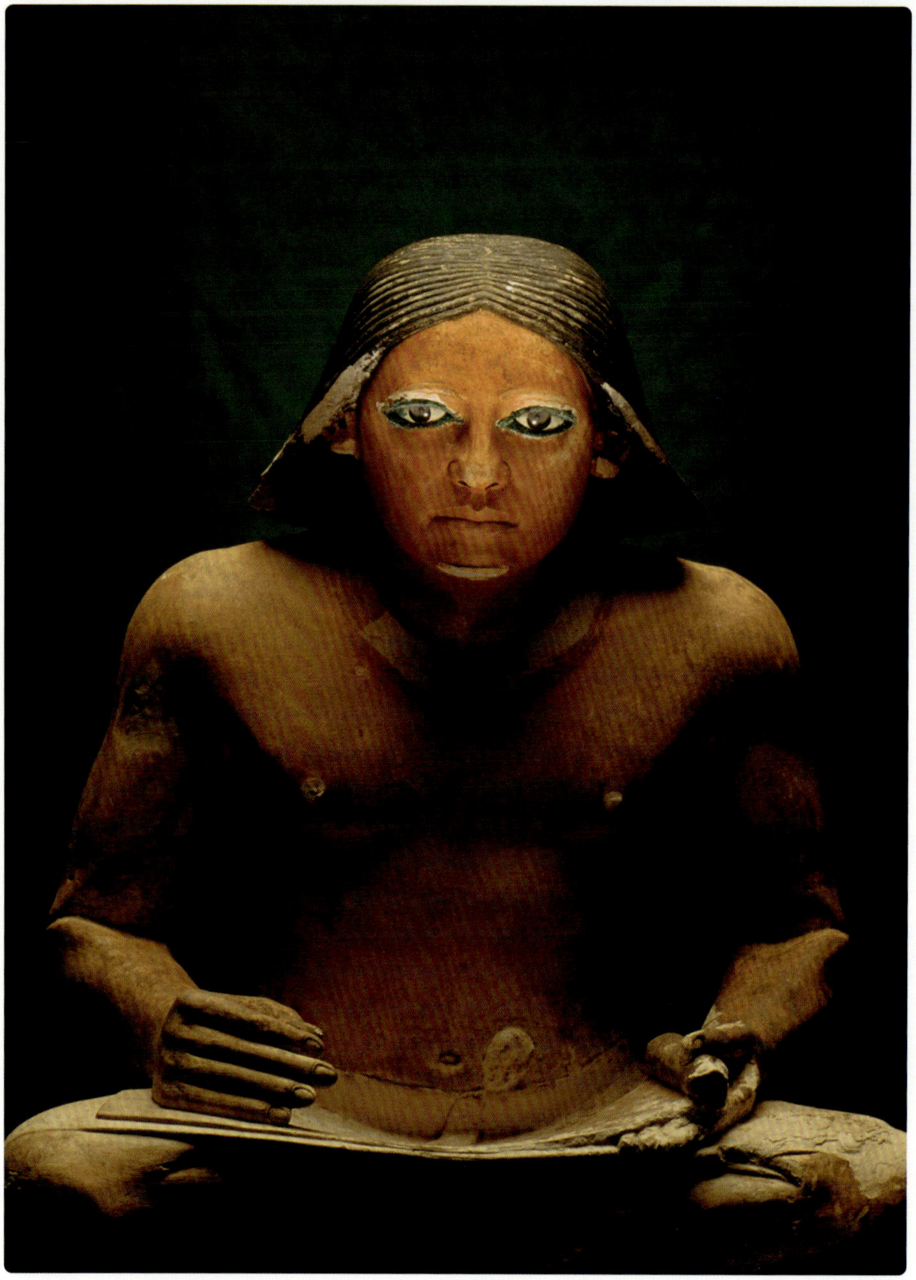

The statue of an anonymous scribe from Saqqara (about 2450 B.C.) appears in a classic pose (above). He holds a papyrus scroll on his lap, but the quill pen in his right hand has been lost.

A guard's light illuminates the tomb of King Unas (about 2325 B.C.) at Saqqara (opposite). The earliest surviving pyramid texts—spells to help the deceased in the afterlife—cover the walls.

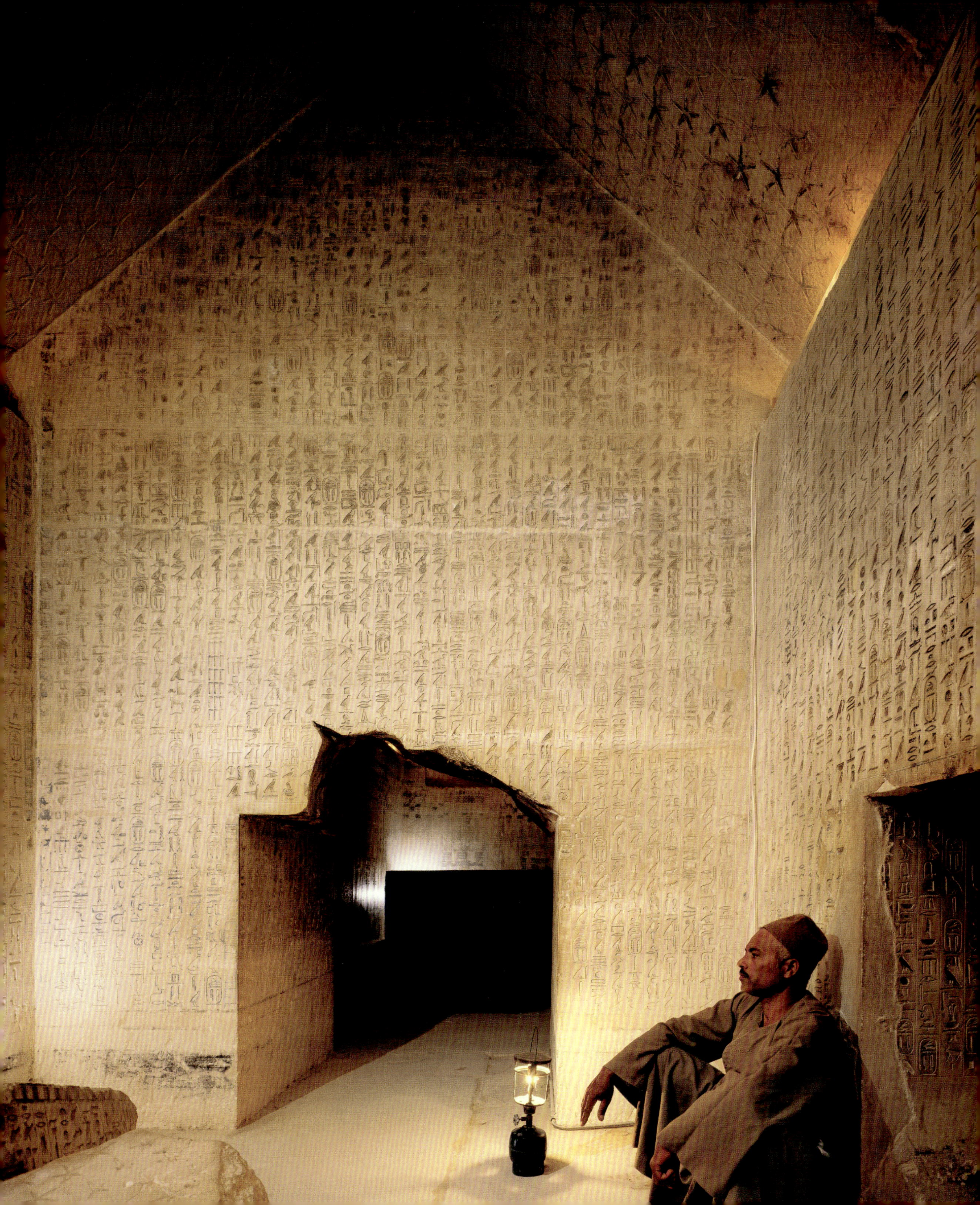

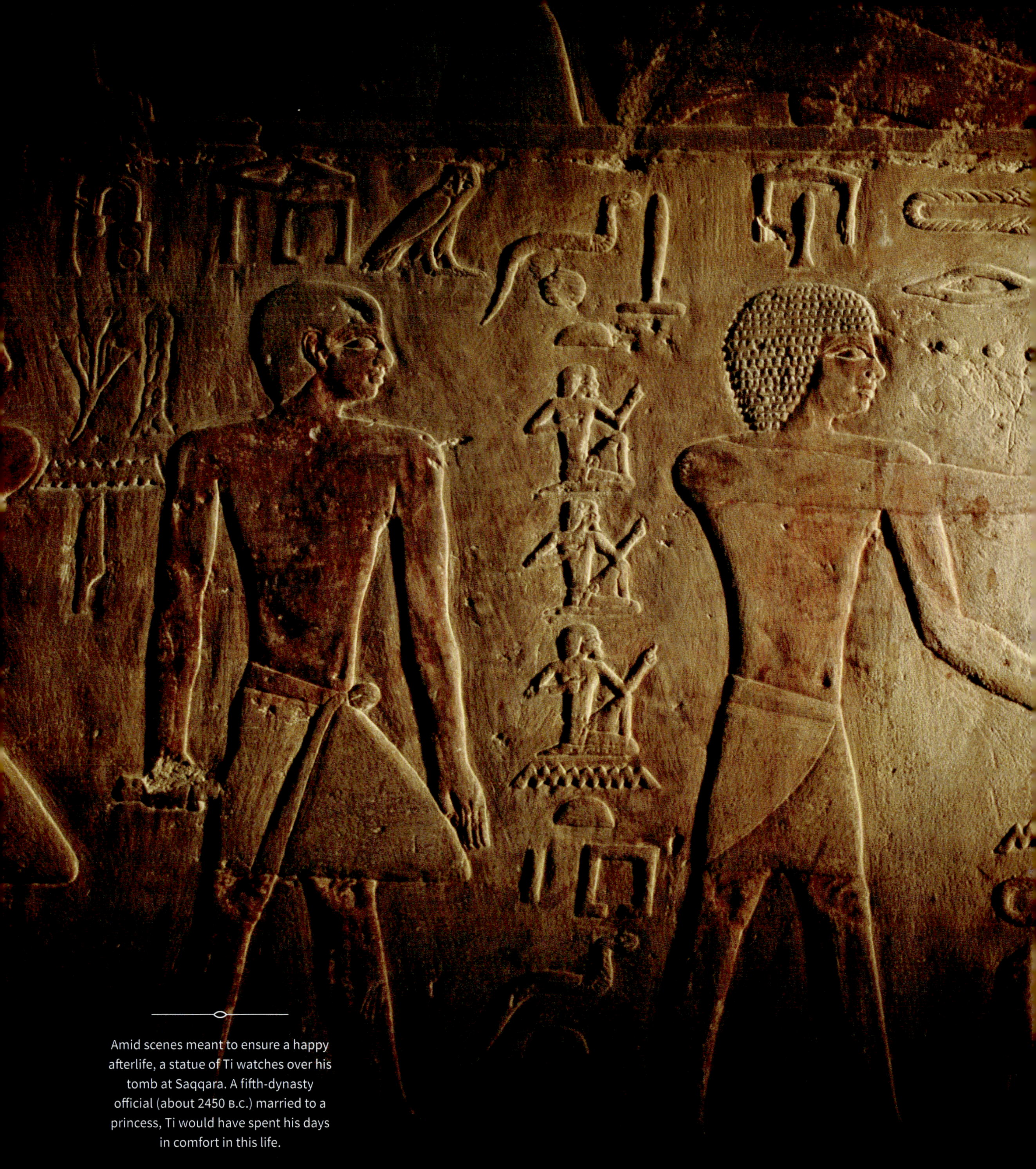

Amid scenes meant to ensure a happy afterlife, a statue of Ti watches over his tomb at Saqqara. A fifth-dynasty official (about 2450 B.C.) married to a princess, Ti would have spent his days in comfort in this life.

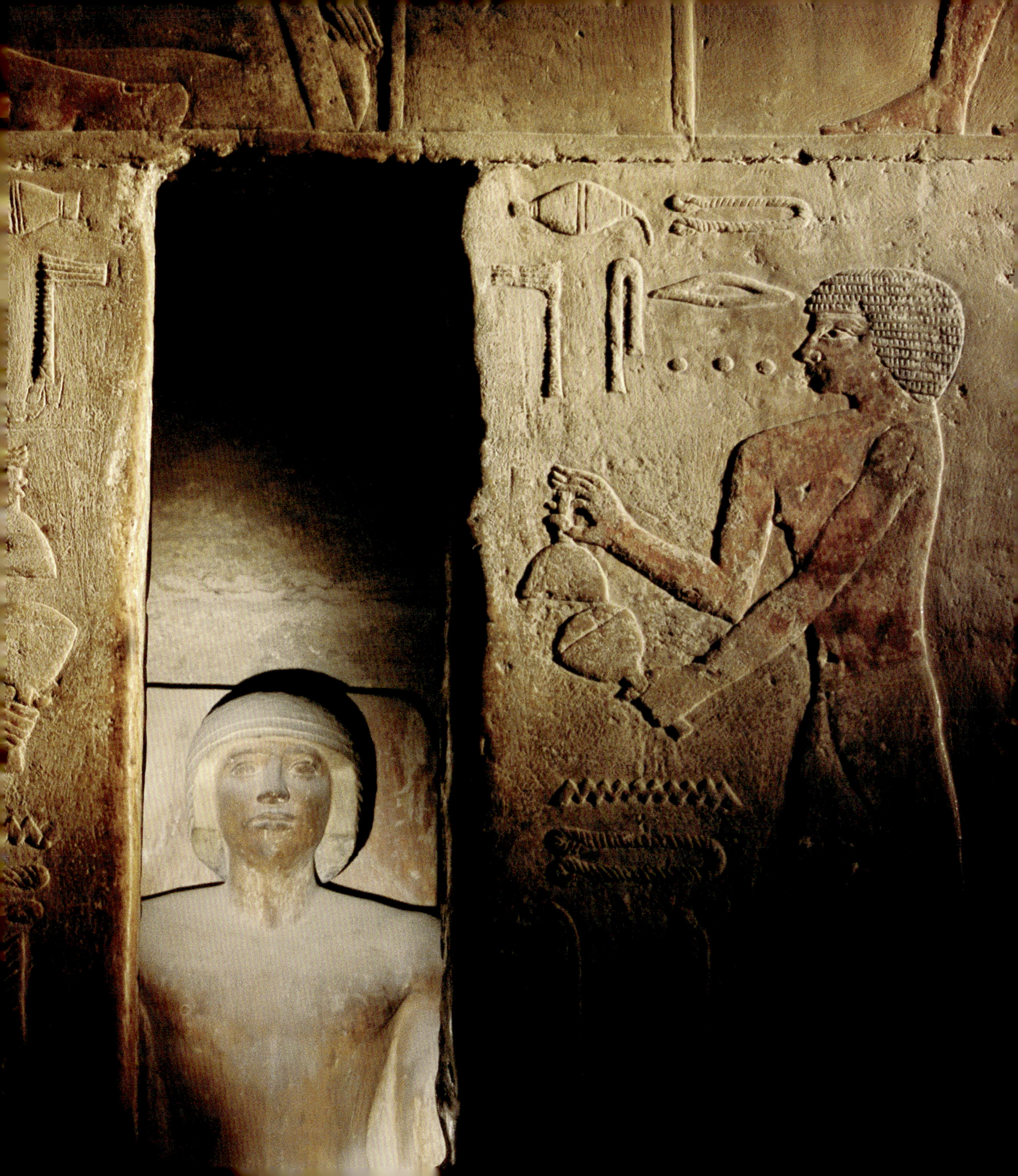

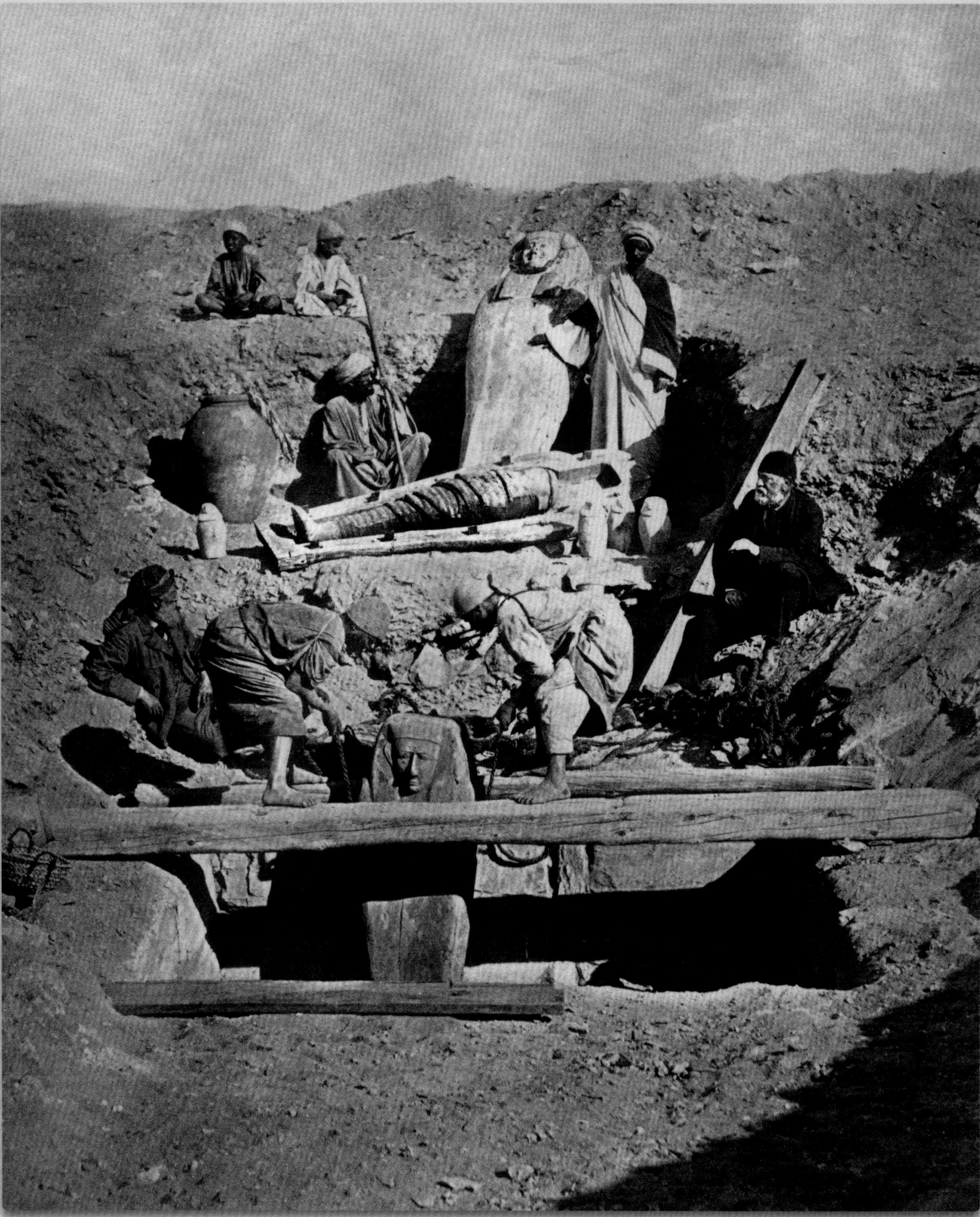

A Pioneer in the Field

AS A YOUNG MAN, Auguste Mariette launched his career in Egyptology by teaching himself how to read hieroglyphs. This led to a position at the Louvre in Paris, where he was tasked with cataloging papyri (inscribed sheets made from the papyrus plant). In 1850, the museum sent him to Egypt to acquire more such documents. But Mariette had a different plan.

He was intrigued with the search for a long-lost temple in Memphis, which Greek writer Strabo (ca. 63 B.C.–A.D. 21) mentioned in a description of the city's ruins: "One finds also a temple of [the god] Serapis in a spot so sandy that the wind causes the sand to accumulate in heaps, under which we could see many sphinxes, some of them almost entirely buried, others only partially covered."

Following this clue, Mariette began to dig. After uncovering traces of the sphinxes, he found catacombs now called the Serapeum, where mummified sacred bulls were once buried.

In 1858, Mariette became the first director of the Egyptian Antiquities Service. He excavated at some three dozen sites, including Saqqara (opposite, ca. 1875.) He also founded the Egyptian Museum in Cairo, on whose current grounds his tomb is now located.

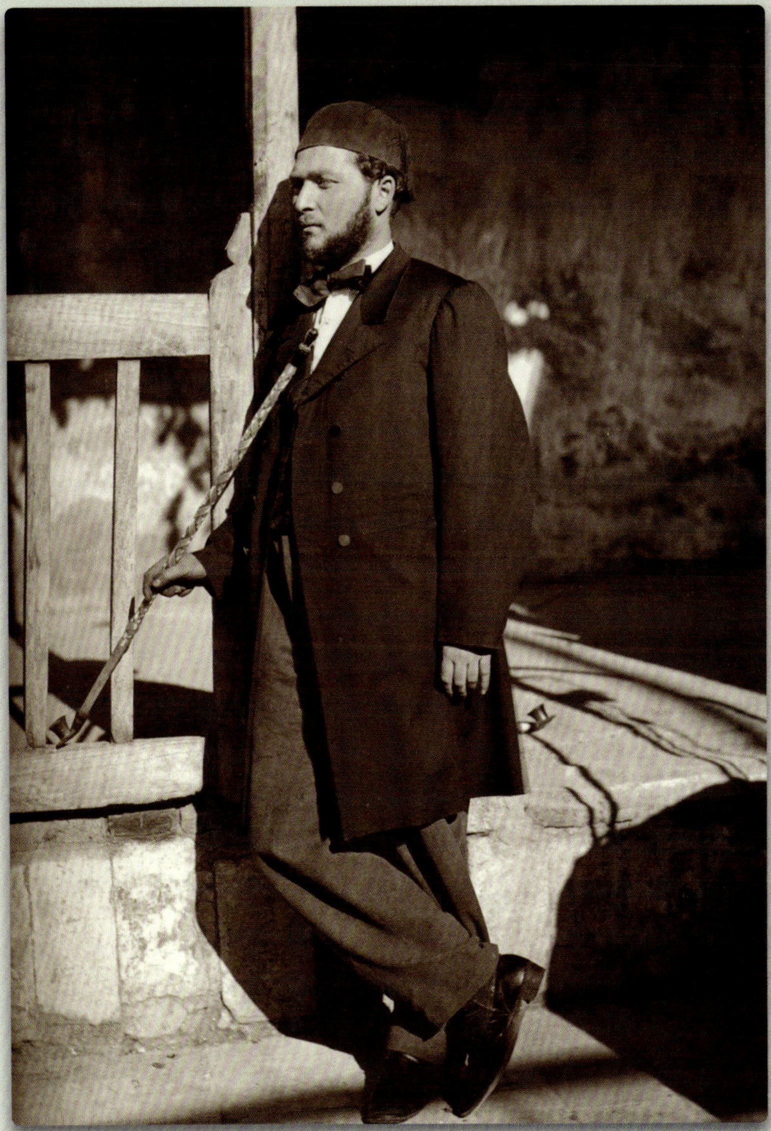

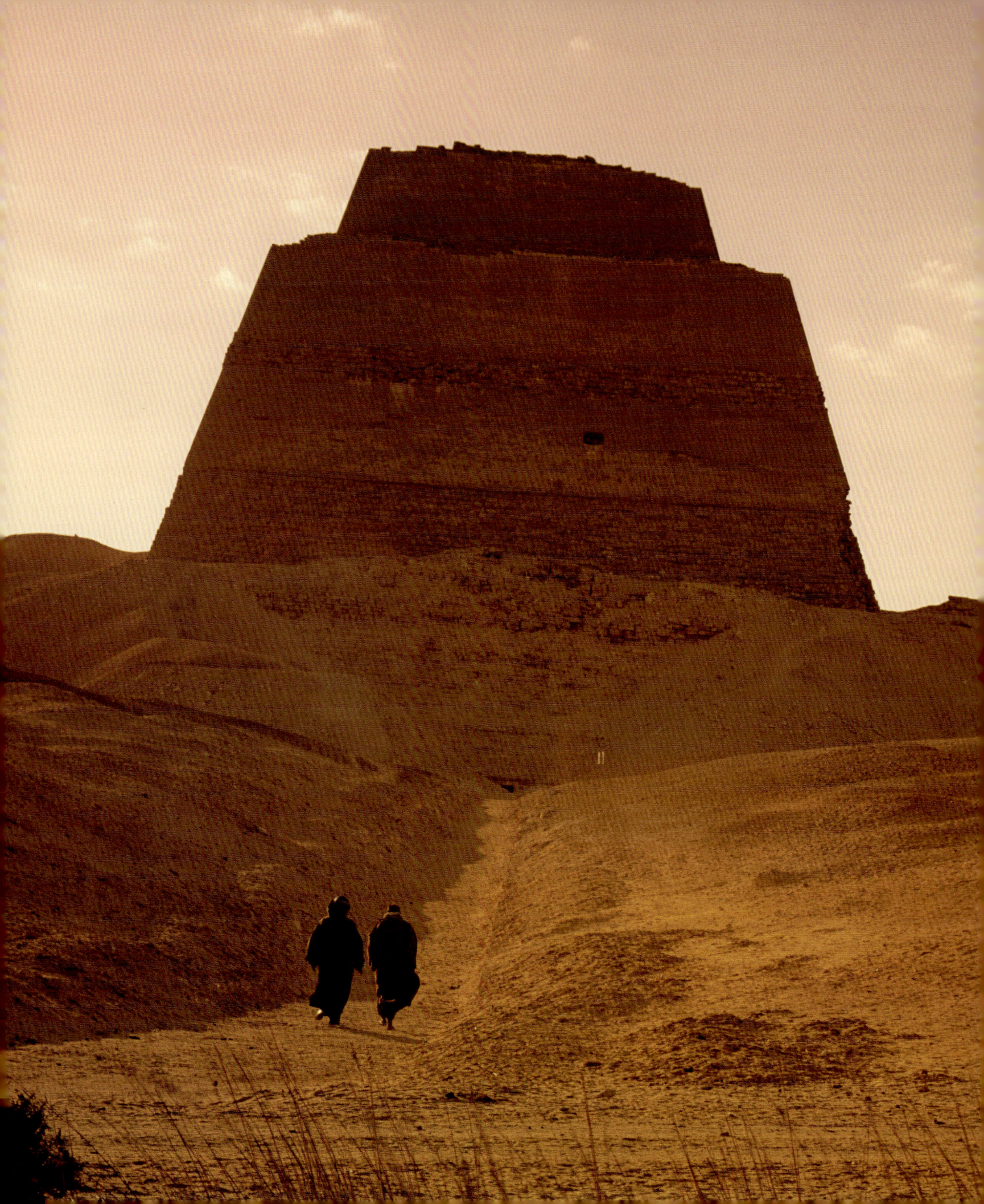

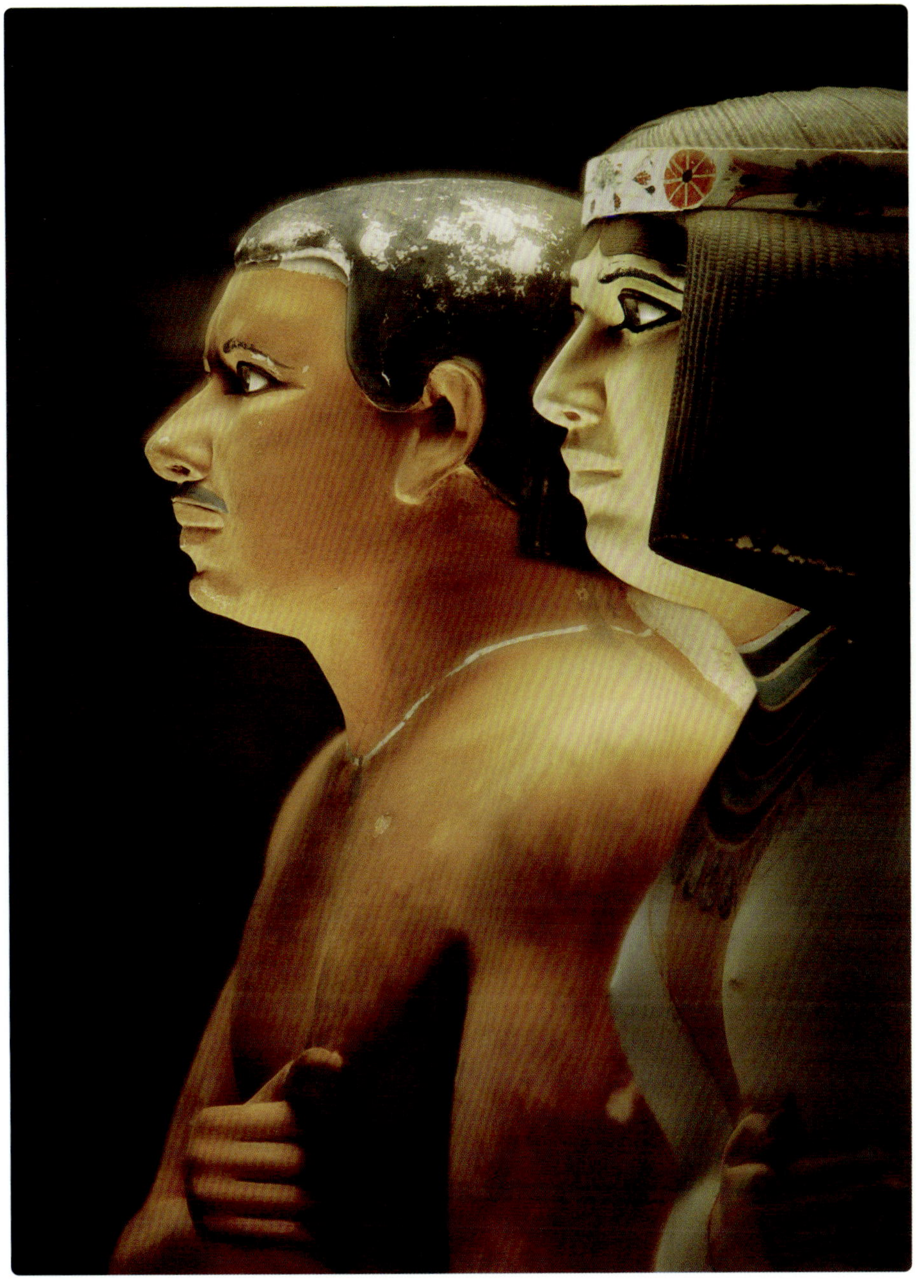

Late in his reign (about 2575 B.C.), King Snefru added stones to his tiered tomb at Meidum (opposite) to give it straight sides. Modern builders have repurposed the outer blocks, revealing the original shape.

Rahotep was a high official and probably Snefru's son. The eerily lifelike statues of him and his wife Nofret (above), when discovered at Meidum, caused the excavation's workers to flee.

DIGGING DEEPER

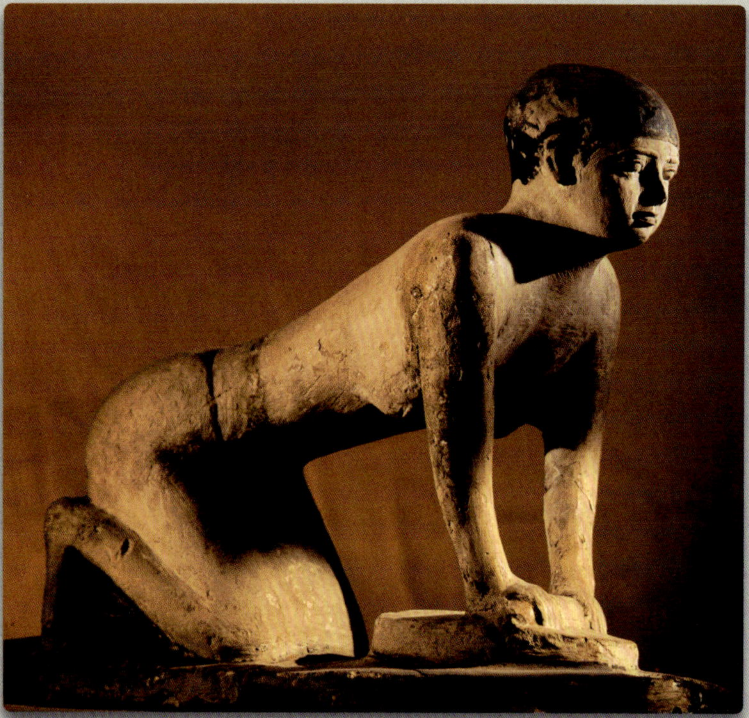

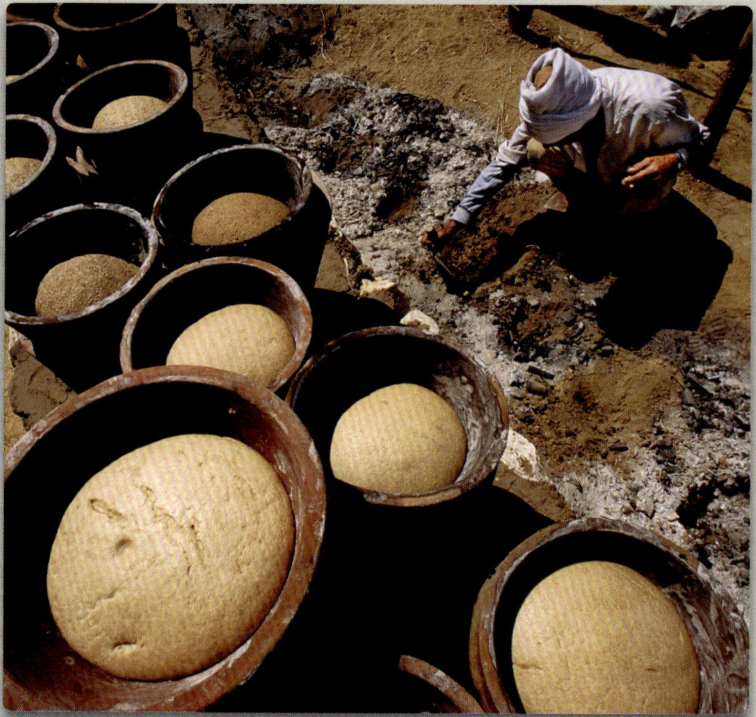

The Daily Bread

DURING THE SEASON when the Nile flooded fields and farmers had time on their hands, kings conscripted people for projects such as building pyramids. Excavations near the iconic royal tombs at Giza have revealed where the workers lived and what they ate. Bones of sheep, goats, and cattle indicate a diet rich in protein that also included fish, lentils, and beans, and the staples of bread and beer.

Archaeologists have also discovered traces of a bakery near a building they believe was a commissary. Using clues from tomb reliefs, sherds of bread pots, and models like this one (above left), which shows a servant grinding grain, a team of experts replicated how bread may have been made there.

Emmer wheat and barley flours, a wild sourdough yeast, and water made up the batter. This was left to rise in the bottom of specially reproduced pots (above right). Meanwhile, the pot tops were heated in a wood fire (opposite). Finally, the hot tops were set on the dough-filled bottoms, and the assembled pots were nestled in the fire's coals. The result? Loaves like the ones the pyramid builders ate 4,500 years ago.

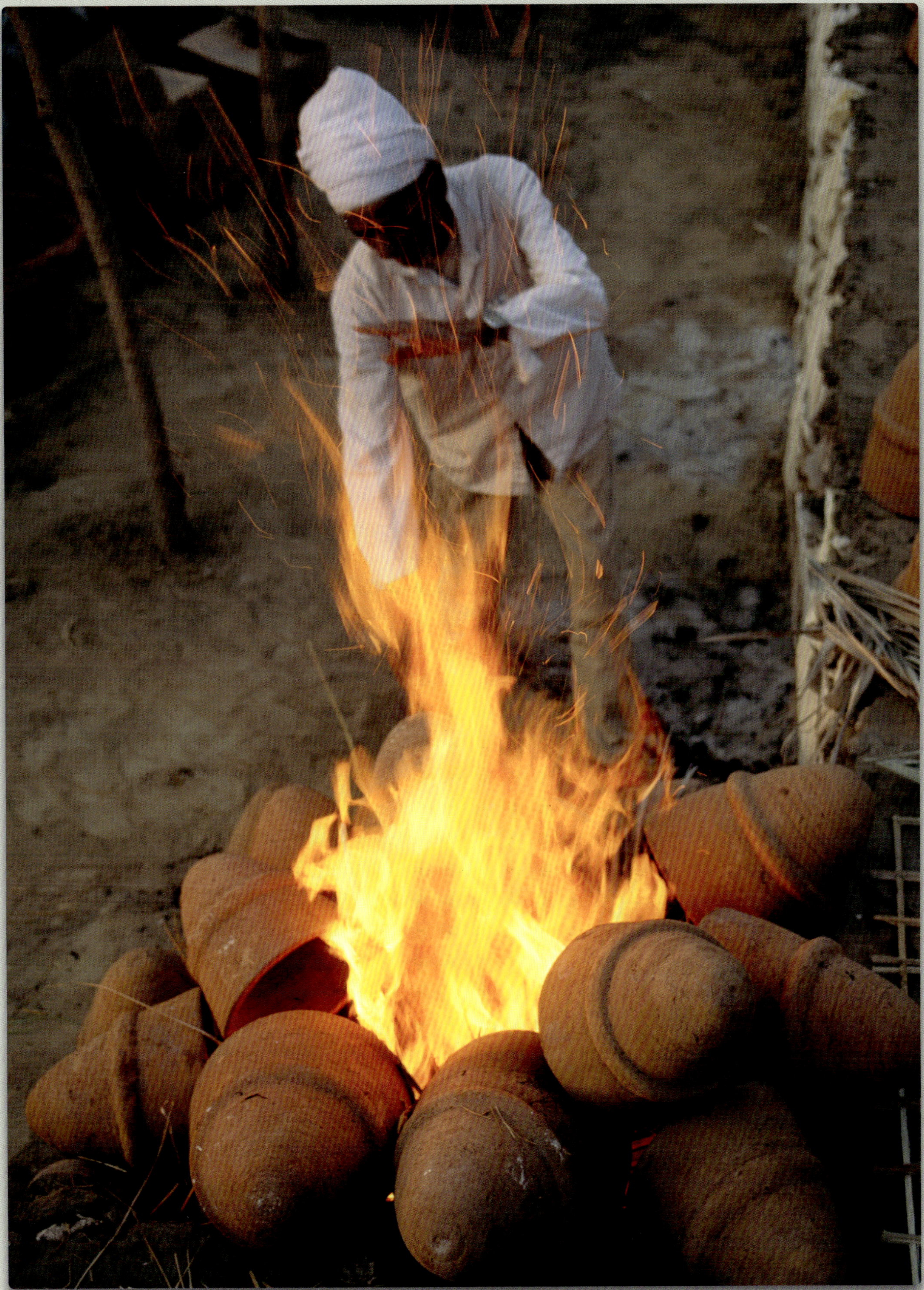

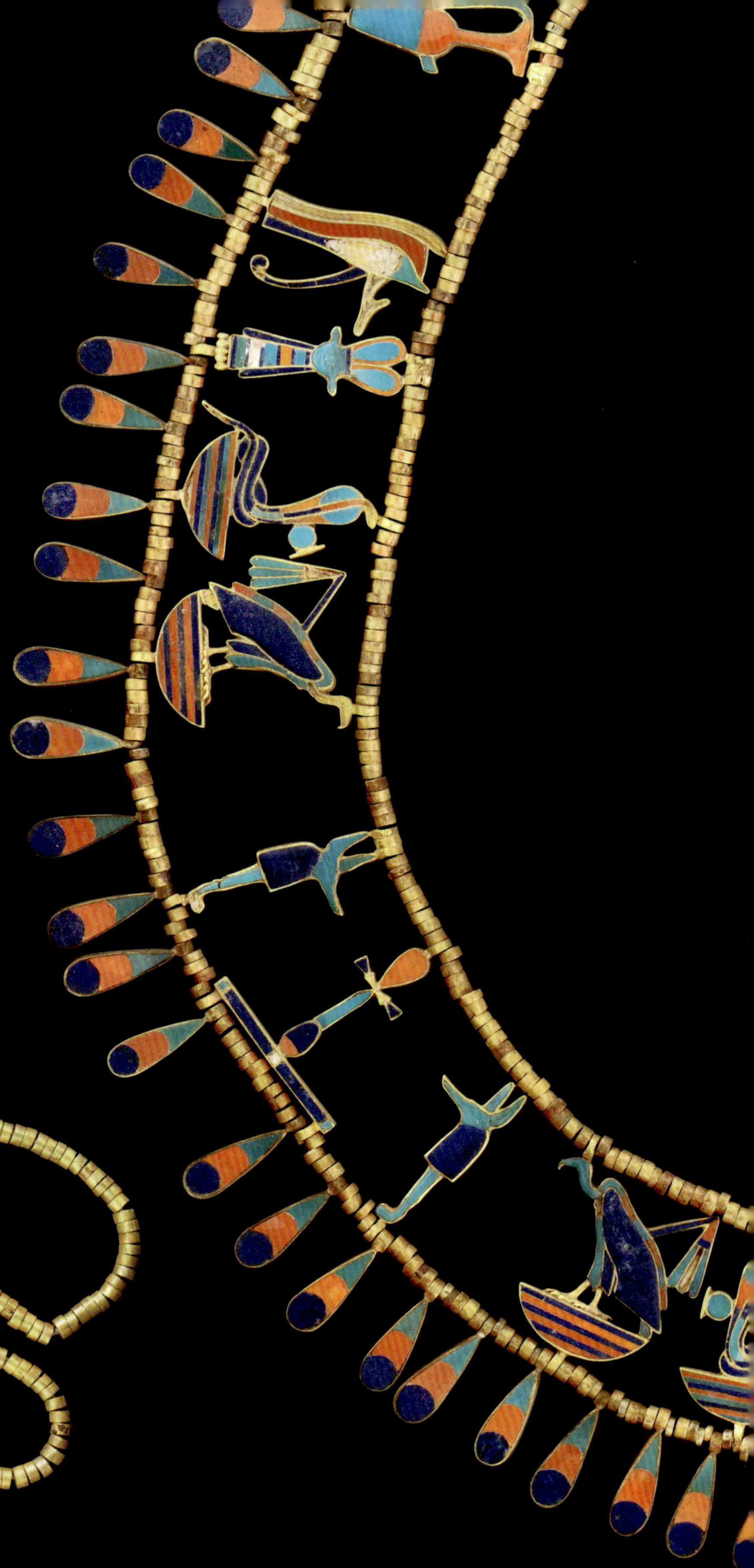

The intact tomb of a daughter of King Amenemhet II (about 1876–1842 B.C.) was found at Dahshur. This necklace (right) lay in pieces on the mummy. Now restored, it includes a central ankh sign, signifying life, and falcon-headed clasps.

The tomb of princess Mereret at Dahshur yielded this pendant (opposite). The griffins defeating Egypt's foes represent her father, Senwosret III (about 1836–1818 B.C.).

A woman named Sithathoryunet was buried beside the pyramid of Senwosret II (about 1842–1837 B.C.) at el-Lahun and was likely his daughter. This necklace (below) was found in a mud-filled niche in her tomb.

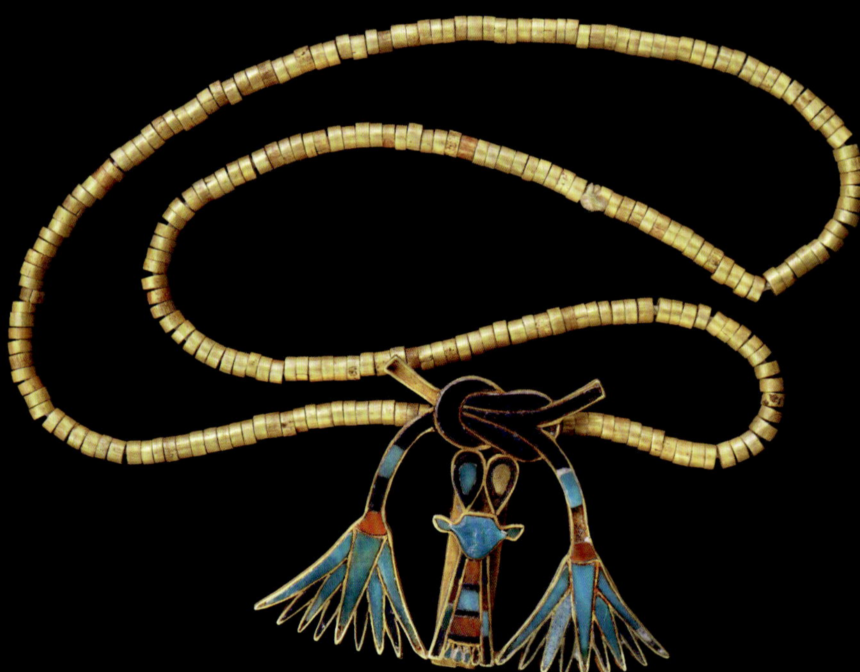

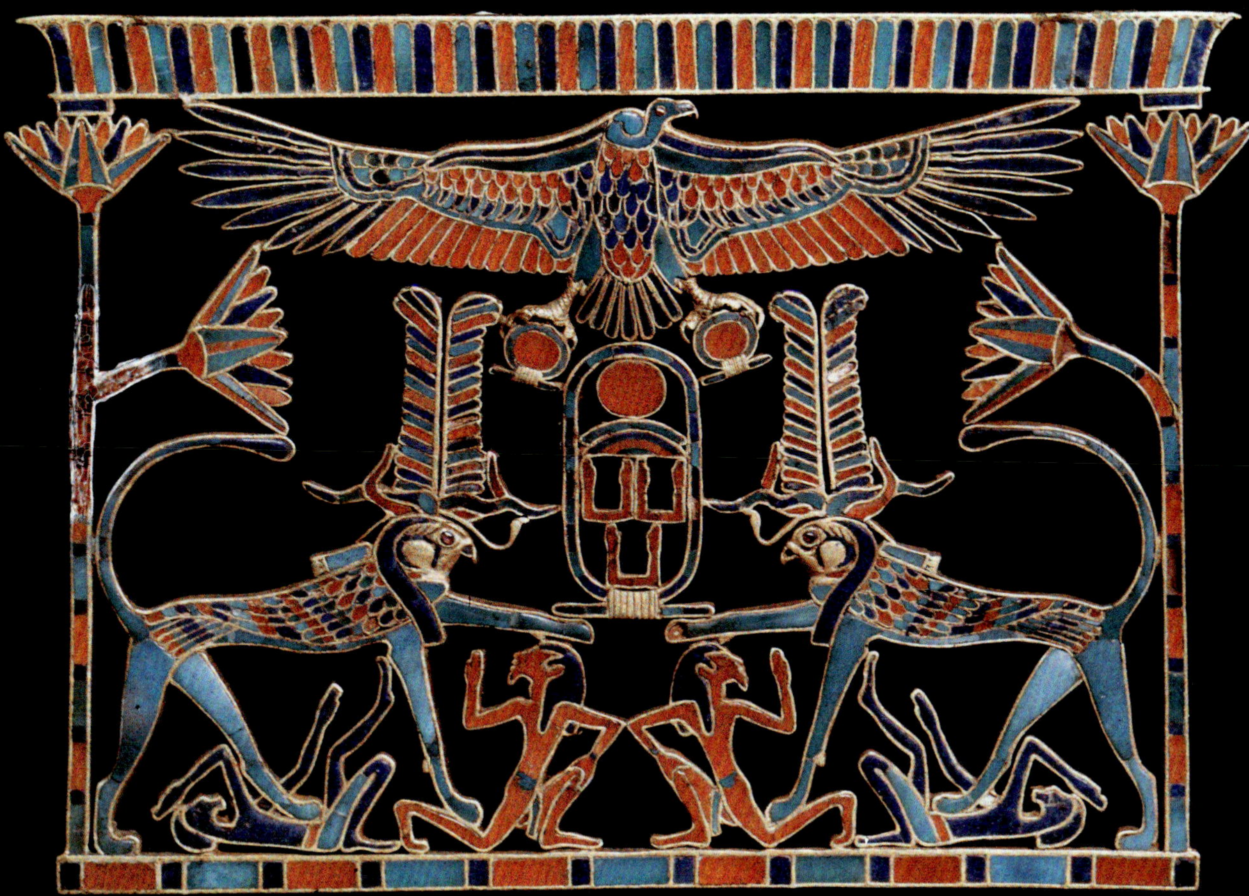

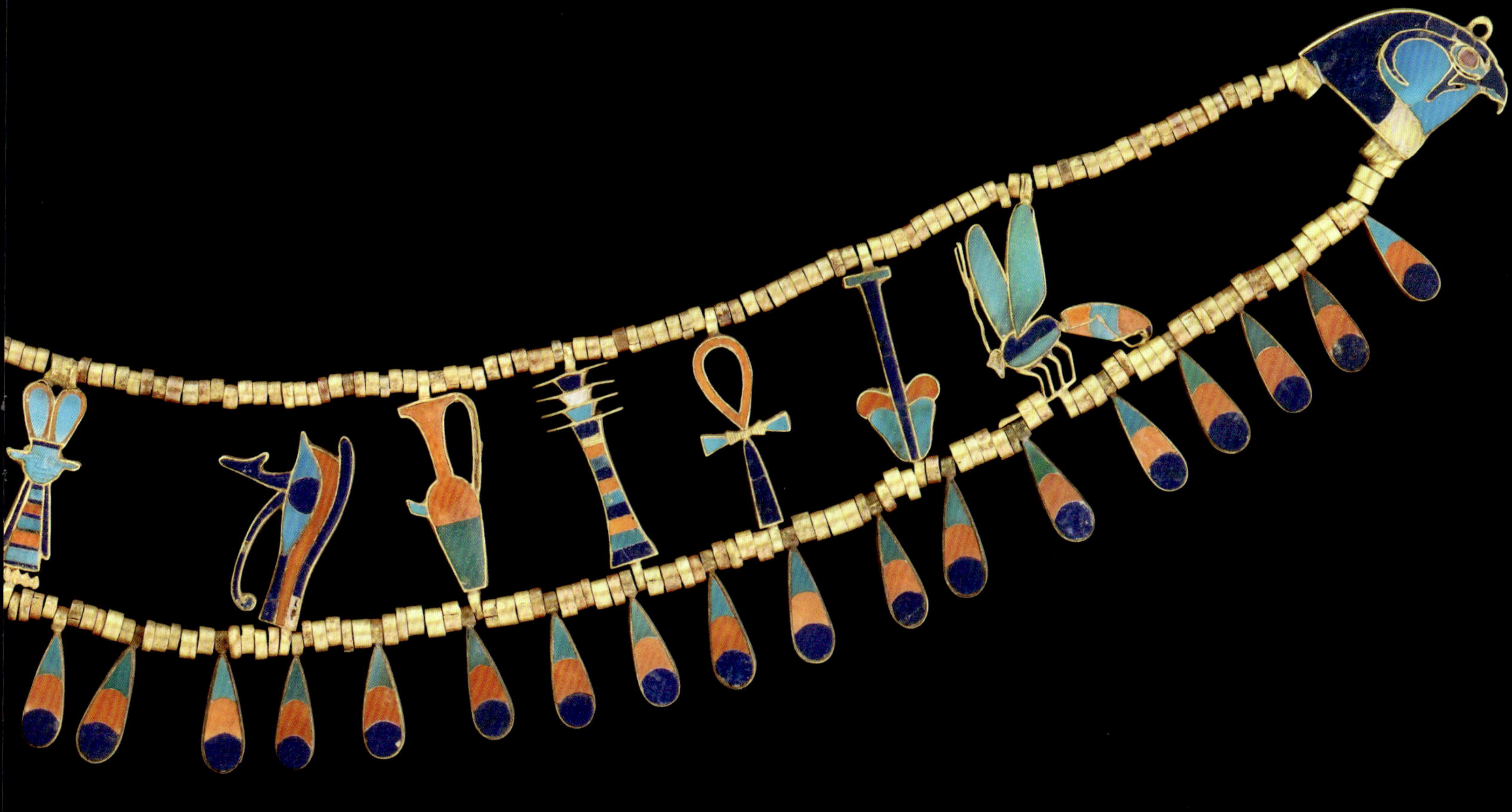

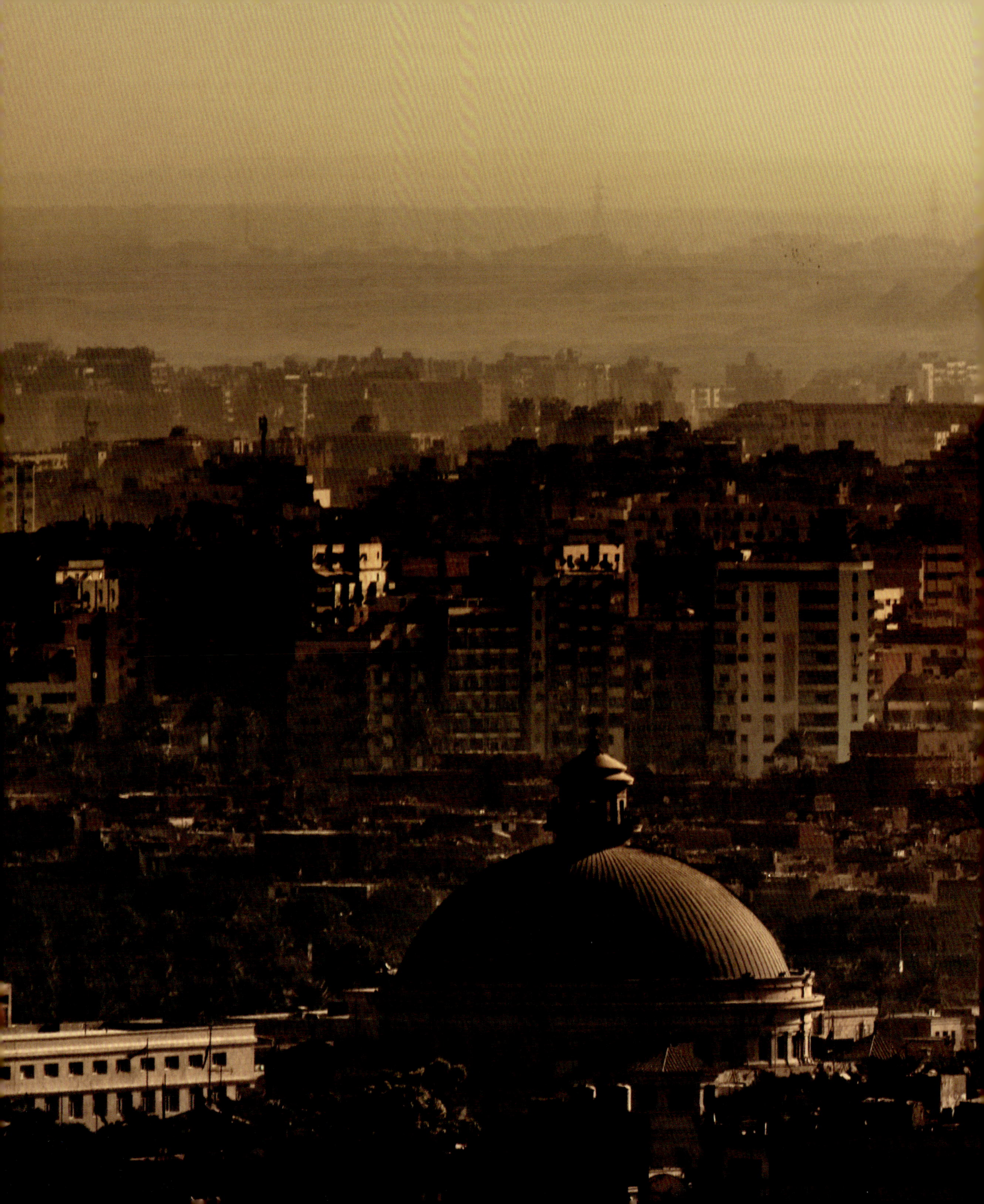

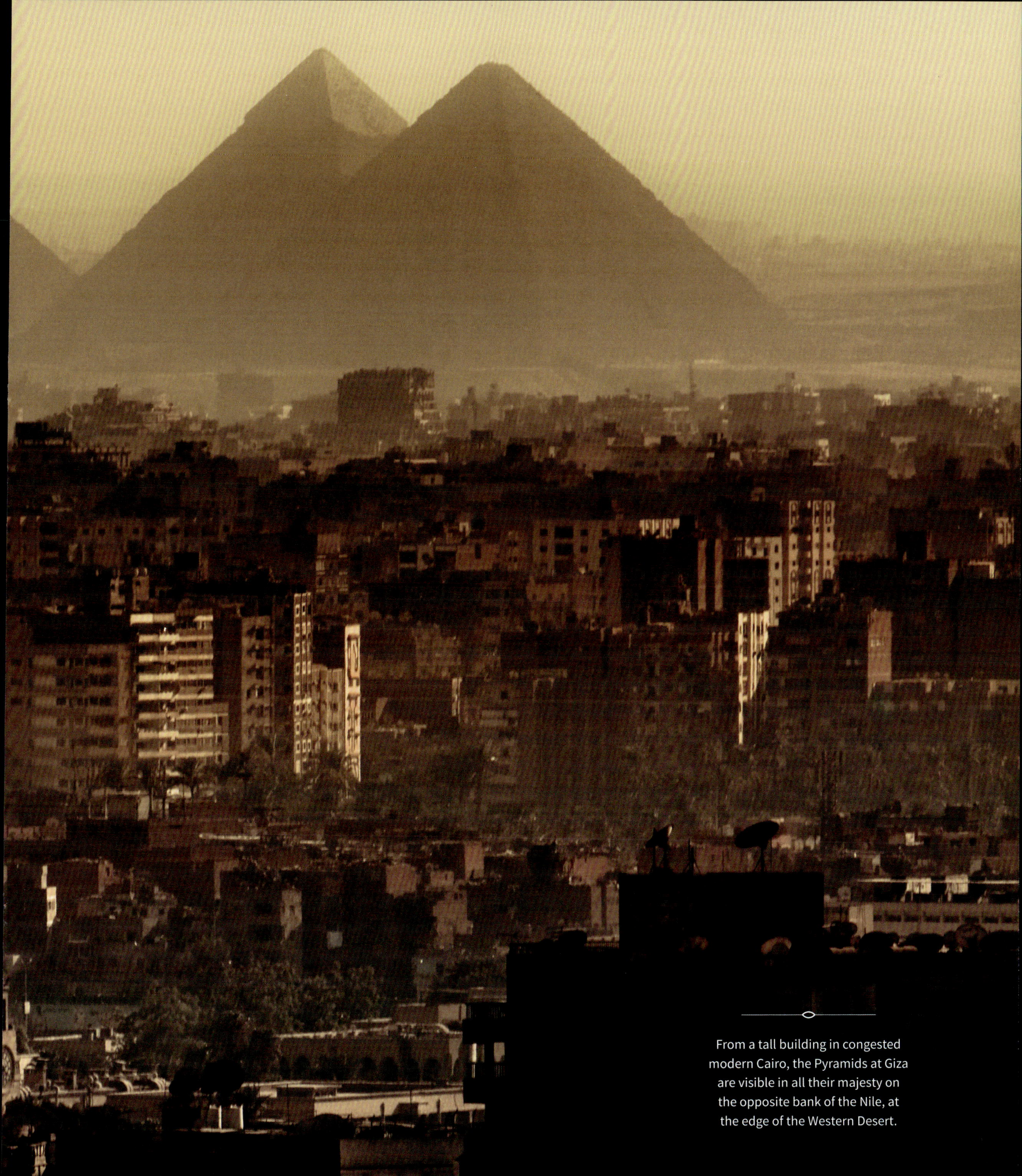

From a tall building in congested modern Cairo, the Pyramids at Giza are visible in all their majesty on the opposite bank of the Nile, at the edge of the Western Desert.

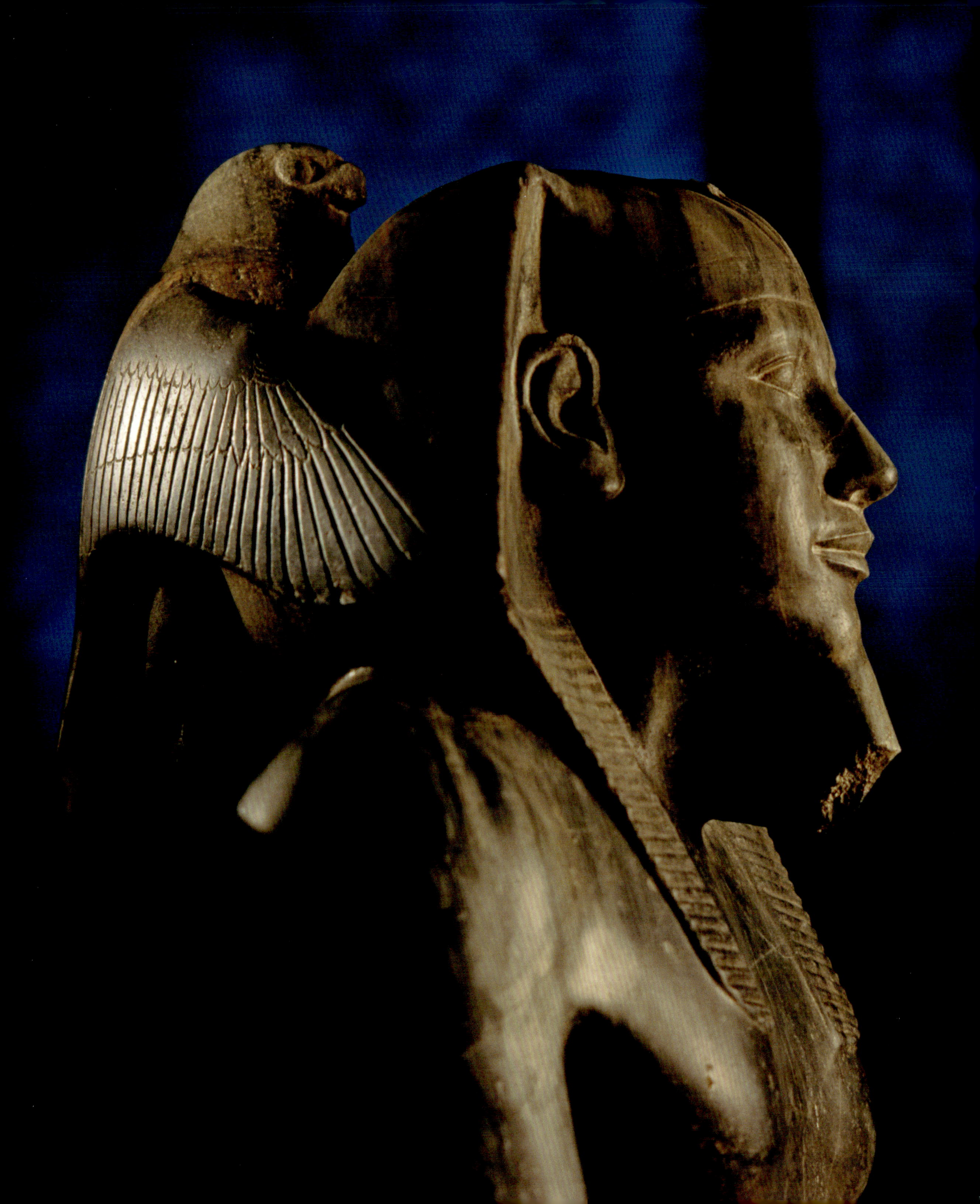

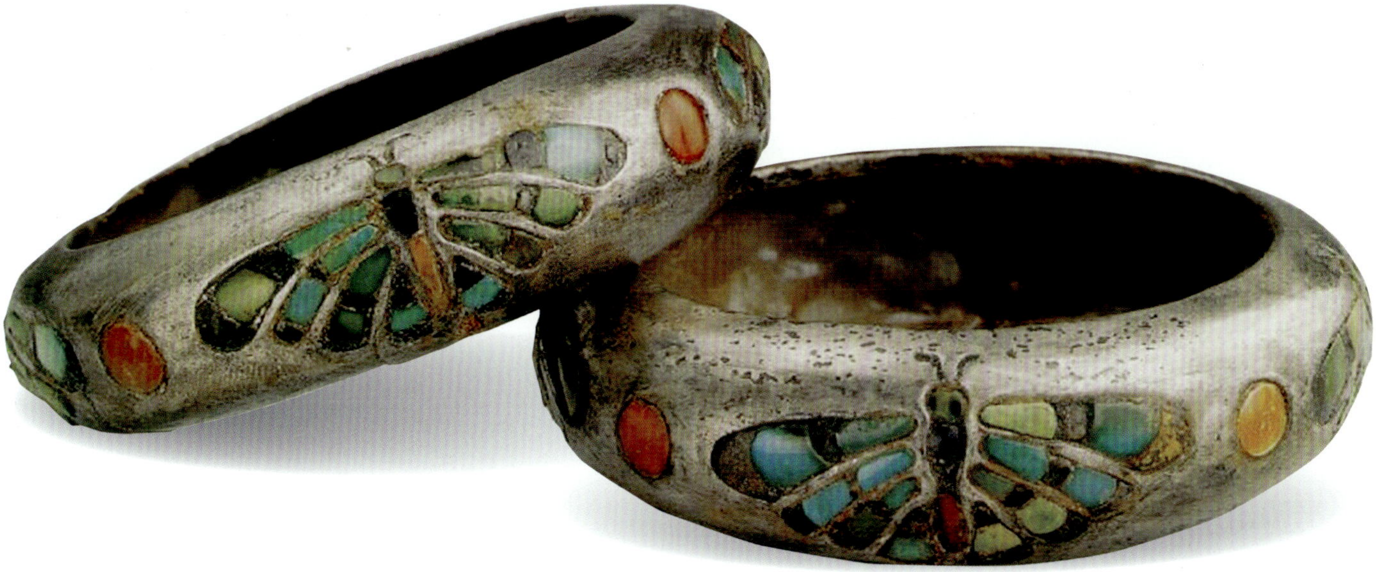

A statue found at Giza (opposite) shows Horus, the falcon god, spreading his protective wings behind King Khafre (about 2550 B.C.), who built the second pyramid at the site.

Khafre's grandmother, Hetepheres, was buried in a shaft tomb at Giza near the pyramid of King Khufu, her son. The artifacts found in her tomb include silver bracelets (above) inlaid with turquoise, lapis lazuli, and carnelian. Silver was rare in ancient Egypt and even more prized than gold.

A museum display (right) shows some of the bracelets in a recreation of the gilded box in which they were discovered.

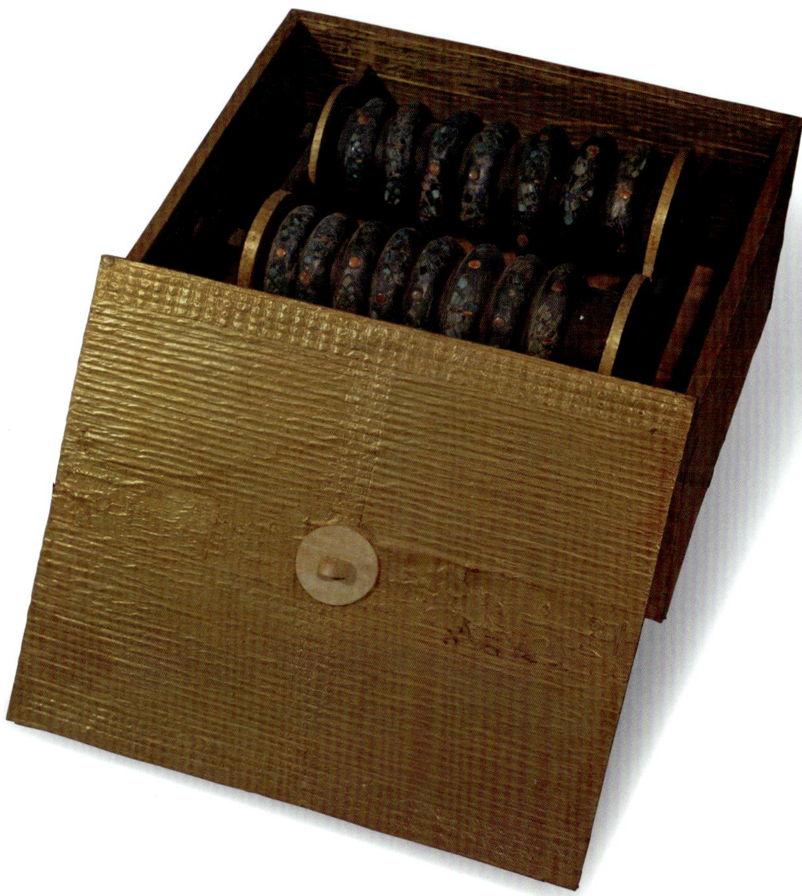

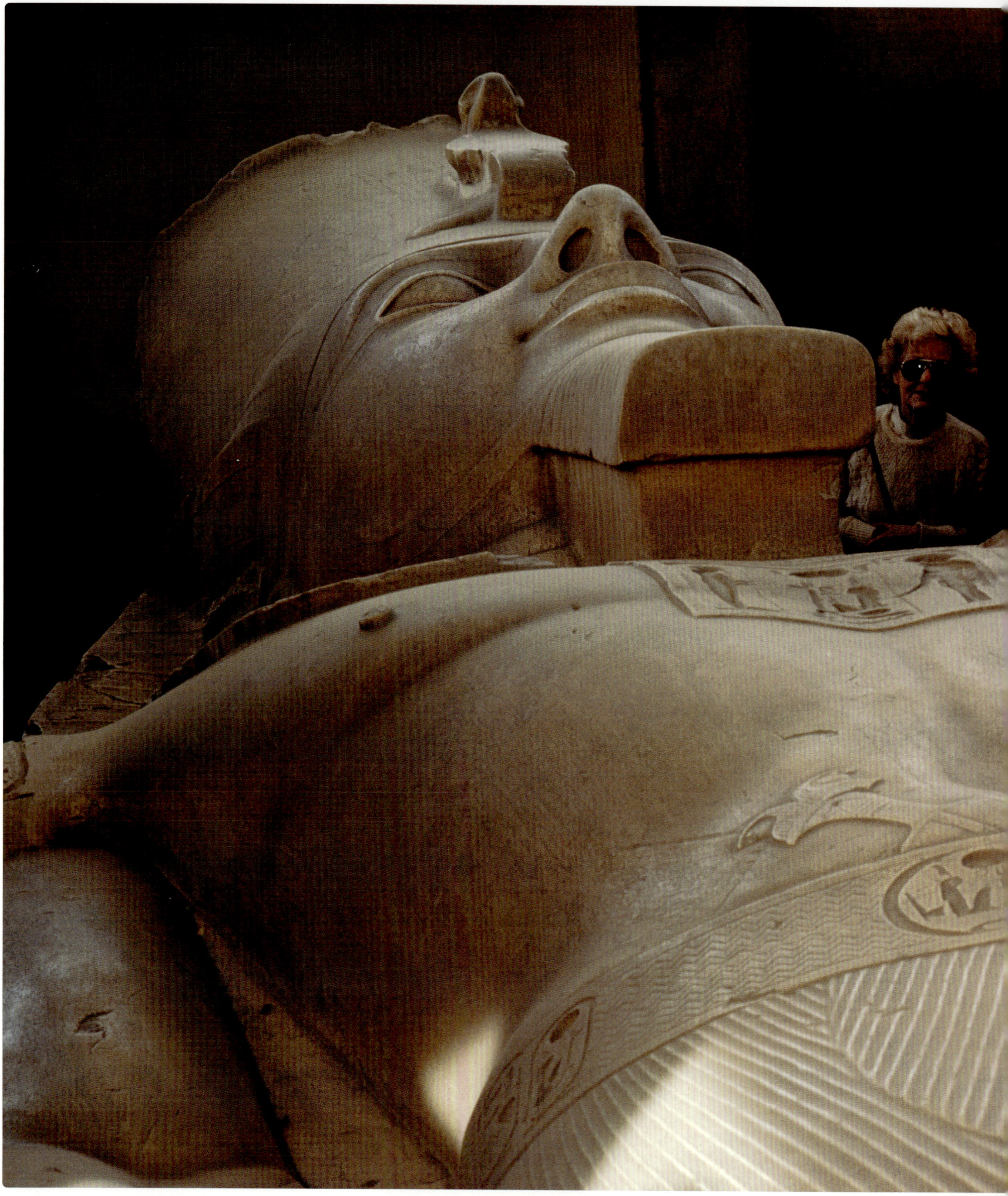

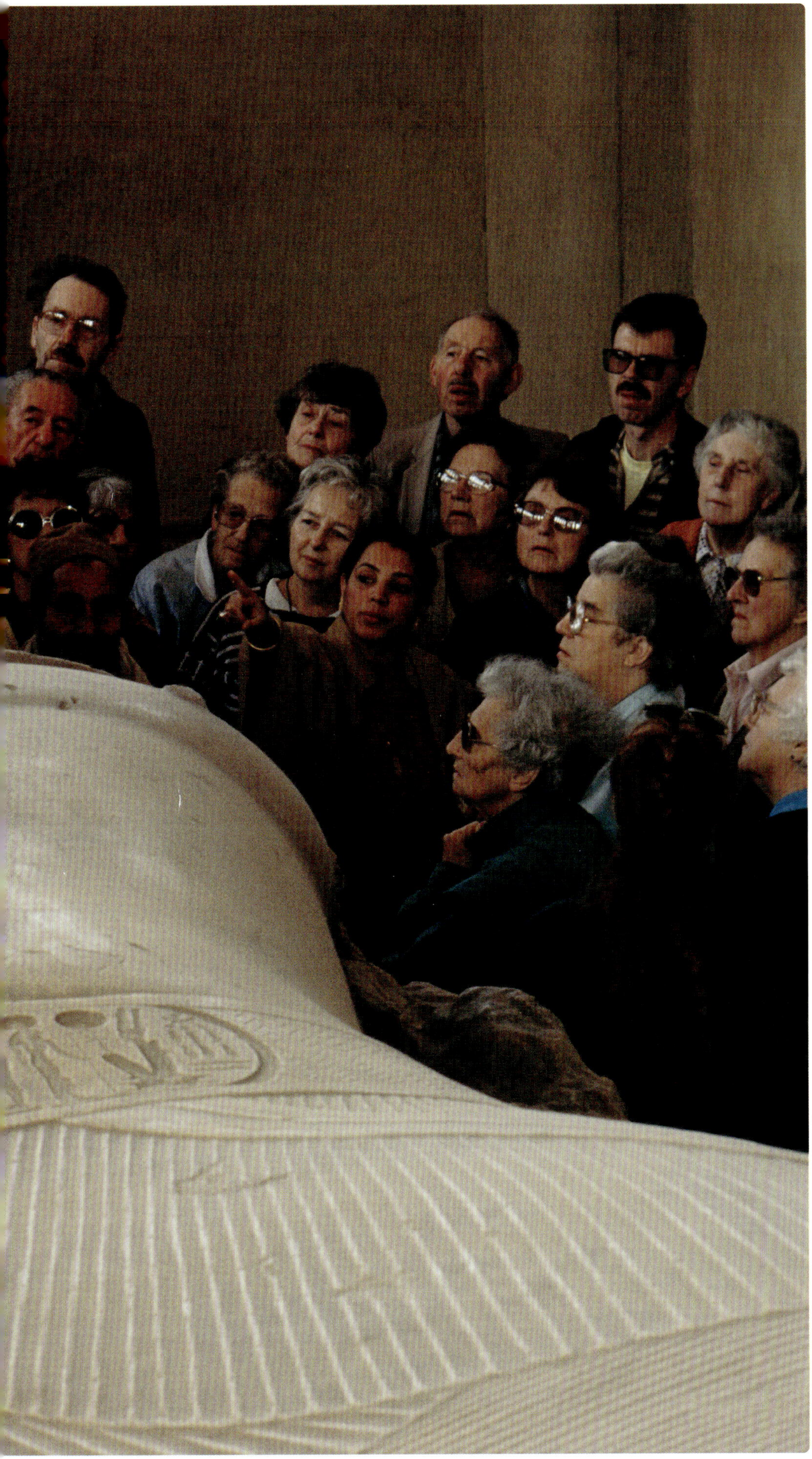

A colossal Ramses II (about 1279–1213 B.C.) draws a crowd in a museum at the ancient site of Memphis. In the 1800s, the British Museum was offered this statue but declined because of the cost of transportation.

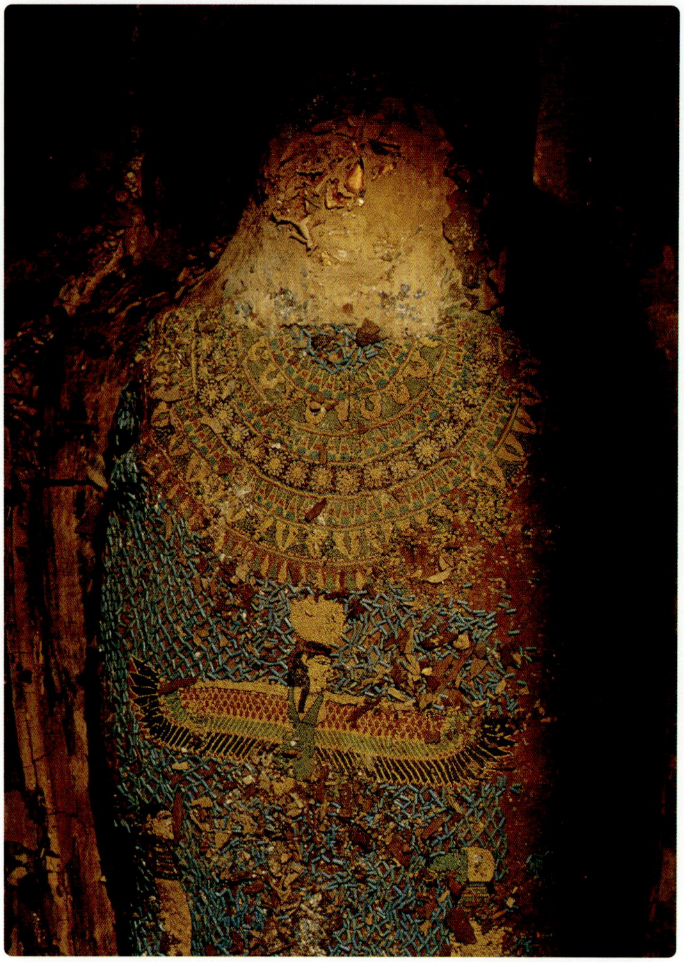

A massive stone sarcophagus (right) held the mortal remains of a priest named Iufaa, who was laid to rest at Abusir in about 500 B.C.

Inside the sarcophagus and a decaying inner coffin of wood, archaeologists found an intricate net of glazed beads lying over Iufaa's mummy (above). Beneath the collar bands, Nut the sky goddess spreads her wings.

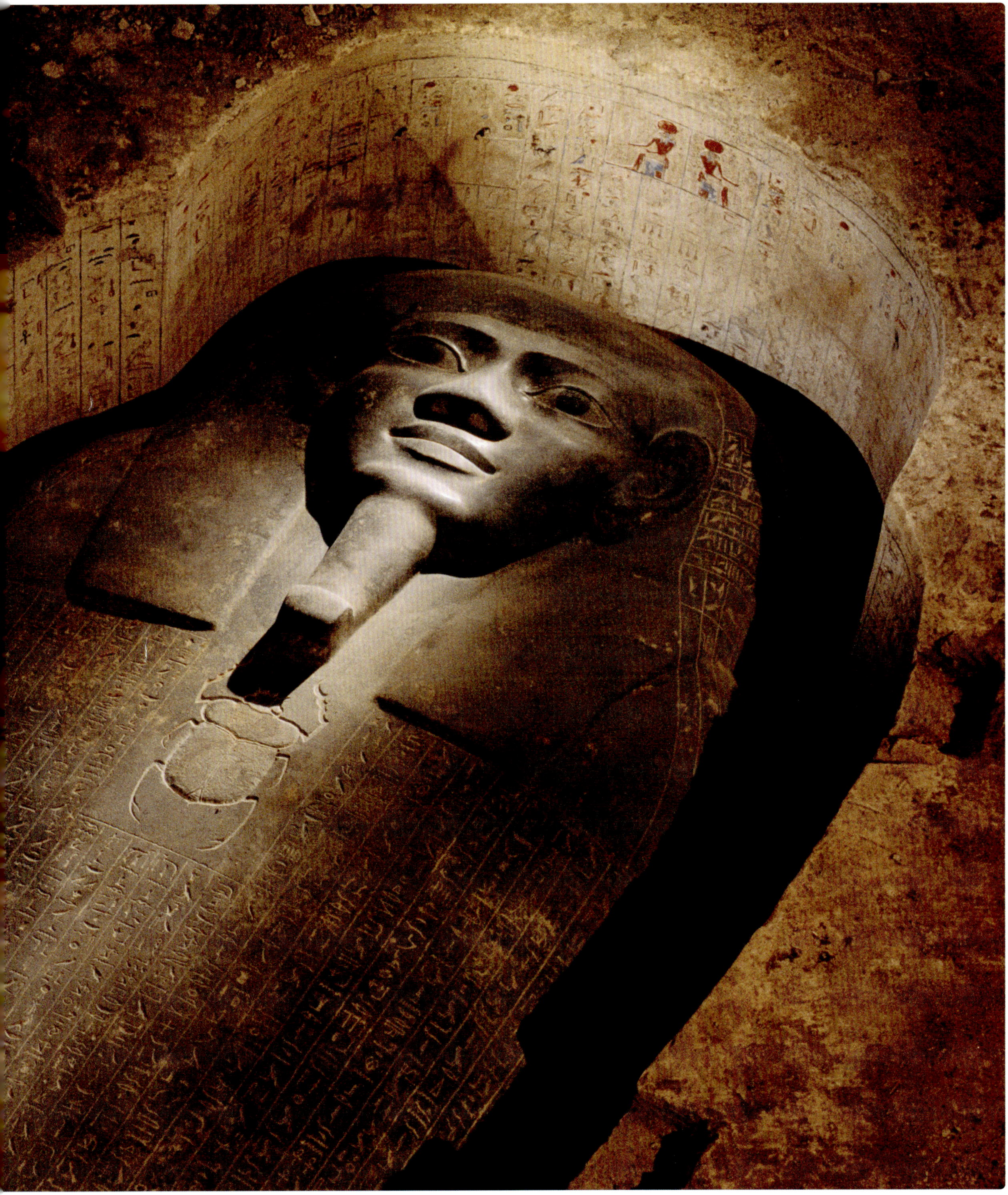

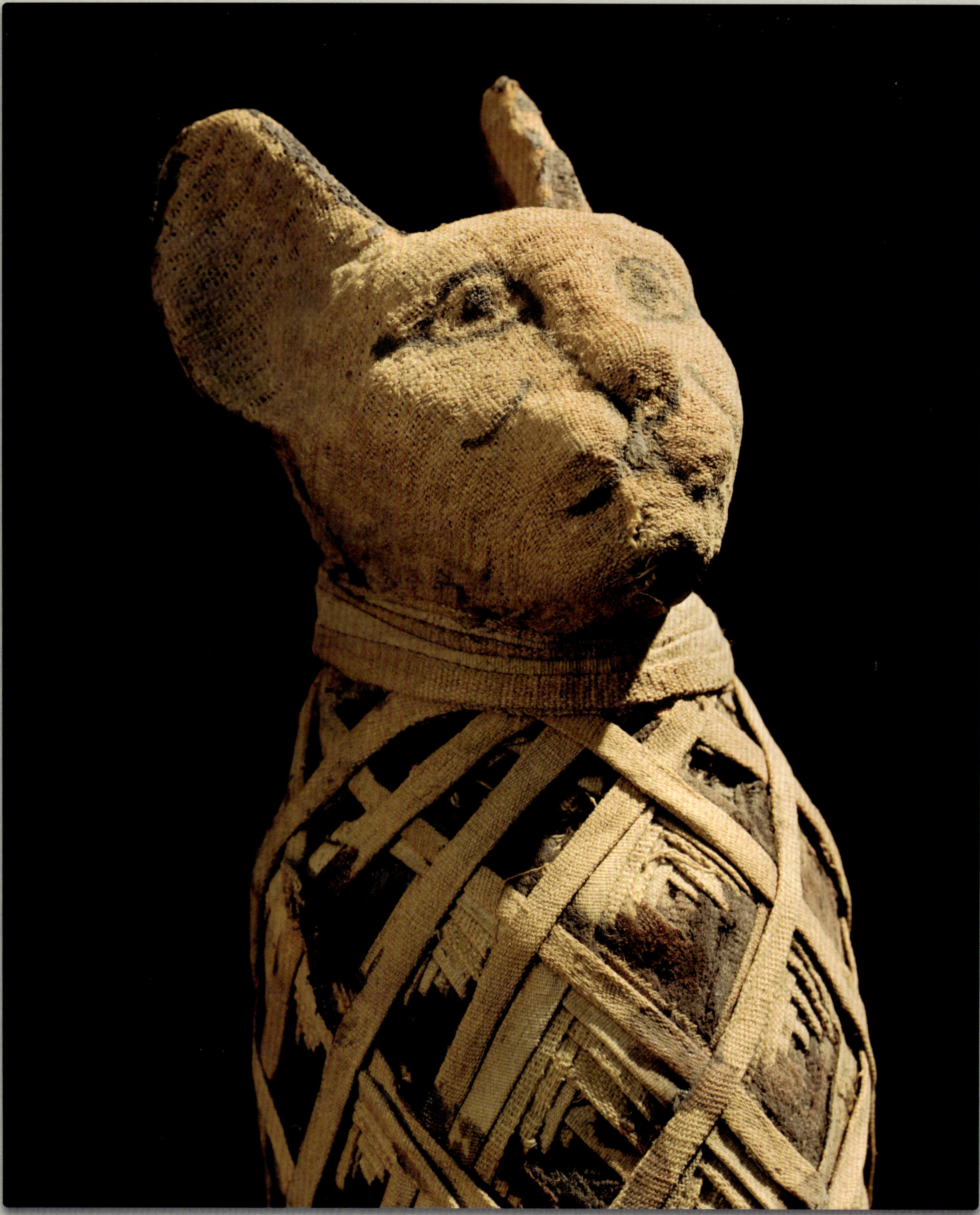

DIGGING DEEPER

Animals Everlasting

BENEATH THE SANDS of Saqqara, large caverns hold a veritable menagerie of animal mummies: cats and dogs, crocodiles and cobras, scarab beetles and ibises, even rare lion cubs. At this and many other sacred locations around Egypt, ancient pilgrims left such creatures as votive offerings. Over time, the deposited mummies could amount to millions. Many were beautifully wrapped in linen like this cat (opposite).

In the Serapeum (below), mummified bulls were buried in massive granite coffins. Each beast, known as an Apis bull, was a sacred animal that represented the physical manifestation of Ptah, the local patron god.

In his lifetime, an Apis bull was pampered and adorned with jewels. When he died, he was mummified and laid to rest with great ceremony. And then the search began for a new Apis bull with just the right markings: a white triangle on his forehead, a scarab silhouette on his tongue, white winged patterns on his shoulders and haunches, and double hairs at the tip of his tail. He too, in turn, would be worshipped by the multitudes for as long as he lived.

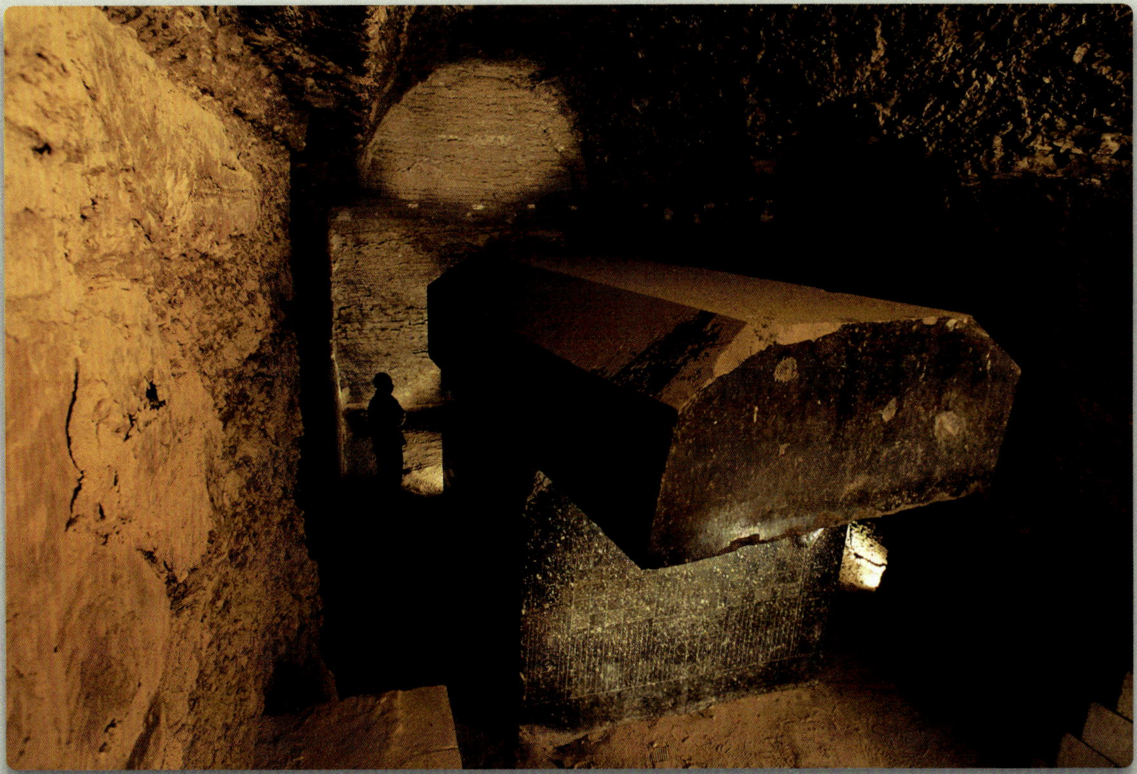

A MENAGERIE OF MUMMIES

A queen's pet gazelle (right) was readied for eternity with the same lavish care as a member of the family. It accompanied its owner to the grave in about 945 B.C., wrapped in blue-trimmed cloth with its own custom-made wooden coffin.

Millions of votive ibis mummies were dedicated in Egypt during the first millennium B.C., including this intricately wrapped specimen (below). It was likely dedicated to Thoth, the god of wisdom and writing.

The lid of a limestone coffin (bottom) identifies the contents: the mummy of a shrew, an animal admired for killing snakes.

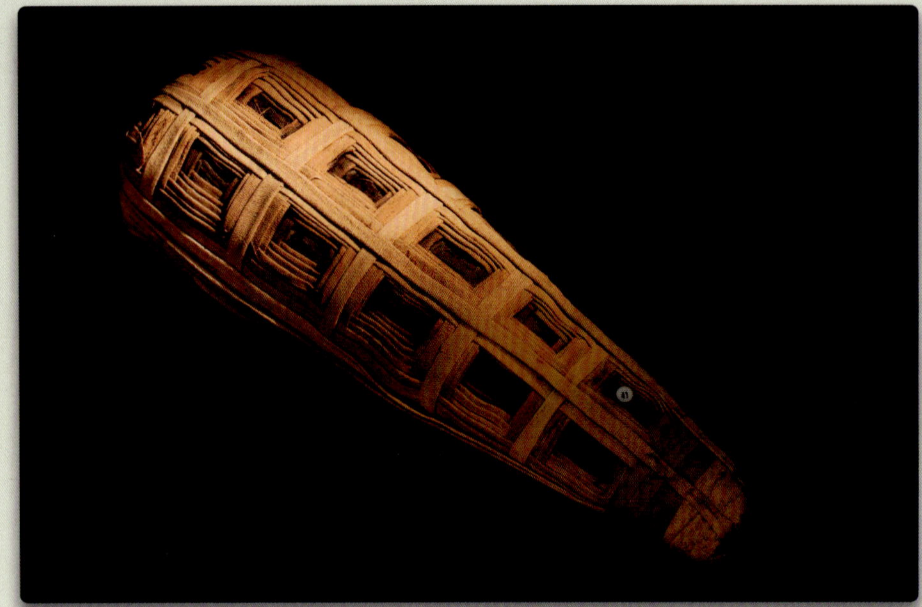

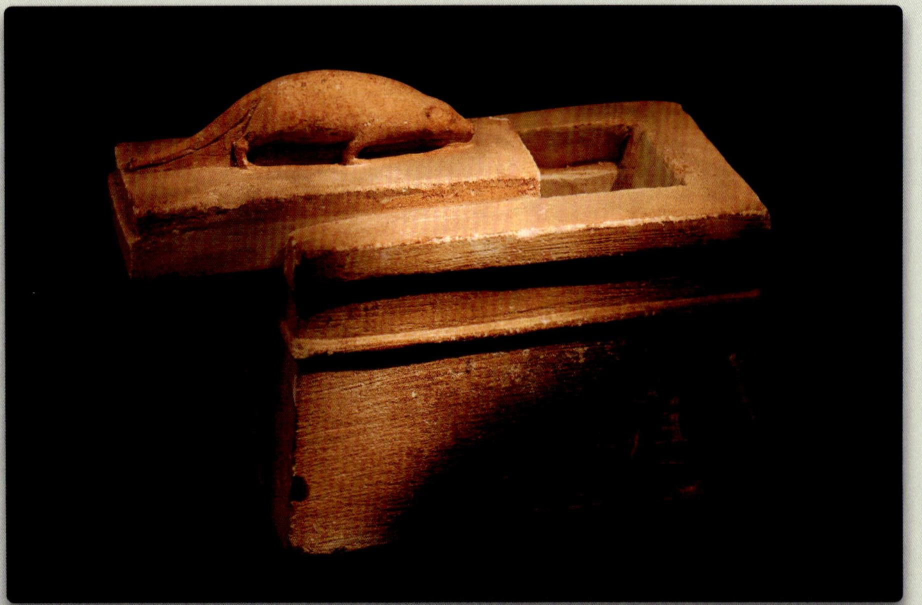

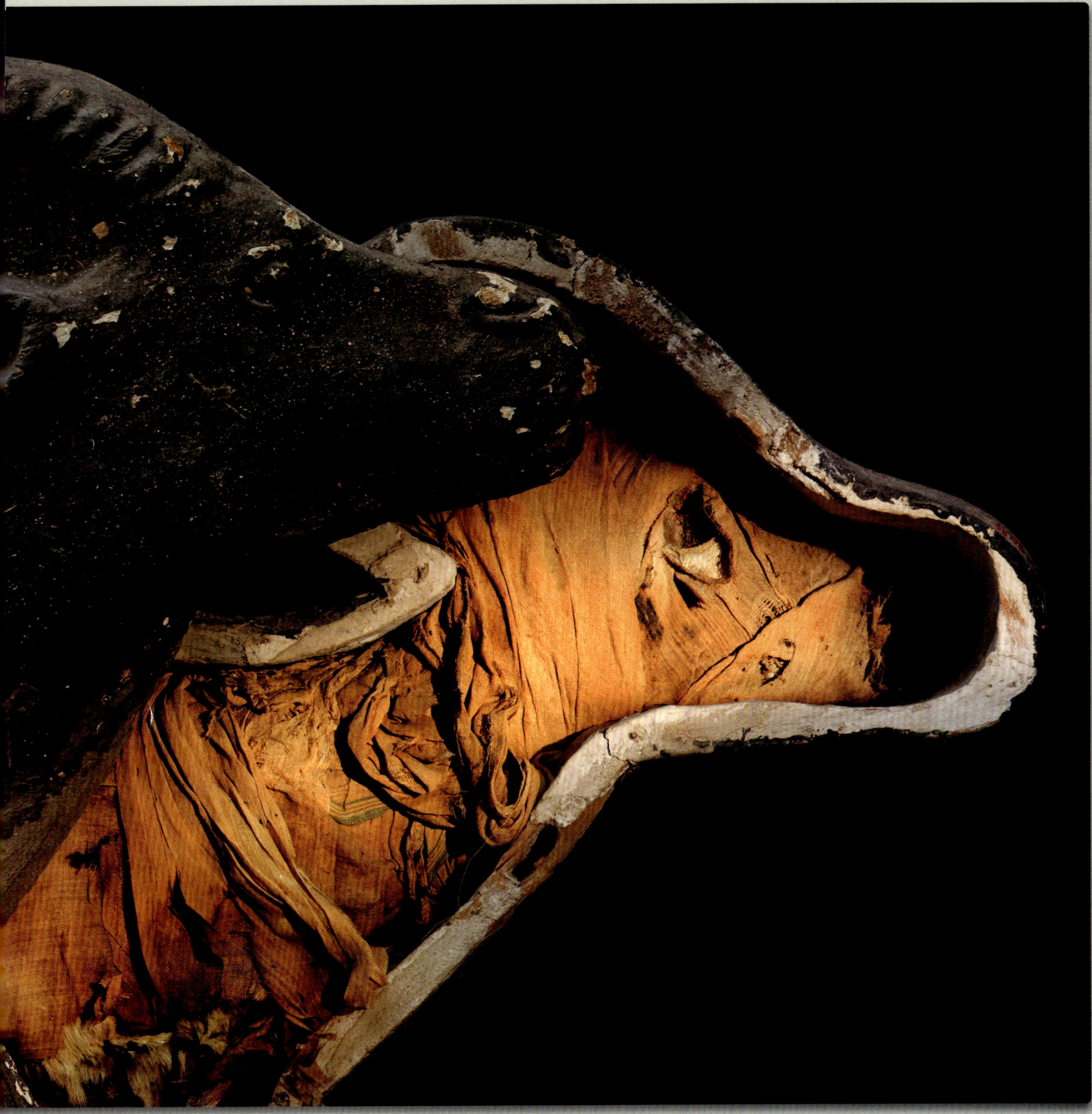

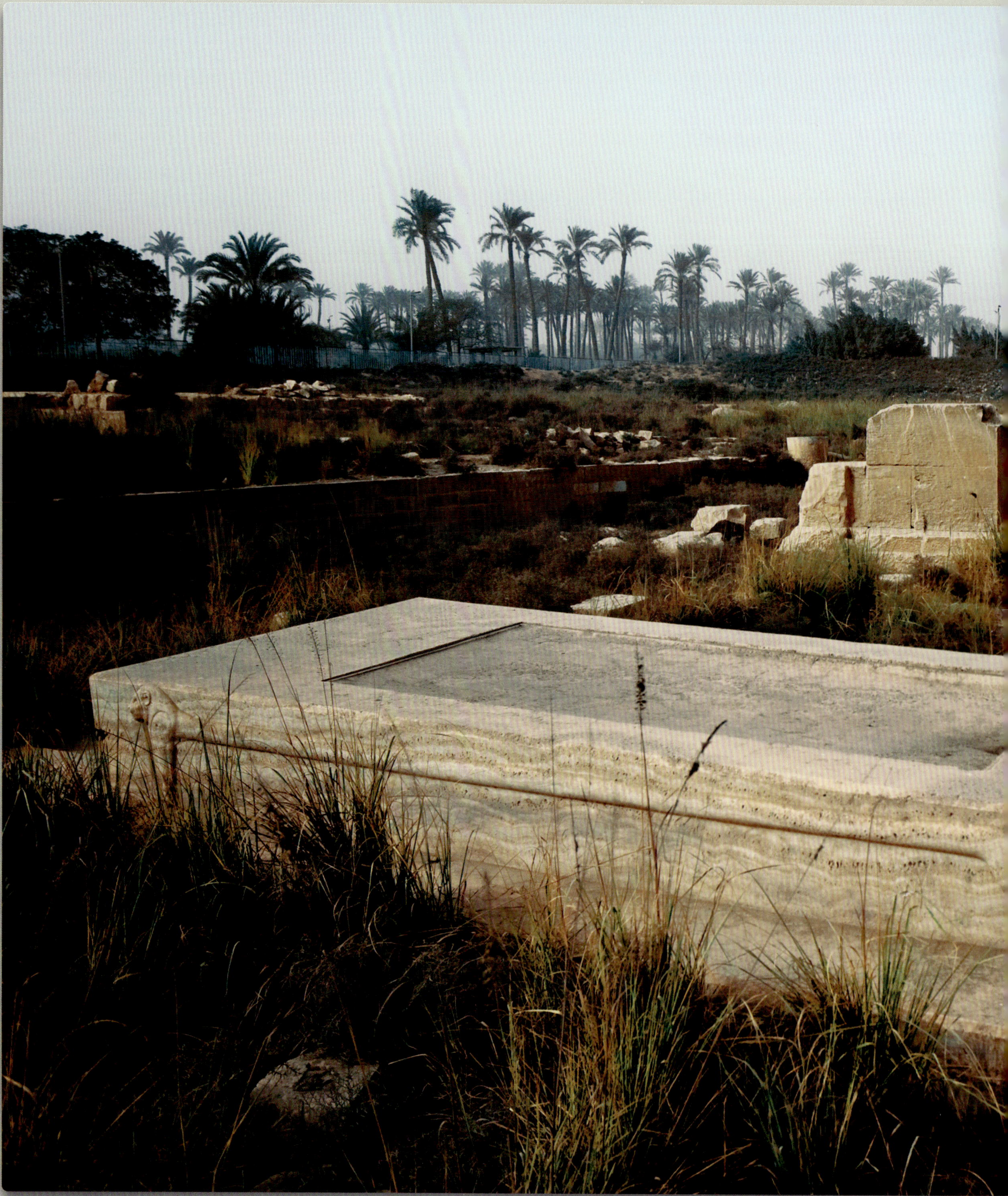

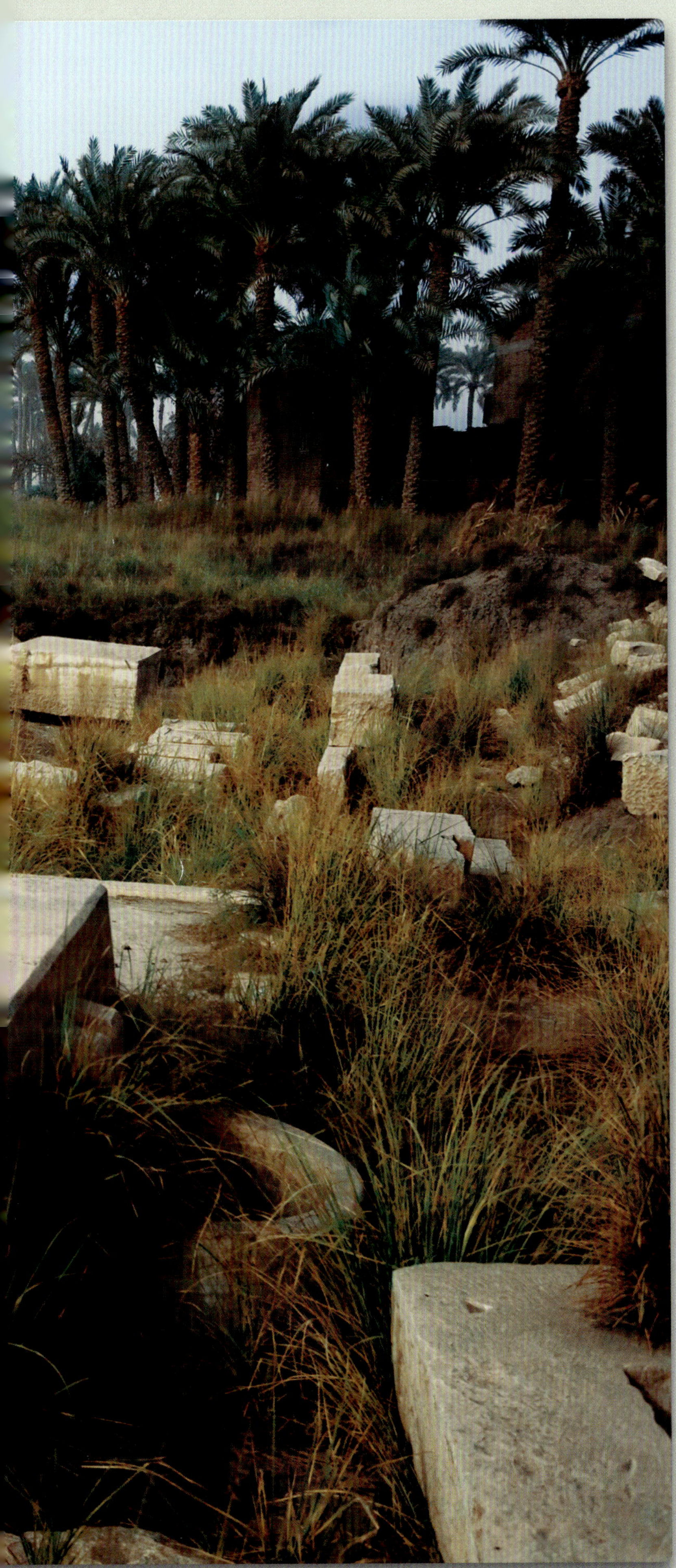

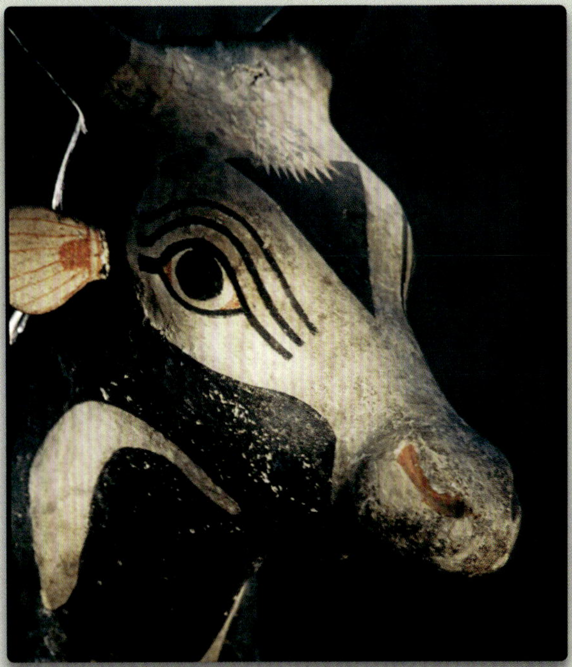

SACRED COWS

This embalming house for Apis bulls—animals revered in the great city of Memphis—survives in ruins near the village of Mit Rahina (left).

In the first or second century B.C., the head of a cow mummy was covered in wood, linen, and painted plaster (above) to represent the Apis bull's mother, an animal worshipped in her own right.

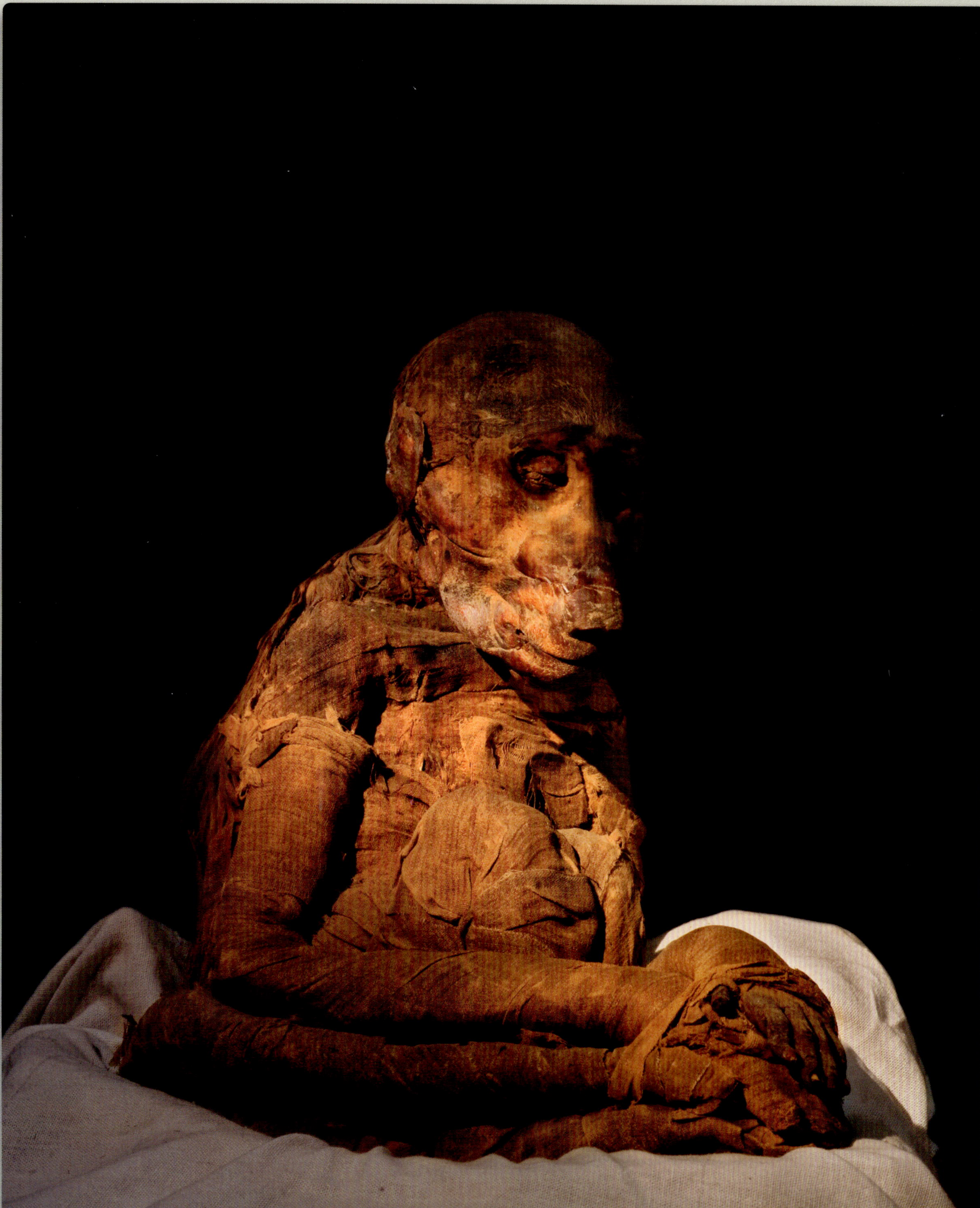

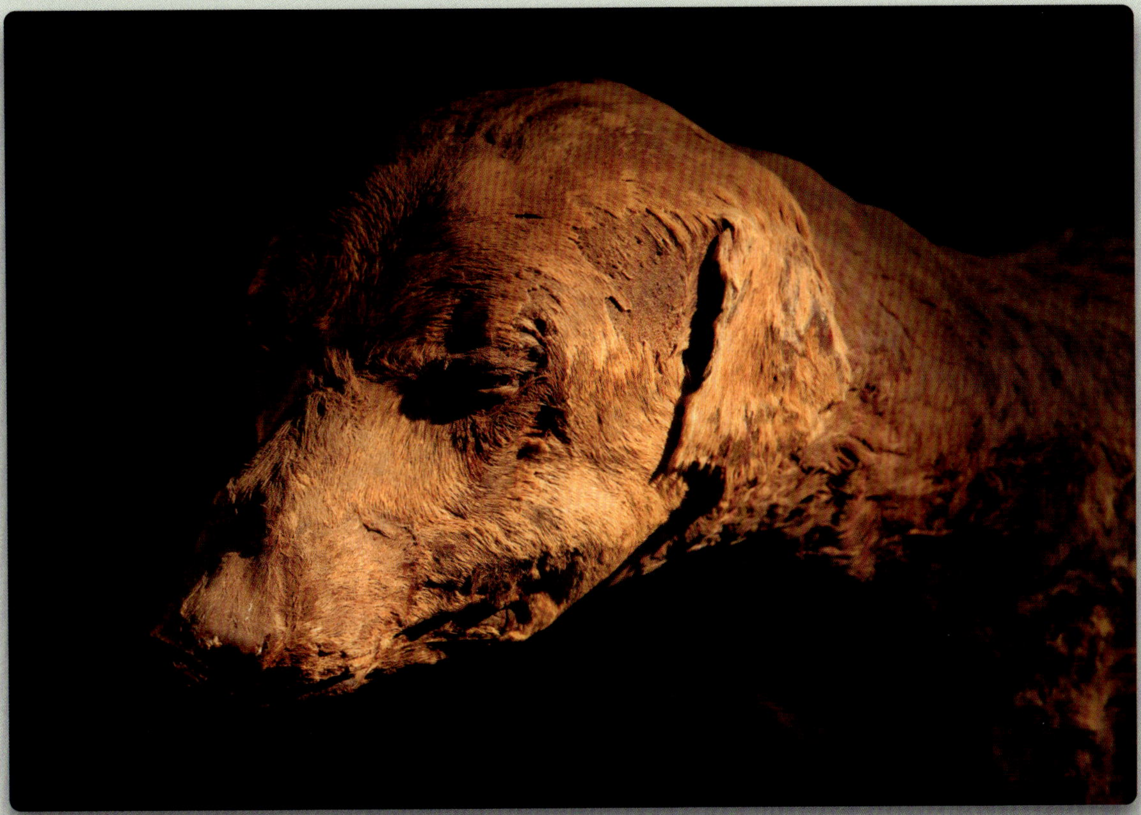

BELOVED BEASTS

Lovingly preserved, this hunting dog (above) likely belonged to a pharaoh and was buried some 3,200 years ago in a specially prepared tomb in the Valley of the Kings.

An x-ray of this baboon (opposite), found with the dog, revealed missing canine teeth. They were probably removed to keep the pet from nipping royal fingers.

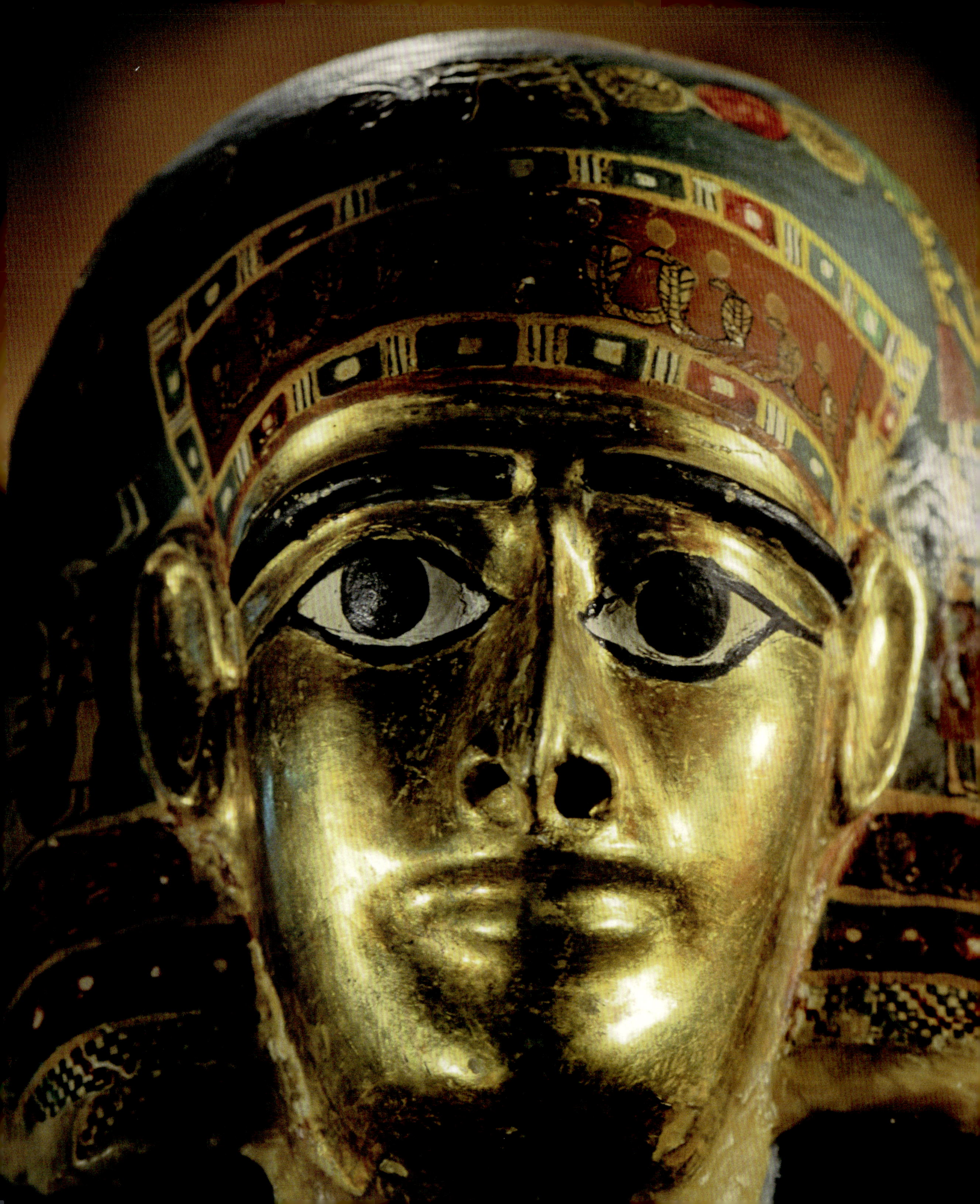

CHAPTER FOUR

THE EASTERN AND WESTERN DESERTS

Lands of Sand and Stone

AMID THE SCORCHED DUNES and rocks of the vast deserts to the east and west of the Nile lie the traces of mines, trading stations, and frontier settlements. These little-known outposts have long been overshadowed by the cities, tombs, and monuments along the river that have claimed the attention of travelers and scholars. But modern researchers are now studying them, and revealing the surprisingly important roles they played in Egyptian history.

"Until archaeologists started looking at these areas, we would have assumed that no one went into the desert, everyone stayed in the Nile Valley," says Egyptologist Salima Ikram. "Now we're looking at a completely different picture, with people trading and traveling and exploring. That's really changing our viewpoint of how the Nile Valley looked at its surroundings, and how the surroundings interacted with the valley."

The ancient Egyptians called the dry part of their realm *deshret,* or the red land. To a certain extent, the difficulties in traveling across it protected Egypt from unwelcome visitors. But it was not impenetrable. Caravan routes crossed the sands even in the early pharaonic era. One text describes an expedition to the kingdom of Punt sent by fifth-dynasty king Sahure in about 2450 B.C. to obtain electrum (an alloy of gold and silver), wood, and myrrh. Punt was somewhere to the southeast, probably reached by crossing the Eastern Desert and then sailing south on the Red Sea.

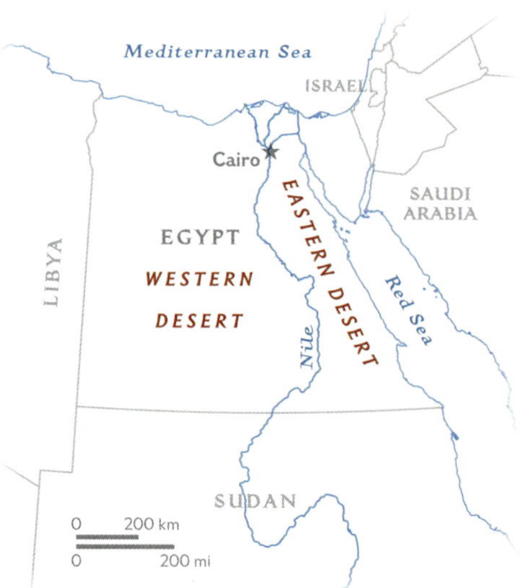

Such expeditions may have begun in Gebtu (modern Qift), a town north of Luxor where an eastward bow in the Nile shortened the desert trek to a hundred miles (160 km). Traders would have followed the ravines carved by infrequent rainstorms. They carried with them all their provisions, plenty of water, and the parts of their ships to be assembled once they reached the coast.

The Eastern Desert was also dotted with mines and quarries that produced all manner of coveted materials: limestone and granite for construction projects, copper for tools, calcite for beautifully translucent vases, gold for jewelry, and a variety of decorative stones, including agate, carnelian, and quartz.

On the opposite side of the Nile, the Western Desert proved to be equally useful, most especially because of the existence of five oases: Siwa, Bahariya, Farafra, Dakhla, and Kharga.

From earliest times, Egyptians appear to have kept in contact with these western springs through a network of trade routes. One, for instance, the Darb el Arba'in, or Forty Days' Road, ran from the central stretch of the Nile Valley through Kharga Oasis and south into Sudan. In more than 270,000 square miles (699,300 km^2) of unforgiving terrain, the oases became vital stops for donkey caravans carrying luxuries such as ebony, ivory, ostrich feathers, leopard skins, and gold from the rest of Africa into Egypt. Piles of rocks still mark the routes, and petroglyphs depict hunting scenes, boats, pharaonic bulls, magical signs, and even the name of an early king.

The oases were expected to send their commodities, often labeled "tribute," to temples in the Nile Valley. An inscription from the tomb of 15th-century B.C. vizier Rekhmire describes

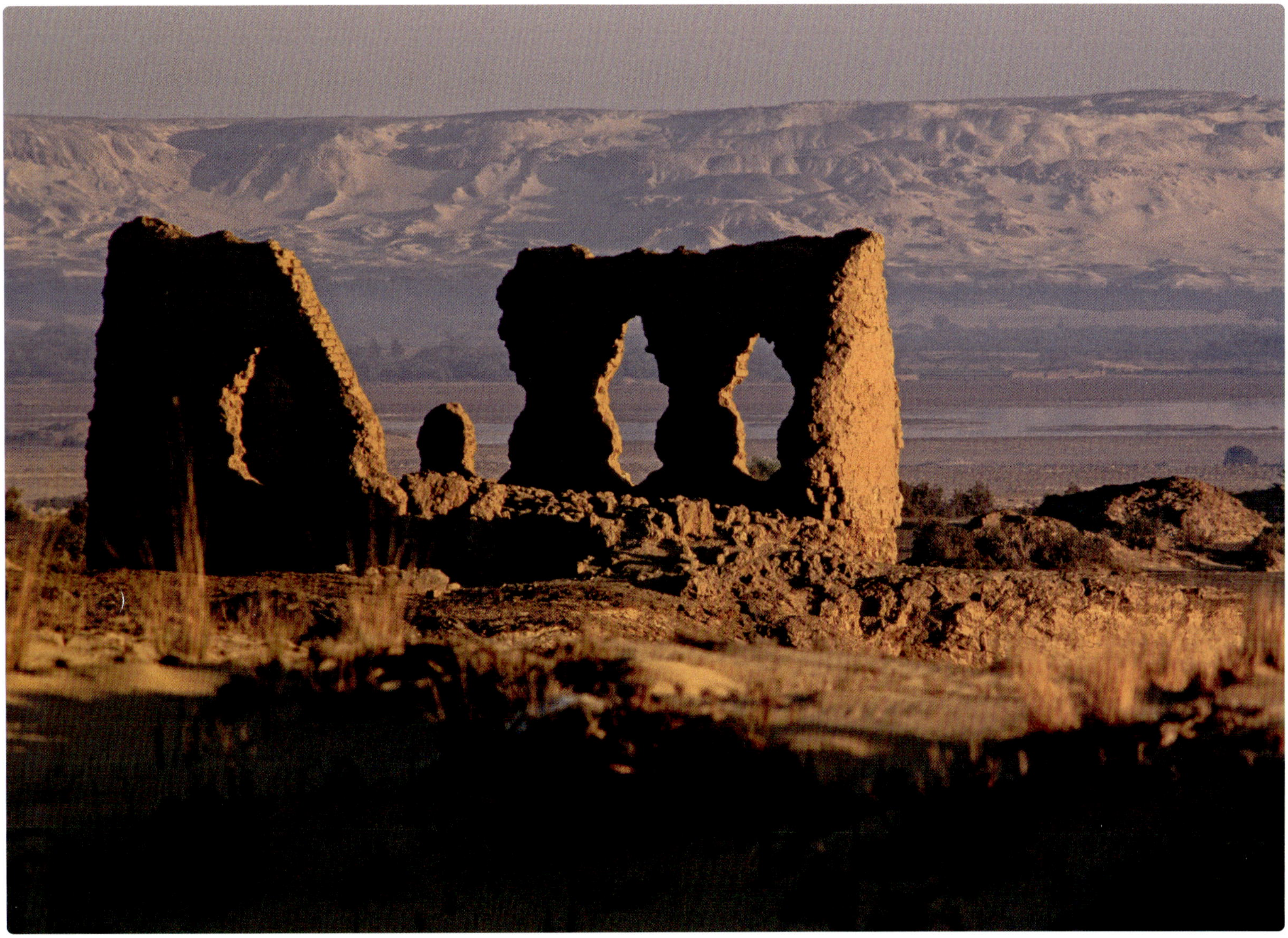

The mud-brick ruins of a Roman fort (30 B.C.–A.D. 395) rise above the Western Desert at Al-Hayz in Bahariya Oasis (above). Traces of a palace and a winery also survive here. Built near sources of water, garrisons like this guarded Egypt's western border, as well as the routes that carried trade to and from other parts of Africa.

PREVIOUS PAGES: A cemetery near a similar building, Qasr el-Labeka, in Kharga Oasis yielded this striking gilded and painted mask, constructed from linen and plaster.

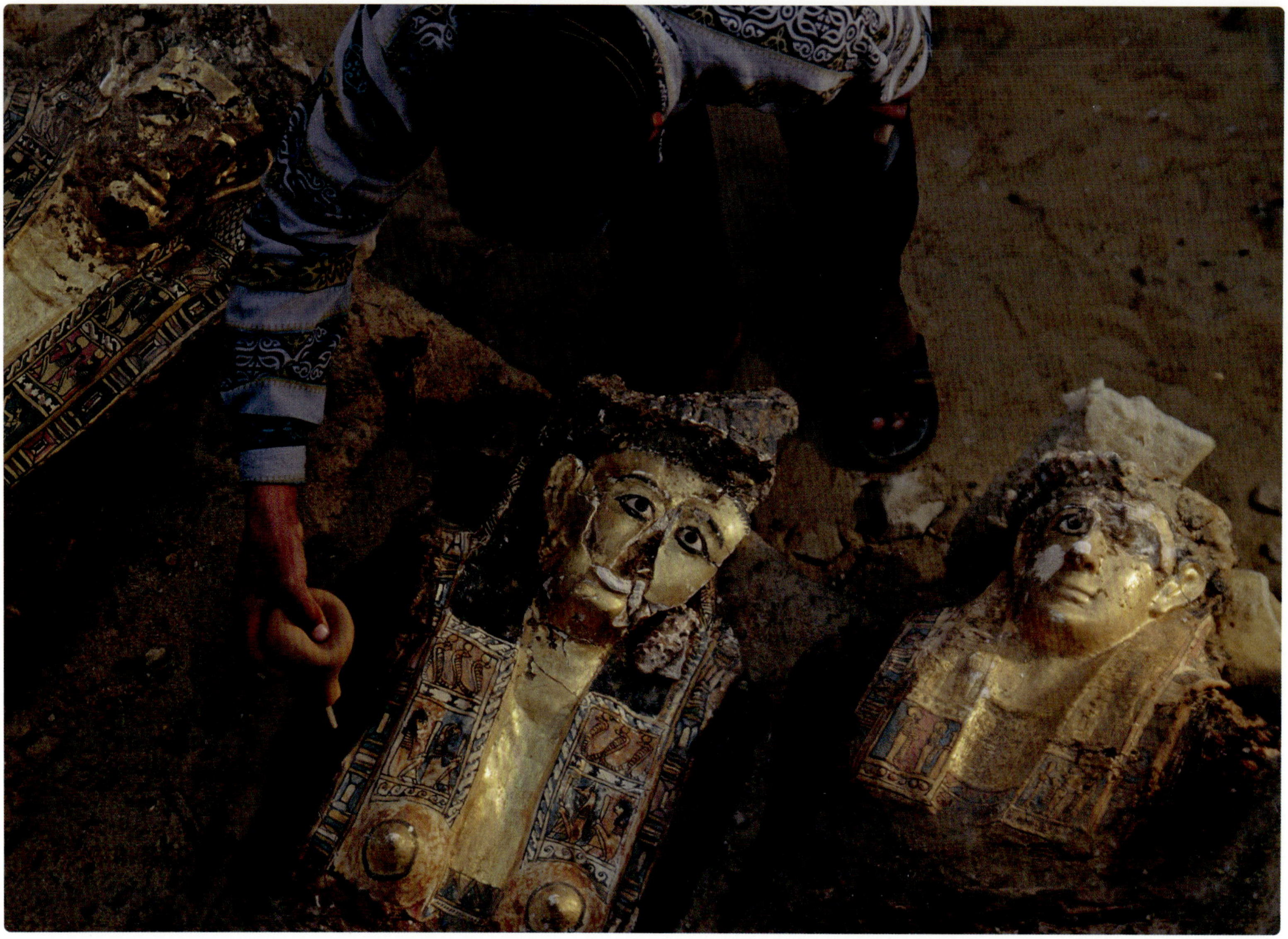

Elaborate, gilded masks from a tomb at Bahariya Oasis testify to the high status of the deceased. A vast Greco-Roman cemetery here (332 B.C.–A.D. 395) has inspired the nickname "Valley of the Mummies."

"receiving the produce of the Southern Oases." His tomb and those of other New Kingdom officials record porters from the oases delivering bales of cloth, baskets, woven mats, and amphorae that likely held wine.

Far removed from the cities and towns connected by the river, the isolated oases became places of exile for Egypt's criminals and renegades. In addition, these garrisoned communities were frequently charged with defending the country against invaders. Kings of the 19th and 20th dynasties became especially concerned about the security of the oases as Libyans pressed in from the west.

After his conquest of the country in 332 B.C., Macedonian general Alexander the Great made an exhausting journey across the desert to the legendary Siwa Oasis. There, the Oracle of Amun declared him a god—and thus the legitimate ruler of Egypt. This led to the foundation of the Ptolemaic dynasty, and eventually to the tragic saga of Queen Cleopatra, her liaisons with Julius Caesar and Mark Antony, and Rome's annexation of Egypt.

Roman rule brought the oases to the height of their prosperity, with the overall population possibly swelling to tens of thousands. Egypt was the empire's breadbasket, reportedly supplying one-third of its grain. Much of this came from the Western Desert, where the oases tapped a deep aquifer that allowed bumper crops to be produced year-round (unlike the single annual harvest in fields along the Nile). Forts were erected at Bahariya, Farafra, Dakhla, and Kharga, and the soldiers stationed at these places provided defense and collected tolls along the trade routes.

At Kharga, Salima Ikram's team found crawl-space caves filled with dog burials, suggesting that Roman soldiers followed the Egyptian cult of Anubis, the canine-headed god of the west. At Dakhla, at least half a dozen stone temples attest to the continued worship of Egyptian gods such as Amun, Mut, and Khonsu.

"'Until archaeologists started looking at these areas, we would have assumed that no one went into the desert, everyone stayed in the Nile Valley,' says Egyptologist Salima Ikram. 'Now we're looking at a completely different picture.'"

Also at Dakhla, archaeologists have uncovered a fourth-century A.D. villa that displays murals with classical scenes, attesting to a life of elegance, luxury, and learning for the wealthiest members of society. Mummies with gilded face masks uncovered at Bahariya offer another glimmer of affluence under the Romans. The four tombs excavated held more than a hundred mummies—likely high-end merchants. The entire cemetery covers about two square miles (5 km^2) and could include an estimated 10,000 additional burials.

In 525 B.C., somewhere between Kharga and Siwa, part of the invading Persian army got caught in a vicious sandstorm. "A wind arose from the south, strong and deadly, bringing with it vast columns of whirling sand, which entirely covered up the troops and caused them wholly to disappear," wrote fifth-century B.C. Greek historian Herodotus. Modern explorers claim to have found traces of these 50,000 men—bones, arrowheads, metal from armor—but the discovery has yet to be confirmed. The location of the lost soldiers is one of the many mysteries still to be solved as archaeologists continue to gather evidence of human activity at the fringes of Egyptian civilization. ▲

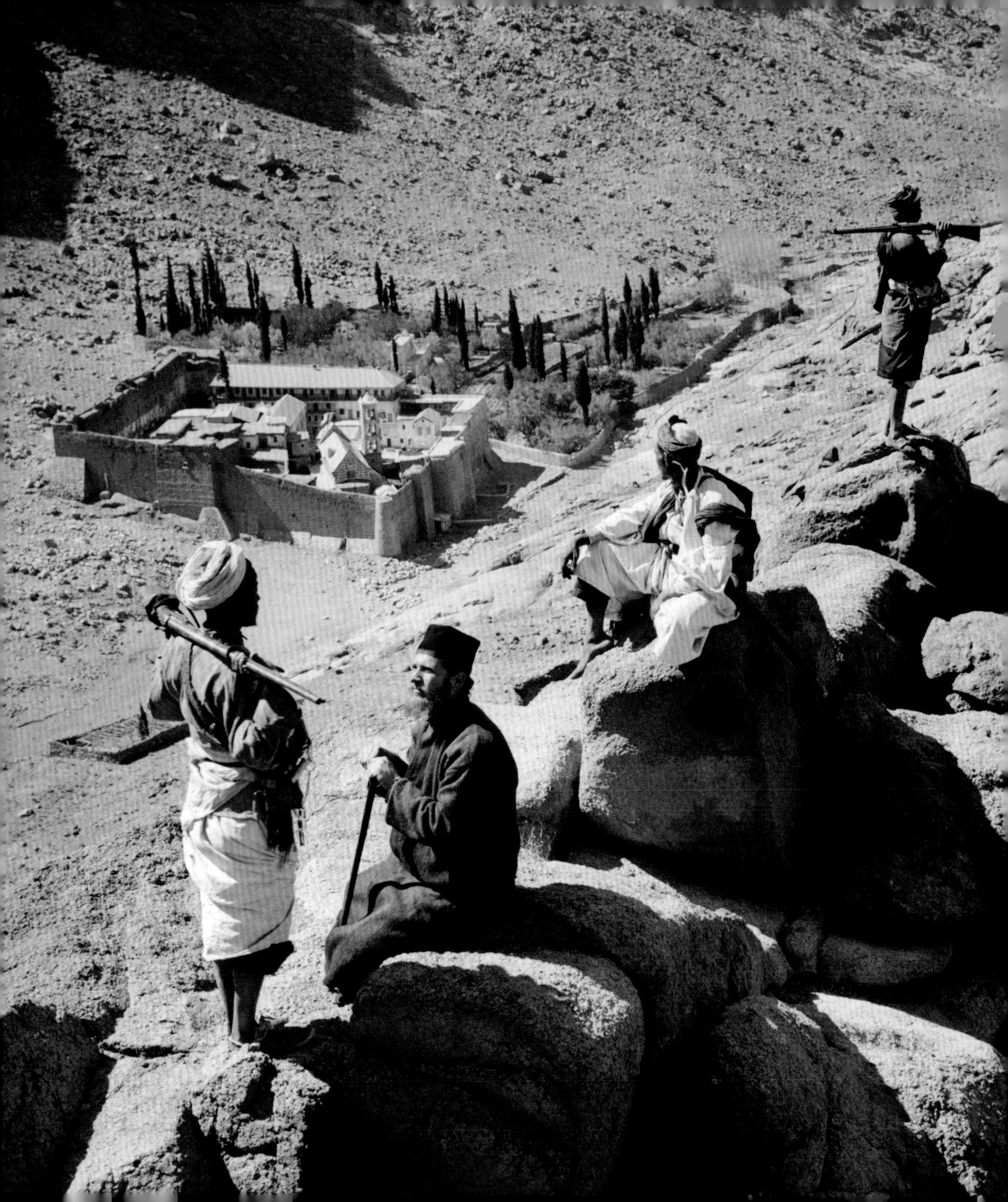

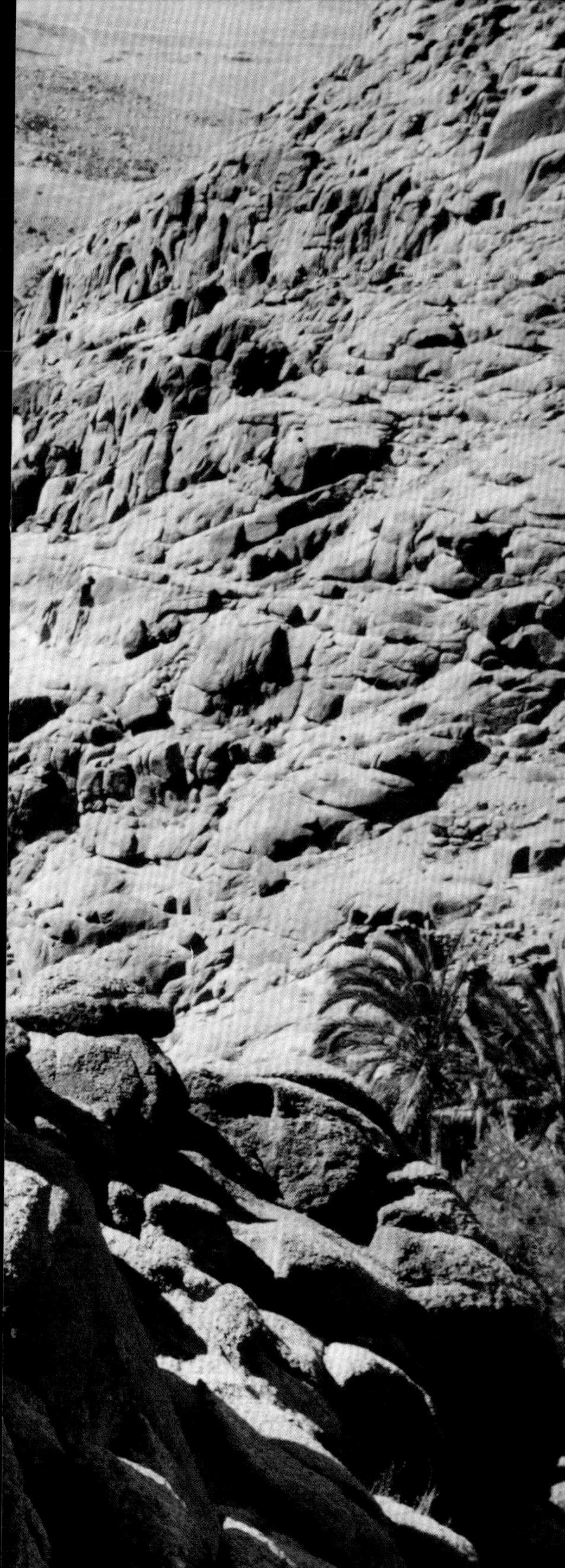

On a hill above his monastery, a Greek Orthodox monk visits with local Bedouin. The December 1912 issue of *National Geographic* included this image in a story entitled "Sunrise and Sunset from Mount Sinai." Established during the rule of Roman emperor Justinian (A.D. 527–565), the monastery is one of the oldest such religious institutions in the world.

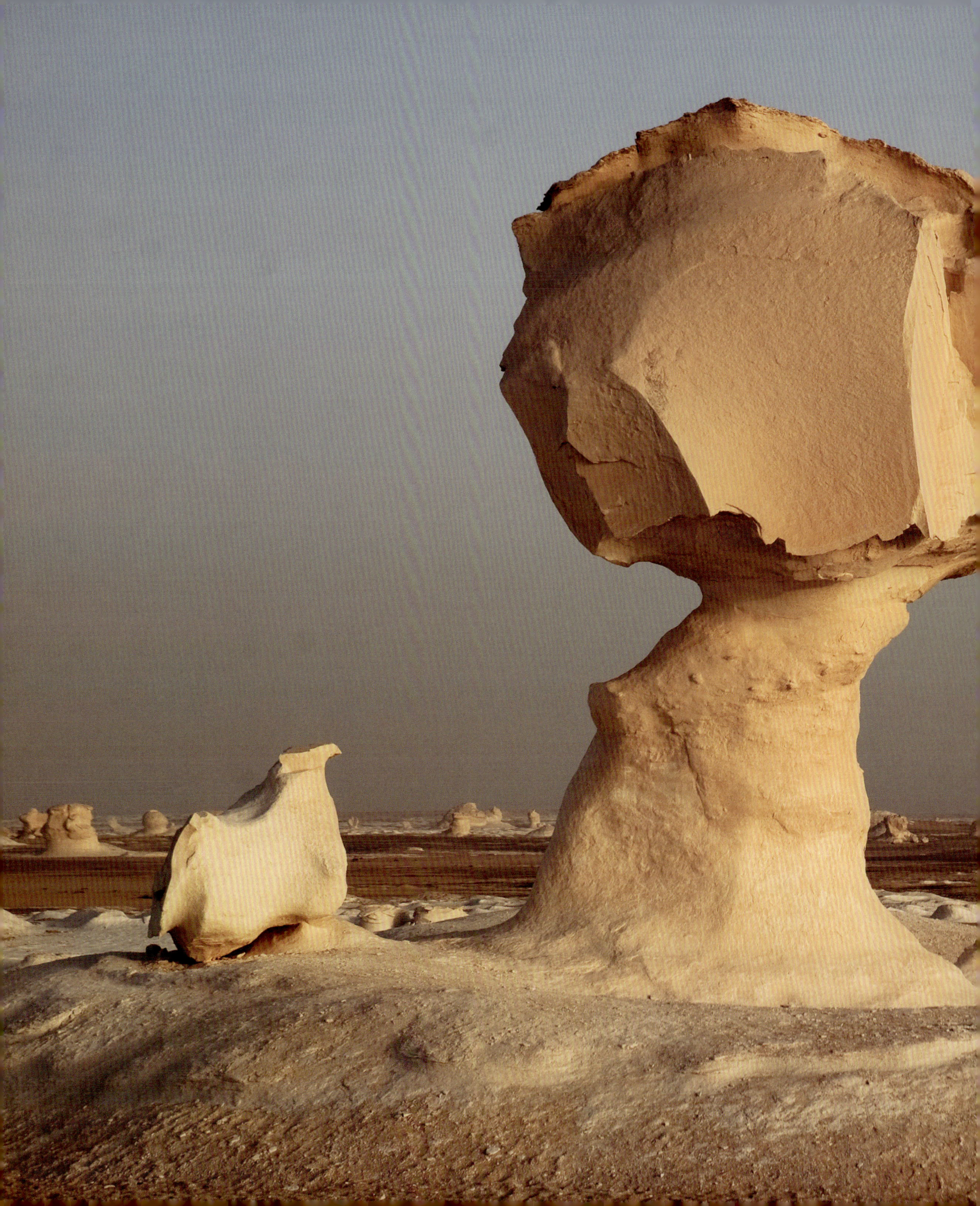

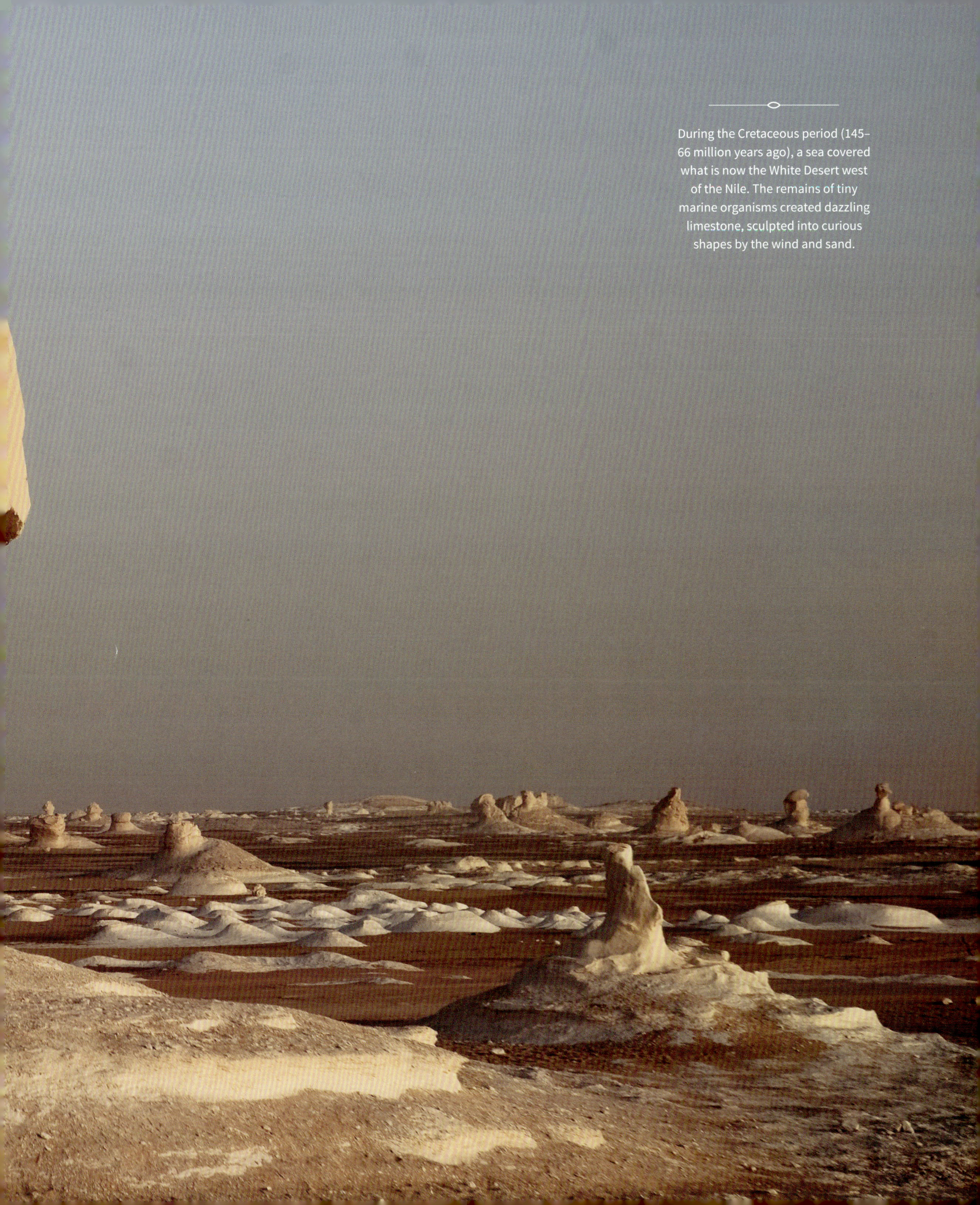

During the Cretaceous period (145–66 million years ago), a sea covered what is now the White Desert west of the Nile. The remains of tiny marine organisms created dazzling limestone, sculpted into curious shapes by the wind and sand.

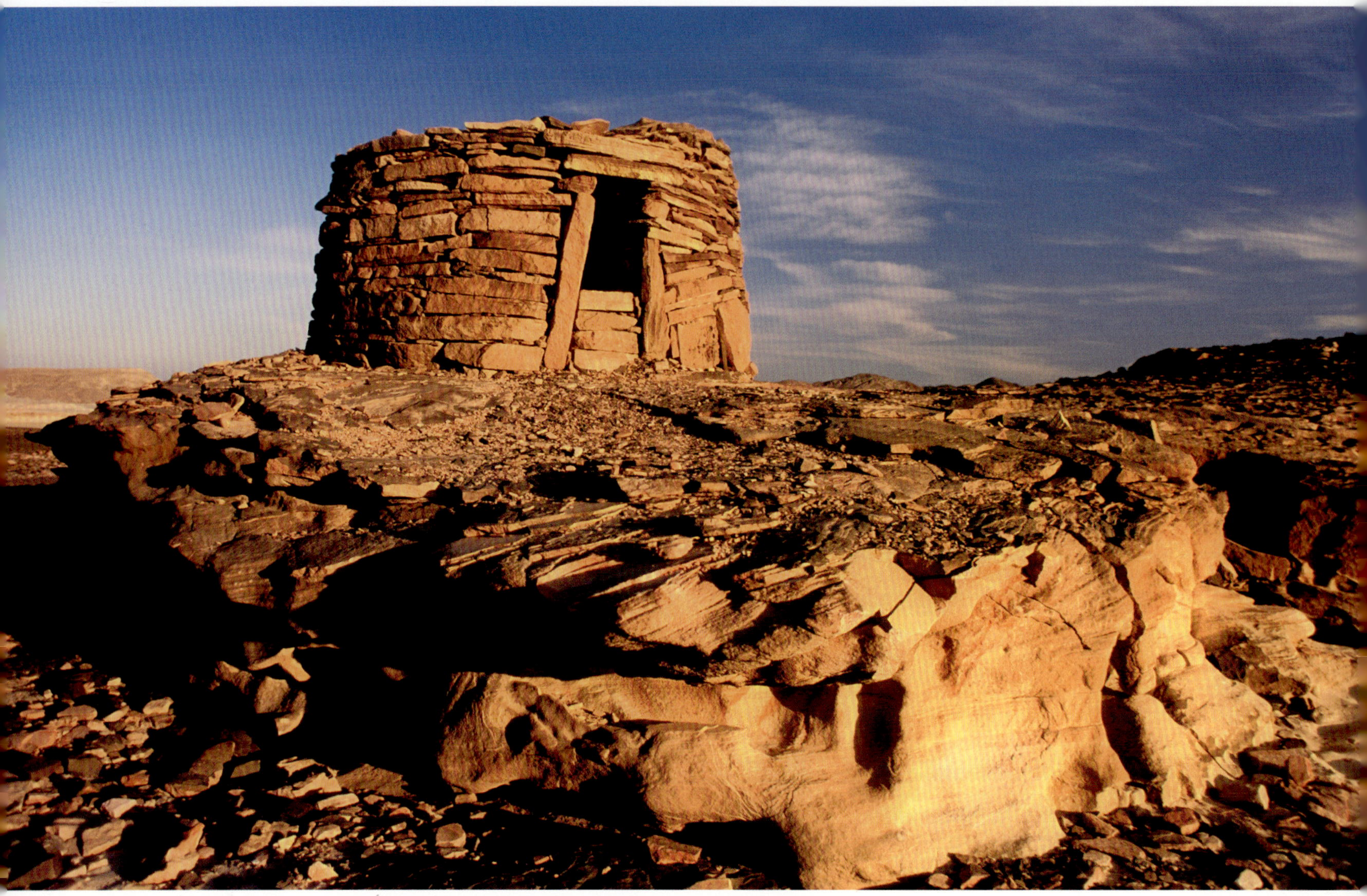

Some 5,000 years ago, nomadic herders in the Sinai Peninsula built circular tombs of stone, now called *nawamis* by the local Bedouin. Like this example, the six-foot-tall (1.8 m) structures usually had a commanding view of the desert.

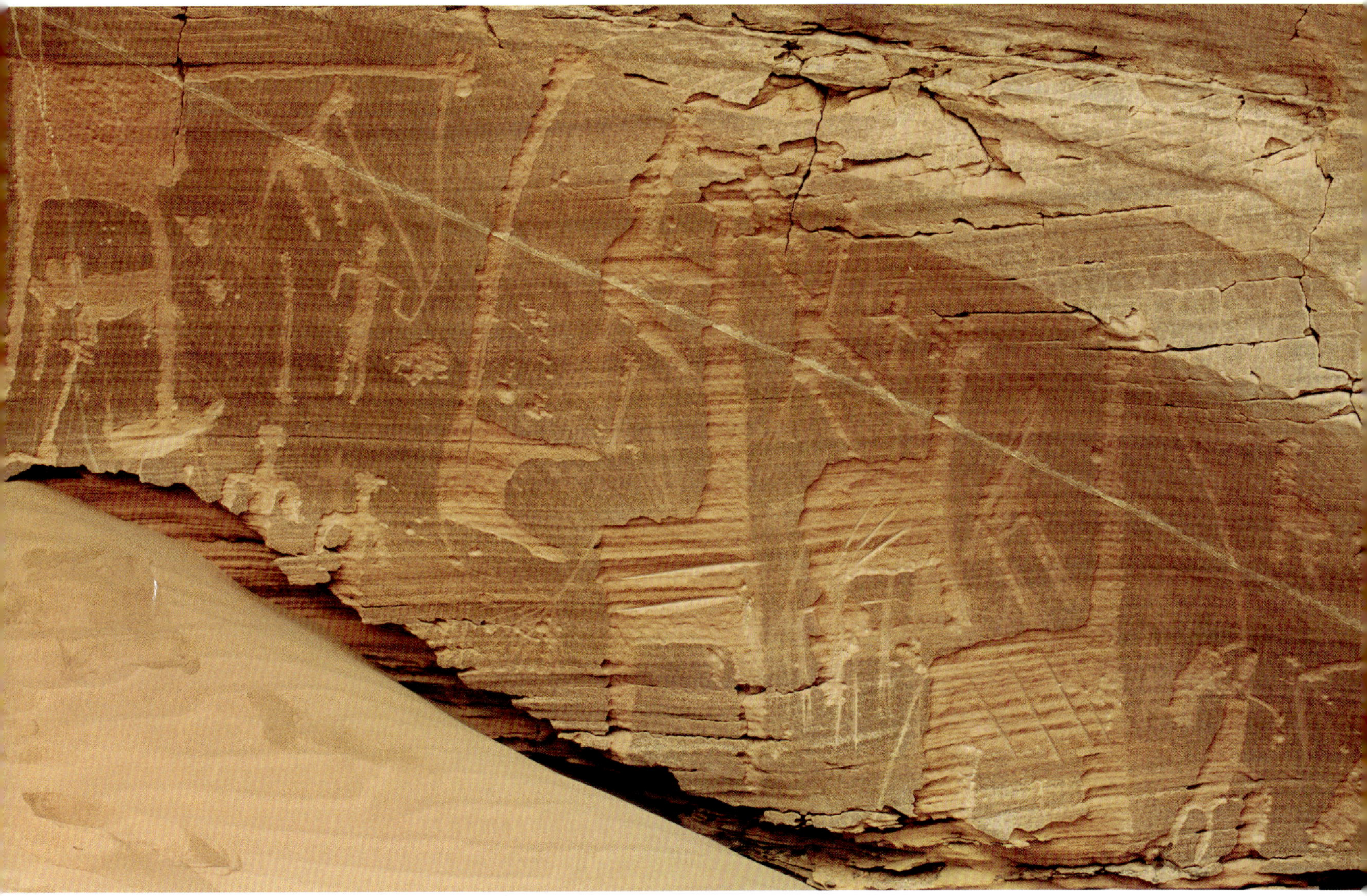

Along an ancient east-west trade route at Kharga Oasis, a parade of leashed giraffes appears on a cliff. Residents probably created the scene around 6000 B.C., when this part of Egypt was still a savannah.

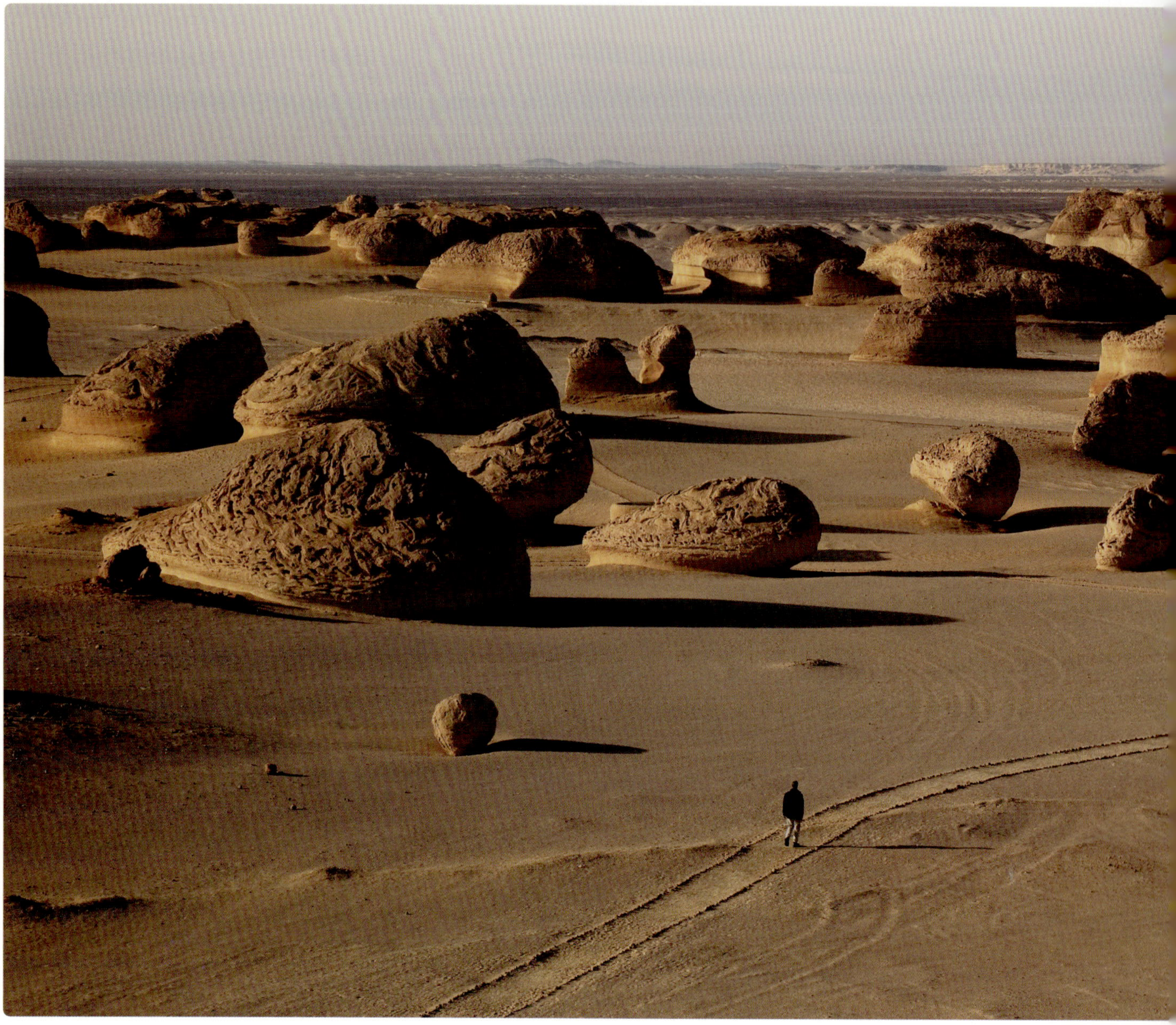

Once lying beneath an ocean, the rock-strewn landscape of Wadi al-Hitan in the Western Desert (above) holds the fossilized remains of sharks, sea urchins, catfish, and prehistoric whales with vestigial legs.

At Kharga Oasis, the name of a previously unknown ruler appears on a rock face along the ancient caravan route called the Darb Ain Amur (opposite). A royal trade mission must have inscribed it there around 3100 B.C.

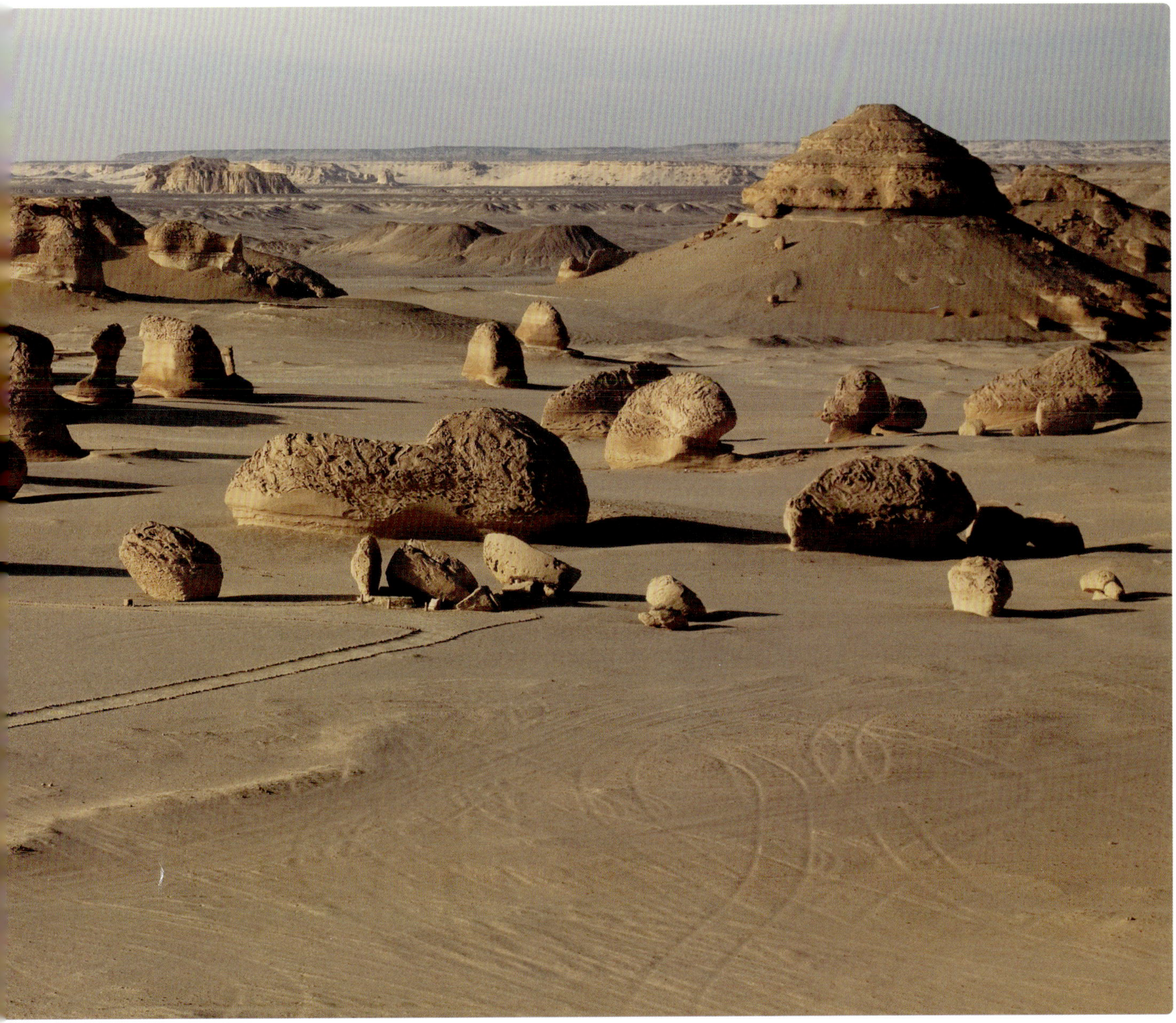

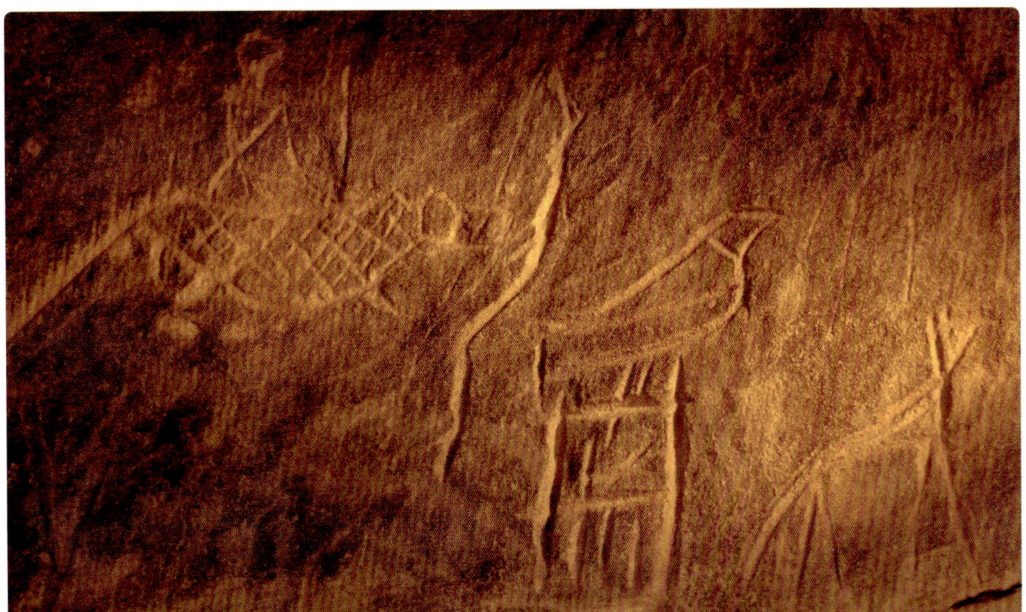

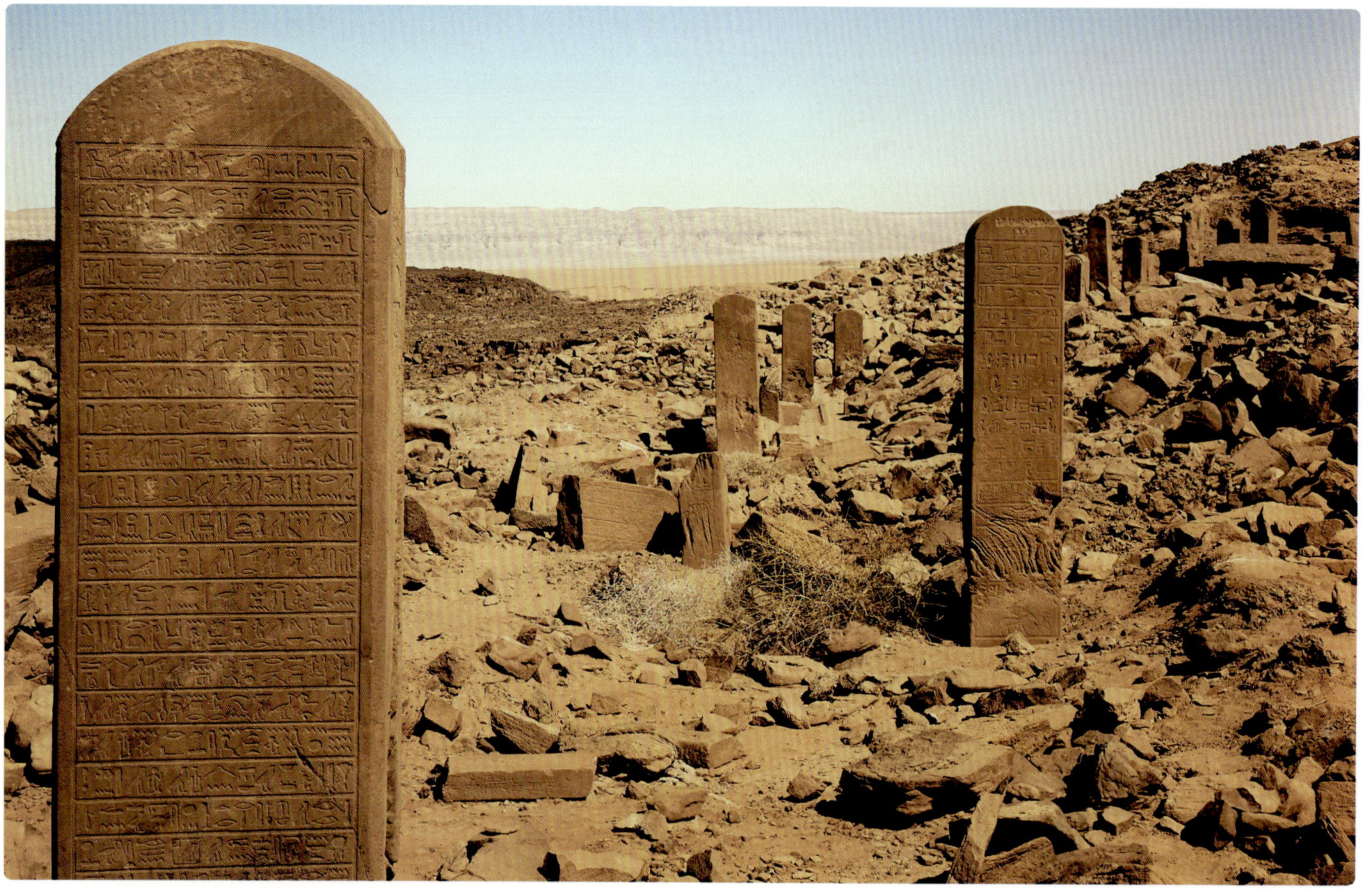

Inscribed stones known as stelae mark the approach to the temple of Hathor at Serabit el-Khadim in the Sinai (above). The structure probably dates to the reign of Amenemhet III (about 1818–1770 B.C.), when the turquoise mine there was especially active. Hathor was the patron goddess of the miners.

This steatite head of Queen Tiy (opposite), once part of a statuette, was found at the temple. Tiy was the powerful wife of King Amenhotep III, who ruled during the 14th century B.C., a time of great wealth for Egypt.

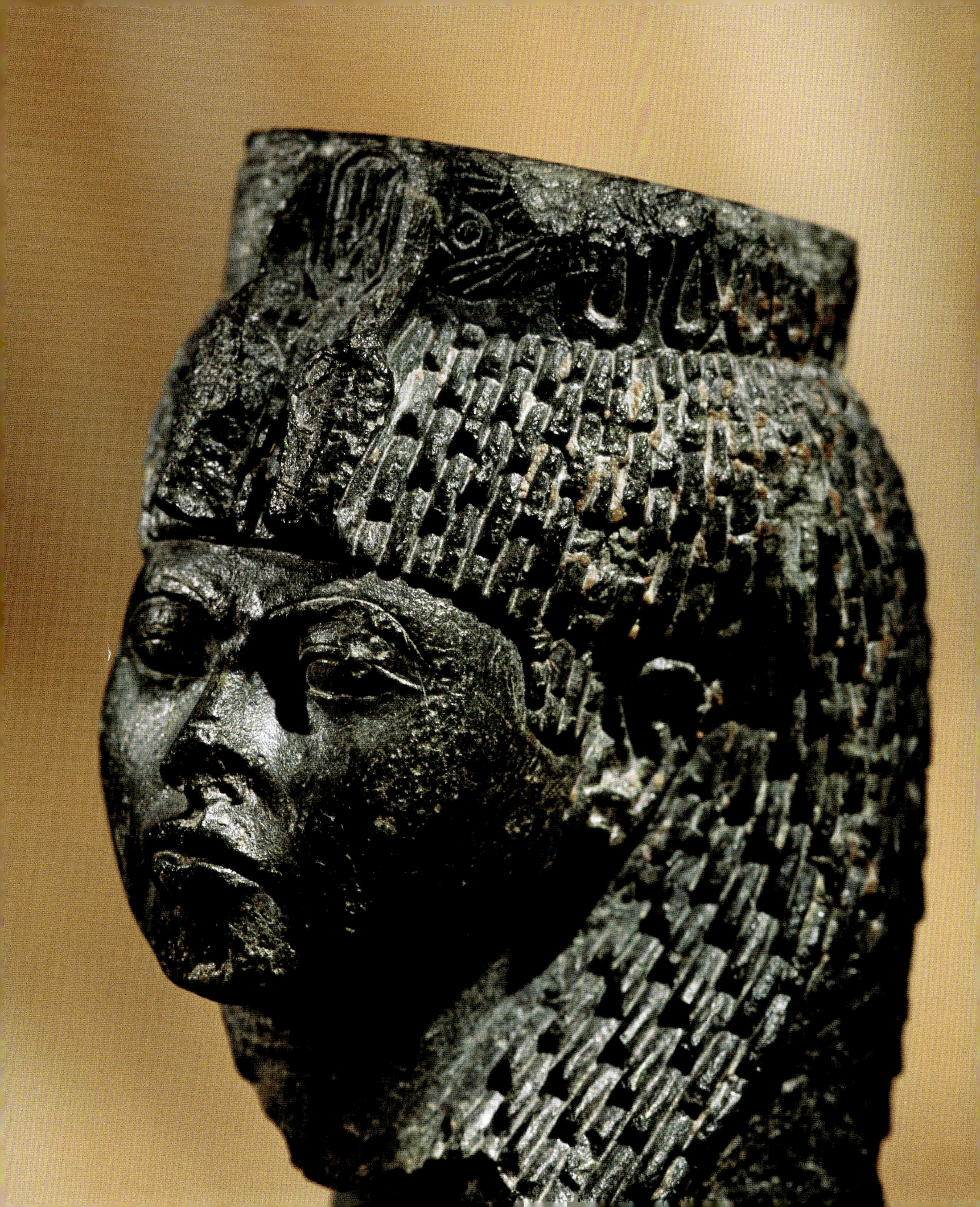

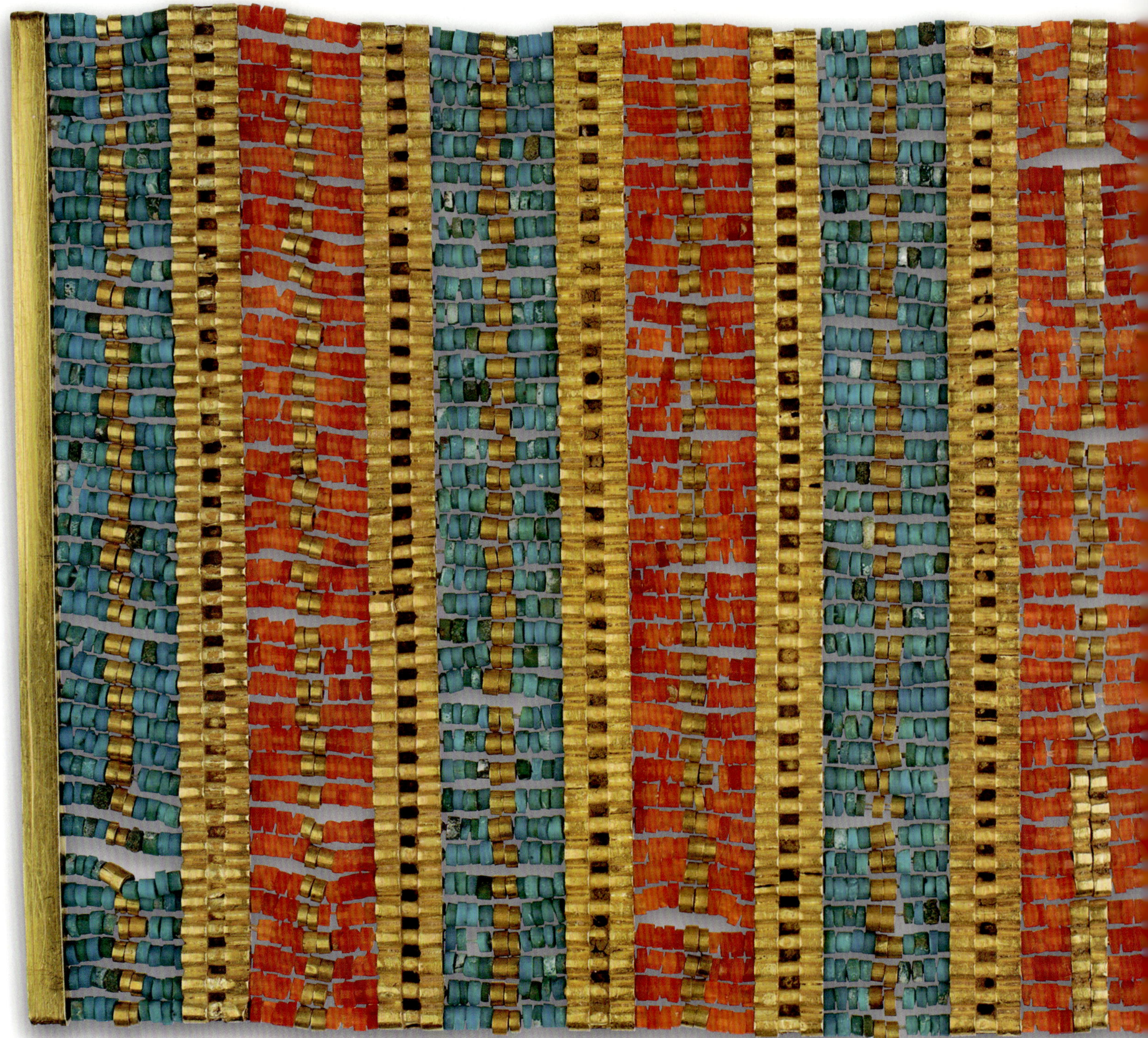

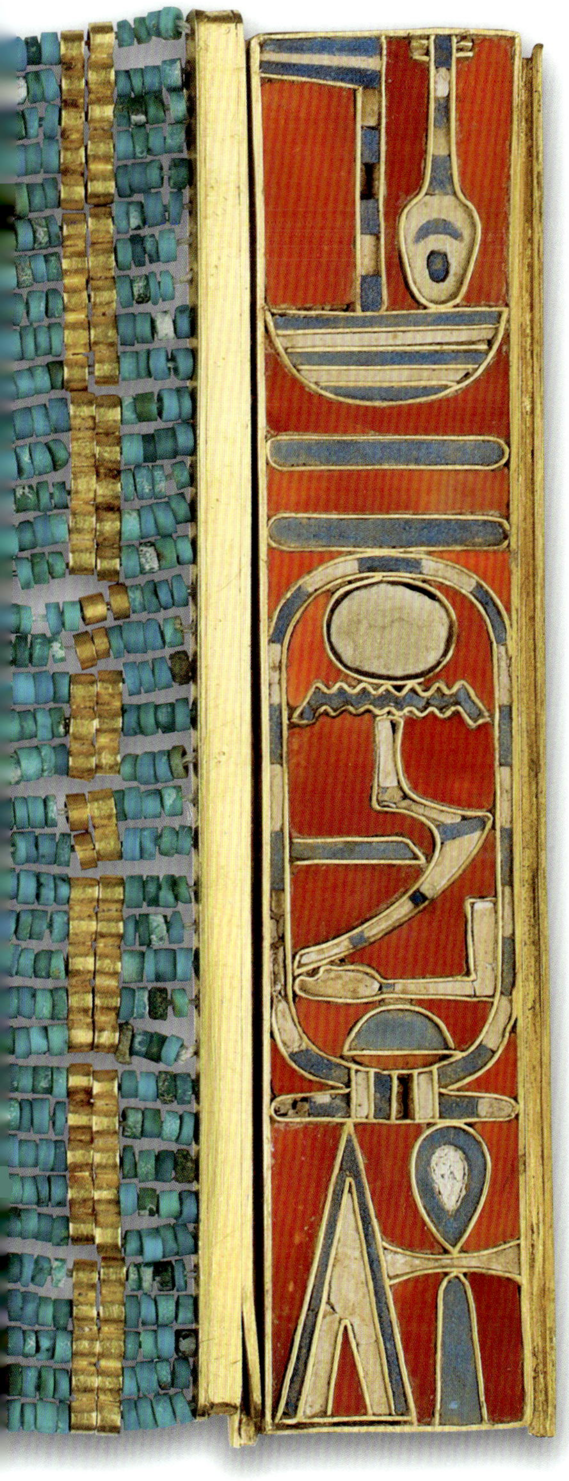

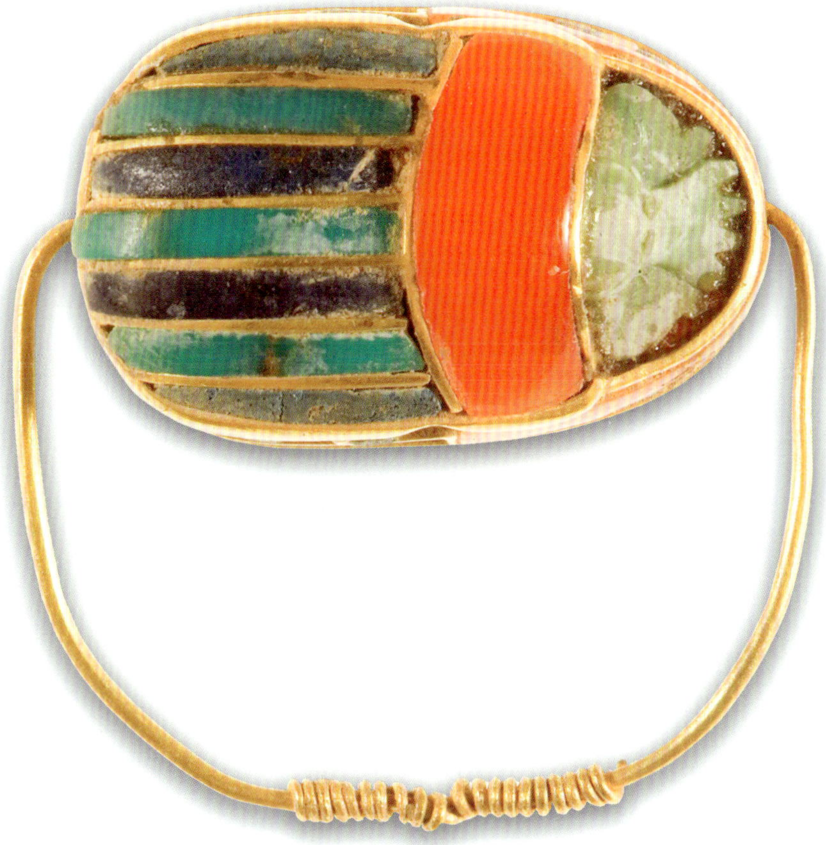

A bracelet (left) belonging to Sithathoryunet, a 12th-dynasty princess (about 1842–1837 B.C.), was buried with her at el-Lahun. Hieroglyphs make reference to the king, her father: "the perfect god."

This scarab ring (above) was also found in Sithathoryunet's tomb. The turquoise may have come from the Sinai Peninsula, or Nubia—also the likely source of the carnelian. Lapis lazuli came from Afghanistan.

A turquoise pendant (below) from the same era was found in a cemetery at el-Lisht.

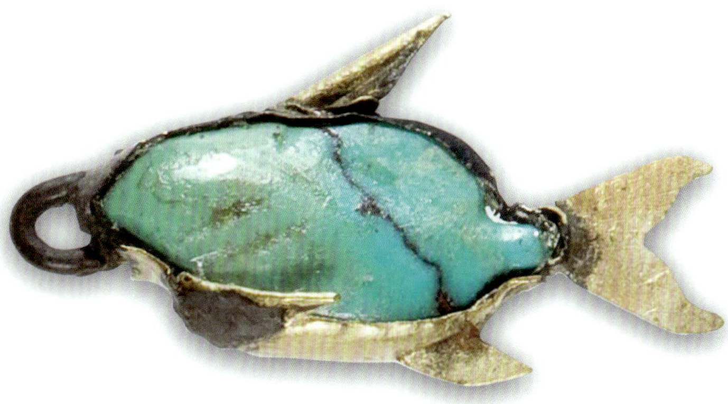

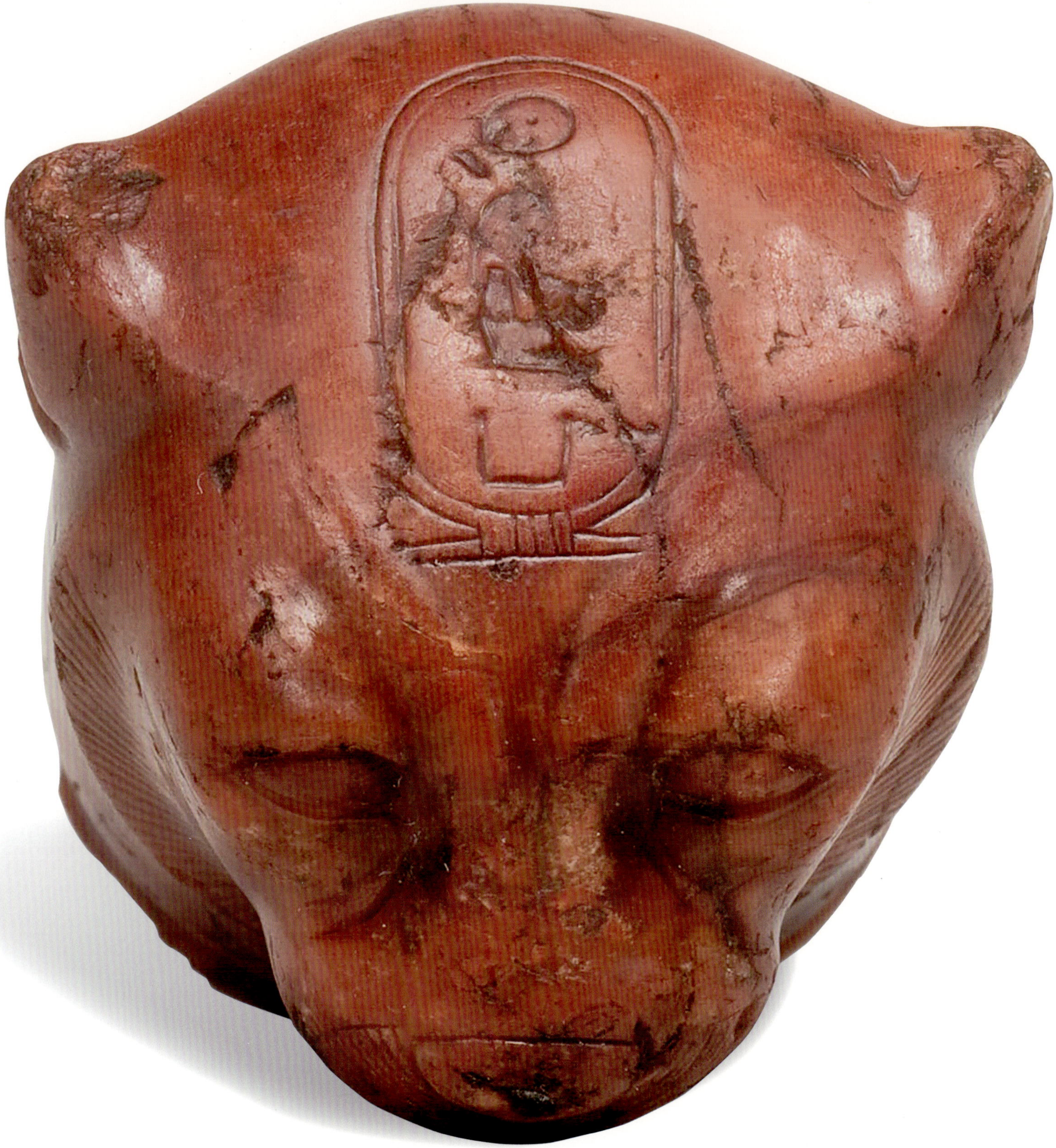

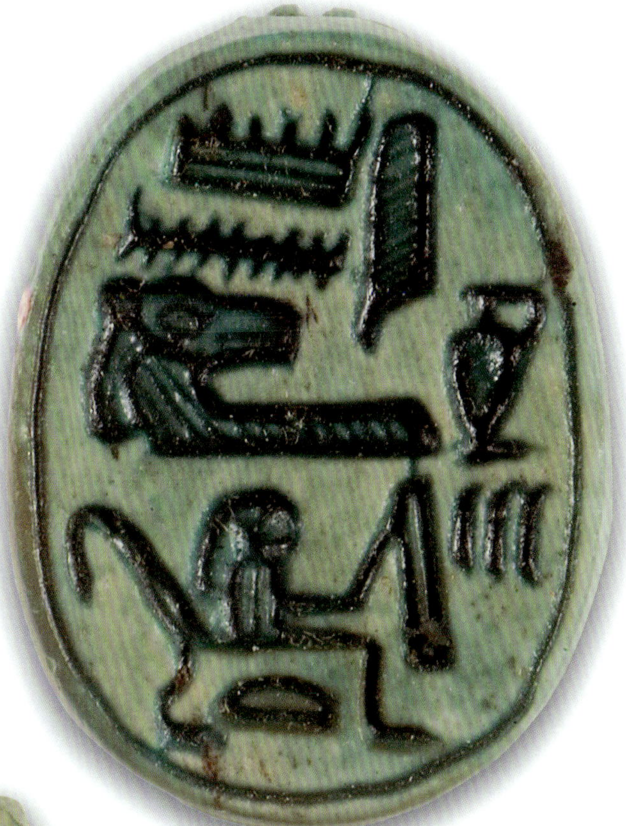

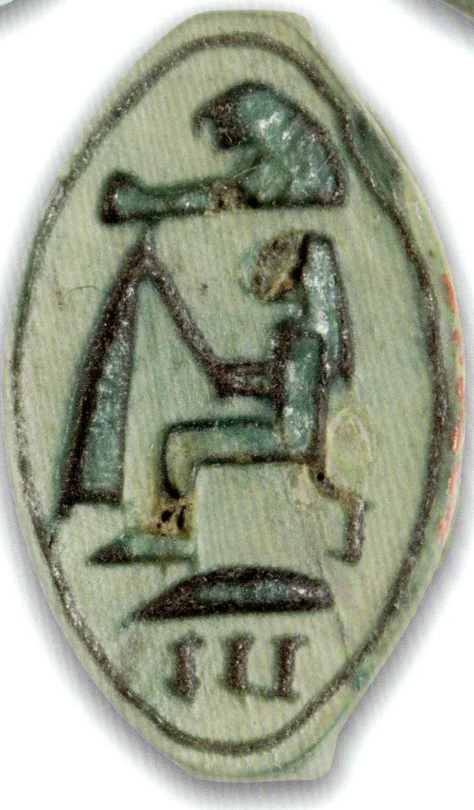

A leopard's head (opposite) inscribed with the name of Hatshepsut (about 1473–1458 B.C.) was likely used to play a board game. It was carved from red jasper, possibly mined in the Eastern Desert, and bears one of the queen's other names, Maatkare.

Several dozen scarabs were discovered in a foundation deposit at Hatshepsut's mortuary temple at Deir el-Bahri. The glazed steatite bases of these three (this page) bear the name Hatshepsut, which means "foremost of noblewomen." Steatite also came from the Eastern Desert.

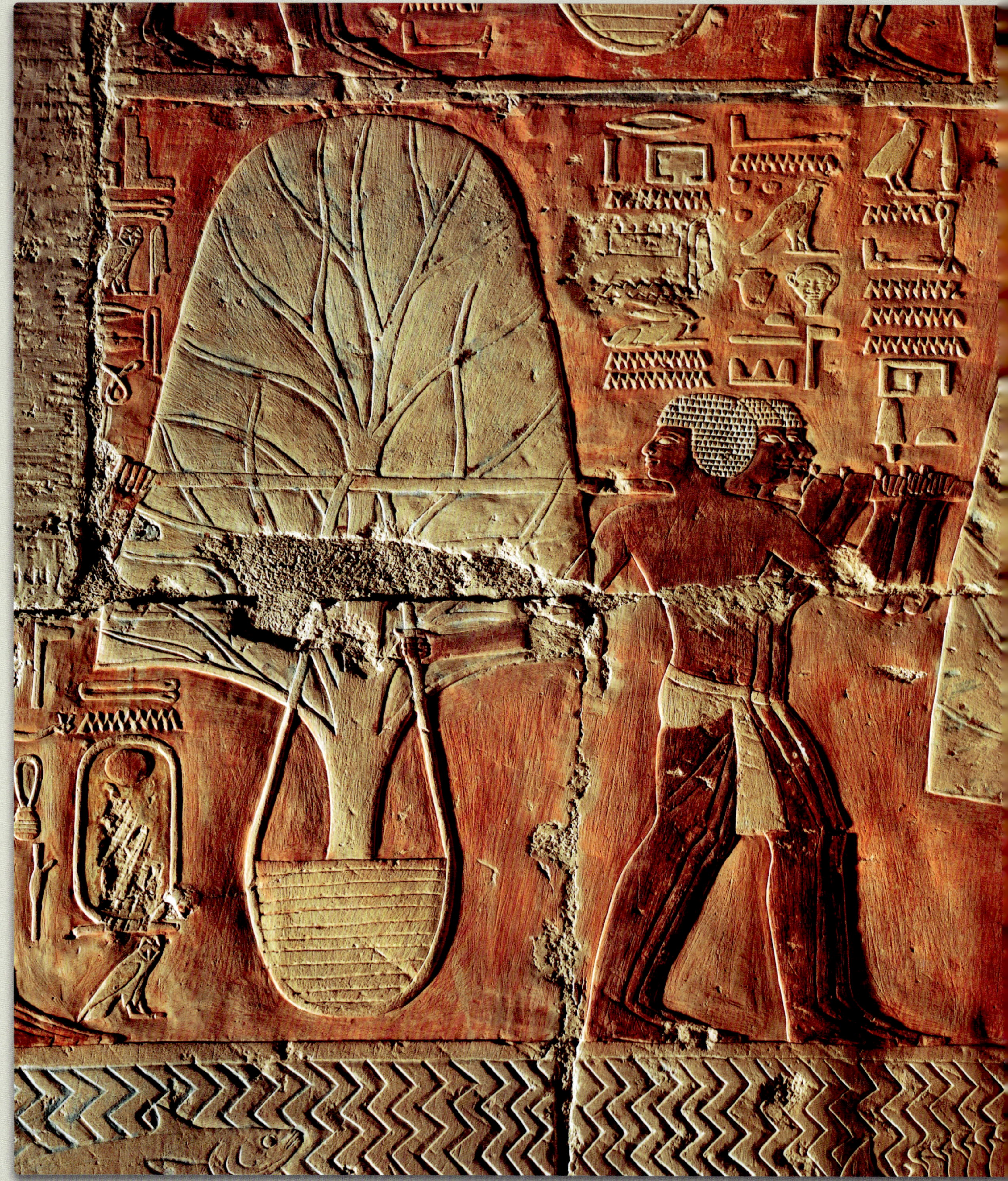

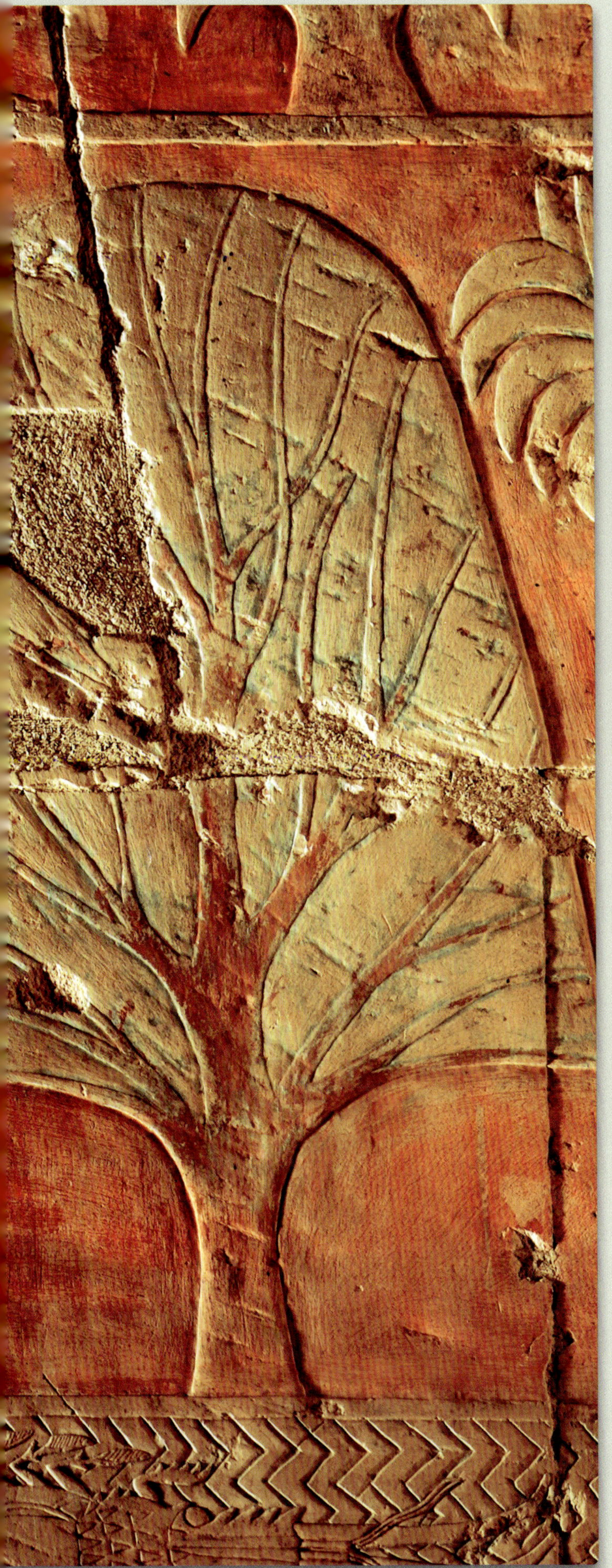

DIGGING DEEPER

The Mysterious Realm of Punt

IN THE 15TH CENTURY B.C., Hatshepsut, a queen who ruled Egypt as a king, sent a trading expedition to the kingdom of Punt. After crossing the Eastern Desert on one of the routes that led from the Nile to the Red Sea, some 200 men boarded five ships and set sail to the fabled land in search of luxury items such as aromatic resins, elephant tusks, and exotic animals. The successful trip was so important to Hatshepsut that she depicted it on a wall in her mortuary temple at Deir el-Bahri. One scene (left) shows a myrrh tree with its roots in a basket, ready for the trip home. “Never since the beginning of the world have the like wonders been brought by any king,” says an inscription at the temple.

But where exactly was Punt? Ancient Egyptian texts don’t say, and modern experts have speculated about various possibilities. Recent research may have solved the puzzle. Isotopes extracted from this 3,300-year-old baboon skull from Luxor (below) and other animals likely imported from Punt suggest that the source was the area of present-day Eritrea, Ethiopia, and northwestern Somalia.

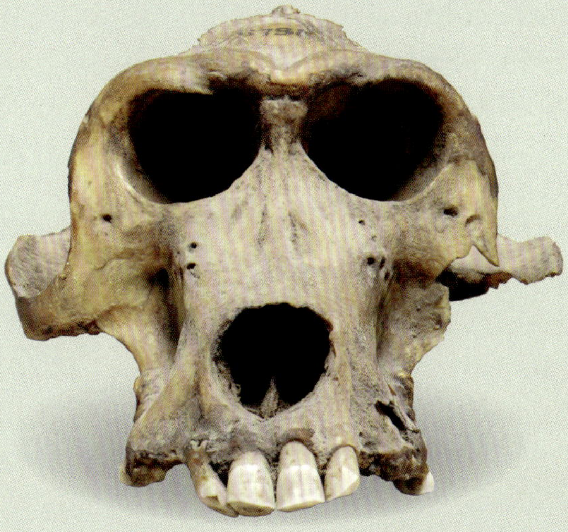

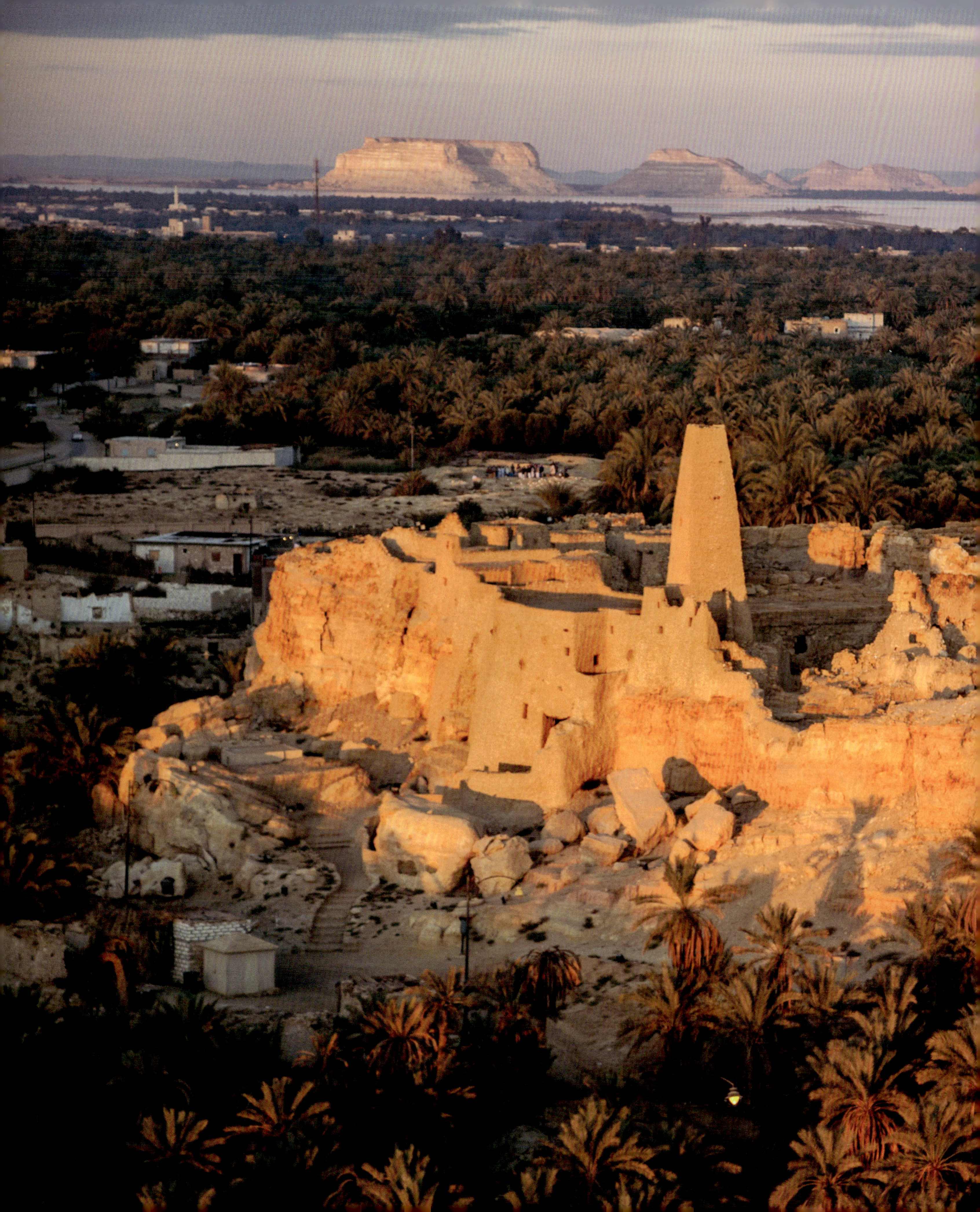

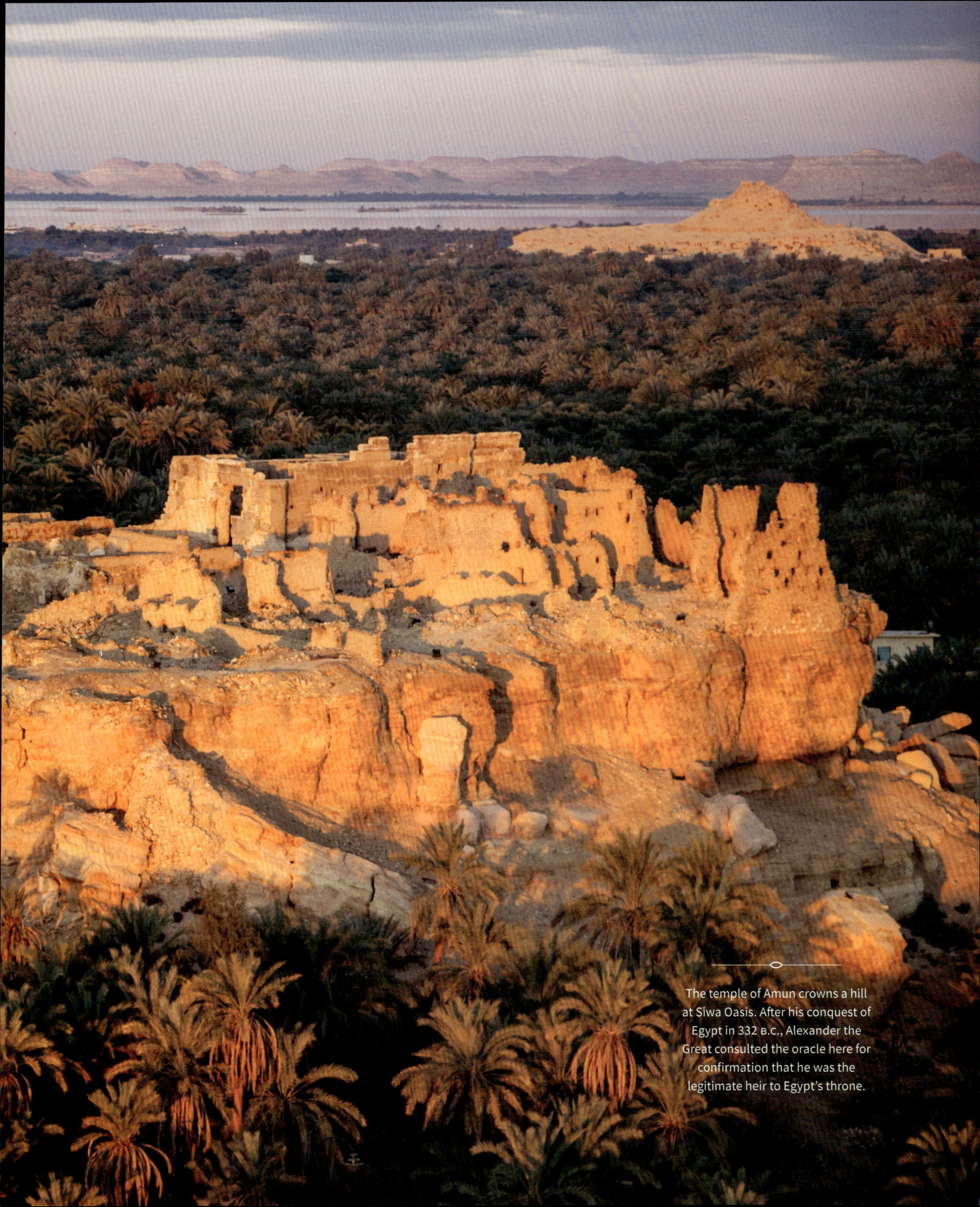

The temple of Amun crowns a hill at Siwa Oasis. After his conquest of Egypt in 332 B.C., Alexander the Great consulted the oracle here for confirmation that he was the legitimate heir to Egypt's throne.

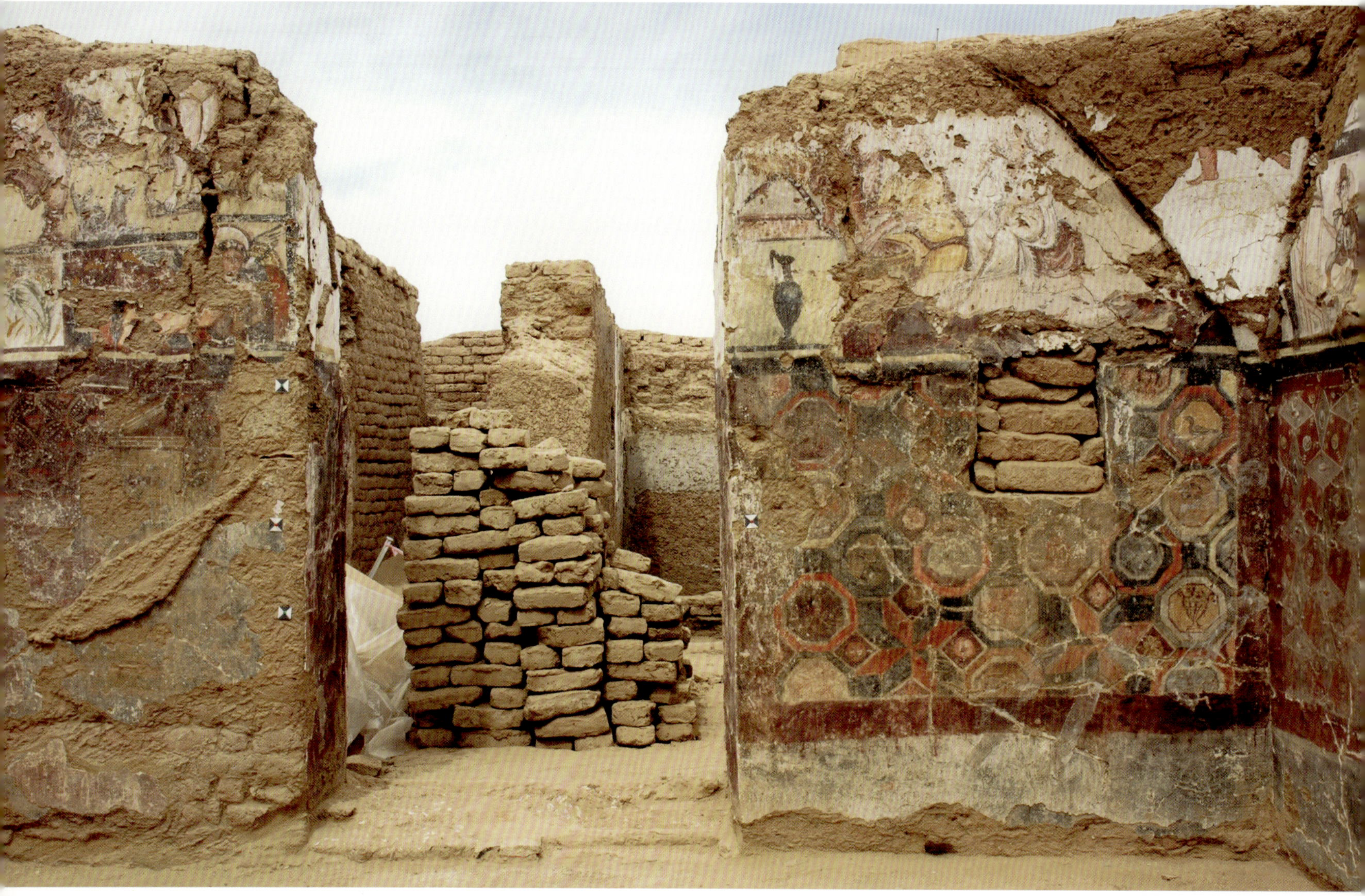

In a Roman city called Trimithis in Dakhla Oasis, an official named Serenos had the mud-brick walls of his home plastered and painted in about A.D. 350. Greek mythology inspired some scenes.

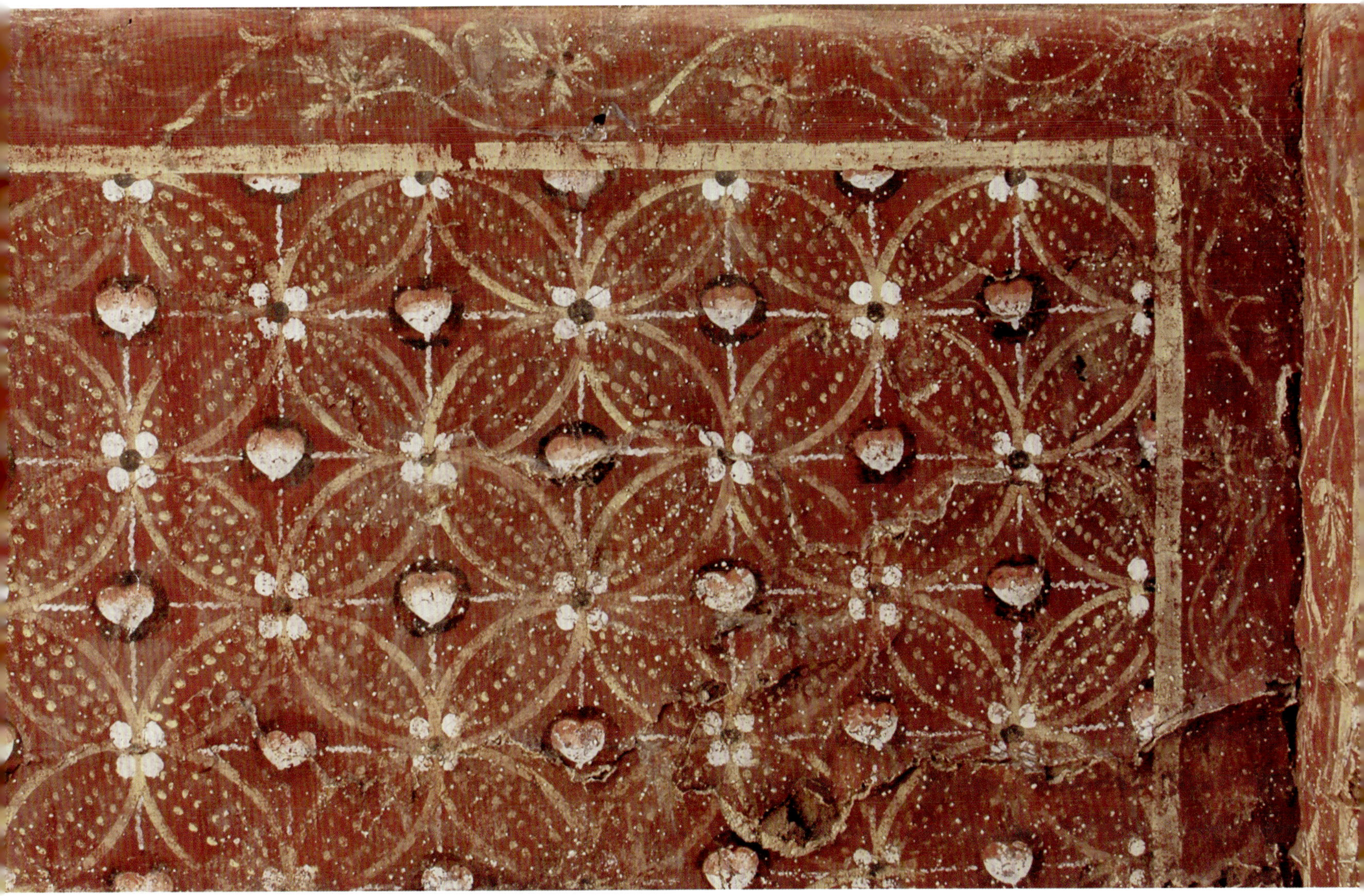

One wall in the home of Serenos bore these bright geometric motifs. Next door was a stable for donkeys, likely used to transport goods such as barley, wine, and dates from nearby farms to his property.

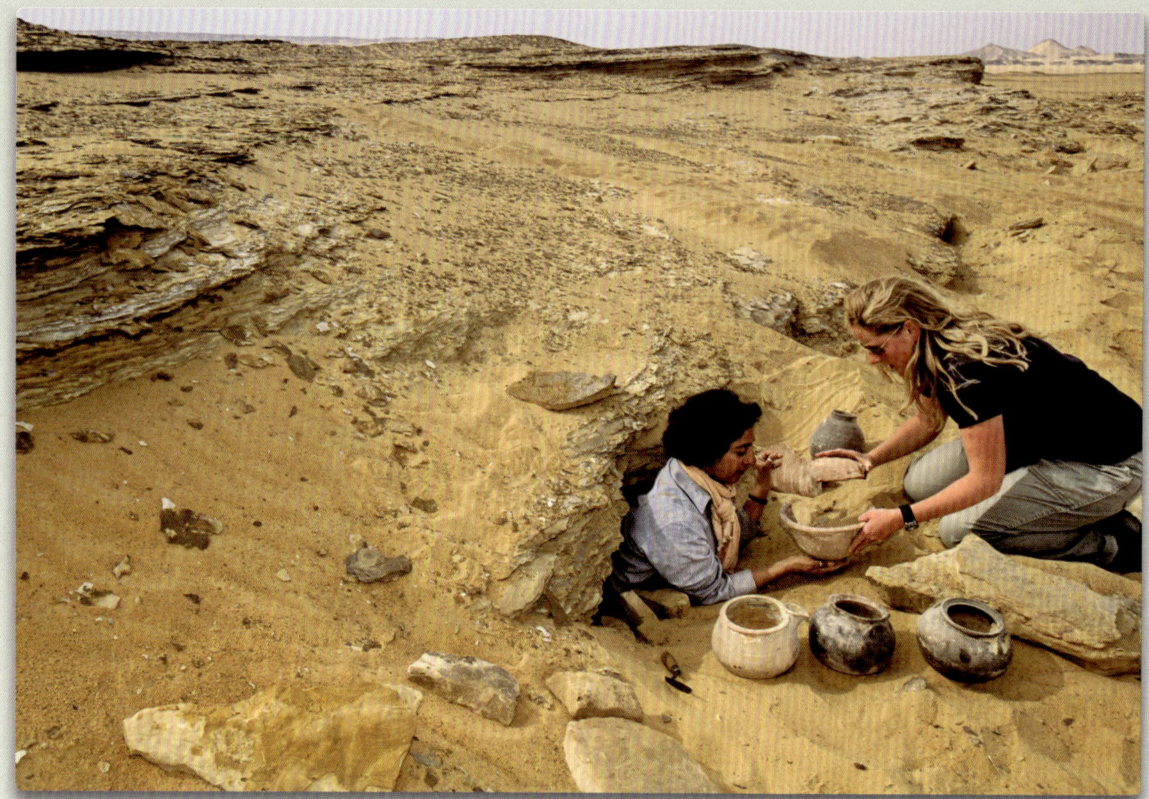

Frontiers in Egyptology

WALKING ACROSS an archaeological site with Salima Ikram is a lesson in animal anatomy. With her eyes always on the ground, she may stop in mid-sentence to pick up a bone, give it a once-over, and name the species it belonged to. A visit to Egypt when she was a child inspired her to study the country's ancient mummies. Now, whenever an excavation uncovers bones, Ikram gets a call for a consultation—and is quickly on her way to the site from her office in Cairo. At Abydos (opposite) she studied an ibis that had been mummified, placed in a ceramic jar, and left in a sacred place as a votive offering.

Beginning in 2001, Ikram also headed a survey of the northern Kharga Oasis, where she and colleague Alison Gascoigne found ceramics in an early-Roman-era tomb (above). "This work very much changed what people know about the oasis," she said. "We actually have a first dynasty royal expedition that is going out to explore. We don't know what they were looking for, but the king must have said, 'What ho! Westward!'"

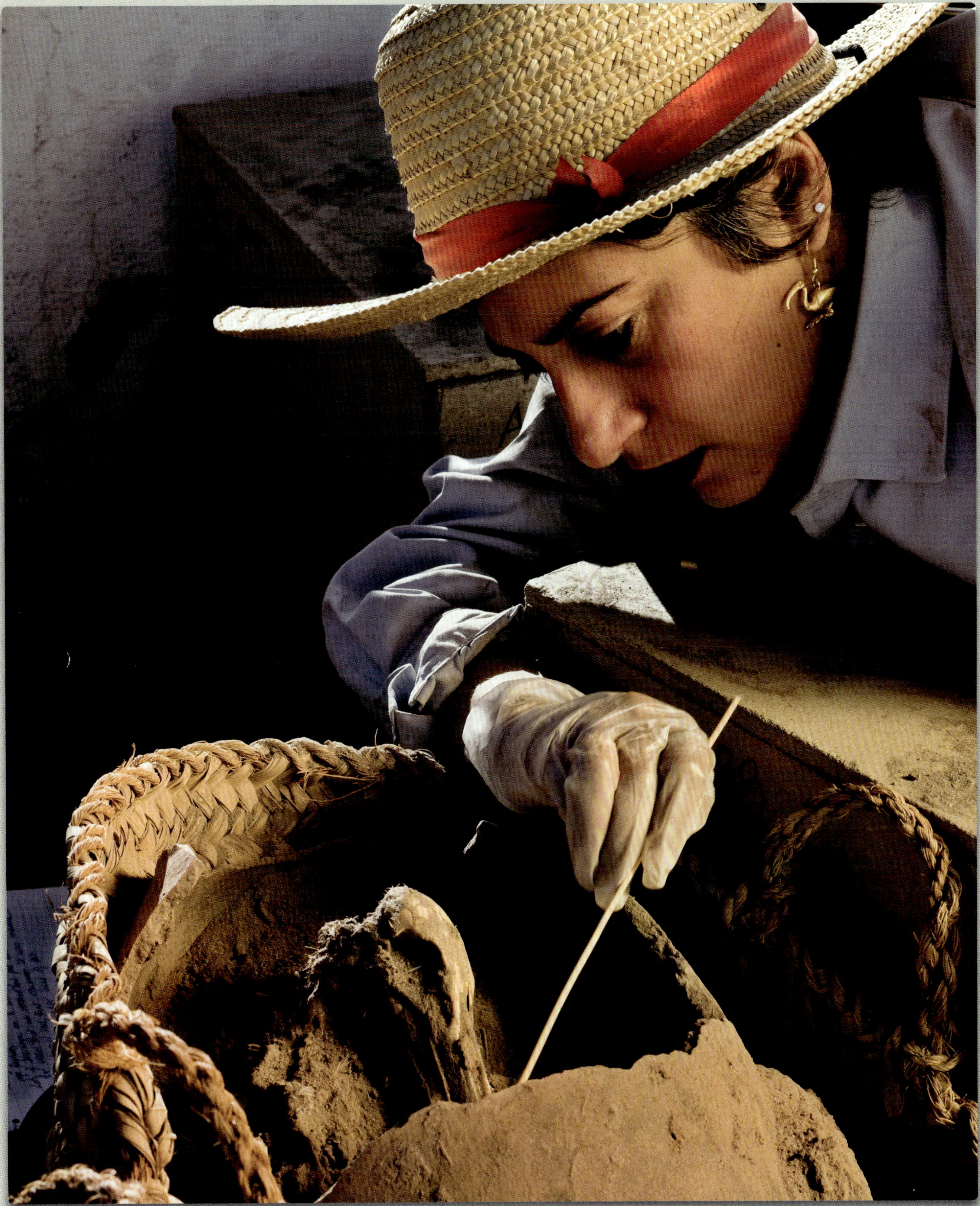

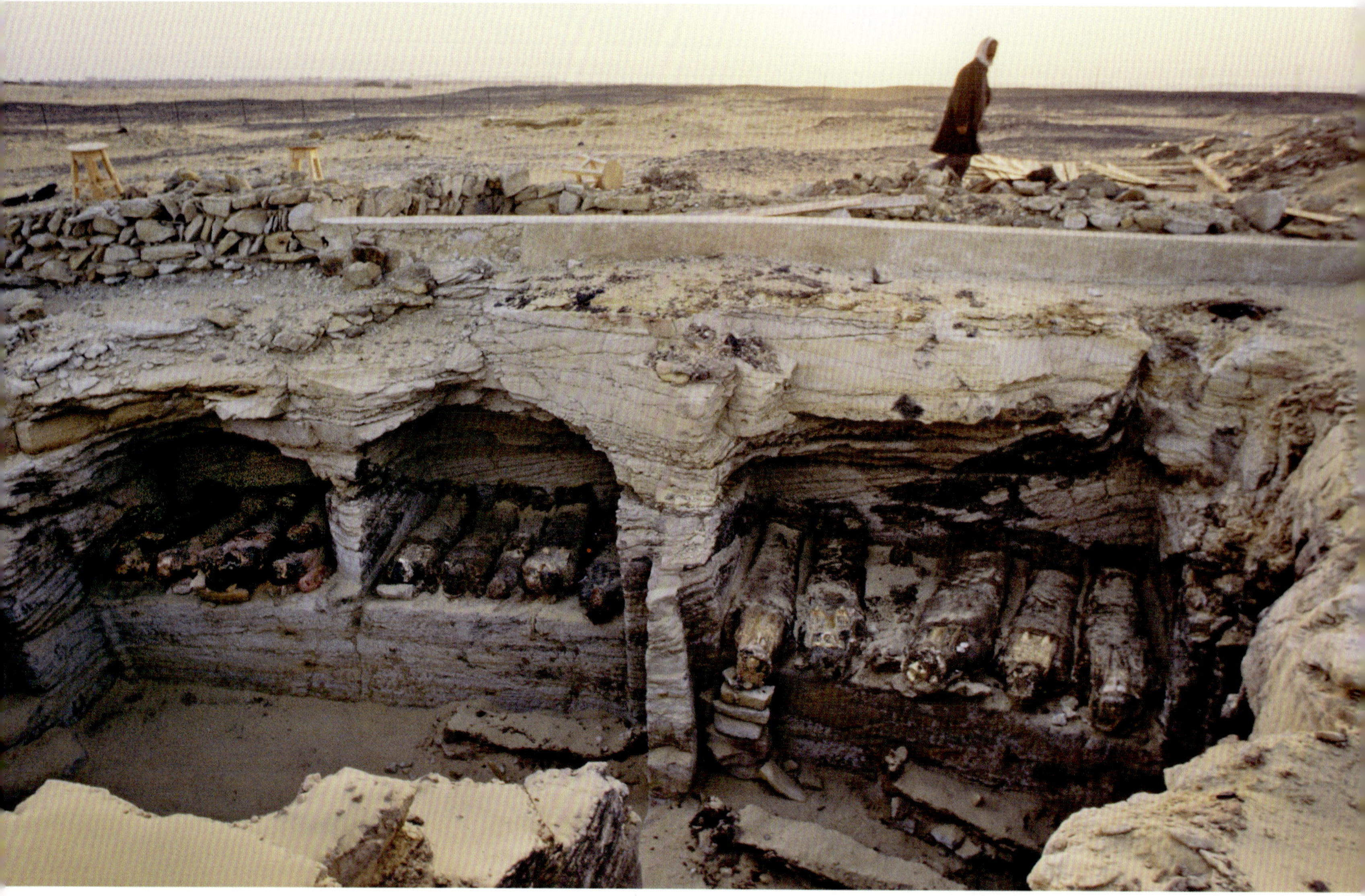

Carved into stone beneath the sands of Bahariya Oasis, a multichambered tomb may have been used by a single family for two centuries. Such burials began there after Alexander the Great's conquest in 332 B.C.

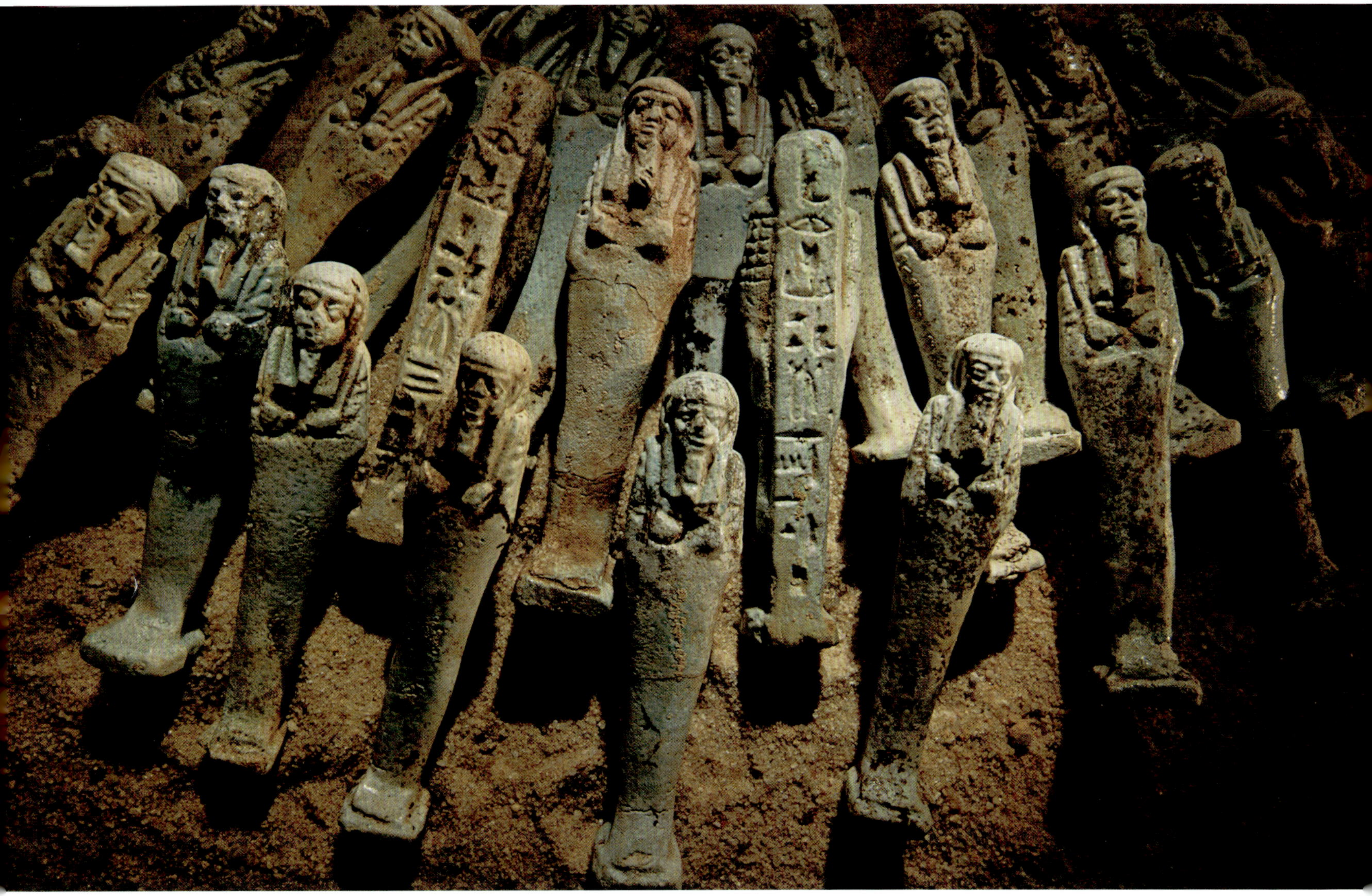

Burials at Bahariya continued the Egyptian tradition of including shabtis among the grave goods. The figurines were meant to work for the deceased in the next life and often bore an inscription to that effect.

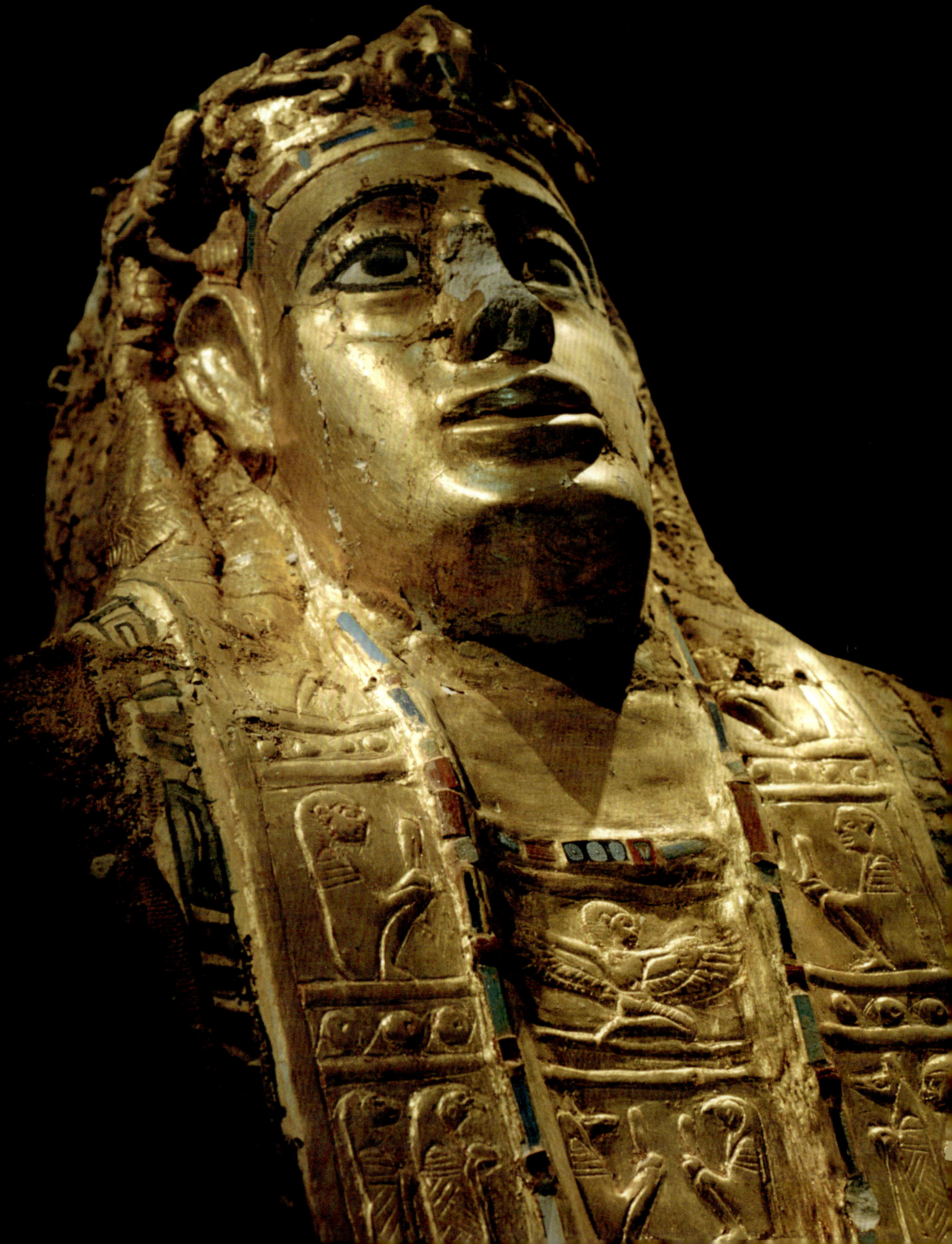

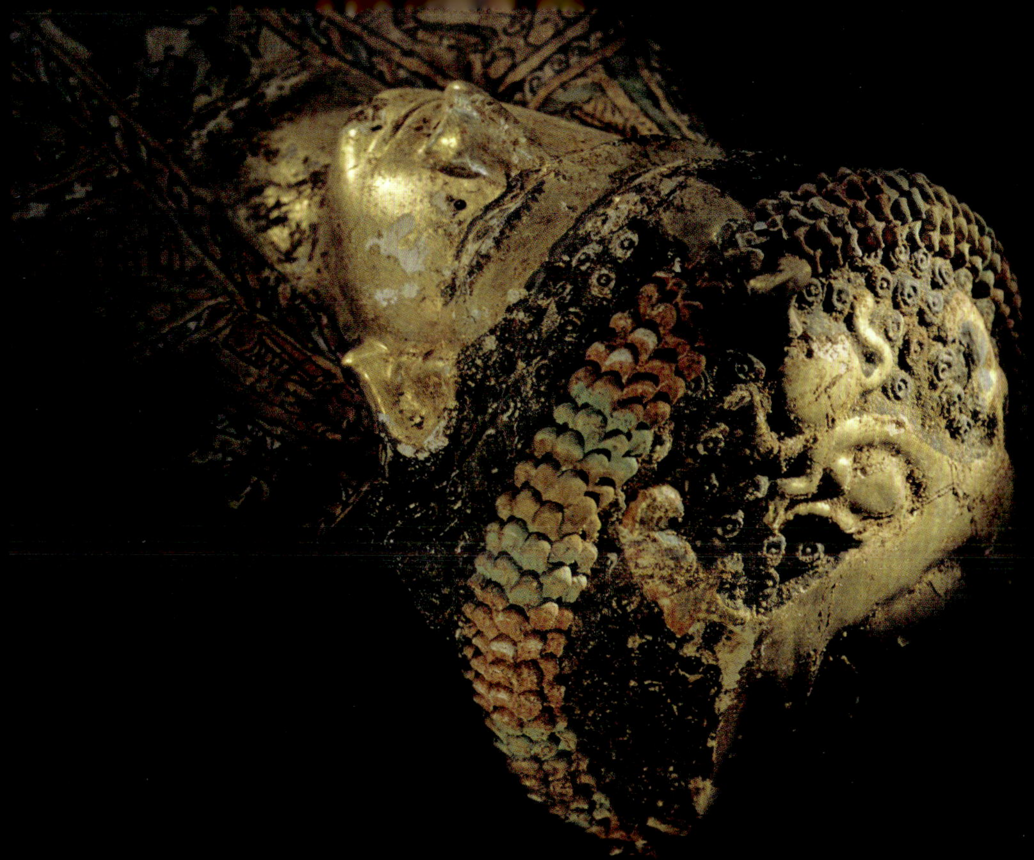

With a gaze fixed on the next world, this mask (opposite) covered the face and chest of a middle-aged man who's the best preserved male mummy found at Bahariya.

Many of the funerary masks from Bahariya, such as this example (below), display tight curls, aquiline noses, and wide eyes, reflecting the influence of Greek sculpture. The deceased were likely merchants or landowners in the oasis.

The circular crown (left) of the same mummy displays a falcon with outstretched wings, a sun disk, and cobras. Once reserved for royalty, the cobra motif had now been adopted by Egypt's elite.

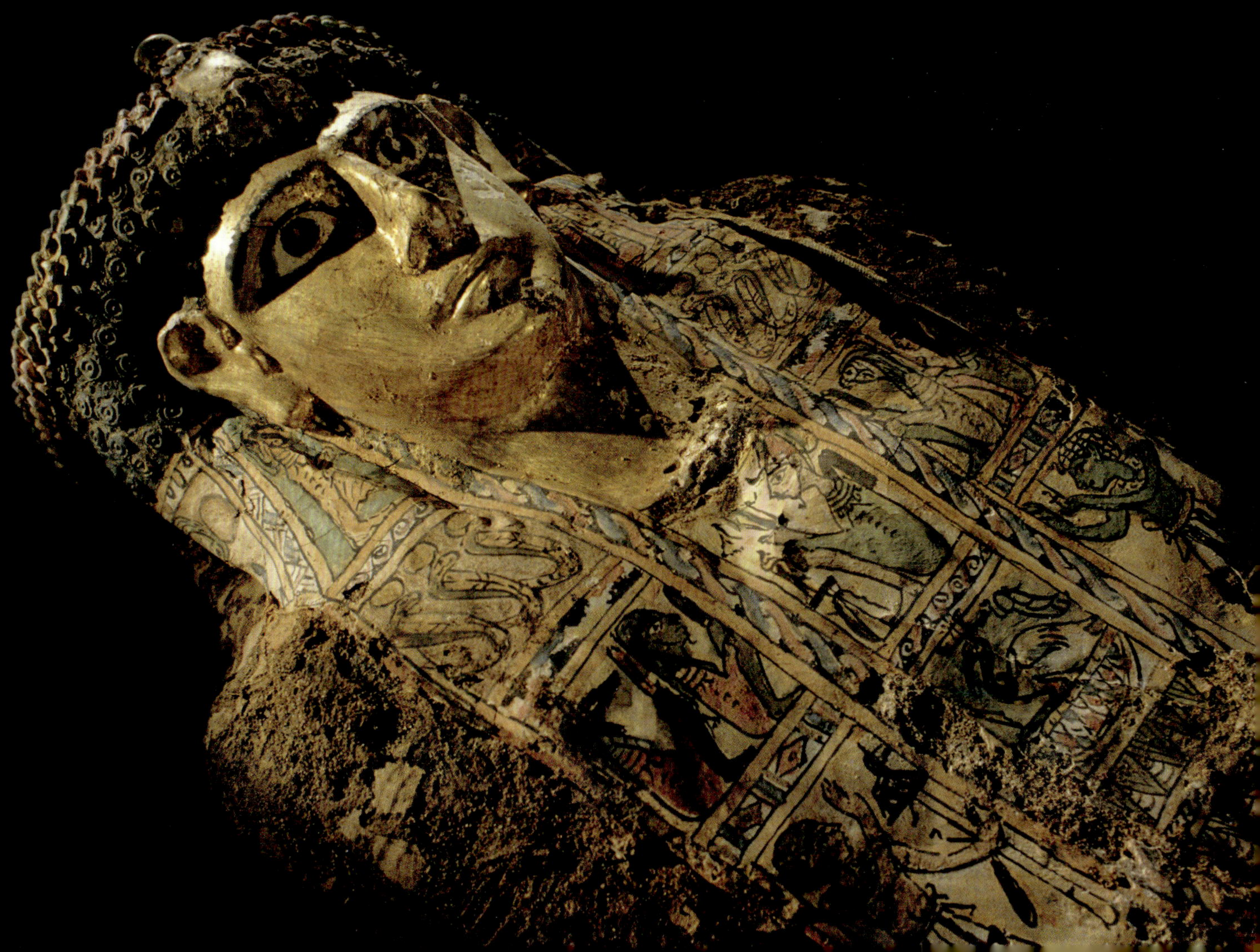

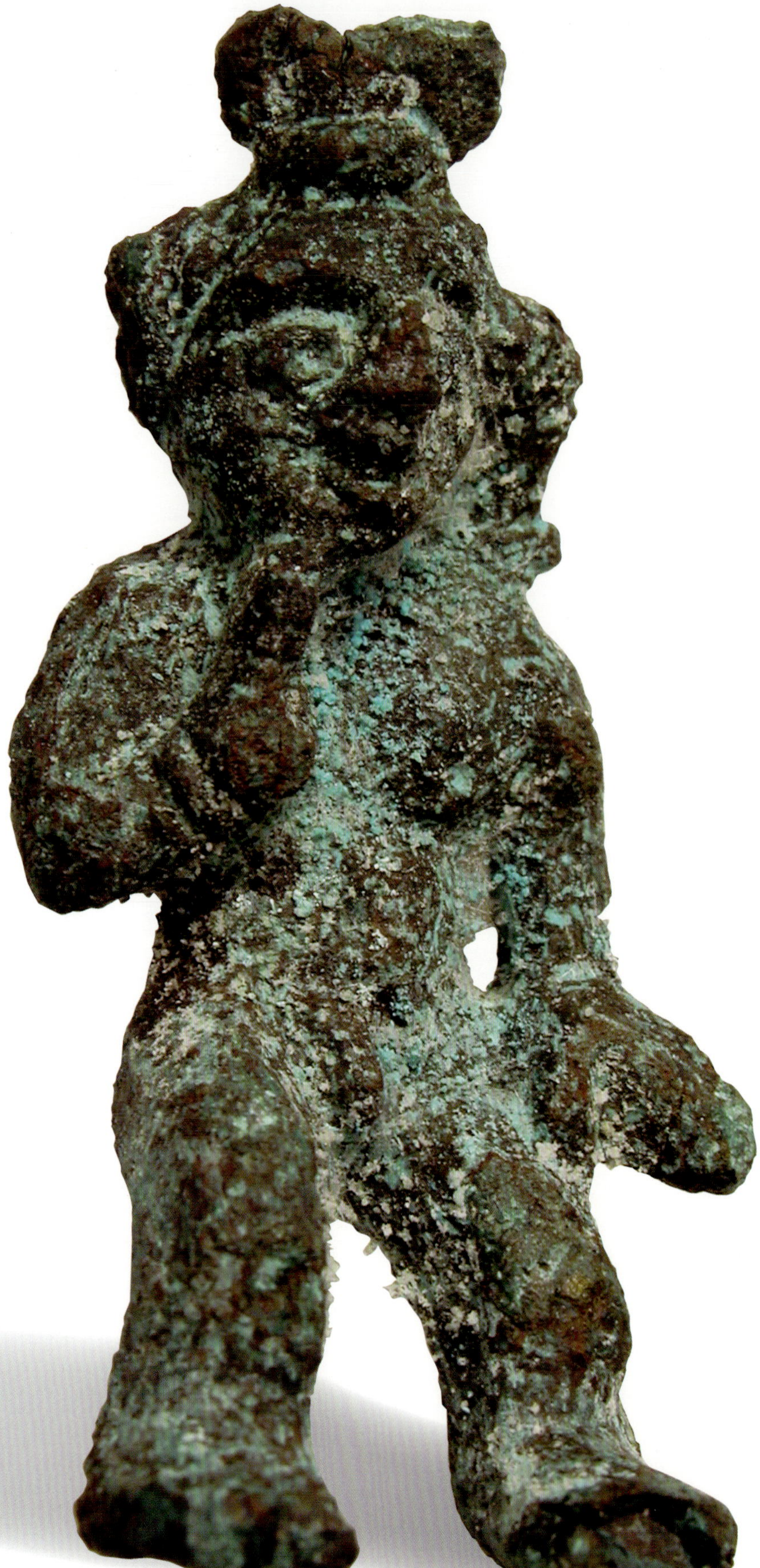

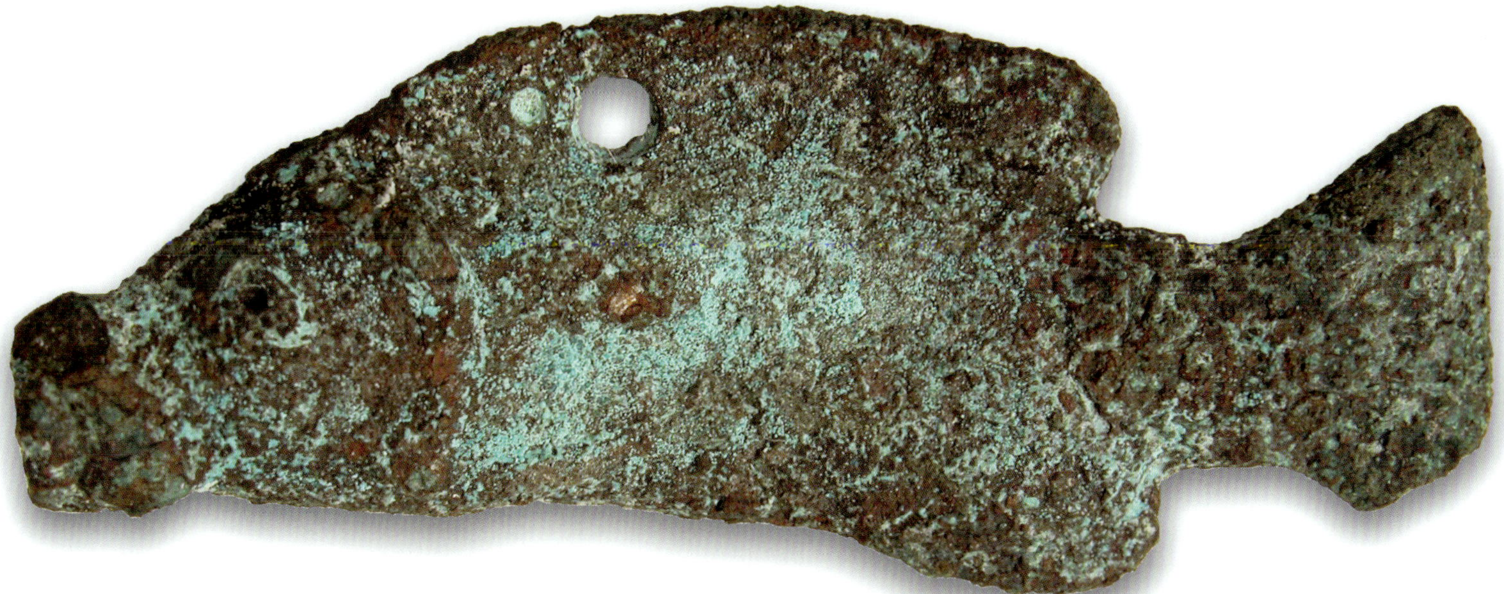

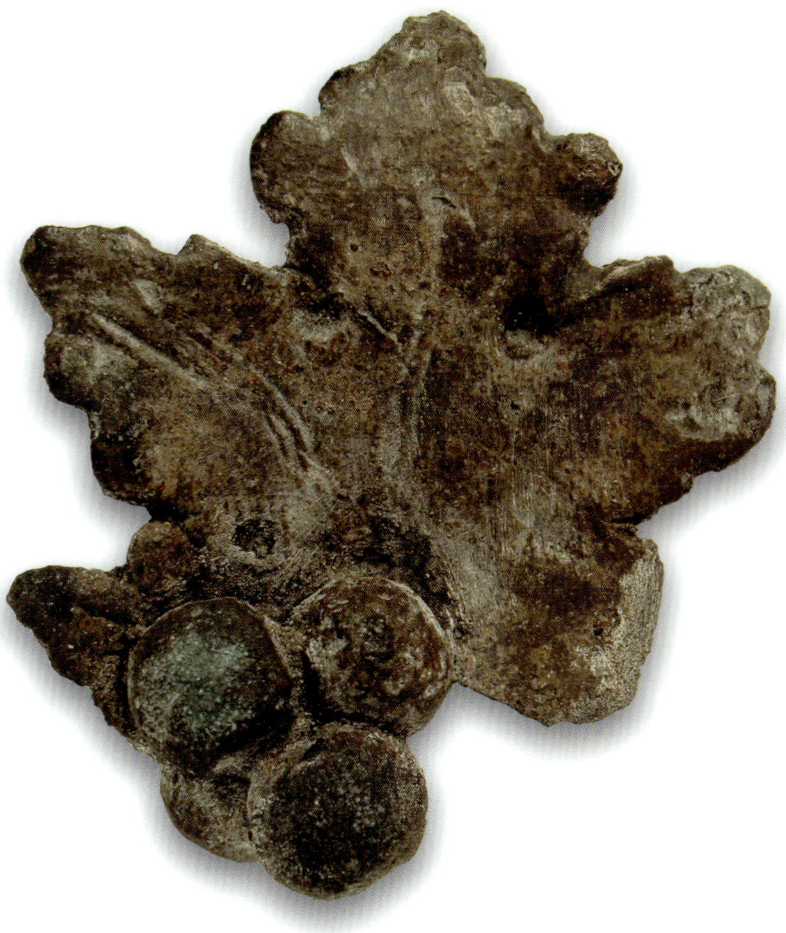

A figurine about one and a half inches (3.8 cm) tall (opposite) was made from a copper alloy in Kharga sometime between the fourth and seventh centuries. The oasis was often a place of banishment, particularly for early Christians. By the year 390, all residents had converted to that faith.

Less than an inch (2.5 cm) long, a copper alloy fish amulet (above), also from Kharga, dates to the same era as the figurine. Egyptian copper had a high concentration of arsenic, making it harder than the pure metal.

A grape leaf and fruit (left), from the third century, may symbolize Kharga's famous wine production.

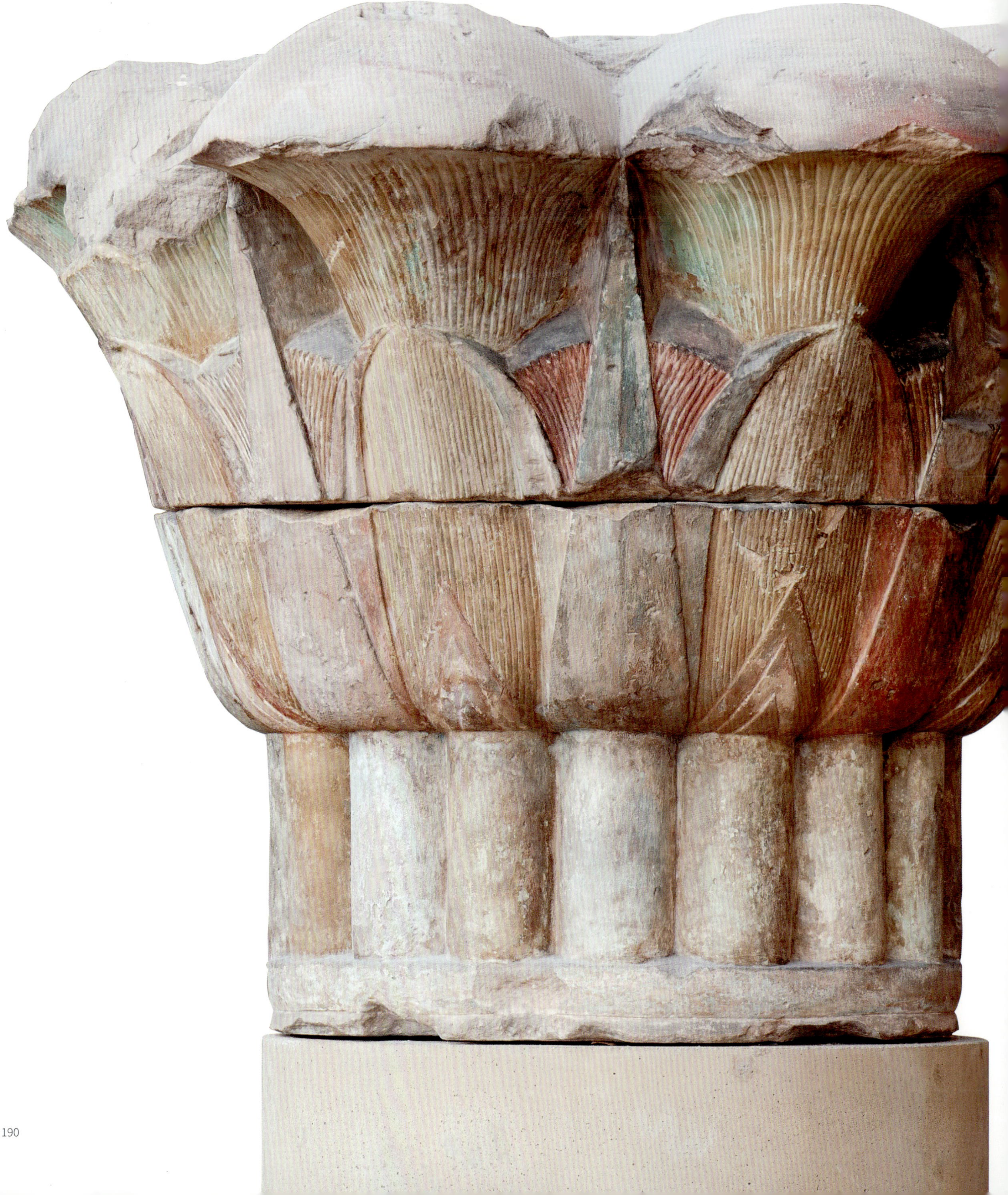

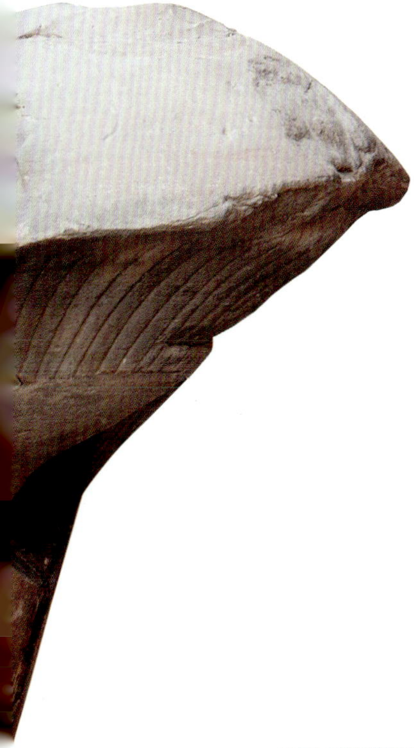

The capital of a column from Hibis in Kharga Oasis (left) incorporates several kinds of plants: the earliest known example of this kind of composition. Nectanebo II (360–343 B.C.) added a colonnade of such columns to a preexisting temple from several centuries earlier.

About 15 miles (24 km) to the south, the temple at Qasr el-Ghueida (below) included an inner sanctuary of stone surrounded by chambers of mud brick. As at Hibis, it was dedicated to the deities Amun, Mut, and Khonsu.

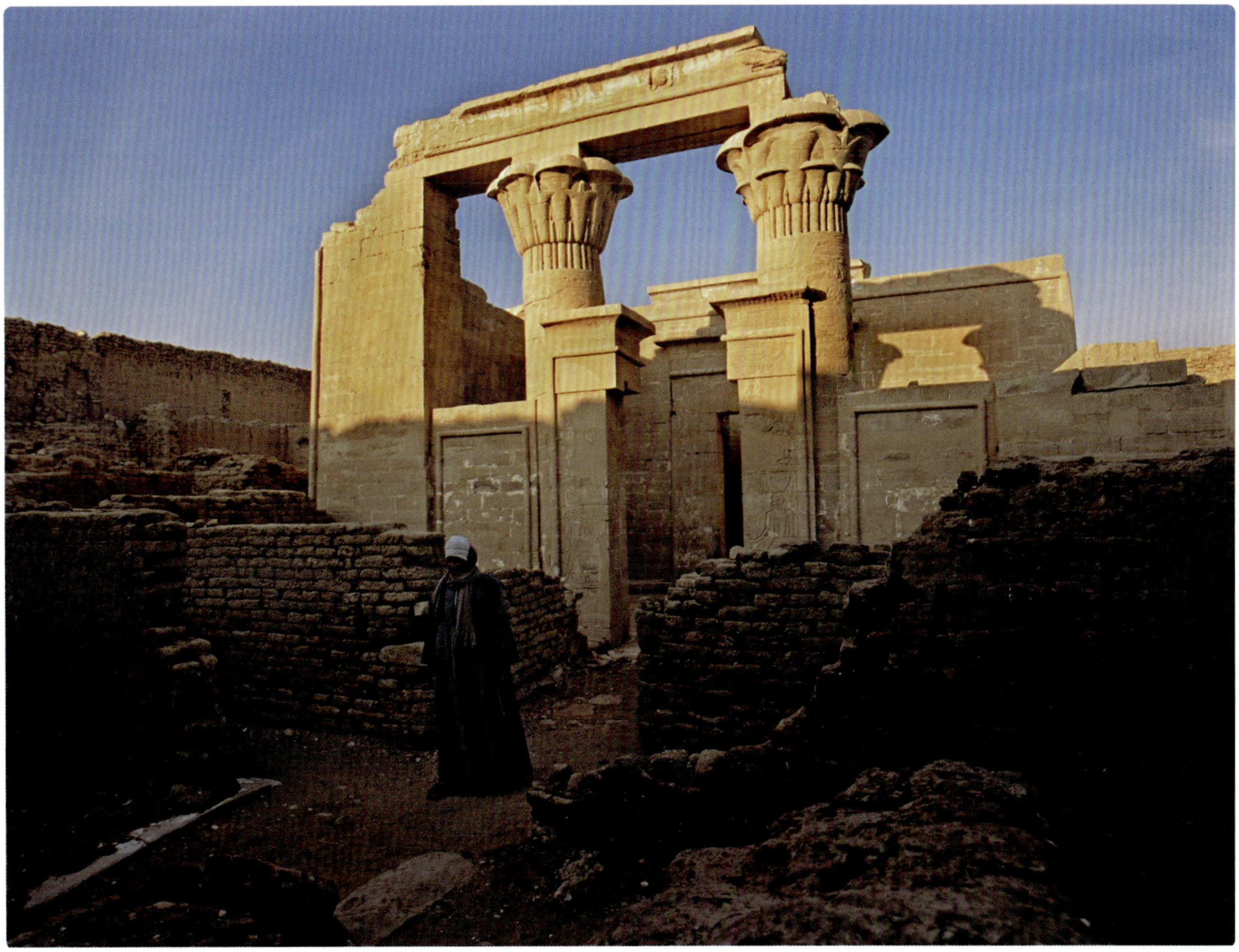

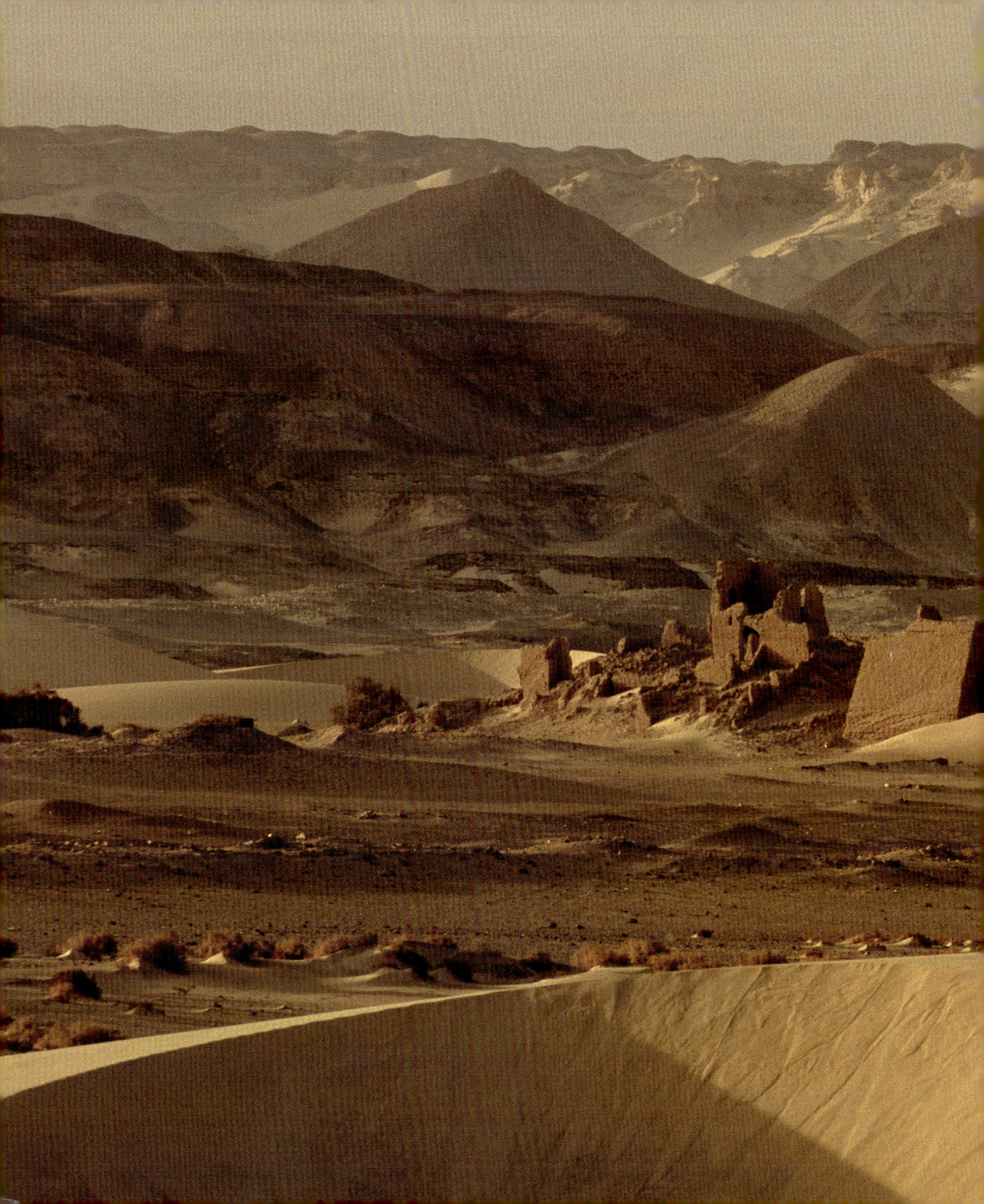

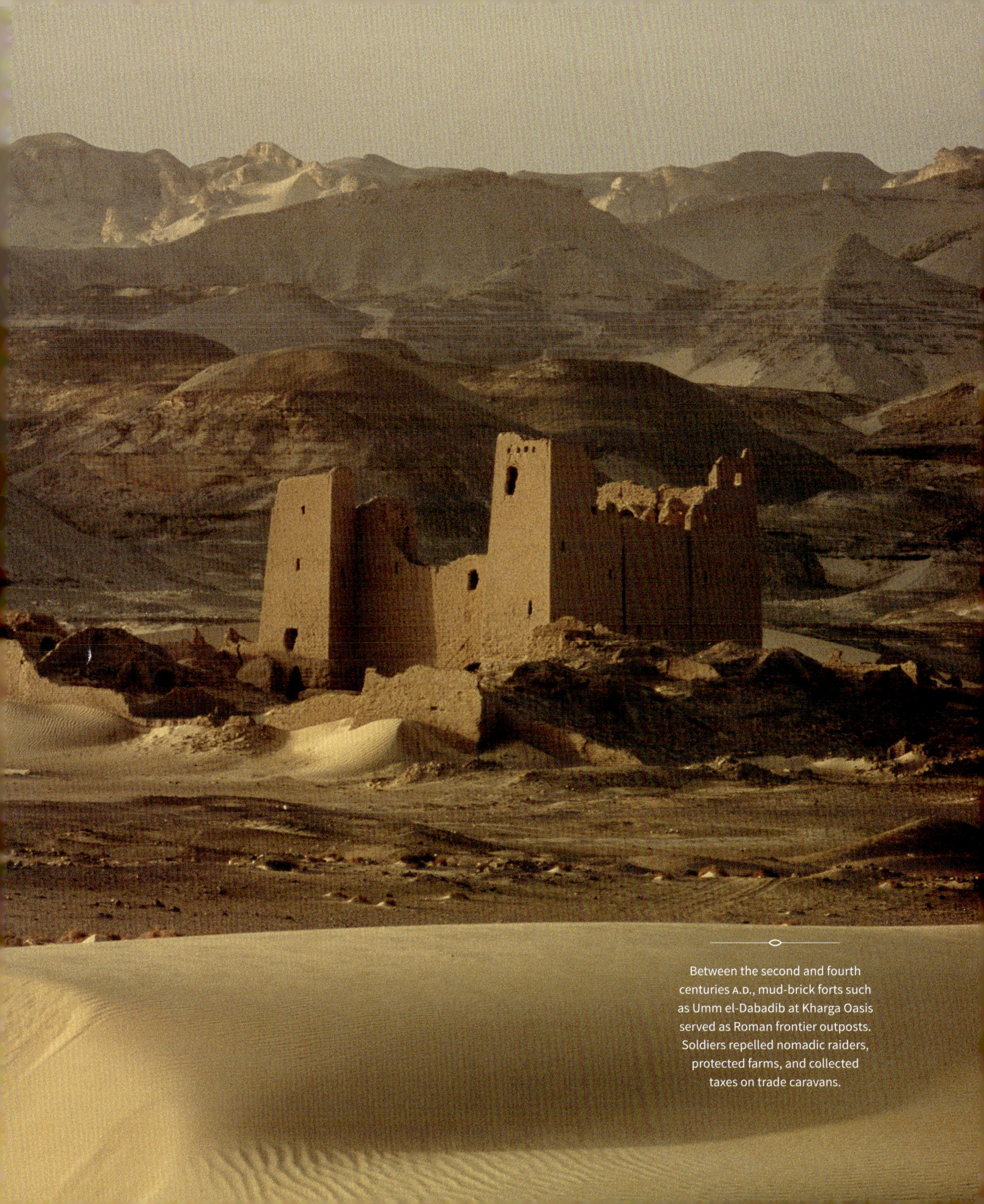

Between the second and fourth centuries A.D., mud-brick forts such as Umm el-Dabadib at Kharga Oasis served as Roman frontier outposts. Soldiers repelled nomadic raiders, protected farms, and collected taxes on trade caravans.

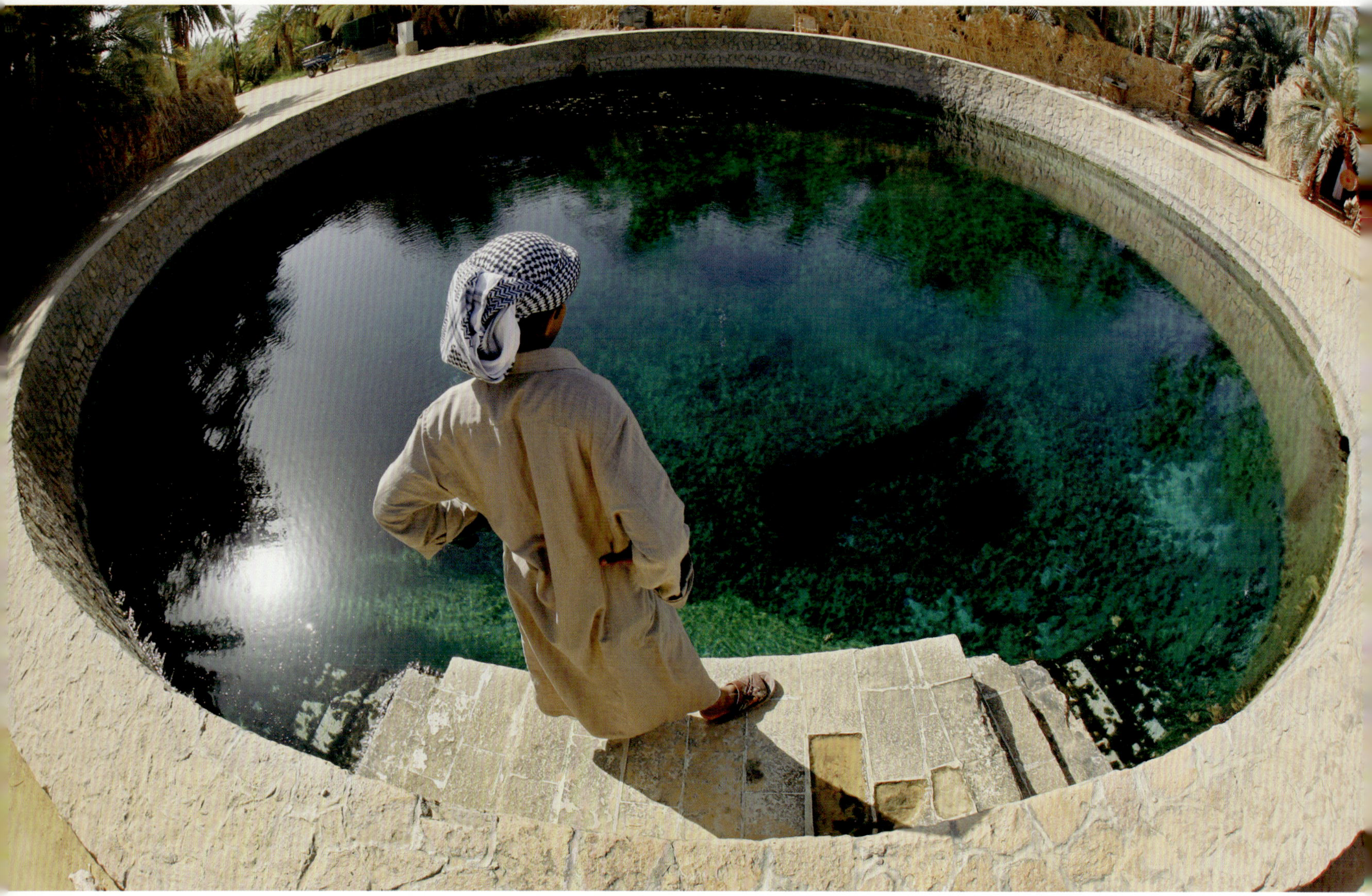

Siwa Oasis is famous for its sparkling waters. Fifth-century B.C. Greek historian Herodotus wrote about this pool, called the "spring of the sun." Legend says Queen Cleopatra (51–30 B.C.) swam here.

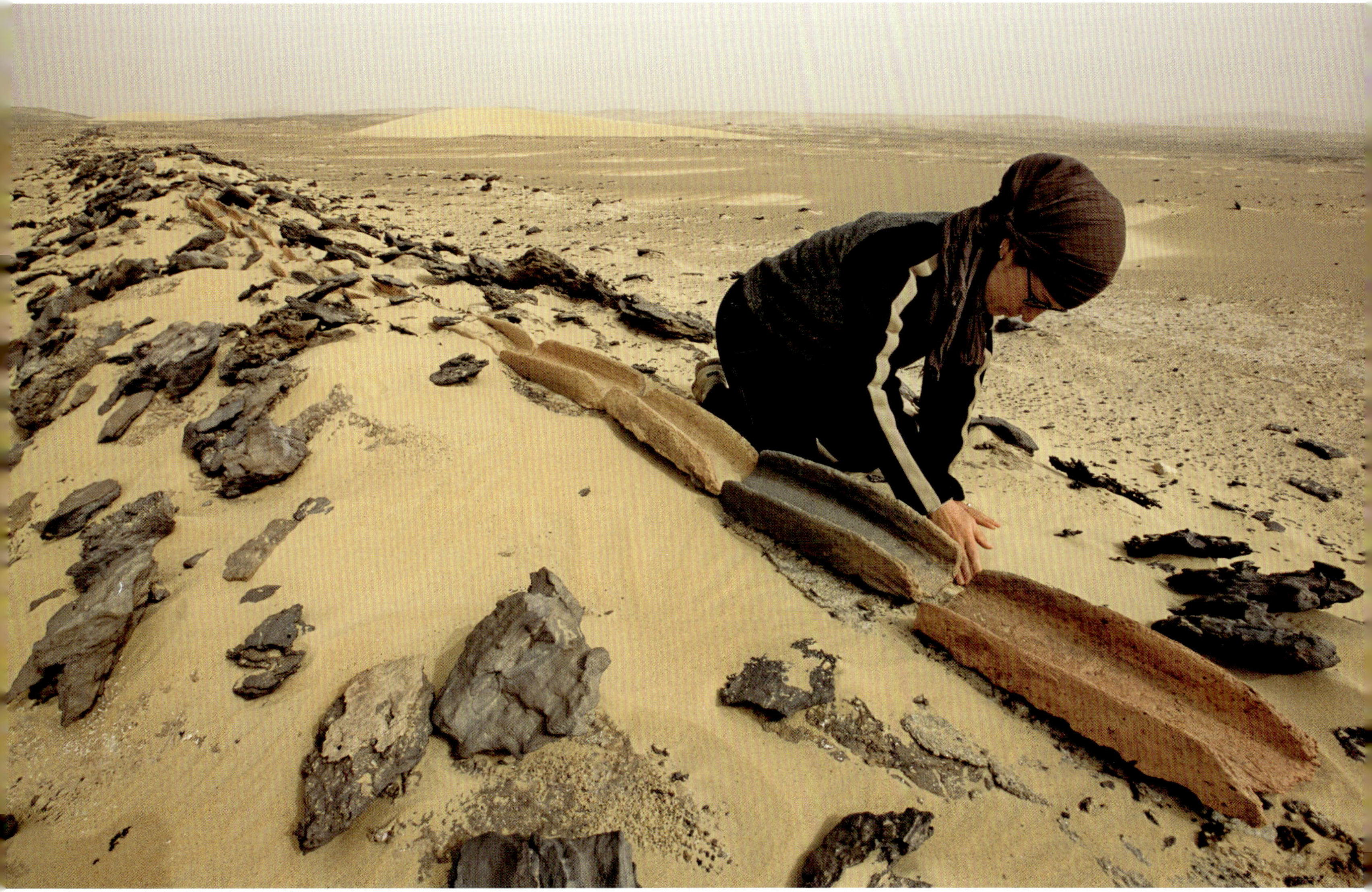

At Kharga Oasis, archaeologist Corinna Rossi inspects a Roman-era ceramic channel that carried water from a nine-mile-long (14.5 km) underground aqueduct to fields planted with wheat and other crops.

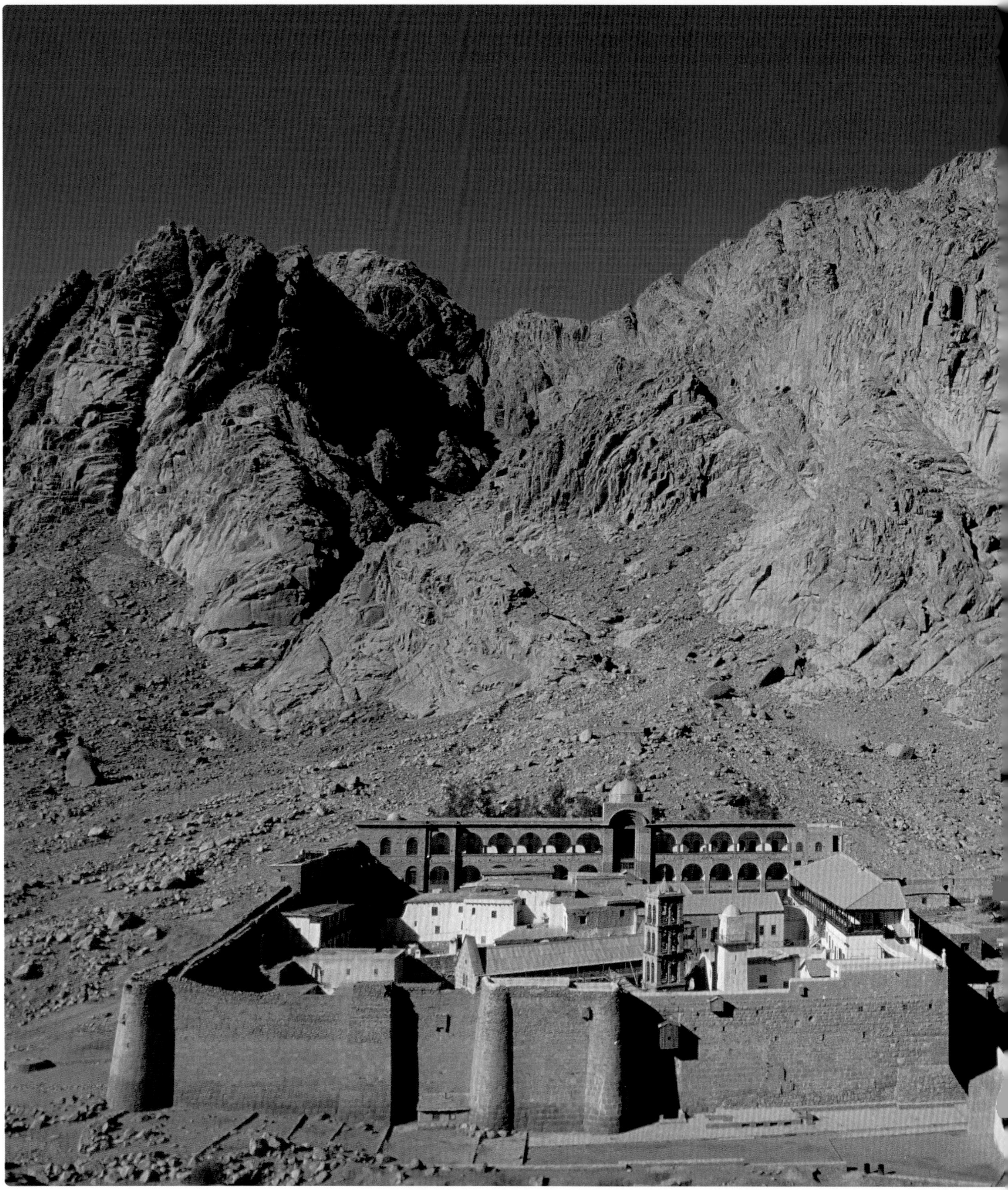

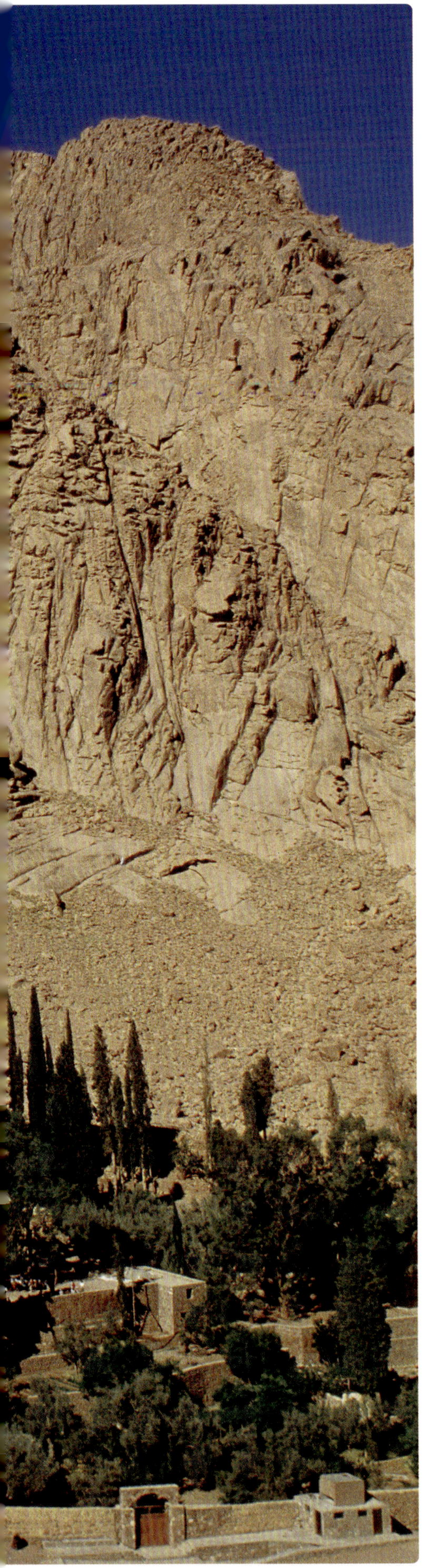

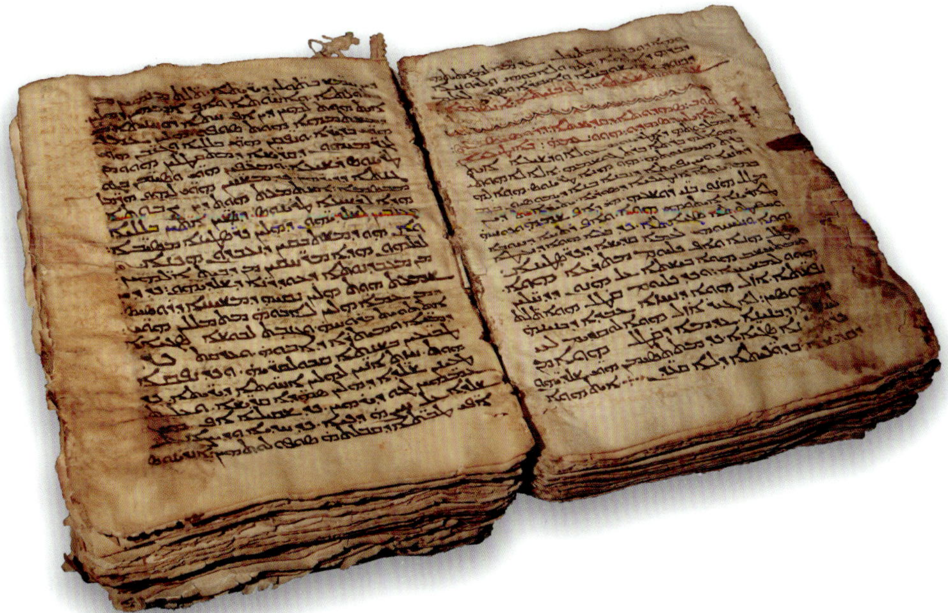

The 1,500-year-old Mount Sinai Monastery (left) still shelters a community of monks, as well as one of the oldest and most important libraries of ancient manuscripts: some 3,500 texts in Greek, Arabic, Hebrew, Latin, Persian, and many other languages. Experts are now digitizing parts of the collection.

This book (above) is a palimpsest: a parchment that was recycled. A fifth-century book of Gospels was erased in the eighth century so another religious work could be added to the pages.

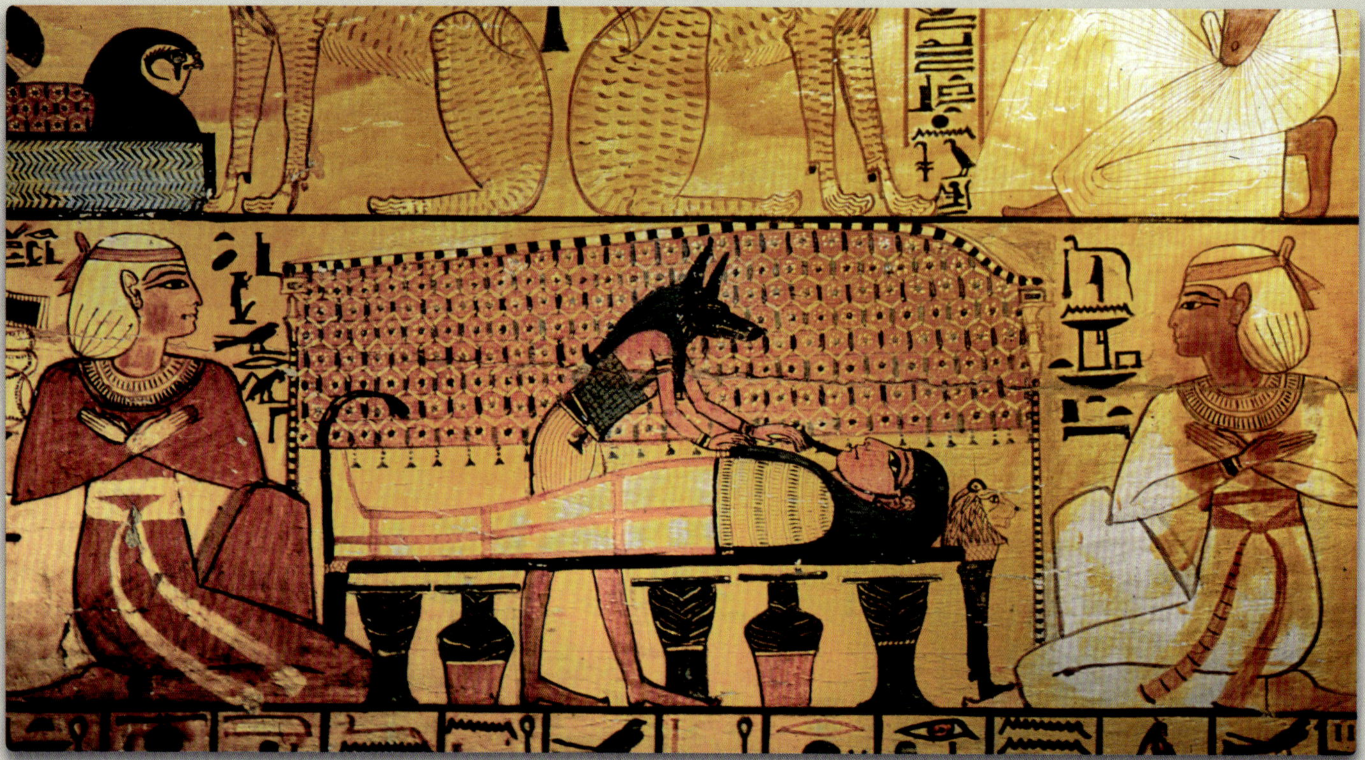

Guardian of the Dead

THE ANCIENT EGYPTIANS believed that the Western Desert was where the sun went every evening to die—and so, it followed that people also went there when they passed from this life. The deceased were called "the westerners," and Anubis, the god associated with them, was "foremost of the westerners."

Anubis was a canine-headed god, as seen in this wooden statue (opposite) found at Qasr el-Labeka, a Roman fort. Possibly imagined as a combination of a jackal and a dog, he frequently appears with a black face—the color of a corpse as it putrefied, and of the fertile earth along the Nile that was a classic Egyptian symbol of rebirth.

The patron god of embalmers, Anubis is often shown attending to the dead, as in this scene (above) from the tomb of Sennedjem in Deir el-Medina, the village of the workmen who built the tombs in the Valley of the Kings.

He was also believed to watch over cemeteries, usually located in the desert. His lookout posts would have been the high desert cliffs, which inspired another of his epithets, "he who is upon his sacred mountain."

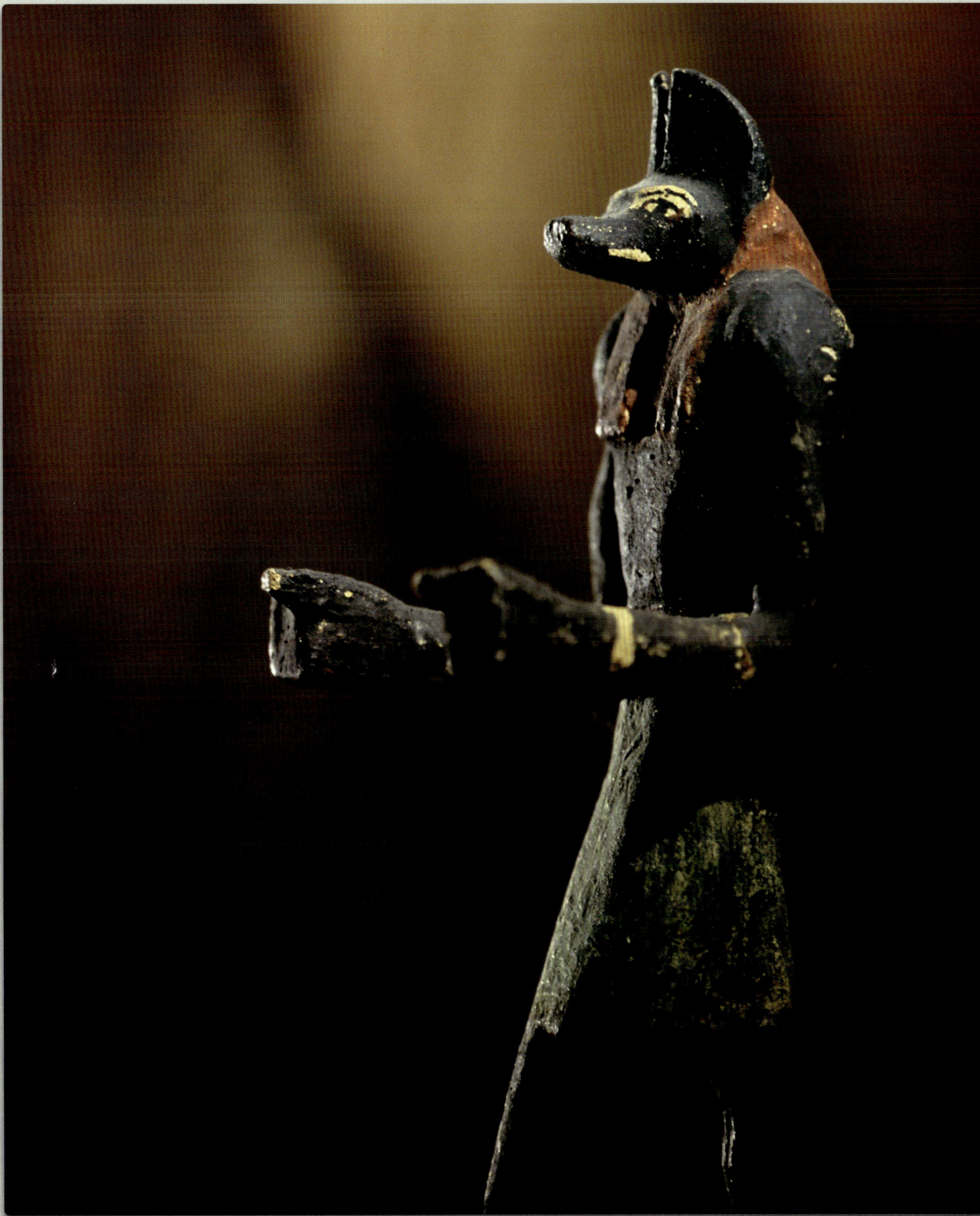

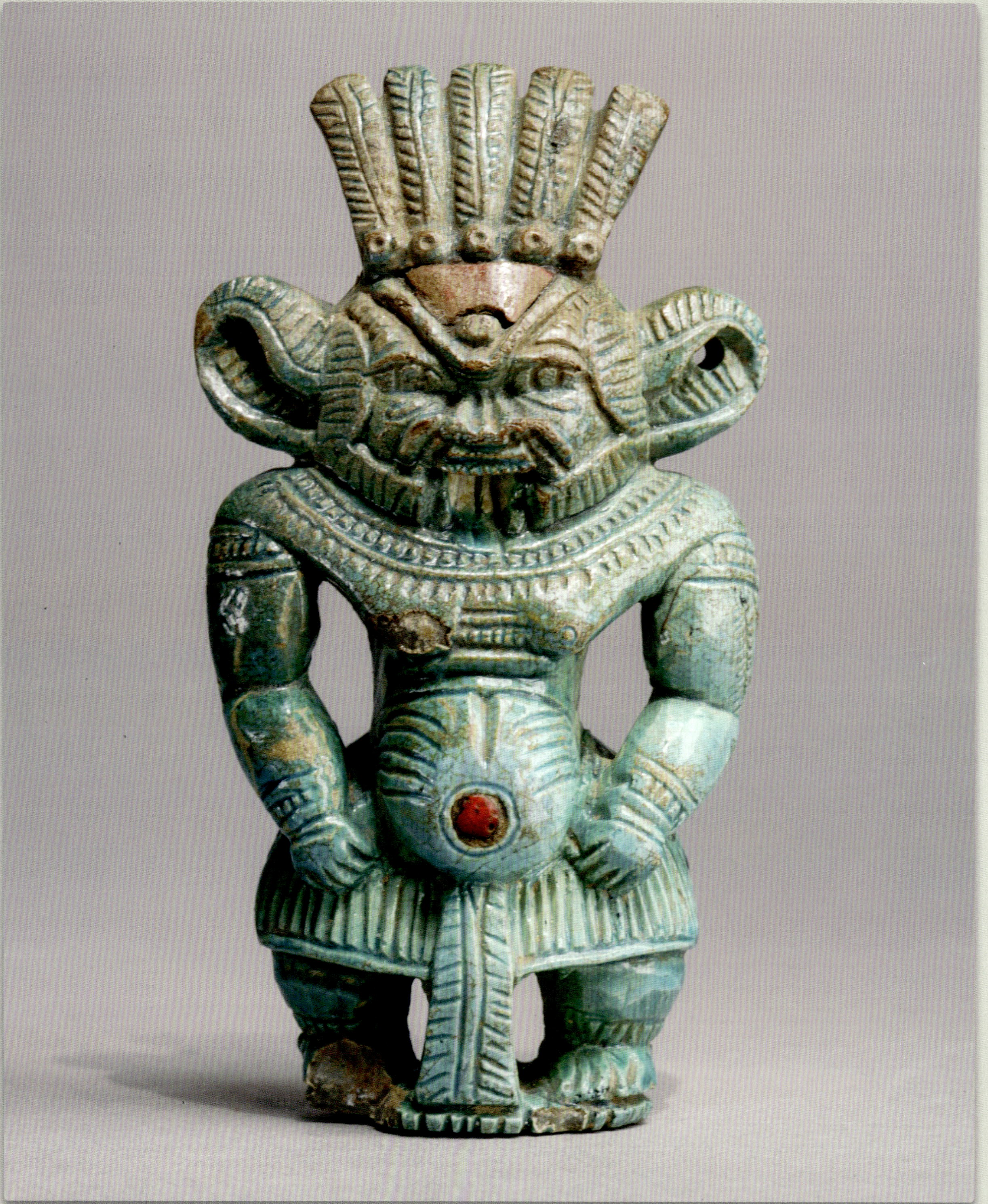

GREAT GODS

Part of a necklace made of faience, a glazed ceramic, includes the head of the goddess Sekhmet (right). The ferocious lioness was believed to breathe fire against her enemies, and the hot desert winds were known as the "breath of Sekhmet."

The god Thoth was sometimes depicted as a baboon (below), a creature that hooted and beat its chest as the sun rose over the Eastern Desert every day. In time, he became associated with writing and scribes.

The grotesque god Bes (opposite) may have begun as a lion deity. He protected families, especially pregnant women.

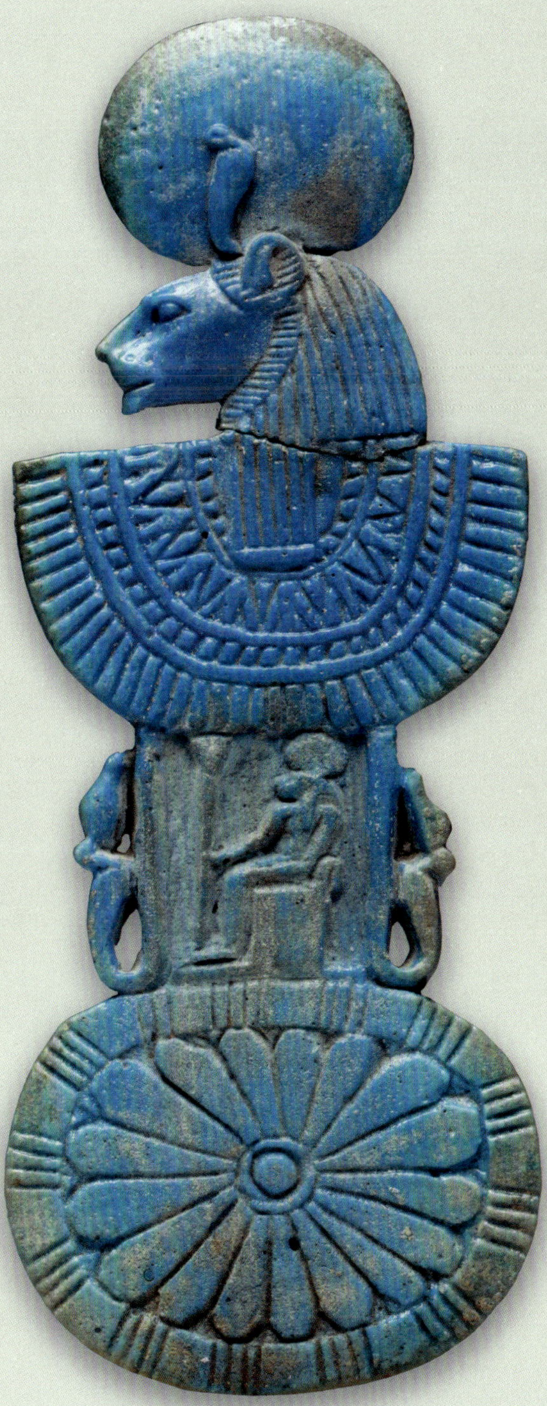

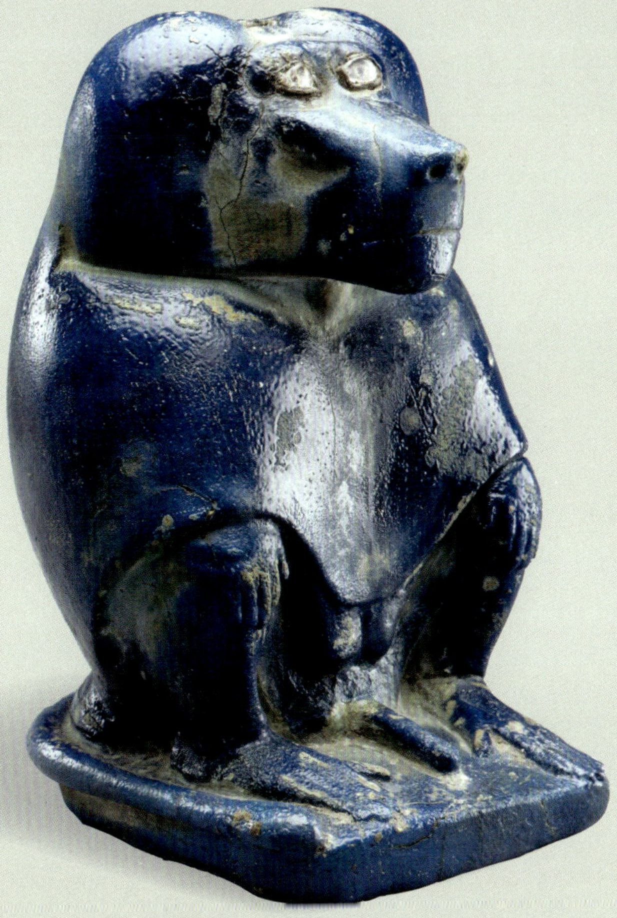

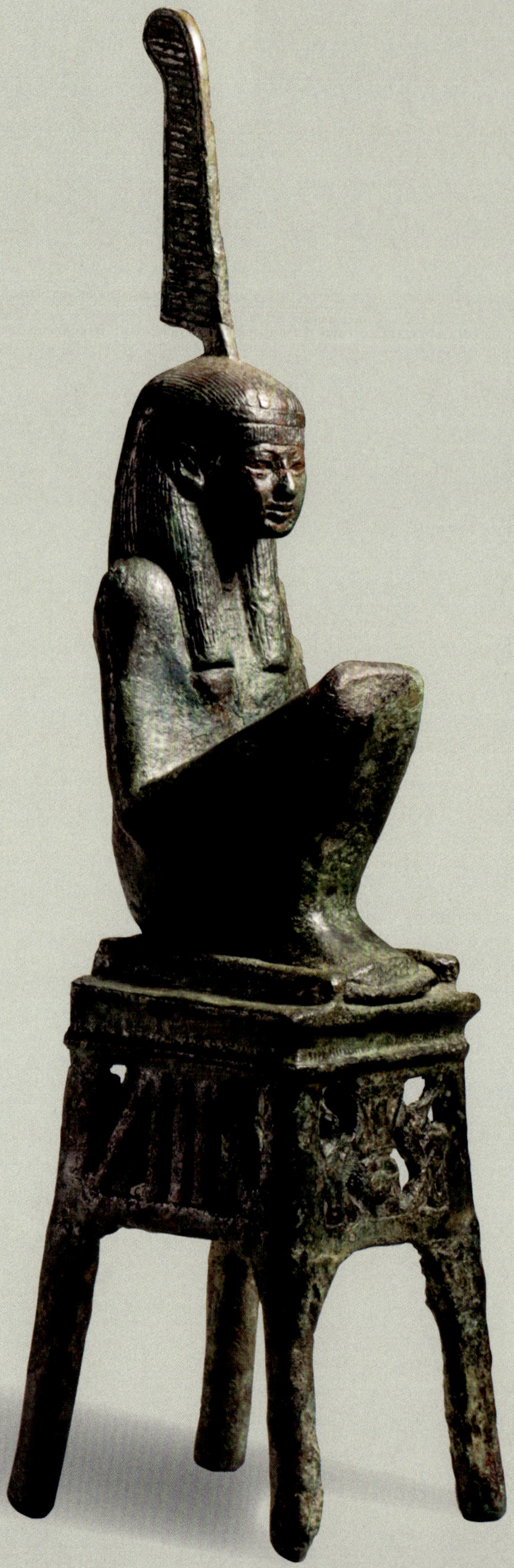

HIGHER POWERS

A bronze statuette from the fifth or six century B.C. (left) represents Maat, the goddess of truth, justice, and the order of the universe. The ostrich feather on her head was sometimes used by itself to represent her.

A painted wooden box (opposite) from the Ptolemaic period (332–30 B.C.) bears the image of the god Thoth in his guise as an ibis.

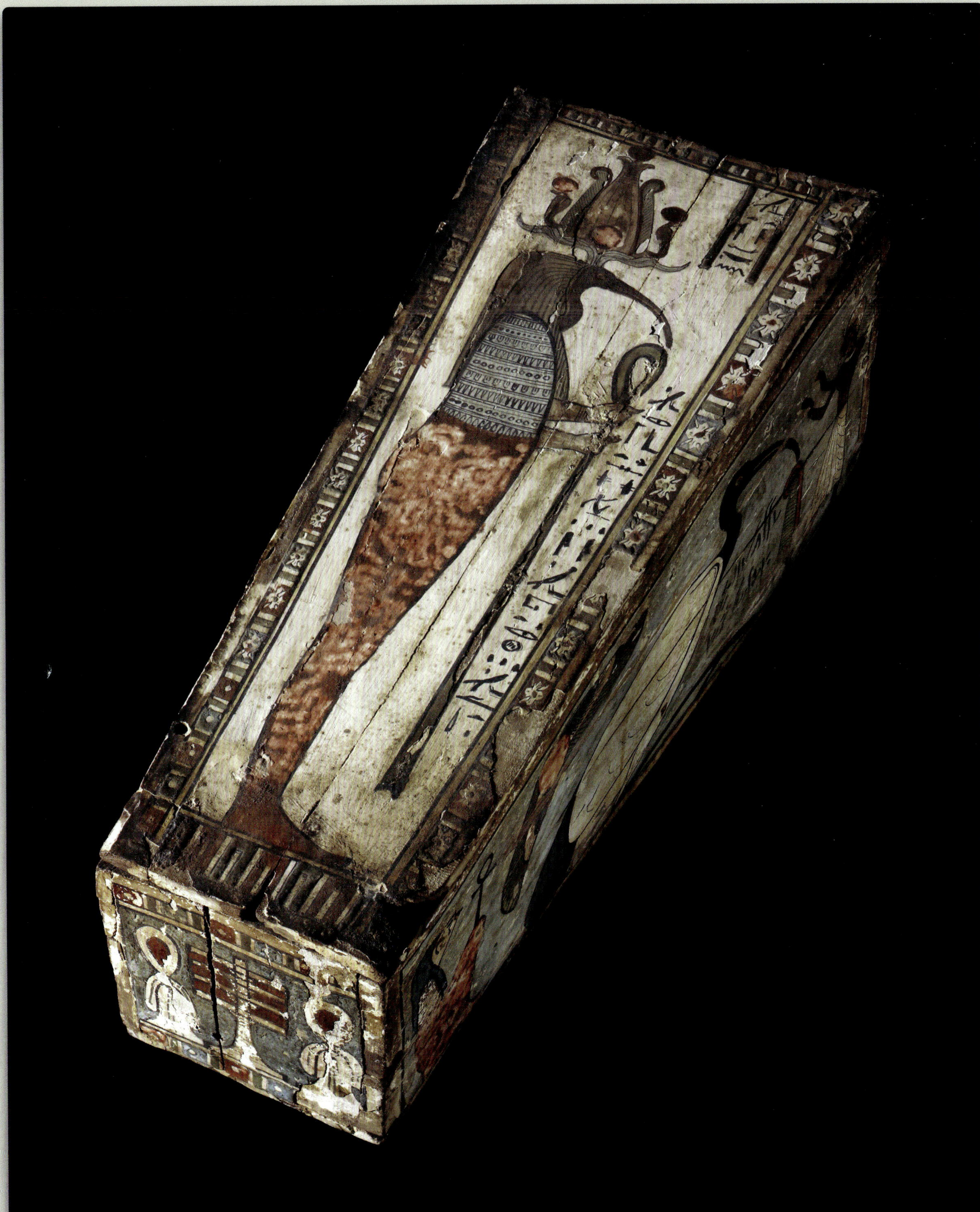

CHAPTER FIVE

LUXOR AND ITS TOMBS

The Golden Age

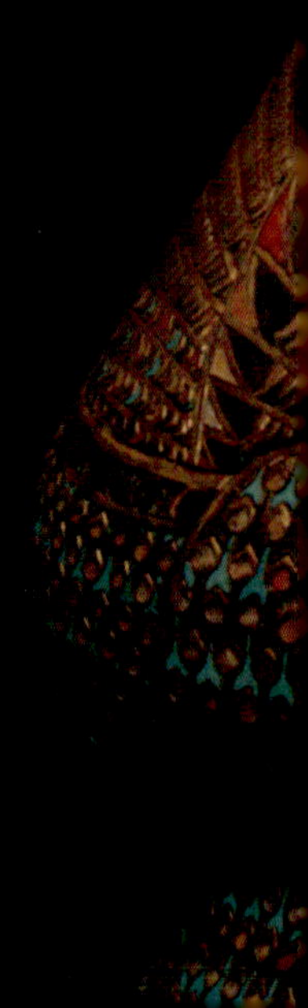

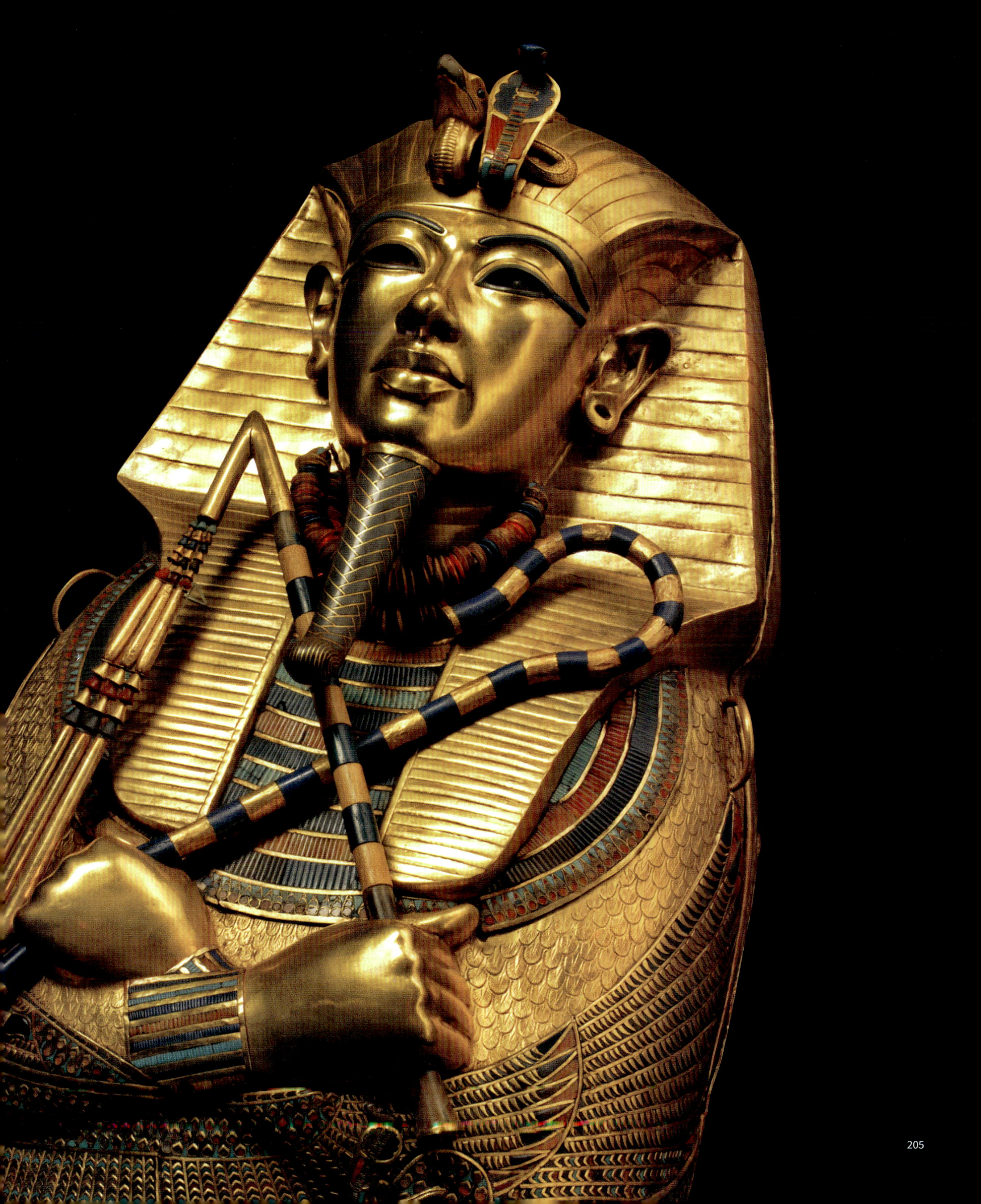

FOUR THOUSAND YEARS AGO, ancient Egyptians called their great city to the south Waset. At some later point, for reasons lost to history, it acquired the name Thebes, like the Greek city. In about the 8th century B.C., the Greek poet Homer described it in the *Iliad*: "In Egyptian Thebes the heaps of precious ingots gleam." Today, its ruins span the city of Luxor, with its impressive New Kingdom temple, and the village of Karnak, about a mile and a half (2.5 km) to the north, with its sprawling collection of temples, statues, obelisks, monumental gates, and shrines.

Construction here began in earnest on the east bank of the Nile at the start of the Middle Kingdom, in about 1795 B.C., when the Theban triad of gods—Amun, his chief wife, Mut, and their son, Khonsu—rose to prominence. Temples at Karnak dedicated to these deities and others accumulated through the centuries as different rulers sought to leave their mark on the sacred landscape. Sometimes that meant a king added to what a predecessor had built, tore it down entirely to make space for his own project, or simply erased a previous ruler's name and substituted his own, thus claiming monumental architecture by just a few strokes of a chisel.

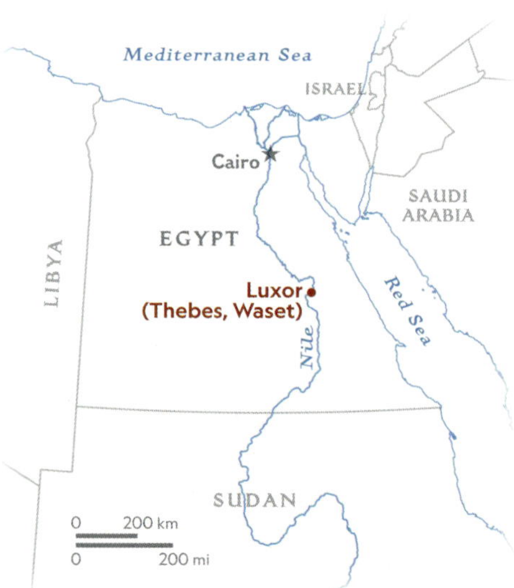

During the New Kingdom, beginning in about 1540 B.C., Egypt's kings made Waset their capital. This was an era of staggering wealth and almost unprecedented royal power, as extensive territories to the north and south of Egypt, which had been conquered by warrior kings, delivered tribute and offered new trading possibilities. The Luxor Temple as we know it today took shape at this time, with King Amenhotep III building much of the interior. Ramses II added the pylon through which visitors pass today, his colossal statues flanking the entrance, along with two obelisks of red granite some 75 feet (23 m) tall. In 1829, Pasha Muhammed Ali, the Ottoman ruler of Egypt, gave one of these obelisks to France; it now stands amid the swirl of traffic at the Place de la Concorde in Paris, replacing a revolution-era guillotine where hundreds of people met their end.

Reliefs at both Karnak and Luxor show scenes from the "Beautiful Feast of Opet." Celebrated in the season of flooding, the festival was a highlight of the year and was linked to fertility, the renewal of the land, and a confirmation of the king's authority. In early versions of the central event, a statue of Amun-Re (a god who combined attributes of Amun with those of Re) was carried from the Karnak complex to the Luxor Temple, where the god visited the version of himself in residence there. The procession followed the route of the Avenue of the Sphinxes, now recently restored.

A century later, the details were slightly different: The statues of Mut and Khonsu joined Amun-Re for the journey to Luxor, which took place via the Nile. Royals, dignitaries, officials, and priests all participated in the festivities. Offerings were made, fat oxen were sacrificed, and the crowds

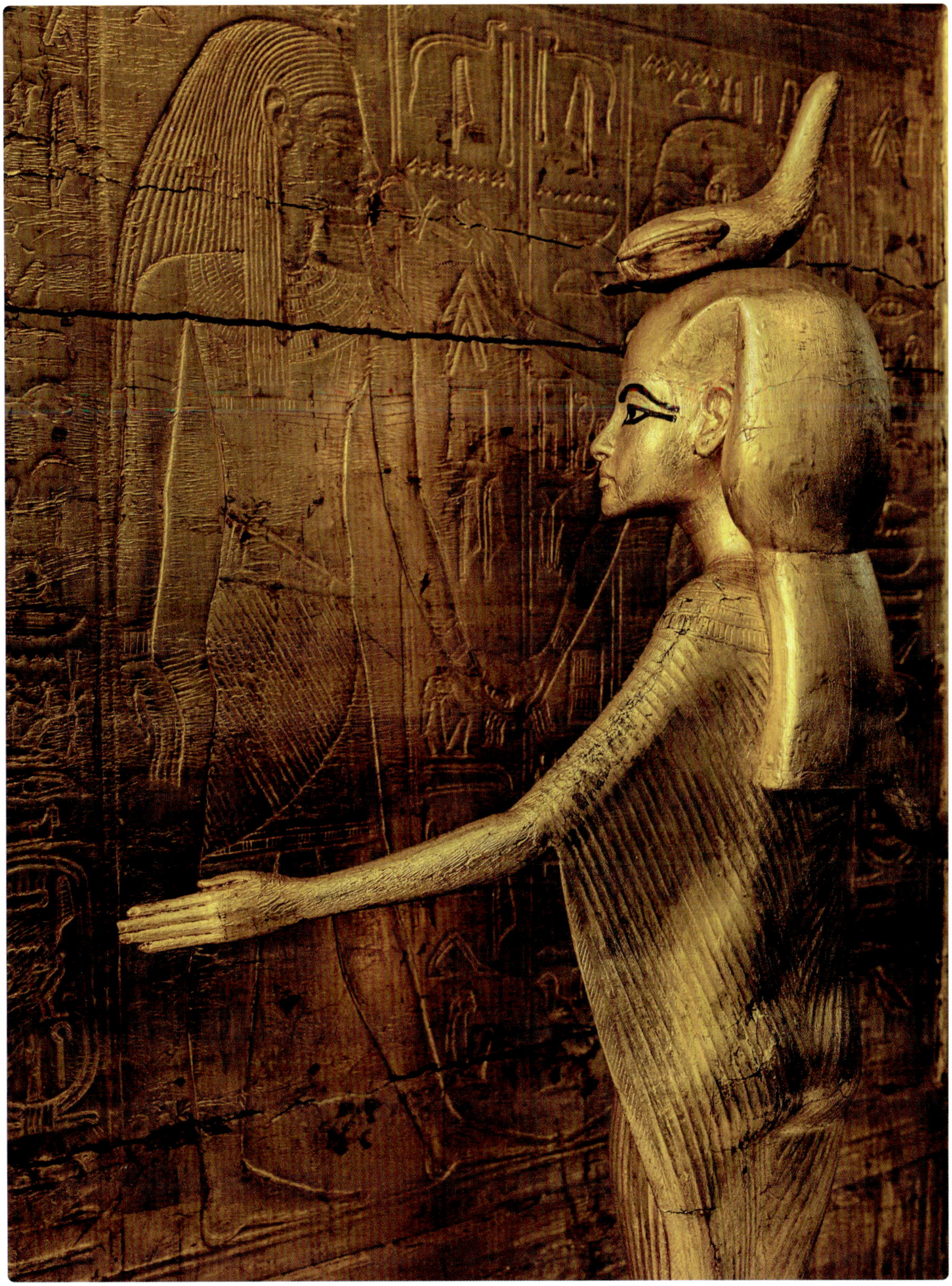

Spreading her arms in protection, a gilded wooden statue of the goddess Selket (above) guards a shrine from King Tutankhamun's tomb. On her head is a scorpion, her identifying feature. Inside the shrine stood a calcite chest containing the jars that held the king's viscera.

PREVIOUS PAGES: After Tut's death, in about 1322 B.C., his mummified remains were interred in this solid gold coffin weighing more than 243 pounds (110 kg). Inlaid semiprecious stones and glass add details.

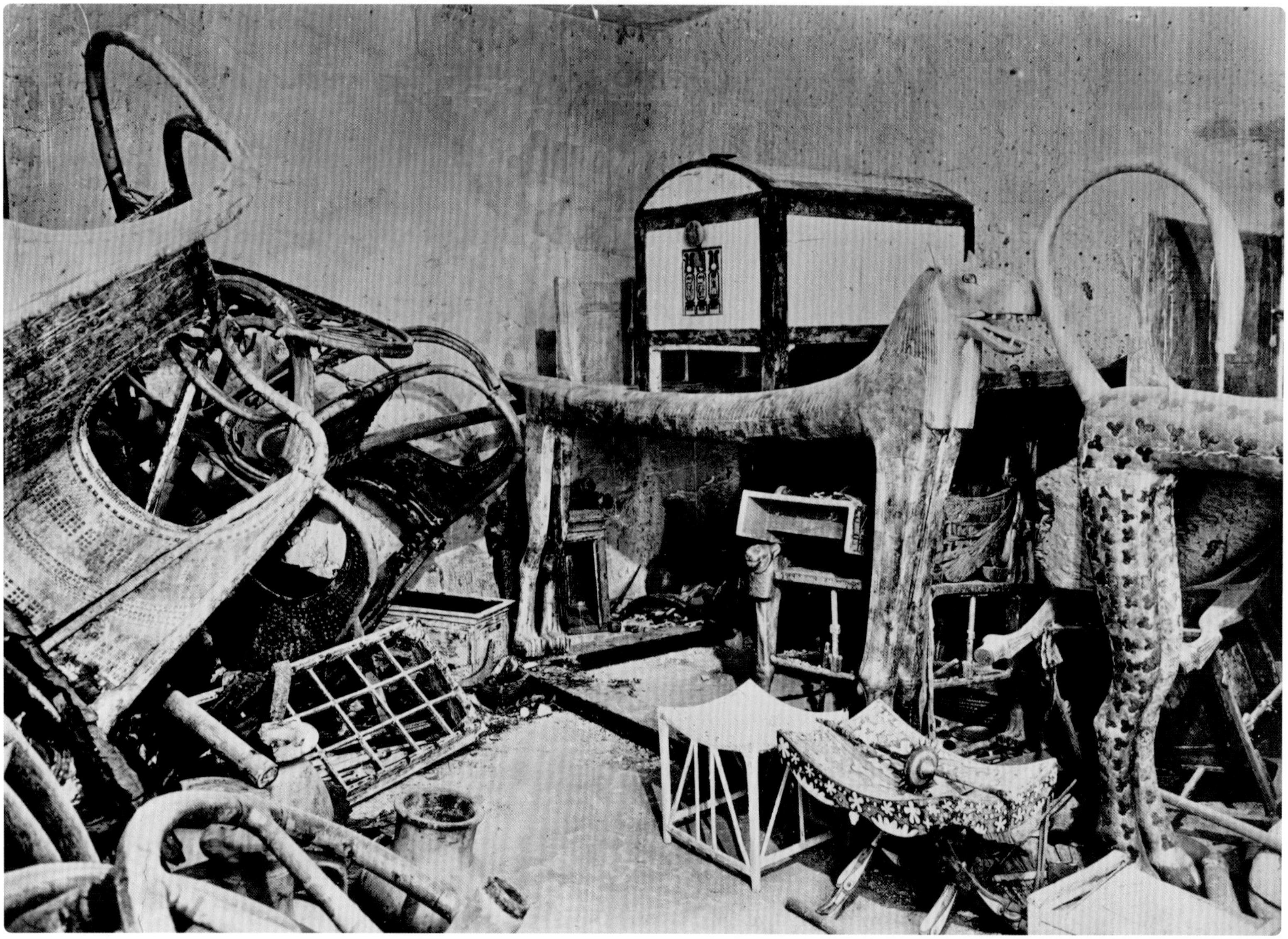

Upon entering King Tut's tomb in 1922, archaeologist Howard Carter first saw the antechamber, filled with a jumble of furniture, chariots, containers of mummified meat, and other supplies for eternity.

enjoyed music, dancing, singing, acrobatic displays, and abundant food for days.

The era's opulence was on display not only in the grand buildings and lavish festivals meant for the living, but in preparations for death as well. Across the Nile to the west, huge numbers of elite tombs were cut into rocky cliffs, decorated beautifully, and equipped for eternity. Areas known now as the Valley of the Kings, Western Valley (or Valley of the Monkeys), Valley of the Queens, Asasif, and Dra Abu el-Naga, among others, belong to a vast cemetery that received the mortal remains of everyone who was anyone for several hundred years.

Nearby, rulers also constructed their mortuary temples—buildings where the deceased could be worshipped, and offerings left, for the rest of time. Queen Hatshepsut, who ruled Egypt between about 1473 and 1458 B.C., claimed a prime location at Deir el-Bahri and poured resources into preparing her own memorial space. Her sweeping, tiered construction, set against a golden desert cliff, is as recognizable around the world today as the Pyramids at Giza.

Early archaeologists, including Auguste Mariette, the first director of the Egyptian Antiquities Service, began to explore the cemetery in the 1800s. In 1905, British Egyptologist James Quibell found the one-chamber burial of Yuya and Tuyu, the great-grandparents of King Tutankhamun. It's now known as KV 46, the 46th tomb uncovered in the Valley of the Kings. The burial was looted more than once in antiquity, with thieves making off with portable items such as jewelry and valuable oils. But what was left offers a look at what wealth and connections could bring to a tomb: ornate chairs and chests, a chariot, gilded coffins and face masks, and two mummies fabulously well preserved by the best embalming money could buy.

"Tutankhamun himself remained a bit of a mystery. Tainted by the heresy of King Akhenaten, who may have been his father, he was omitted from standard lists of Egypt's rulers."

Tutankhamun himself remained a bit of a mystery. Tainted by the heresy of King Akhenaten, who may have been his father, he was omitted from standard lists of Egypt's rulers. But his name was not unknown. It appeared on buildings, monuments, and artifacts that came to light at various sites in the early years of archaeology, as well as on a few items uncovered in the Valley of the Kings. After finding several dozen royal tombs in the valley, archaeologists were closing in on Tut when archaeologist Howard Carter and his patron, George Herbert, the fifth earl of Carnarvon, took up the hunt early in the 20th century. By a combination of luck and sheer persistence, Carter made one of the most famous discoveries of all time: the treasure trove of King Tut's tomb, KV 62.

Looters must have hit the high-end Theban tombs almost before the paint was dry. Until KV 62 was found, archaeologists saw only tantalizing glimpses of royal wealth in burials that had mostly been cleaned out. In fact, KV 62 was robbed on a couple of occasions, but fortunately the losses were minor. Still, the people who sought to hide their final resting places here in the rocky crevasses of the Western Desert must have hoped the location would offer some protection. And it cannot have been an accident that a high cliff overlooking the cemetery had been shaped by eons of wind and weather into a rough pyramid. ▲

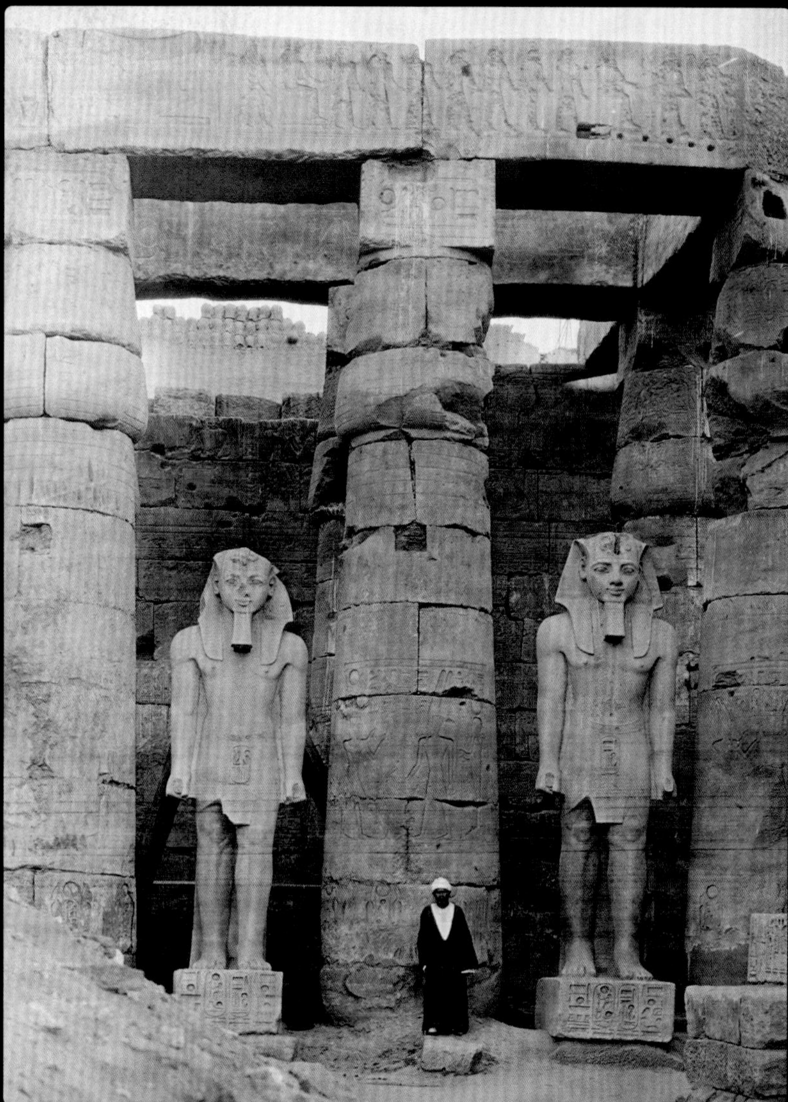

King Ramses II (about 1279–1213 B.C.) was a prolific builder. His additions to the Great Temple at Luxor include a colonnade with colossal statues of himself, as seen in this image from 1913 (above).

A photo shot in the mid-1800s (right) shows Ramses II's mortuary temple, now known as the Ramesseum. The king, depicted in the form of the god Osiris, stands at each pillar of the portico.

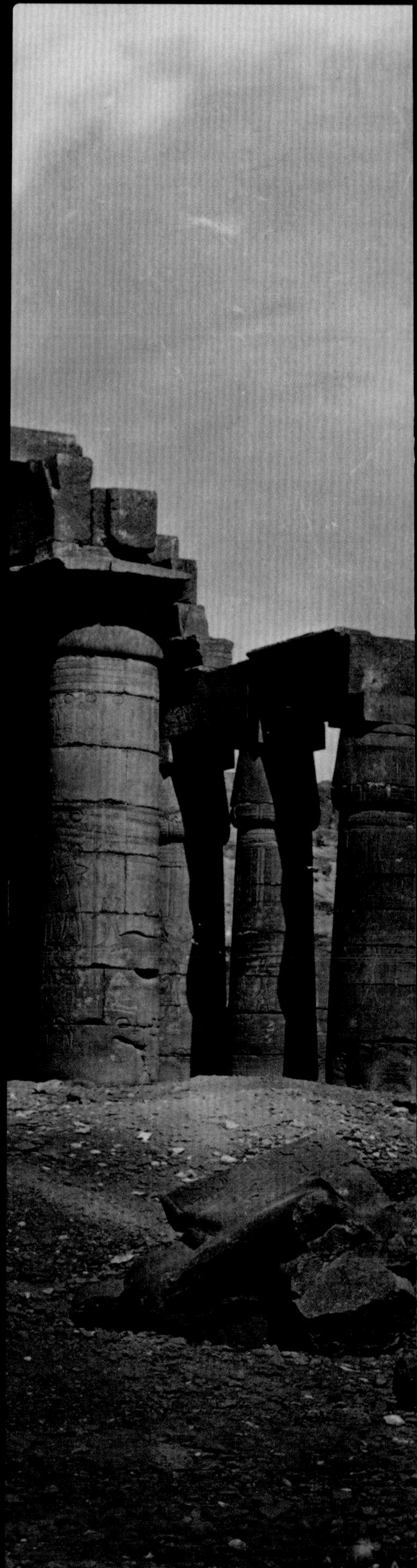

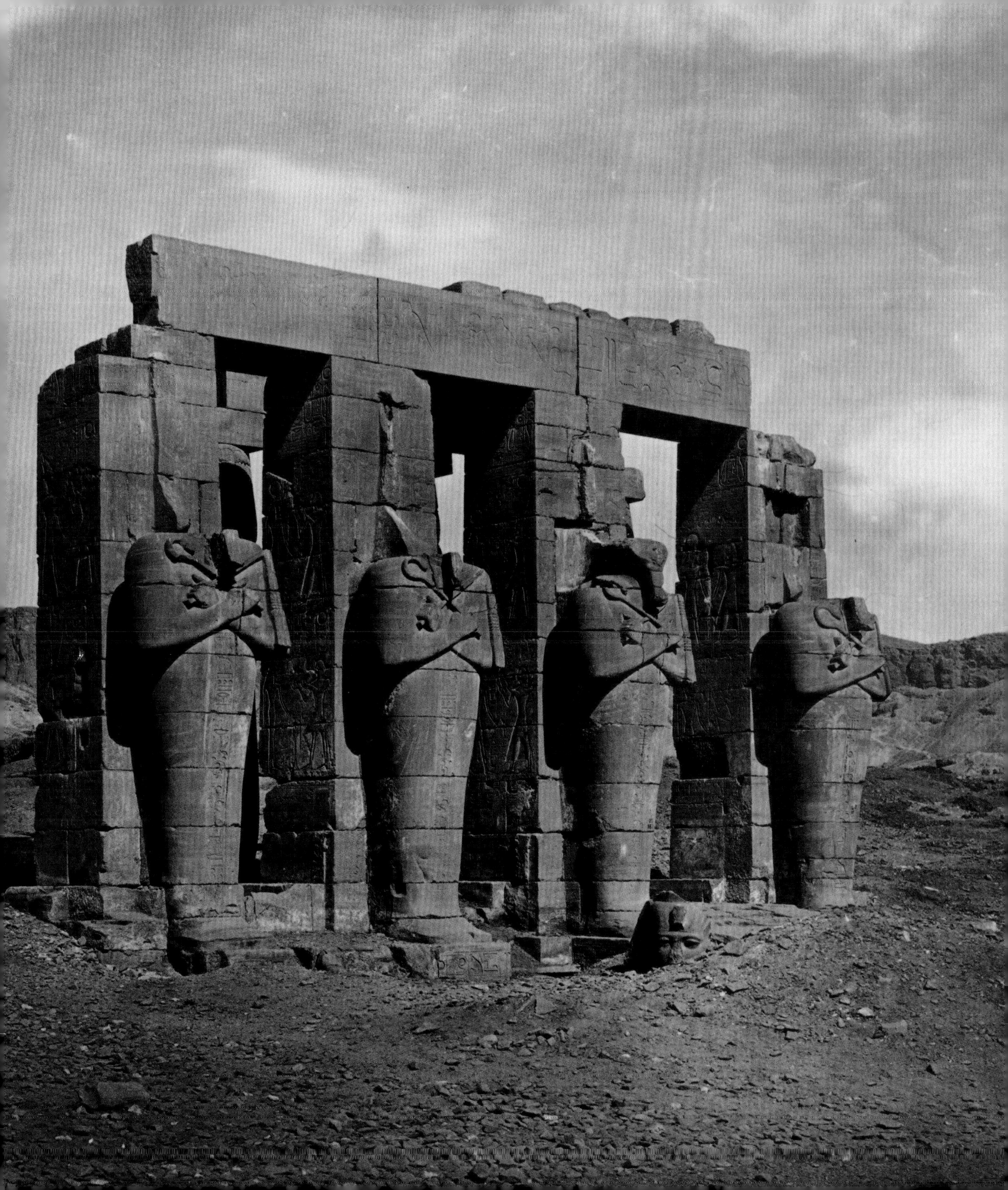

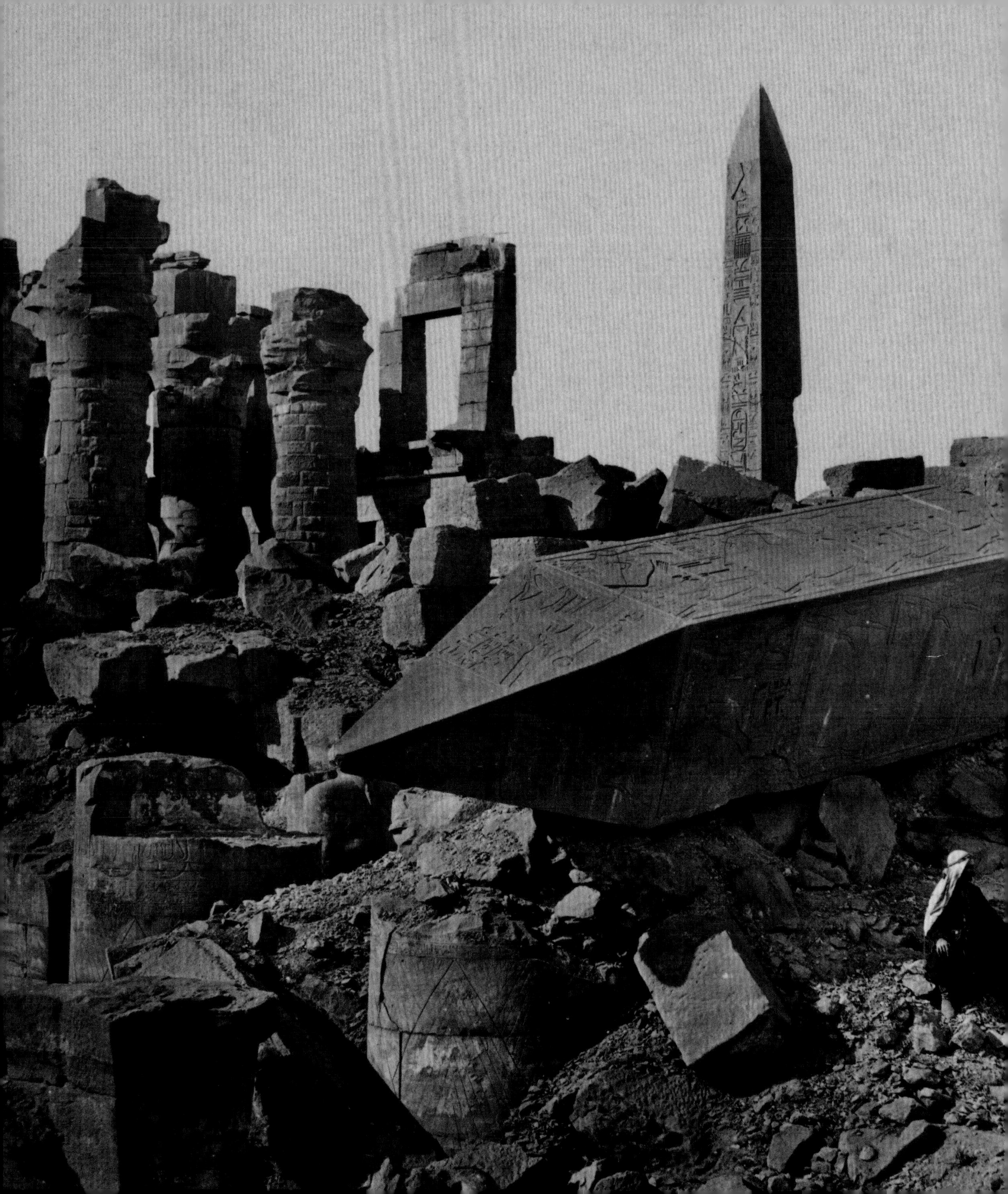

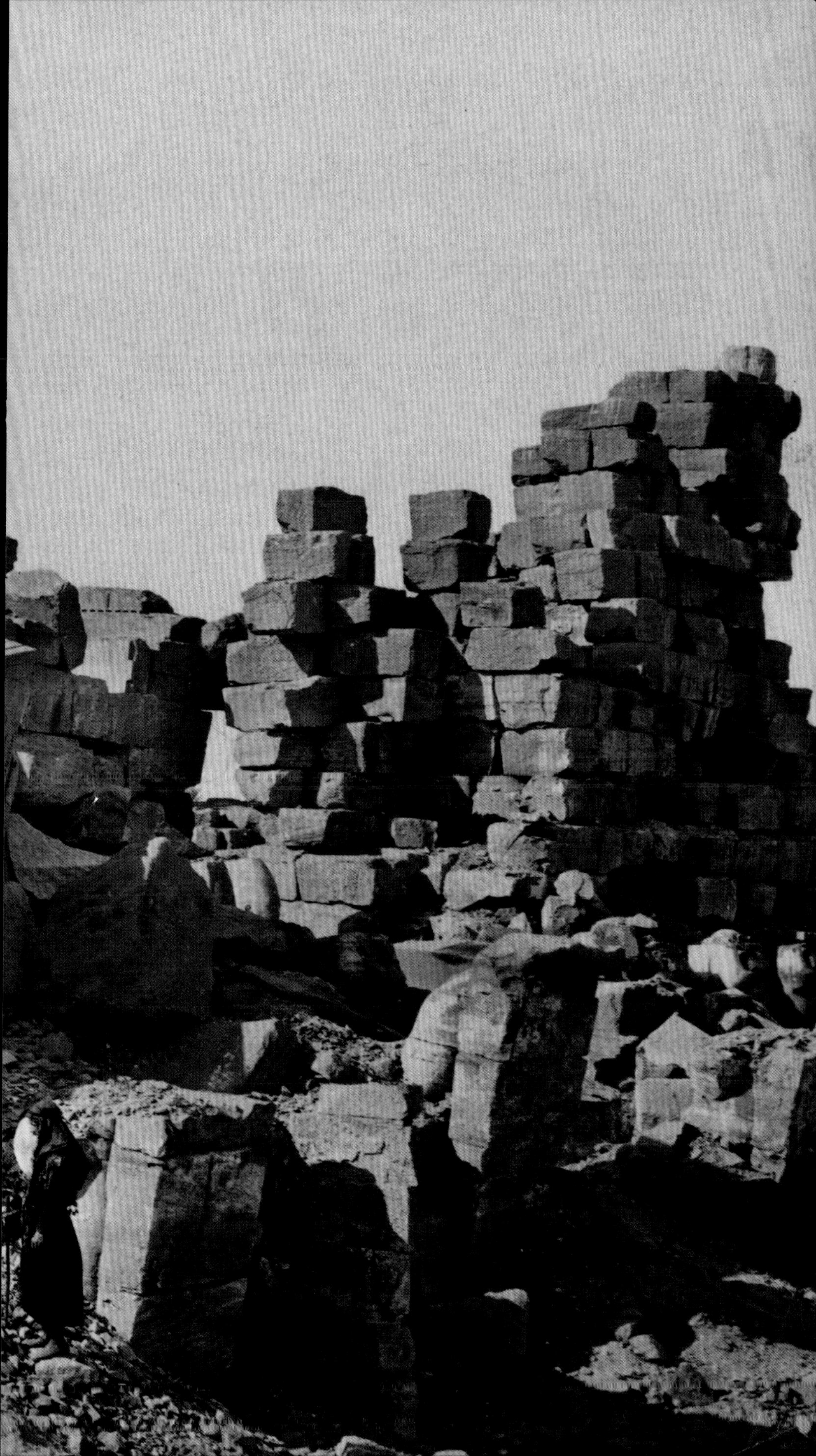

By the 1850s, a red granite obelisk erected by Queen Hatshepsut (about 1473–1458 B.C.) in the Amun temple at Karnak had long since toppled. A similar monument from her father's reign was still standing.

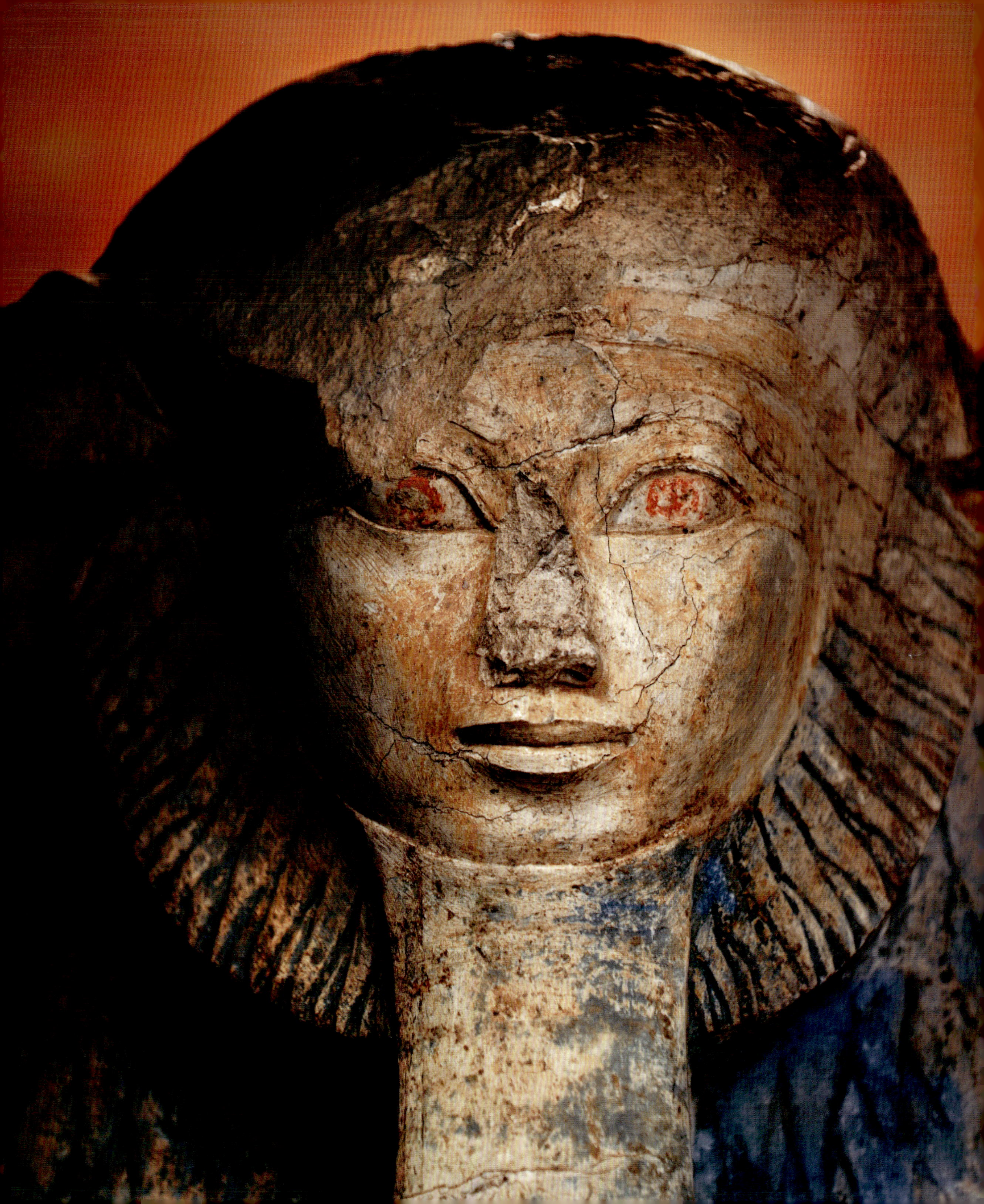

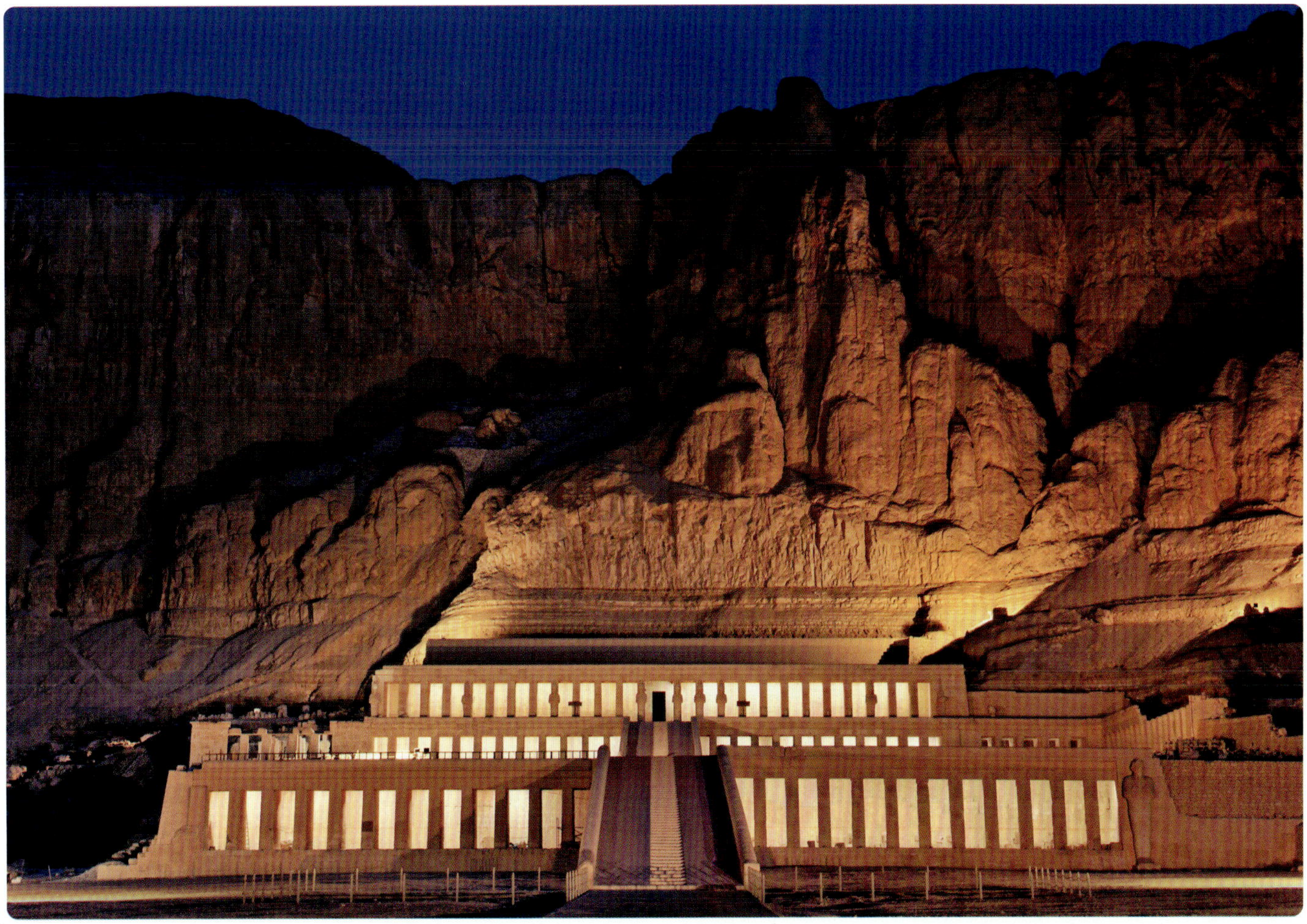

After the death of her husband, Thutmose II, in about 1479 B.C., Queen Hatshepsut became regent for her stepson. She then slowly took on the trappings and power of a king. In this painted limestone statue (opposite), she appears as a male lion with a full mane.

This statue once graced the queen's mortuary temple at Deir el-Bahri (above), which was known in antiquity as Djeser-djeseru, "holy of holies."

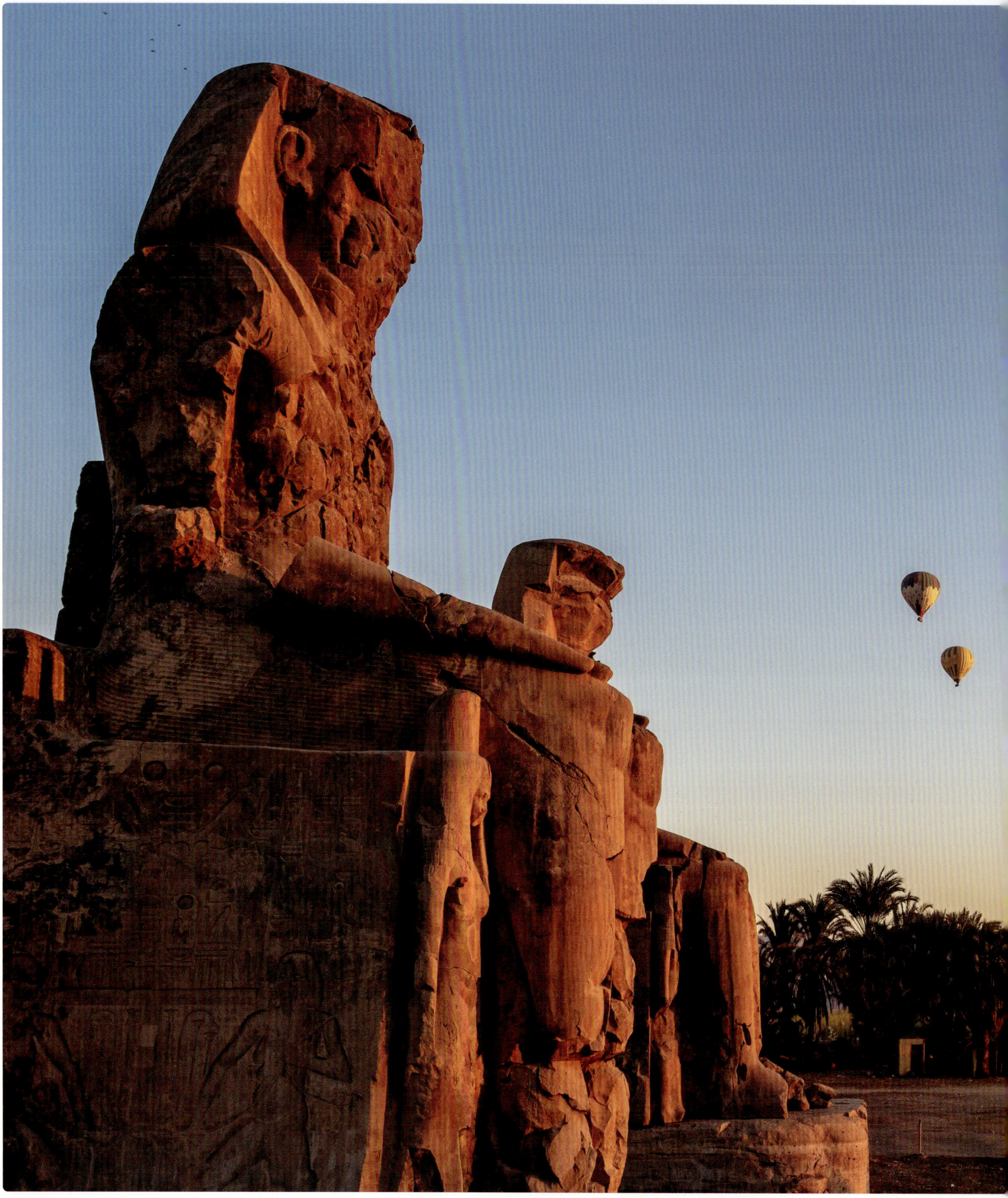

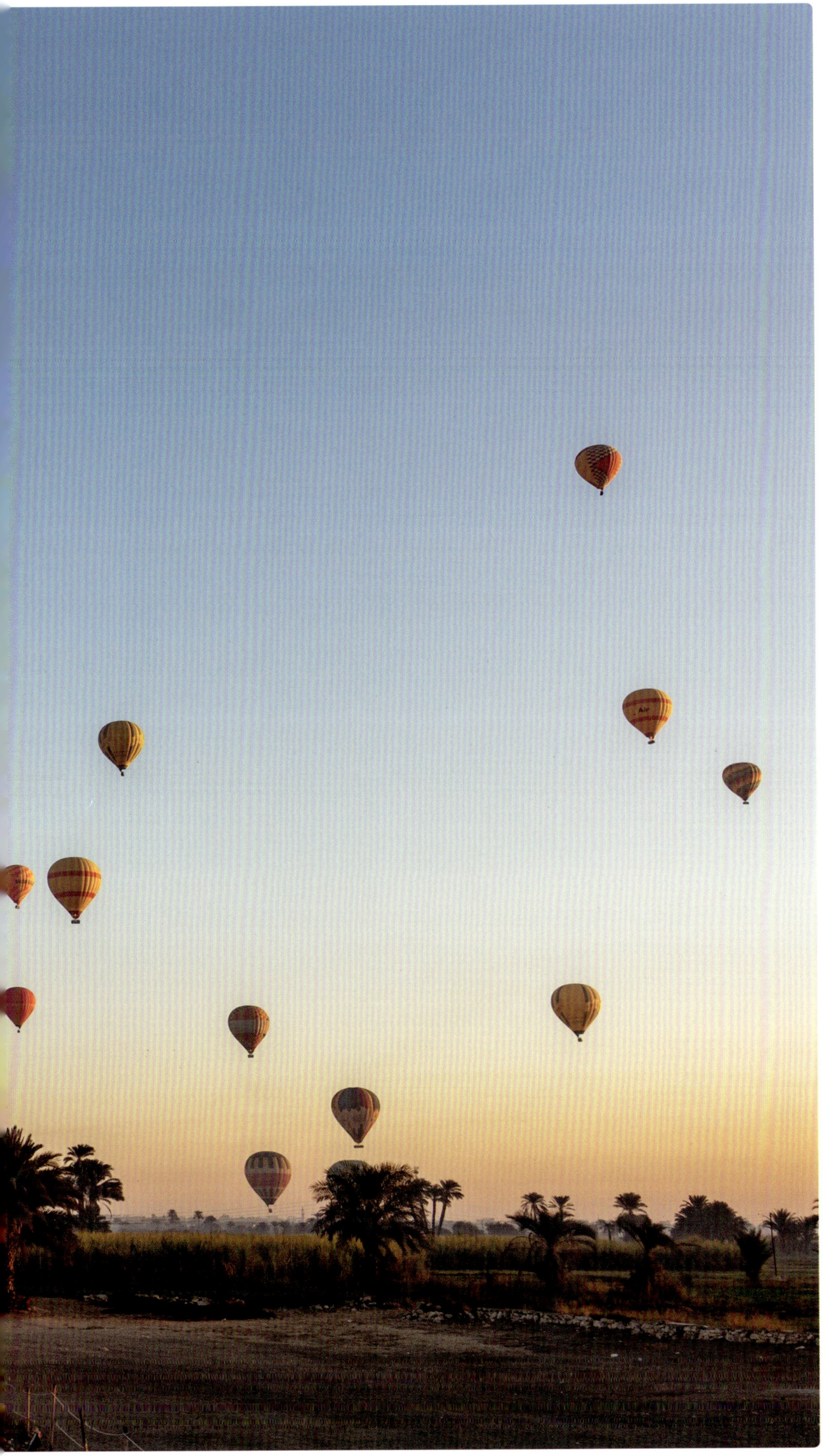

Near Luxor, hot-air balloons float in the sky at dawn to give tourists a bird's-eye view of the Colossi of Memnon: reconstructed statues of Amenhotep III (about 1390–1353 B.C.) at the site of the king's mortuary temple.

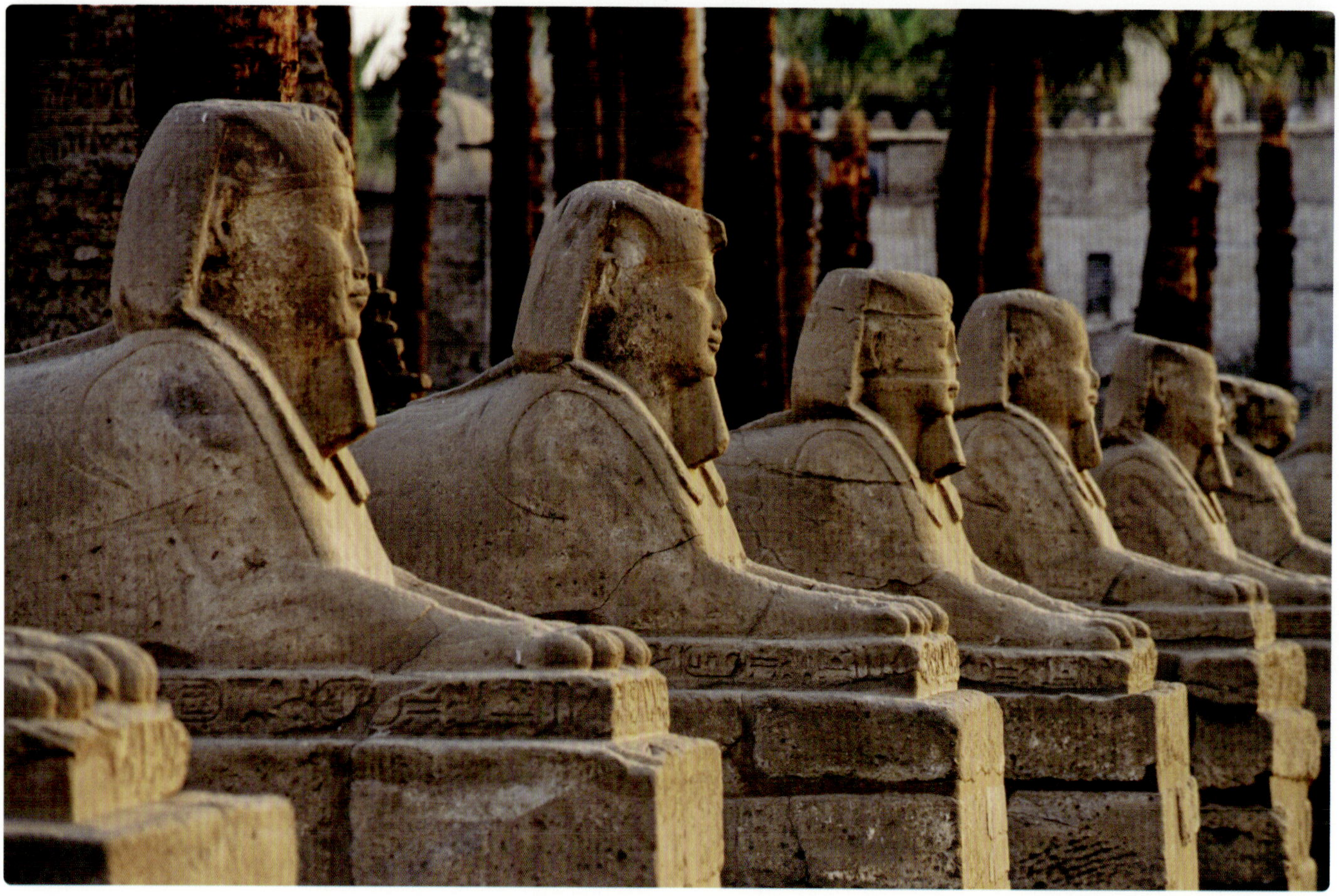

Sandstone sphinxes (above) bearing the head of King Nectanebo I (380–362 B.C.) line a 1.2-mile-long (2 km) processional avenue that connects the temples of Karnak and Luxor. The statues replaced earlier ones that had fallen into ruin.

Taking the shape of stylized papyrus plants, the monumental columns in the temple of Amun at Karnak (opposite) rise to more than 49 feet (15 m).

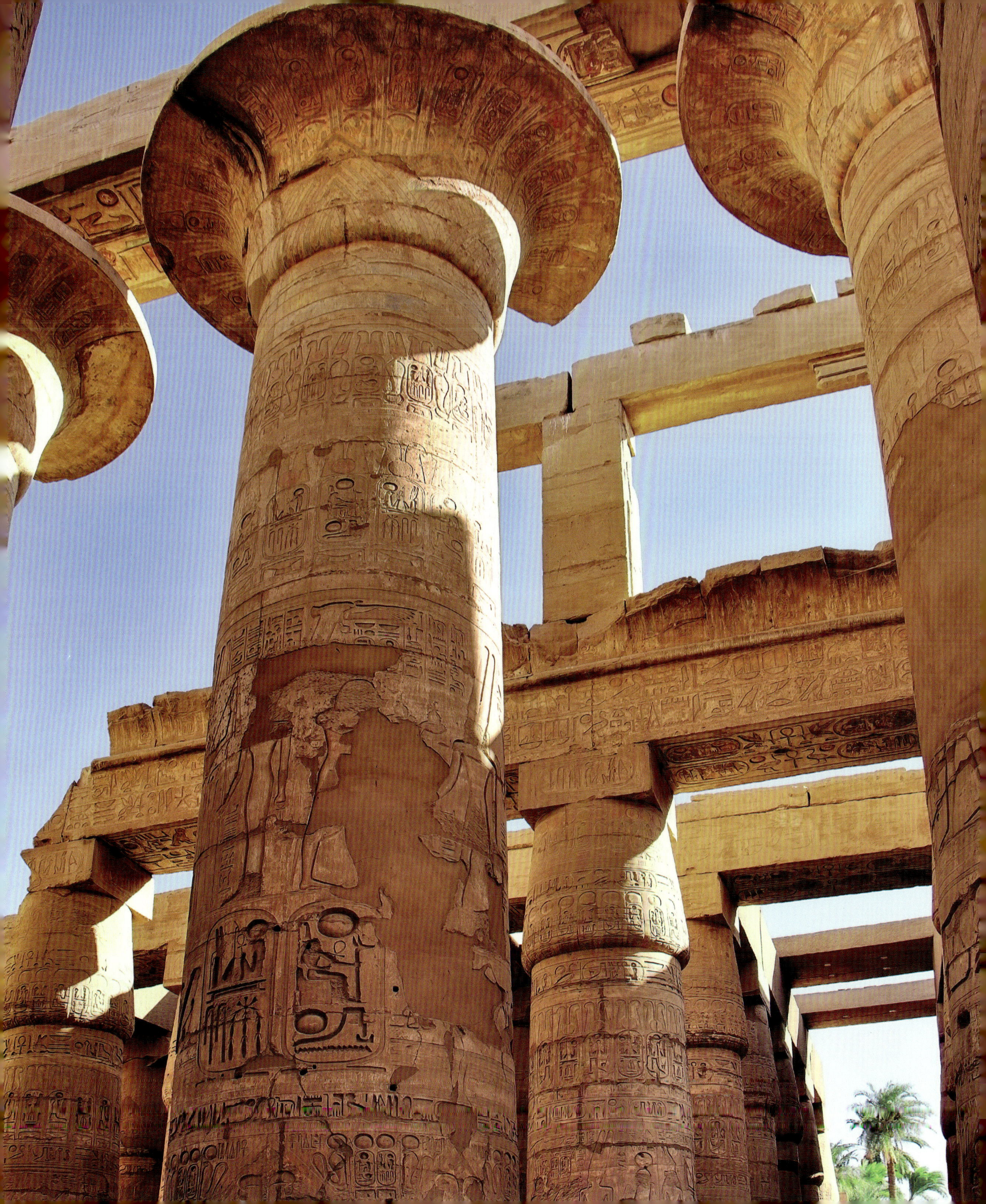

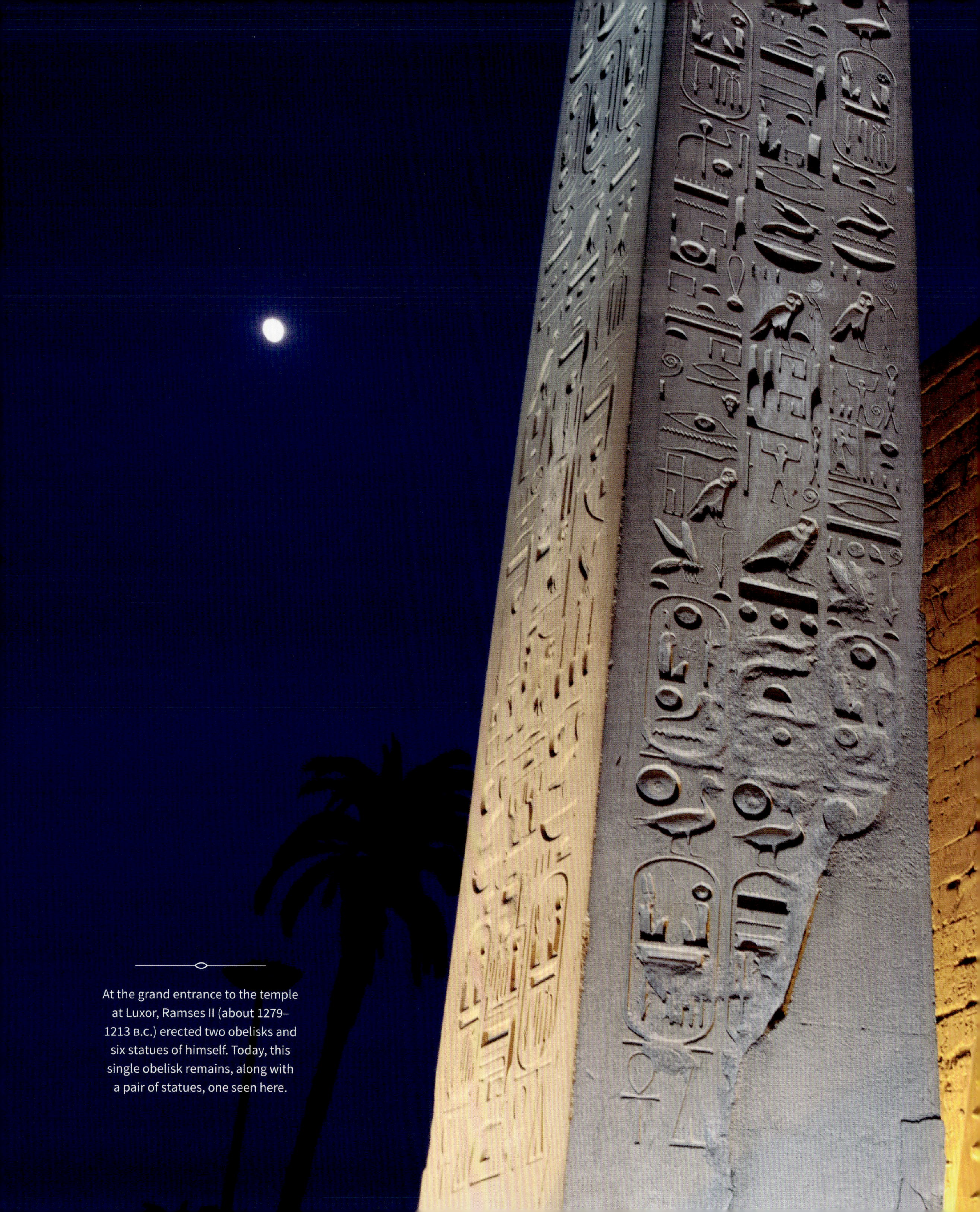

At the grand entrance to the temple at Luxor, Ramses II (about 1279–1213 B.C.) erected two obelisks and six statues of himself. Today, this single obelisk remains, along with a pair of statues, one seen here.

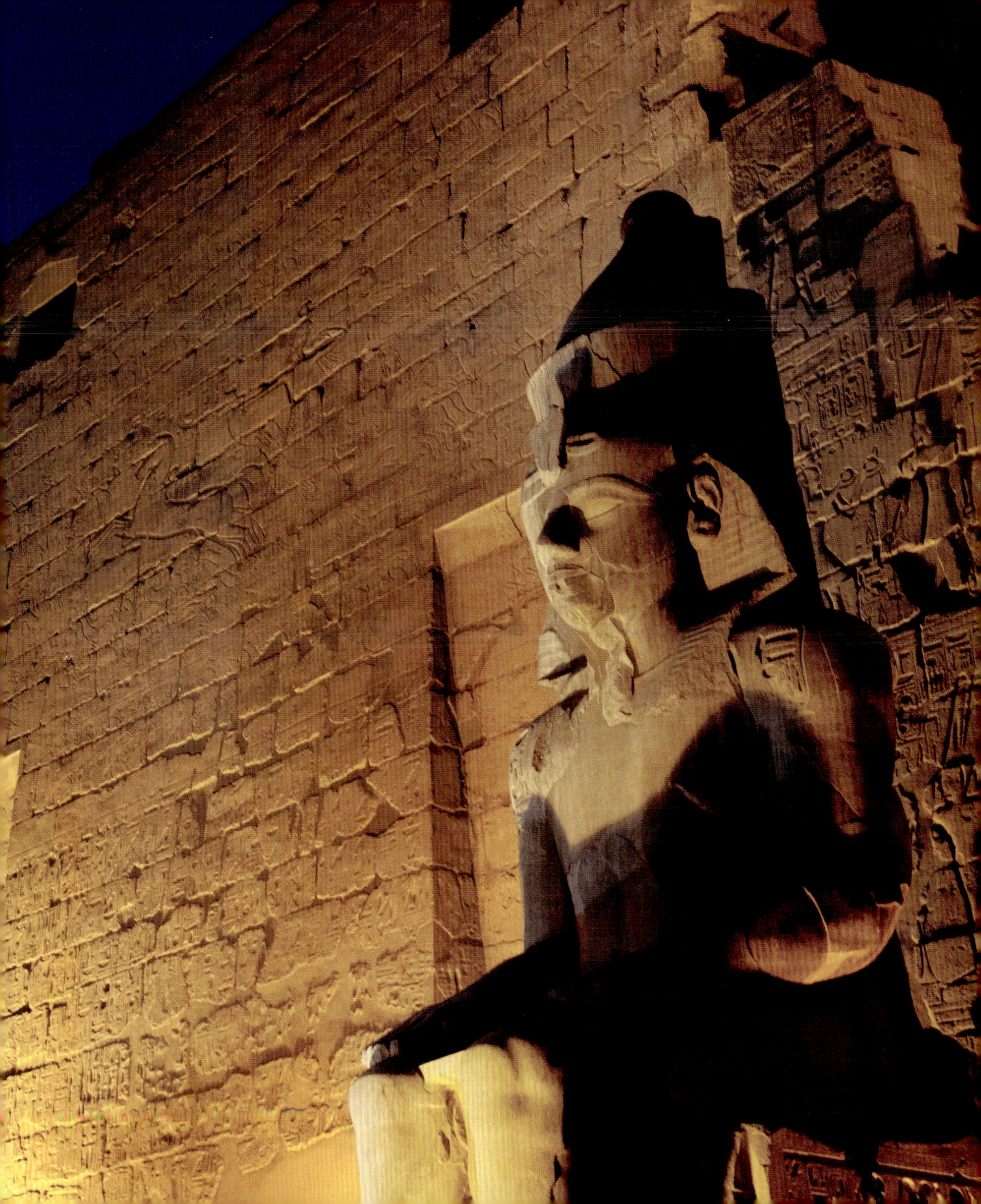

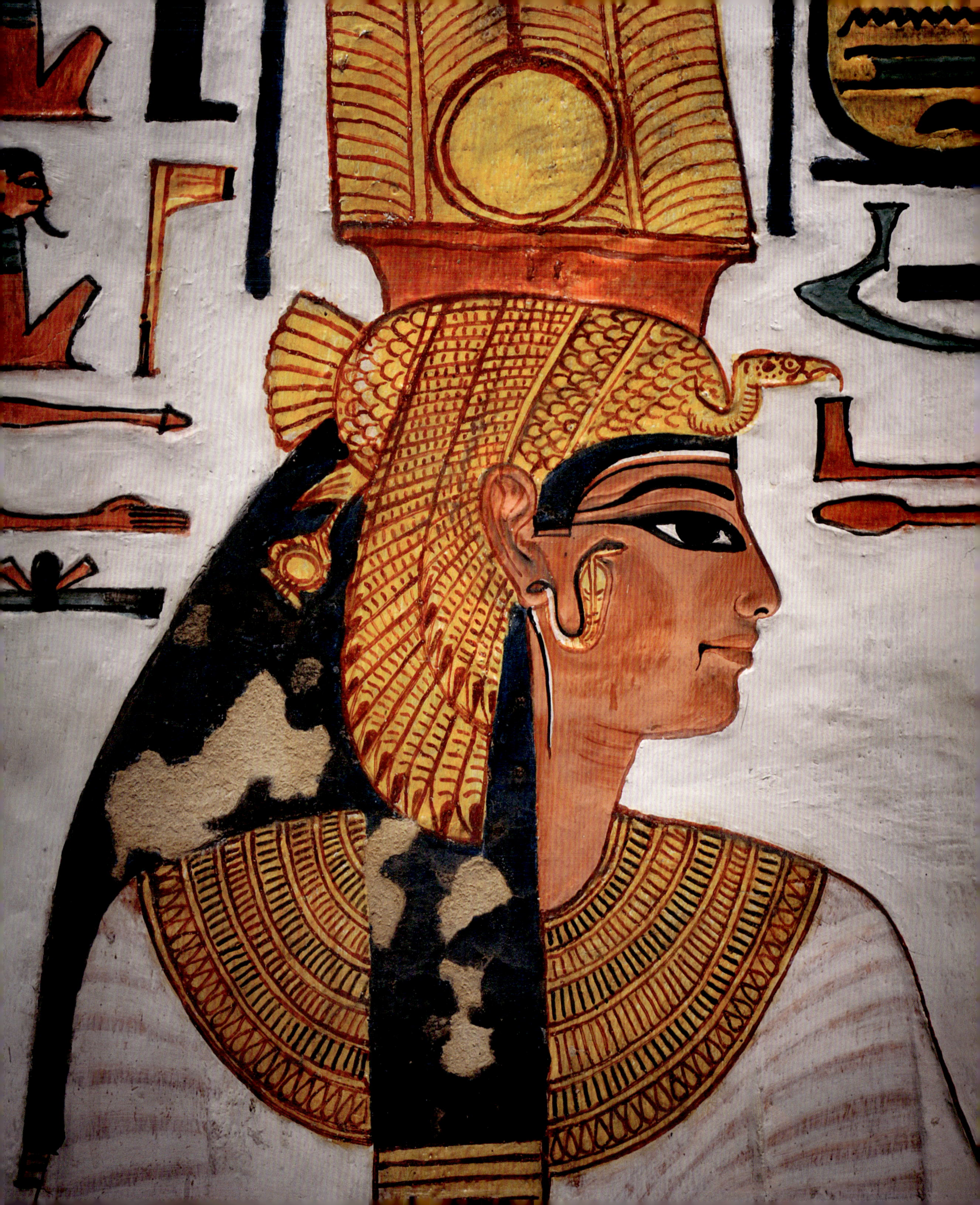

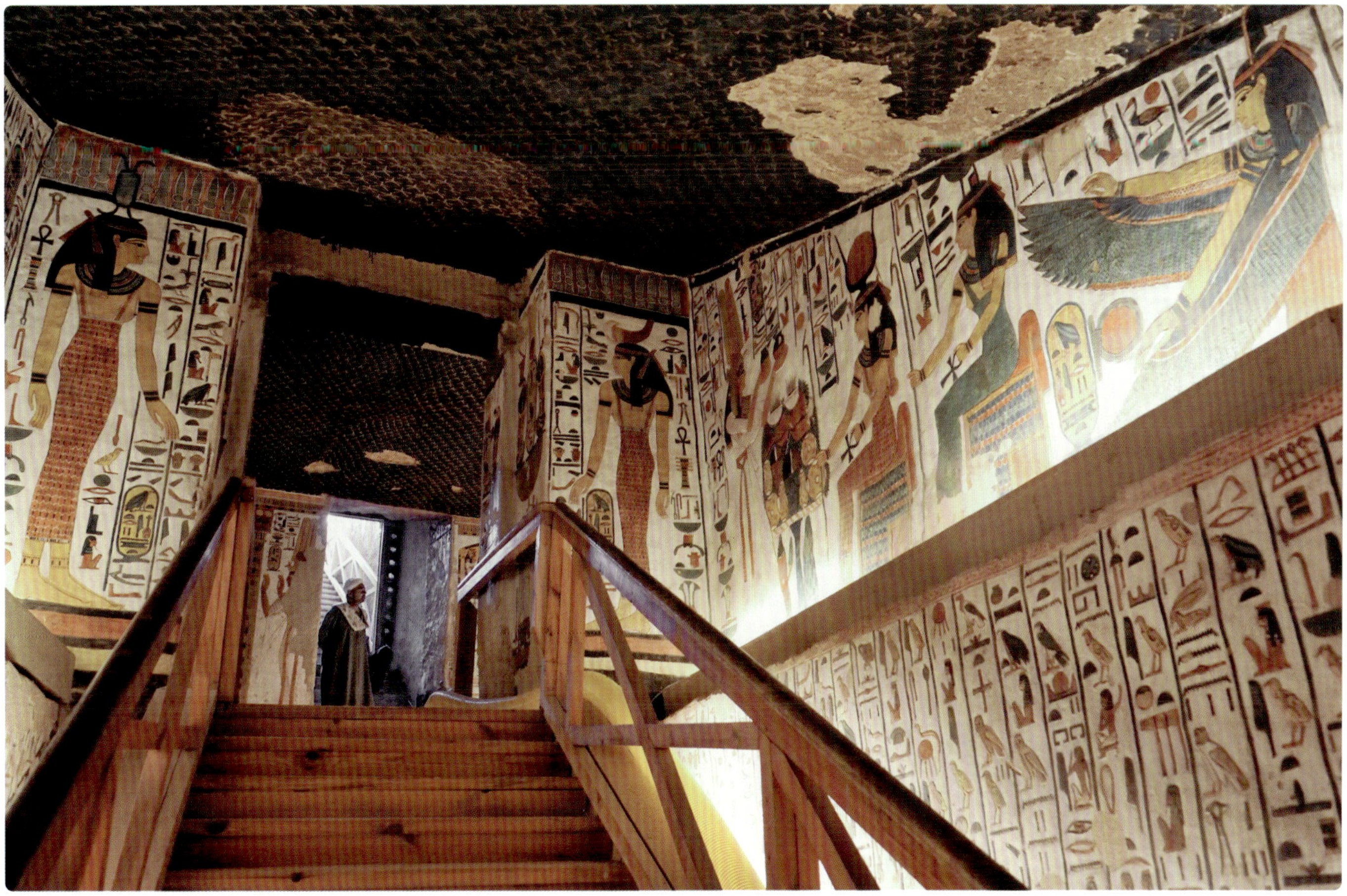

In her spectacular tomb near Luxor, Nefertari, the principal wife of Ramses II, wears a headdress in the shape of the protective vulture goddess, Nekhbet (opposite).

The same artisans who created royal tombs in the Valley of the Kings must have prepared Nefertari's final resting place (above), carving rock chambers, plastering walls, and painting every available surface.

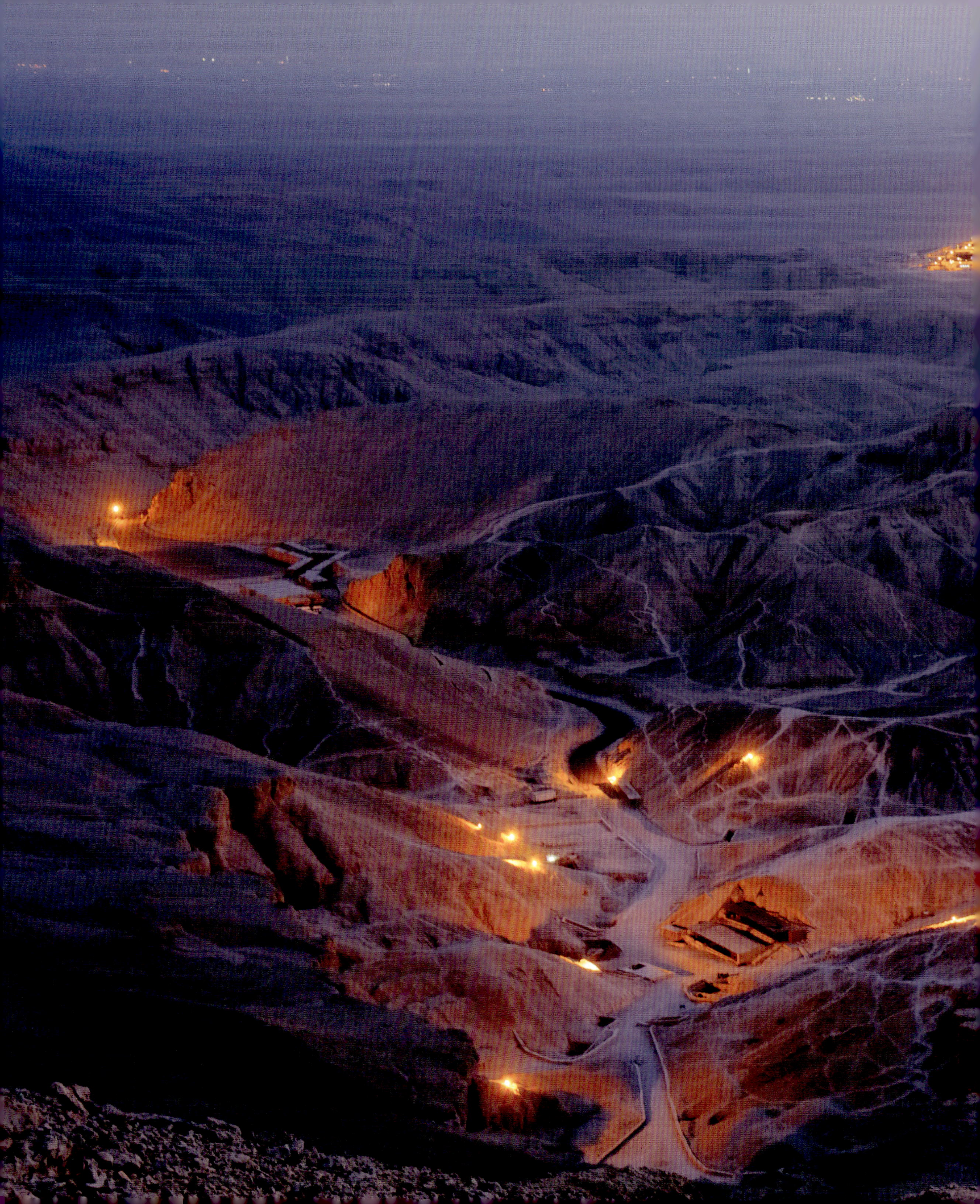

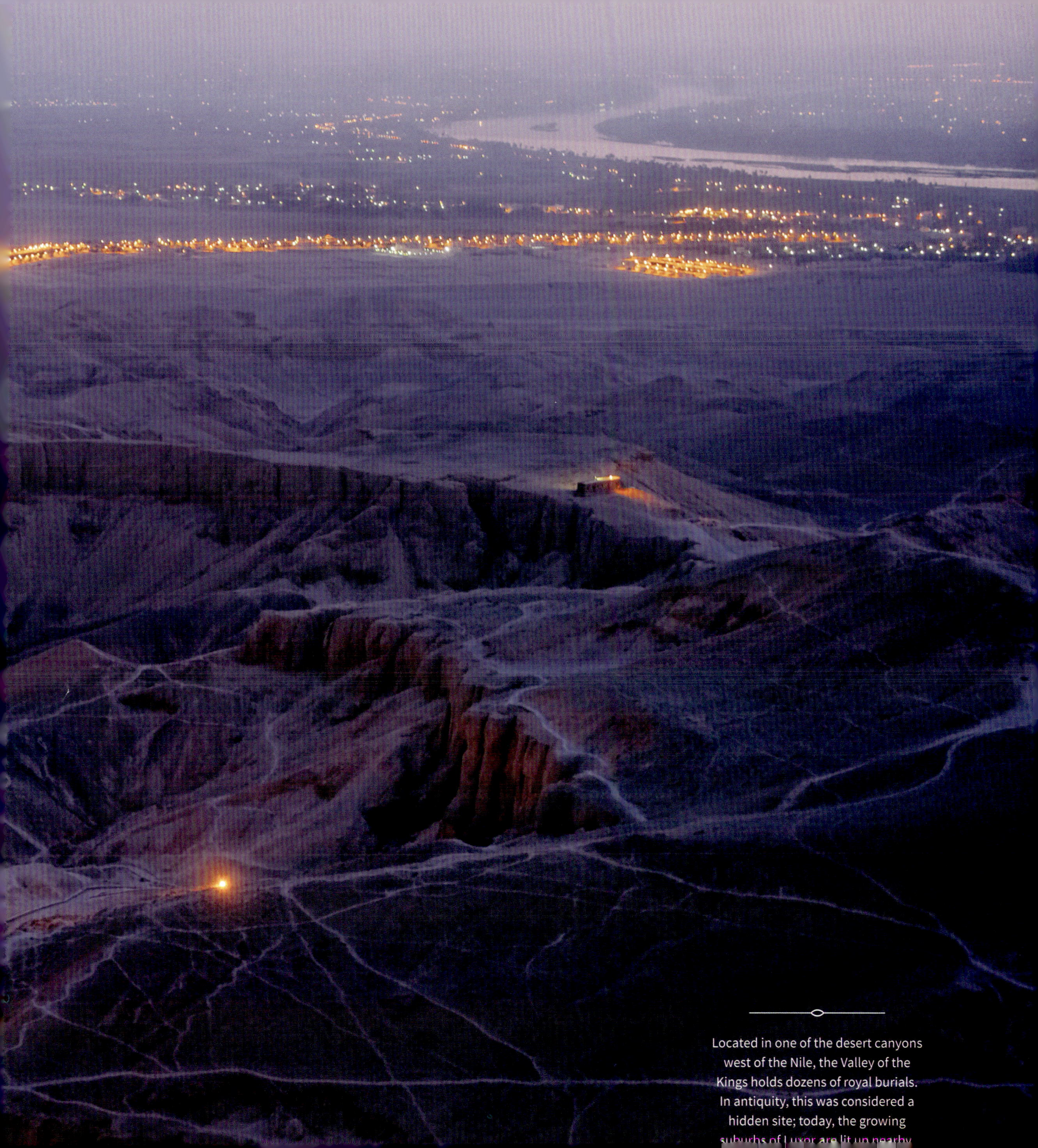

Located in one of the desert canyons west of the Nile, the Valley of the Kings holds dozens of royal burials. In antiquity, this was considered a hidden site; today, the growing suburbs of Luxor are lit up nearby.

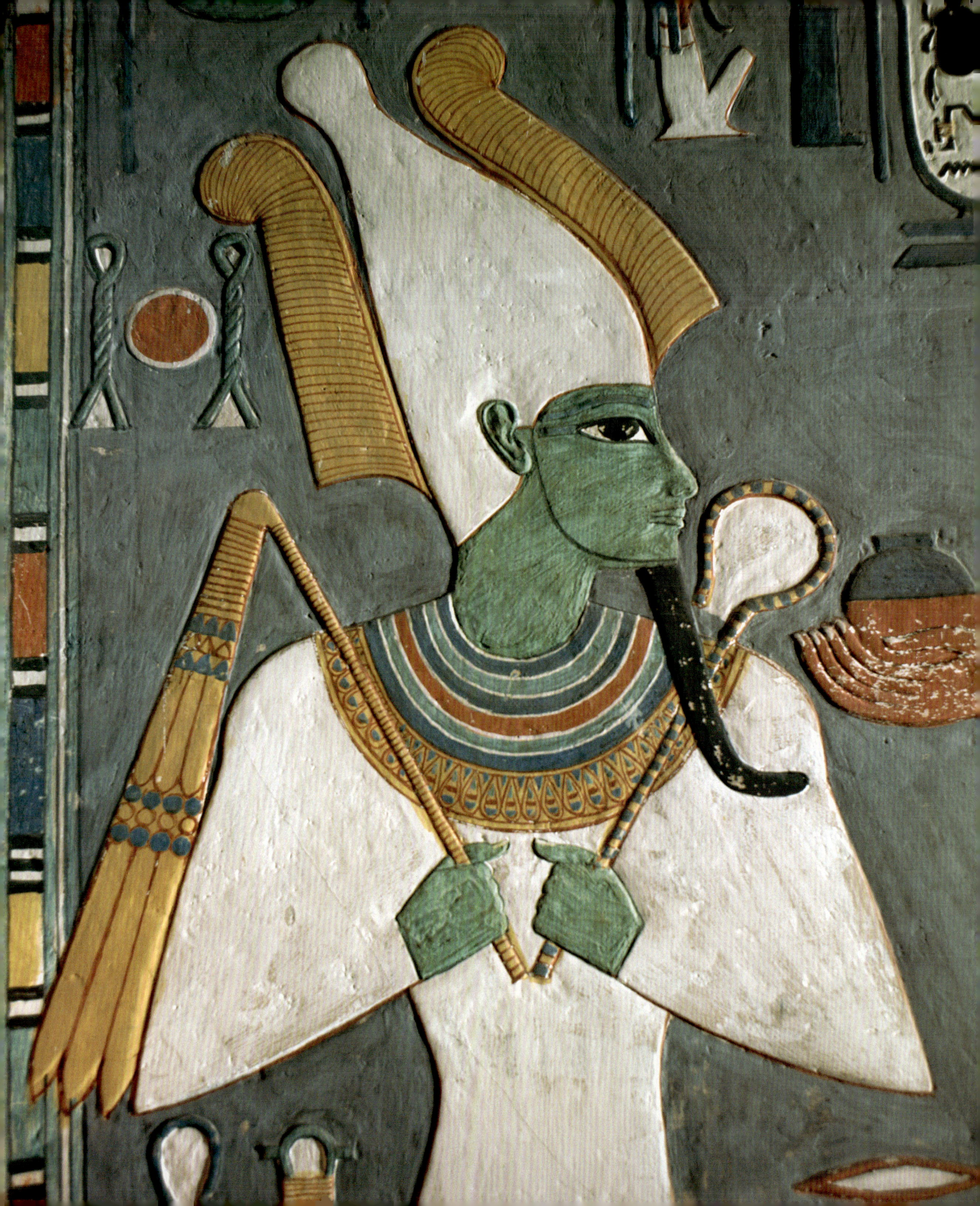

Still showing gilded and painted details, this servant figurine of cedar (right) was found in the tomb of Yuya and Tuyu. As the parents of Queen Tiy, the principal wife of King Amenhotep III (about 1390–1353 B.C.), the pair secured a burial in the Valley of the Kings.

An ornate jewelry box (below) was another of Yuya and Tuyu's grave goods. It was found empty, though; thieves had taken whatever it held.

An army general who became king, Horemheb (about 1319–1292 B.C.) was buried in the same royal cemetery in a large, lavishly decorated tomb (opposite).

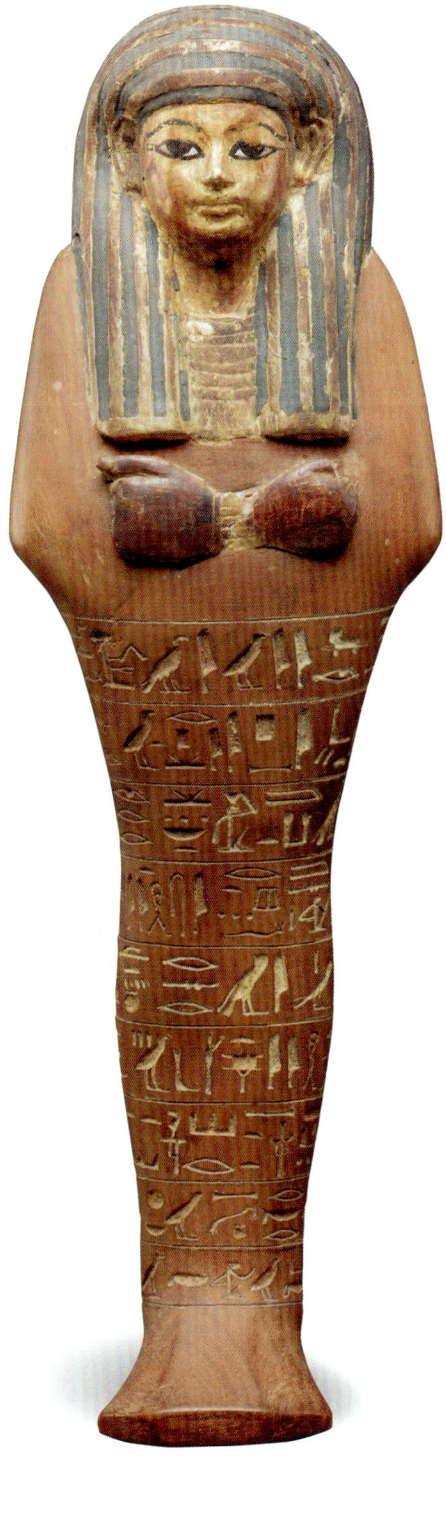

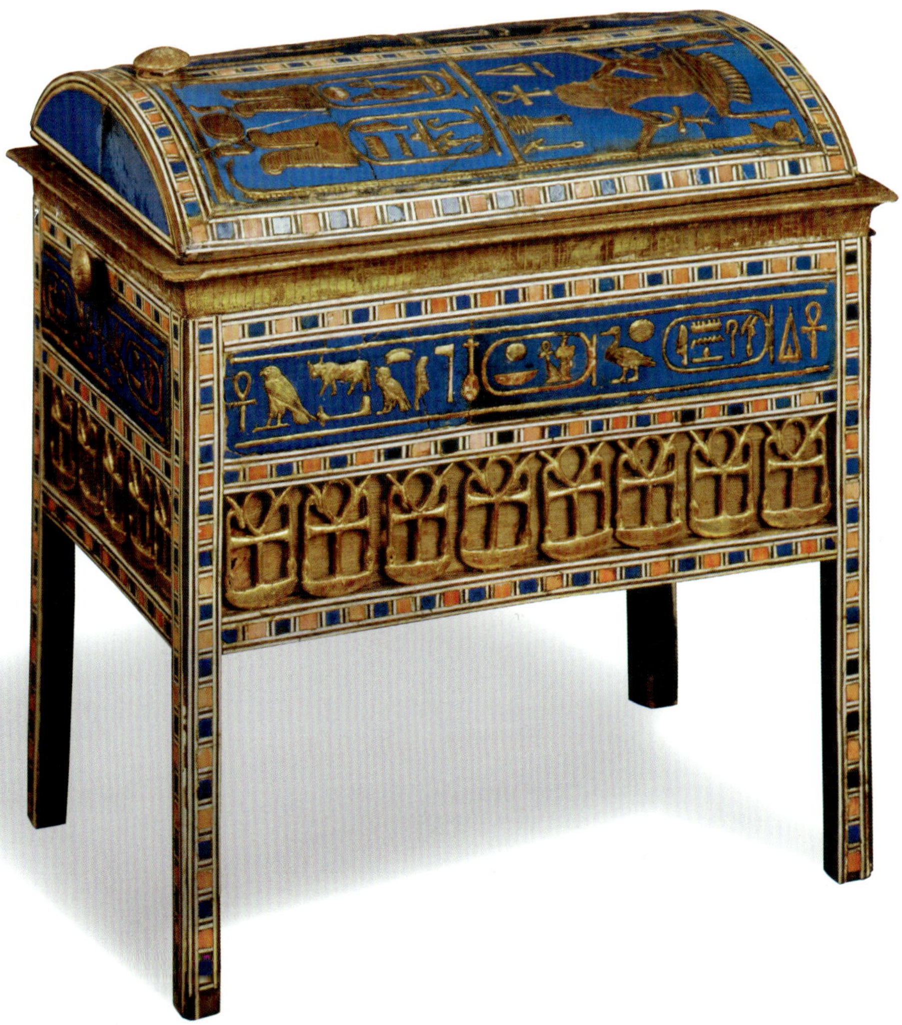

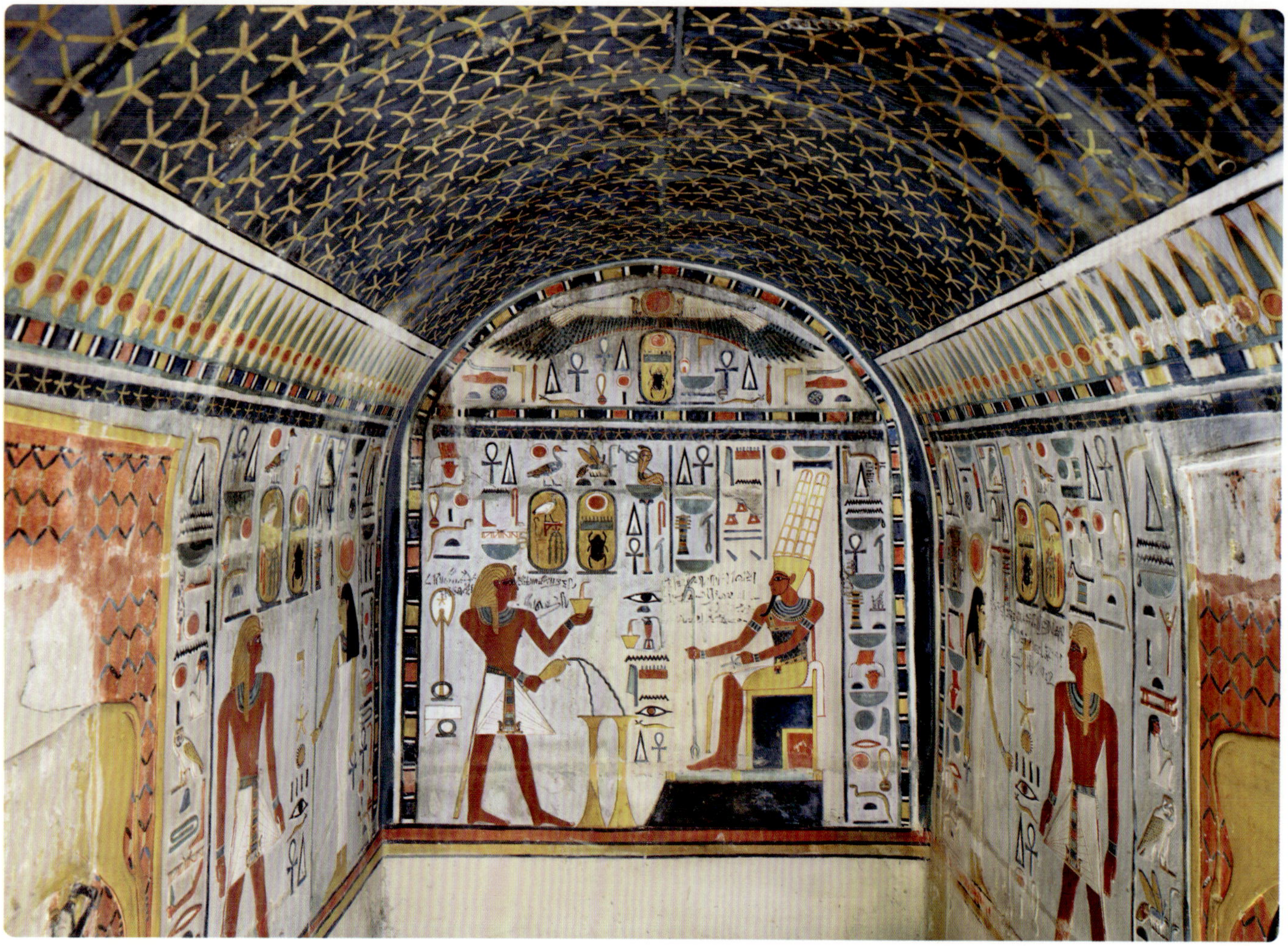

On the back wall of a Deir el-Bahri chapel (above), King Thutmose III (about 1479–1425 B.C.) pours a liquid offering to the god Amun-Re.

In the 13th century B.C., a man named Khonsu was interred in these coffins (opposite), one nesting inside the other, at Deir el-Medina. He shared a burial space with relatives, including his father, Sennedjem, an artisan who created tombs in the Valley of the Kings.

FOLLOWING PAGES: The goddess Nut was believed to arch over the sky, swallowing the sun in the evening and giving birth to it at dawn. As symbols of eternal life, two images of her span the ceiling of the burial chamber of King Ramses VI (about 1145–1137 B.C.).

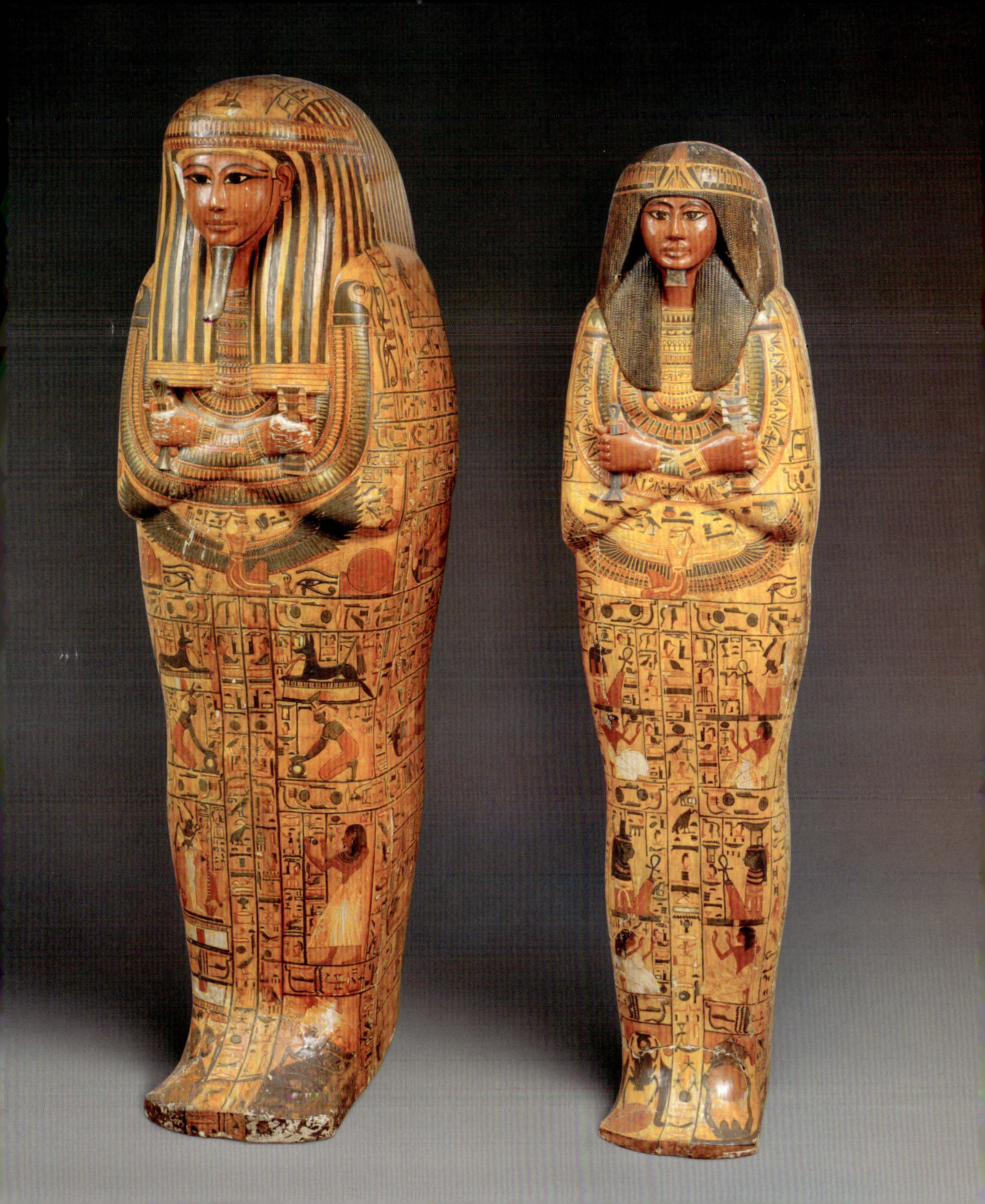

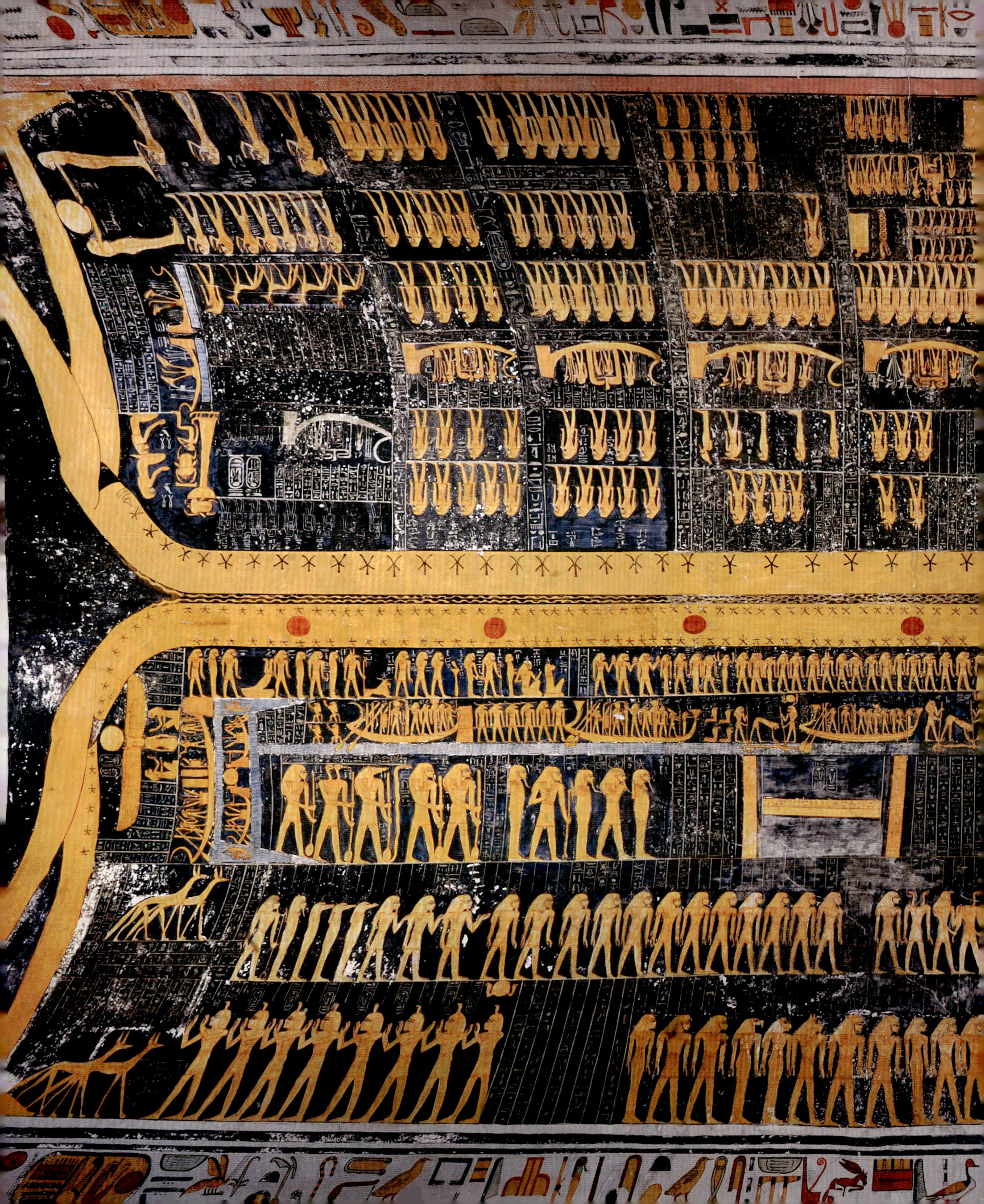

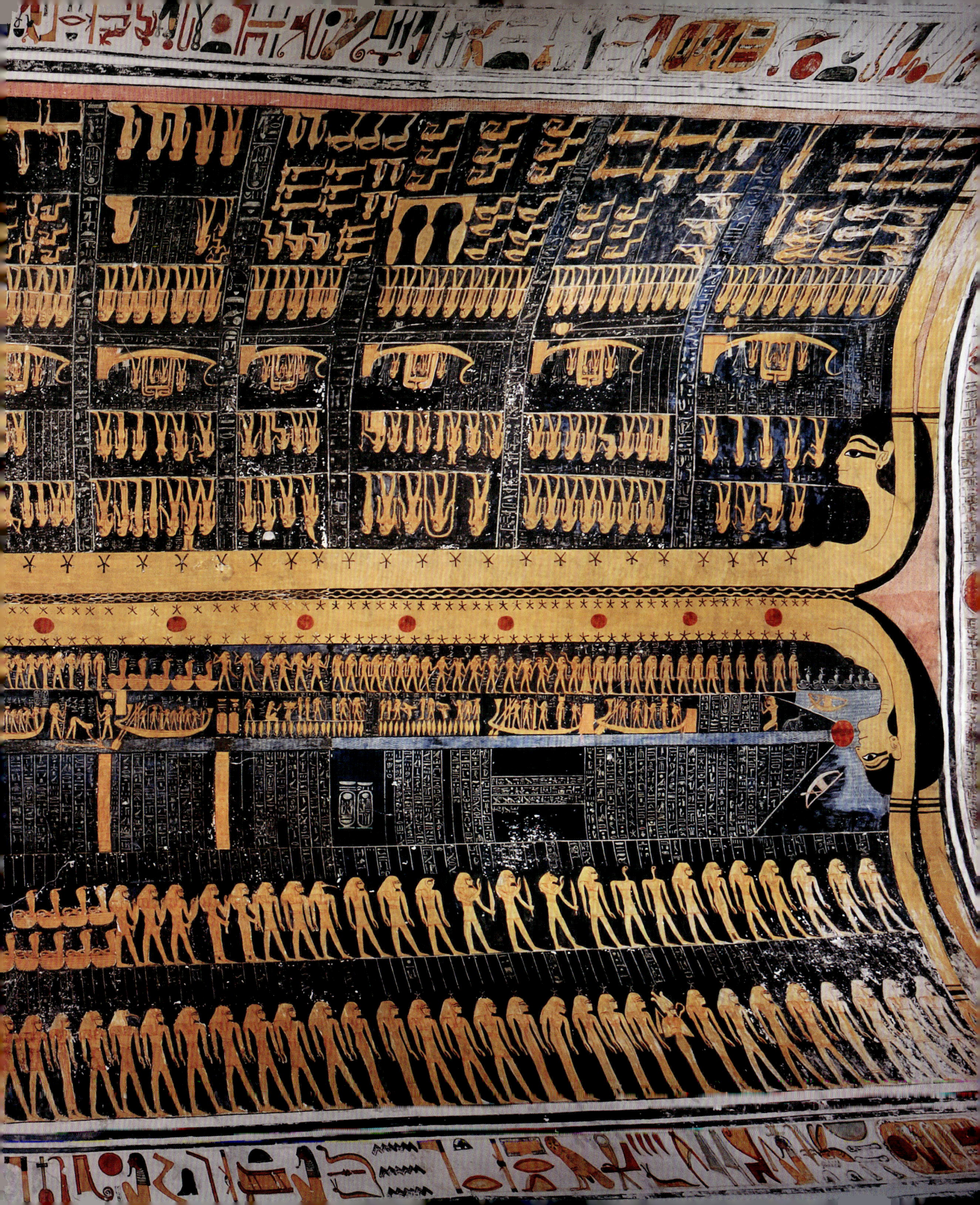

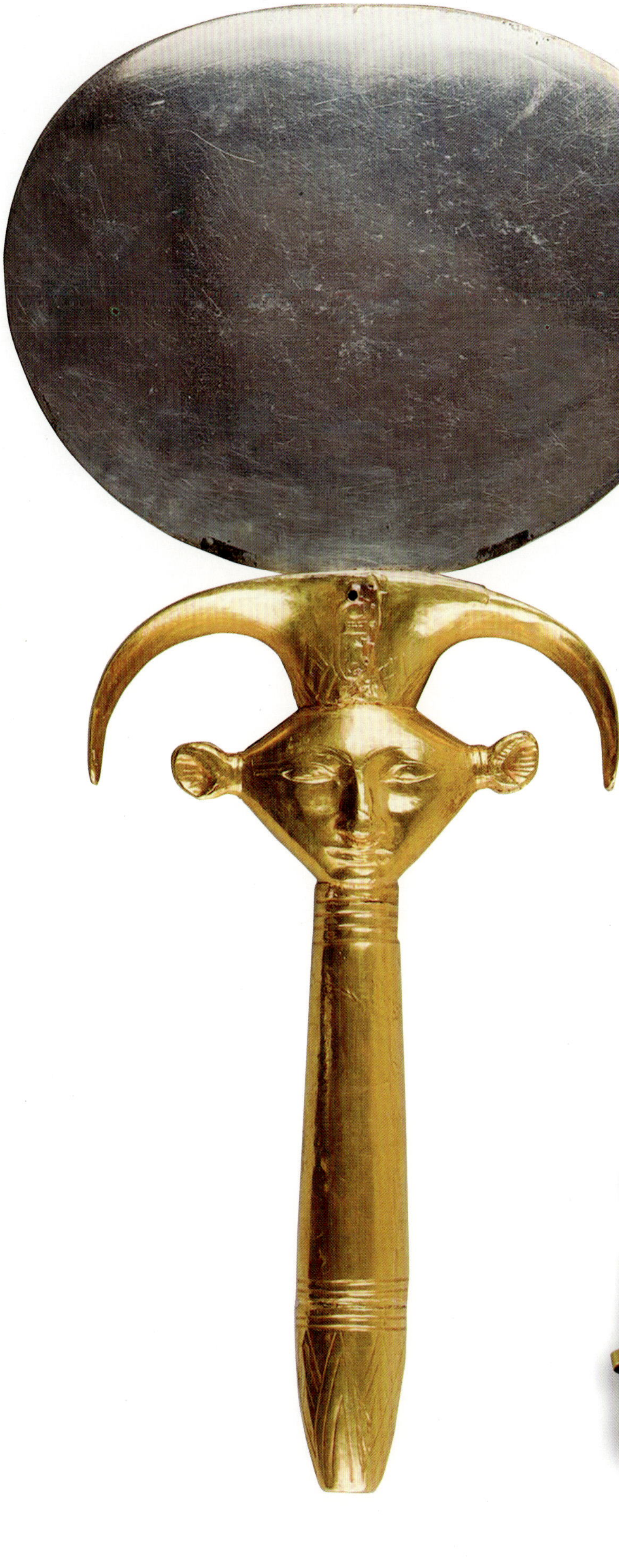

The harem of King Thutmose III (about 1479–1425 B.C.) included three foreign-born wives: Menhet, Menwi, and Merti. Villagers living near Luxor found their tomb in 1916 and sold some of its contents, including these items.

A mirror (left) displays the king's cartouche above a cow's head, likely symbolizing the goddess Hathor.

A diadem of gold (opposite) is decorated with two gazelle heads, as well as rosettes of glass and carnelian.

A bracelet of gold, carnelian, lapis lazuli, and glass (below) is adorned with cats, animals that often represented the goddess Bastet.

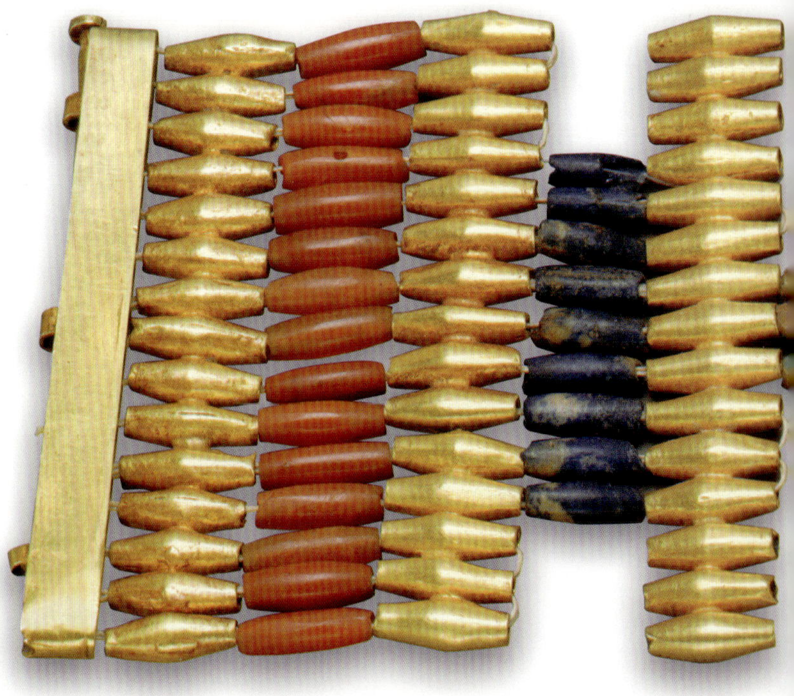

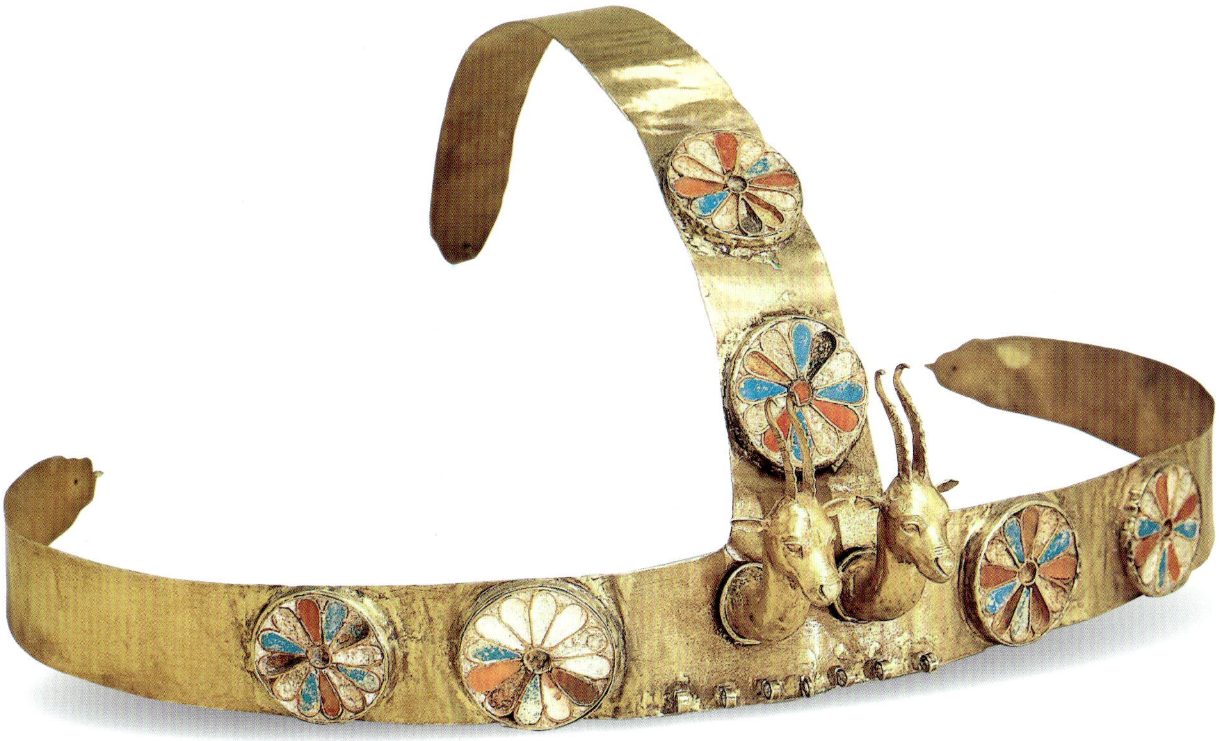

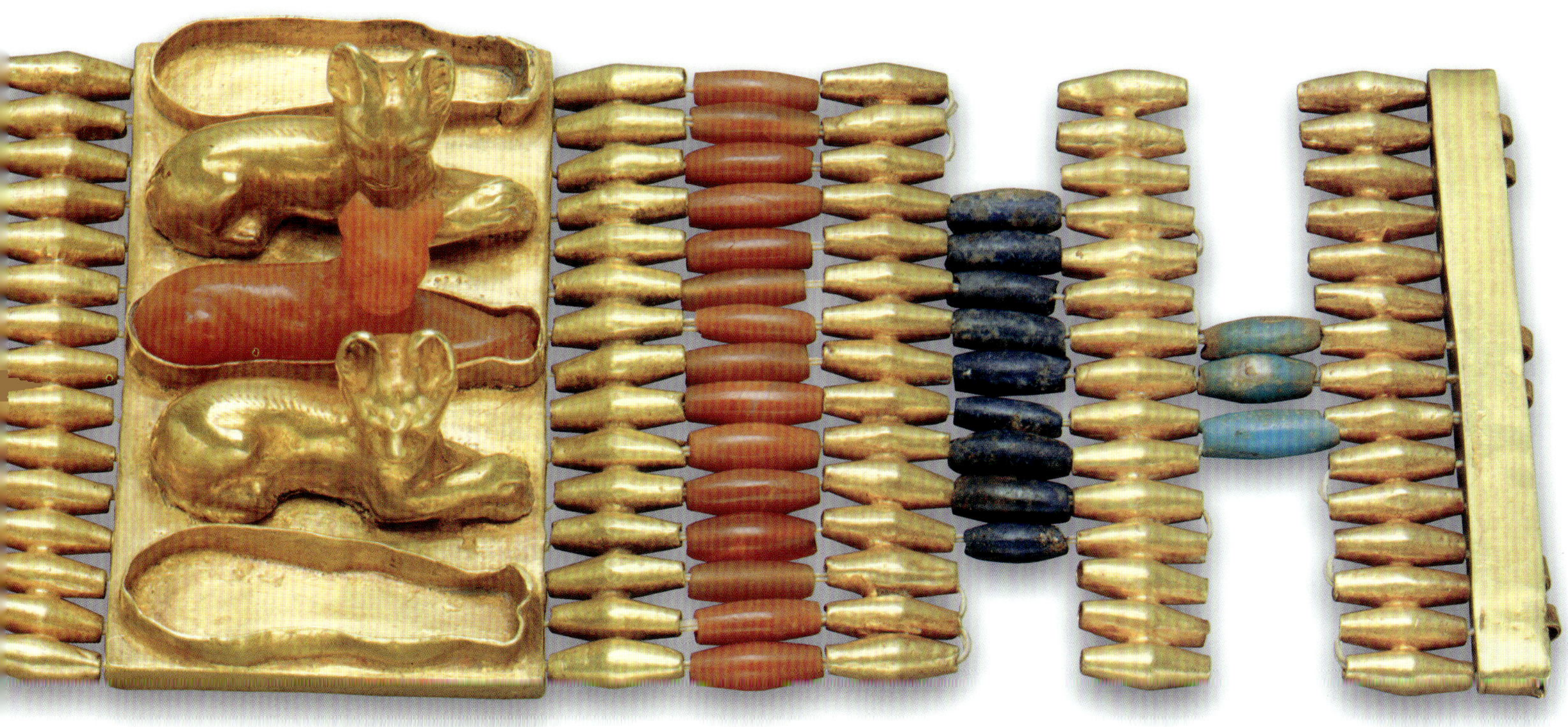

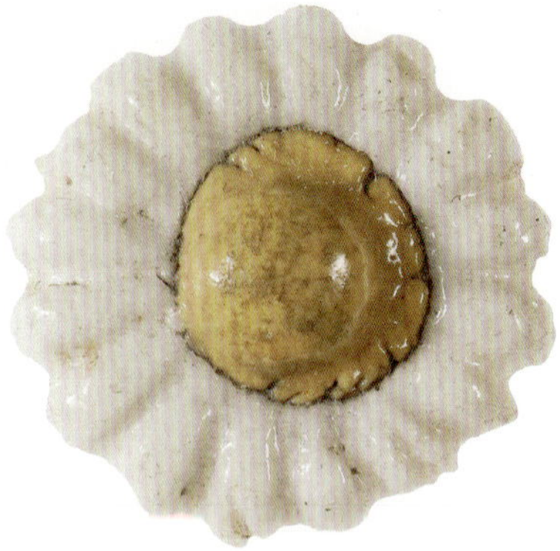

Daisy

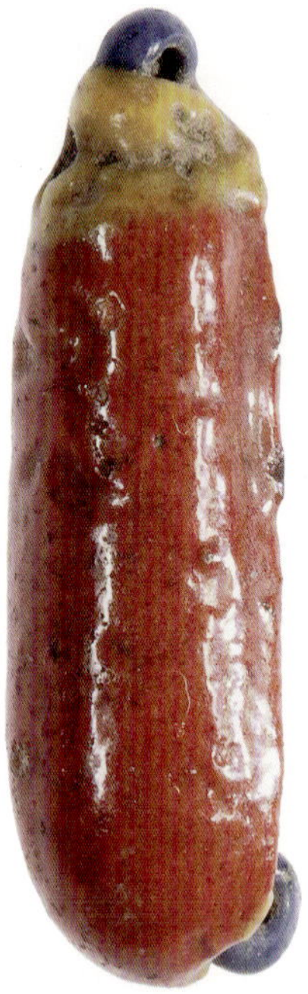

Date

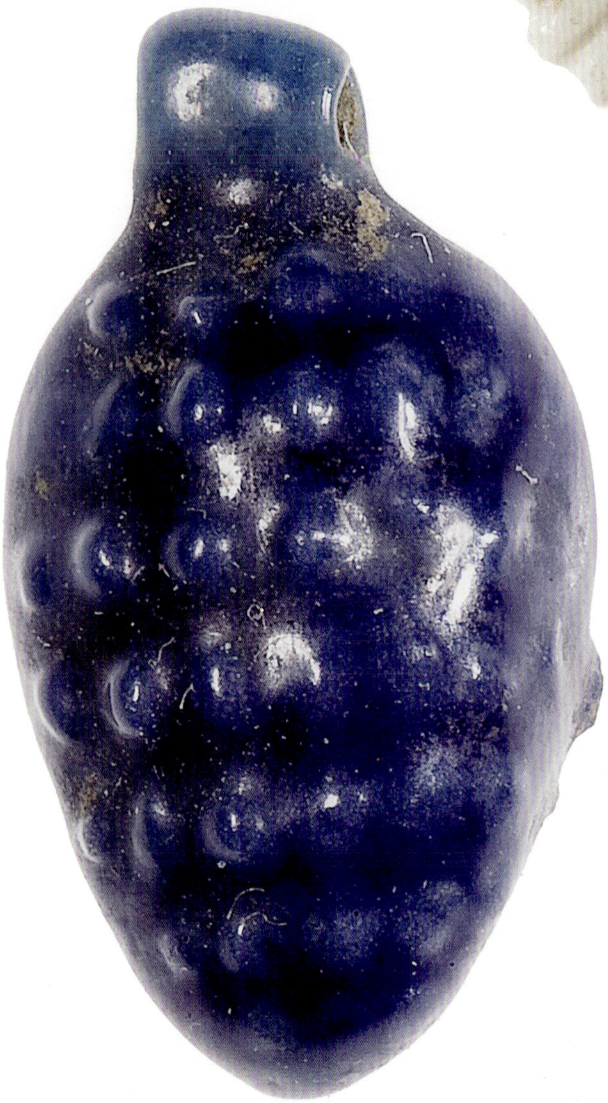

Grapes

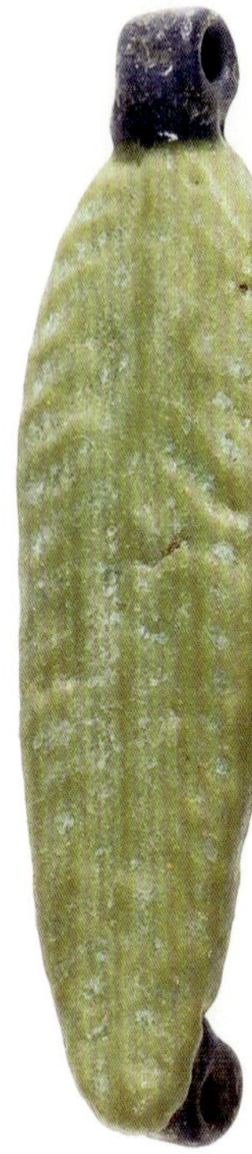

Leaf

To celebrate his 30th year on the throne, King Amenhotep III (about 1390–1353 B.C.) constructed a festival city across the Nile from Waset, the modern city of Luxor. Buildings included palaces, offices, and ceremonial structures, as well as housing for the many artisans and servants involved in the endeavor.

These beads and pendants were uncovered in the ruins of one of the palaces, at the archaeological site called Malqata. Made from a ceramic called faience, they all measure less than an inch (2.5 cm) in diameter.

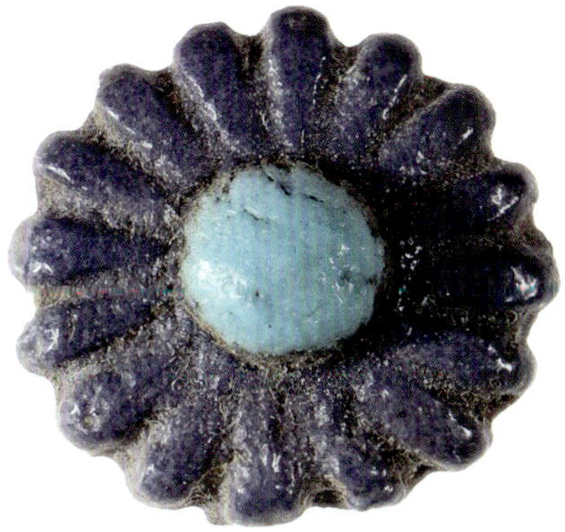

Daisy

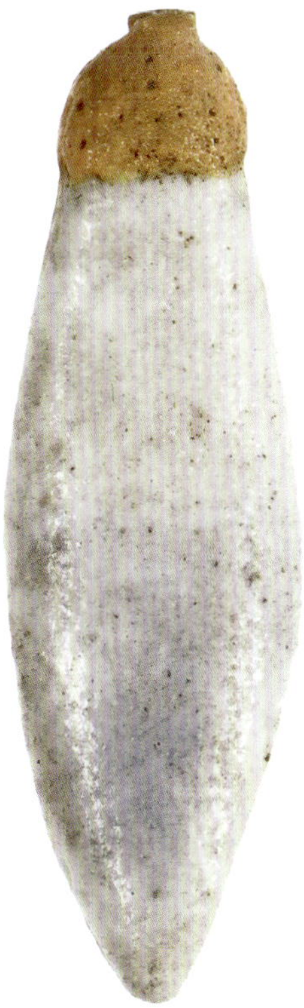

Lotus petal

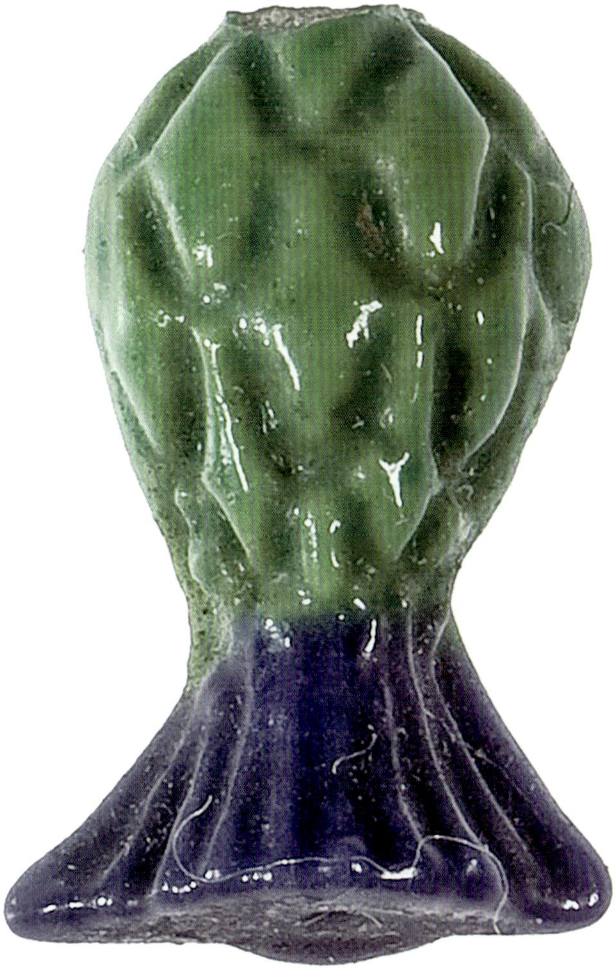

Cornflower

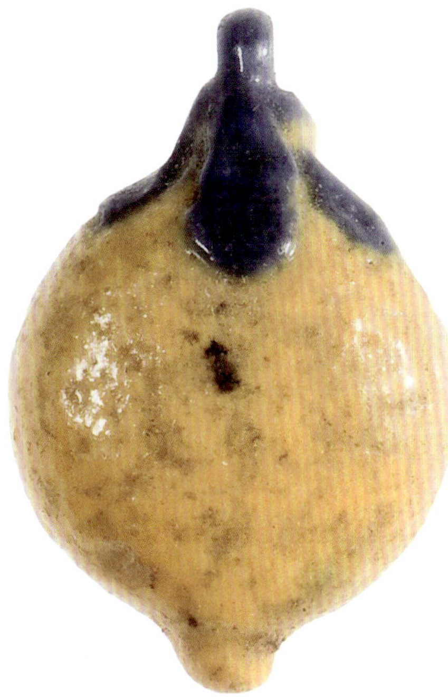

Persea fruit

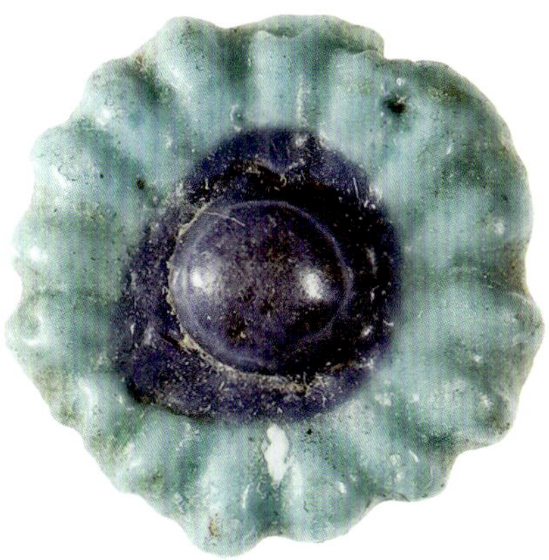

Daisy

An Improbable Path to Fame

HOWARD CARTER FIRST WENT to Egypt as an artist, not an archaeologist. Growing up in Norfolk, England, he was inspired by his father, an *Illustrated London News* artist. Carter's talent soon came to the attention of a well-connected neighbor. When he was 17, the neighbor introduced him to Egyptologist Percy Newberry, who in 1891 hired Carter to copy tomb paintings at Beni Hasan.

Carter would move on to other sites, including Tell el-Amarna. There he worked for the legendary William Matthew Flinders Petrie, whose insistence on collecting archaeological evidence with scientific rigor surely had an impact.

In 1907, Carter began working for Lord Carnarvon, a wealthy patron of archaeology in Egypt. That same year, the team of American businessman Theodore Davis uncovered a cache of embalming objects, some bearing the name Tutankhamun. But after finding a looted burial nearby, Davis declared, "I fear the Valley of the Tombs is now exhausted."

Carter and Carnarvon would famously prove him wrong, discovering the treasure-filled tomb of the teenage pharaoh in November 1922. Carter would spend the next decade meticulously cataloging every artifact—coffins (below) and all. Petrie himself could not have done better.

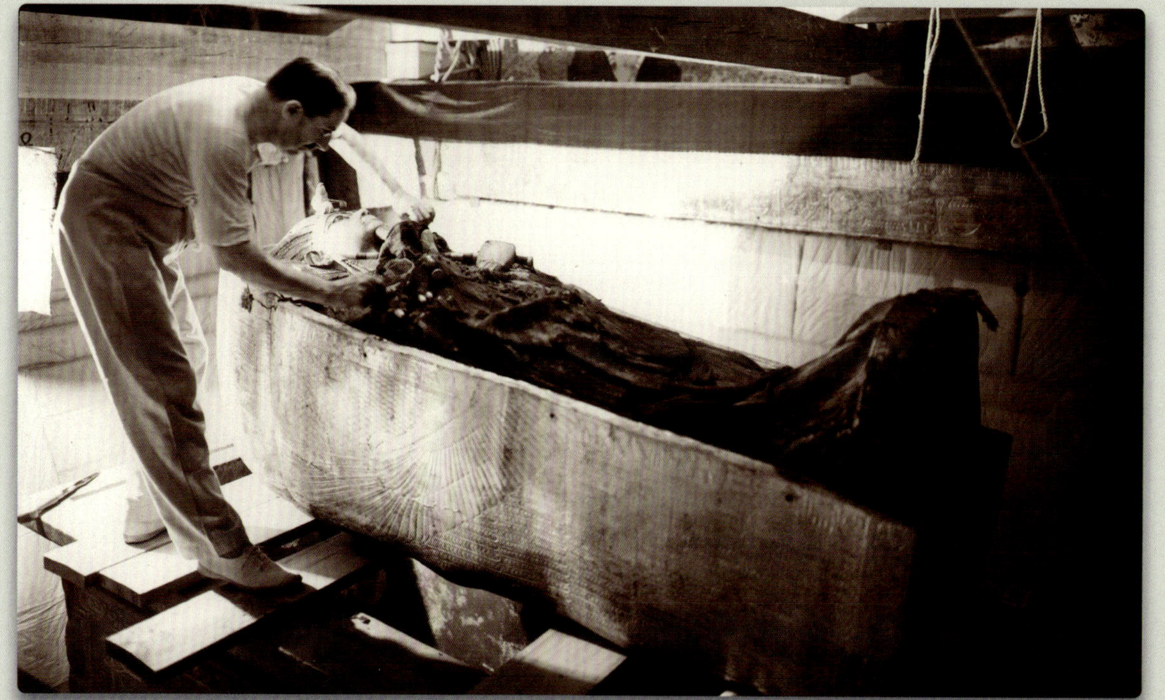

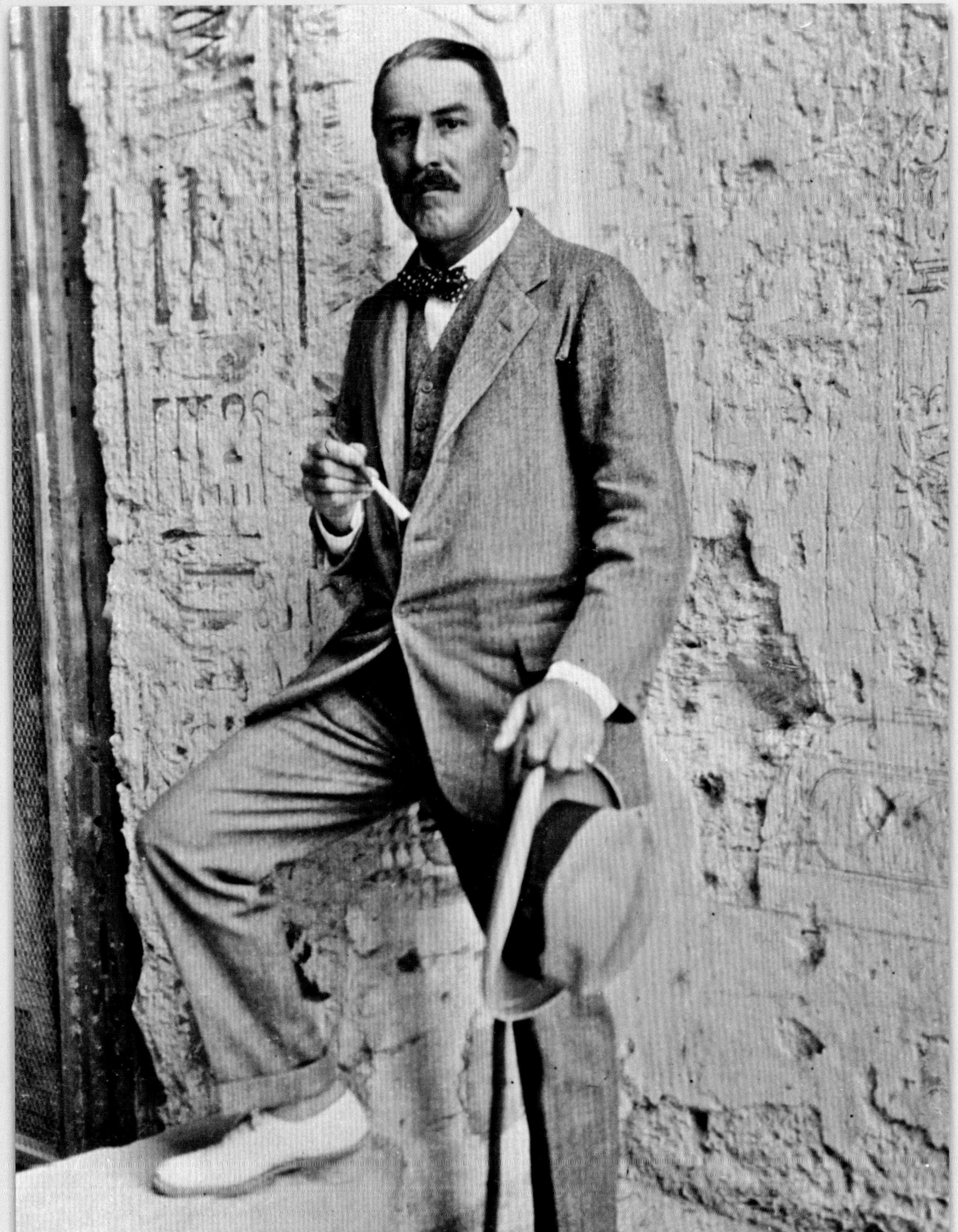

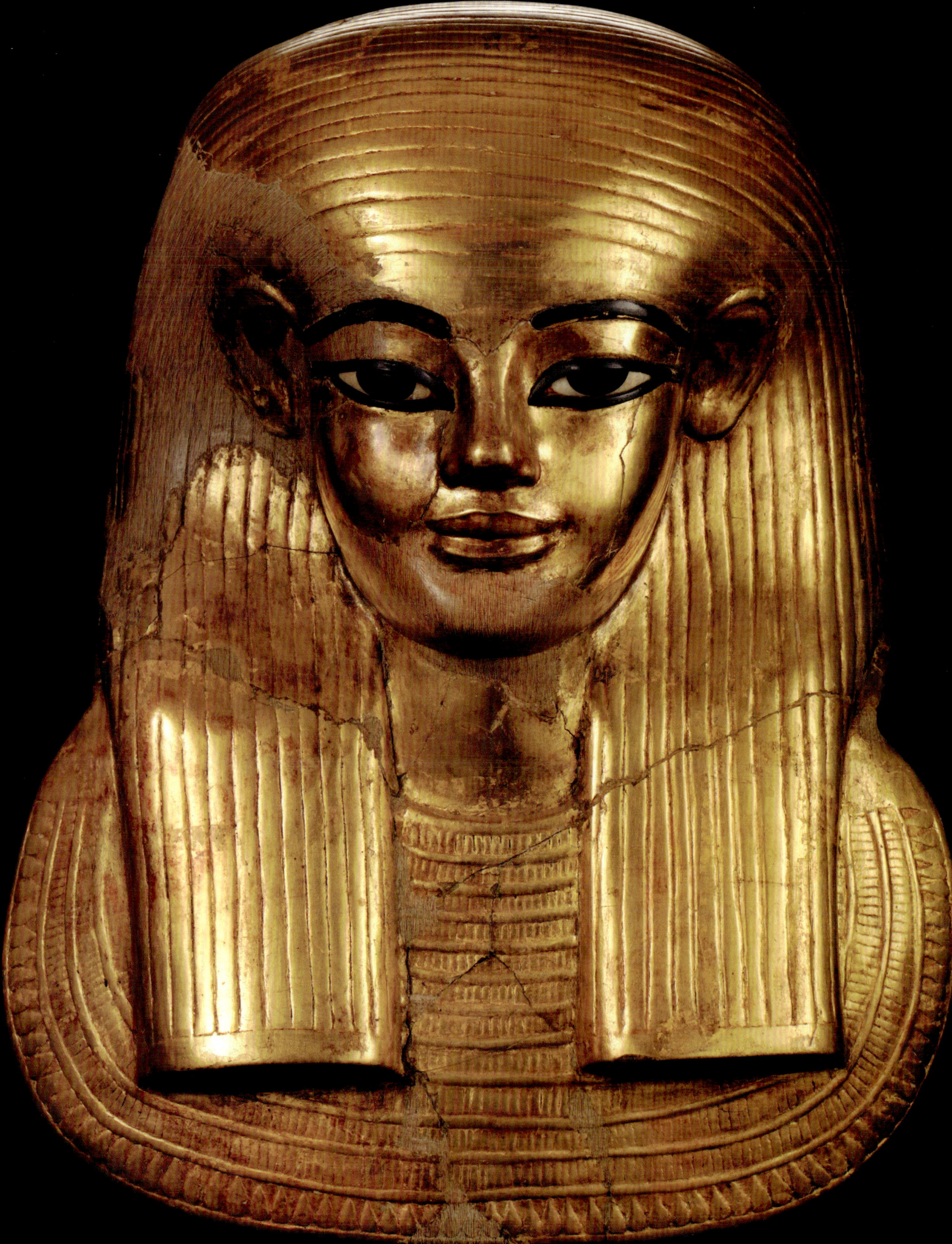

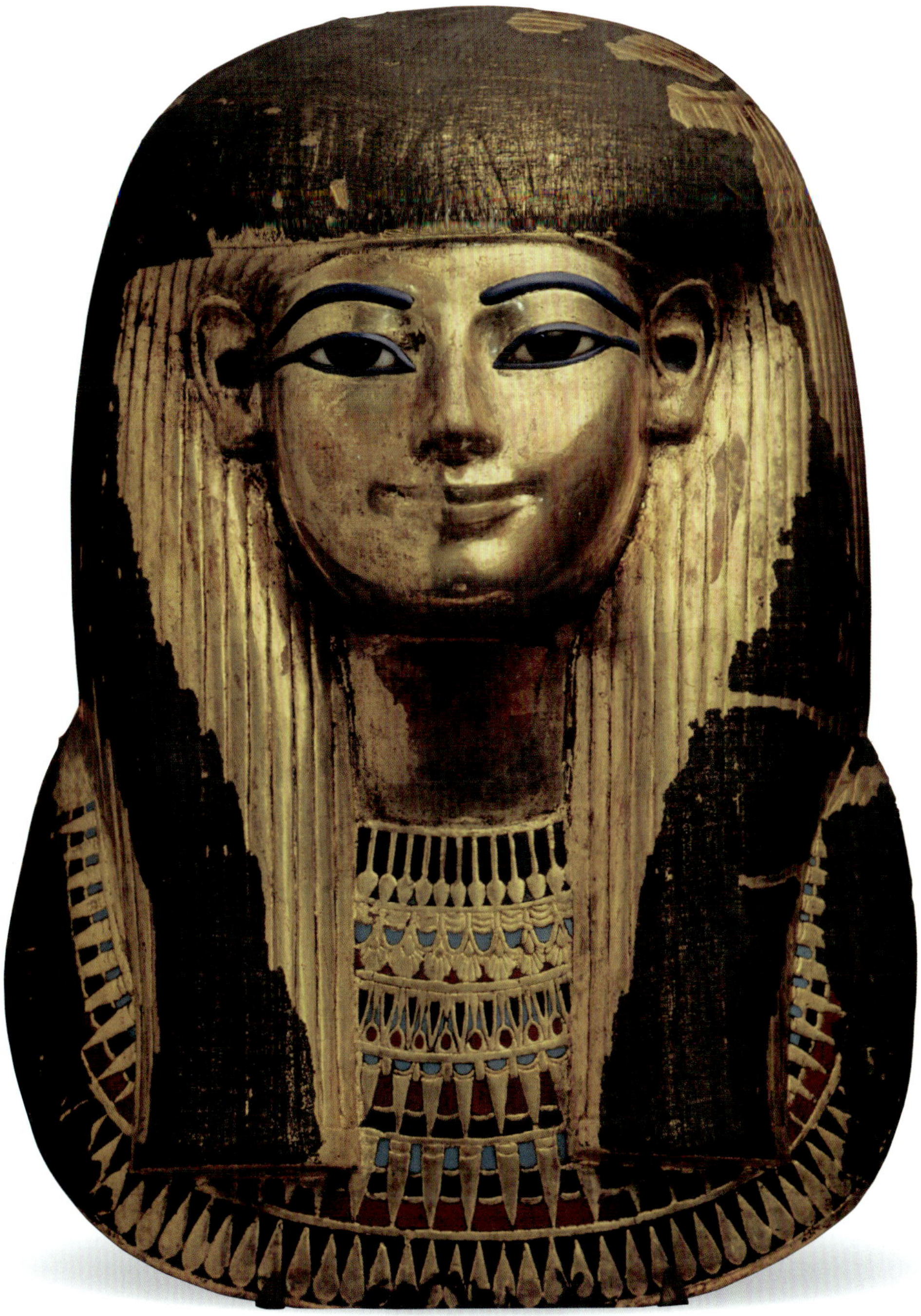

Yuya (opposite) and Tuyu (above), the in-laws of King Amenhotep III, were laid to rest wearing these masks made of linen and plaster. At the time of burial, a dark, gauzy veil was draped over Tuyu's mask. Parts of it are now stuck to the gilded surface.

The couple seems to have benefited from their royal connections even after death. Wonderfully skilled embalmers prepared their remains for the afterlife. Their mummies are still surprisingly well preserved, some 3,400 years after their burial.

DIGGING DEEPER

Everywhere the Glint of Gold

FOR DECADES, King Tutankhamun's personal effects resided on the second floor of the Egyptian Museum in Cairo. Large glass cases in open galleries held the gilded chariots and the once nested burial shrines that still smelled of cedar some 3,350 years after they had been created. Smaller vitrines held everything from ornate thrones and fully rigged model boats to pairs of sandals and a petrified piece of bread in a loosely woven basket.

In a closed side room always crowded with visitors, cases held the stunning pieces of gold—bracelets and pendants inlaid with colorful glass and stones, Tut's innermost mummiform coffin, and the mask (right) that covered the young pharaoh's head and shoulders.

During the Arab Spring protests in neighboring Tahrir Square in early 2011, the theft of several of King Tut's artifacts after a museum break-in highlighted the treasures' vulnerability. But by then, a new home was already under construction—the Grand Egyptian Museum on the Giza plateau. There, on the second floor, rooms were built to display all of Tutankhamun's funerary goods—more than 5,000 total—reuniting them for the first time since they were removed from his tomb.

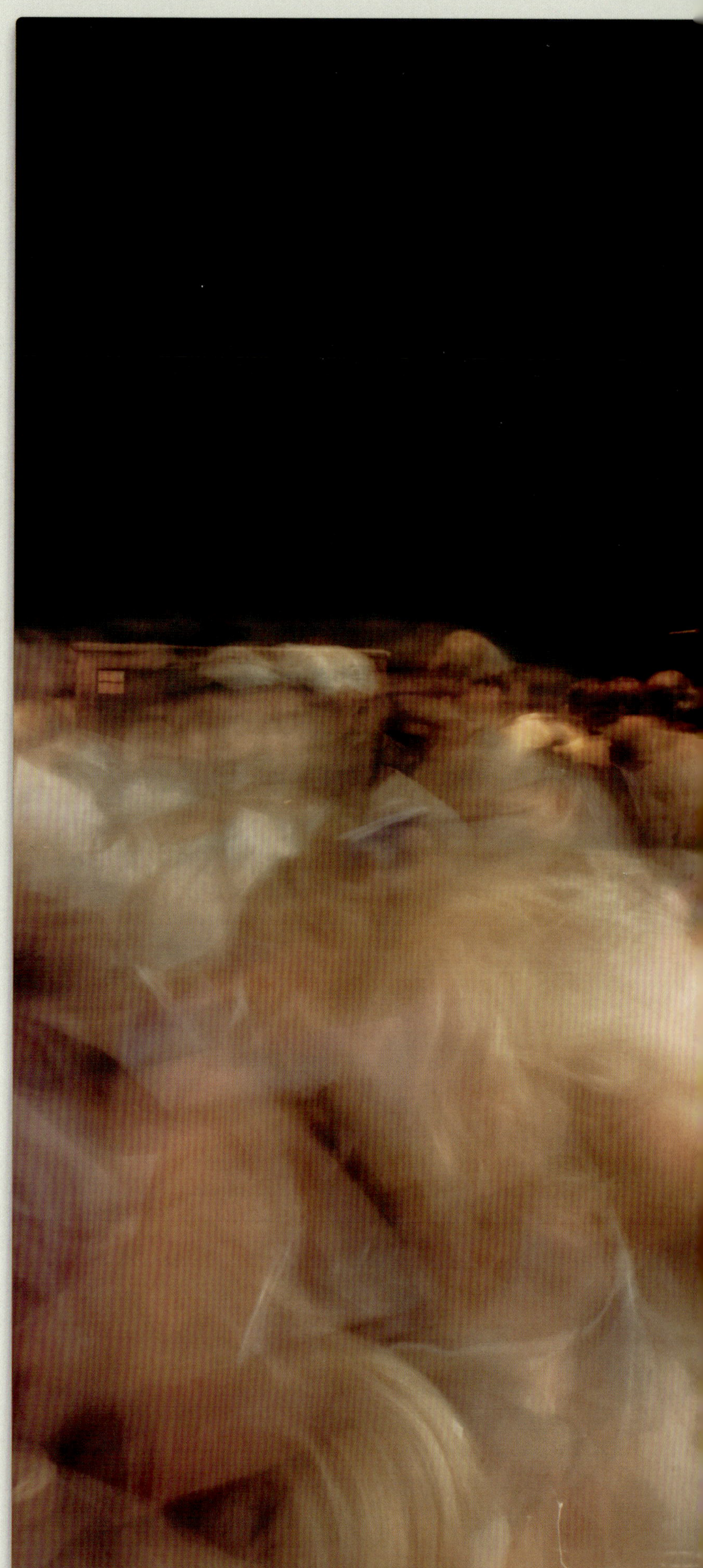

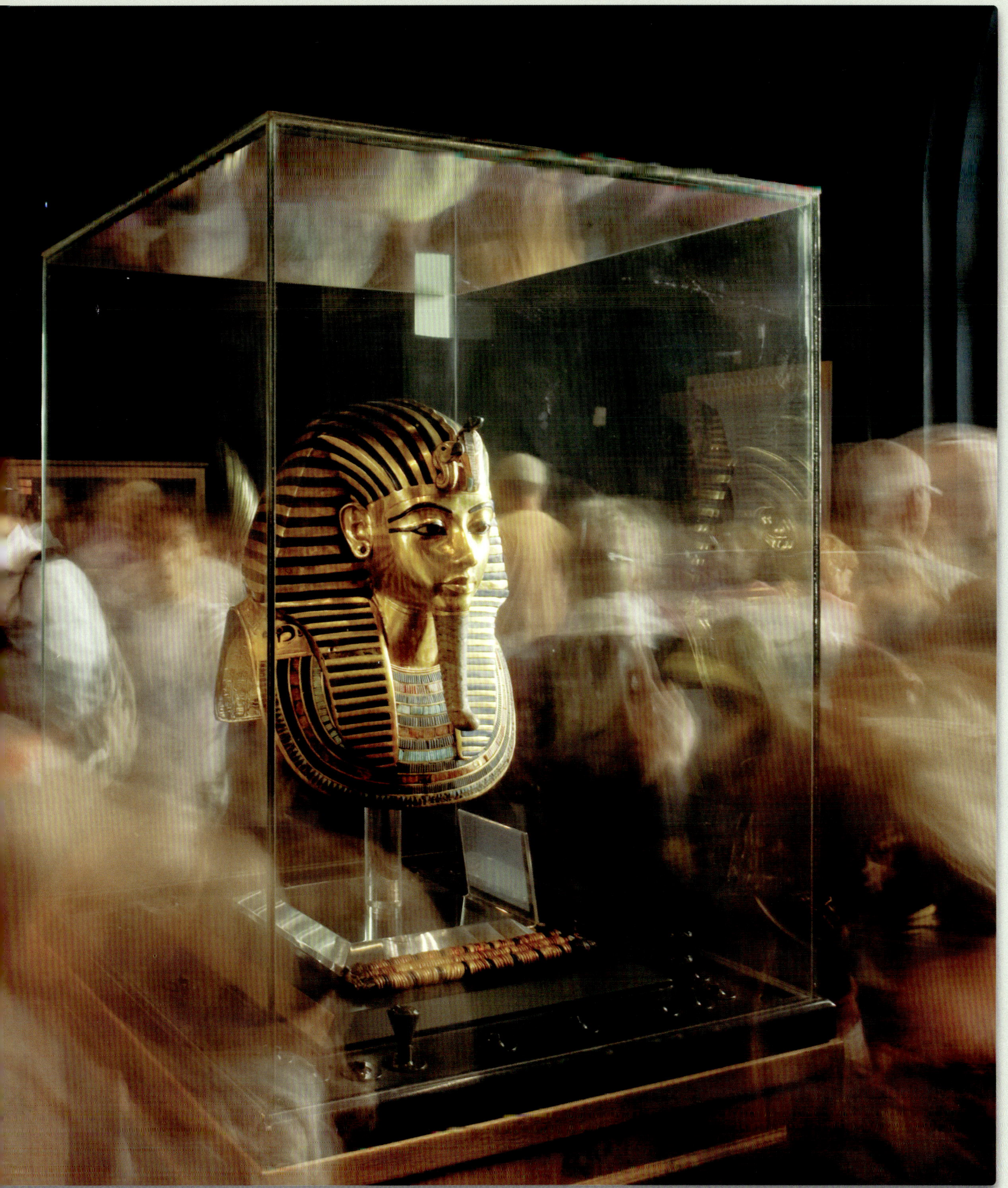

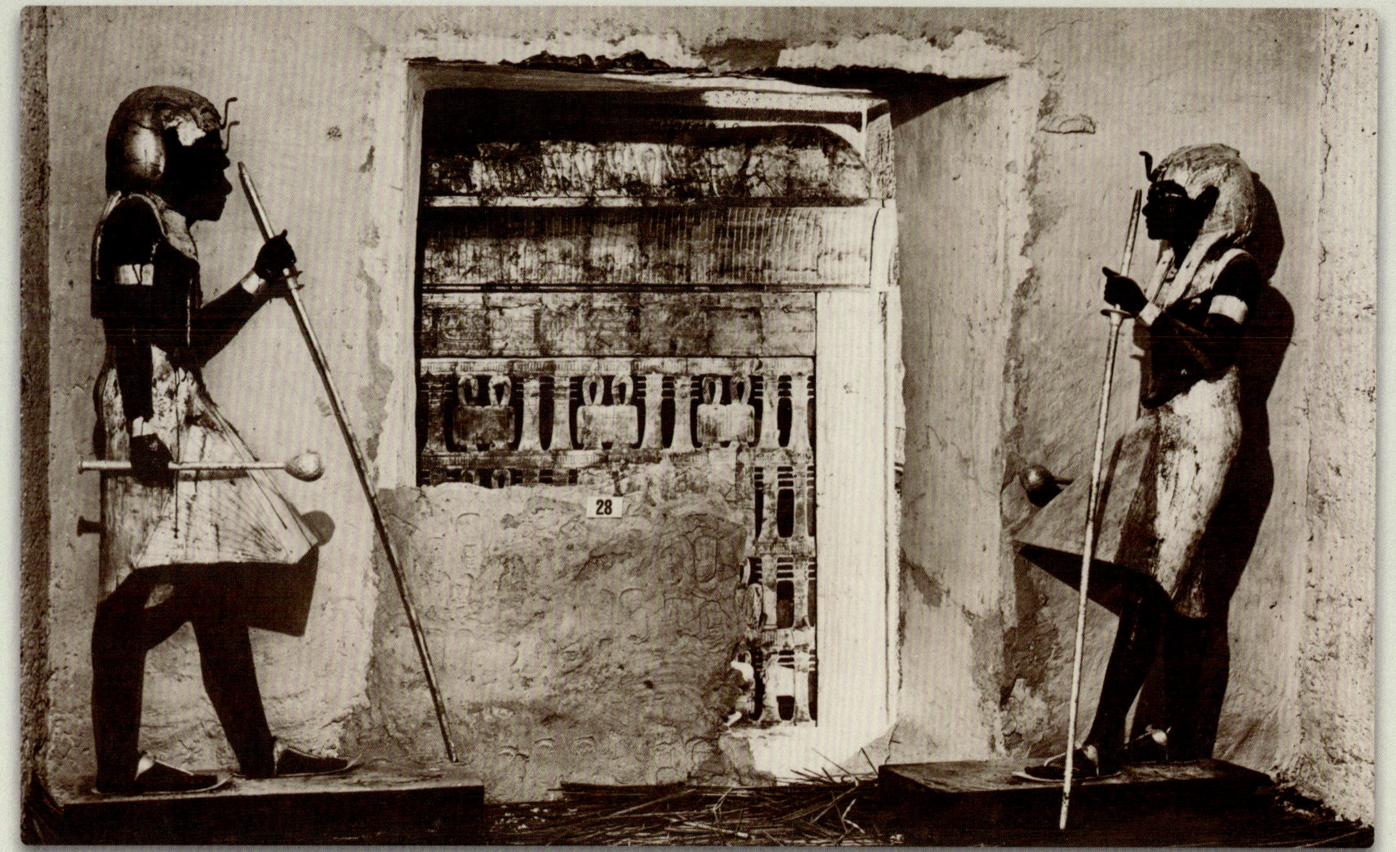

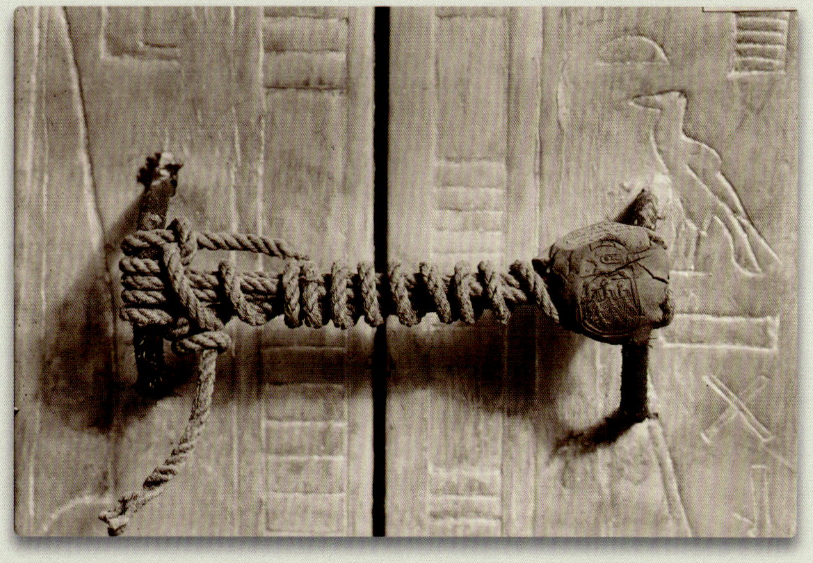

THE MOMENT OF DISCOVERY

When Howard Carter broke through the sealed doorway into King Tut's burial chamber, the first thing he saw was one of four nested funerary shrines (above). Statues of Tut's *ka*, or spiritual essence, stood guard.

The outermost shrine had been opened in antiquity. But the next one had remained closed for 3,200 years. An intact seal (left) bore an official imprint: a jackal above nine bows that symbolized the enemies of Egypt.

Gilded reliefs such as this one (opposite) cover the shrines inside and out. They bear the king's cartouches as well as scenes and texts to assist him after death.

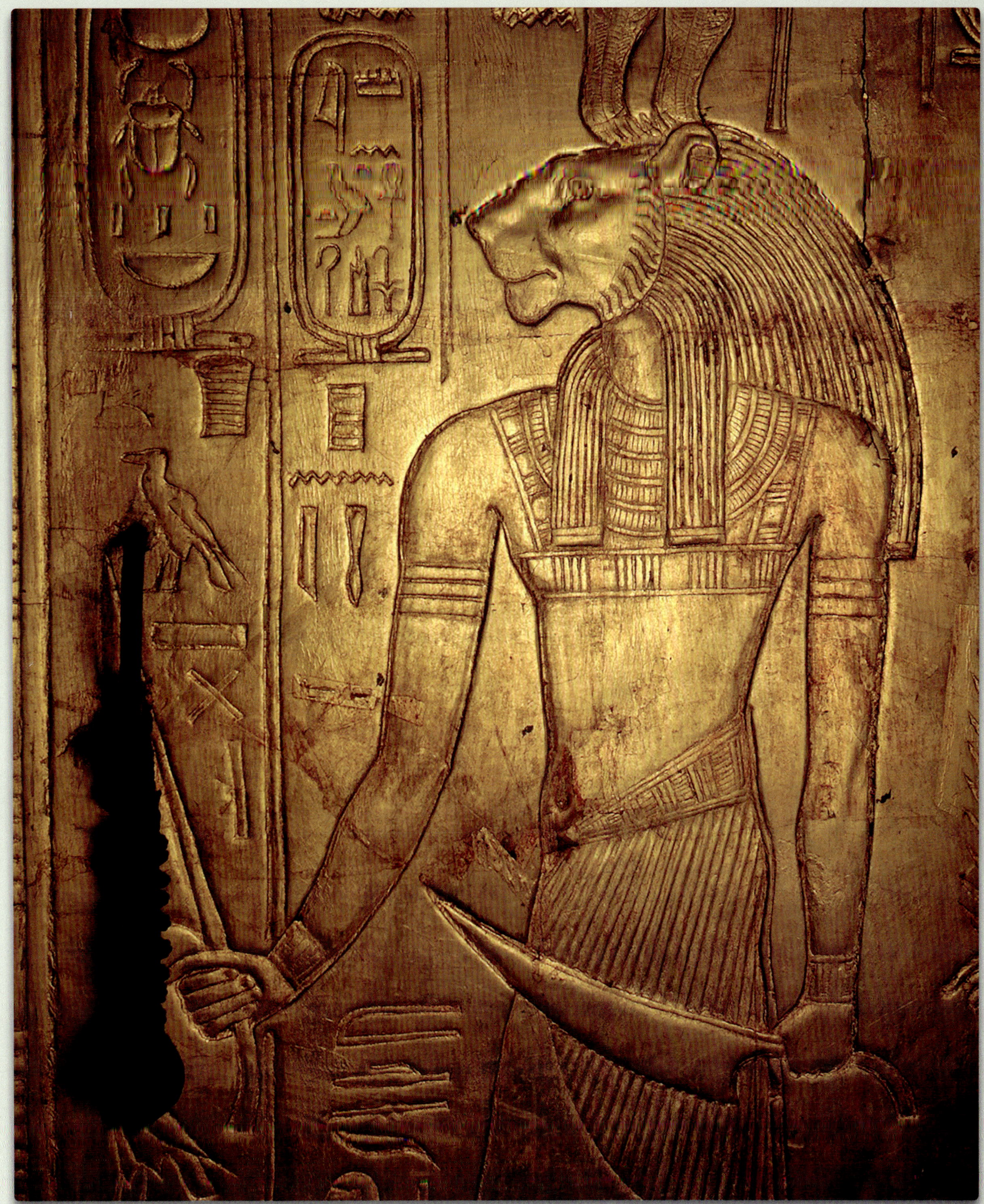

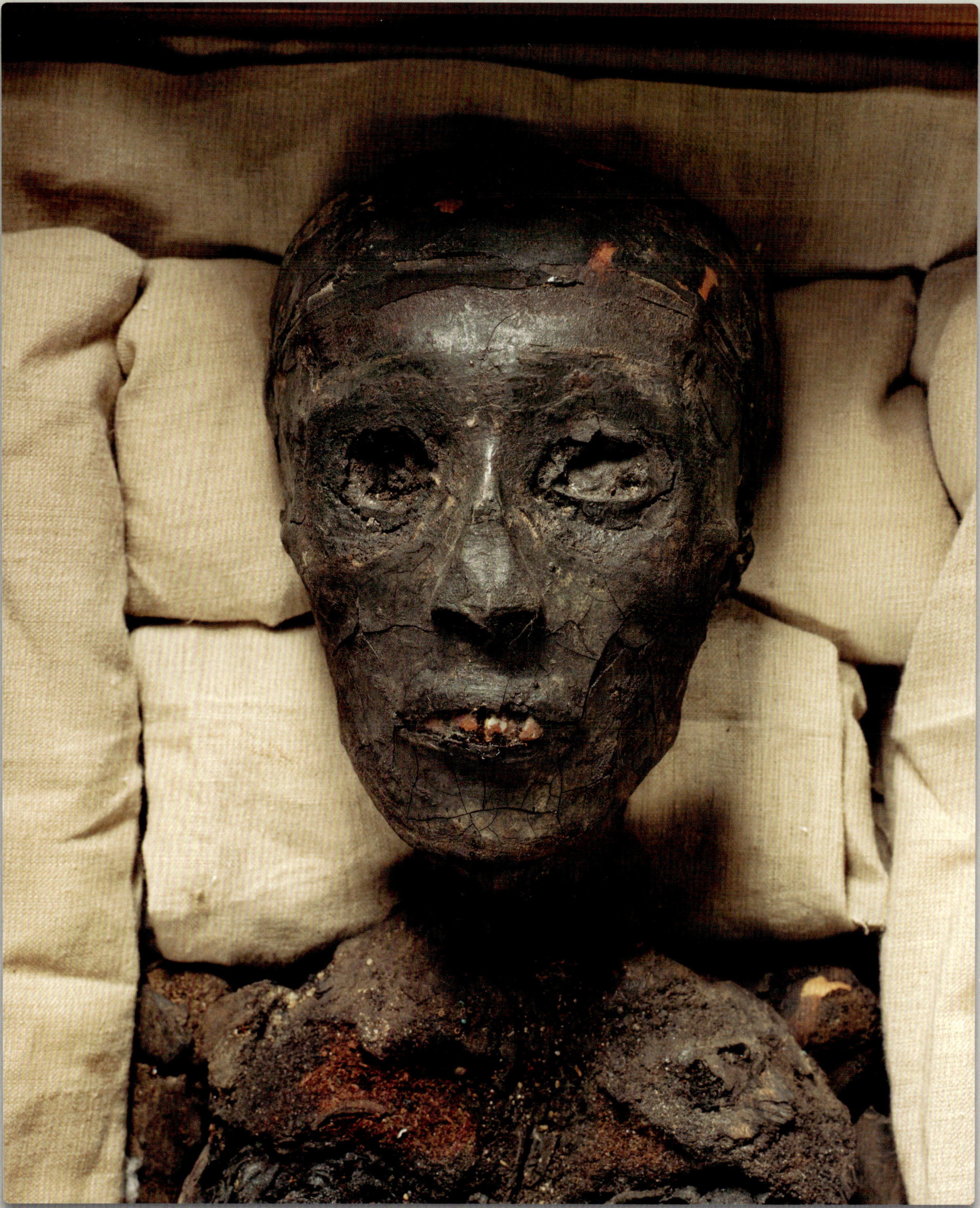

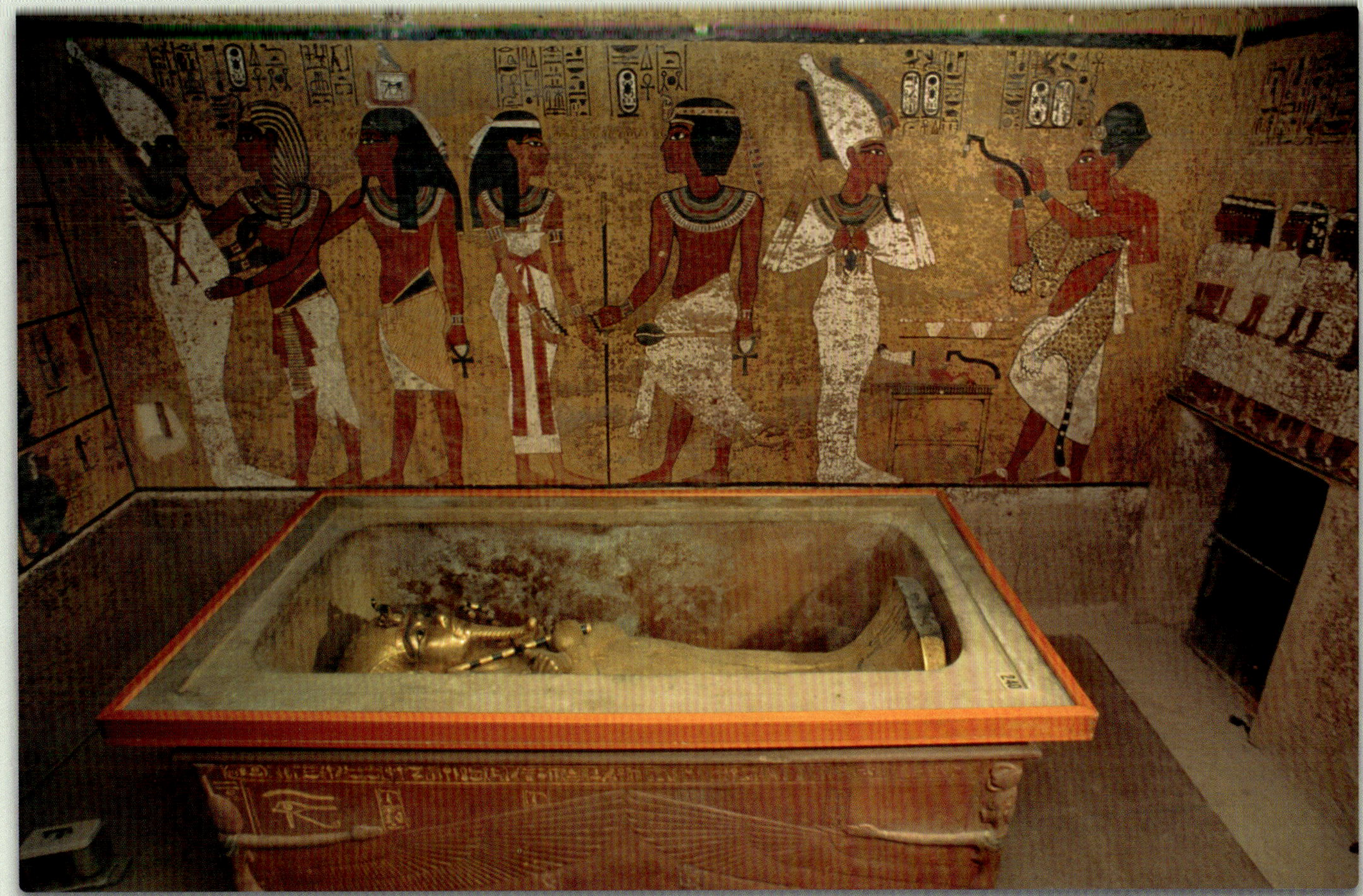

THE ROYAL BURIAL

Five-foot-six (1.7 m) and slightly built, King Tut (opposite) was only 19 when he died. One theory about his death suggests that he broke his left leg above the knee, and a lethal infection set in.

In the burial chamber (above), Tut's stone sarcophagus holds one of his three coffins—this one of gilded cedar. Scenes painted on the chamber walls were meant to help the teenager on his dangerous journey to the afterlife.

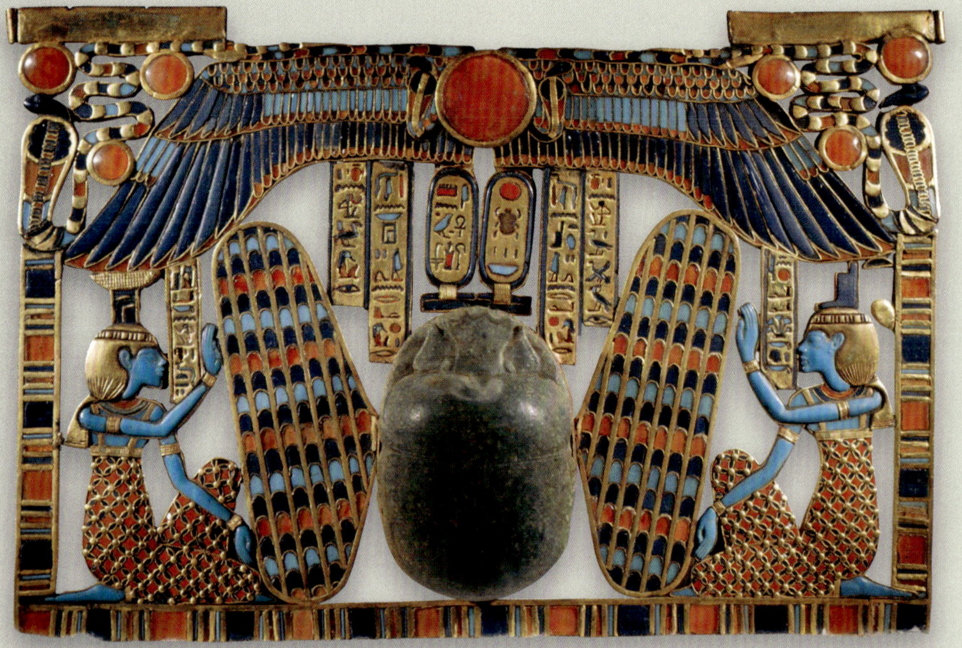

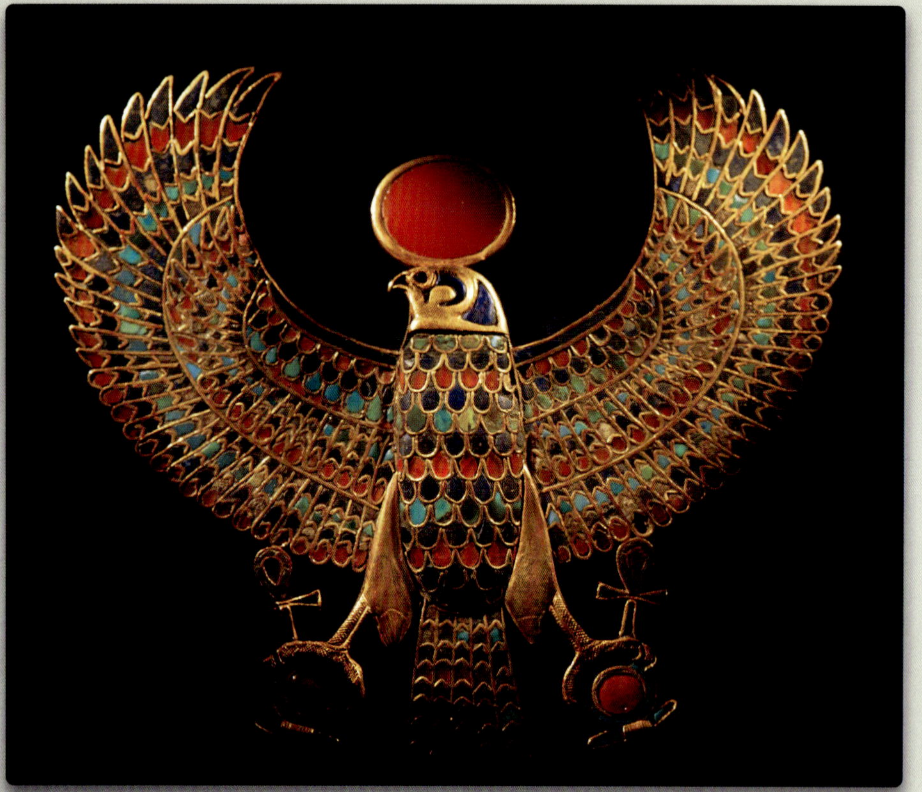

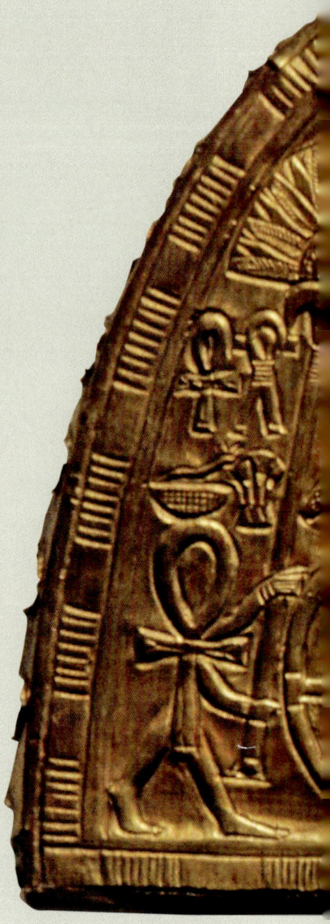

TUT'S BLING

The teenage pharaoh took a fortune in jewelry to the next life. Not only was his mummy decked out with astonishing pieces, but others were tucked away in chests. One pendant (top left) shows the goddesses Isis and Nephthys flanking a scarab. Another (bottom left) takes the shape of a falcon whose claws clutch the hieroglyphs for eternity.

The gilded base of a fan (right) bears a visual pun: Tut is hunting an ostrich, the kind of bird whose plumes once crowned this artifact.

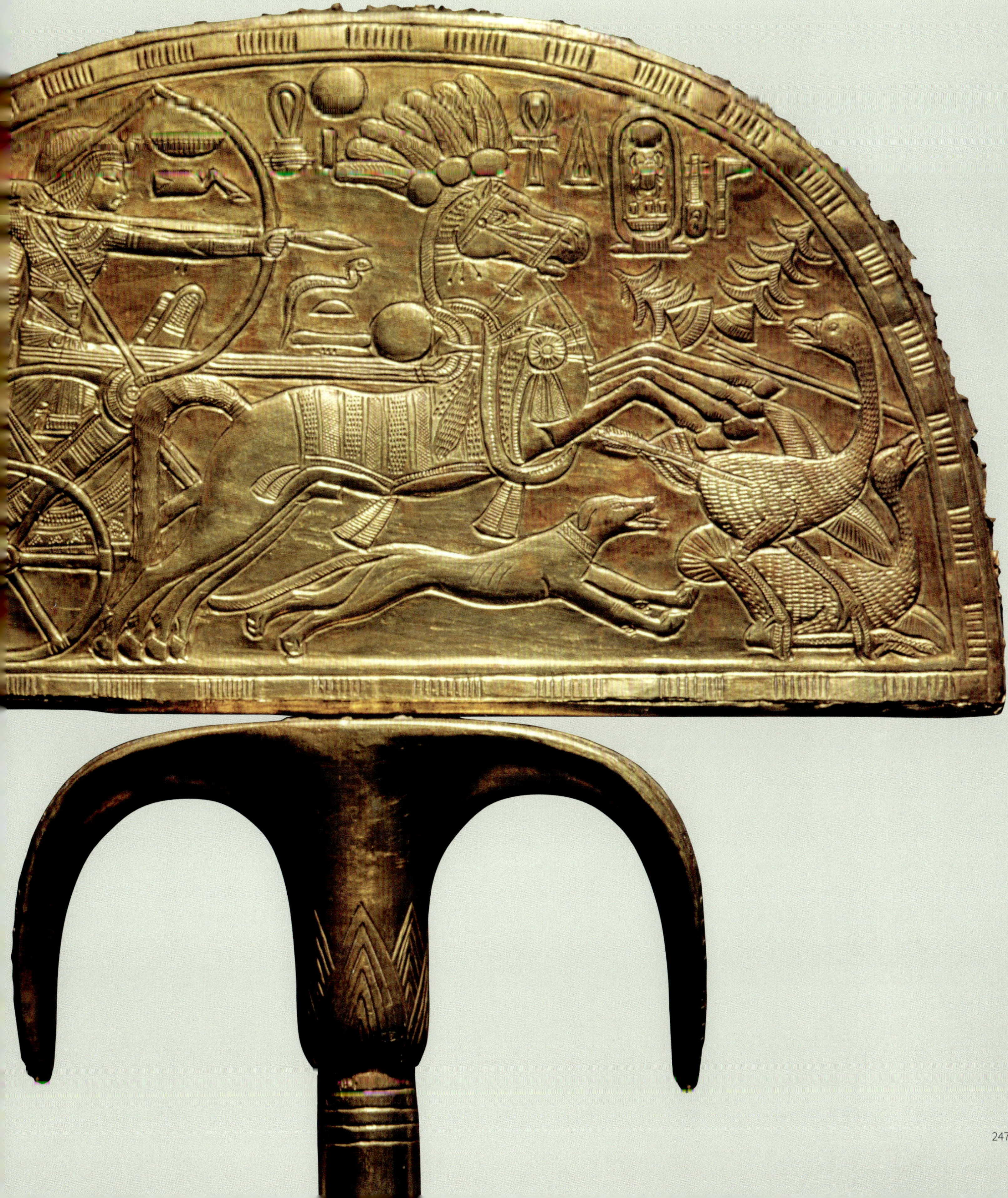

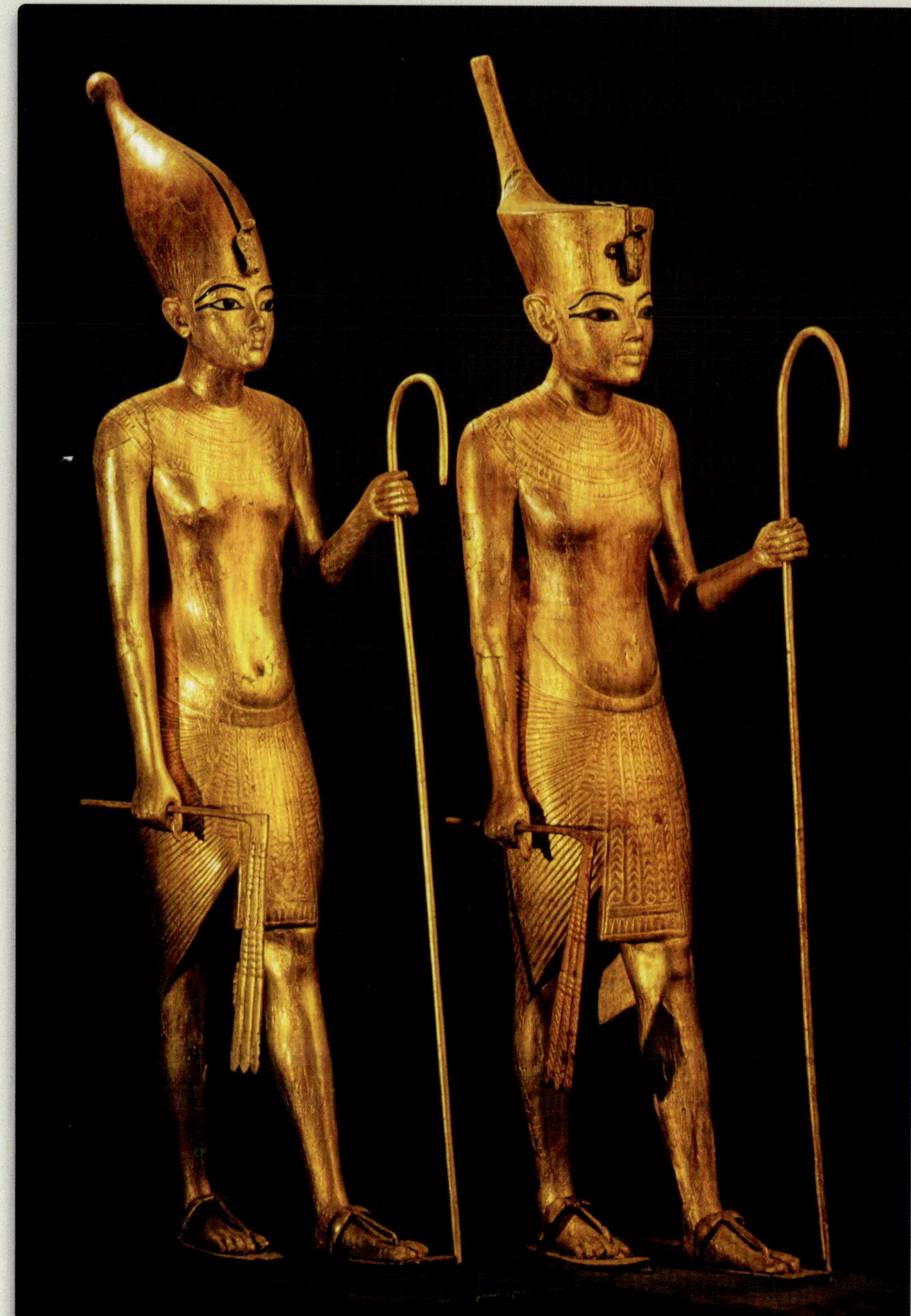

ROYAL PORTRAITS

Gilded wooden figures from King Tut's tomb (above) show the pharaoh wearing crowns from the two lands that Egypt's earliest rulers united: the tall, conical crown of the south and the flatter crown of the north.

The luminous, inlaid back of a chair (opposite) depicts Tutankhamun with his wife, Ankhesenamun, who is applying perfumed oil to his arm.

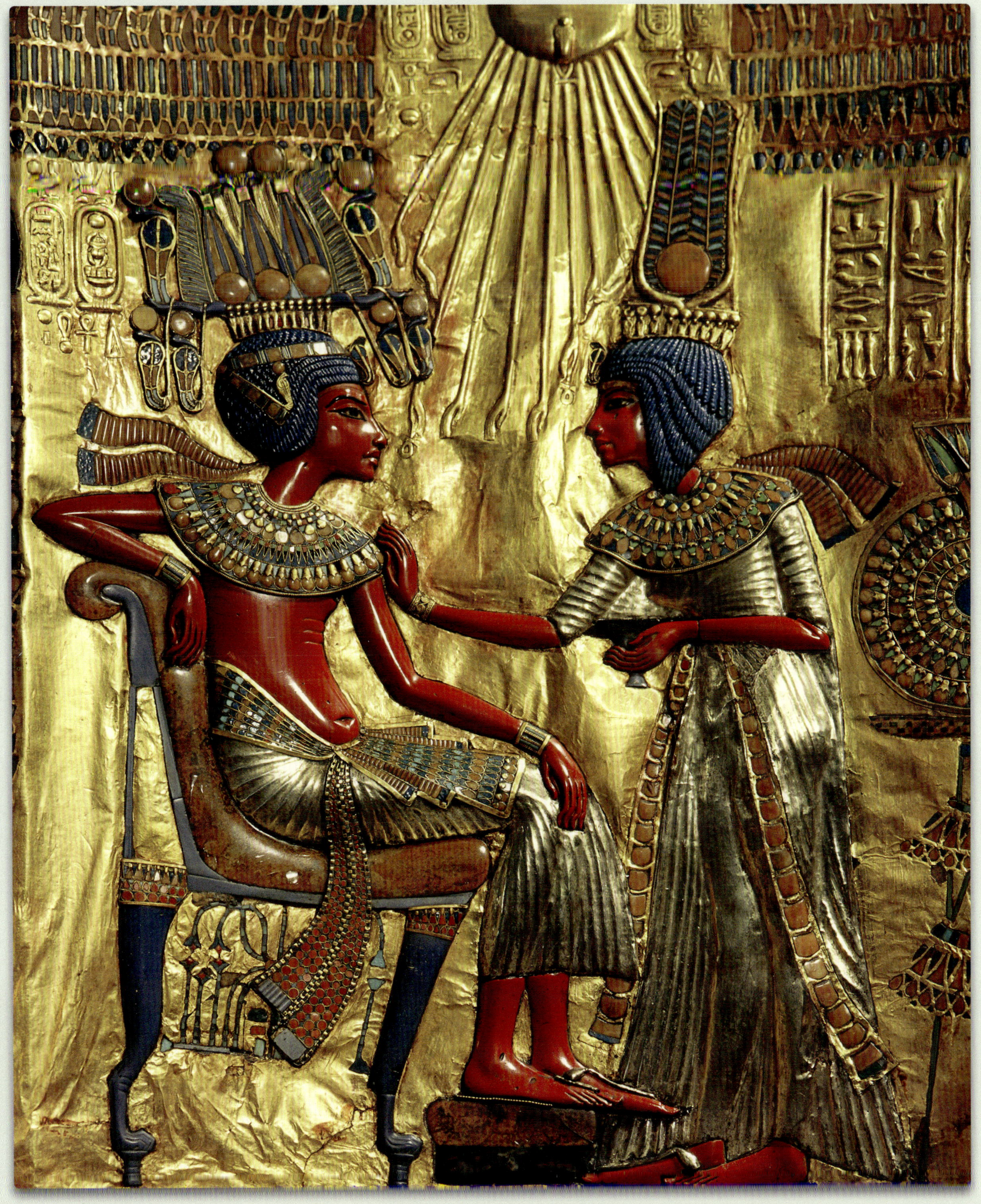

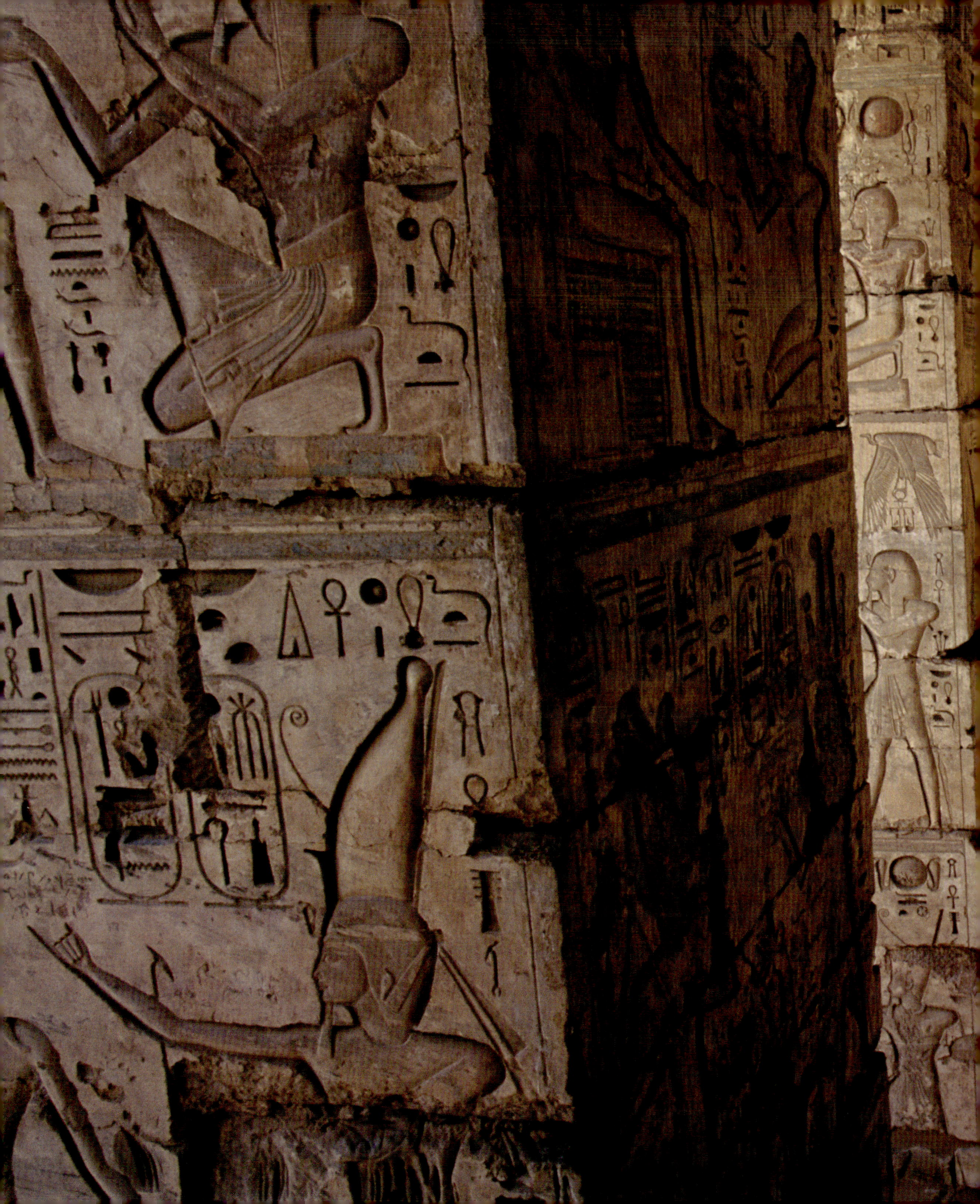

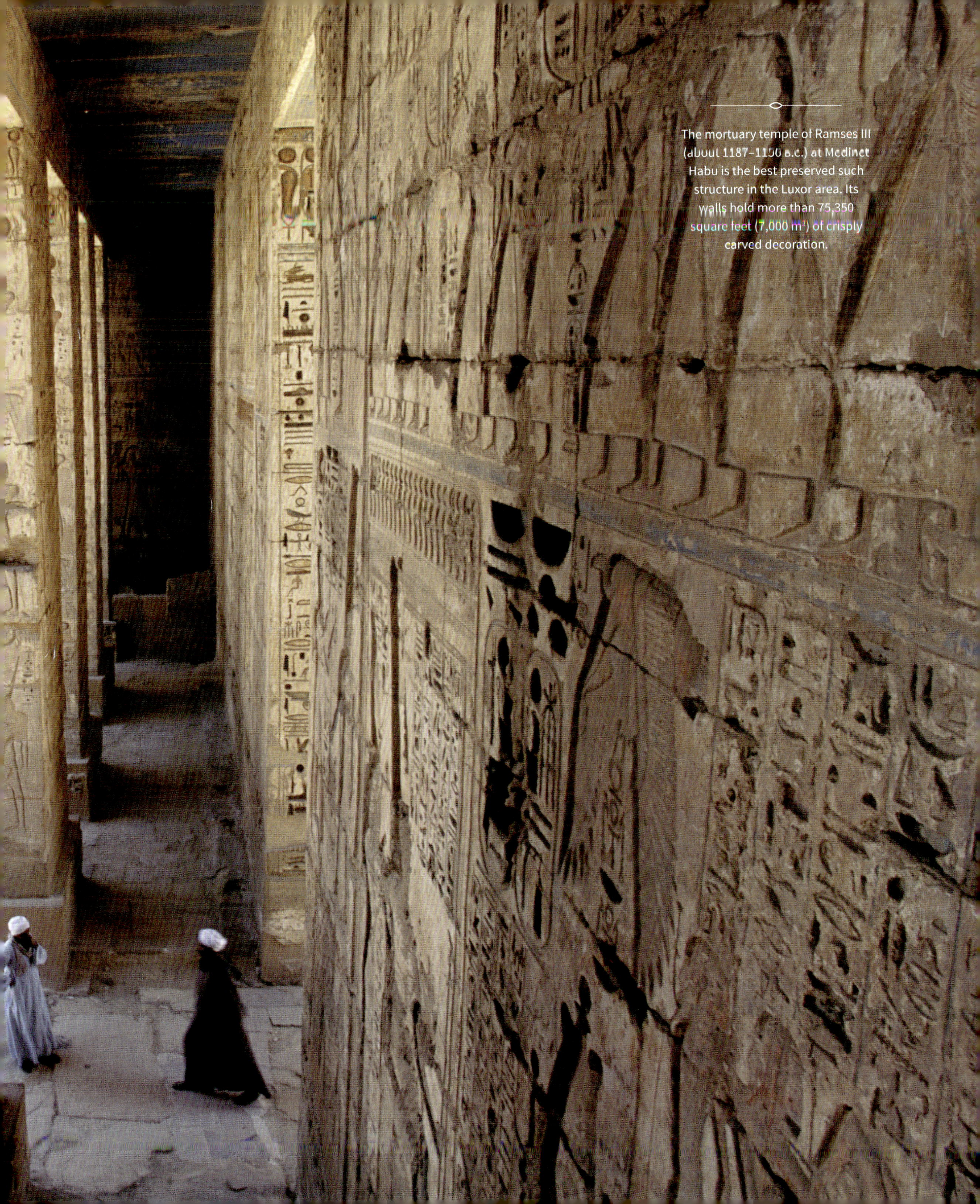

The mortuary temple of Ramses III (about 1187–1156 B.C.) at Medinet Habu is the best preserved such structure in the Luxor area. Its walls hold more than 75,350 square feet (7,000 m^2) of crisply carved decoration.

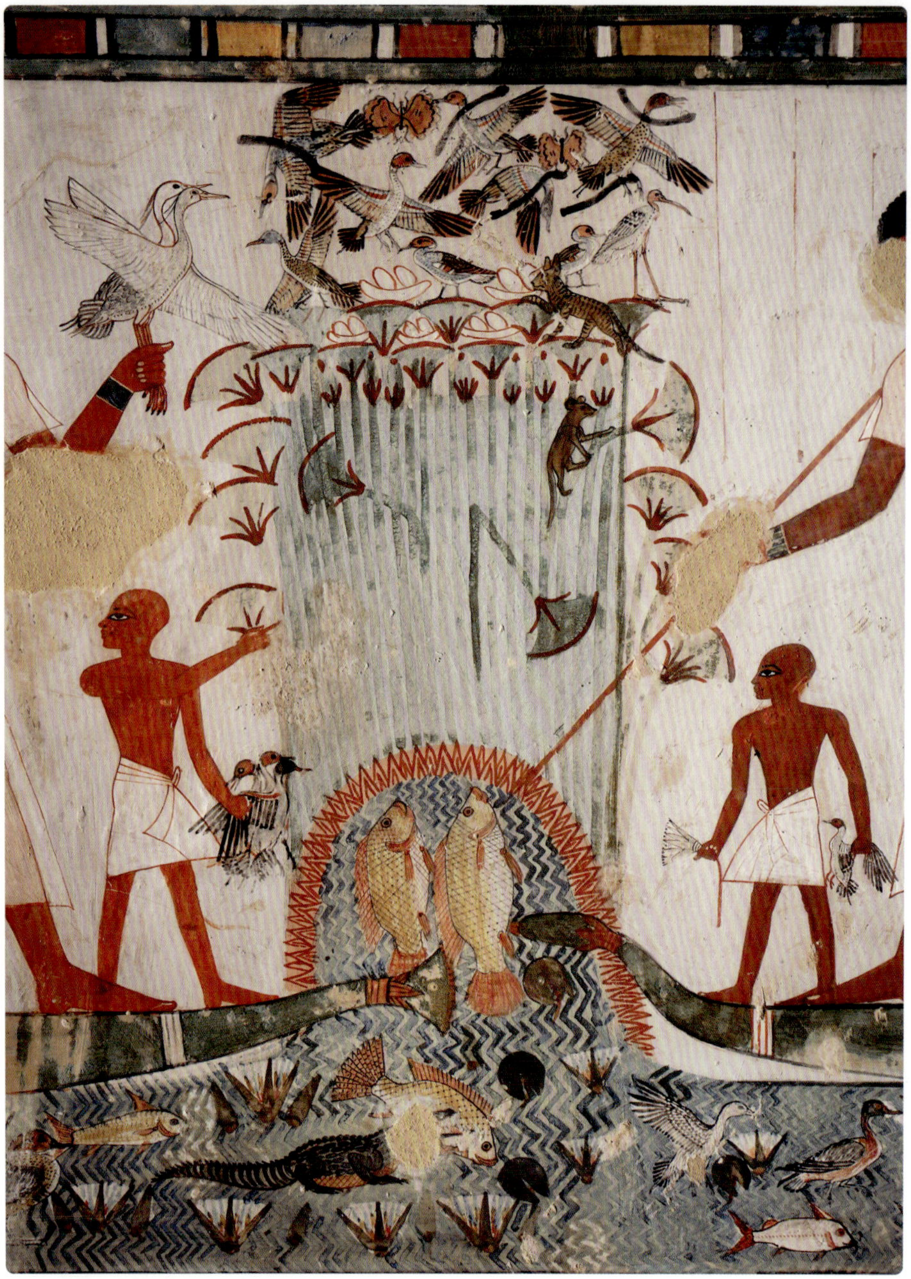

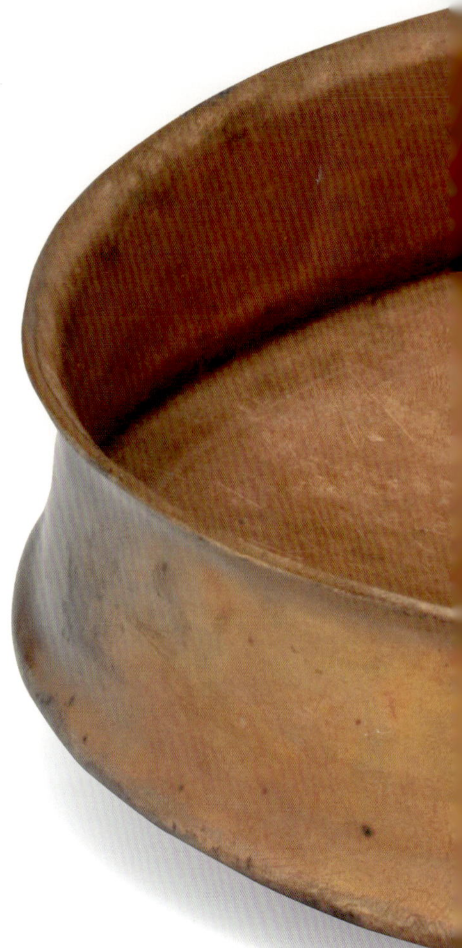

A votive bowl (right) from the tomb of Rekhmire, a vizier to Kings Thutmose III and Amenhotep II (about 1479–1400 B.C.), attests to Egypt's cattle-raising tradition.

A scene of hunting and fishing (above) adorns the tomb of Menna, an early 14th-century official. He called himself the "eyes of the King in every place," but the name of that ruler is unknown.

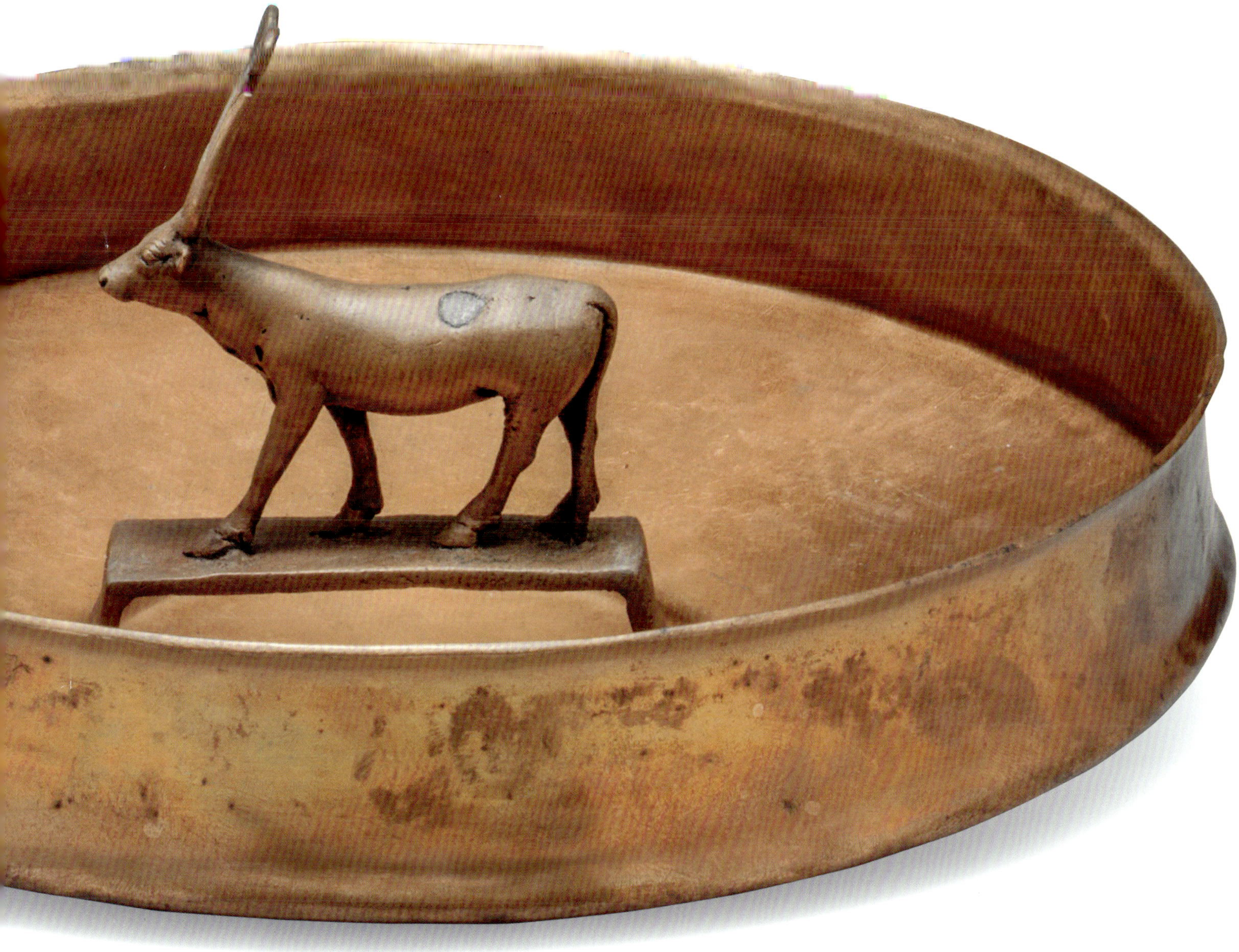

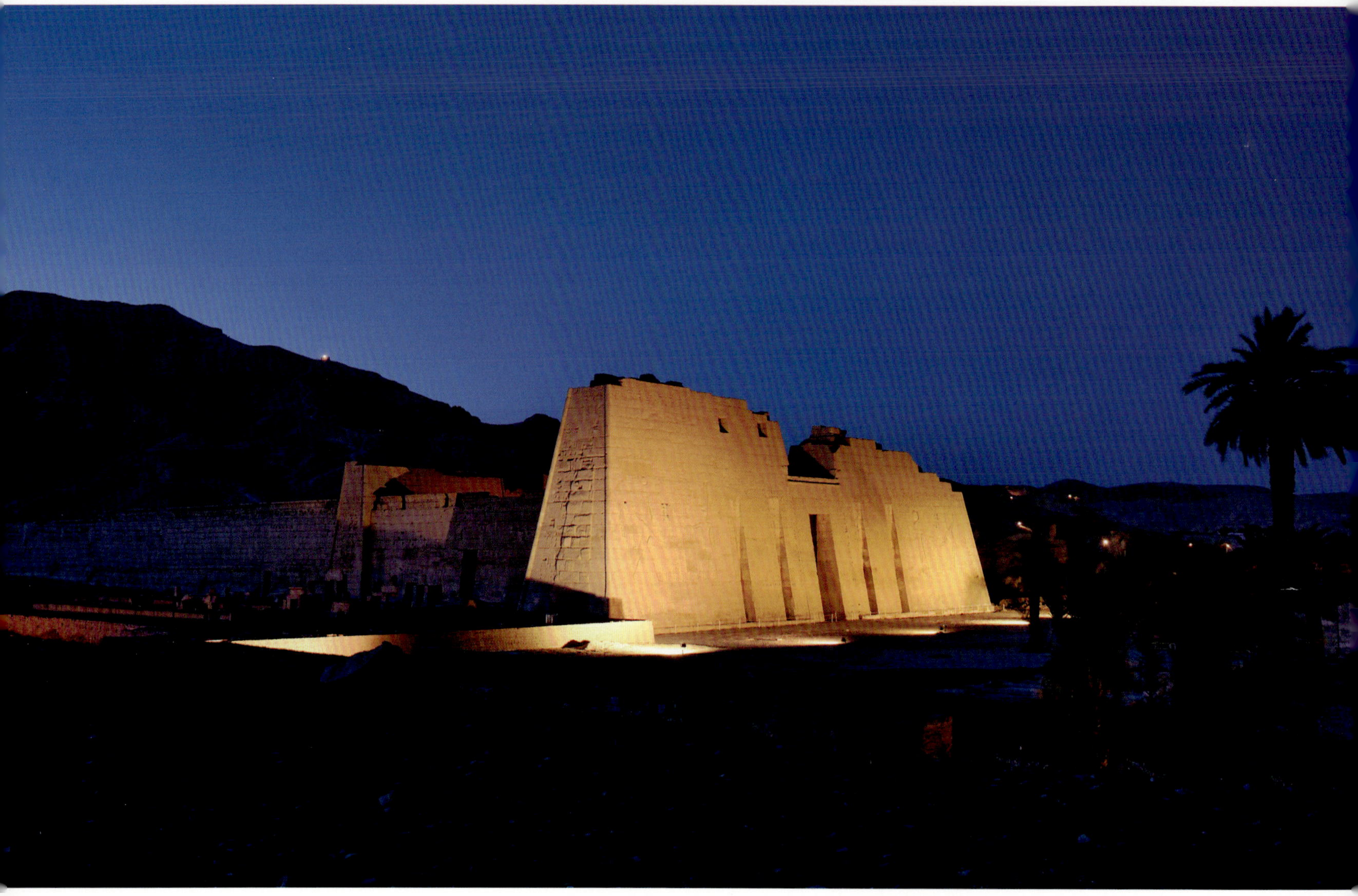

The impressive entryway to Ramses III's mortuary temple at Medinet Habu displays monumental reliefs of the king, in the presence of gods, annihilating the enemies he has captured.

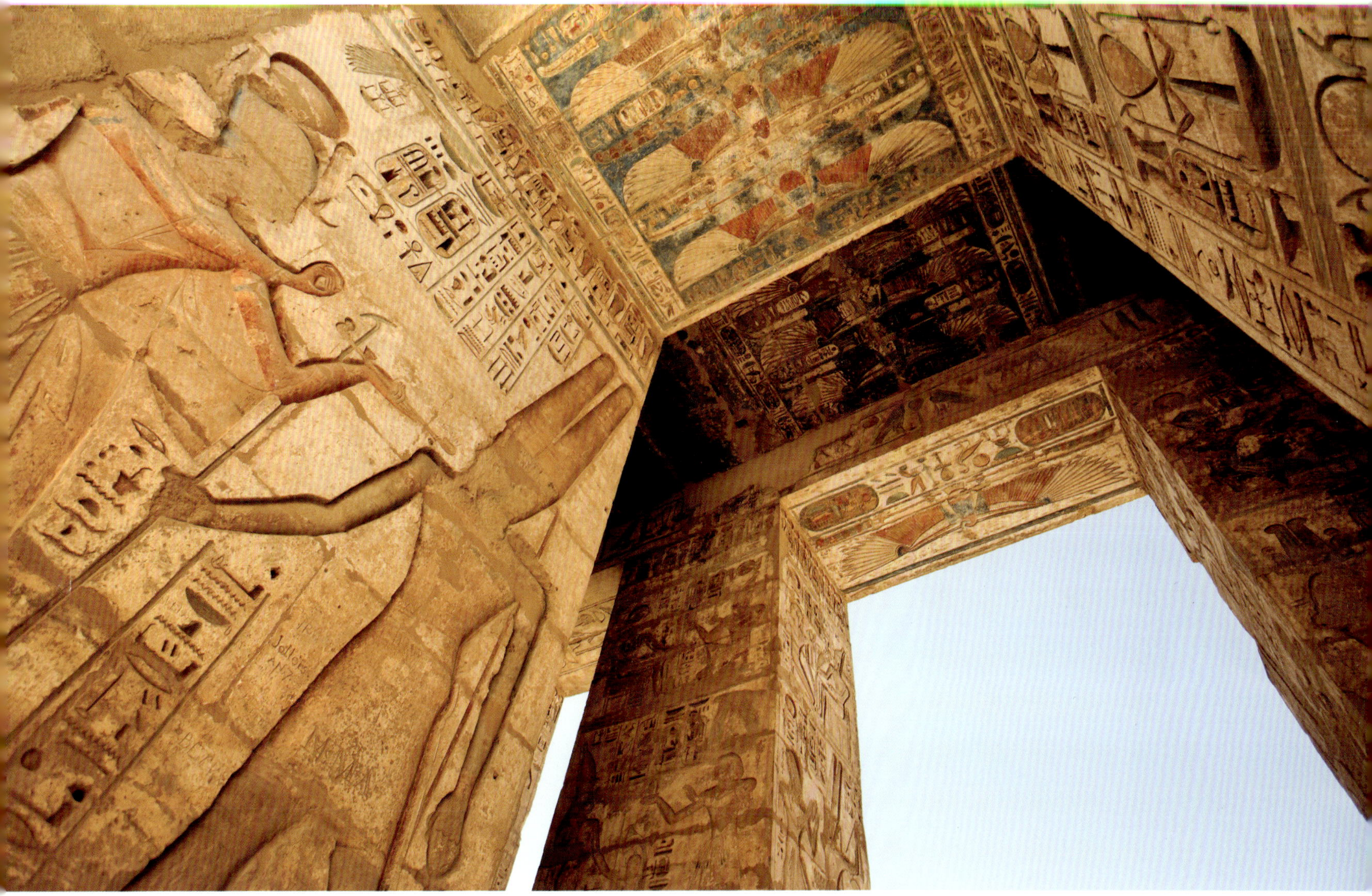

For hundreds of years, the Medinet Habu temple complex served as an administrative center in the Luxor area. Modern conservators have removed an accumulation of soot to reveal some of the original bright paint.

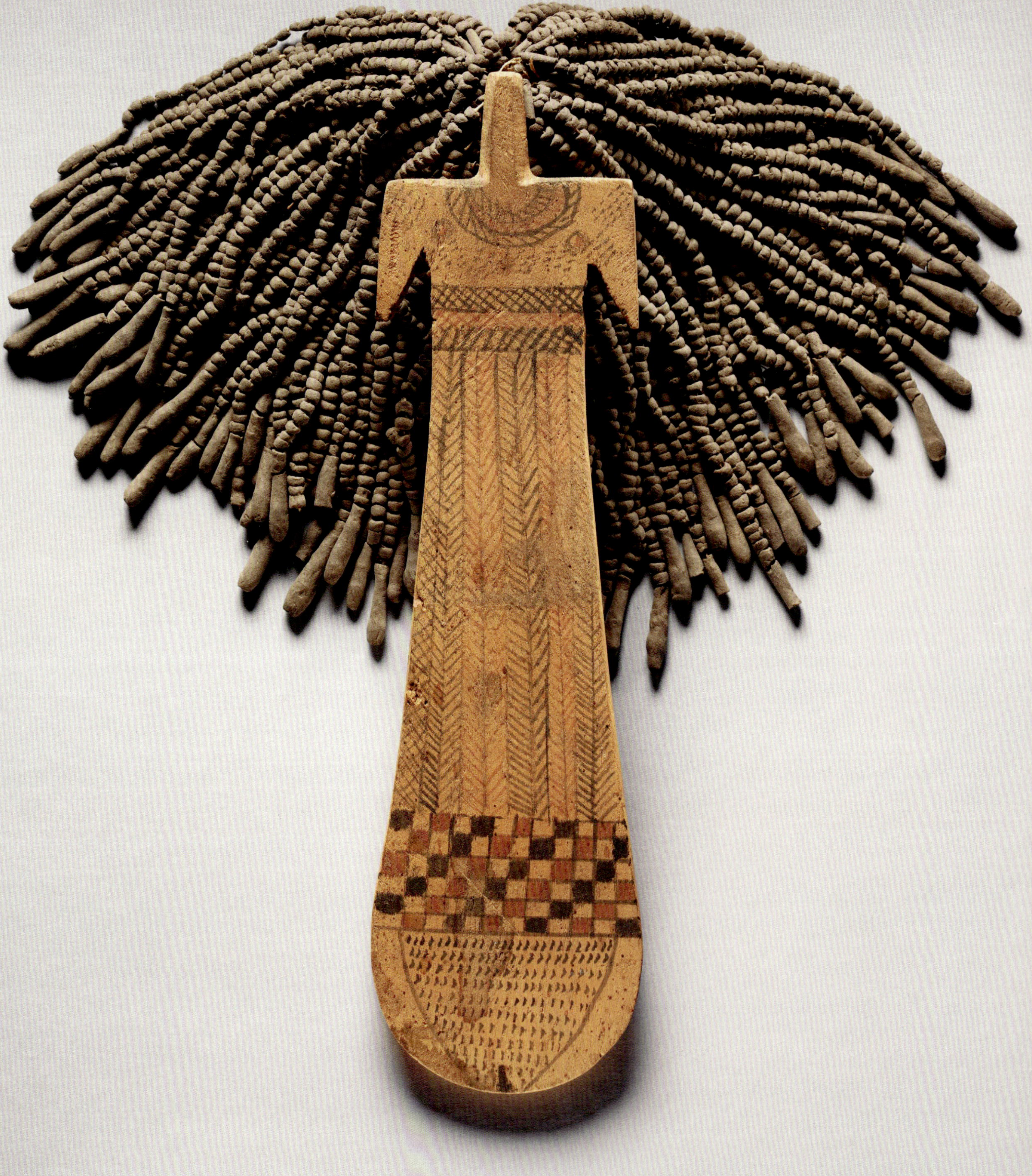

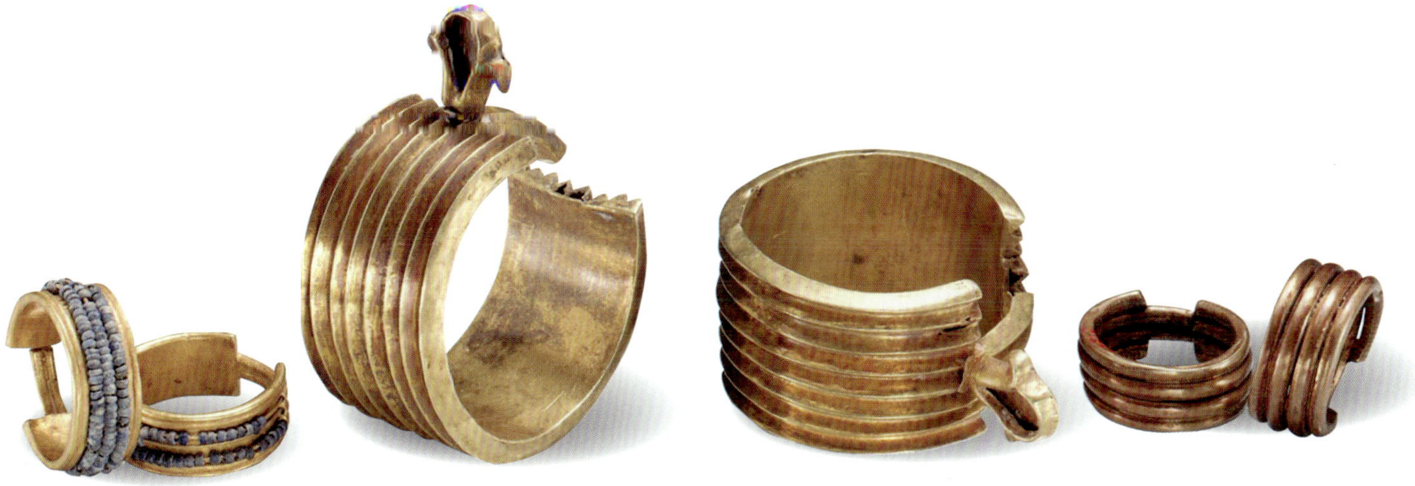

Excavations at the ancient cemetery of Asasif, near Luxor, have turned up all manner of curious things. This paddle figurine from about 2030–1802 B.C. (opposite) may have been used during religious ceremonies. The rattling of its beads was believed to please the gods.

Gold earrings (above) would have adorned elite Egyptians during the late 16th and early 15th centuries B.C.

This beautifully carved game of ebony and ivory from the late 19th century B.C. (right) includes a board shaped like an ax blade, and counters in the form of hounds and jackals.

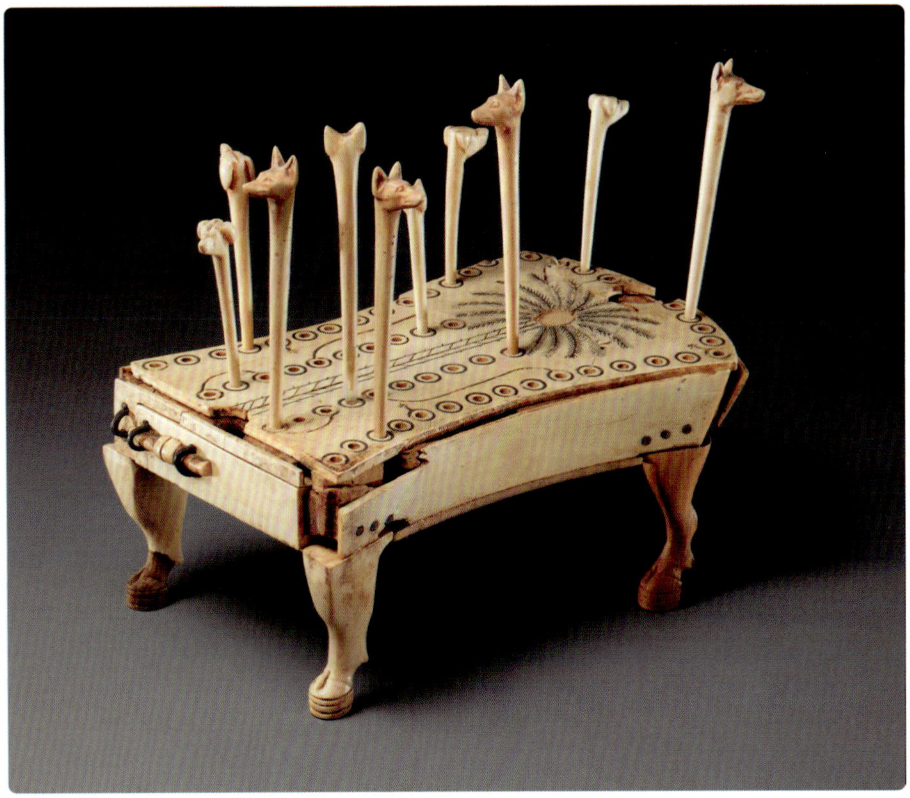

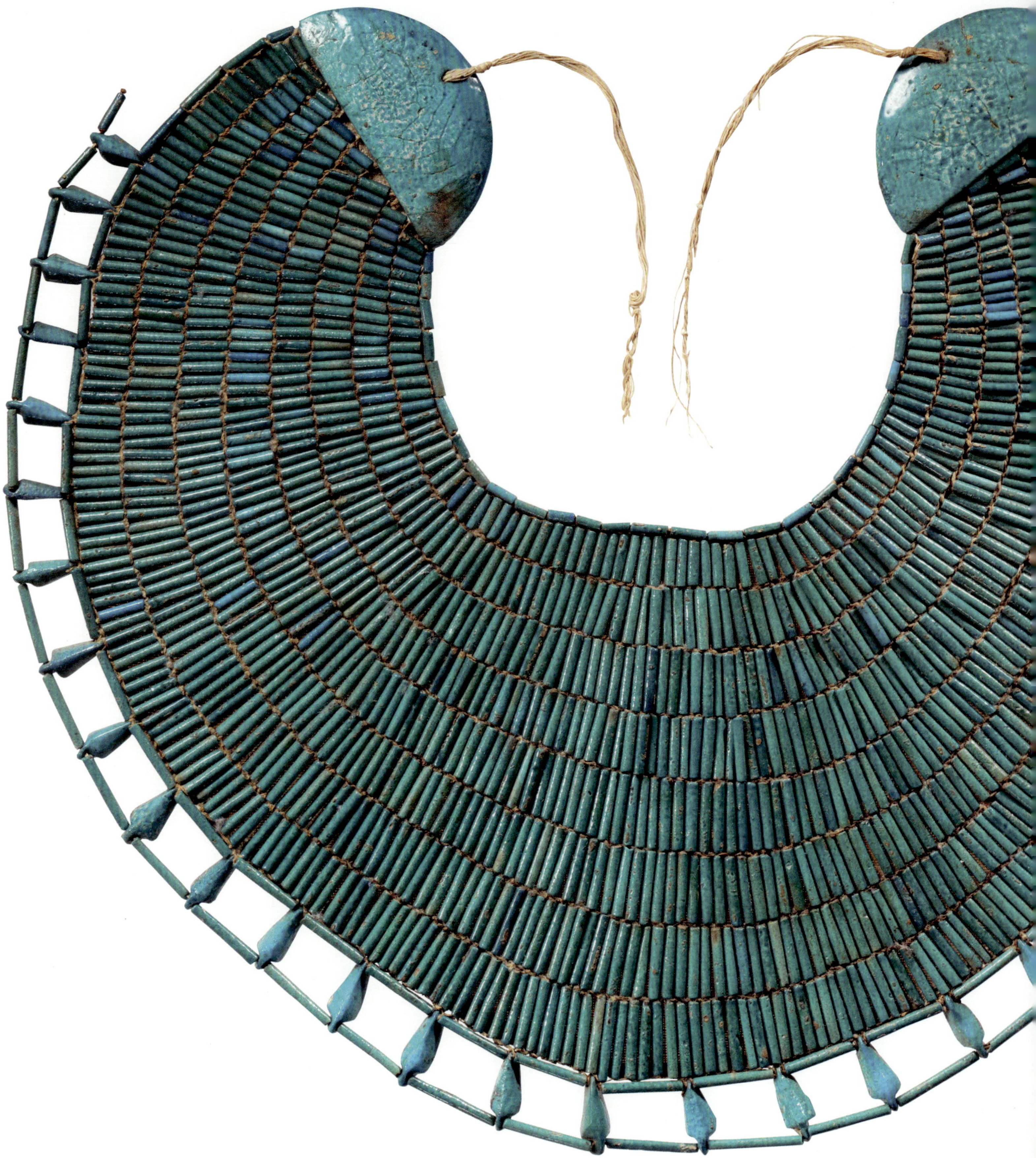

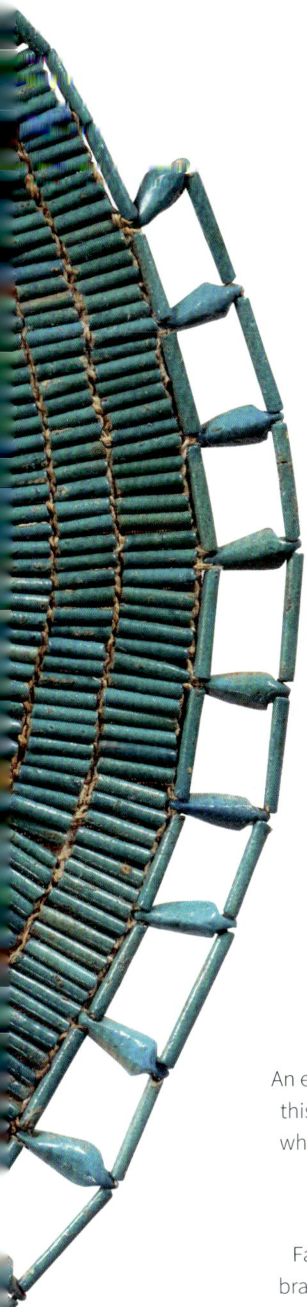

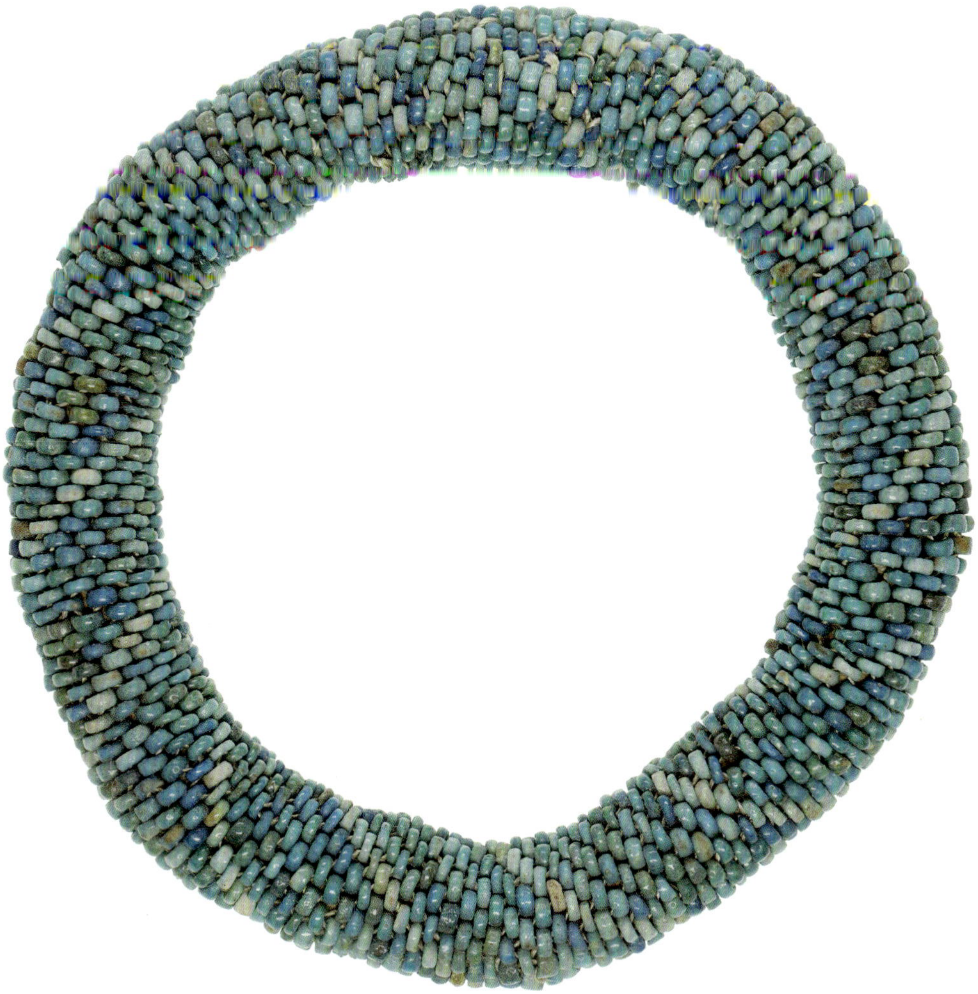

An estate manager named Wah wore this necklace of faience beads (left) when he was buried at Asasif in the 20th century B.C. Most of the stringing is original.

Faience beads also make up this bracelet (above), buried with a man named Baki in a tomb he shared with relatives. Among the deceased was Neferkhawet, his father or father-in-law, who had worked as a scribe and treasurer for Queen Hatshepsut (about 1473–1458 B.C.).

A box of wood inlaid with faience (right) lay in the burial of Neferkhawet's wife Rennefer, in that same tomb complex.

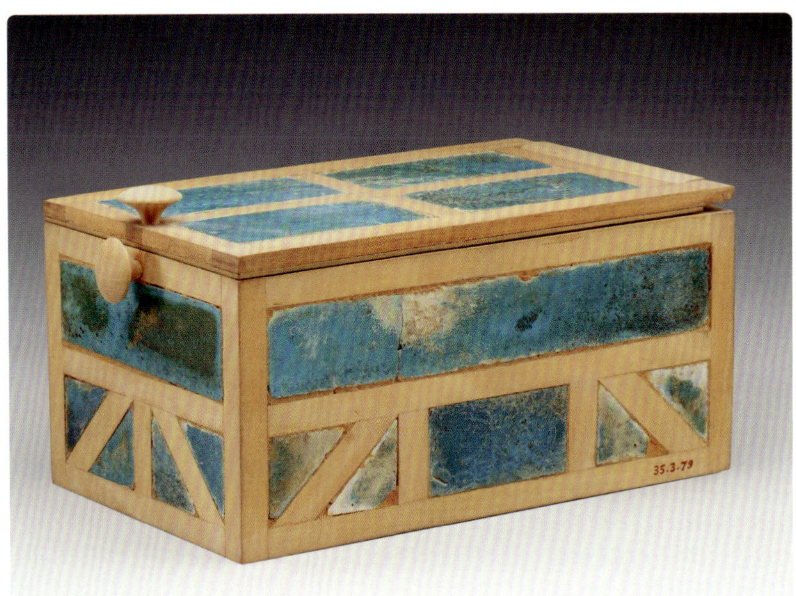

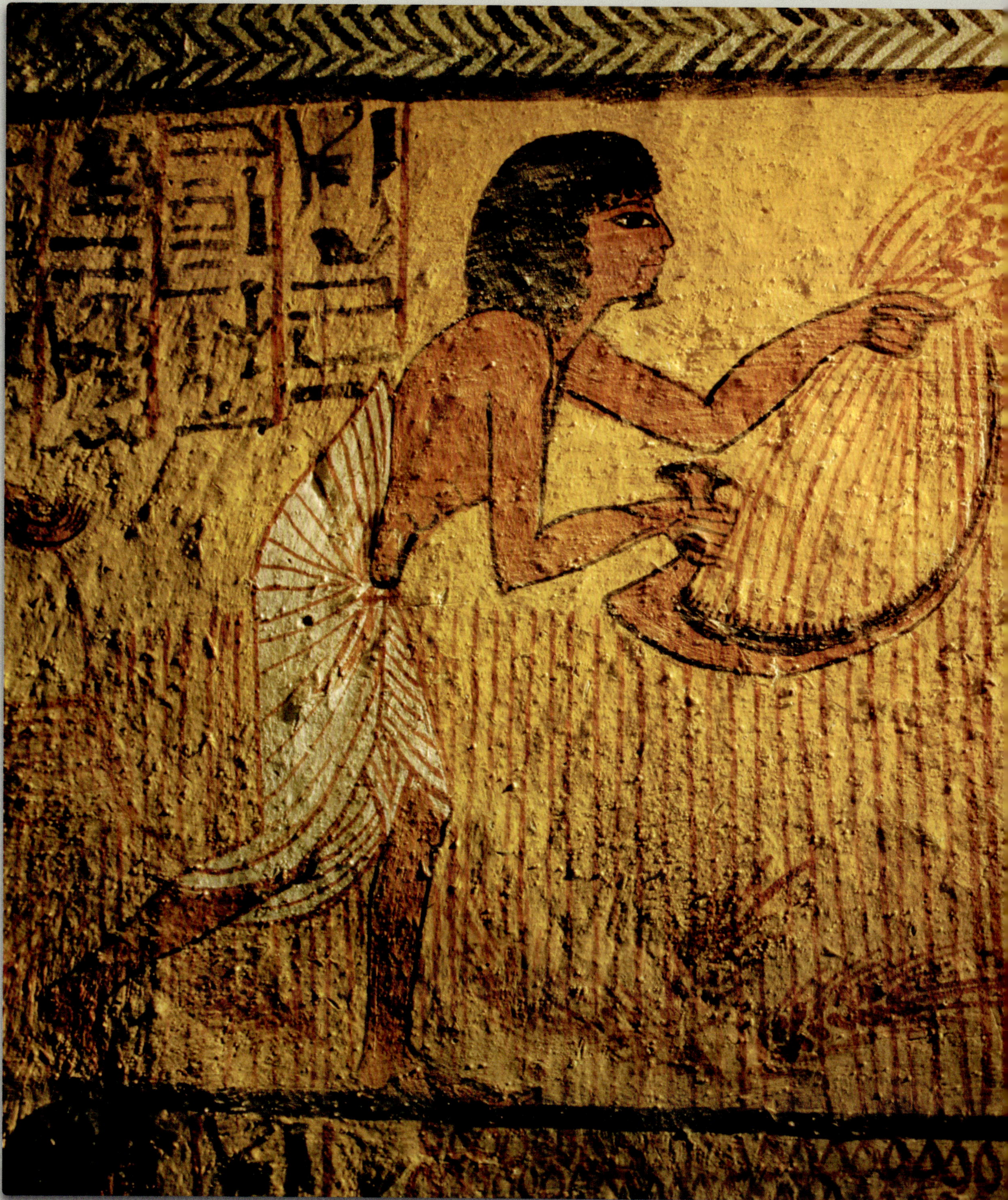

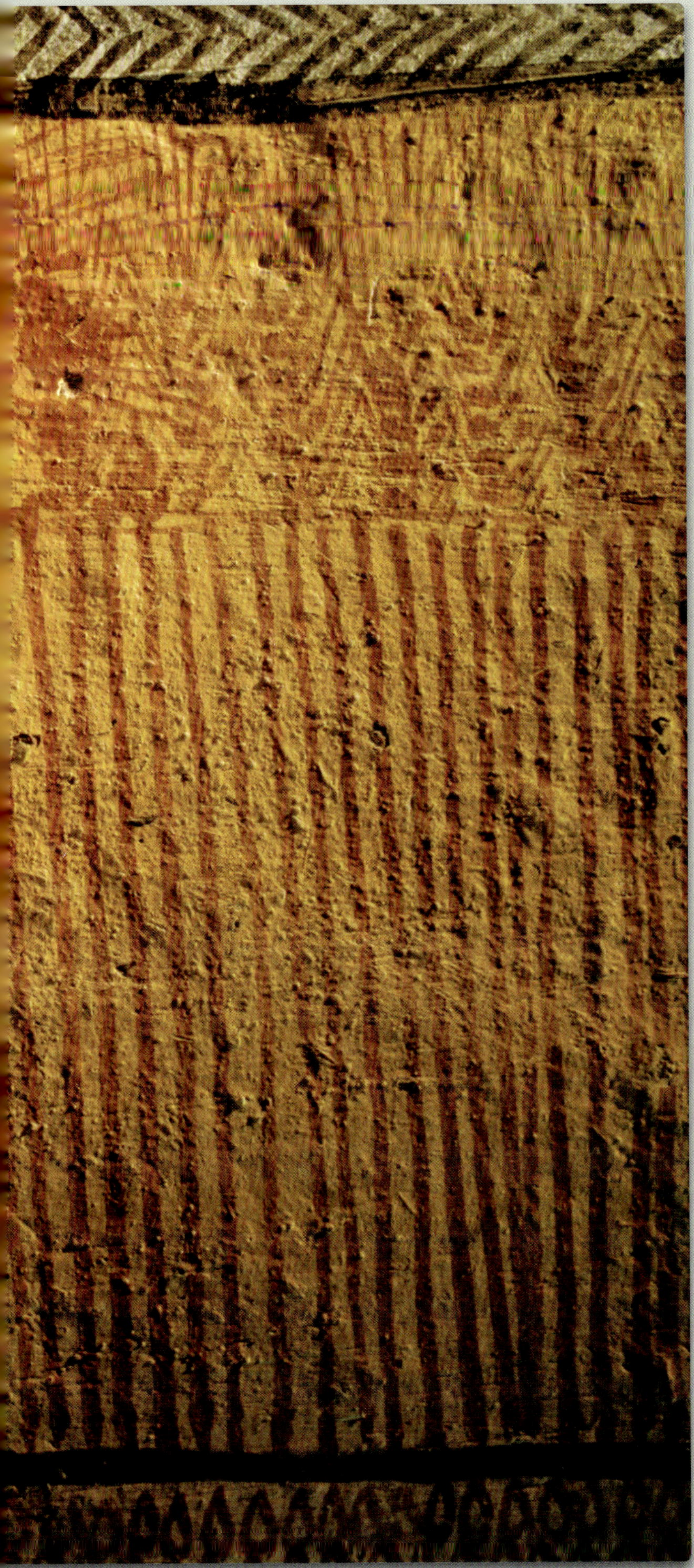

DIGGING DEEPER

Taking It All With You

FOR THE ANCIENT EGYPTIANS, the great beyond featured all the beautiful aspects of life on Earth without any of its unpleasantness. To make sure they had access to everything enjoyable during their eternal journey, they were buried with an array of items. King Tutankhamun had food and furniture, luxuries and fresh linen underwear. Those with lesser assets included whatever they could afford.

In King Tut's time, people might also place texts on the walls of their tombs to help their journey to the hereafter. They also could include scenes they believed would become magically accessible after death: good times from this life, their status expressed as titles, workers providing them with bread and beer, cattle, and produce. There are also scenes showing the abundance of the next life, as in this vignette in a tomb at Deir el-Medina (left): Sennedjem, one of the craftsmen who built the royal tombs in the Valley of the Kings, symbolically harvests his vast field of wheat in his new domain. Of course, he wouldn't really work in paradise. Servant figurines, called shabti, were brought along to do the actual labor.

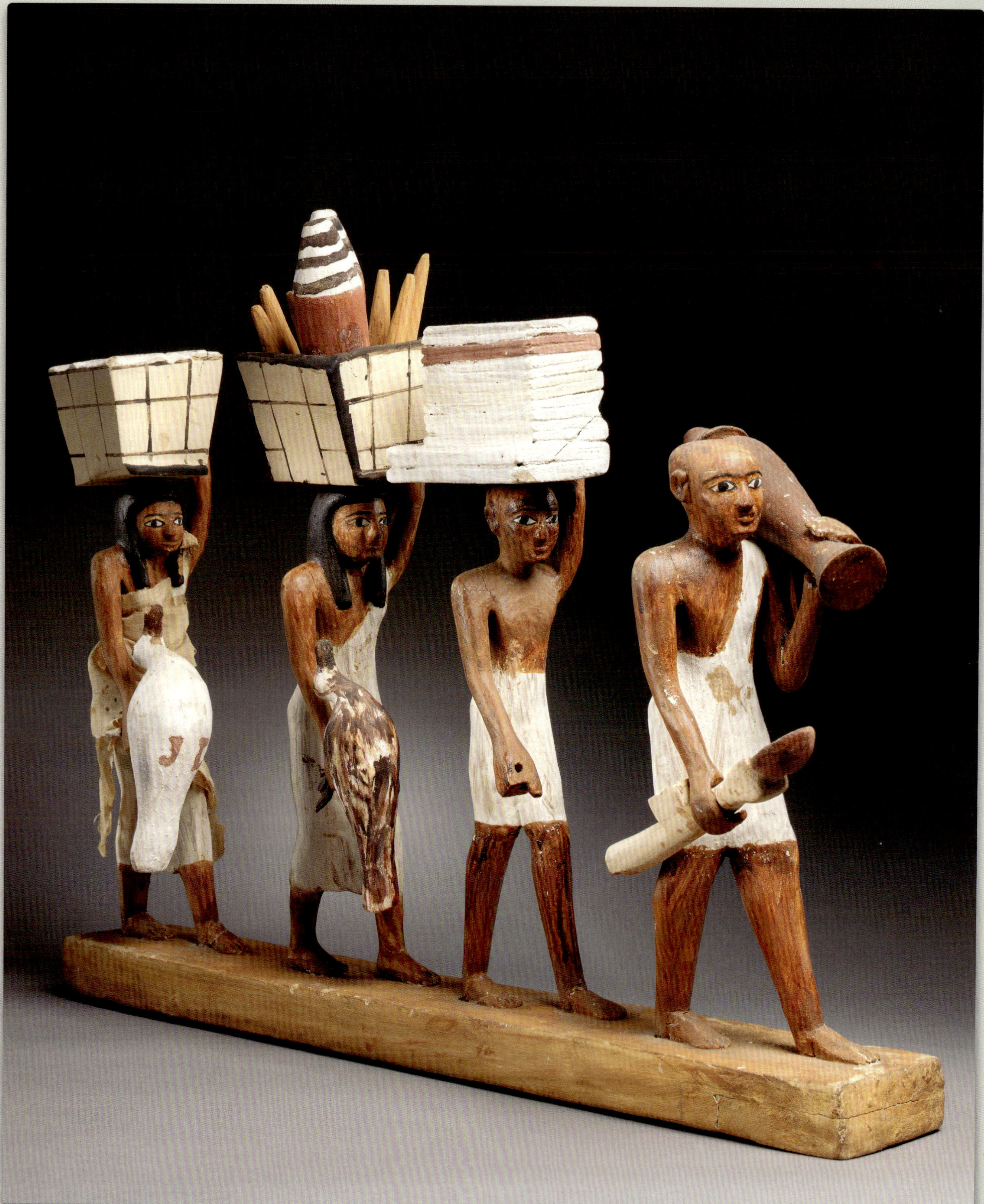

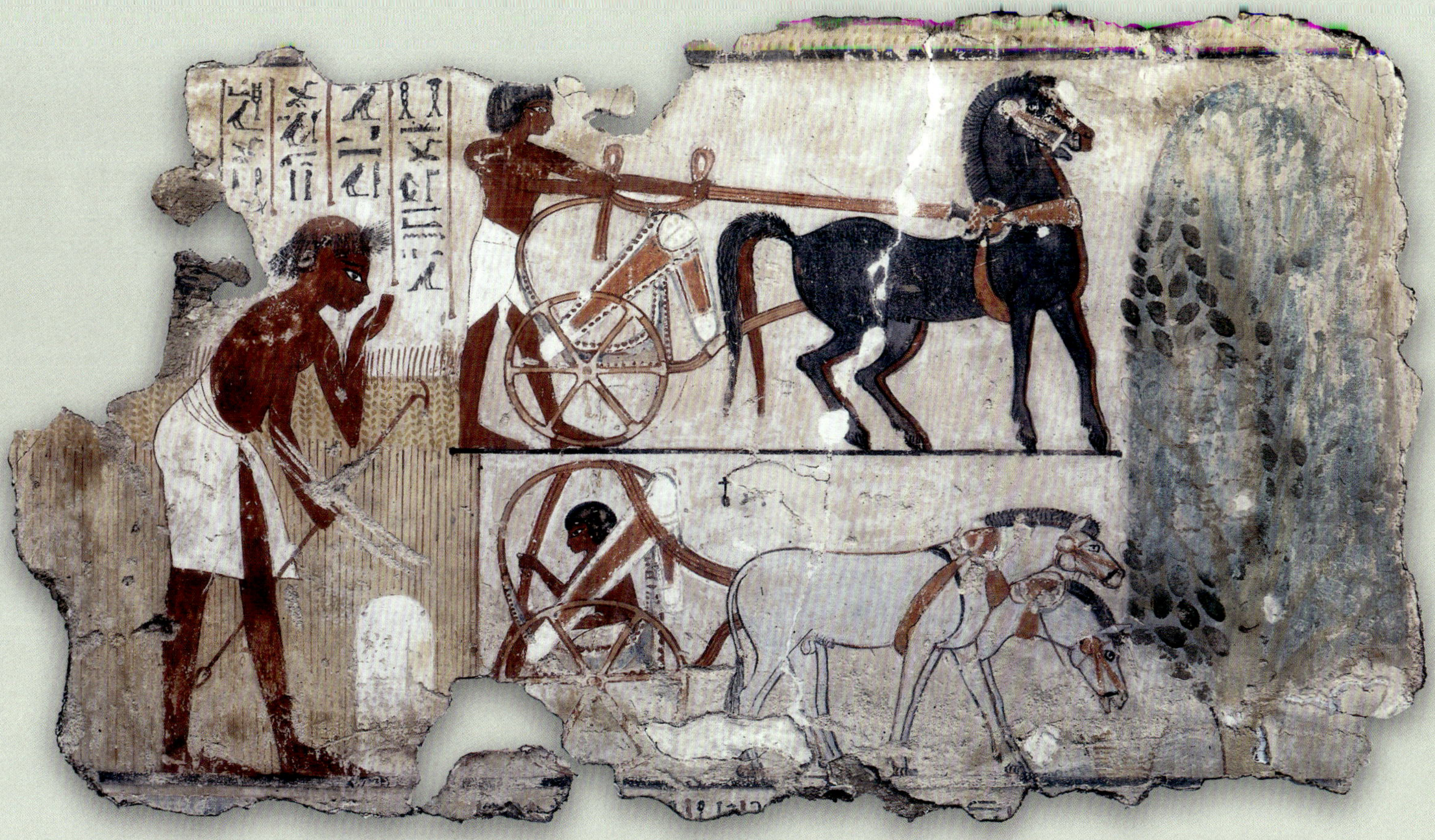

ELITE PURSUITS

A royal chief steward named Meketre was laid to rest in the 20th century B.C. near the Valley of the Kings. His tomb held two dozen painted wooden models like this one (opposite), which shows a procession of people bearing offerings—a libation vase and an incense burner, a stack of linen, baskets of beer and bread, and plump birds. Meketre's tomb was looted in antiquity, but archaeologists found the models hidden in a small chamber under a floor.

A wealthy 14th-century scribe named Nebamun also prepared his tomb near the fabled cemetery of kings. This scene from one of the walls (above) shows a worker inspecting one of Nebamun's fields and officials arriving in chariots.

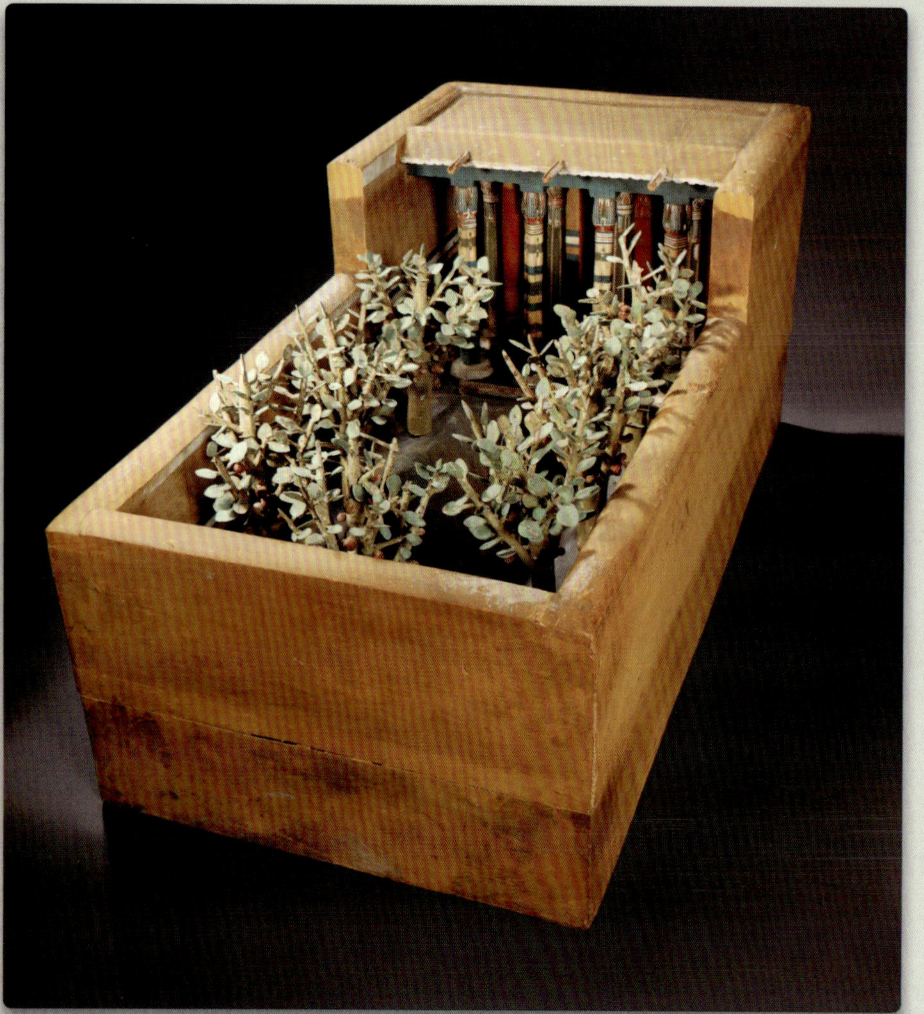

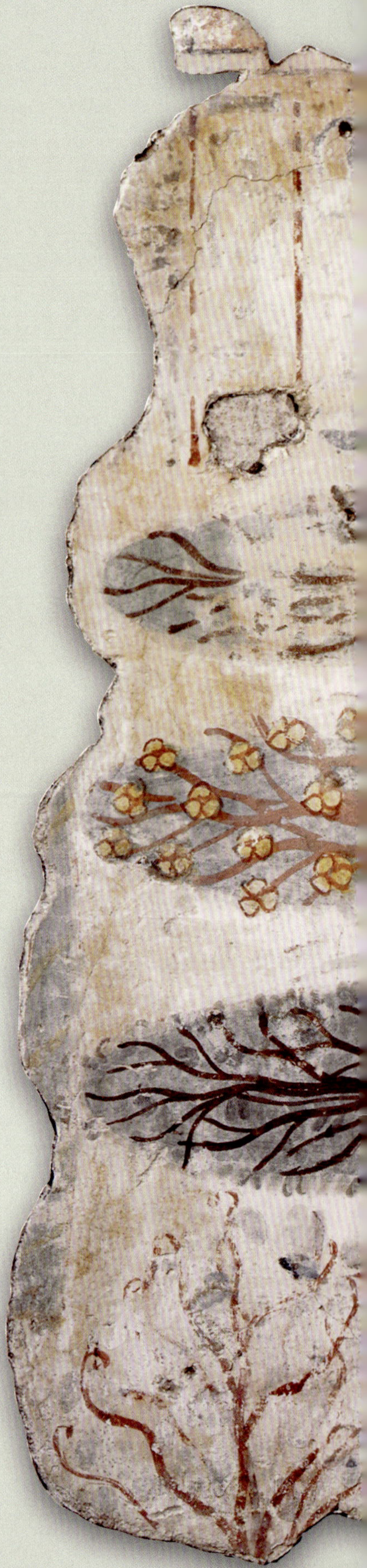

EARTHLY DELIGHTS

Meketre's tomb also yielded this libation basin (above) in the form of a pond set in a lush garden. Sycamore fig trees laden with fruit surround the pond.

The paintings in Nebamun's tomb include this glimpse of a garden on his estate (right). Date palms, sycamores, and mandrakes surround a pond well stocked with fish and fowl. The goddess Hathor, in a guise associated with the sycamore tree, appears with harvested fruits at upper right.

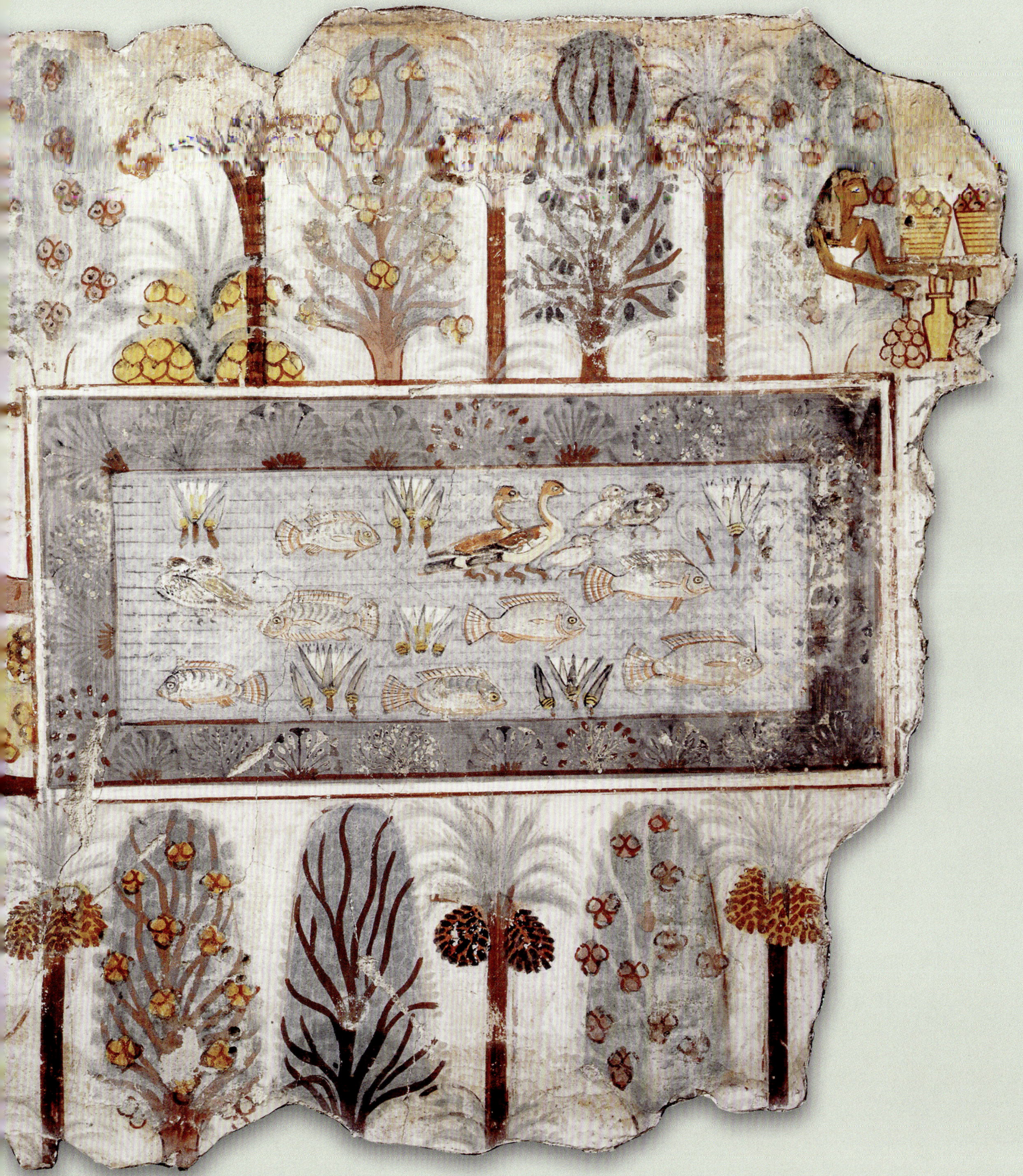

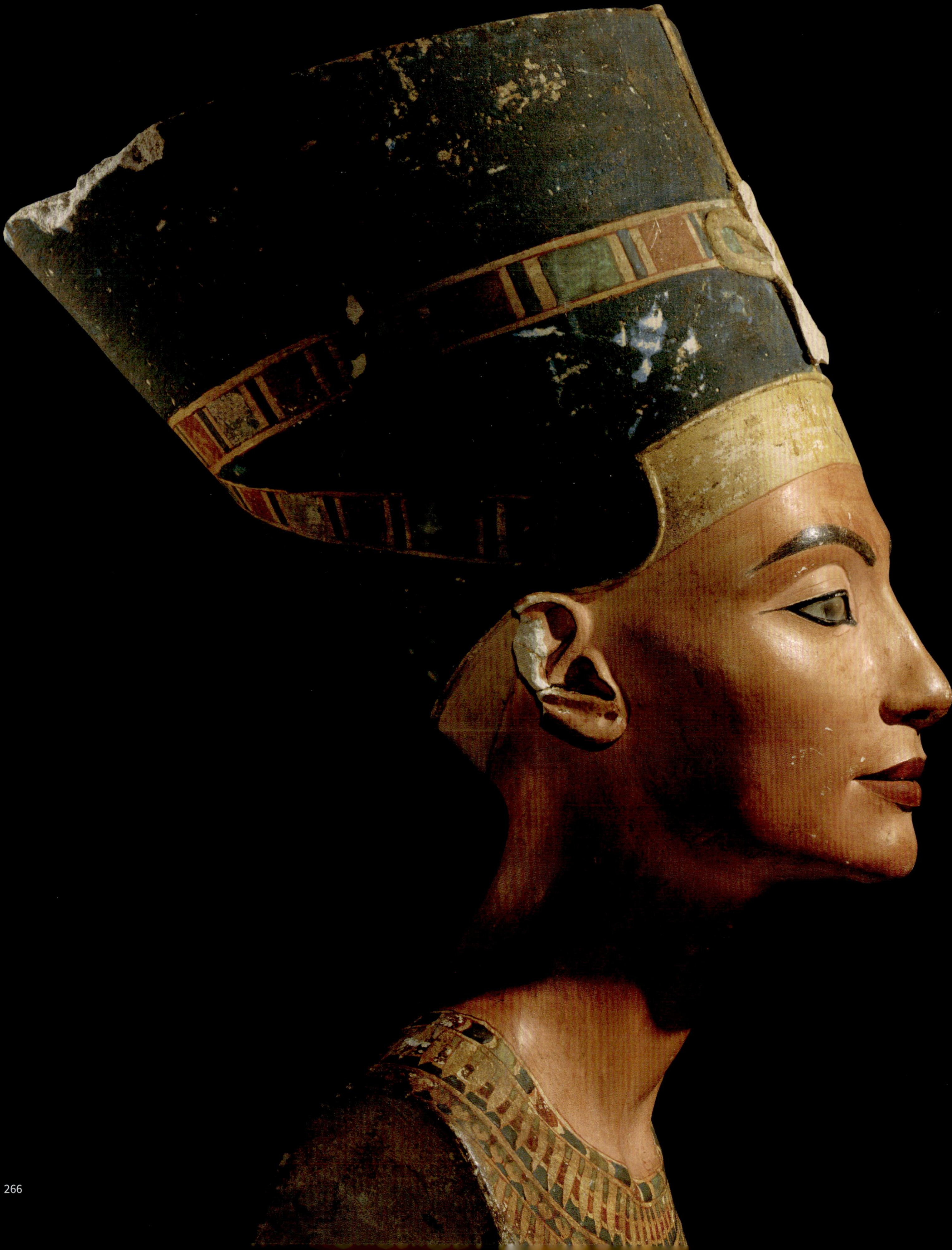

CHAPTER SIX

AMARNA

A Radical Experiment

IN THE 3,000 YEARS of pharaonic history, King Akhenaten's reign has to be one of the strangest. In just a few years, he threw Egypt into turmoil by upending traditional religion, changing his name, adopting a weird portrait style, and building a new capital far from Waset, his family's seat of power. (The ruins of Waset, now often called Thebes, are located in modern Luxor and Karnak.) "It must have been a horrific time," says Ray Johnson, director of the University of Chicago's research center in Luxor. "The family that had ruled for centuries was coming to an end, and then Akhenaten went a little wacky."

The roots of this chaos lay in the reign of Akhenaten's father, Amenhotep III. Archaeologists know the broad outlines of this preamble, but many details are still unknown, leaving frustrating gaps for historians trying to reconstruct his son's disastrous rule and the murky line of succession.

Amenhotep III, one of the 18th dynasty's great warrior kings, had inherited a strong, wealthy country. Territories stretched into Lebanon and Syria to the north, and Nubia in the south. Trade was booming, and the king had plenty of resources to support the arts and build temples.

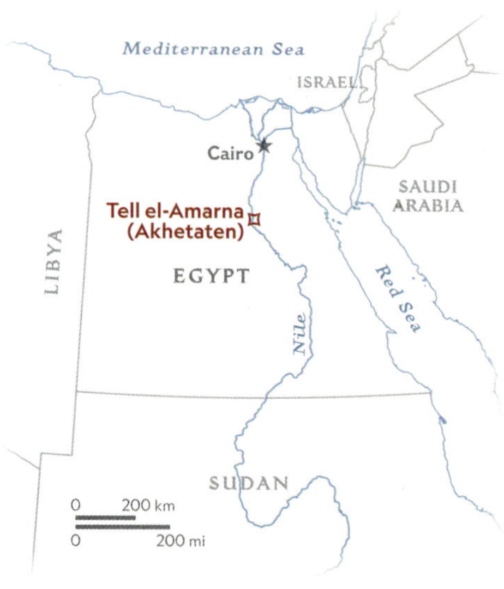

Fortunately, he and his chief wife, Tiy, had at least two sons. The first born, Tuthmosis, died early, which moved a son named Amenhotep into the line of succession. Some Egyptologists believe that Amenhotep III created a co-regency with his namesake, and there is evidence that the son's radical new art style started to emerge toward the end of his father's reign.

In its full expression, the art is a unique marker of the son's years on the throne. His colossal statues show an elongated face with narrow eyes and full lips, and a body with breasts, wide hips, and a fleshy belly likely meant to evoke fertility. Reliefs show the king and queen playing with their children in scenes of unprecedented royal family intimacy. Paintings of the natural world depict beautifully realistic birds in flight, nodding stands of papyrus, fish in ponds, and cavorting bulls.

Amenhotep III died in about 1353 B.C. after a rule of almost four decades. Amenhotep IV began his own reign with a typical coronation at the temple of the god Amun at Karnak and a marriage to a well-connected woman named Nefertiti. But ruptures with the past soon followed. In his fifth year on the throne, the new king changed his name: Amenhotep, which means "the god Amun is content," became Akhenaten, "servant of the god Aten."

The king began to focus his religious fervor on a single god, the Aten, symbolized by the disk of the sun. He suppressed other gods and even closed the temples of Amun, appropriating their significant resources for his own use. In year six of his reign, he abandoned Waset to build a new capital on a vacant site some 200 miles (320 km) to the north.

On the Nile's east bank, the new city nestled in a crescent-shaped bay of cliffs about eight miles (13 km) long and three miles (5 km) wide. Ordinary buildings were made of mud brick, while official buildings were constructed of distinctive

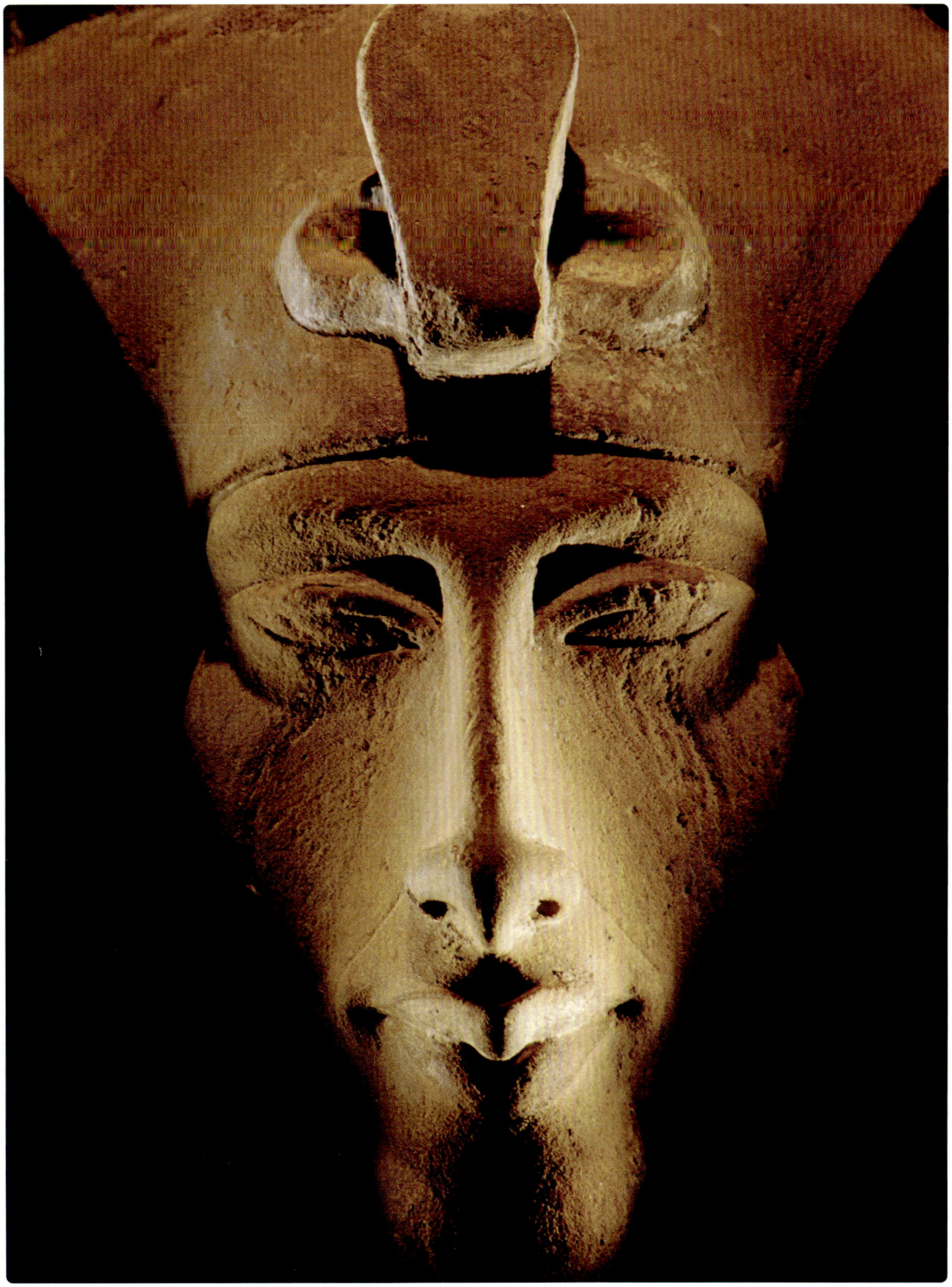

The heretic king Akhenaten (about 1353–1336 B.C.) promoted an unusual new style of art as part of his radical religious agenda. This sculpture (above), showing him with traditional regalia but unprecedented androgynous features, was created for the temple he built at Karnak to his god, the Aten.

PREVIOUS PAGES: One of the world's most famously beautiful faces, this portrait of Nefertiti, Akhenaten's chief wife, was found in the ruins of Akhetaten, the pharaoh's new capital.

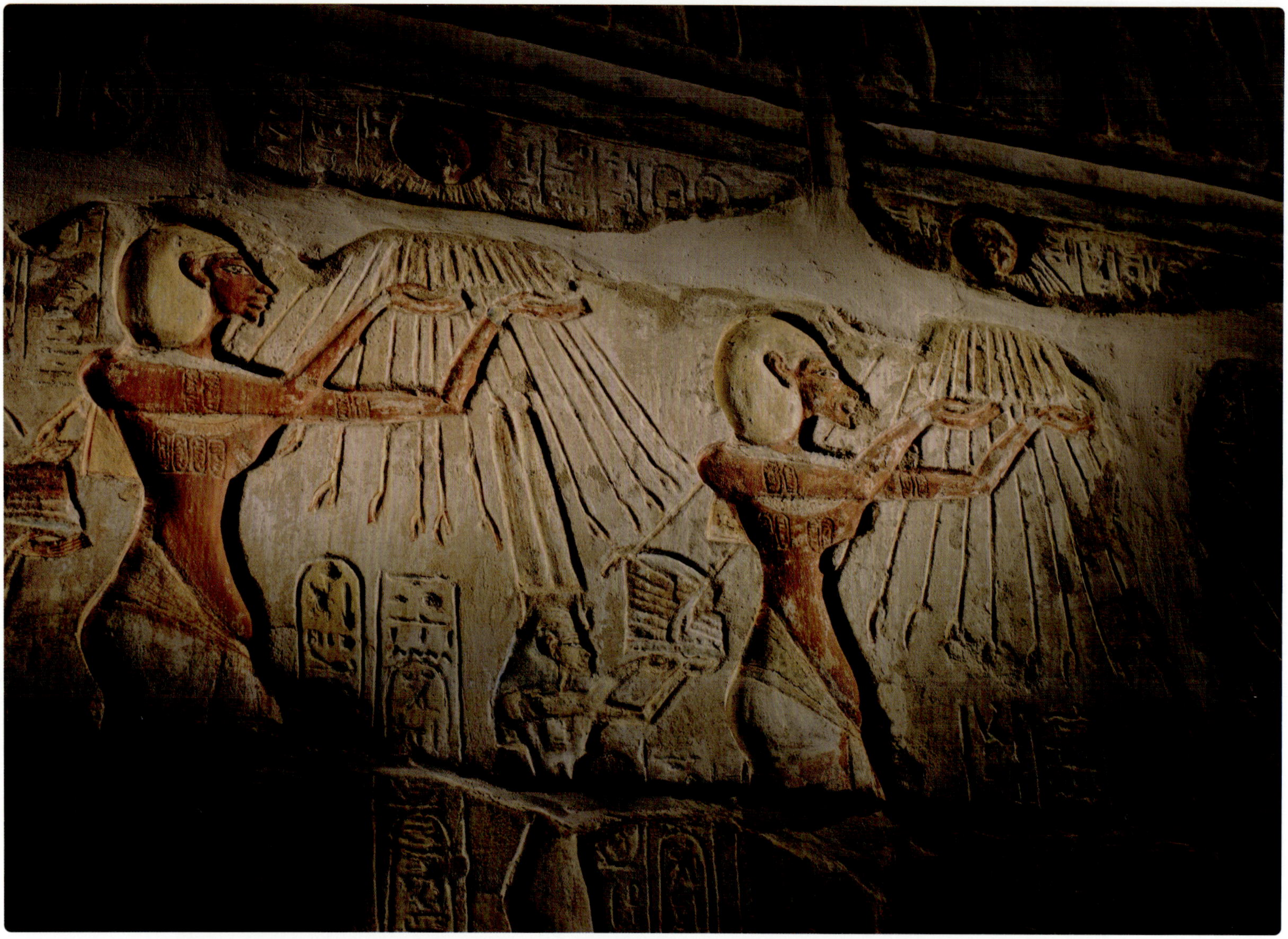

In a classic scene from Akhenaten's reign, the king and his family are bathed in light from their god, the Aten: a sun disk whose rays end in hands that deliver goodness and eternal life.

sandstone blocks now called *talatat*. Measuring about 20.5 by 10.25 by 9.5 inches (52 x 26 x 24.1 cm), the blocks were much smaller than what had been used in earlier royal construction projects, allowing them to be set in place more quickly so the monumental architecture could rise in record time.

The king called his new city Akhetaten, "horizon of the Aten," which is now the archaeological site of Tell el-Amarna. His family, courtiers, and officials were all forced to move there and could not have been happy amid the noisy turmoil of construction far from the comforts of Waset.

Only about 10 percent of the city's population were the uncomfortable elite, though. Many of the other 20,000 people were laborers. Skeletons uncovered at one of the city's cemeteries suggest that they were abused and thoroughly miserable. Children suffered from malnutrition, scurvy, and rickets, and were worked hard. Adults' bones also showed signs of heavy toil, including high rates of arthritis and fractures.

An enormous temple to the Aten marked the center of the city. Unlike the typical roofed temples with dark interiors built by previous kings, this structure was open to the sky so that rays of light could pour in. The temple's courtyards were filled with rows of tables displaying food offerings for the Aten to consume and enjoy.

Several palaces also graced the city. One, constructed of limestone and surrounded by a wall of mud brick, is among the largest buildings known from the ancient world, at 162,000 square feet (15,050 m^2). Another had gardens, pools, and storerooms. An administrative building held the royal archives of clay tablets. Most were diplomatic correspondence written in cuneiform in the Akkadian language, the lingua franca of the time. In the late 1800s, a local villager digging up ancient mud bricks to use as fertilizer uncovered a cache of these tablets. Illegal excavations turned up more, which were sold on the antiquities market. Today, 382 tablets are known, held by various museums in Egypt and Europe.

"In his fifth year on the throne, the new king changed his name: Amenhotep, which means 'the god Amun is content,' became Akhenaten, 'servant of the god Aten.'"

In late 1912, German archaeologists uncovered the ruins of the home and workshop of Thutmose, a royal sculptor. Tools, stones such as steatite and granite, and plaster casts of statues came to light, along with one of the most striking pieces of art ever created: the famous bust of Queen Nefertiti. "In front of us at about knee height first a skin-coloured neck with painted red ribbons was laid bare," wrote excavation director Ludwig Borchardt about the moment of discovery. He did not get to bed, he noted, until 12:40 a.m. "after this dizzy day."

After just 17 years of rule, Akhenaten died. Who succeeded him is unclear. Nefertiti had been a powerful figure in her husband's administration, and she may have rounded up support to rule on her own for a while. She may even have taken a masculine throne name to make this unconventional move more acceptable. A mysterious man named Smenkhkare is another possibility, either as Akhenaten's successor or as a replacement for Nefertiti.

But the king everyone remembers from this transition is a nine-year-old named Tutankhaten. Heeding his advisers, he would change his name to Tutankhamun, leave the city of Akhetaten, and bring back the old-time religion, restoring what the ancient Egyptians called *ma'at:* things as they should be. ▲

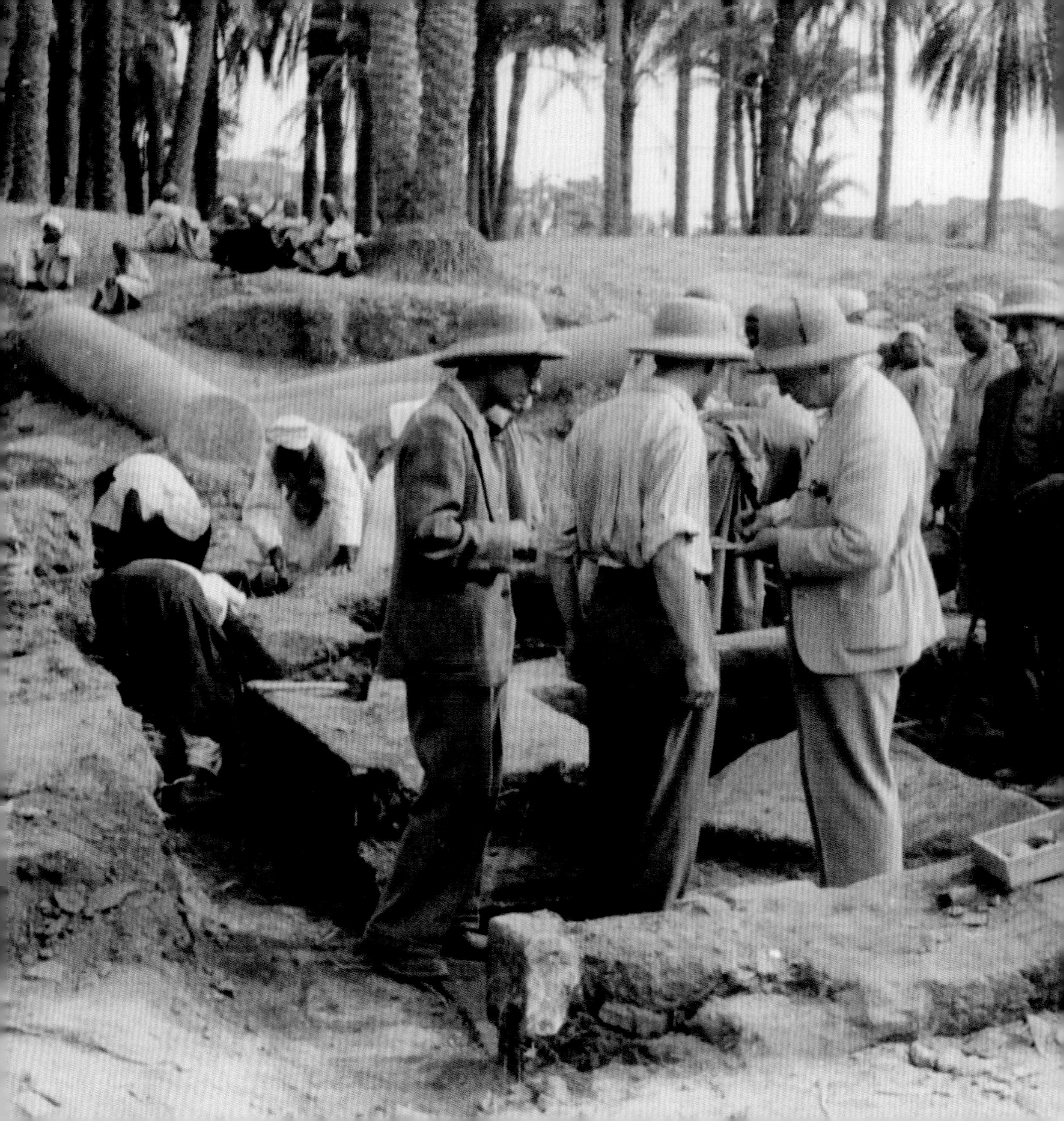

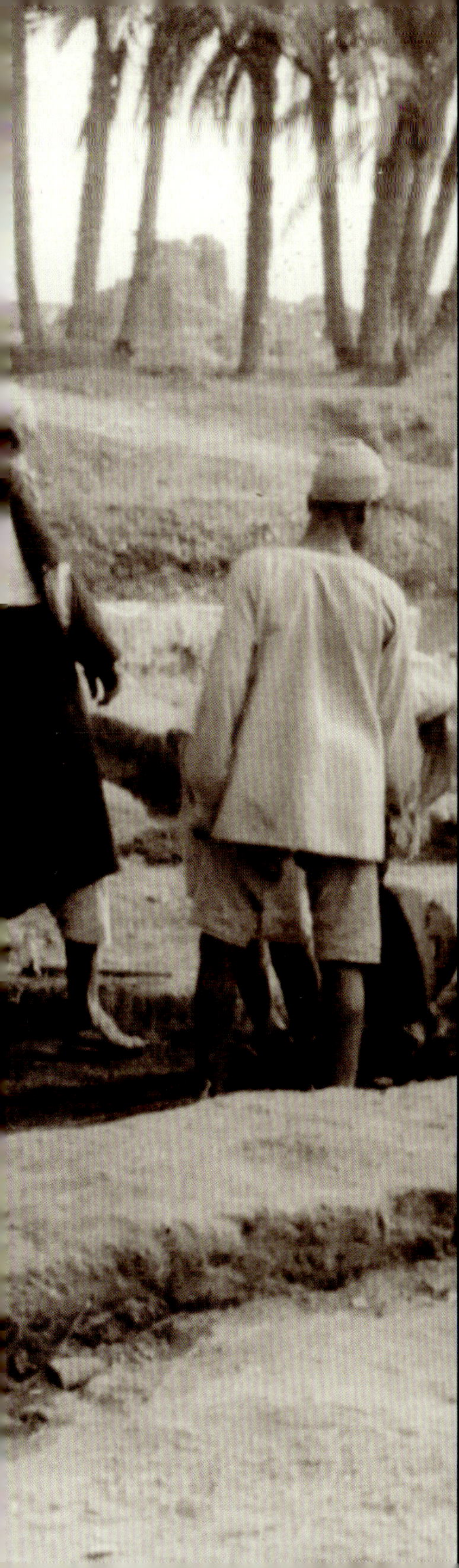

In the 1930s, excavations at el-Ashmunein (left) uncovered some 2,000 recycled stone blocks from the site of Akhenaten's capital just a few miles away. After the heretic king died, his city was abandoned and became a quarry for later builders.

Today, columns of a fifth-century Christian basilica mark the site (below), which the Greeks named Hermopolis Magna.

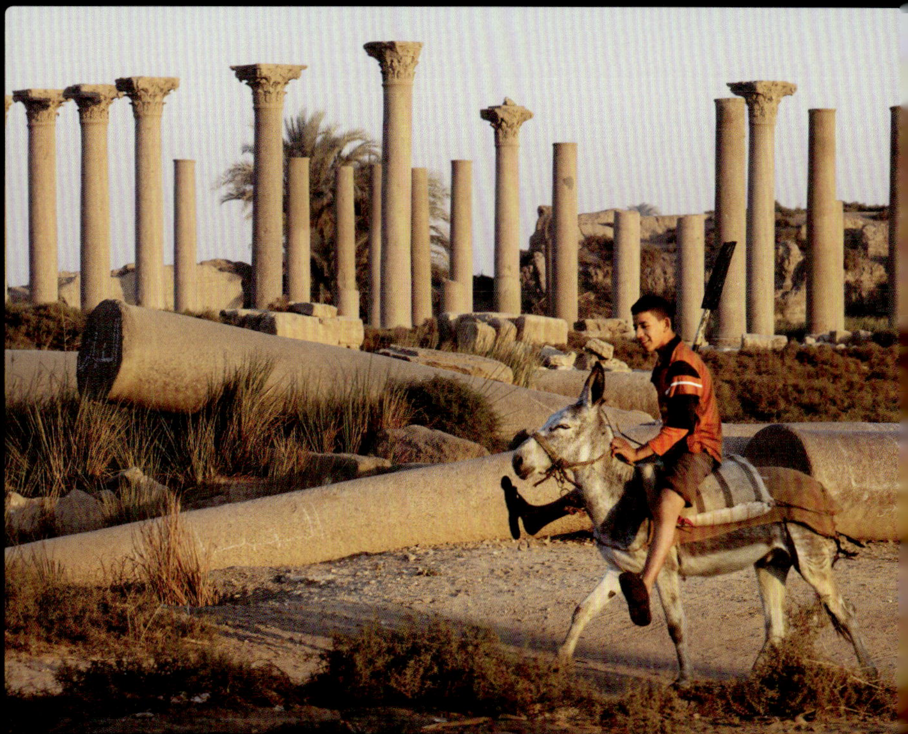

“I shall make Akhetaten for the Aten, my father, in this place,” declared King Akhenaten in 1348 B.C. of the site he chose along the Nile where his new capital would rise.

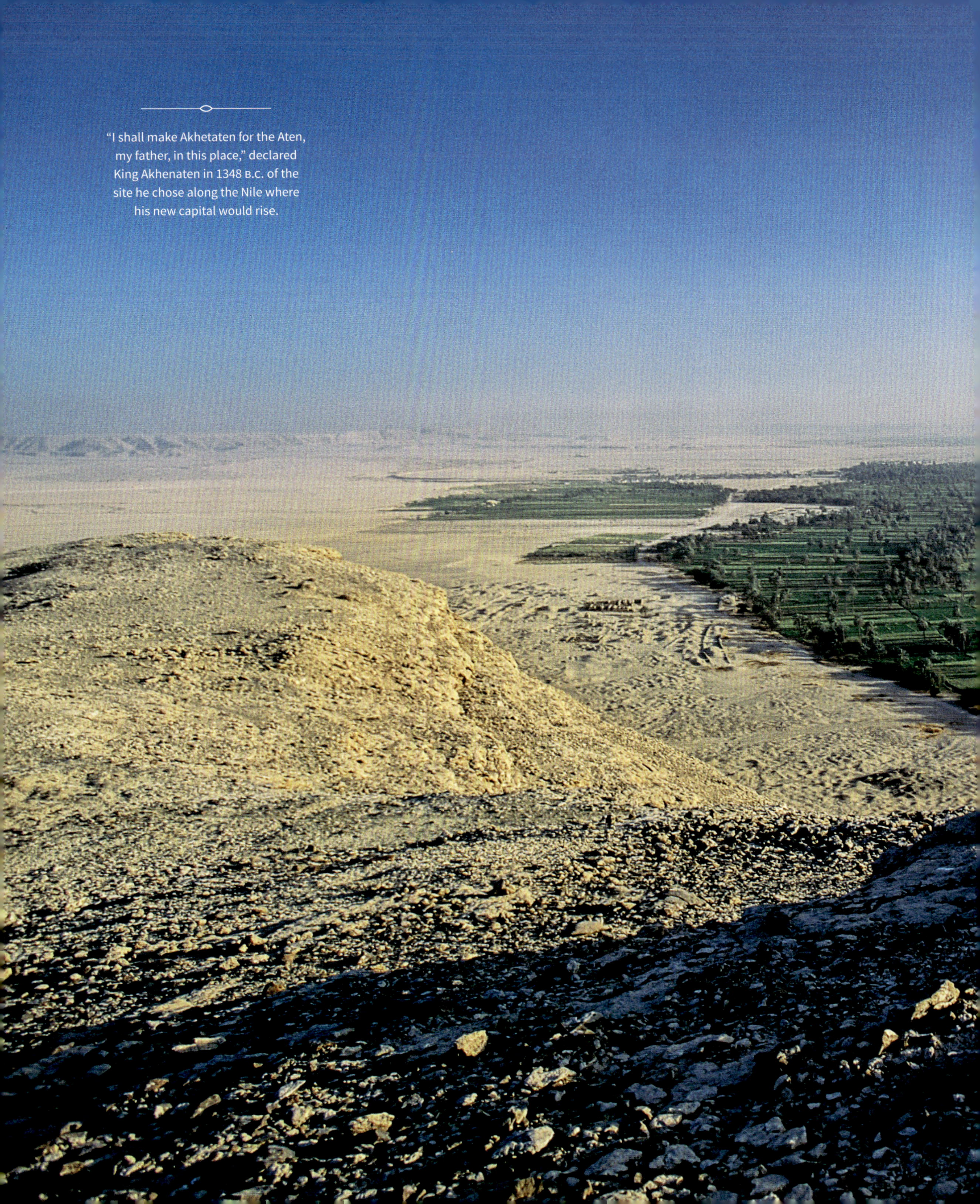

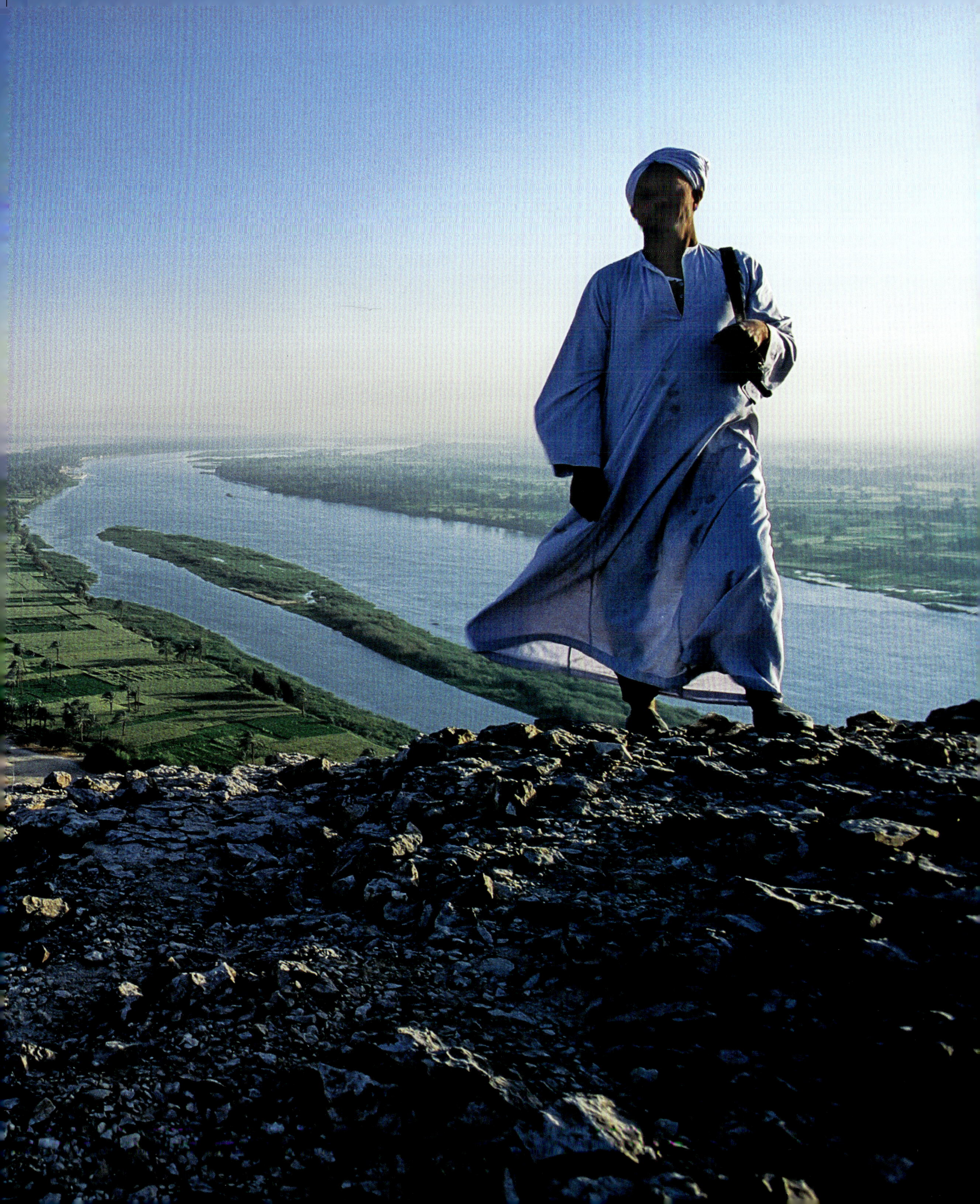

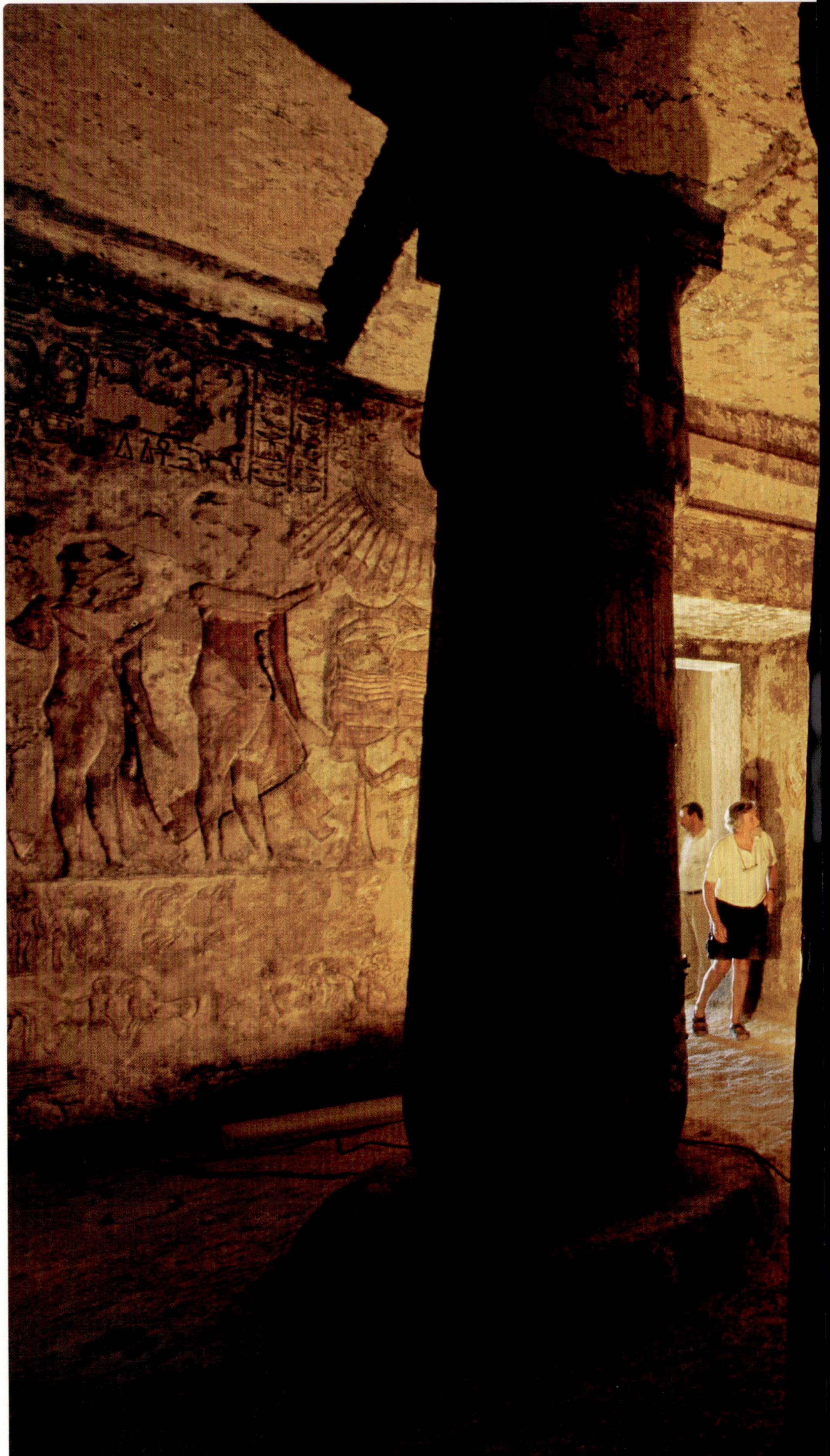

Carved into a cliff at Akhetaten, the tomb of Meryre, a high priest of the Aten, retains vivid reliefs that detail the new capital's architecture, royal events, and the king's role as his subjects' link to the supreme deity. The quality of the art attests to the high status of the deceased in the royal court.

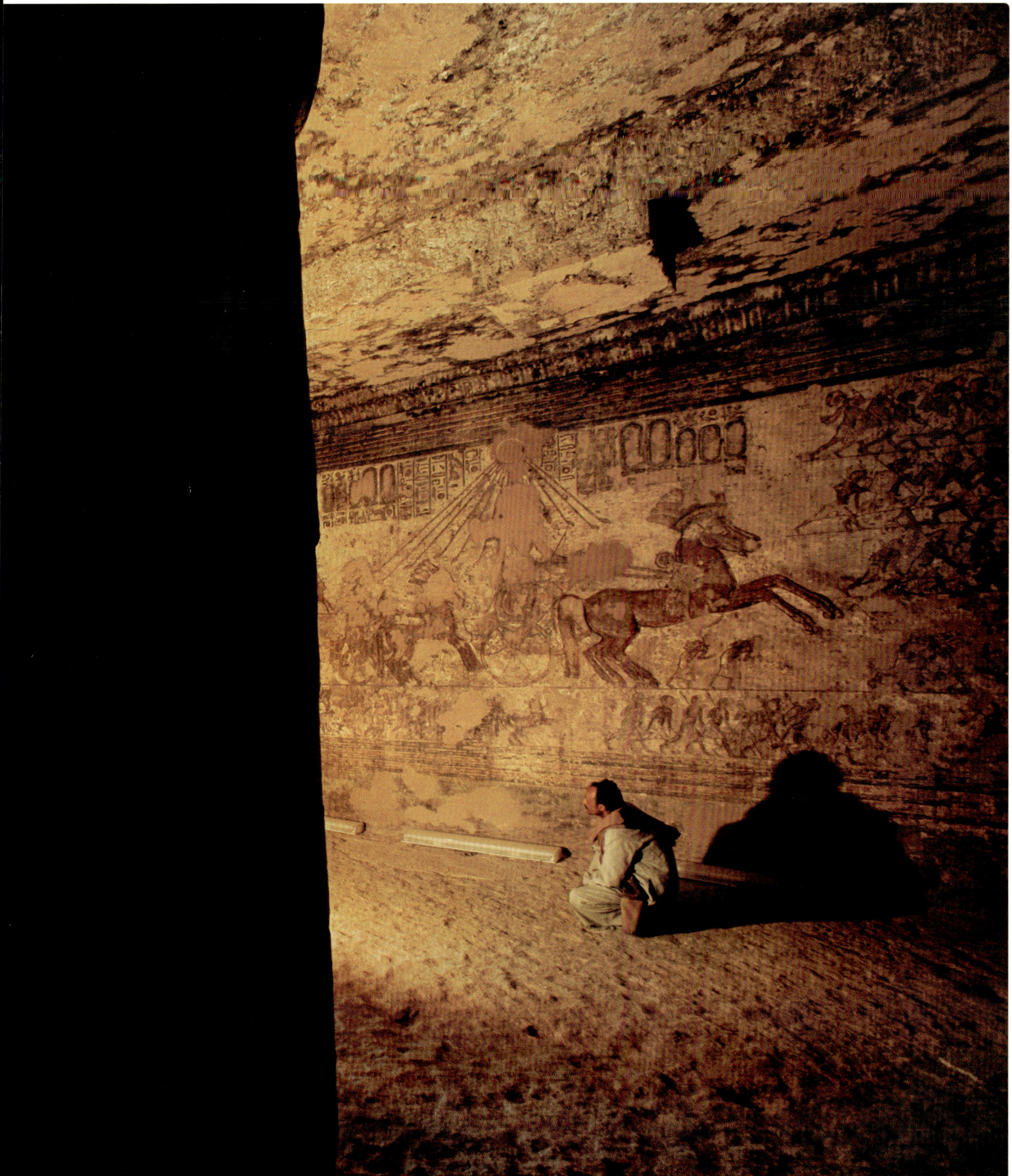

A Master of Detail

BORN IN 1810 in what is now Germany, Karl Richard Lepsius visited Egypt only three times—but his impact on Egyptology was immense. A pioneer of methodical, scientific archaeology, he recorded many ruins that were later altered or destroyed. He also provided history-changing insights about Akhenaten and his reign.

Lepsius learned to read Egyptian hieroglyphs after studying classical archaeology. He was a university lecturer when he was chosen to lead a three-year research expedition to Egypt and Sudan sponsored by Prussian king Friedrich Wilhelm IV.

In September 1843, Lepsius spent three days exploring the ruins of Akhenaten's capital; in June 1845, he returned for another nine days. During these brief visits, he uncovered two essential truths. Previous scholars had believed Akhenaten was female, but Lepsius realized he was a male shown with feminized features. Lepsius was also the first to recognize the nature of Akhenaten's religious upheaval, centered on the sun disk.

Published between 1849 and 1856, Lepsius' 12-volume *Monuments of Egypt and Ethiopia*—which includes this illustration (right) of an inscription at Tuna el-Gebel carved at Akhenaten's command—is still an important reference for scholars today.

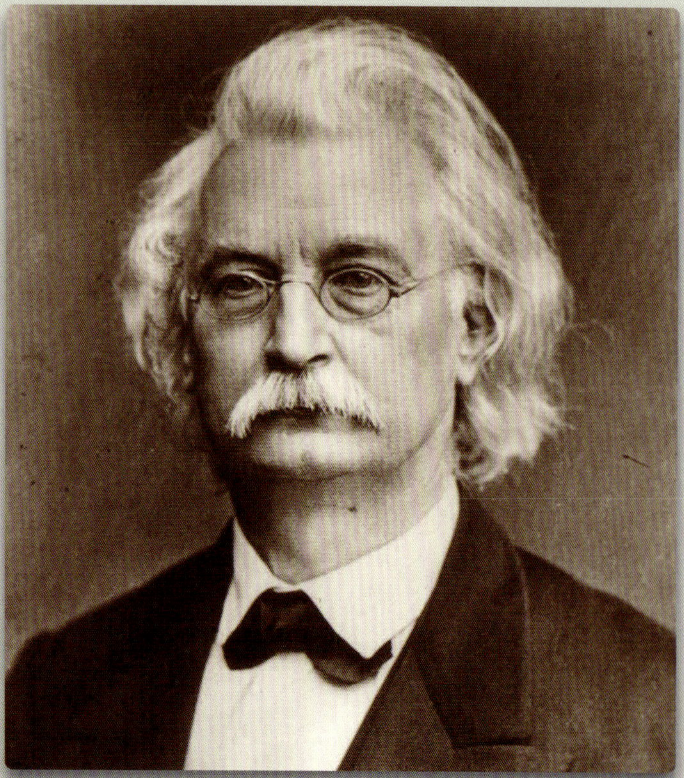

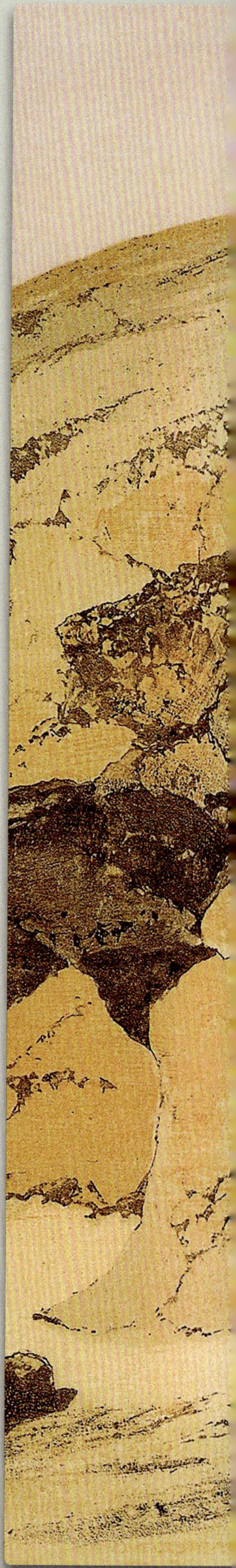

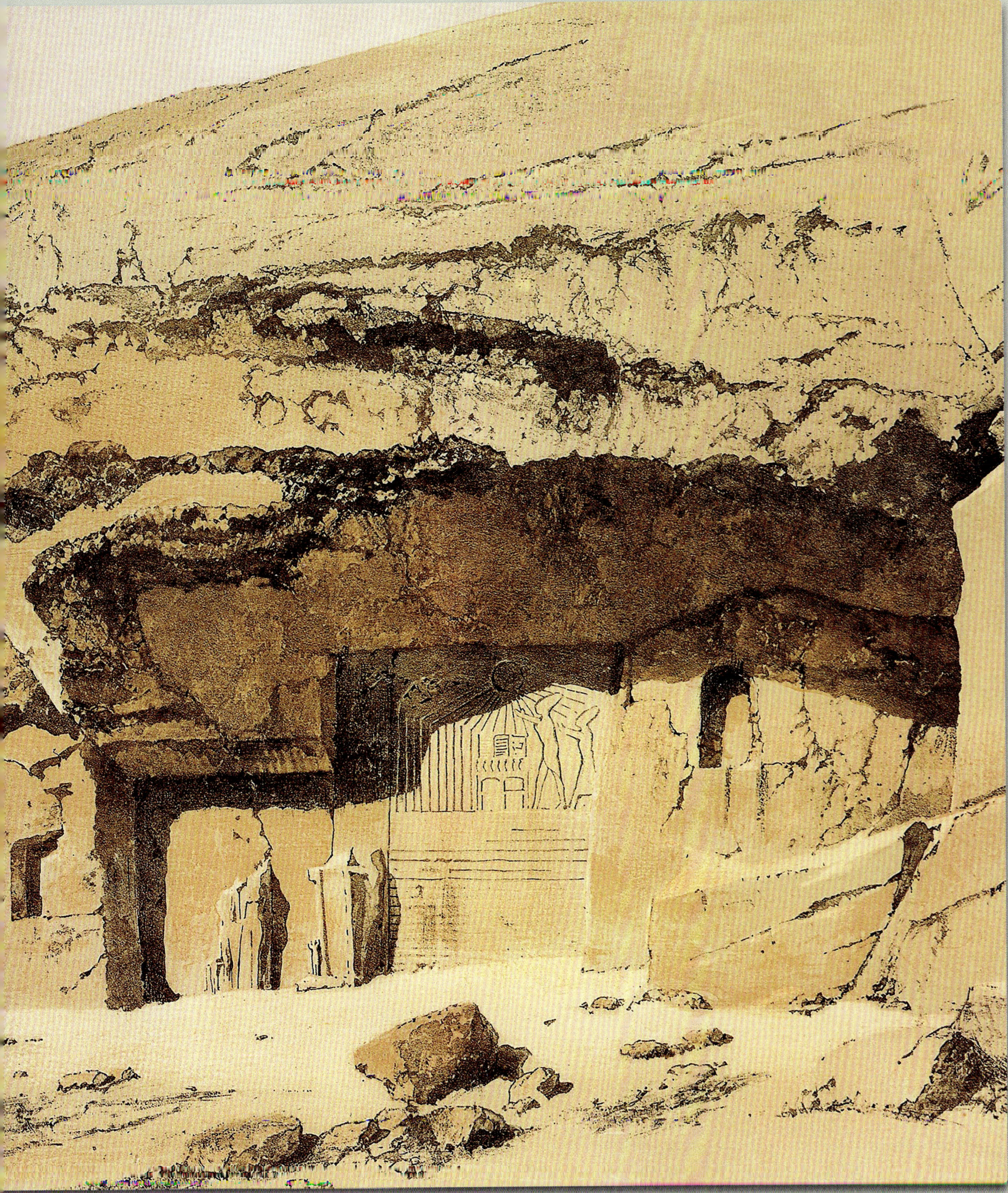

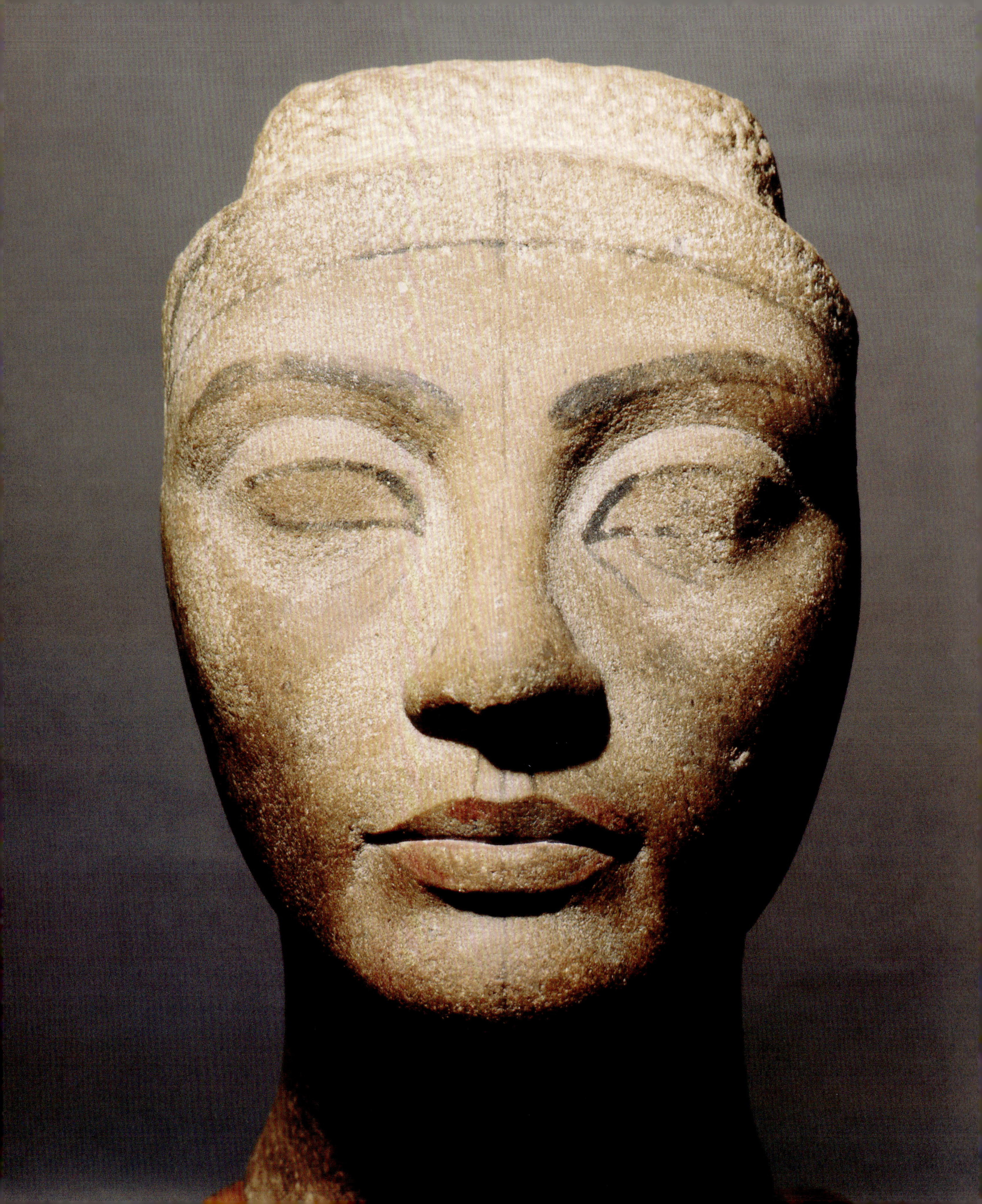

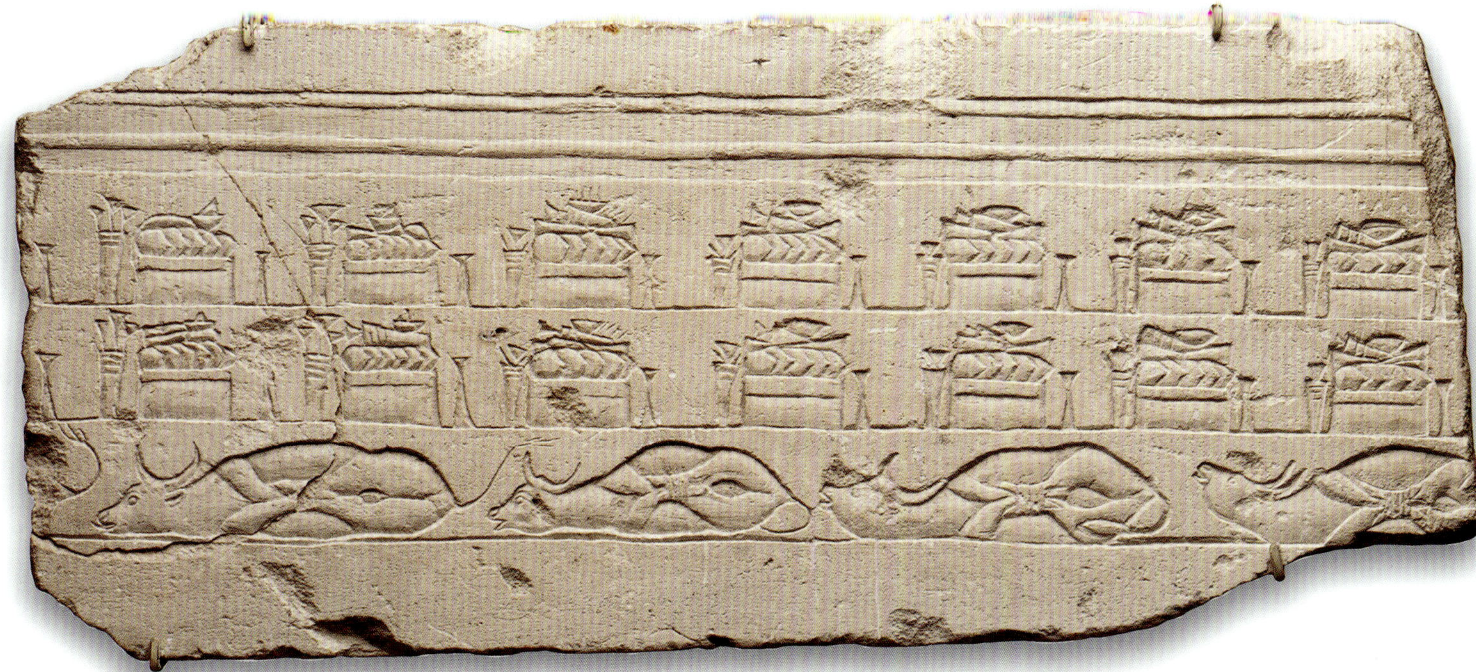

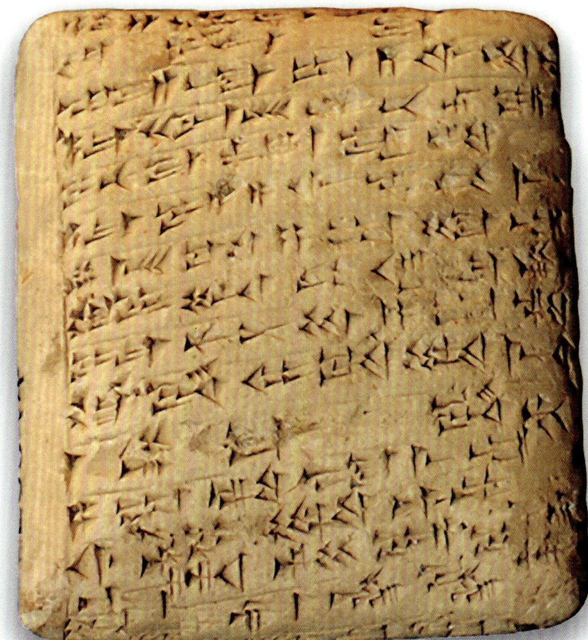

Capturing Nefertiti's aloof beauty, an unfinished sculpture (opposite) was found at Akhetaten in the workshop of a royal artist named Thutmose.

A building block from the ruins of the Great Temple at Akhetaten (above) shows offerings made to the Aten—rows of tables with loaves of bread, bouquets of flowers, and bowls of incense. Cattle prepared for sacrifice appear at the bottom.

A clay tablet bearing a text in Akkadian cuneiform, the common international language of the day (right), is one of 382 surviving diplomatic letters from Akhenaten's reign.

During Akhenaten's rule, portraits exaggerated his family's characteristic long skulls. This head (right) may depict Meritaten, the king's oldest daughter. It too came from Thutmose's workshop.

Informal family scenes were also hallmarks of the era. This fragment of a wall painting (below) shows young princesses, likely part of a scene that included the king, queen, and other sisters.

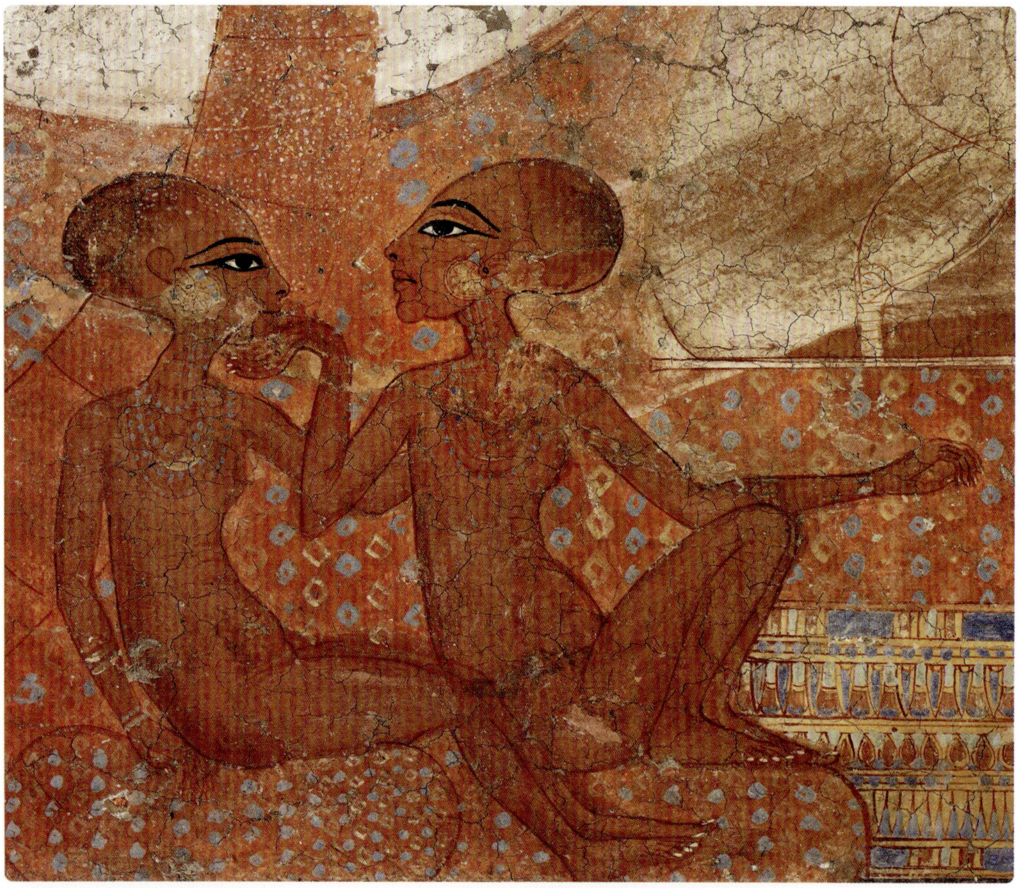

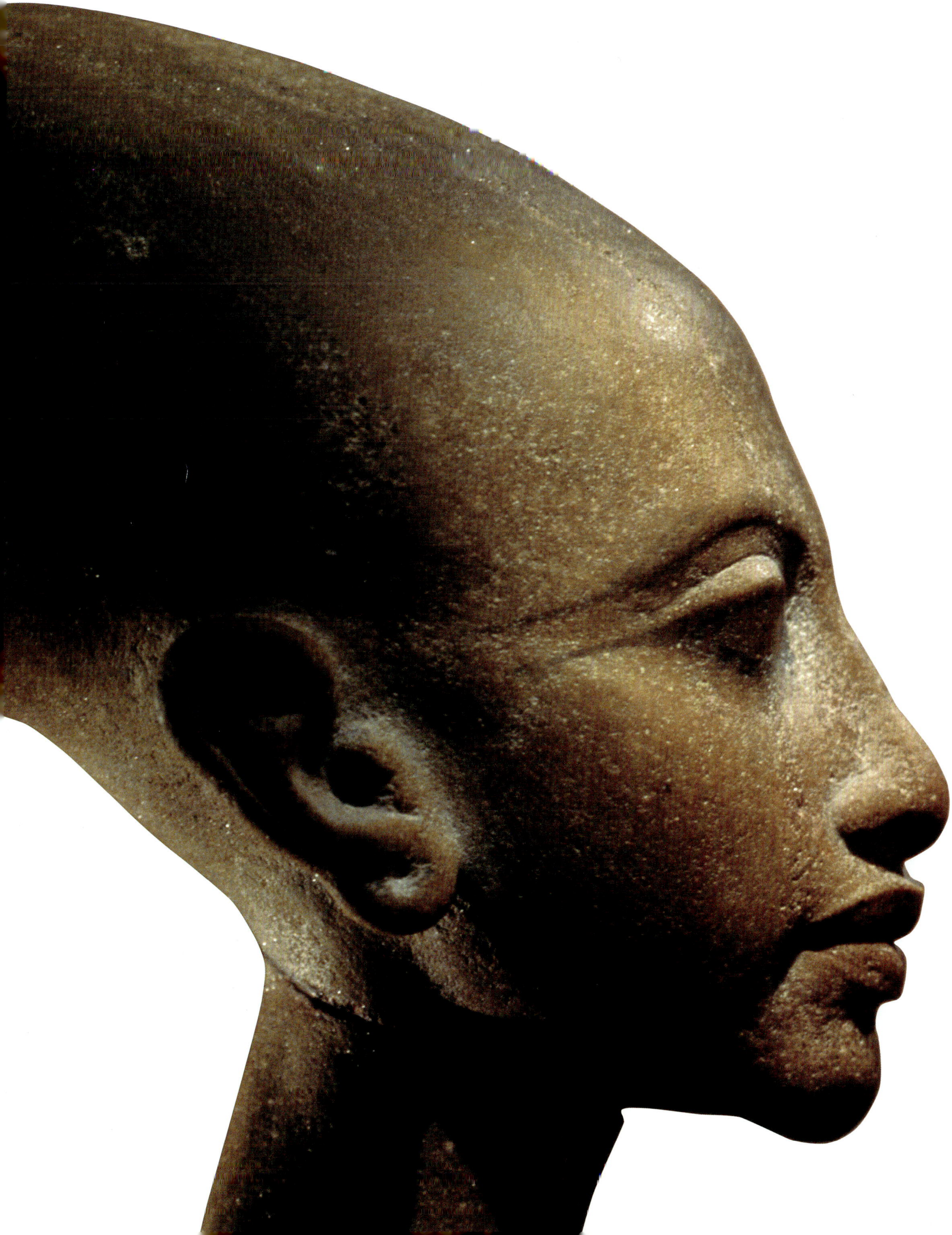

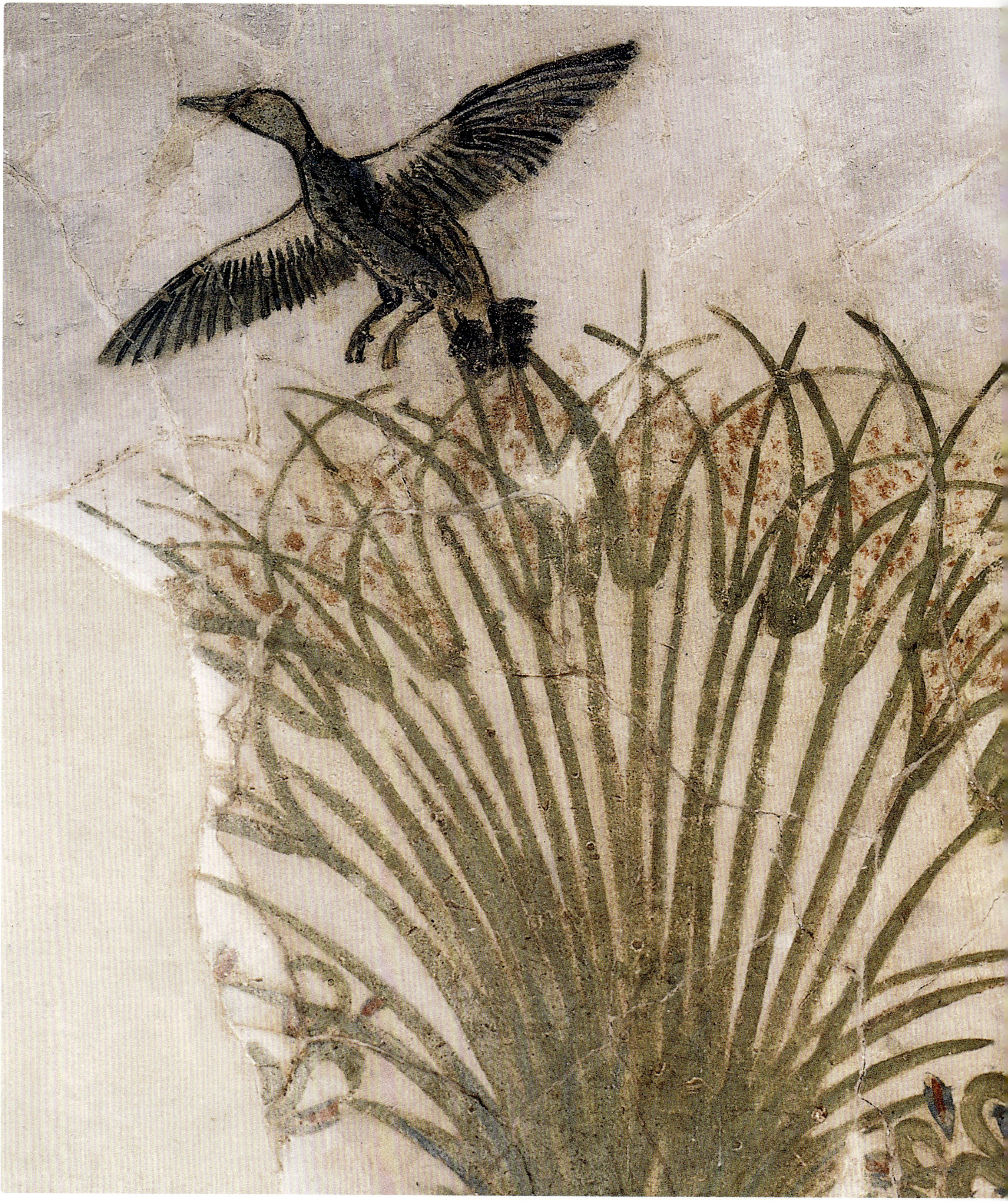

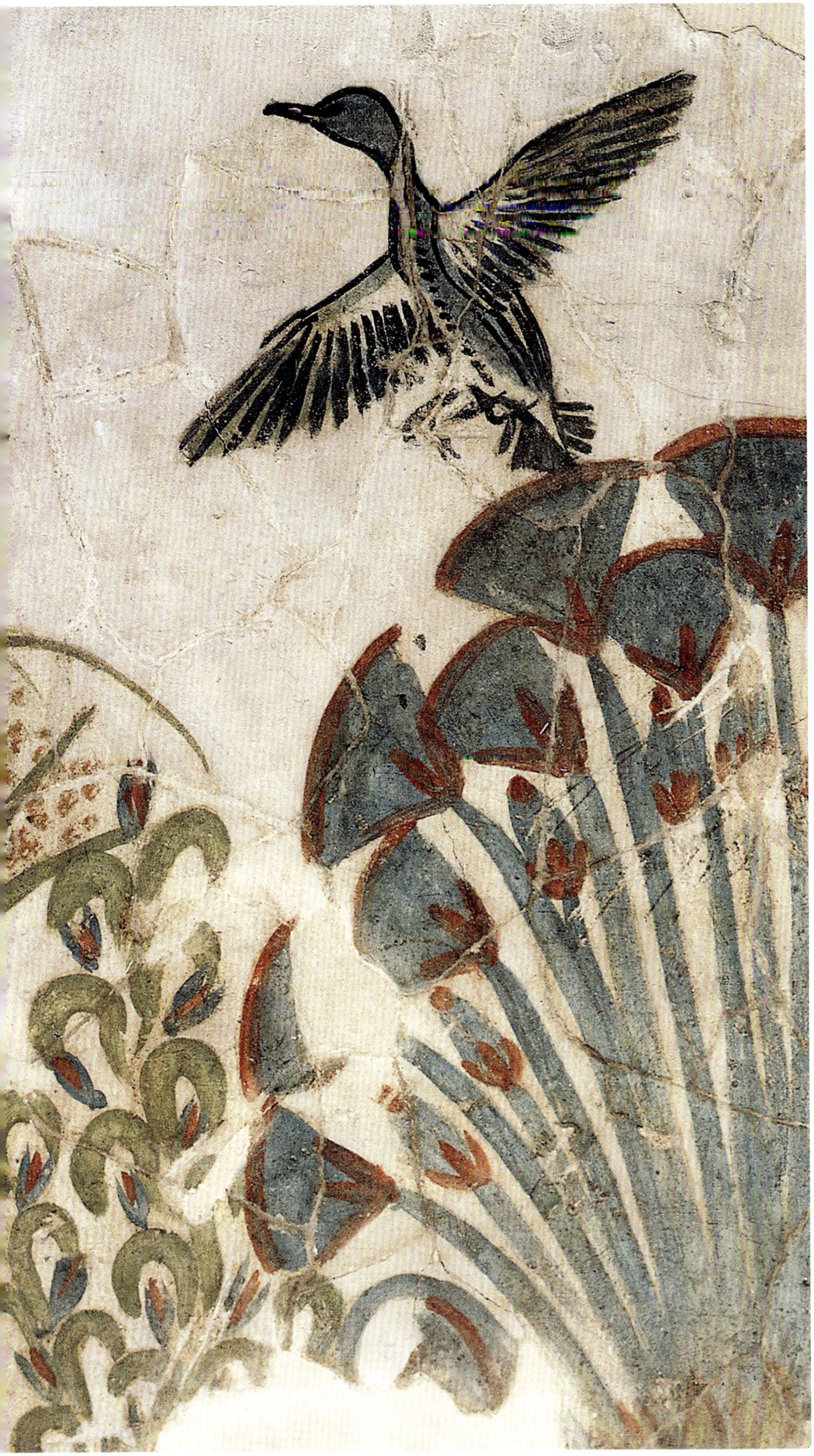

Wild ducks take flight over stalks of papyrus and other marsh plants in a fragment from a palace floor at Akhetaten. Such realistic scenes from nature were popular during this time.

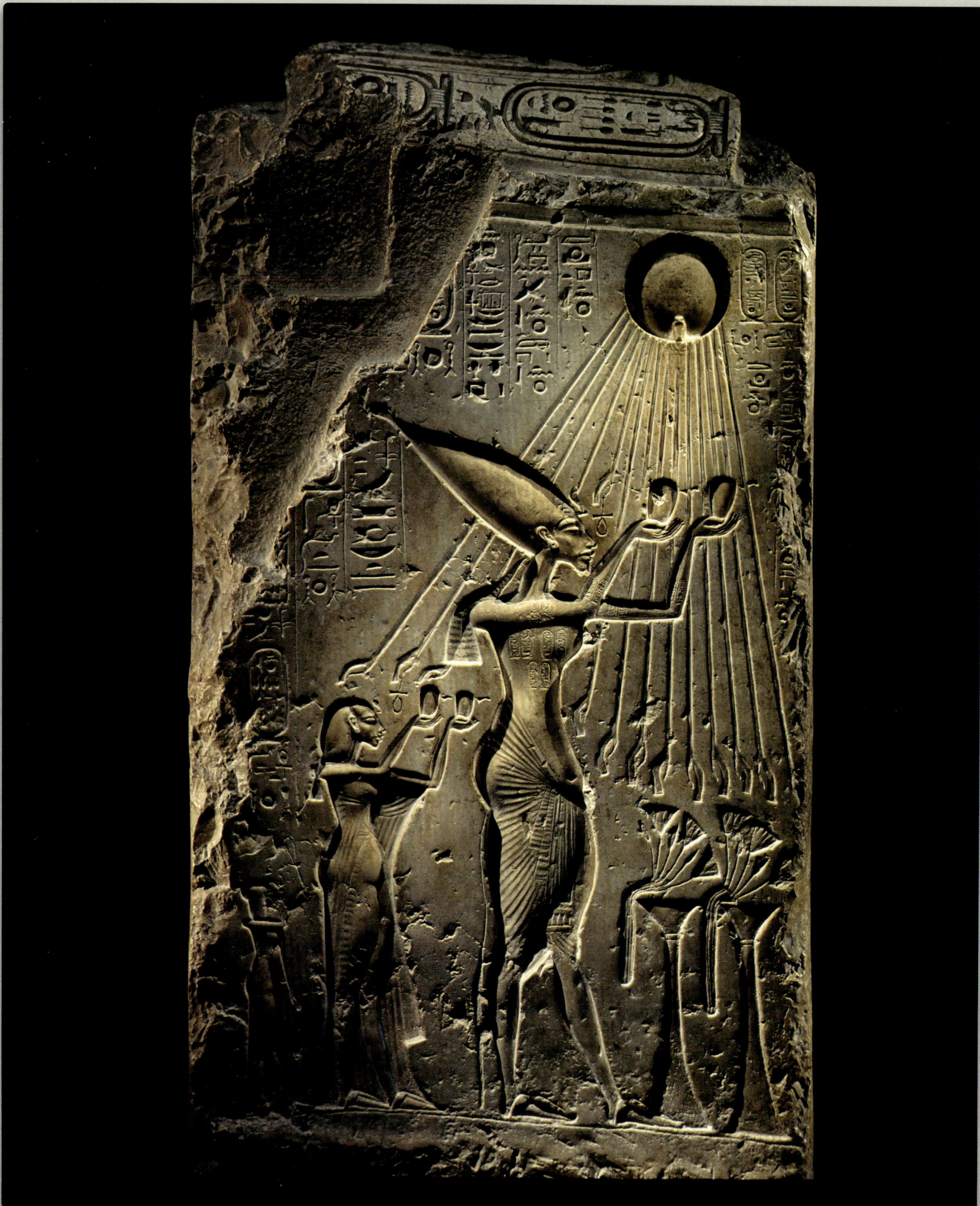

The Aten Revolution

"BEAUTIFULLY YOU APPEAR from the horizon of heaven, O living Aten who initiates life," began a hymn to the sun disk deity written around the time of Akhenaten (right) and sometimes attributed to him.

Akhenaten was not the first king to recognize this god; the Aten had been worshipped from at least as early as the 19th century B.C. But by Akhenaten's time, some five centuries later, the god's importance had grown. In fact, "radiance of Aten" was one of the epithets of Akhenaten's own father.

Once Akhenaten became king, he made the Aten Egypt's main god. Aten temples were built in several cities, including two in the new capital. Royal art showed Akhenaten and his queen, Nefertiti, bathed in the Aten's light, whose rays end in caressing hands (opposite). The worship of Amun—previously the most prominent god—was banned, and other deities were diminished in stature.

Akhenaten was hardly cold in his grave when Egyptians returned to their traditional religious beliefs. The Aten temples were torn down and, ironically, many of their stones were used to restore or expand temples of the gods the heretic king had persecuted.

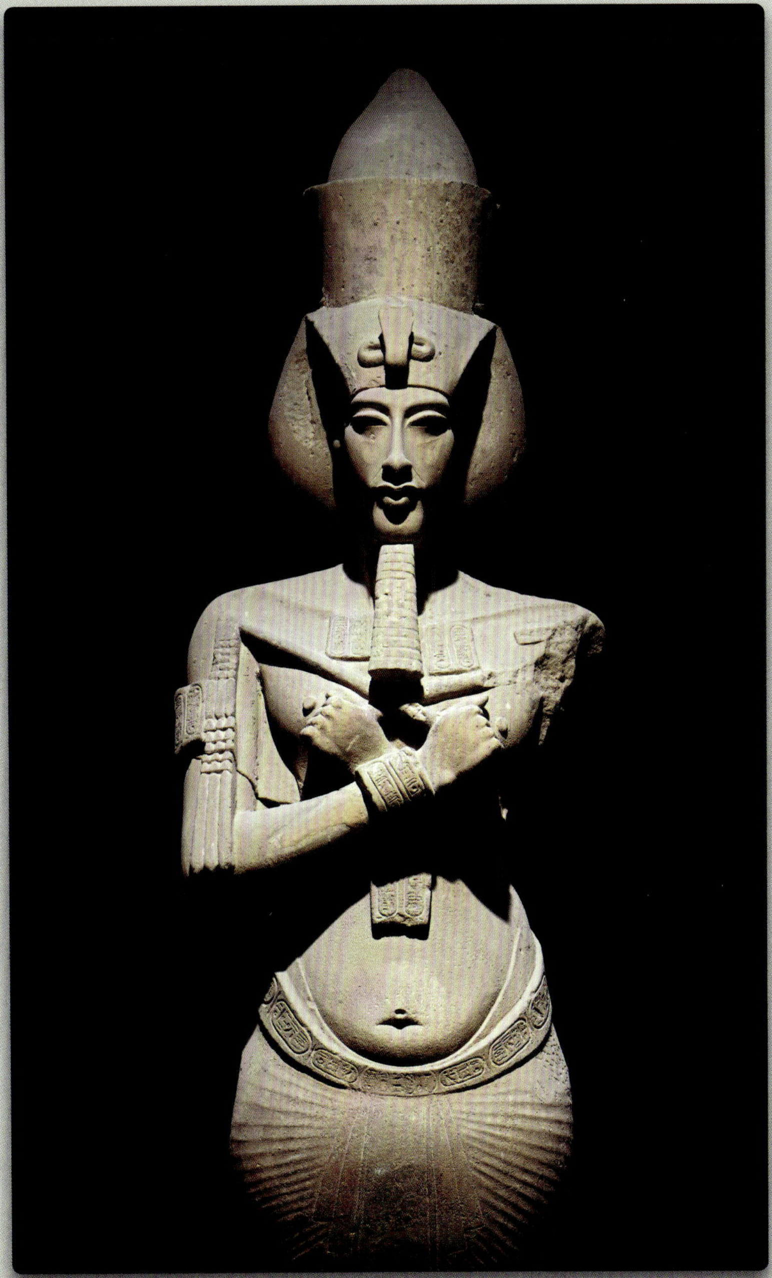

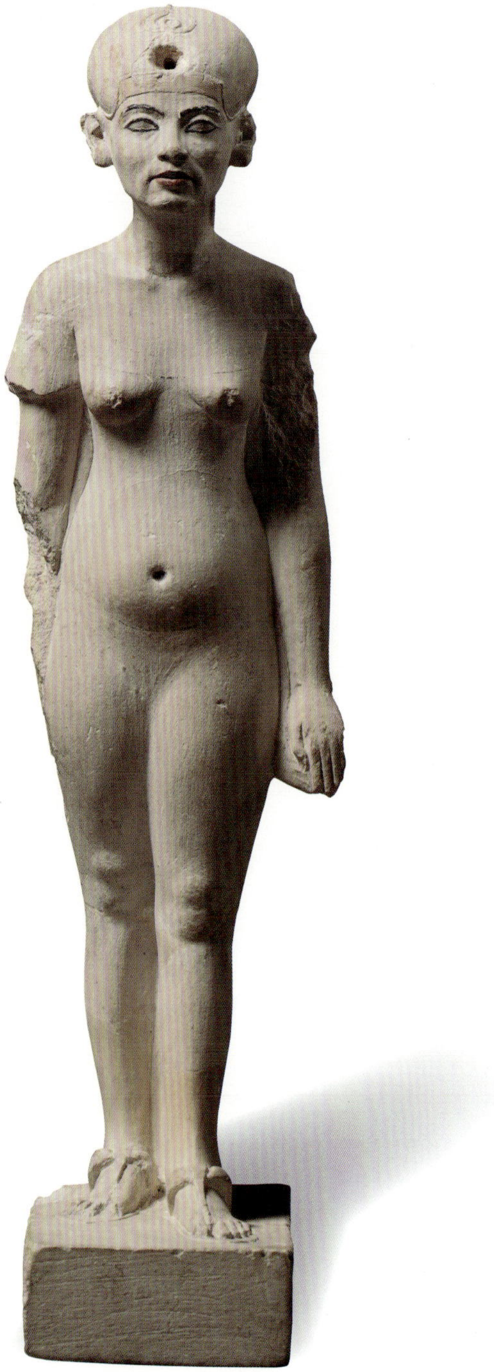

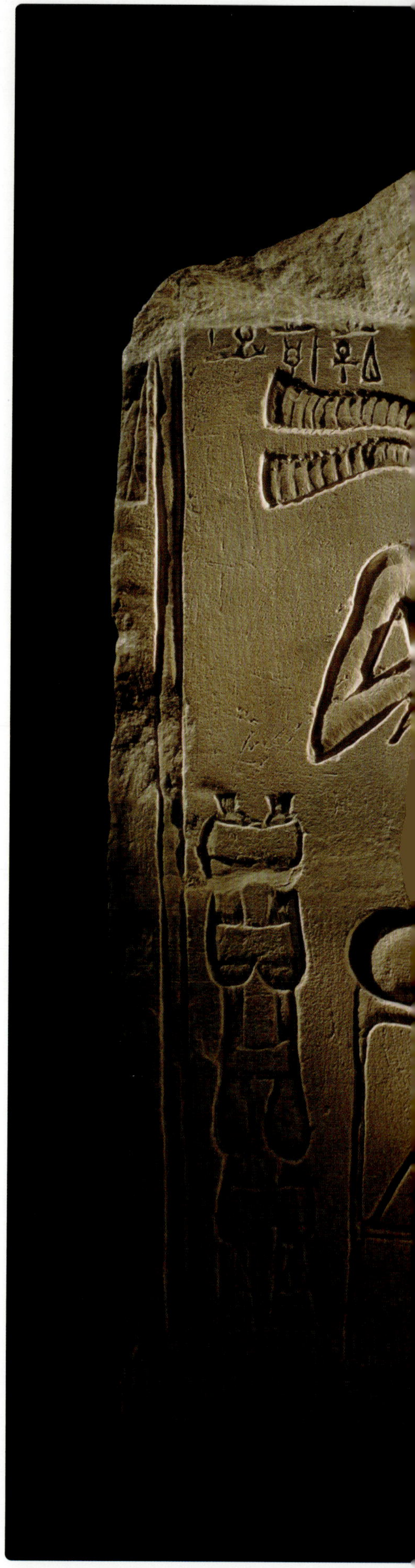

In an intimate scene embodying Akhenaten's new religious and artistic vision (right), the king and queen cuddle their daughters as they form a life-giving triad with their god.

The queen wears a barely there diaphanous robe and sandals in a limestone sculpture (above) that was found in pieces in Thutmose's workshop and reassembled.

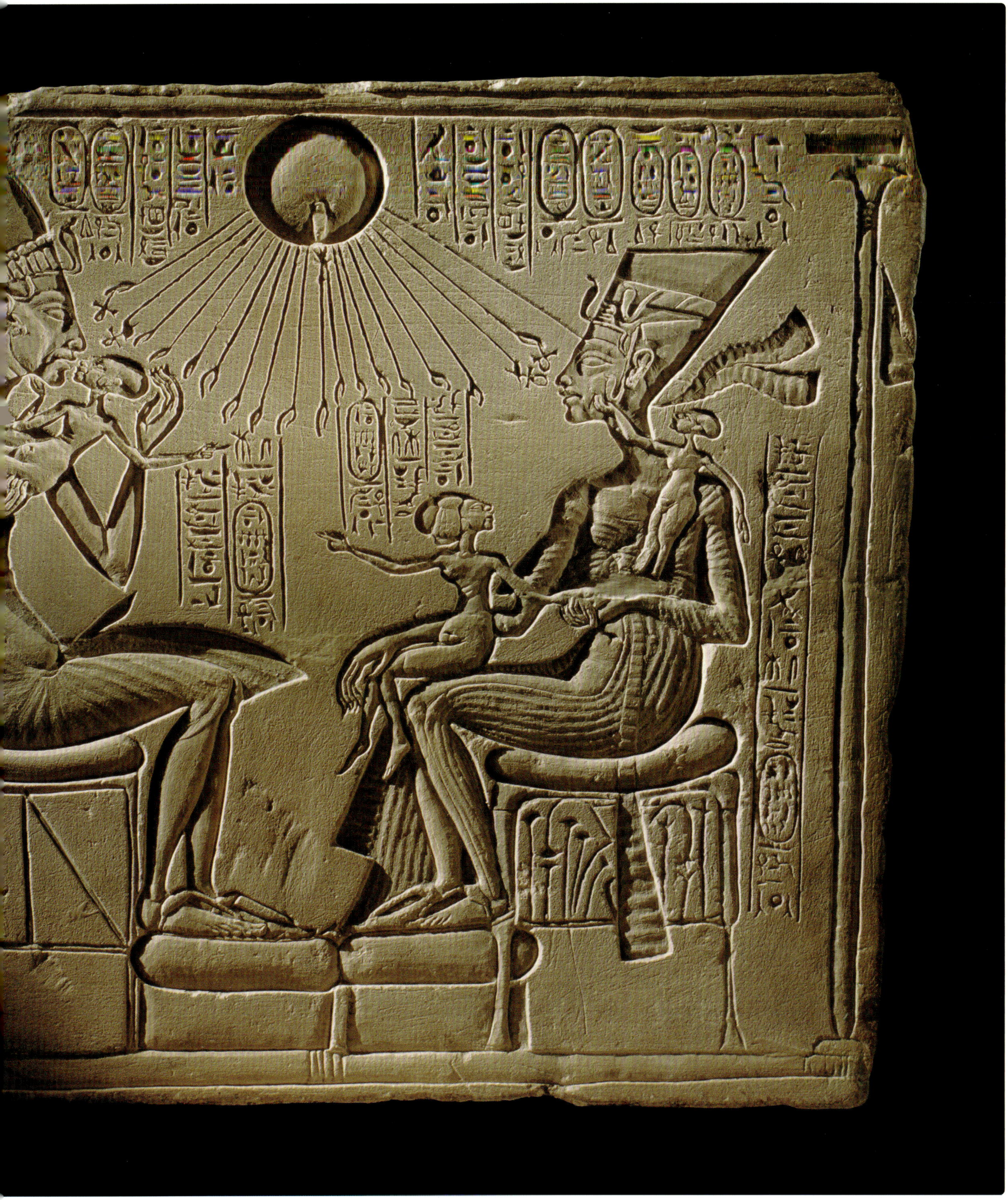

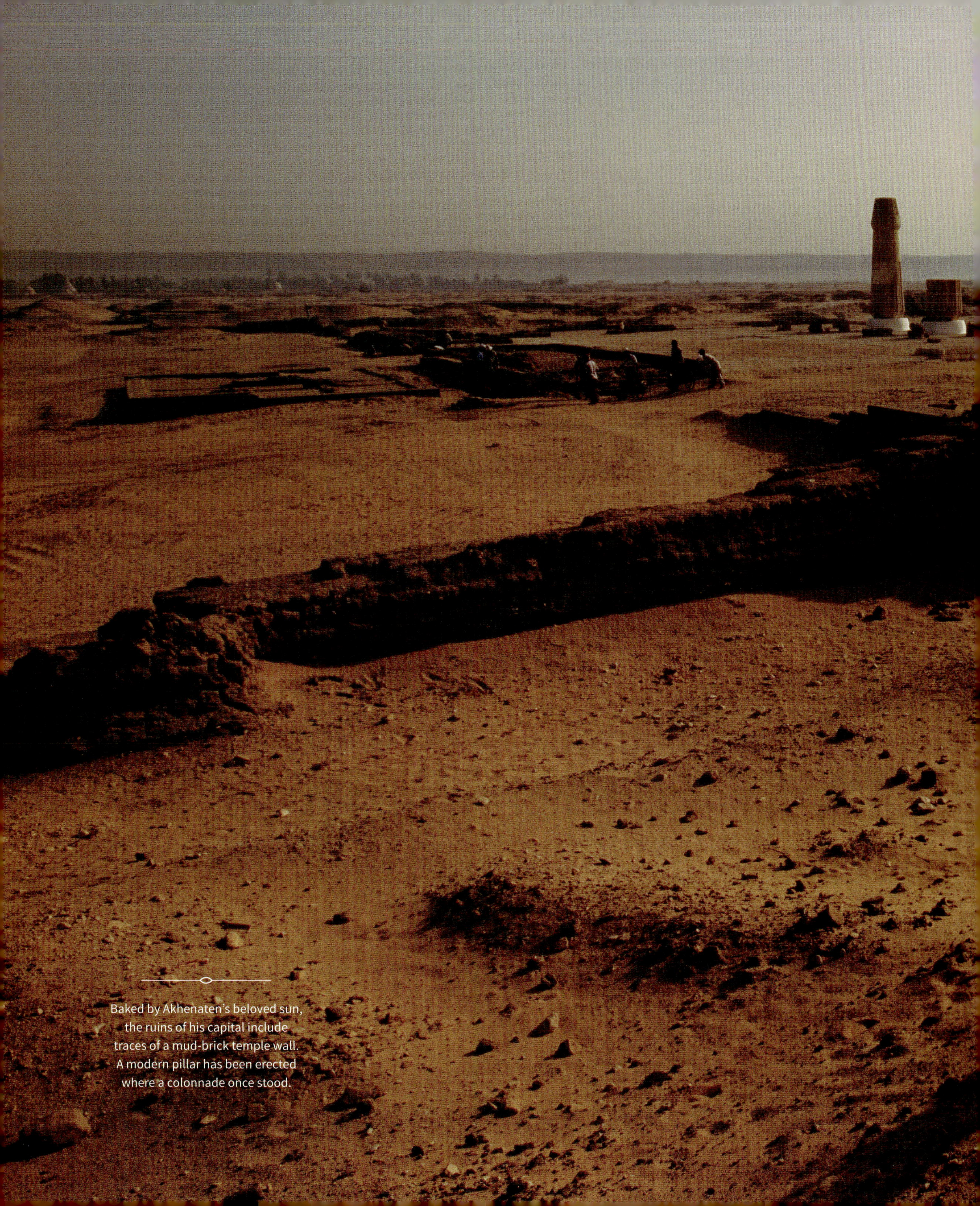

Baked by Akhenaten's beloved sun, the ruins of his capital include traces of a mud-brick temple wall. A modern pillar has been erected where a colonnade once stood.

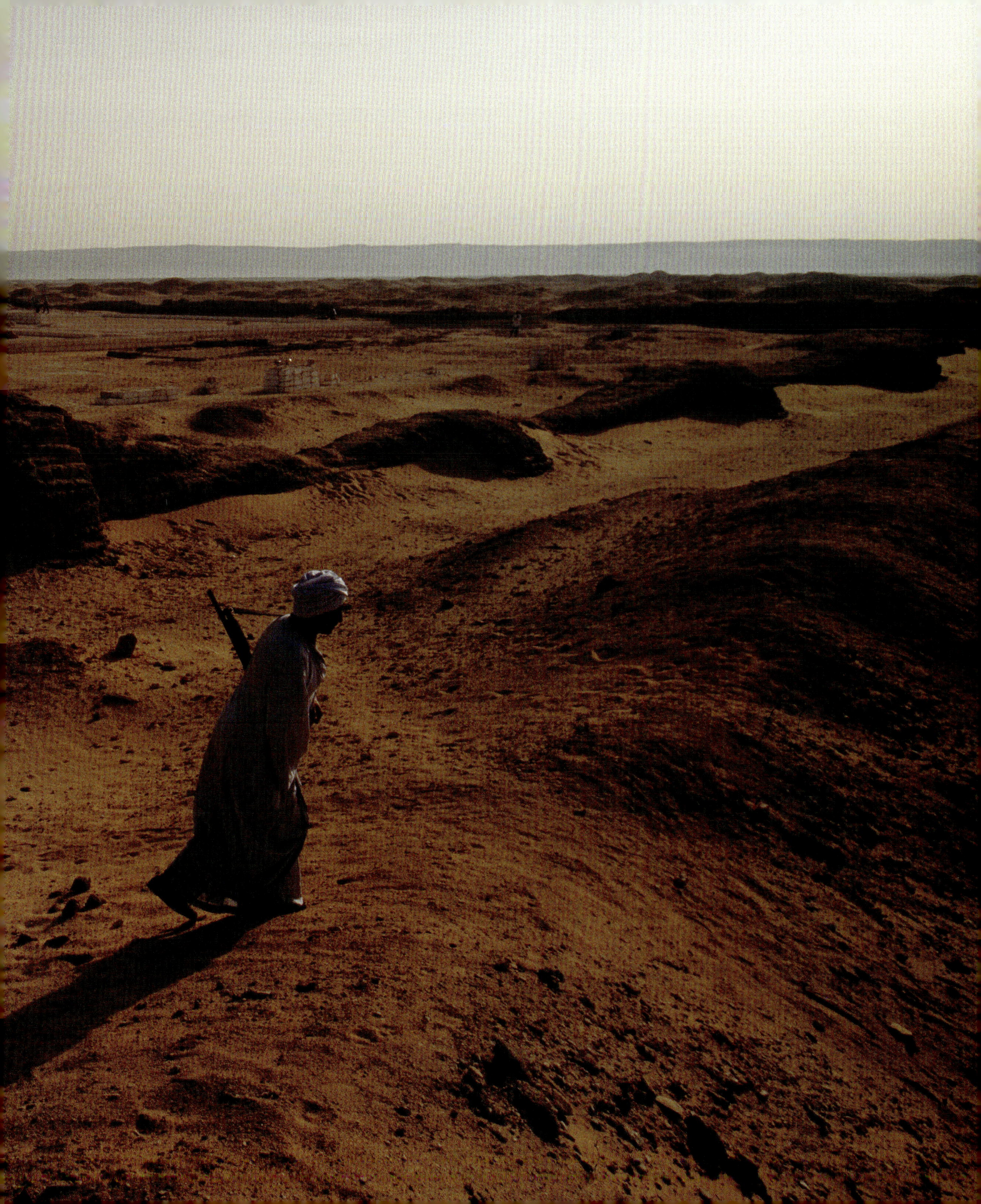

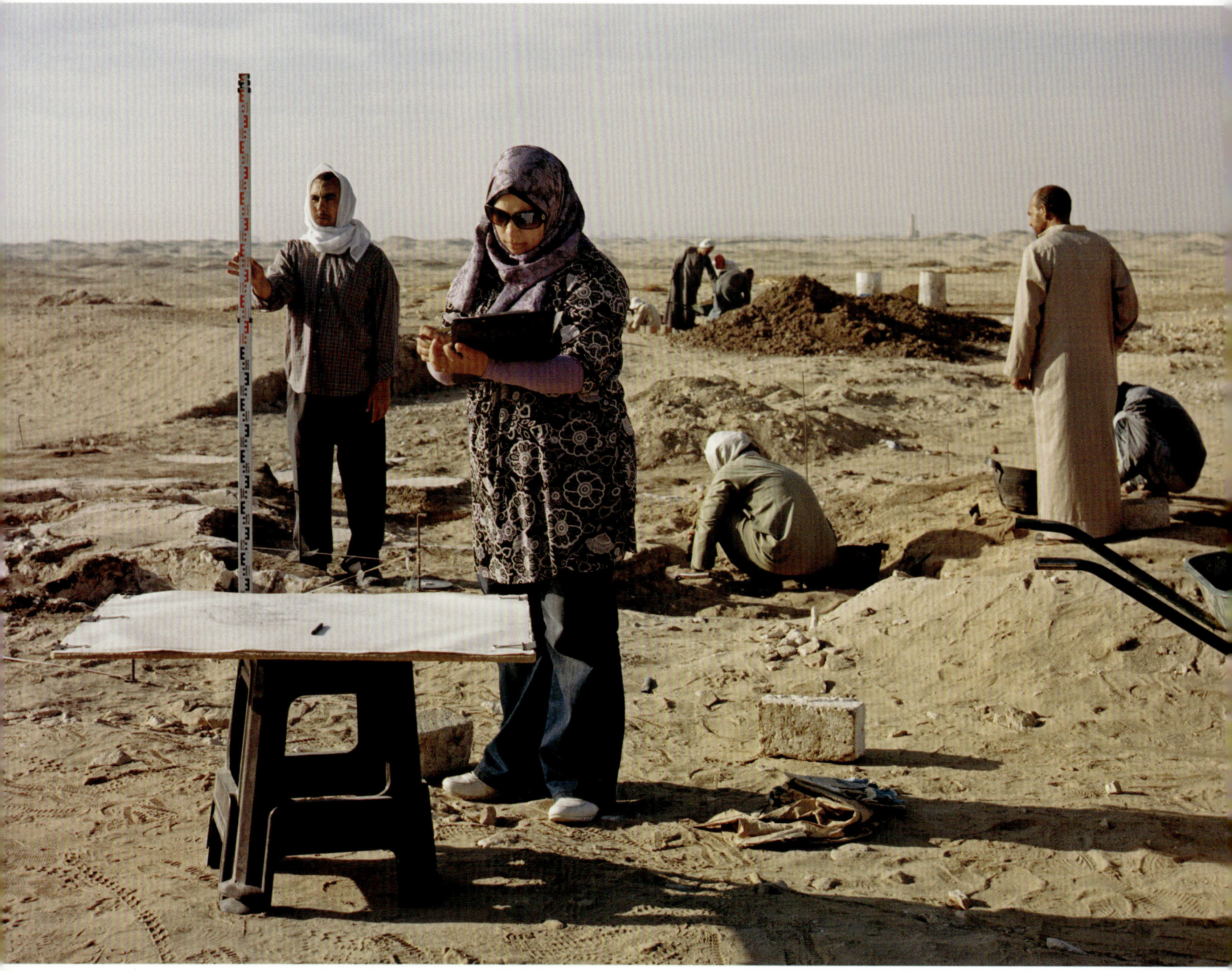

Excavation of the larger of Akhetaten's two Aten temples has revealed traces of six courtyards. Each was once filled with stone tables, for a total of more than 700 offering surfaces.

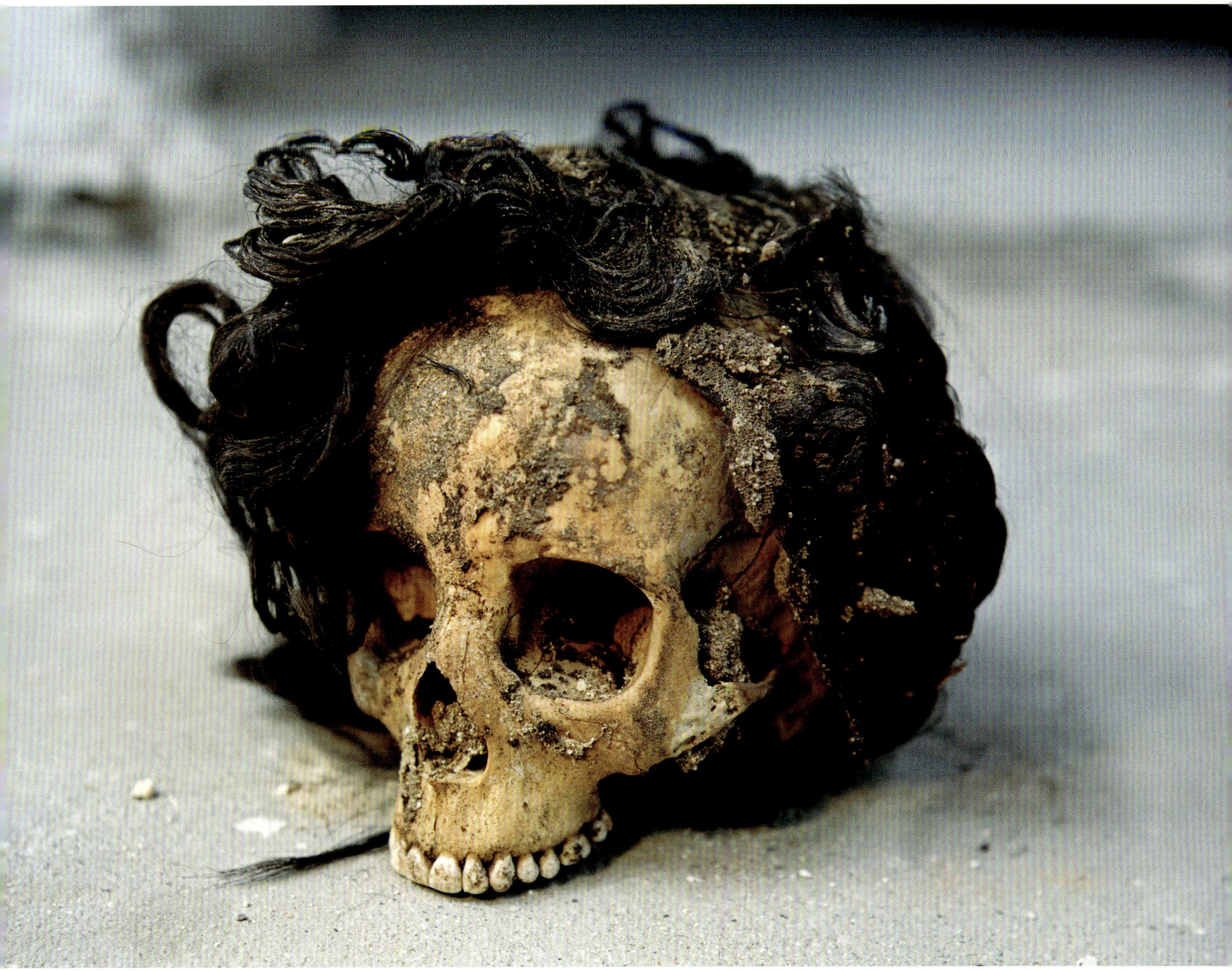

Despite a life of hard work, residents of Akhetaten apparently took time to create elaborate hairstyles. Human remains from a cemetery there display curls, coils, and braids, all held in place with fat.

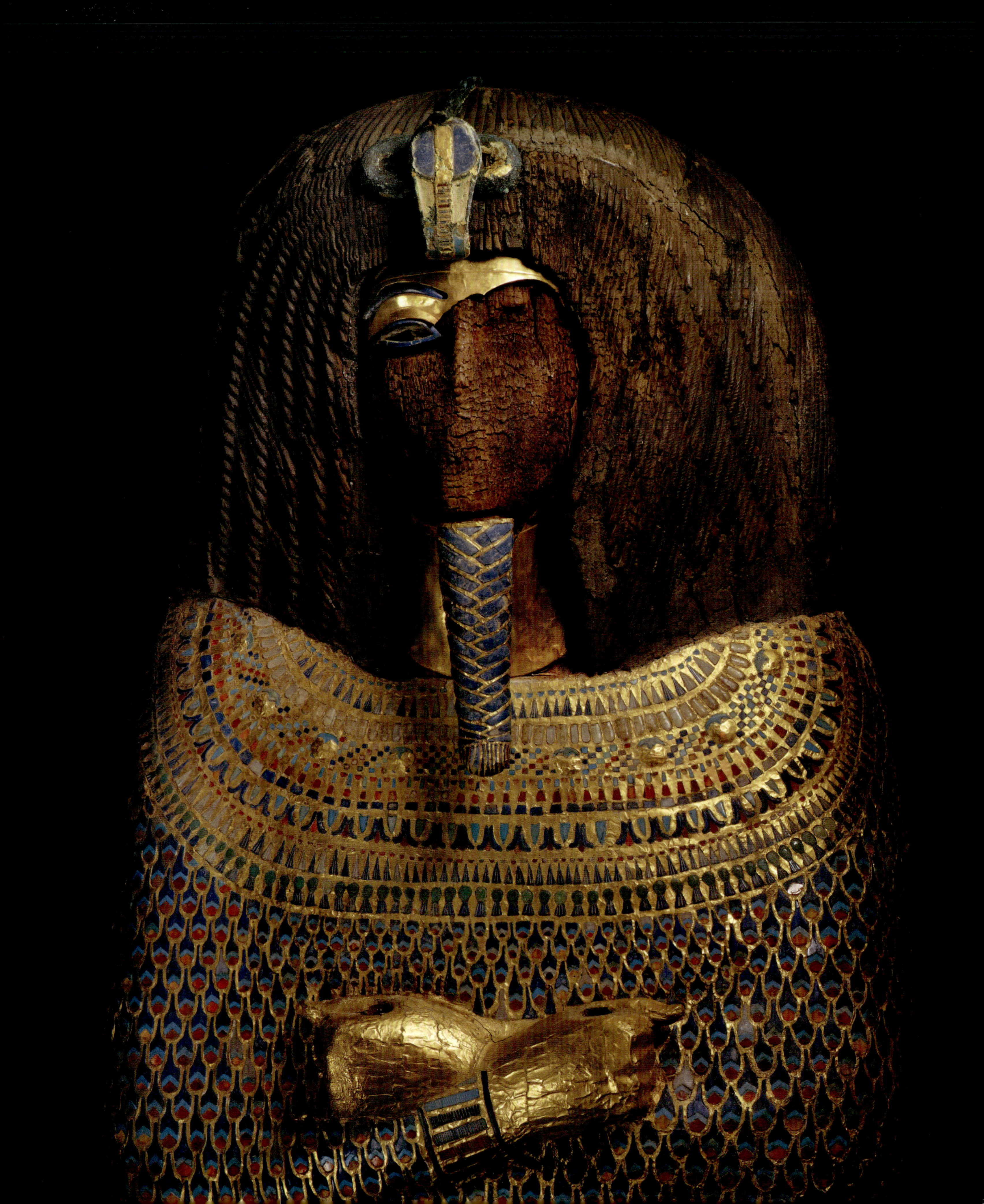

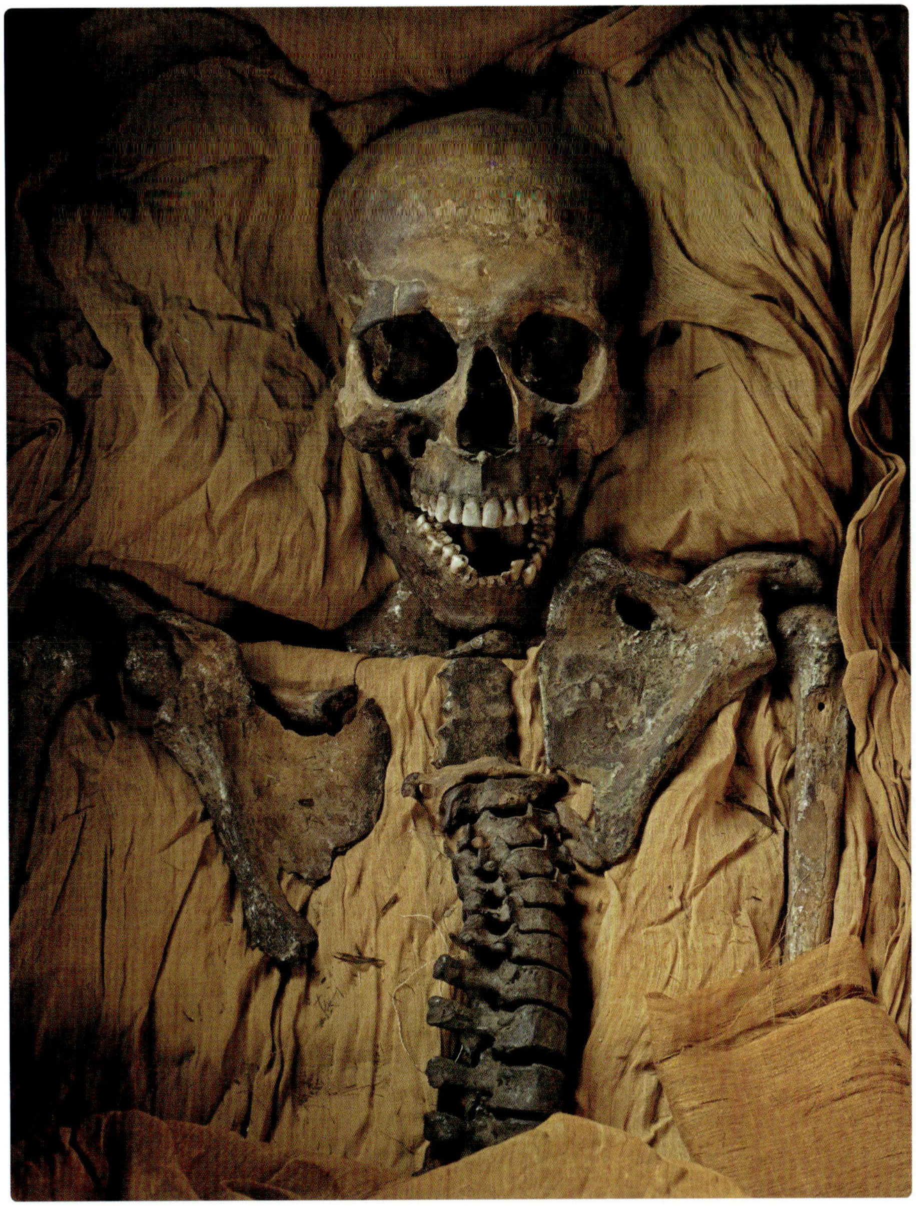

Buried in the Valley of the Kings, a richly decorated coffin (opposite) was likely made for a female, but the human remains it held upon discovery were male. The face and inscribed royal names had been deliberately destroyed in antiquity.

DNA testing suggests that the bones in the coffin (above) were those of Akhenaten, but the identity has not been confirmed for certain.

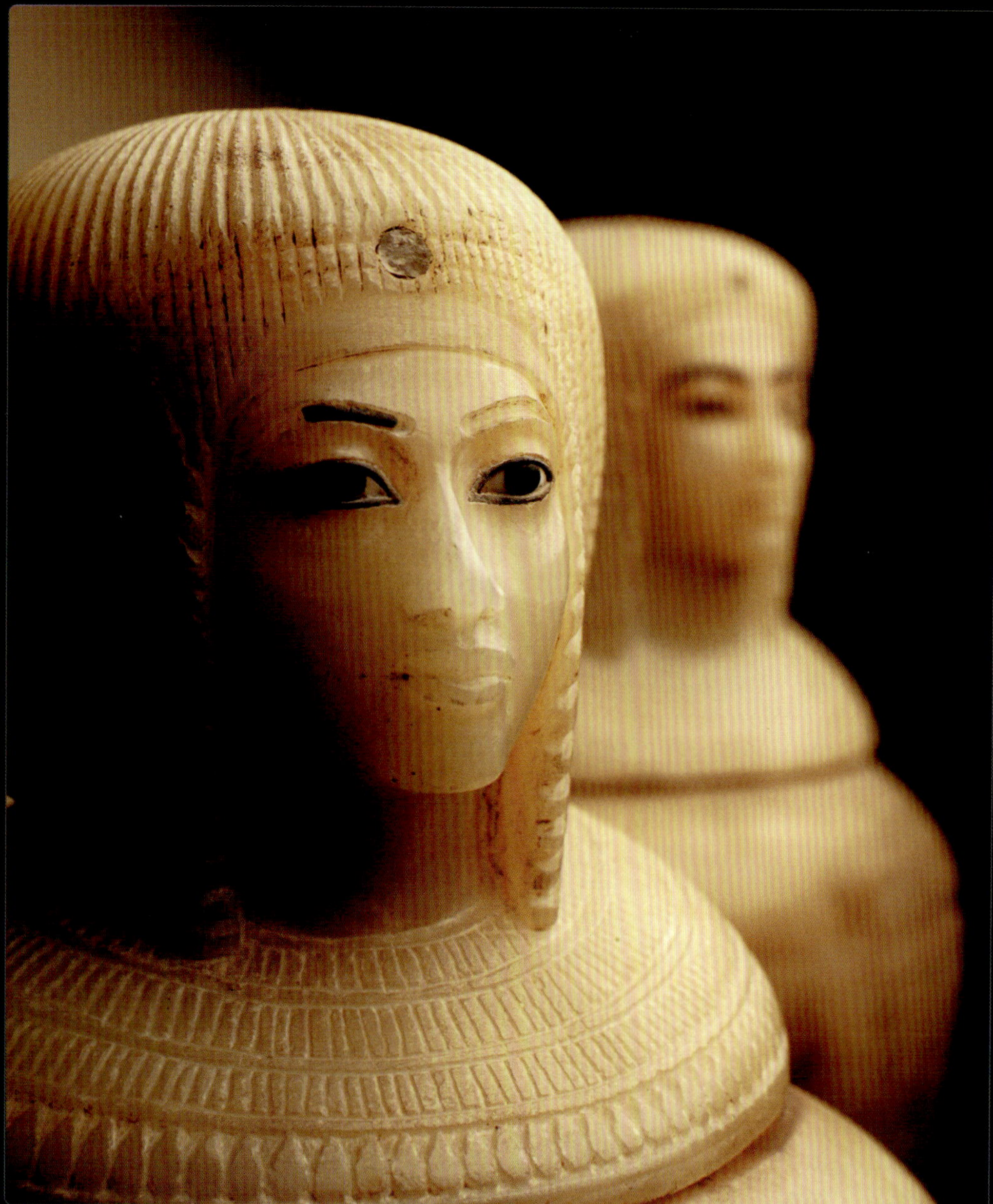

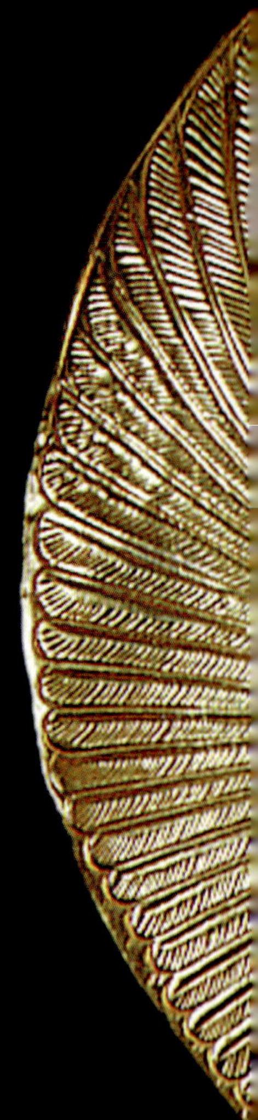

The purported tomb of Akhenaten, known as KV 55, held a strange collection of royal artifacts, likely brought from the abandoned city of Akhetaten. These stone canopic jars (above) may have been carved for a royal wife named Kiya.

A gold collar in the shape of Nekhbet (right), a protective goddess, was found in the same tomb. In her claw, the vulture holds the hieroglyph for eternity.

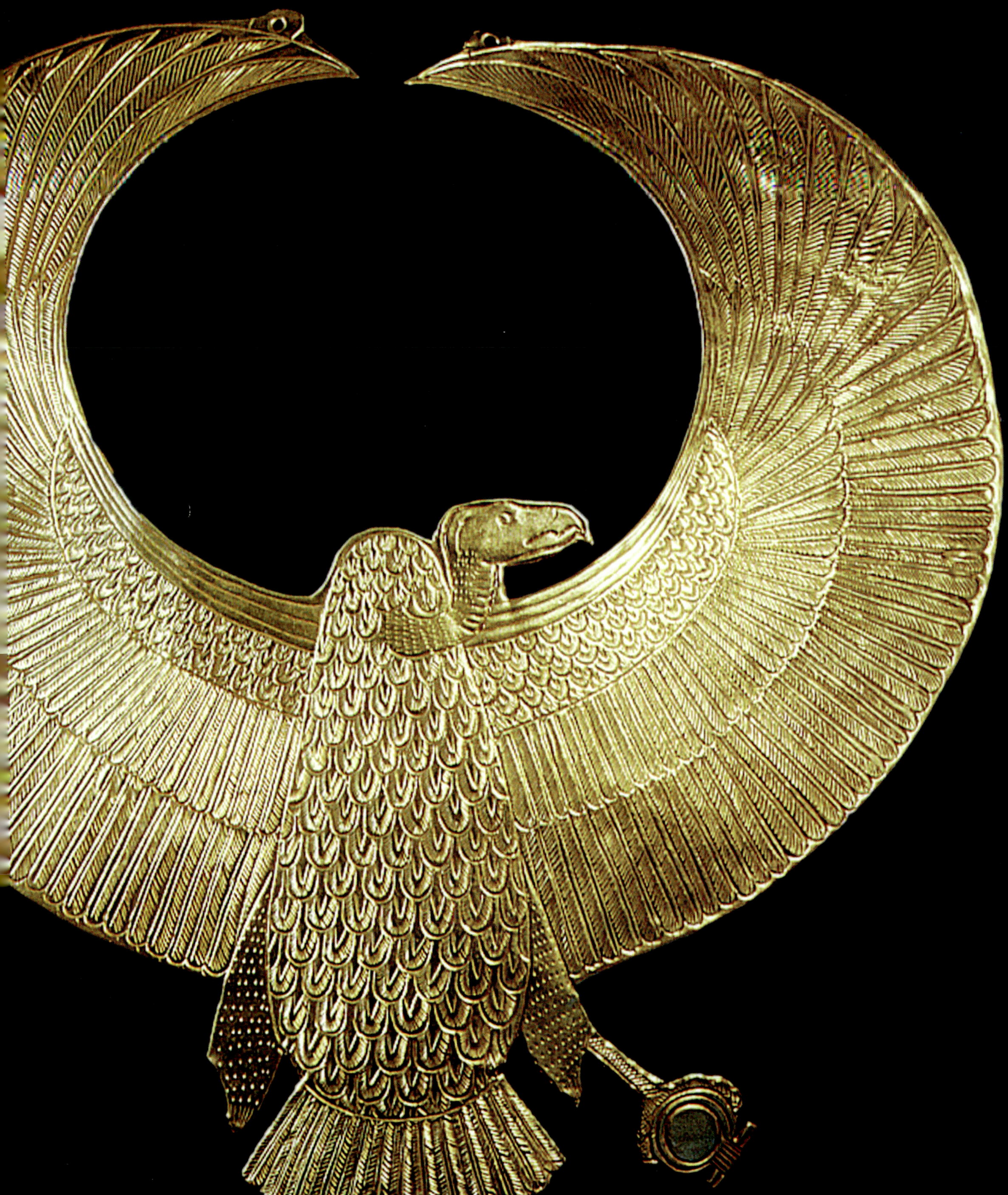

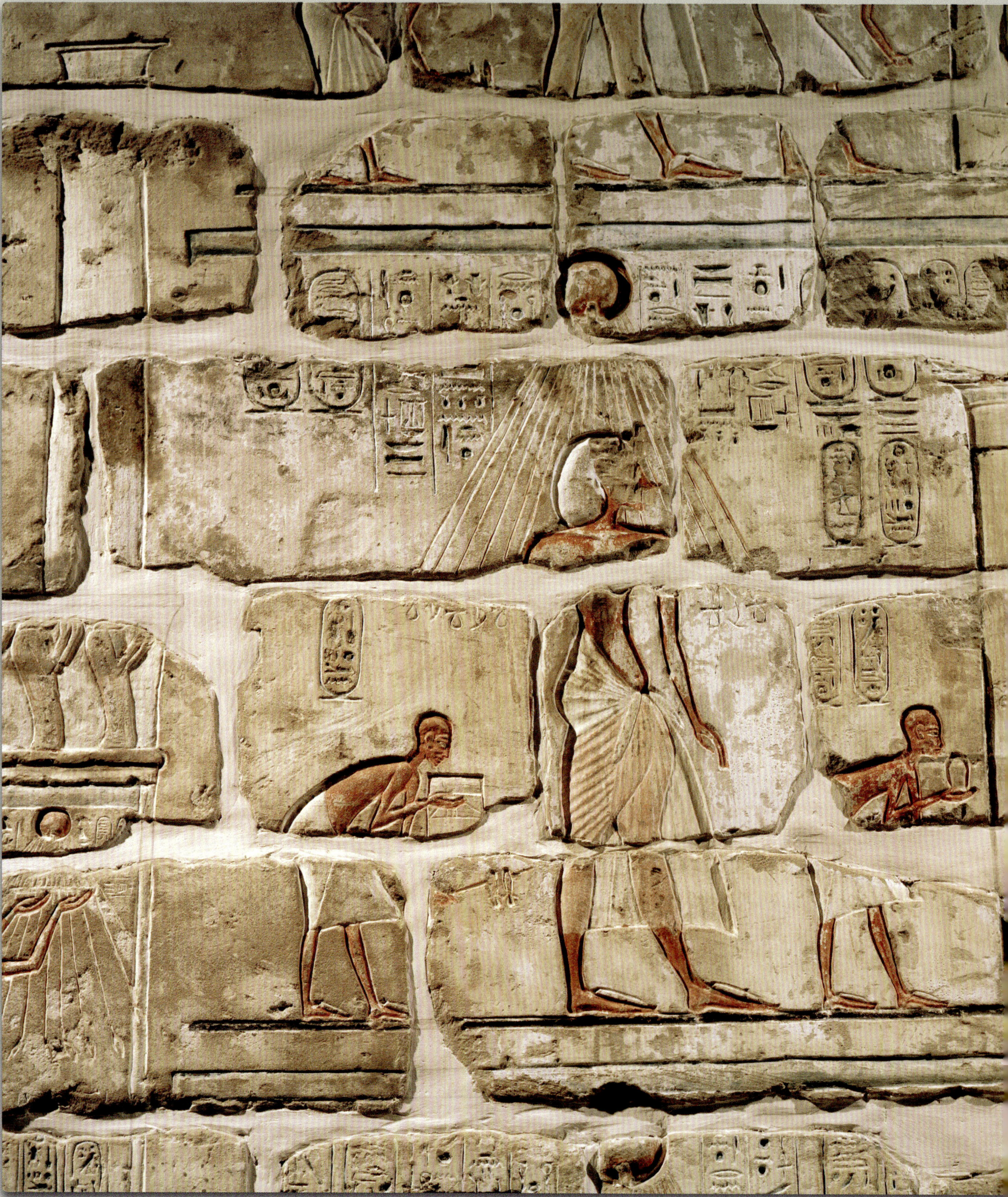

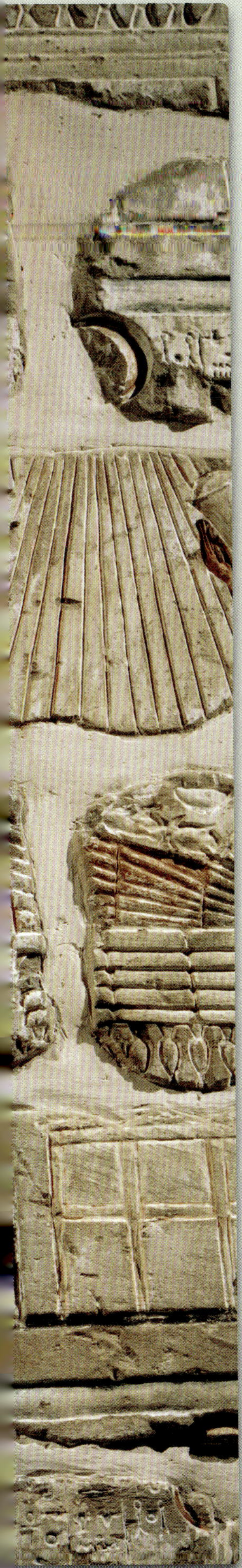

DIGGING DEEPER

Building Faster

WHEN AKHENATEN DECIDED to radically remake Egypt, he wanted to do so as quickly as possible. Building crews had to work faster than ever to create architecture expressing the king's new message. By greatly reducing the size of stones used in construction, they saved considerable time.

The stones used to build the pyramids at Giza weigh 2.5 tons (2.3 metric tons) or more. But Akhenaten's temples and palaces took shape with *talatat*, stones weighing only 120 pounds (55 kg) that were much easier to maneuver. No other pharaoh built with blocks this size, so whenever they turn up—often bearing distinctive reliefs—archaeologists know they belong to Akhenaten's reign. In a visual pun, one block (below) even shows workers building with talatat.

Akhenaten first made his mark by constructing a temple complex at Karnak; next, he started on the monumental buildings in his new capital. But what went up so quickly came down just as fast. When the king died, his city was demolished, and the talatat were reused in new construction. To recreate this wall showing the king with bowing courtiers (left), experts had to puzzle out the correct order of its recovered pieces.

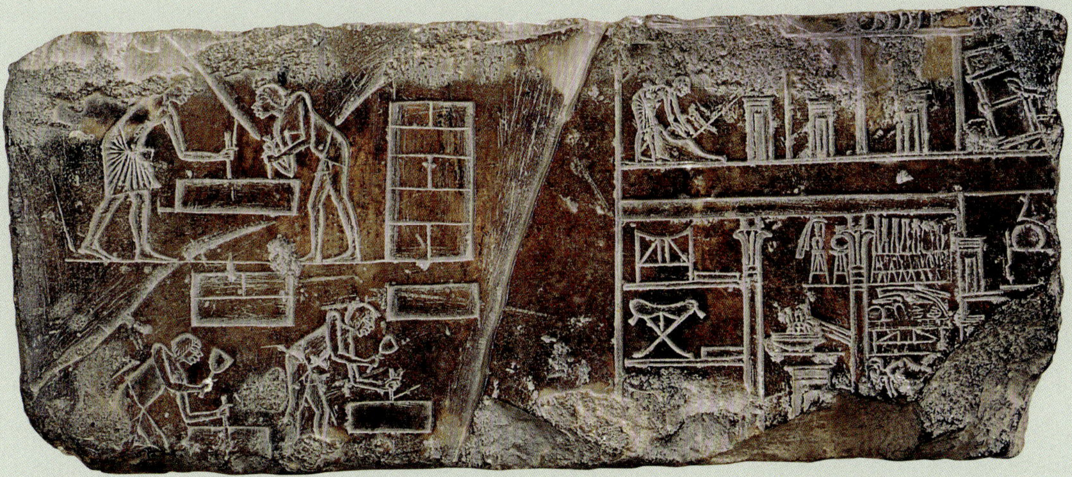

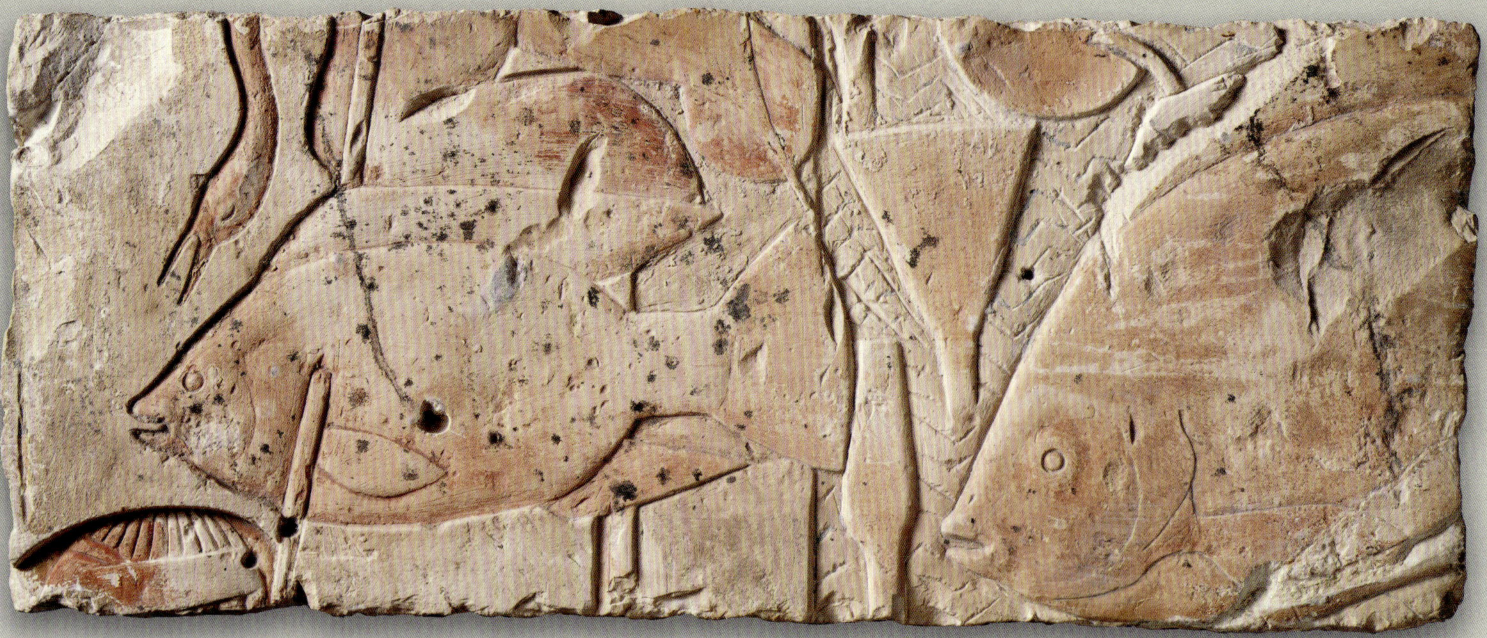

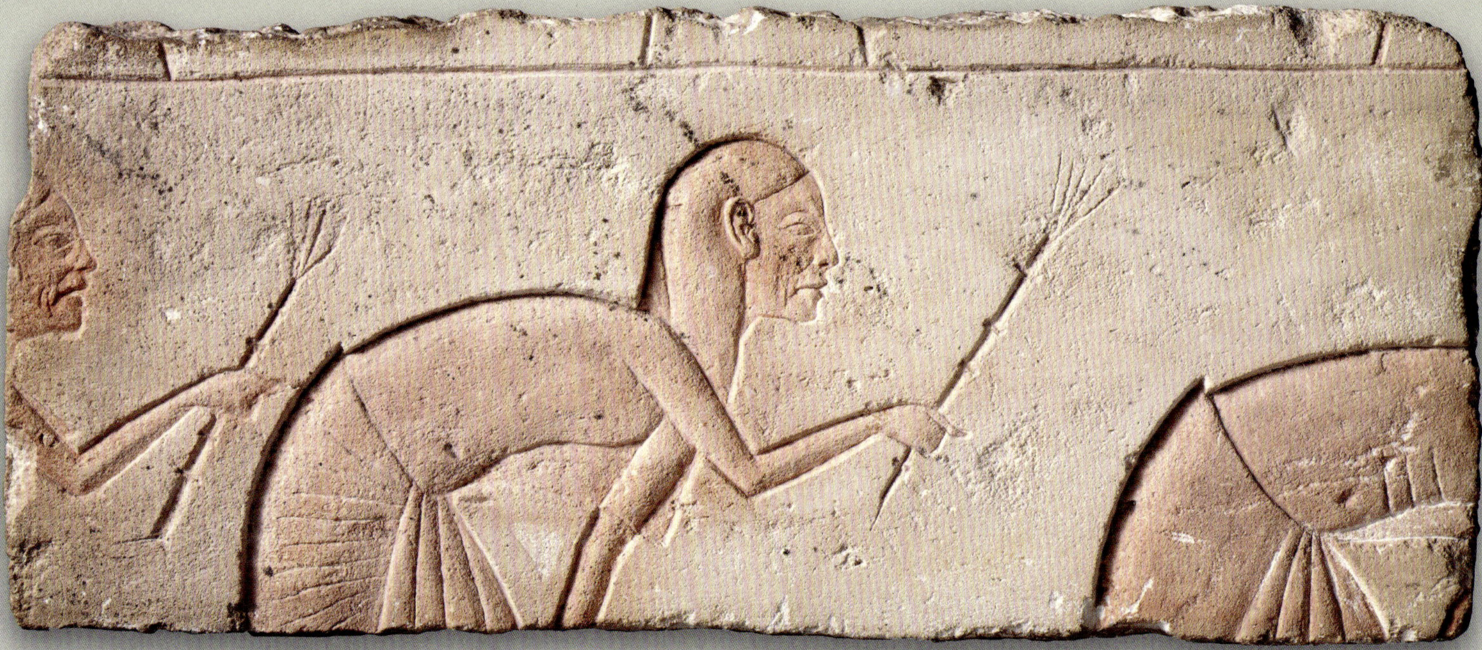

CONSTRUCTION BLOCKS

Some of the *talatat* used in Akhenaten's building projects bear reliefs that offer glimpses of elite life during this turbulent time. The subjects depicted on these examples are (clockwise from upper left) a pond with lily plants, the head of a duck, and fish—one of which has been speared; court ladies riding chariots in a procession; Nefertiti making an offering to the Aten; and bowing attendants possibly taking part in a religious or palace ritual.

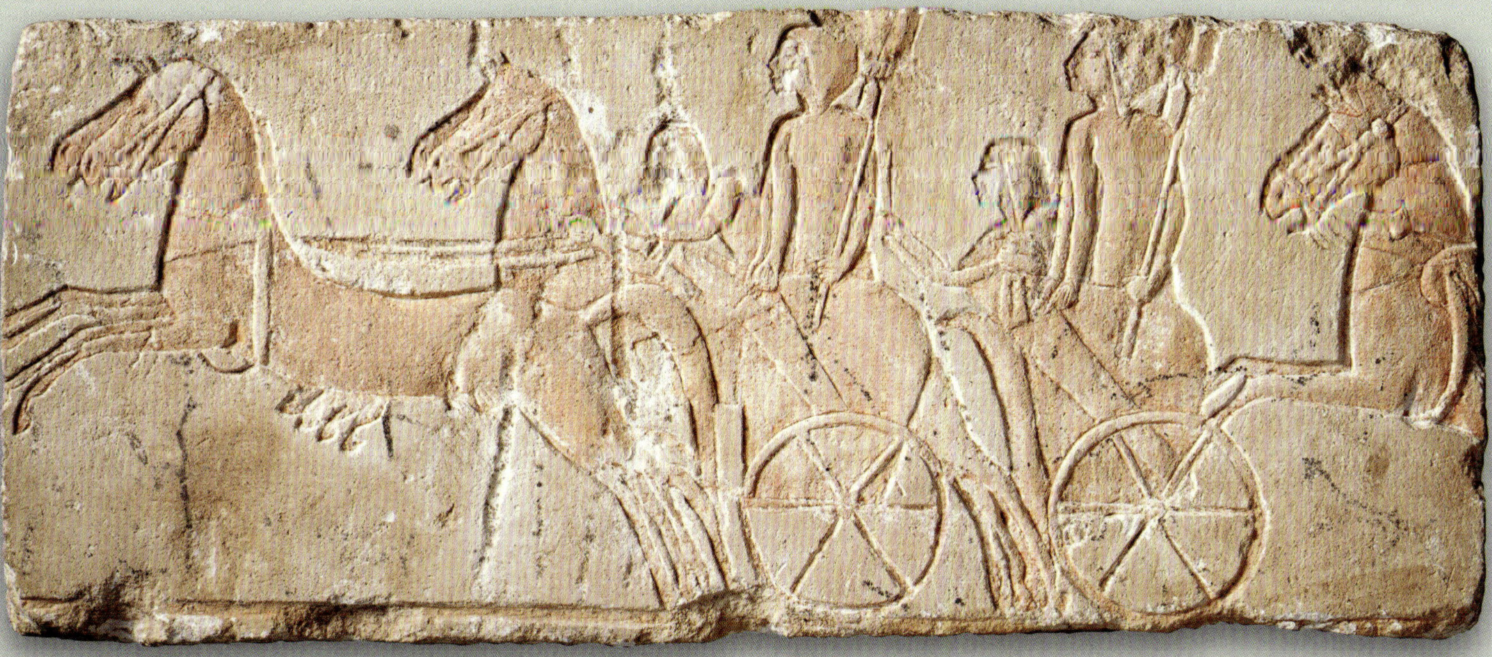

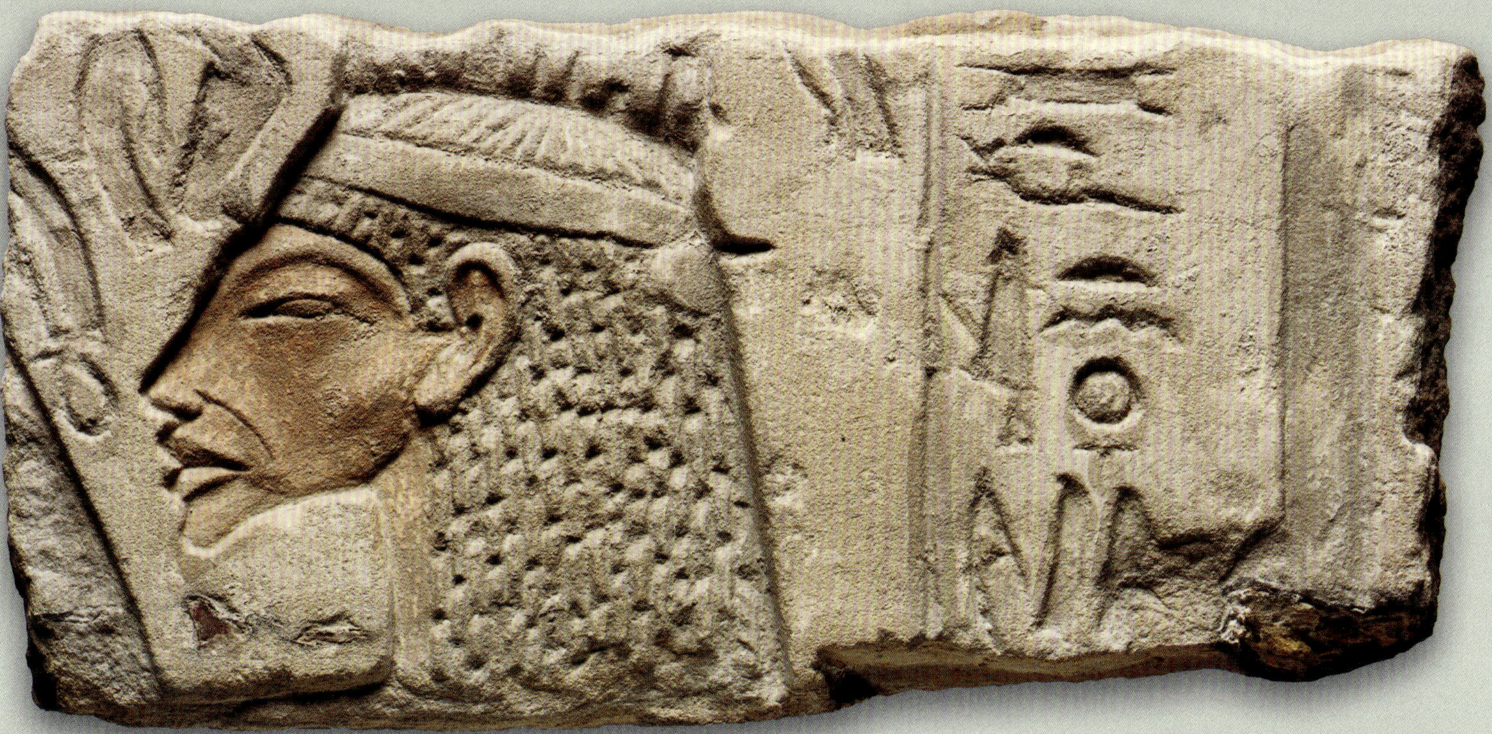

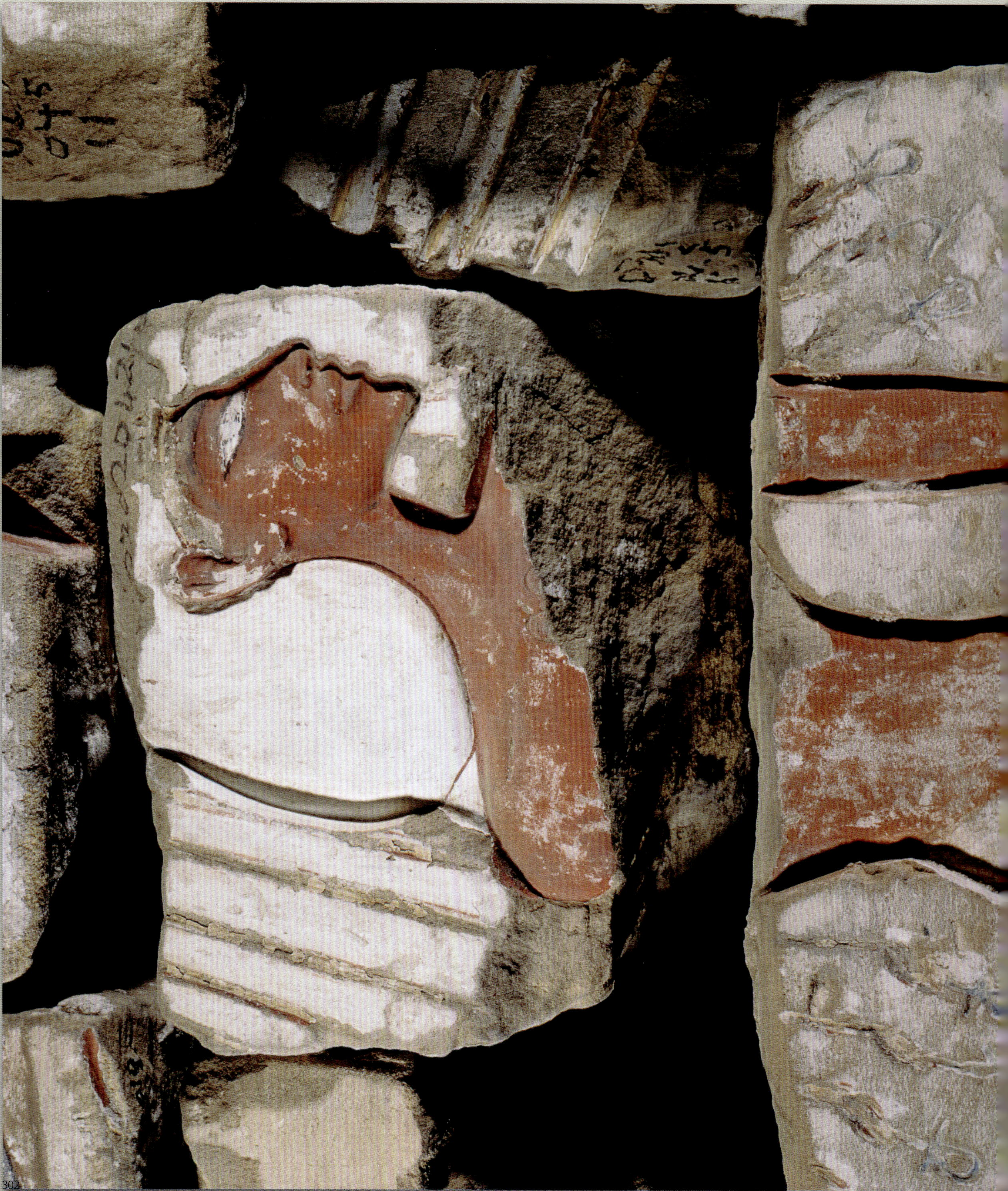

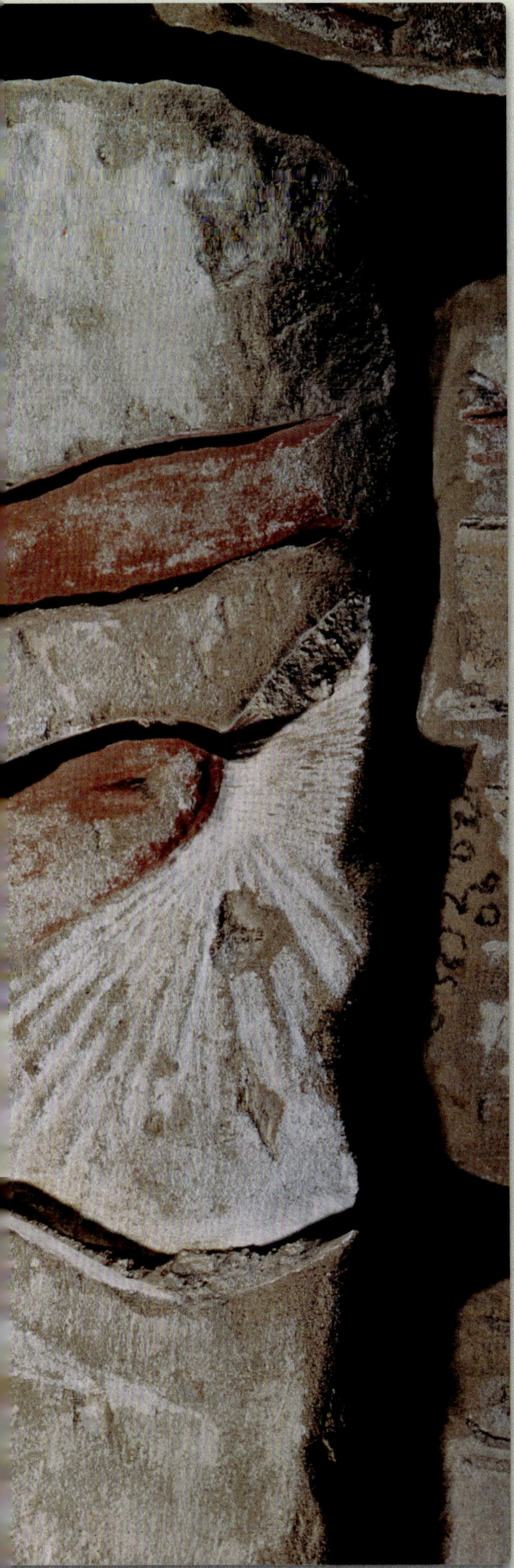

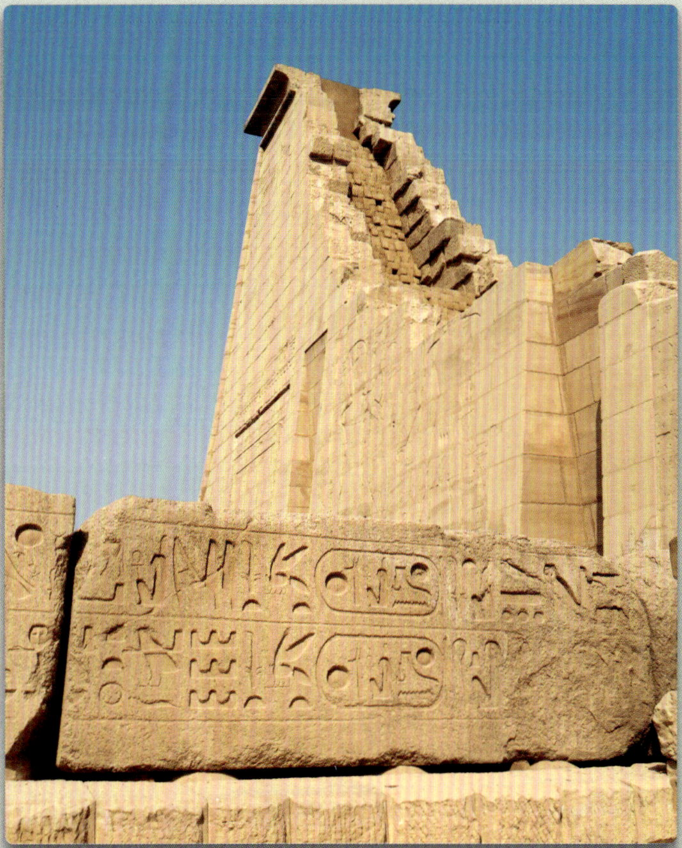

MASONRY REPURPOSED

The core of a monumental gate at Karnak (above) is filled with recycled building stones. King Horemheb (about 1319–1292 B.C.) dismantled temples that Akhenaten had built and used the materials for his own projects like this.

A portrait of Akhenaten appears on these stones inside the gate (left). More than 50,000 such blocks have been identified at Karnak and Luxor.

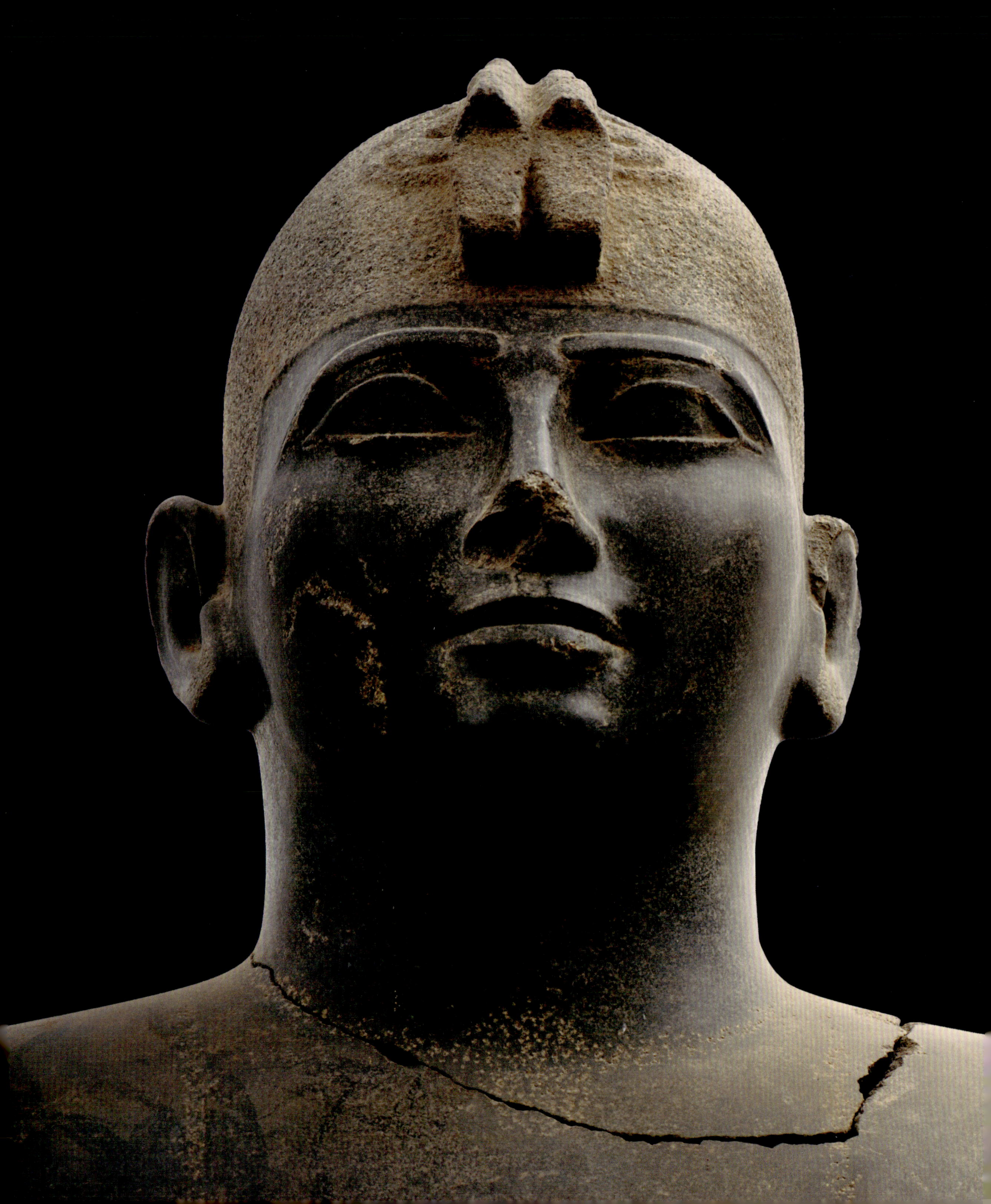

CHAPTER SEVEN

THE LEVANT AND KUSH

Conquered Territories

FOR MUCH OF ITS DYNASTIC history, Egypt was protected by its geography. Deserts to the east and west buffered the Nile Valley. Six rock-strewn rapids, known as cataracts, interrupted the Nile between what is now Aswan and Khartoum, preventing ships from sneaking in from the south. The Mediterranean Sea to the north and Red Sea to the east deterred everyone but skilled sailors.

But protected didn't mean isolated. Even before kings had unified the country, Egypt's citizens had ties to the outside world. Such artifacts as a knife from Gebel el-Arak, dated to about 3200 B.C., offer tantalizing clues to connections with foreign lands: The flint blade's ornate handle was carved from hippopotamus ivory in a style likely influenced by the Levant or Mesopotamia.

By the fourth dynasty, around 2575 B.C., trade was already flowing between the Levant and Egypt. As part of his funerary preparations, King Khufu had two enormous boats of Lebanese cedar buried near his pyramid tomb at Giza. One of the boats included timbers more than 72 feet long (22 m) and five and a half inches (14 cm) thick. Since at that time the Egyptians employed neither wheeled vehicles nor large beasts of burden, the wood must have been transported by sea through the port of Byblos. Commodities such as resins, olive oil, and wine also may have been imported.

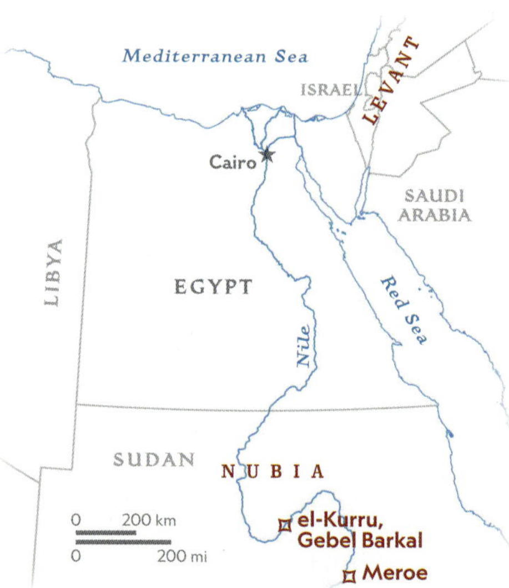

Egypt had connections with lands in Africa as well—especially Kush just to its south. Luxuries like sub-Saharan elephant ivory traveled to Egypt through Kush; copper and other goods came from Kush itself. It was the country's deposits of gold, however, believed to be the flesh of the gods, that especially attracted Egypt's interest.

From at least the time of Khufu, the Egyptians called their neighbor Yam. It was also often referred to as "vile Kush" and presented as one of Egypt's enemies, while its people were portrayed as uncivilized and unsophisticated. The term Nubia came into use in the fourth century A.D., perhaps inspired by "nbw," the Egyptian word for gold.

Before the time of Alexander the Great, ancient Egypt didn't possess a currency system as we know it. Barter was frequently used for foreign trade, with each side laying out goods until both agreed that a fair balance had been reached. In other instances, goods were exchanged in the guise of diplomatic gifts, which kings and other elites could then give to their underlings as rewards for loyalty.

Representing early rulers, Egyptian officials began to launch trading expeditions. During the reign of Pepi II, around 2200 B.C., a man named Harkhuf, a governor of southern Egypt, made several trips into Kush. Traveling on the "ivory road," he explored future trade possibilities and procured exotic merchandise. On a wall of his tomb, he recorded what he brought back: "300 donkeys laden with incense, ebony, oil, aromatics, panther skins, ivory carvings, throw sticks for hunting, and all good products."

As the centuries wore on, though, commerce sometimes turned into conquest. According to inscriptions found in the Ptah Temple at Memphis, 12th-dynasty king Amenemhet II

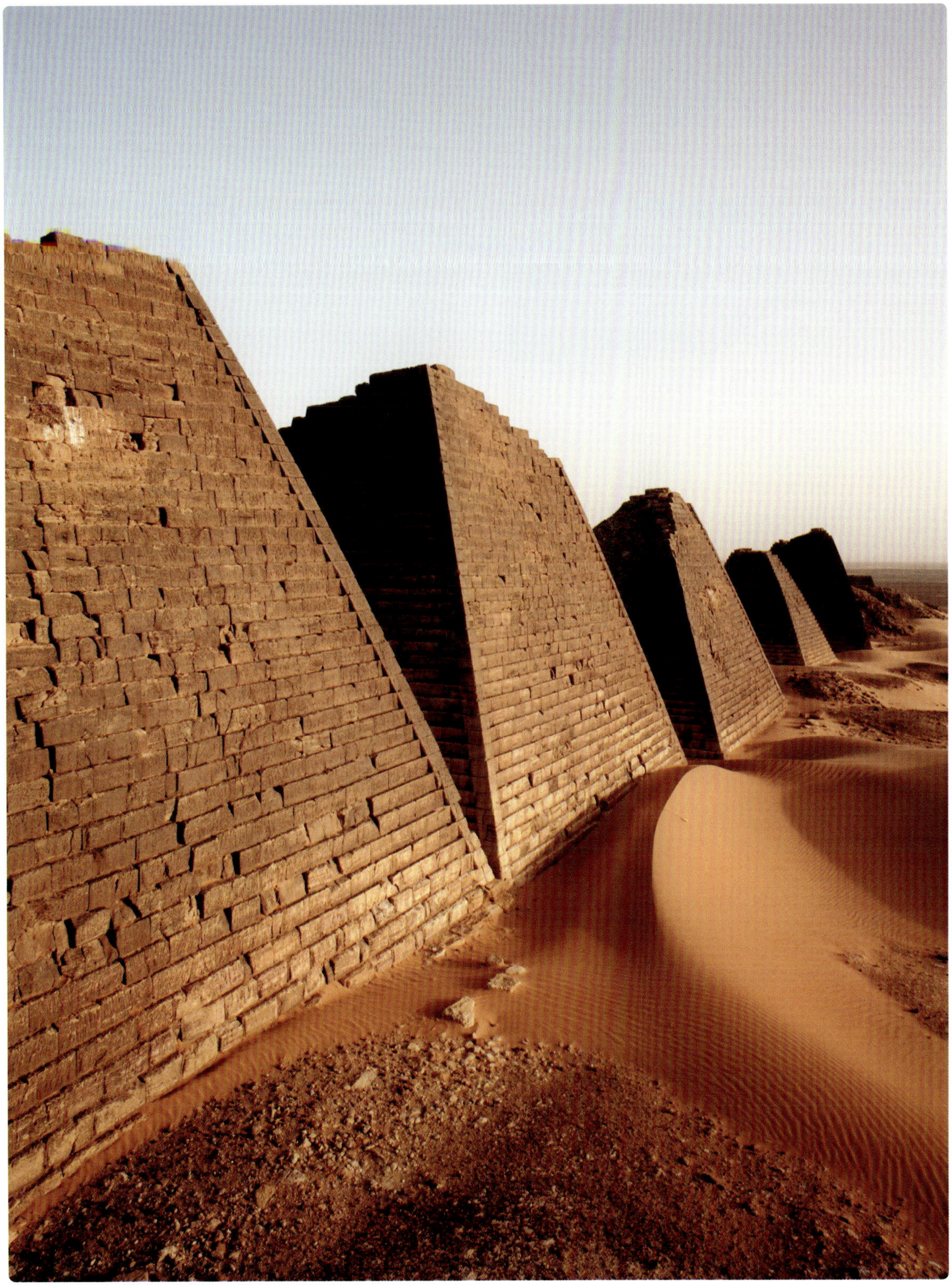

Inspired by Egypt, their neighbor and sometime overlord to the north, the kings of Kush built pyramids to mark their graves starting in about 750 B.C. At Meroë (above), an administrative center and then a capital in antiquity (now in Sudan), some 200 such structures rise from the sand.

PREVIOUS PAGES: Also around 750 B.C., kings of Kush conquered Egypt and ruled there for a century. Taharqa, here wearing a typical royal Kushite cap, inherited the throne in about 690 B.C.

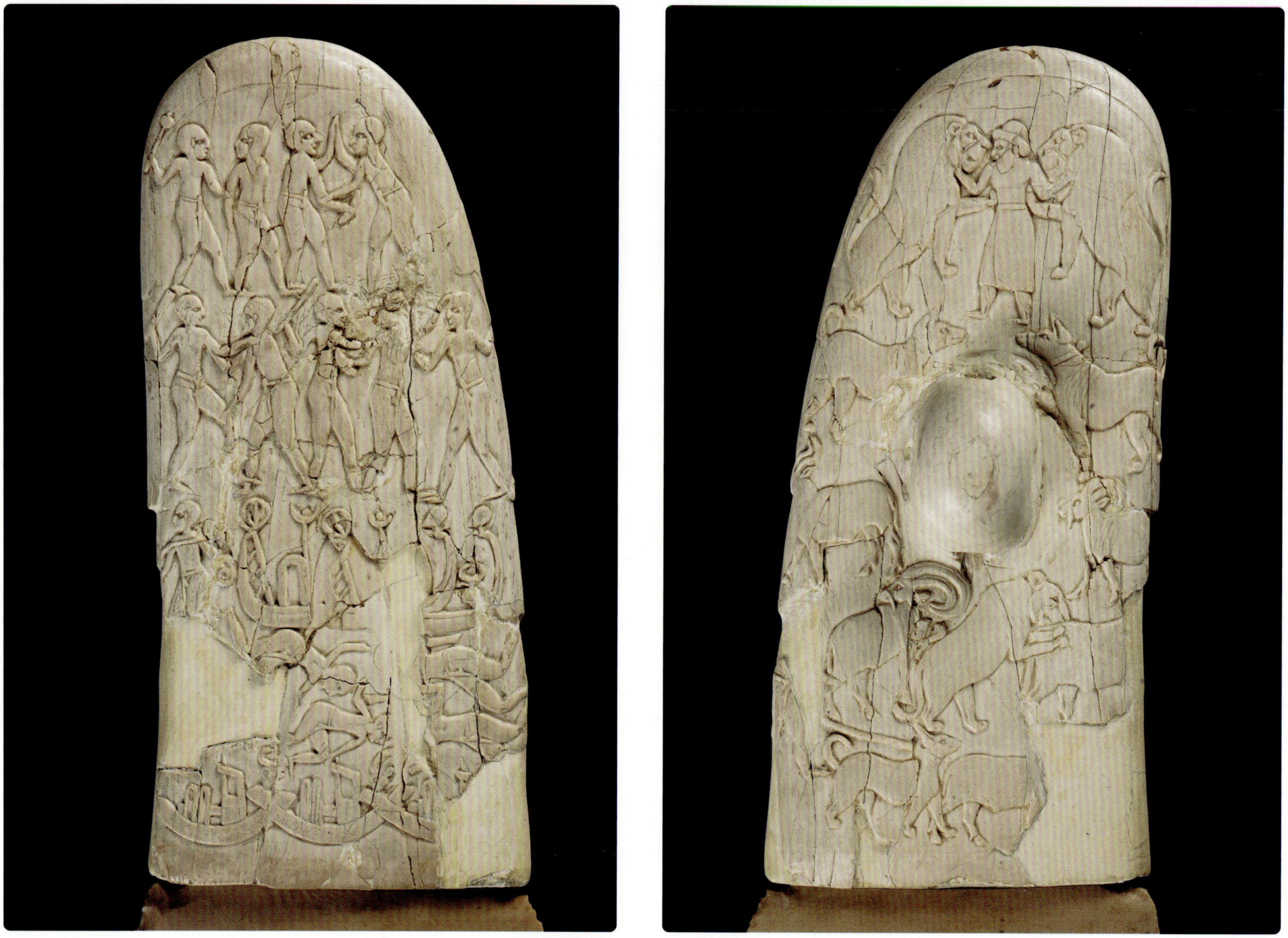

The hippopotamus-ivory handle of a flint knife displays Mesopotamian-style carving. Purchased at Gebel el-Arak, Egypt, in 1894, it dates to about 3200 B.C., the predynastic period.

launched military campaigns into the southern Levant after 1876 B.C. During the reign of that same king and Senwosret II, his successor, an official named Khnumhotep II served as "doorway of the foreign lands": essentially, a customs officer. One painted scene in his tomb at Beni Hasan shows a procession of foreigners identified in hieroglyphs as Aamu, or people from the Levant. Possibly tribute bearers, they are delivering galena, an ore that may have been smelted for silver or used as high-quality eye paint. Symbolically, the Aamu may also have evoked the idea of Egypt subduing foreigners, viewed as the embodiment of *isfet,* or chaos.

During the New Kingdom, Egypt continued to make incursions into the Levant, at one point controlling the Mediterranean coast, with its lucrative ports and markets, even past the border of modern Turkey. In 1275 B.C., Ramses II famously fought a battle at Kadesh, a site now in Syria. His enemy was the Hittite king, marching south from central Turkey. In reliefs displayed like billboards on monumental buildings, Ramses the Great claims to have personally led his troops and brought about victory. The reality was probably less heroic, and in 1259 B.C., he and the Hittites agreed to a peace treaty.

To the south, in Kush, Egypt was smelting copper at a site near the second cataract as early as the fourth dynasty. By the 12th dynasty—about 1950 B.C.—it had built a series of forts between the second and third cataracts in an attempt to control the region's wealth and the trade with places farther south.

Under the empire-building warrior kings of the 18th dynasty, Egypt pushed even deeper into Africa. Eventually, its domain reached past the fourth cataract. Egyptian troops were stationed in Kush to maintain control, and native Kushites known as the Medjay served throughout Egypt as elite infantry.

It was during this period that the title viceroy of Kush began to be used—an indication that the region was being governed and administered, rather than merely occupied. Egypt now concentrated on building temples, rather than forts; Ramses II had two cut into a cliff at Abu Simbel—one for himself and the other for his favorite wife, Nefertari.

"During the New Kingdom, Egypt continued to make incursions into the Levant . . . In reliefs displayed like billboards on monumental buildings, Ramses the Great claims to have personally led his troops and brought about victory. The reality was probably less heroic."

In the 1960s, one of the greatest engineering feats in the history of cultural heritage preservation took place there. As the Aswan High Dam was built to tame the wild annual flooding of the Nile, these two temples—and others such as the complex at Philae—were disassembled and moved to higher ground, away from the impending waters of Lake Nasser.

As the New Kingdom came to an end, around 1075 B.C., Egypt saw its power fade and its territory contract. It then suffered the ultimate indignity: a series of incursions by foreign powers, including Kush, which defeated its former overlord in about 750 B.C. The Kushites—the so-called Black pharaohs of the 25th dynasty—ruled for about six decades, viewing themselves as restorers of ancient Egyptian traditions. But they, too, would lose control, to a dynasty backed by the Assyrians in Mesopotamia. Two Persian invasions followed, and then the fateful conquest by Alexander the Great. Egypt would not gain independence again until after the 1952 revolution. ▲

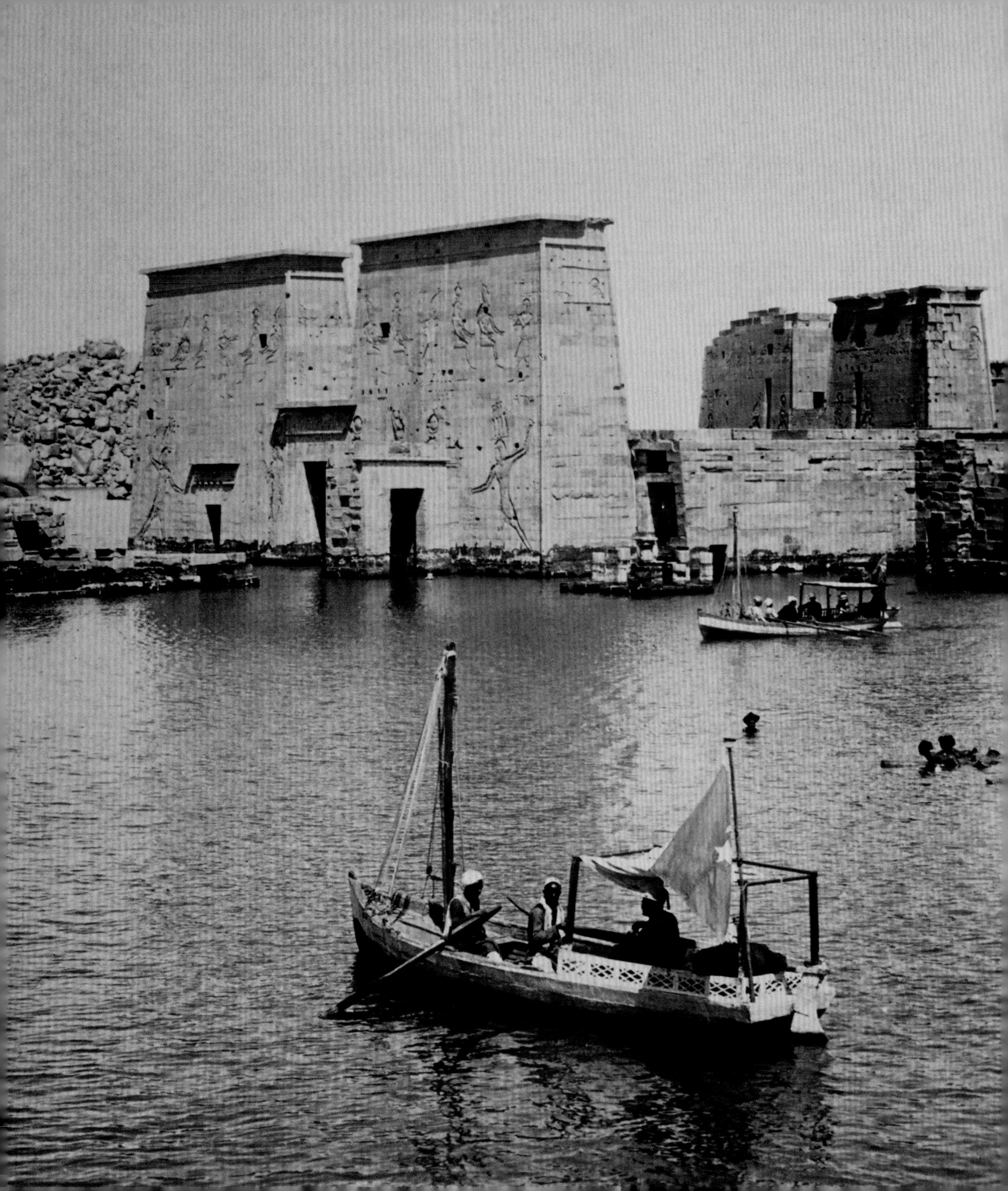

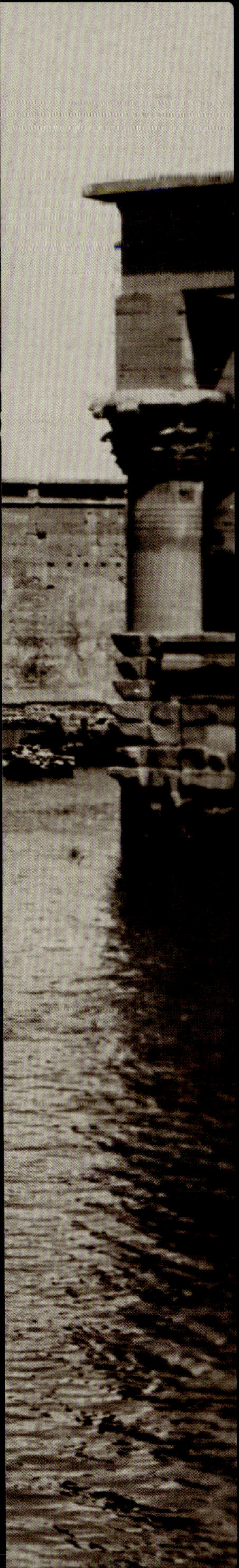

FIRST PHOTOS

A photo of the island site of Philae from about 1903 (left) shows the flooding produced by the construction of an early dam on the Nile at Aswan. The swamped temples date from about 380 B.C. to A.D. 300.

Once the Aswan High Dam was completed in 1970, and the waters began to rise at Philae, the entire complex was transported to higher ground (below) on the island of Agilqiyya.

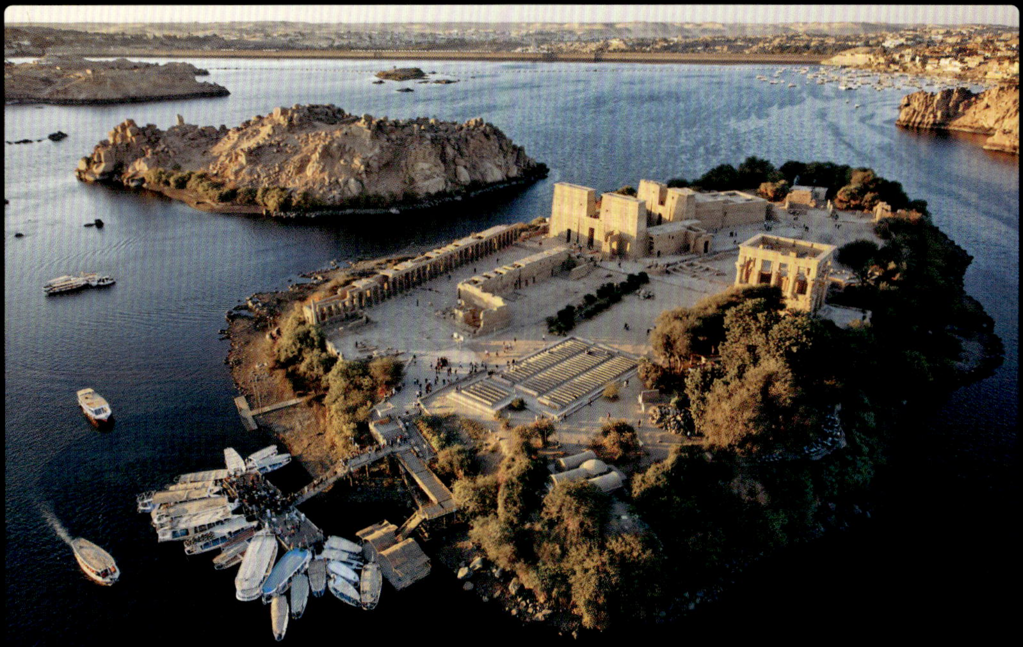

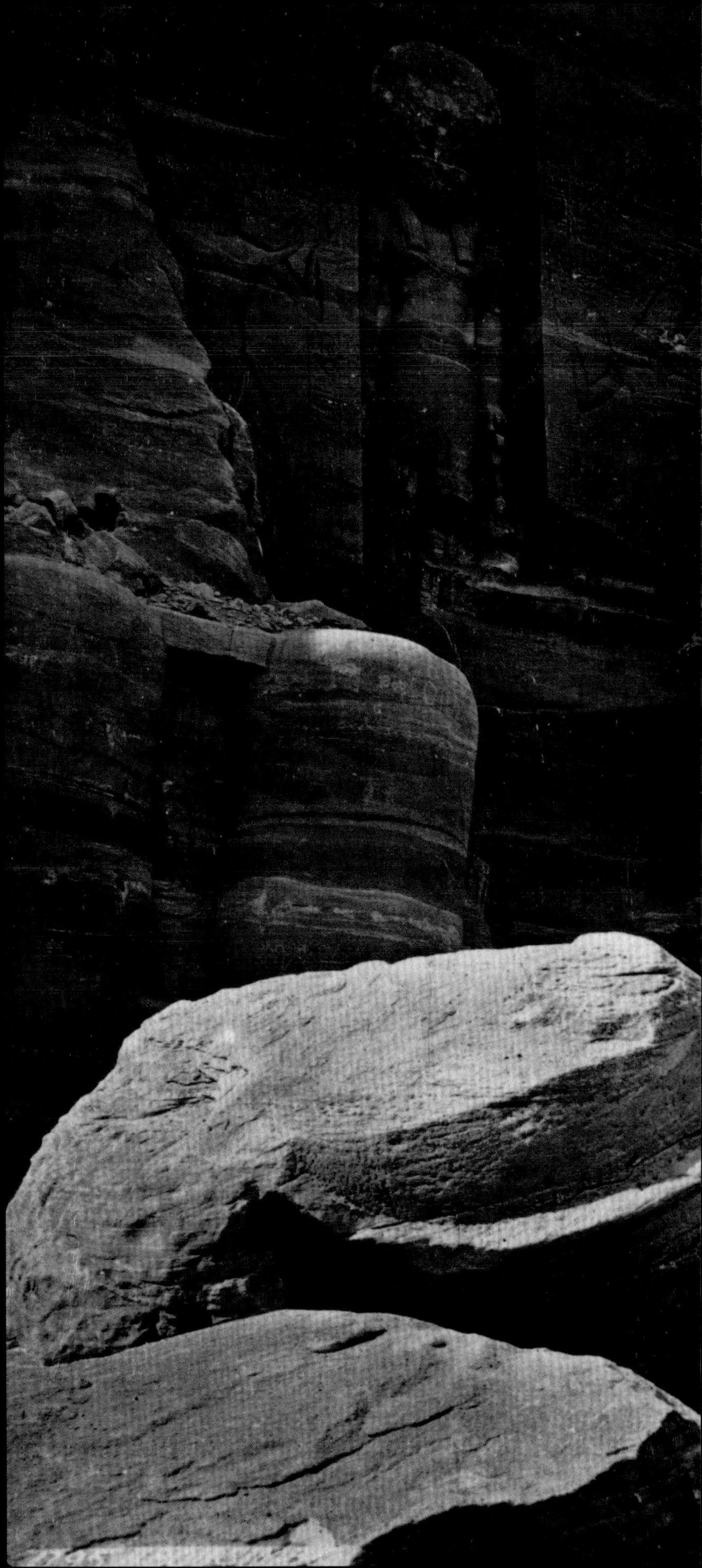

Sand cascades around the colossal figures of Ramses II at his temple at Abu Simbel in a photo from the 1850s. The monument and its iconography were meant to demonstrate the Egyptian king's control of Kush in the 13th century B.C.

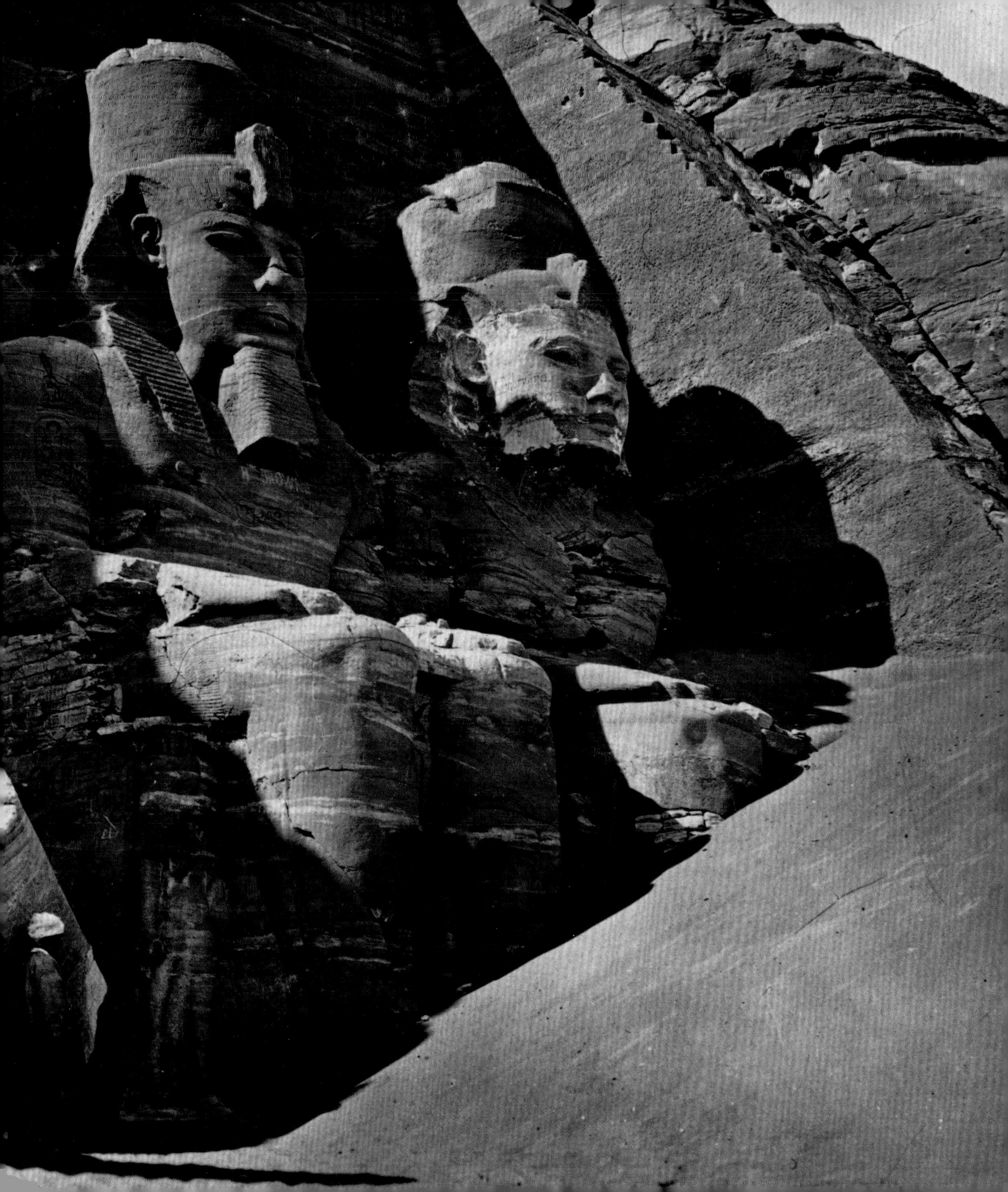

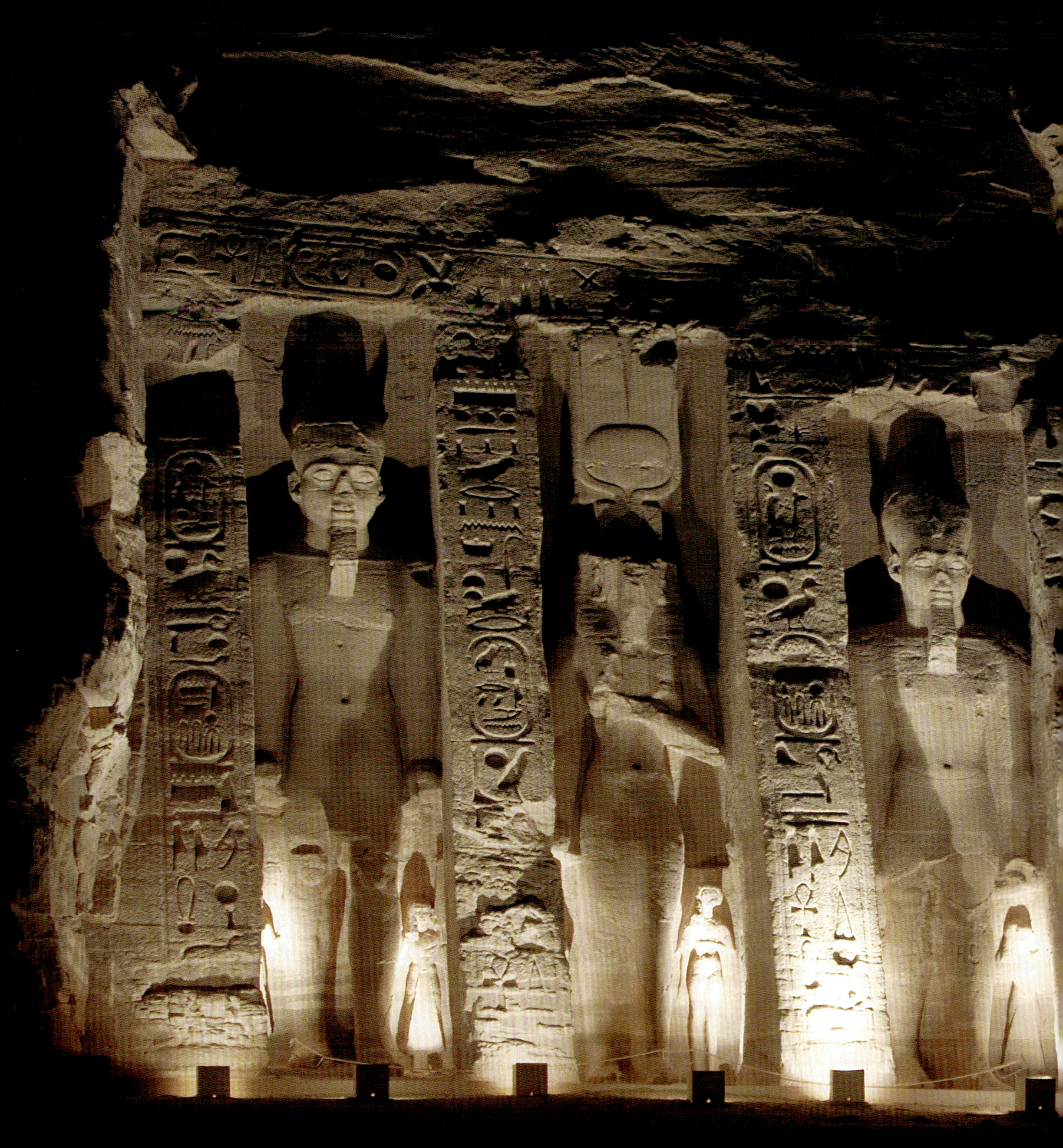

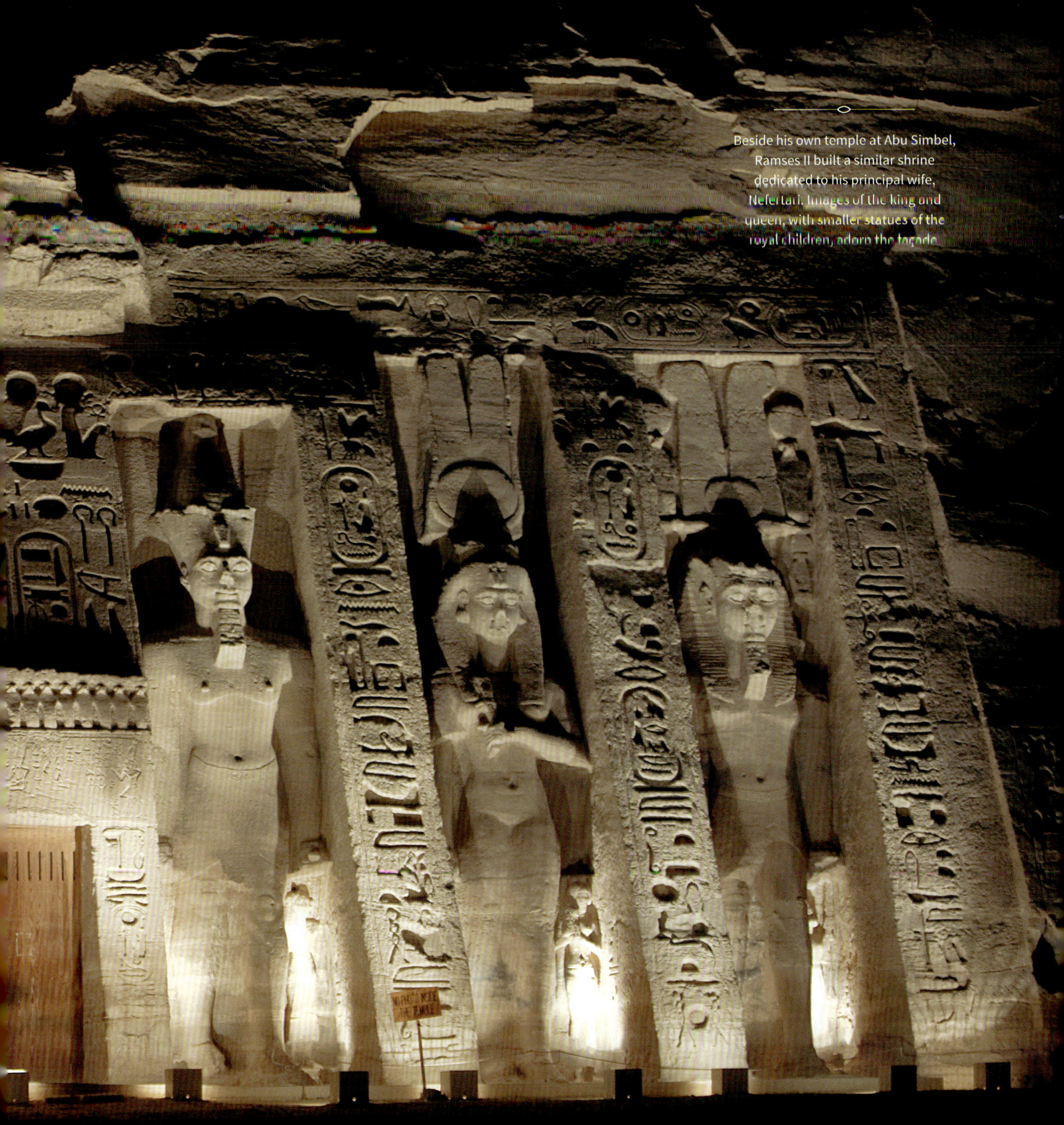

Beside his own temple at Abu Simbel, Ramses II built a similar shrine dedicated to his principal wife, Nefertari. Images of the king and queen, with smaller statues of the royal children, adorn the façade.

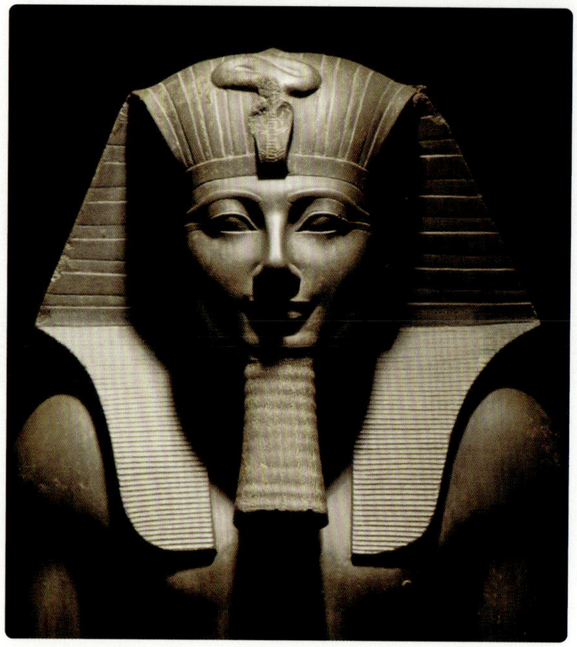

King Thutmose III (above) conquered territory from Gebel Barkal in Kush to the Euphrates River in Mesopotamia in the 15th century B.C.

A gold collar (below) from a 19th-century B.C. royal grave in the trading city of Byblos was likely made locally. The falcon with wings spread wide, and the heads of the falcon god Horus at the clasp, are Egyptian motifs.

Ceramic coffins (opposite) from the 14th–13th centuries B.C. were uncovered at Deir el-Balah, now in Israel. The mummy-like figures show Egyptian influence.

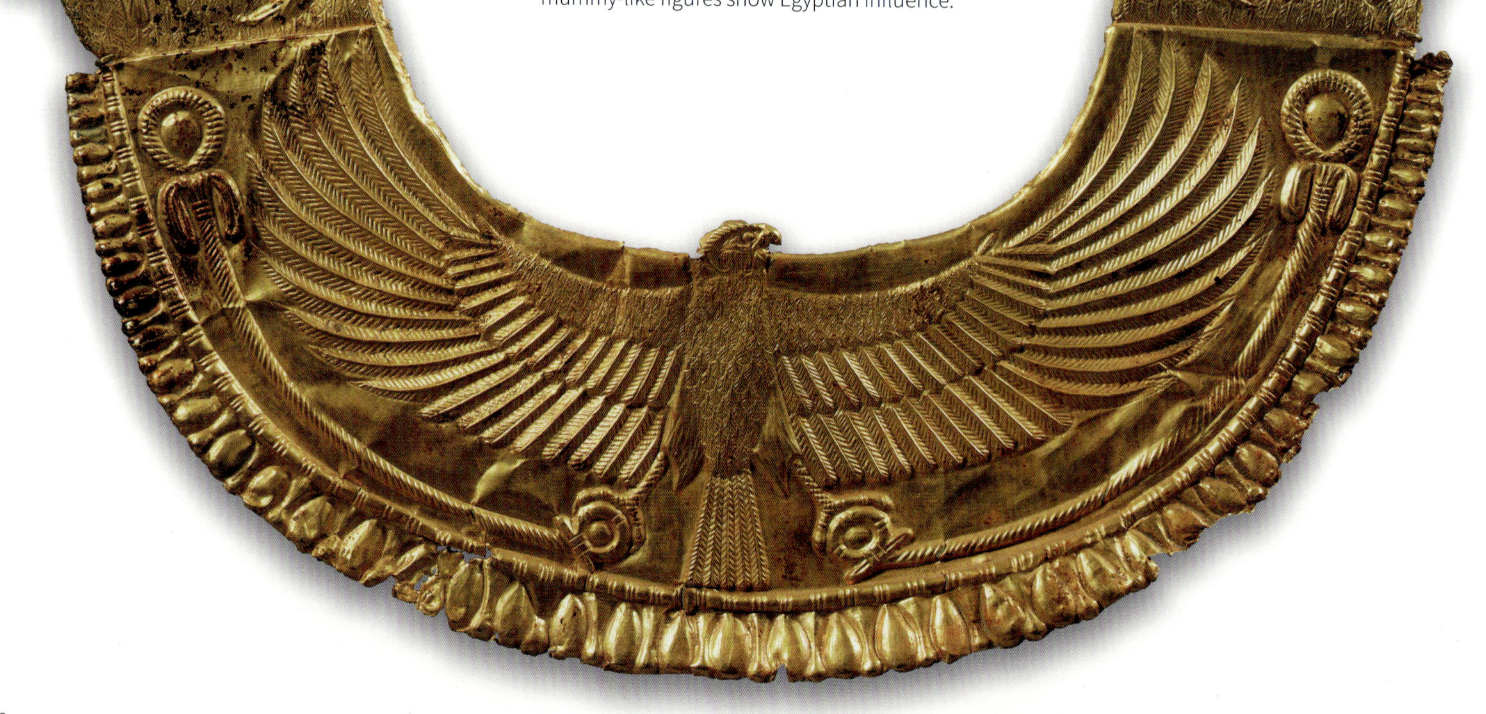

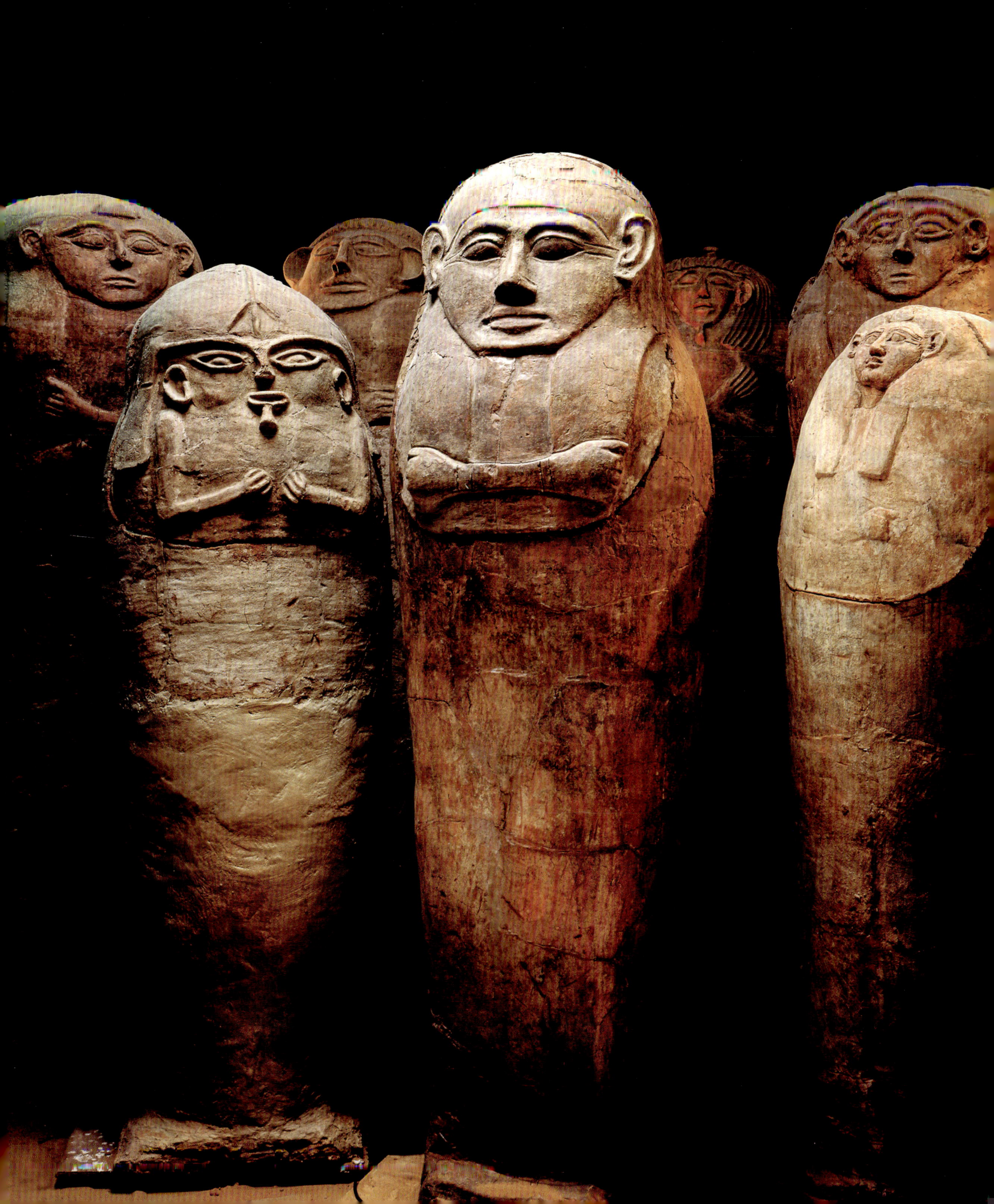

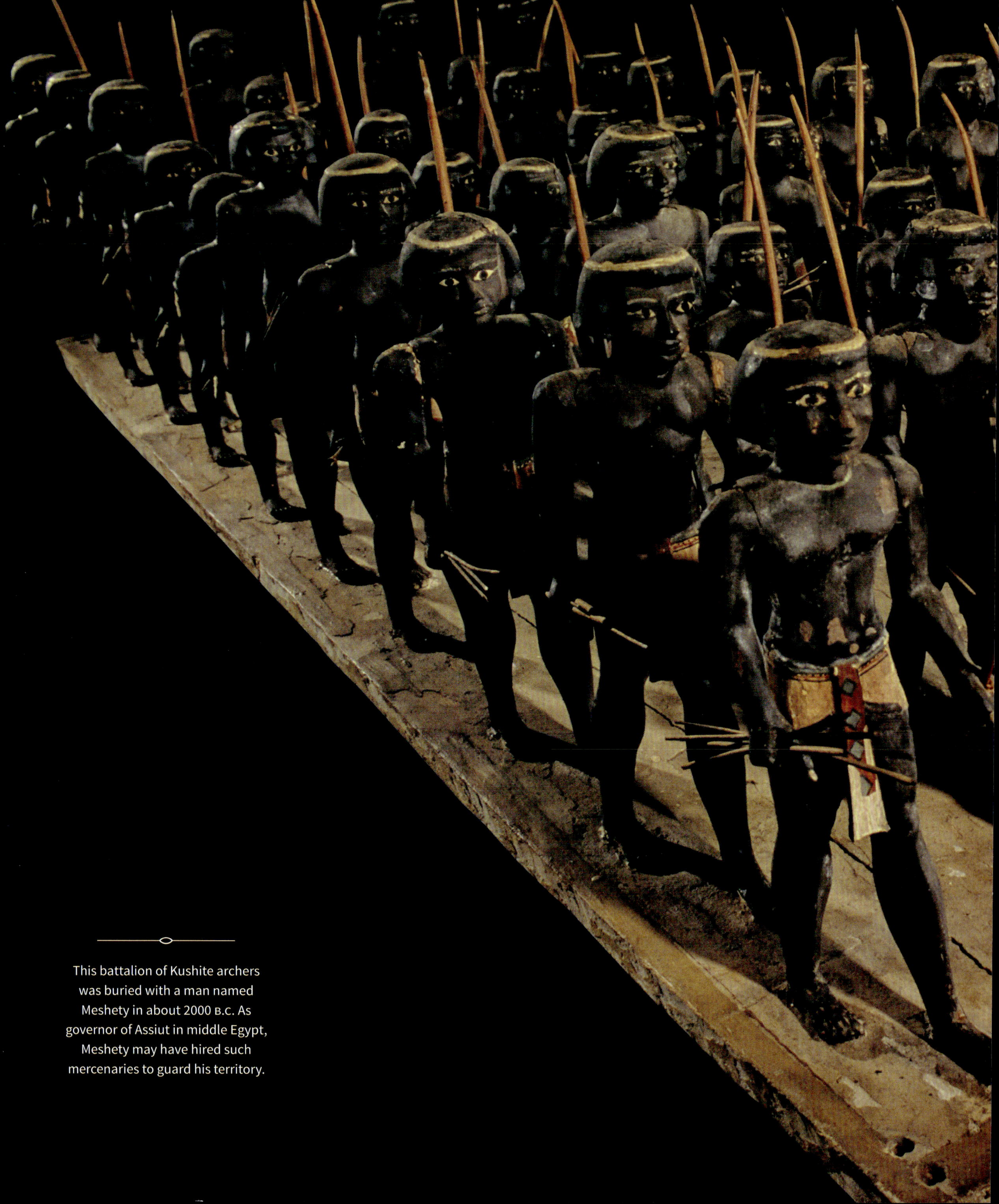

This battalion of Kushite archers was buried with a man named Meshety in about 2000 B.C. As governor of Assiut in middle Egypt, Meshety may have hired such mercenaries to guard his territory.

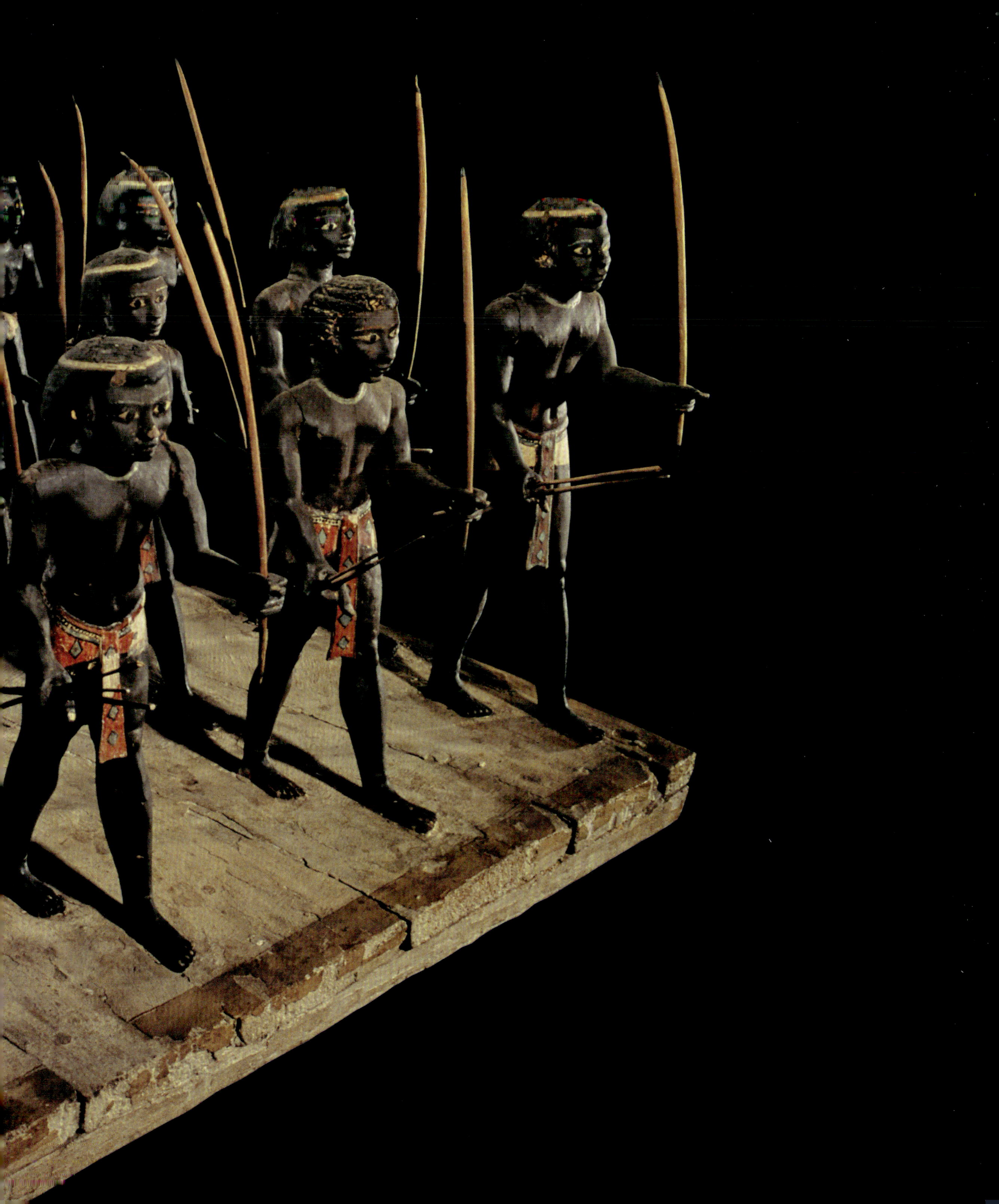

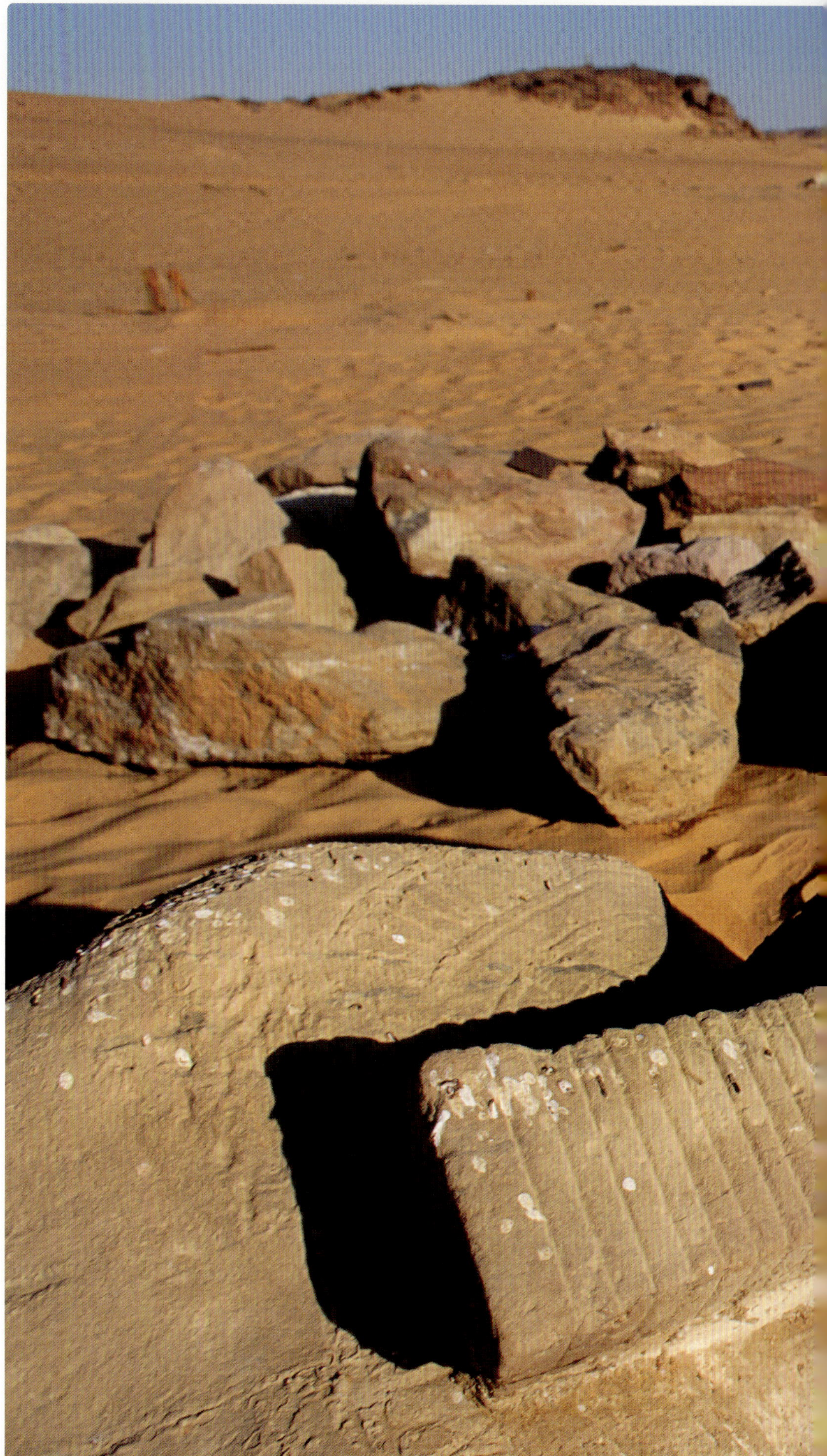

The Wadi es-Sebua ruins, about 70 miles (110 km) south of Aswan, include a fallen statue of Ramses II. In the 13th century B.C., the king built a temple to Amun there and restored Amenhotep III's temple from a century earlier.

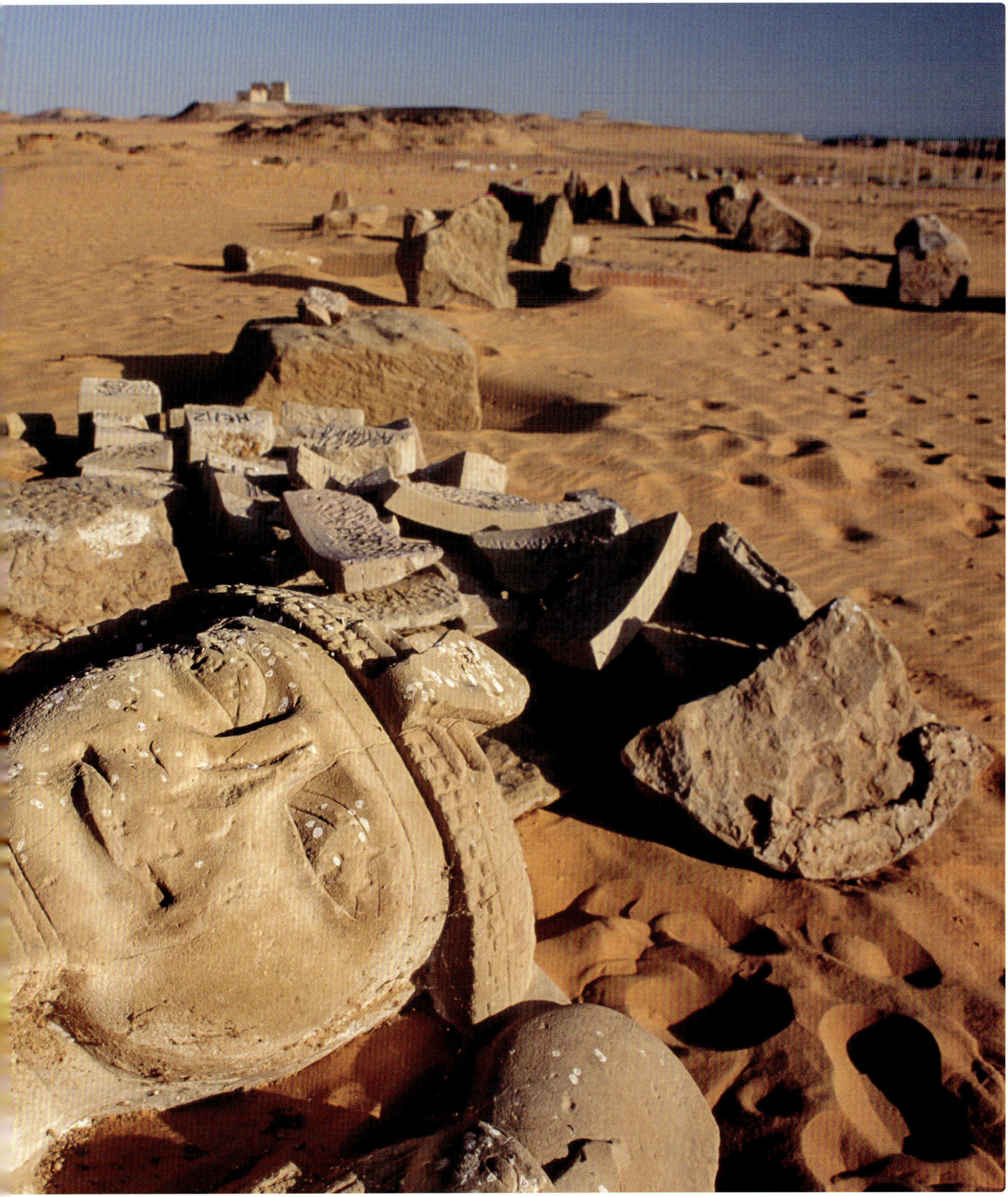

DIGGING DEEPER

A Triumph of Engineering

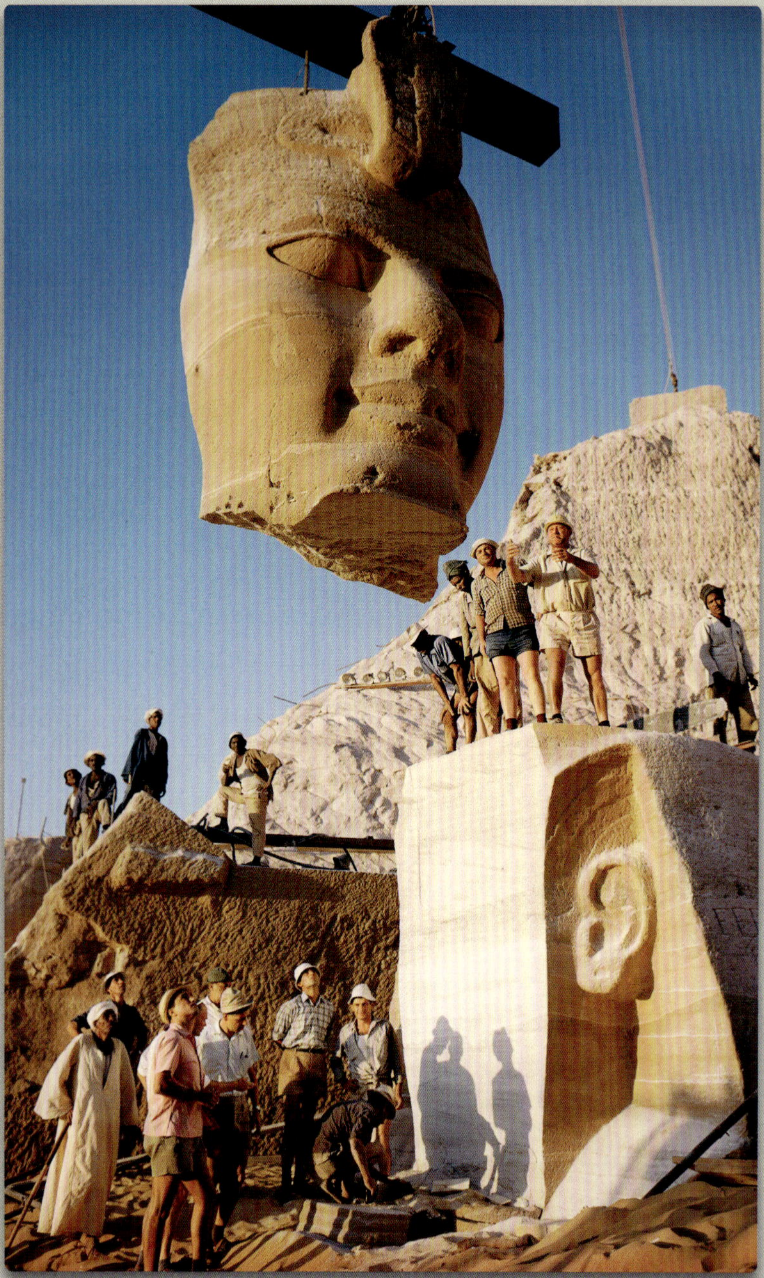

IN THE 13TH CENTURY B.C., King Ramses II had two temples cut into a sandstone cliff at a place along the Nile now called Abu Simbel. One was dedicated to the deified version of himself and other gods. The façade displays four statues of the seated pharaoh, each some 65 feet (20 m) tall. The building was meant to express the king's piety, as well as his domination of Kush, Egypt's southern neighbor. A smaller temple nearby was dedicated to Nefertari, Ramses's principal wife.

In 1960, Egypt began to build the Aswan High Dam to generate hydroelectric power and control the Nile's annual flooding. But the lake created by the project would overwhelm many ancient sites, including Abu Simbel.

An international effort to rescue the Abu Simbel temples began in 1964. Fragile details were reinforced with resin (opposite) before the buildings were cut up. This colossal head (left) and almost a thousand other sculpted pieces were then moved to higher ground for reassembly. Ramses II's recreated temple is so faithful to the original that twice a year the rising sun illuminates the innermost chamber just as it did in antiquity.

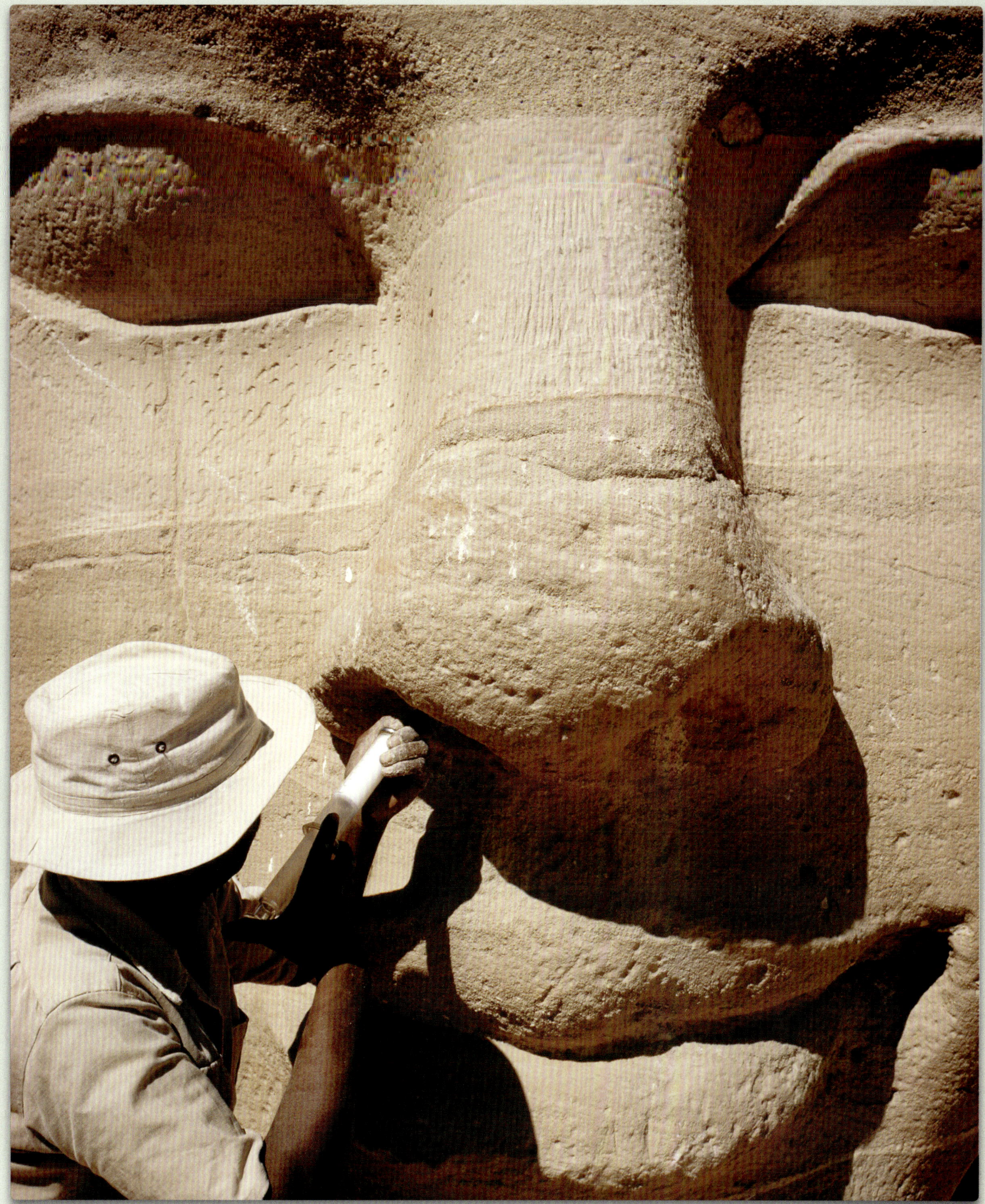

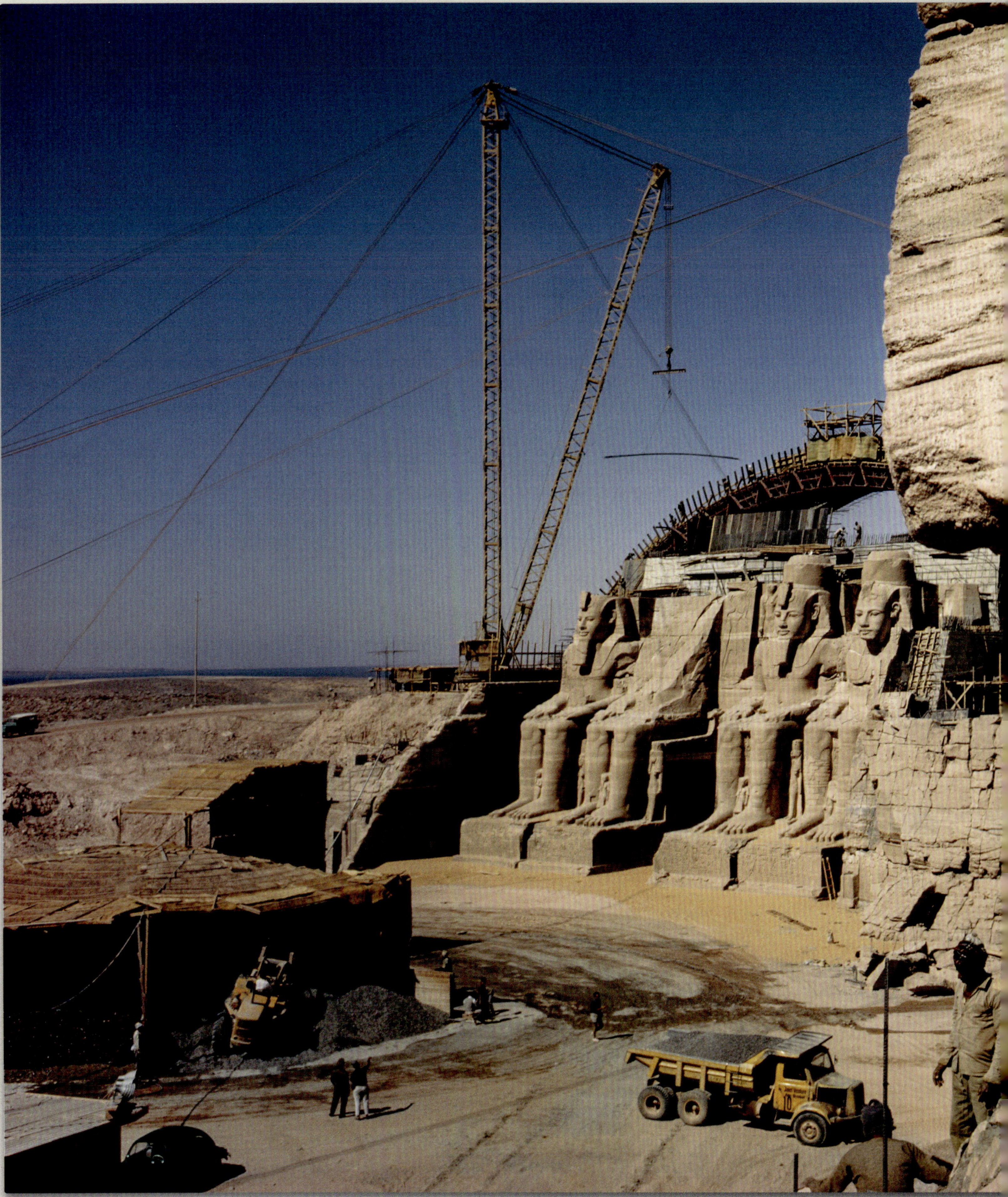

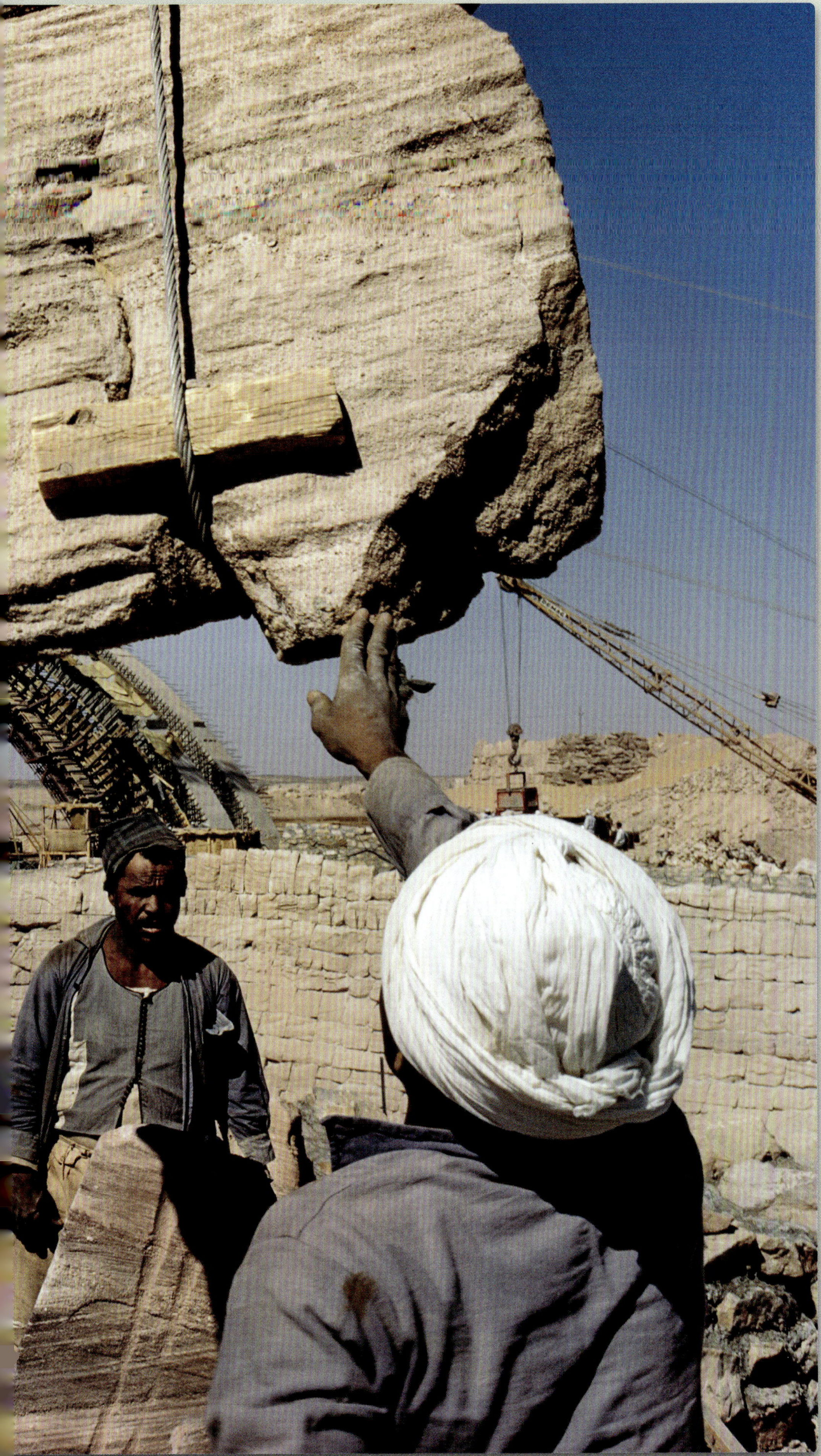

A MODERN MARVEL

At the new site of the Abu Simbel temples, a workman guides a chunk of stone into place. In the background, scaffolding arches over the future home of Ramses II's temple. At the old site, the temple's chambers were carved into a cliff; here they will be protected by a concrete dome poured in some 300 sections.

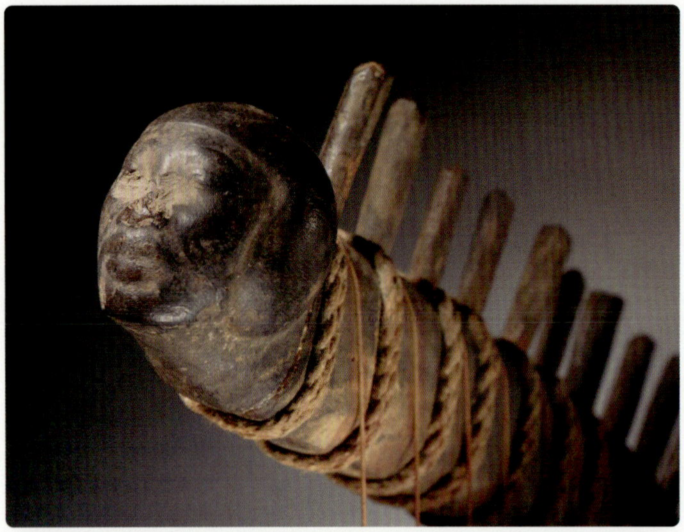

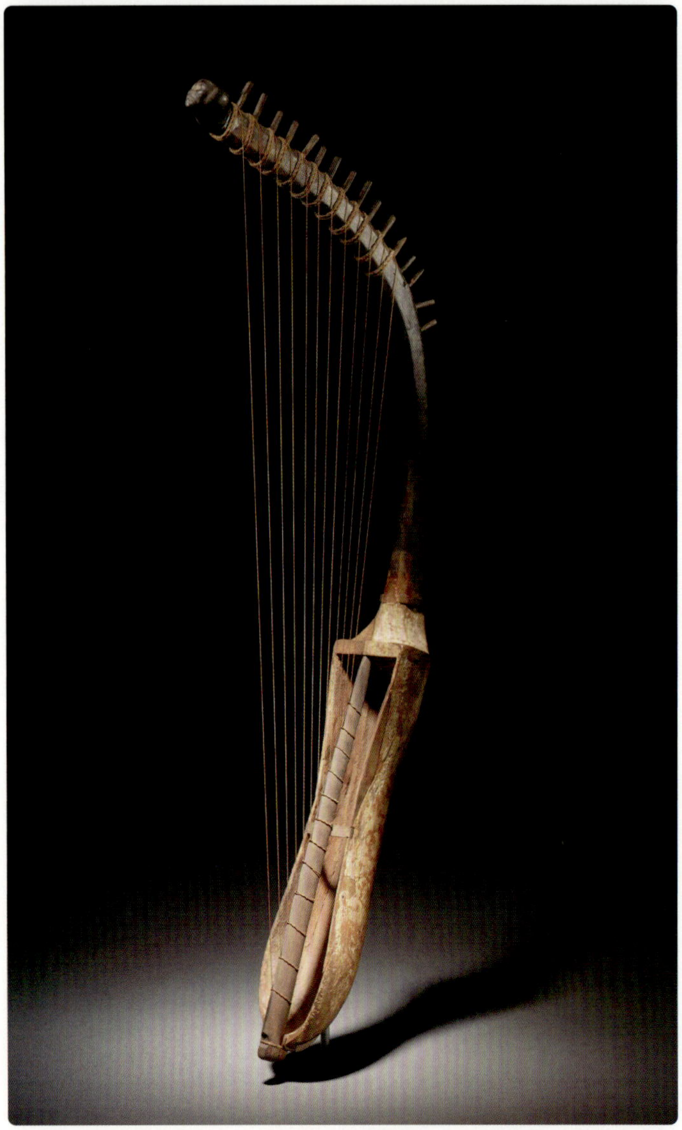

King Tutankhamun was buried with more than 130 walking sticks in about 1322 B.C. Some are quite elaborate, like this one with a handle in the shape of a Nubian (opposite). When grasped by the king, the symbolic enemy of Egypt would be upside down and rendered powerless.

A wooden harp from about the same time was carved with a Nubian's face at one end (top left). The strings bind the figure (bottom left), just as the king's captives would have been bound. Popular instruments, harps were played along with rattles and clappers.

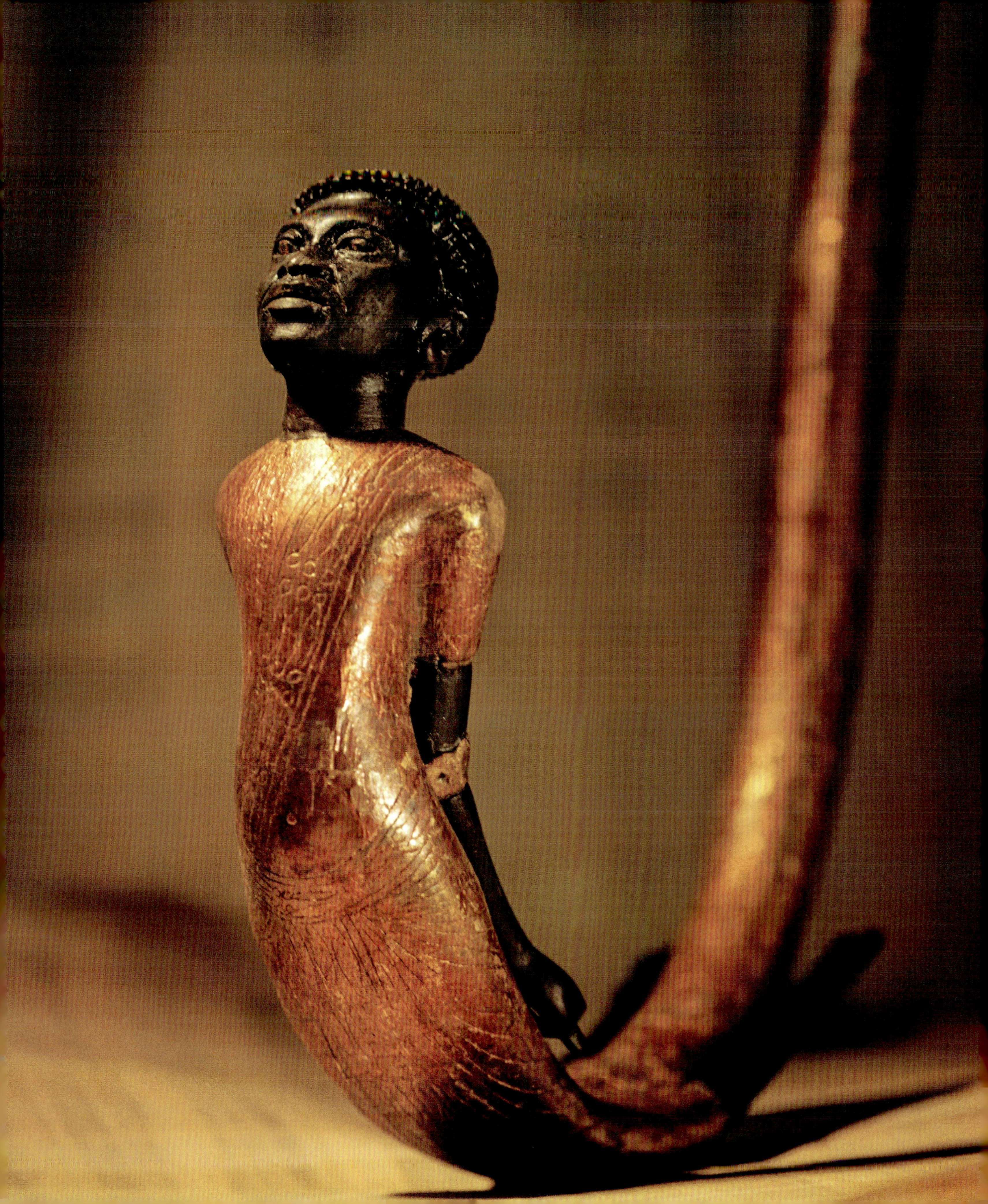

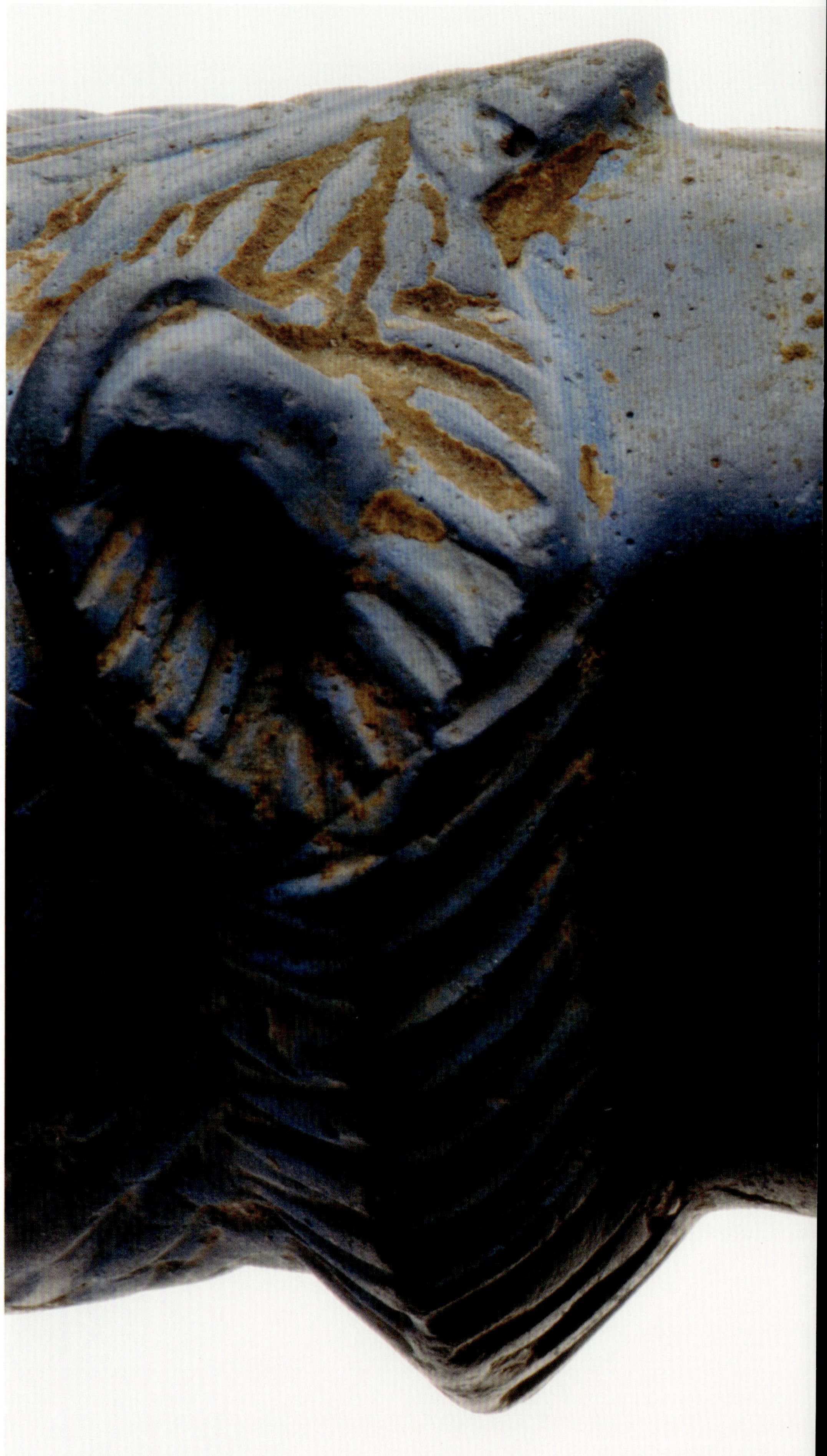

A lion symbolizing the pharaoh devours a Nubian in this artifact made of faience and gold. Dated to the 13th century B.C., it may have served as the handle for a fly whisk or a whip.

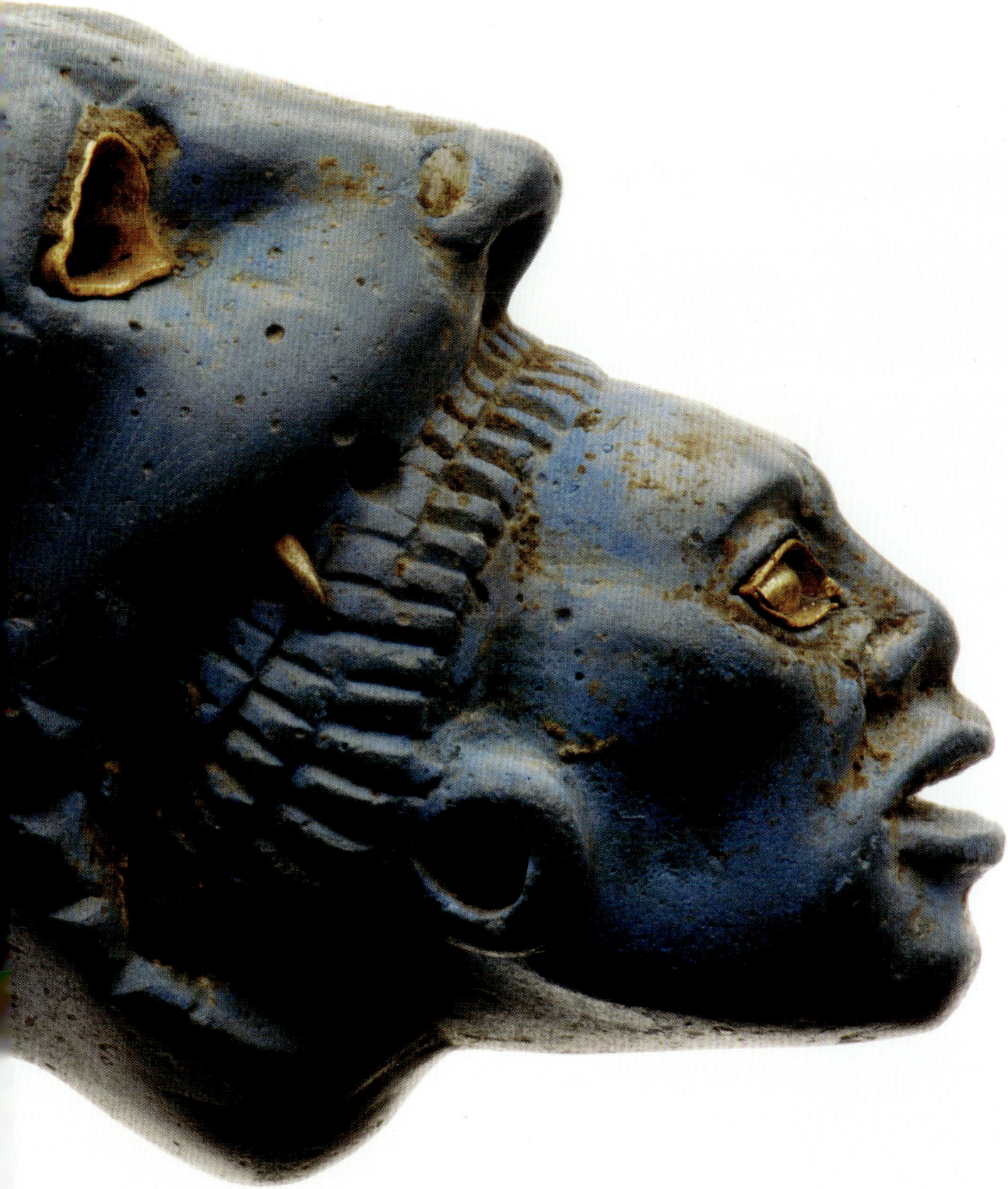

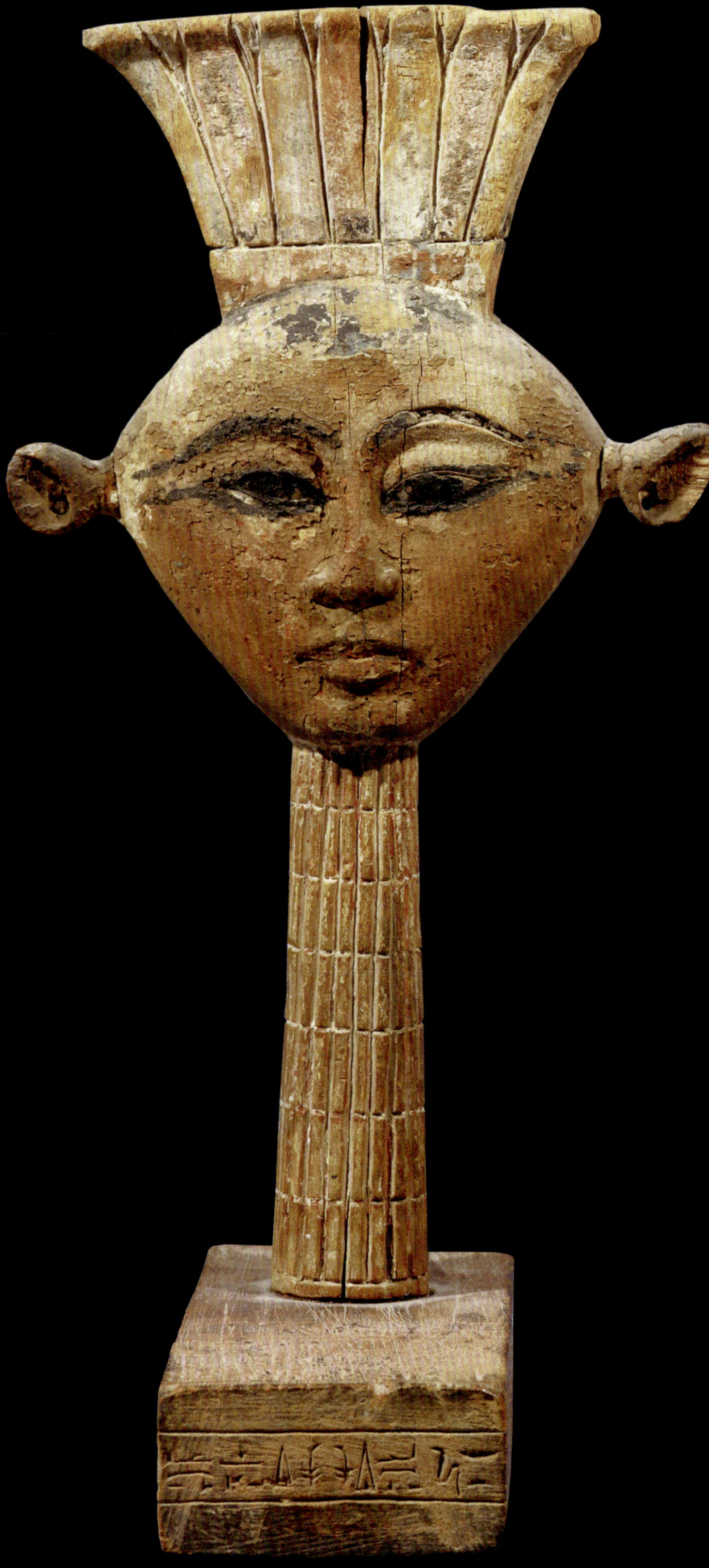

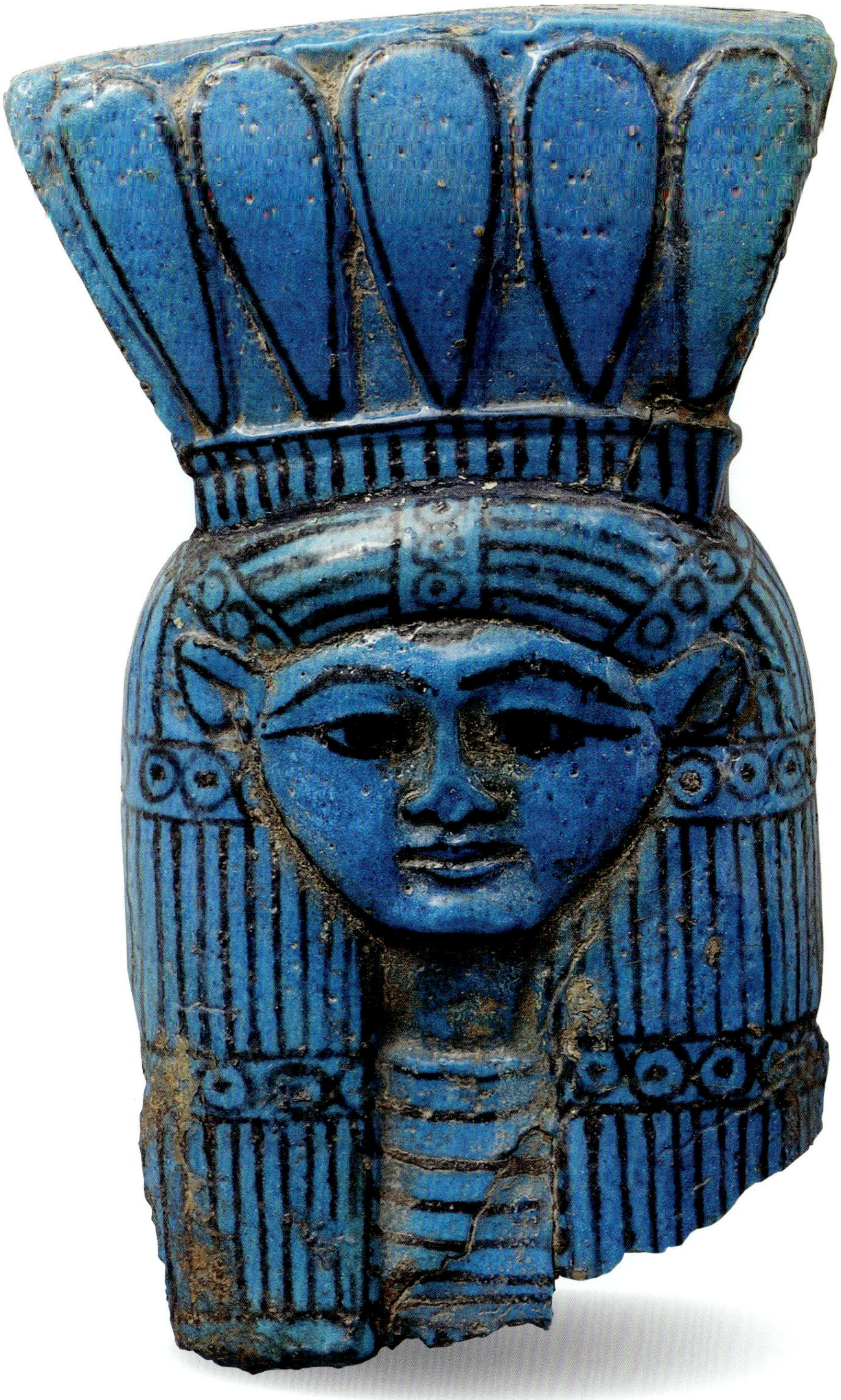

A faience emblem of the goddess Anukis (above) dating to about 1292–1190 B.C. was discovered at the temple of Satet on Elephantine Island near Aswan. Anukis was the daughter of the deities Satet and Khnum.

This wooden artifact from the same era (opposite) also depicts Anukis, who was associated with Egypt's southern border and the rocky outcroppings that interrupt the Nile in that area.

A Life of Adventure

GIOVANNI BATTISTA BELZONI'S EXPLOITS were as large as the man himself. Born in Italy, he was a Capuchin novitiate, a religious trinket salesman, and—at six feet seven inches (2 m) tall—a circus performer called the "Patagonian Samson." Traveling to Egypt in 1815 as a hydraulic engineer, he met British consul Henry Salt, who engaged him to collect antiquities for shipment to England.

Belzoni also got to know fellow adventurer Johann Ludwig Burckhardt, who had discovered the temple of Ramses II at Abu Simbel. Inspired by Burckhardt's description, Belzoni visited the site himself, but found the temple entrance buried in 30 feet (9 m) of sand. He eventually got workers to clear the way and, once inside, collected a few statues for Salt.

Belzoni did things that make modern archaeologists cringe. He battered through walls, carved his name into monuments such as the Ramesseum in Luxor (below), and clumsily crushed mummies, whose airborne fragments were "rather unpleasant to swallow," he noted. But he did document his work, and he helped popularize ancient Egypt by publishing an account of his discoveries. He died in 1823 in Benin while searching for the source of the Niger River.

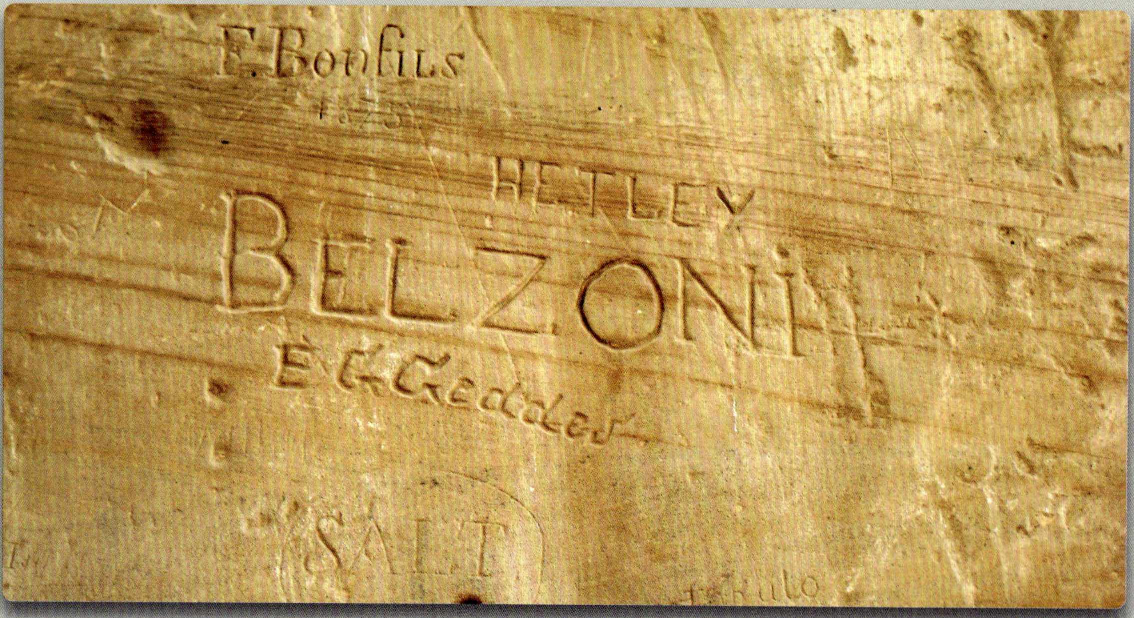

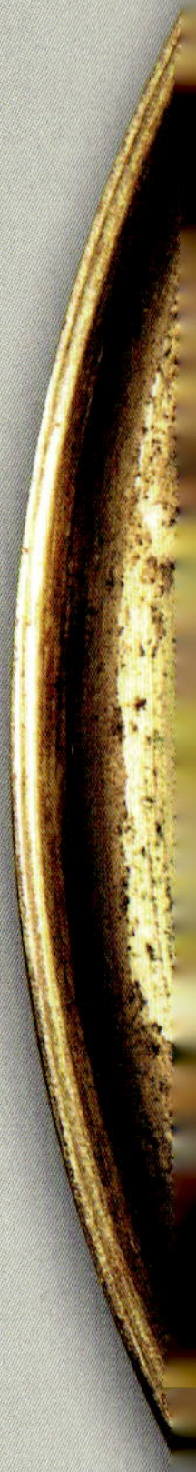

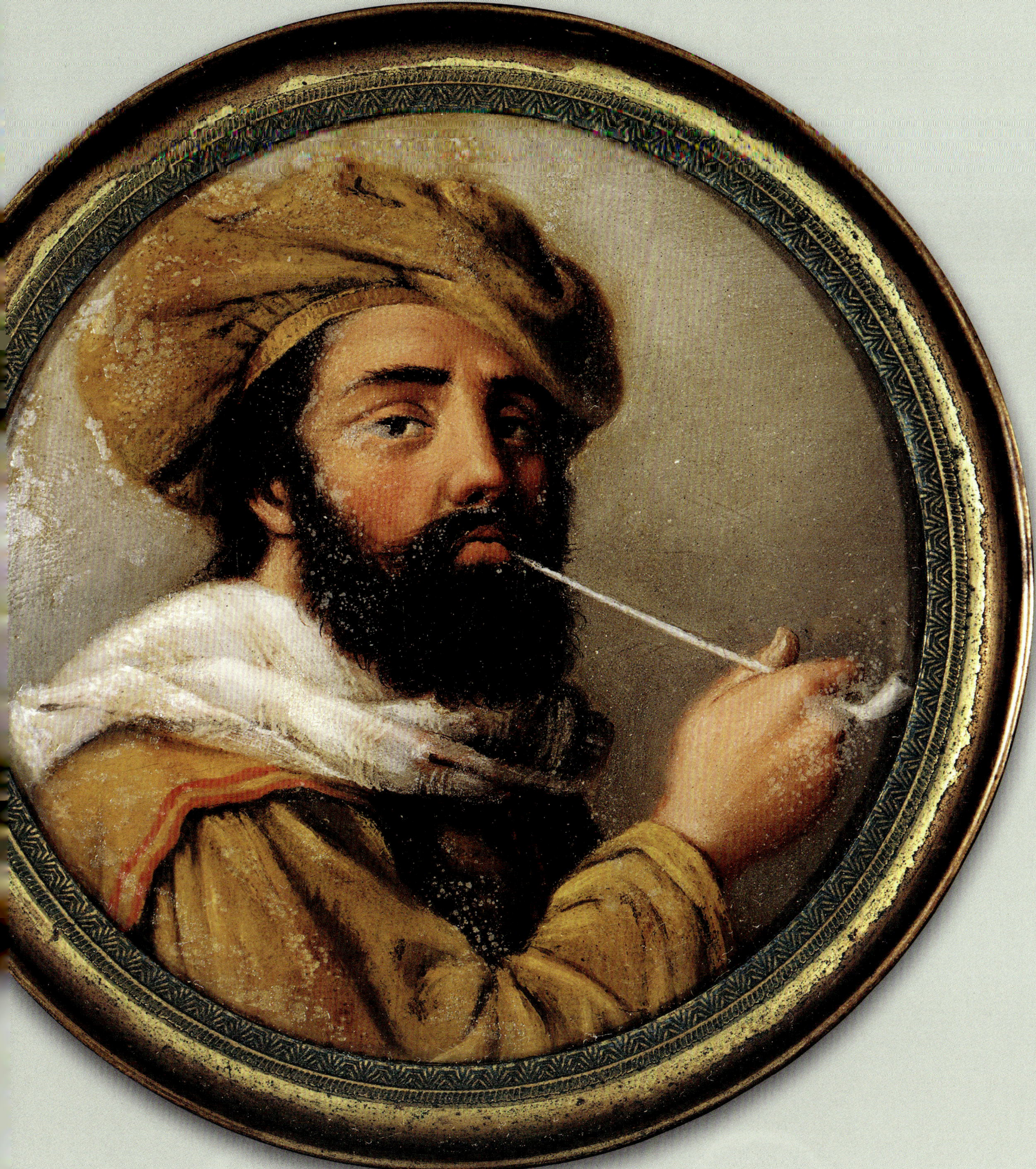

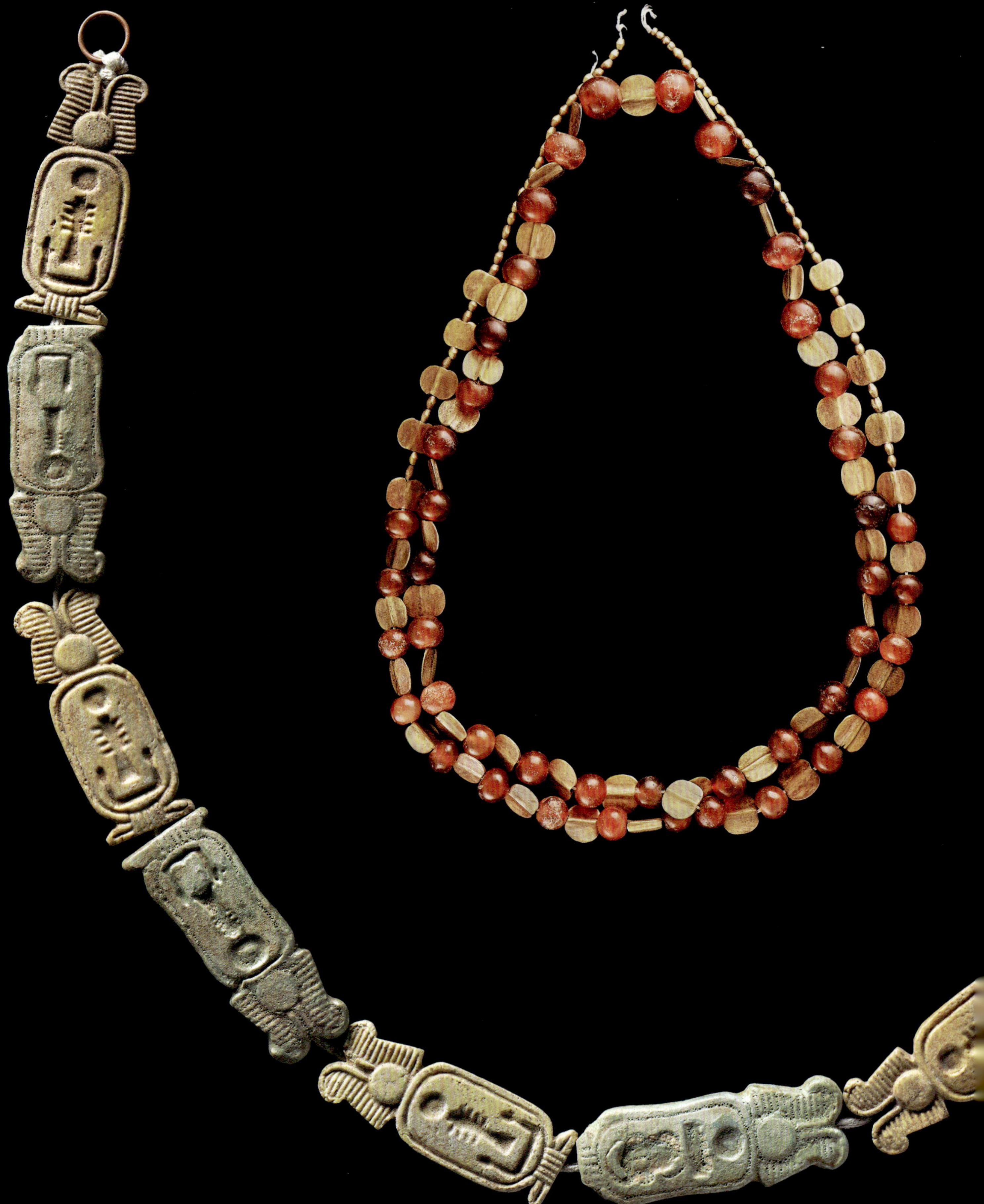

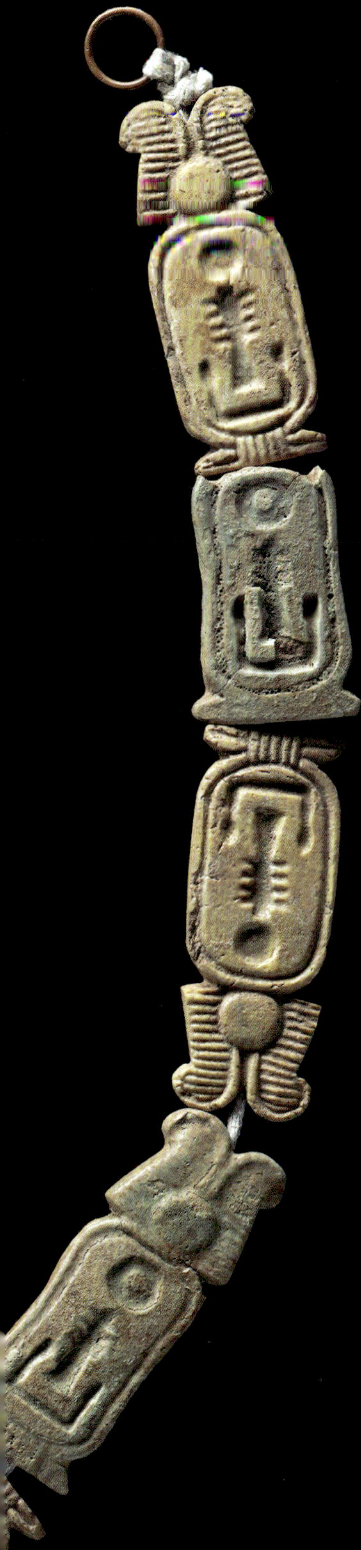

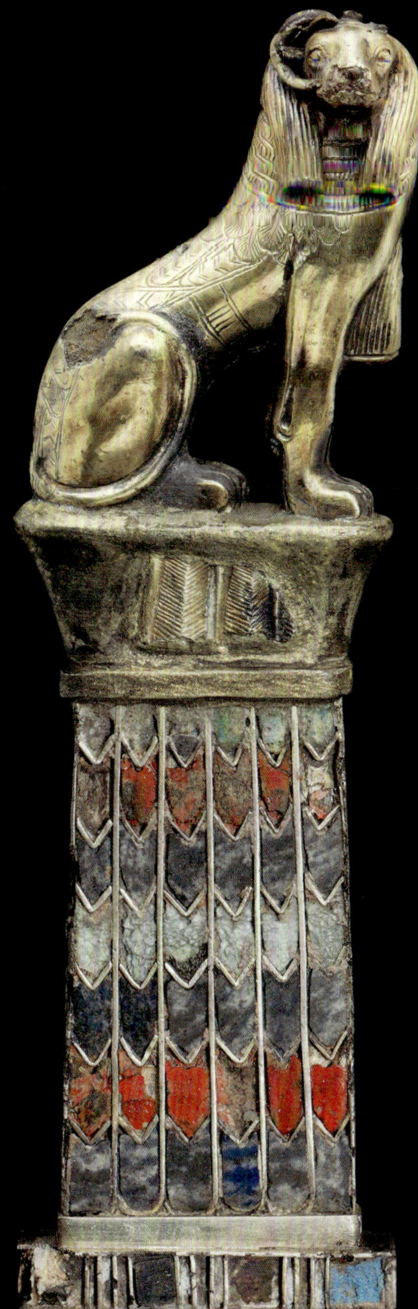

The tombs at el-Kurru, Sudan, the earliest Kushite royal cemetery, yielded intriguing jewelry. This amulet in the shape of a ram-headed sphinx crouched on a column (above) was found in an eighth-century B.C. grave.

Among several necklaces uncovered in another tomb, these strings of beads (opposite top) pair gold with carnelian.

One of two dozen horse graves yielded these beads from an equine's trappings (opposite bottom). They bear the cartouche of Shebitku, a Kushite ruler of Egypt in the seventh century B.C.

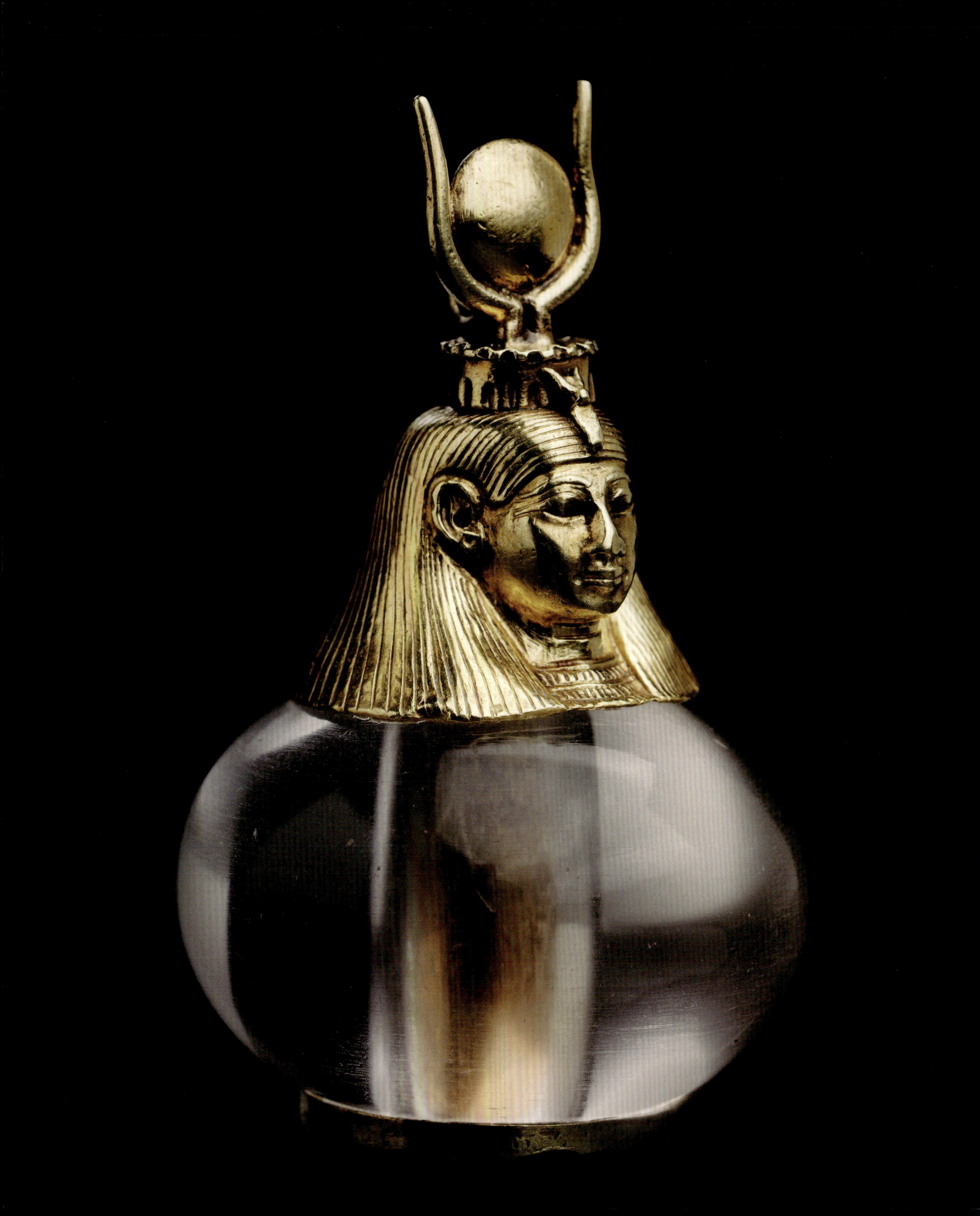

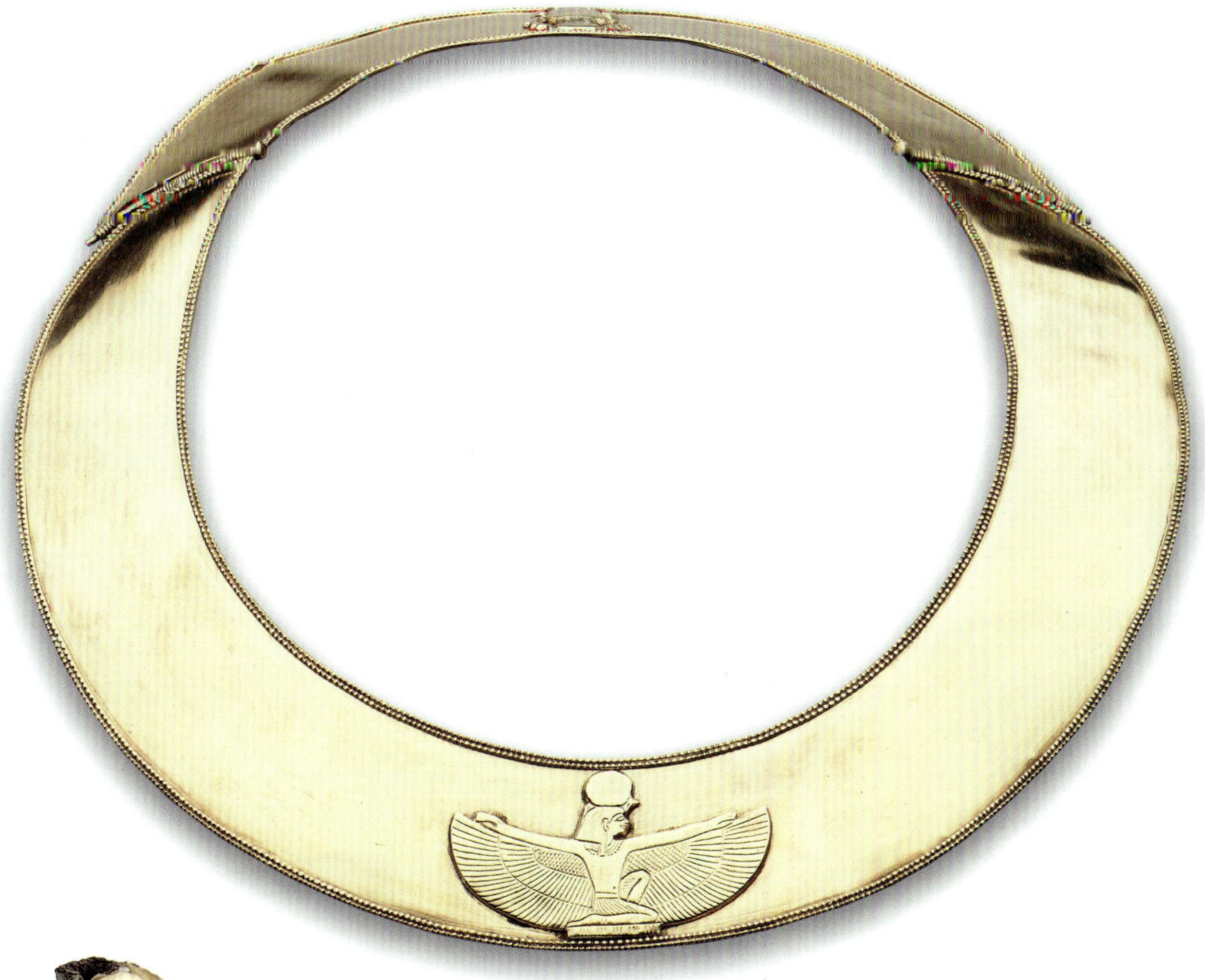

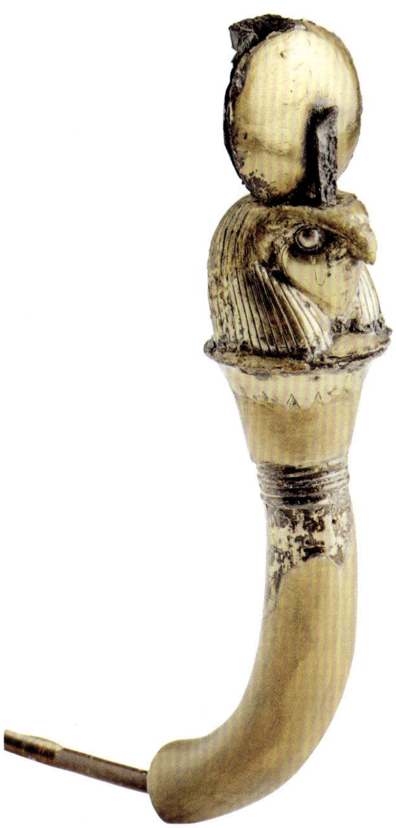

El-Kurru's treasures include these three dazzling artifacts: A gold head of the goddess Hathor (opposite) tops a crystal globe to form a pendant. The owner may have been a queen of Piye, the first Kushite king to rule Egypt (about 750–715 B.C.).

A queen of King Shebitku probably wore this gold collar (above) embossed with an Egyptian-style winged goddess wearing a disk and cobra on her head.

A horse grave yielded this plume holder of gilded silver that was once attached to a bridle (left). A papyrus capital supports a falcon's head, also adorned with a disk and cobra.

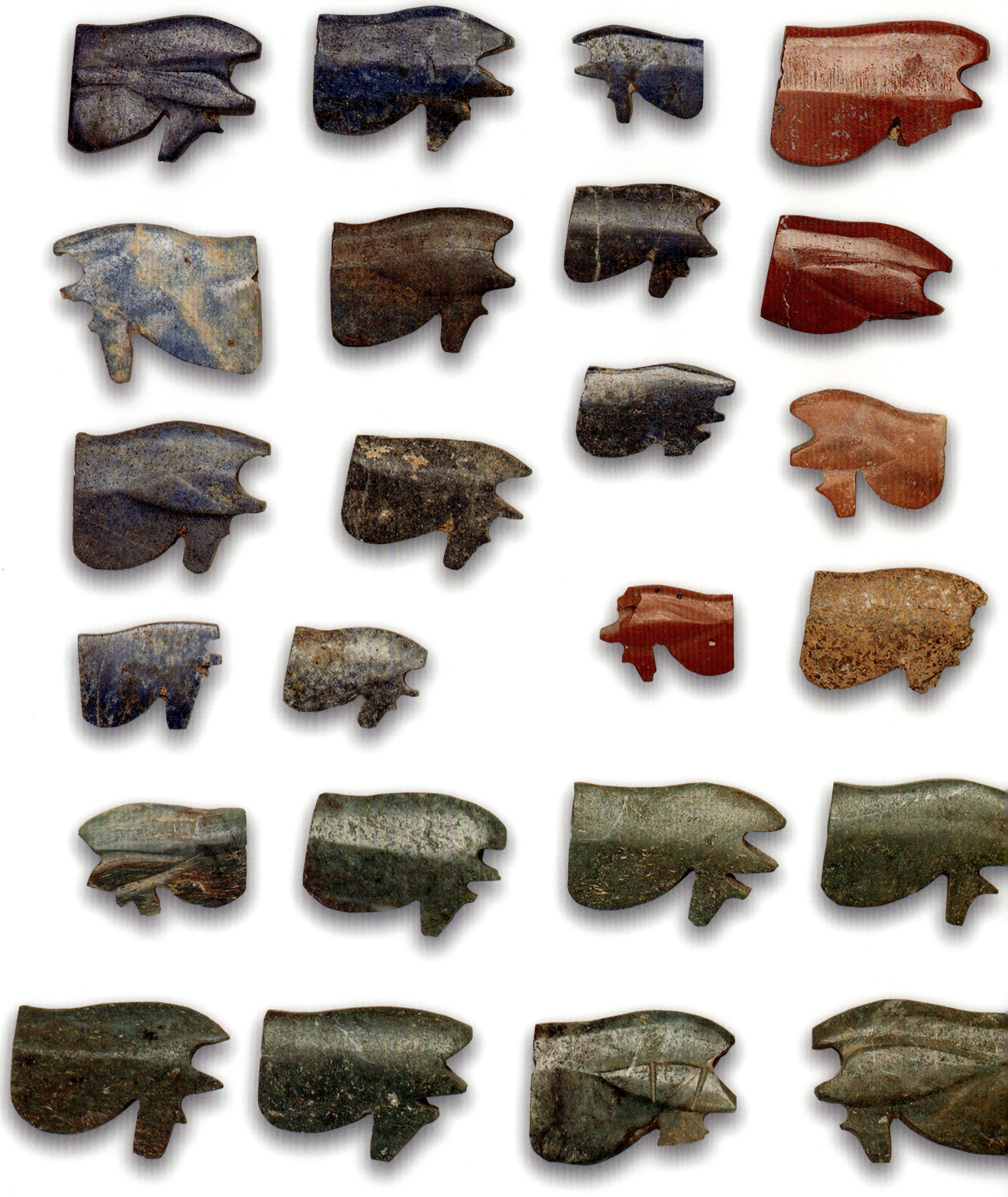

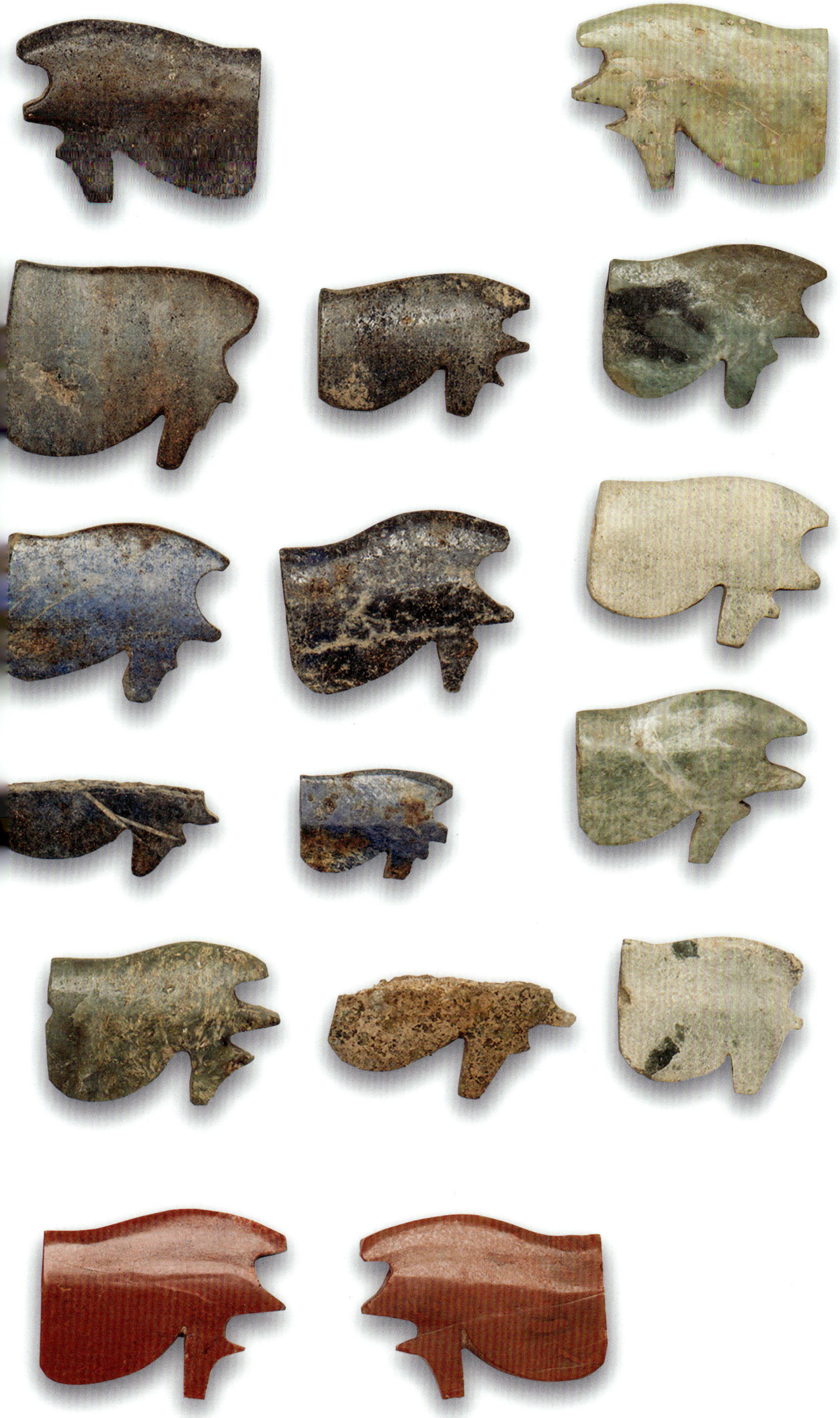

In the tomb of King Shabaka (about 715–700 B.C.) at el-Kurru, archaeologists found a cache of 120 amulets, including these. Made of materials such as gold, silver, lapis lazuli, beryl, red jasper, and malachite, they have the shape of the eye of Horus, or *wedjat,* a symbol of healing, strength, and protection.

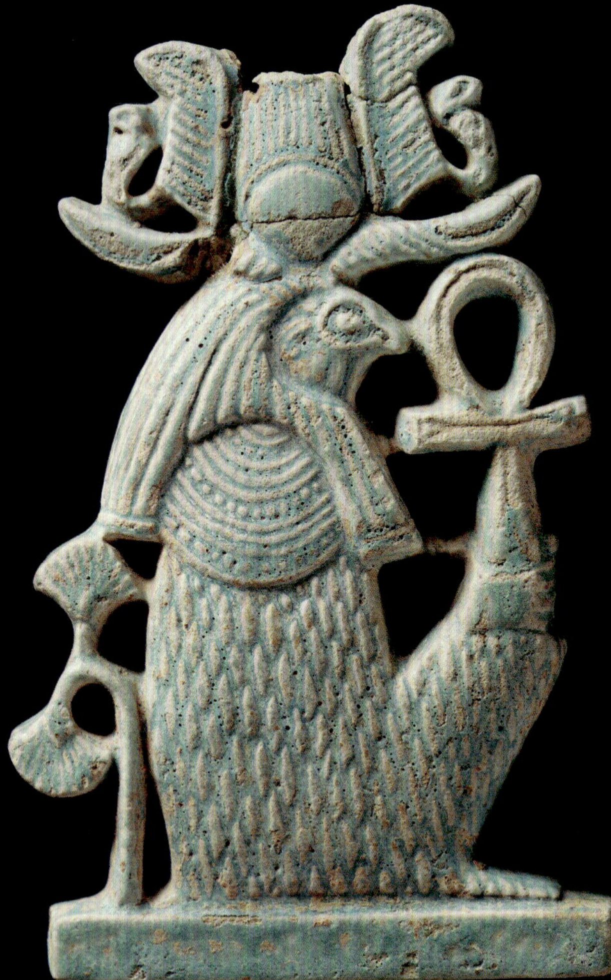

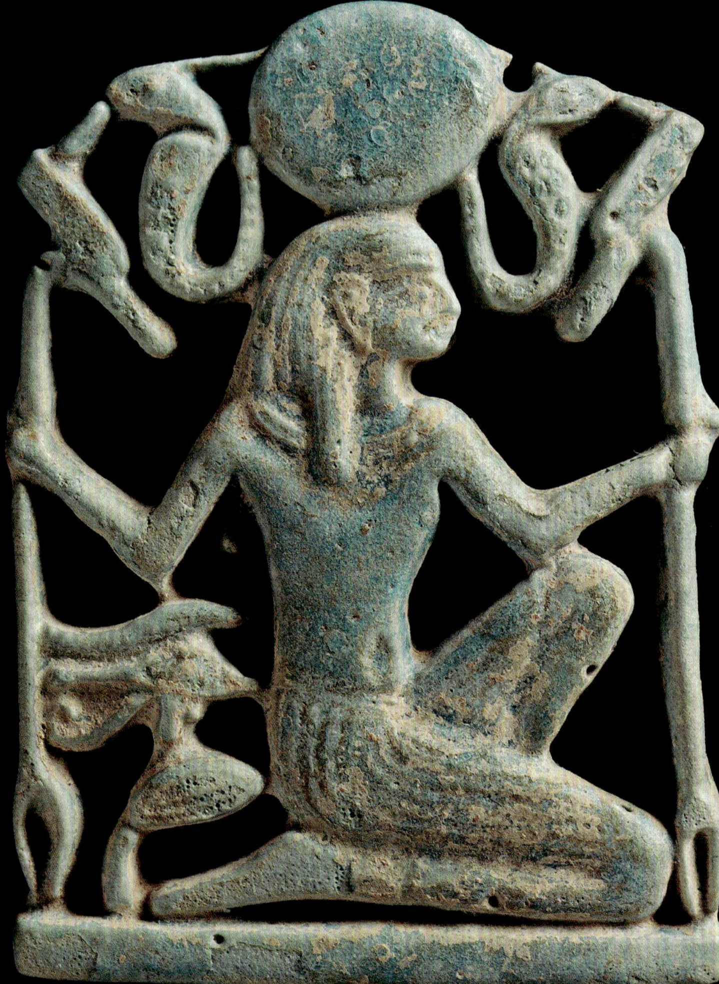

Intricate faience amulets were buried with Kushite queens at el-Kurru in the eighth century B.C. Representing one of Egypt's falcon-headed gods, this example (above left) includes the hieroglyphic symbol for "life."

The god Heh (above right) personified the concept of eternity. The hieroglyphs in his hands are the signs for "years."

The identity of this winged lioness deity (opposite) is a mystery, but her characteristics were inspired by Egyptian mythology. Plaques like these were often worn as pendants on necklaces.

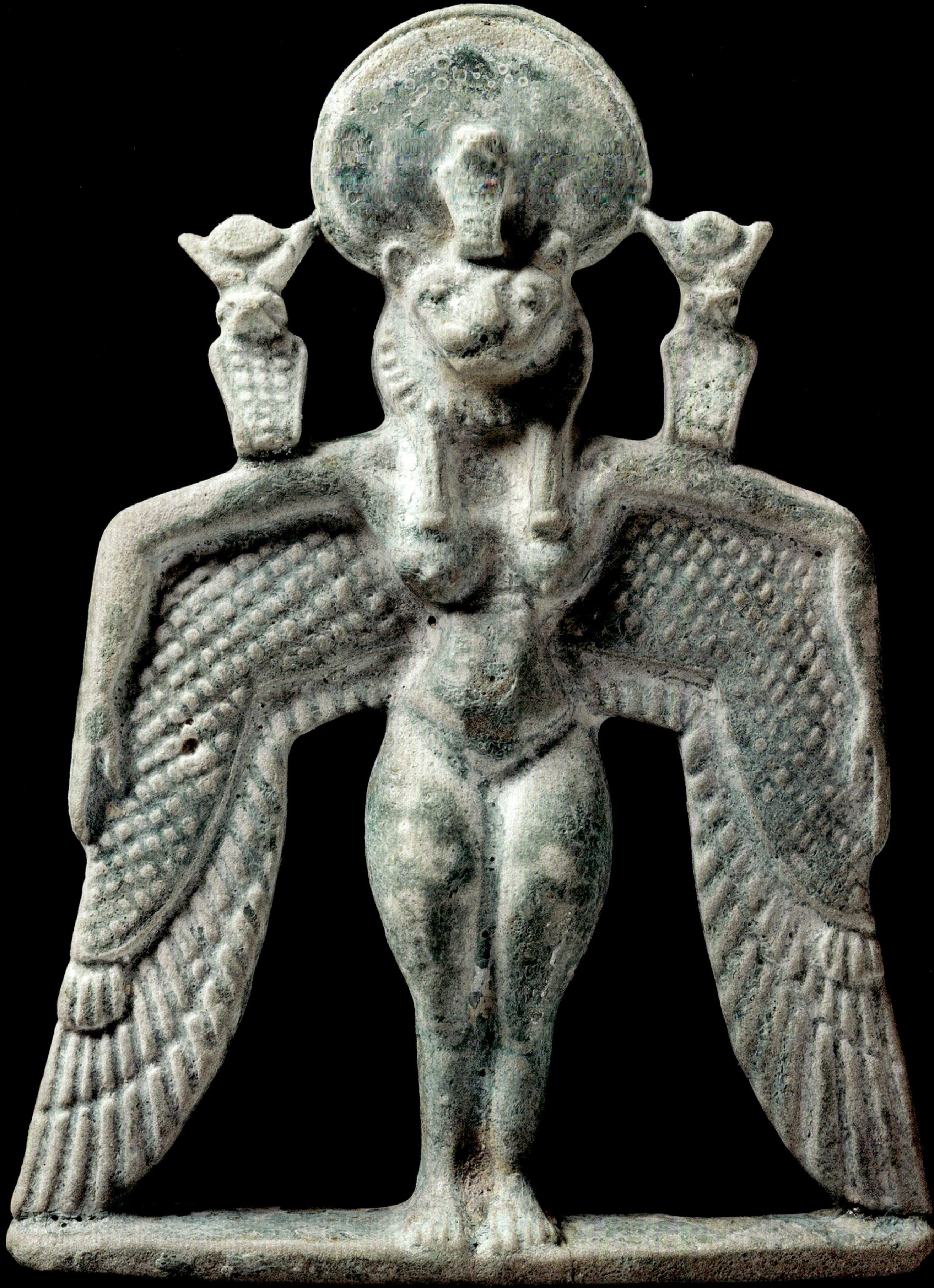

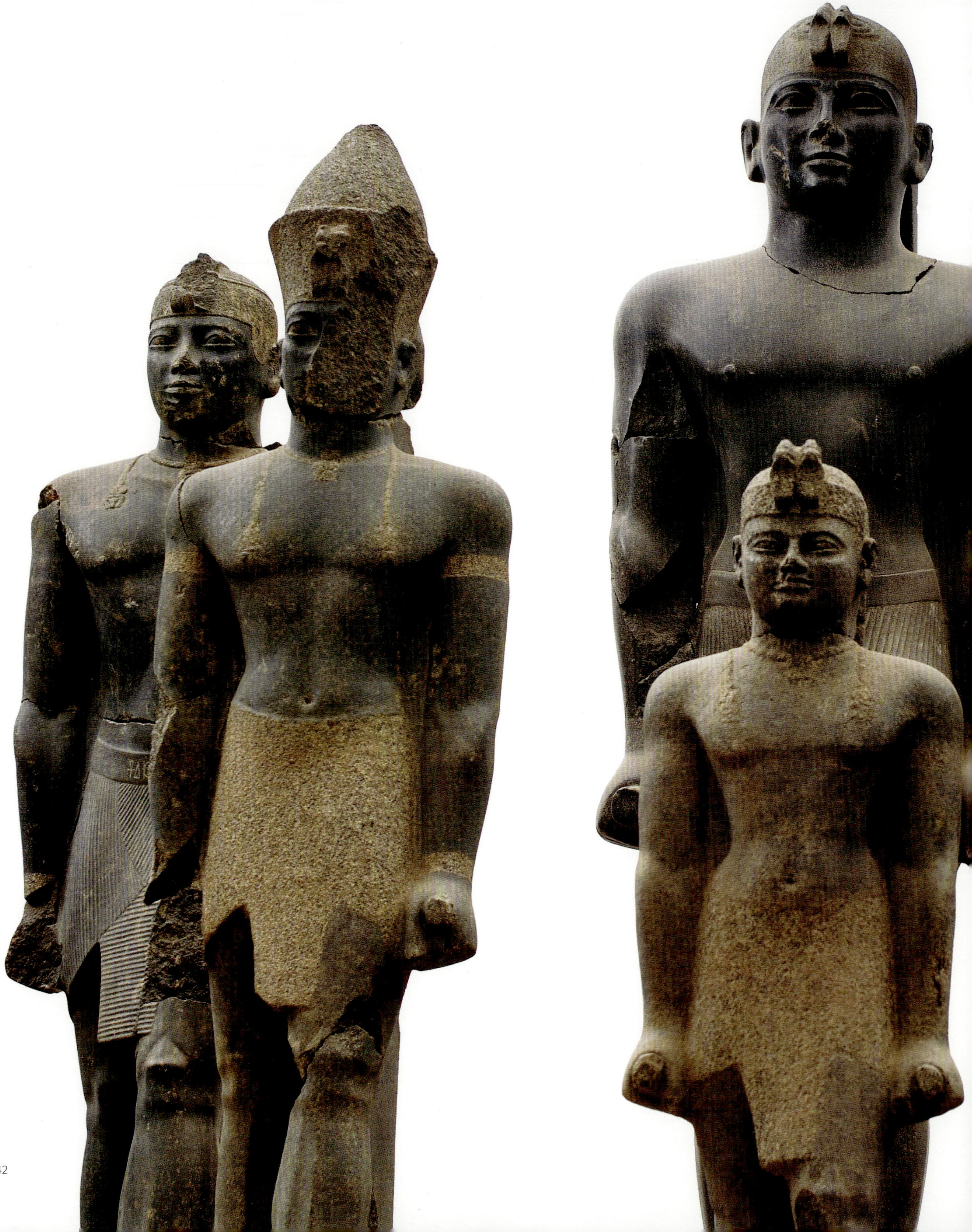

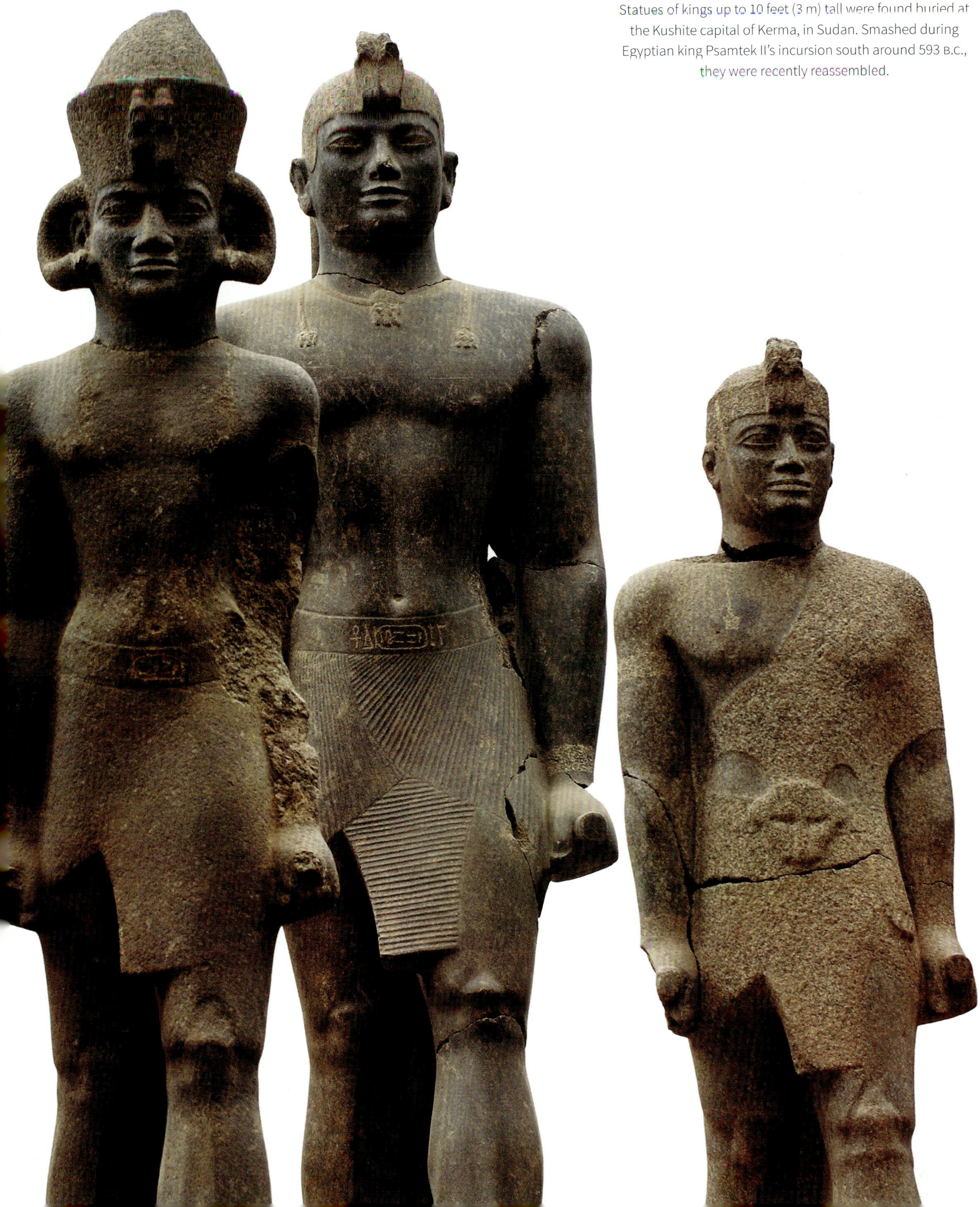

Statues of kings up to 10 feet (3 m) tall were found buried at the Kushite capital of Kerma, in Sudan. Smashed during Egyptian king Psamtek II's incursion south around 593 B.C., they were recently reassembled.

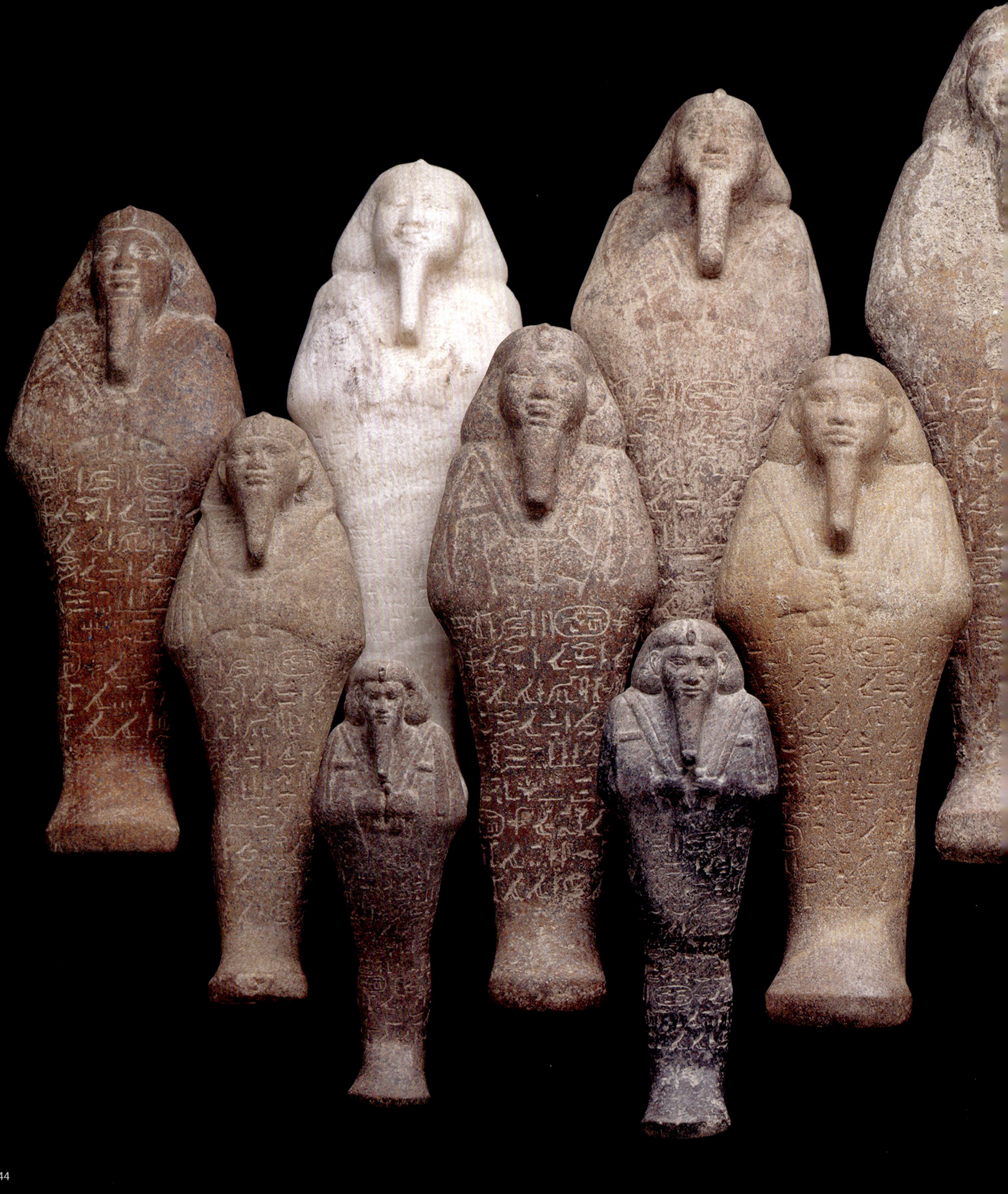

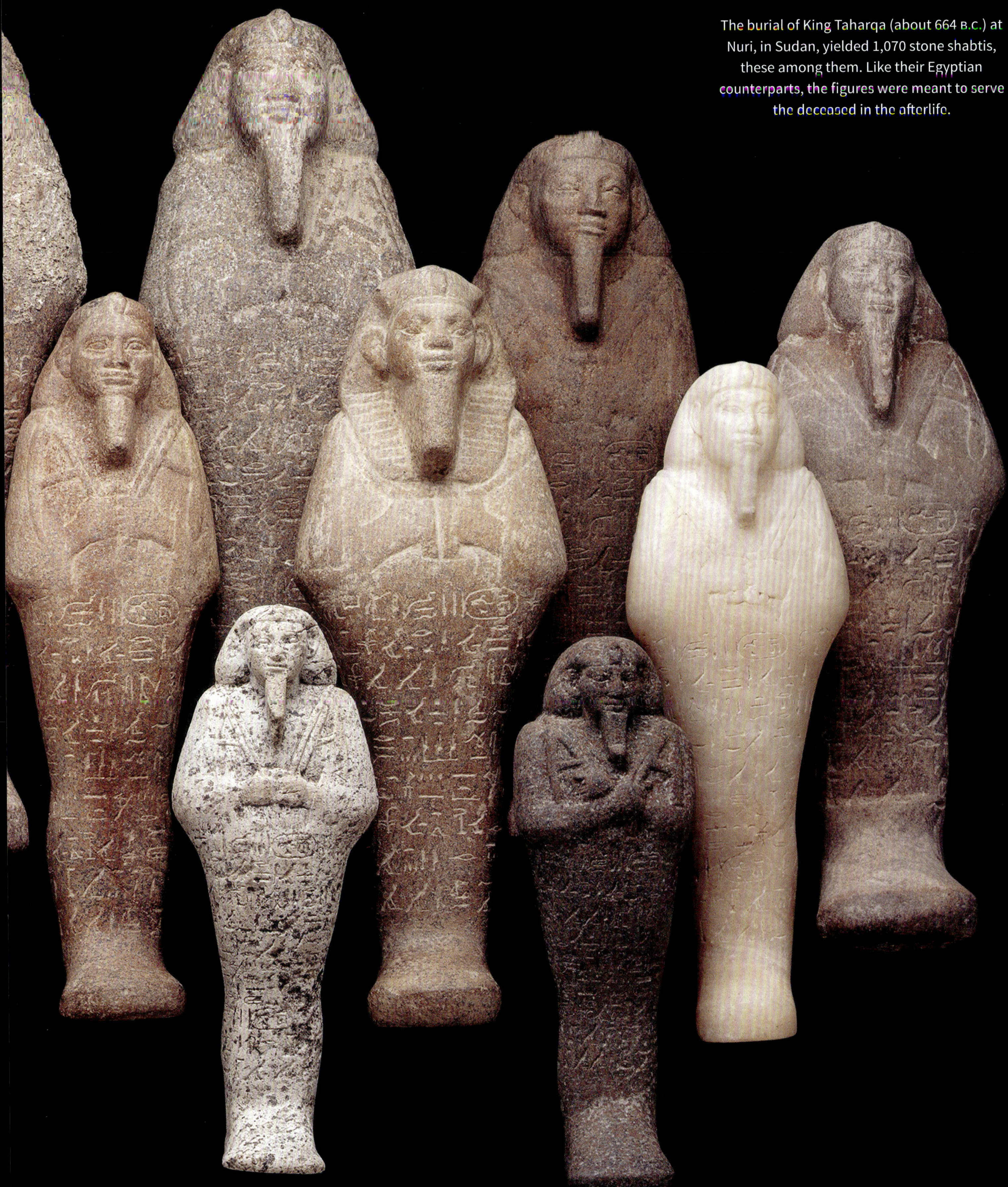

The burial of King Taharqa (about 664 B.C.) at Nuri, in Sudan, yielded 1,070 stone shabtis, these among them. Like their Egyptian counterparts, the figures were meant to serve the deceased in the afterlife.

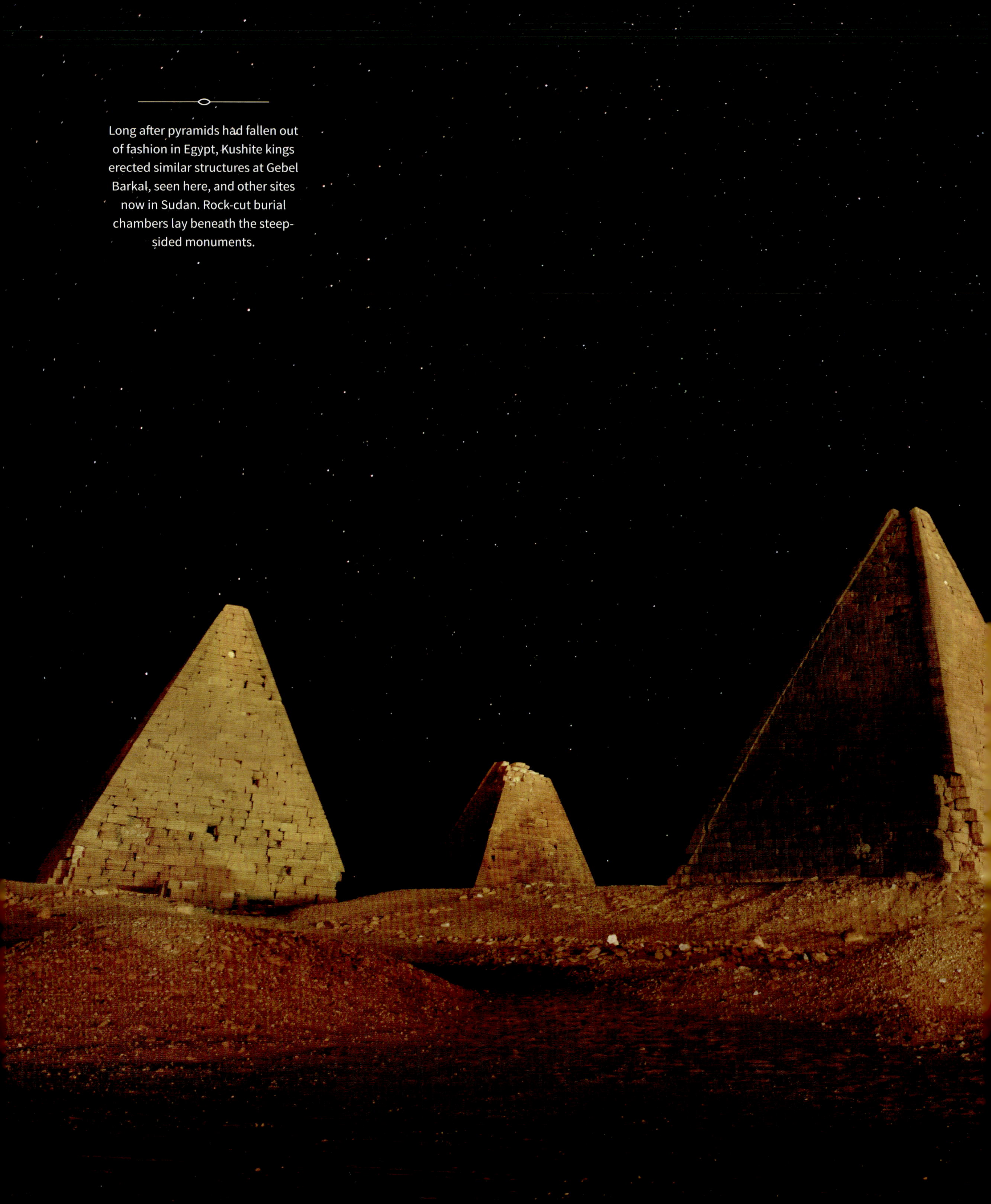

Long after pyramids had fallen out of fashion in Egypt, Kushite kings erected similar structures at Gebel Barkal, seen here, and other sites now in Sudan. Rock-cut burial chambers lay beneath the steep-sided monuments.

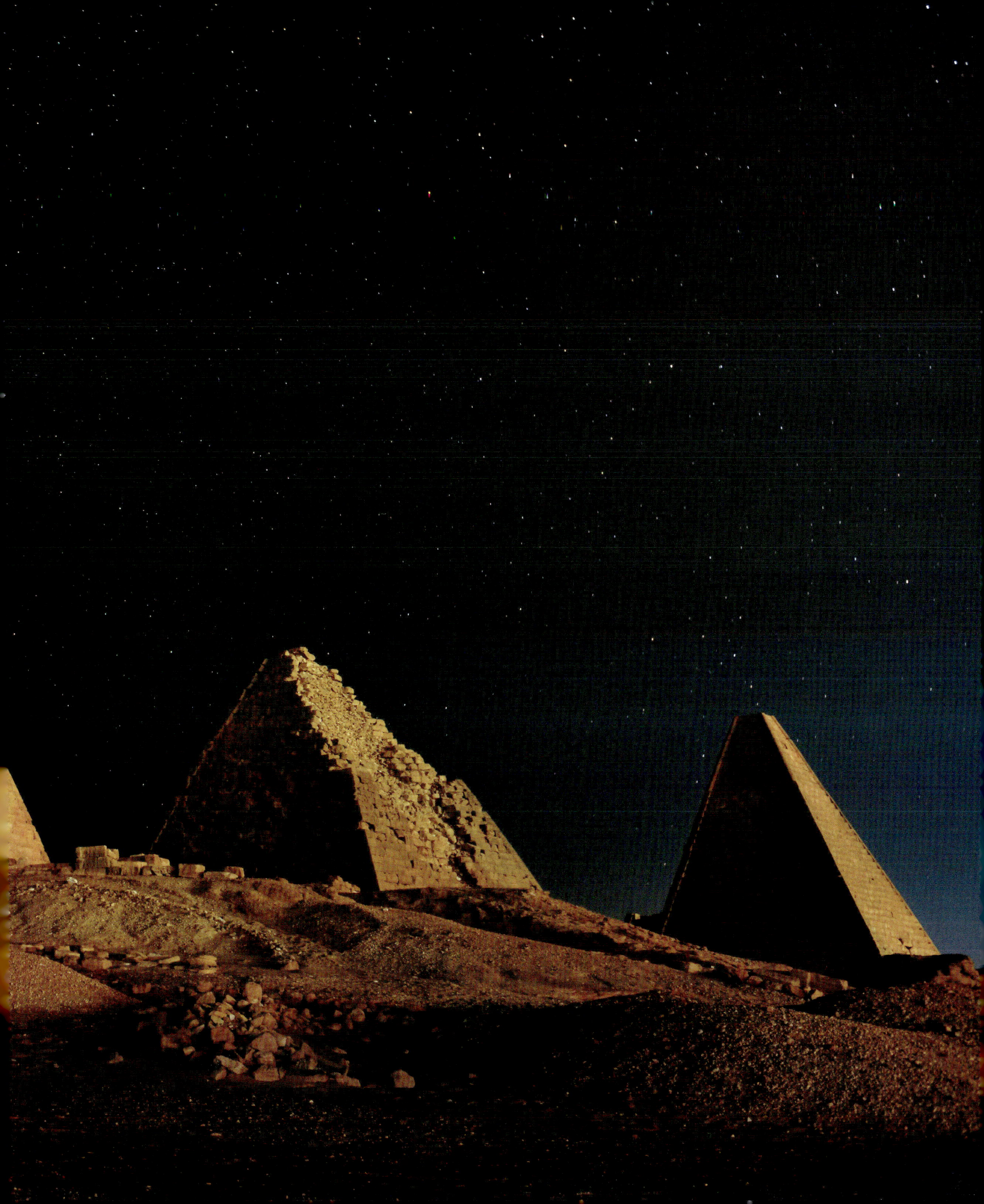

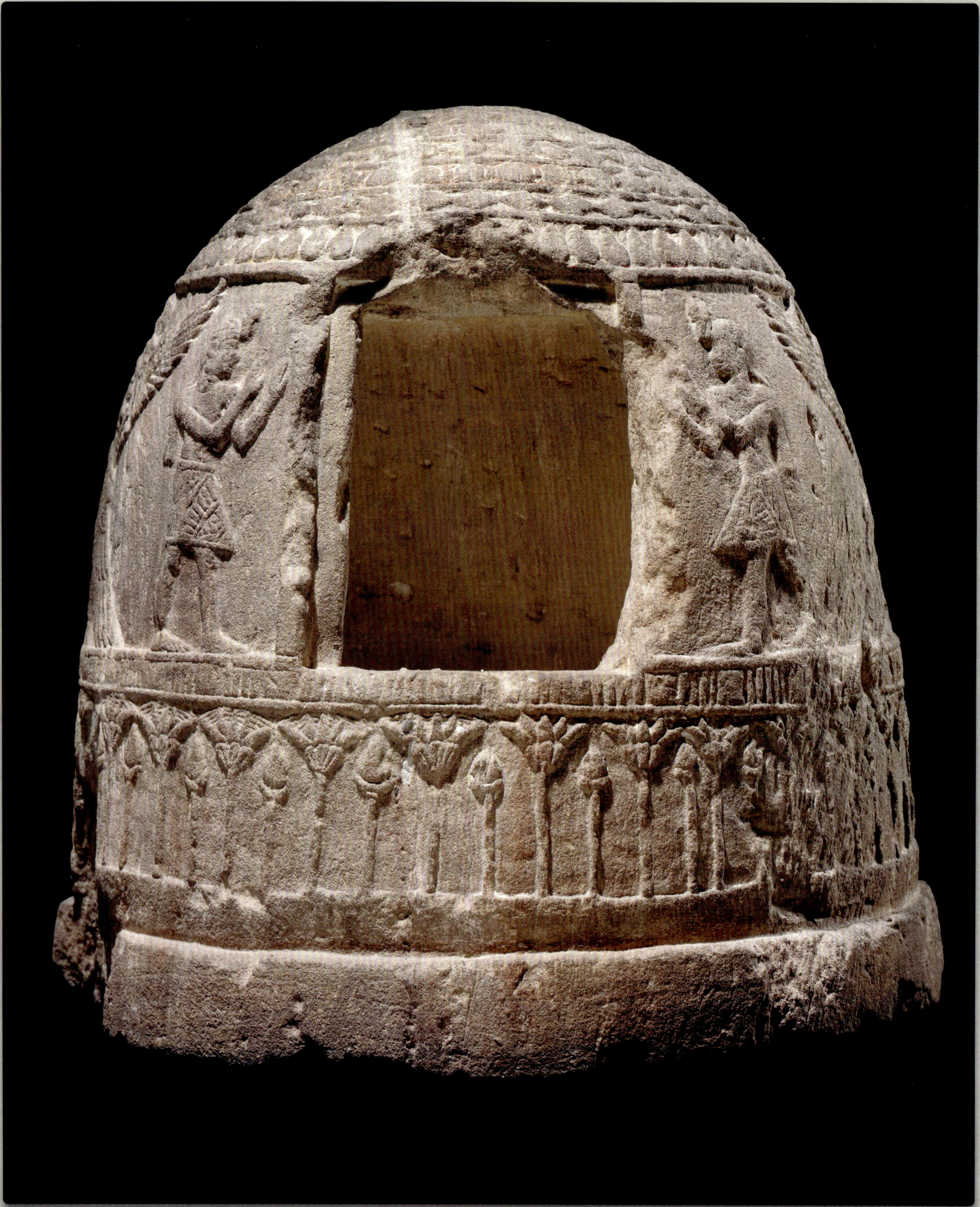

A Southern Sanctuary

AT THE SITE of Gebel Barkal, some 500 miles (800 km) south of Aswan, a cliff with an intriguing spire towers over the sand. Viewed from a certain angle, the spire resembles a rising cobra, evoking the serpent goddess placed on the crowns of Egyptian kings for protection.

In about 1500 B.C., Egypt's army marched south to conquer new territory. Arriving at Gebel Barkal, soldiers and the accompanying priests saw the spire as a sign that the site was the birthplace of Amun, Egypt's supreme god.

The Egyptians called the cliff Dju-wa'ab, "pure mountain," and began to build a religious center at its base. Eventually, more than a dozen temples stood there, including one dedicated to Mut (right), Amun's wife. Pot sherds now litter the ground, many from the bread molds used every day to bake loaves for the gods.

Natives of the region also considered the site sacred. Beginning in the fourth century B.C., local royalty built pyramid tombs there. This model from the second century A.D. (opposite) imitates a local hieroglyph for the mountain. Experts believe it originally may have had a brass door adorned with a rising cobra.

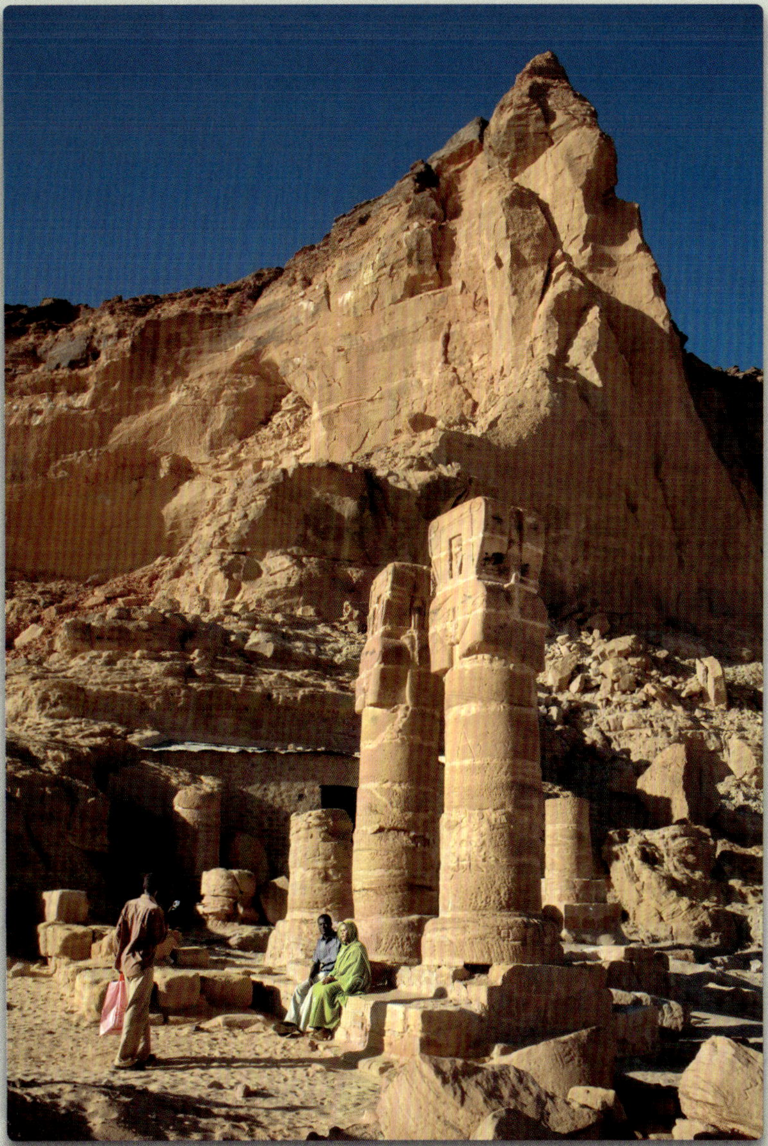

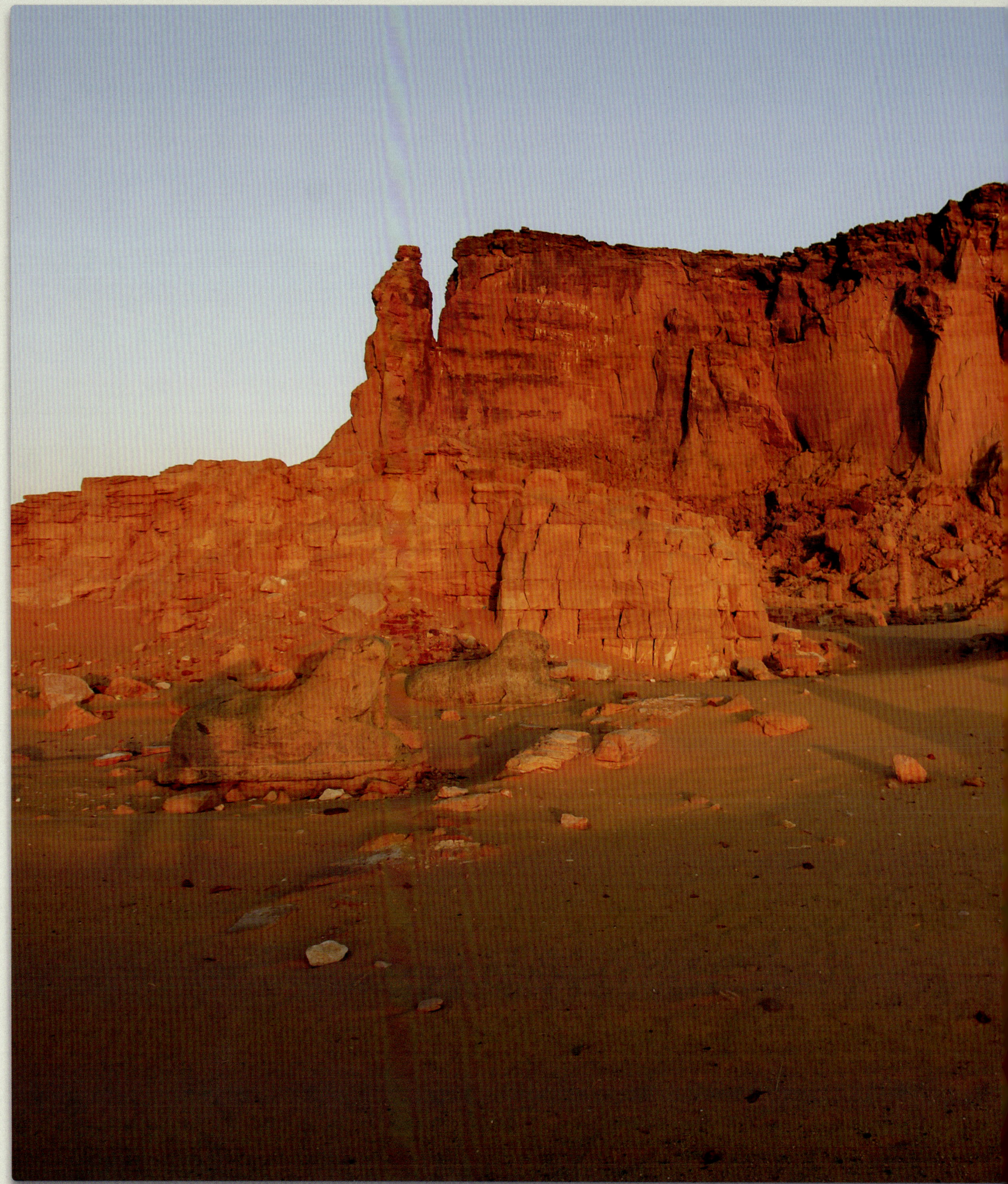

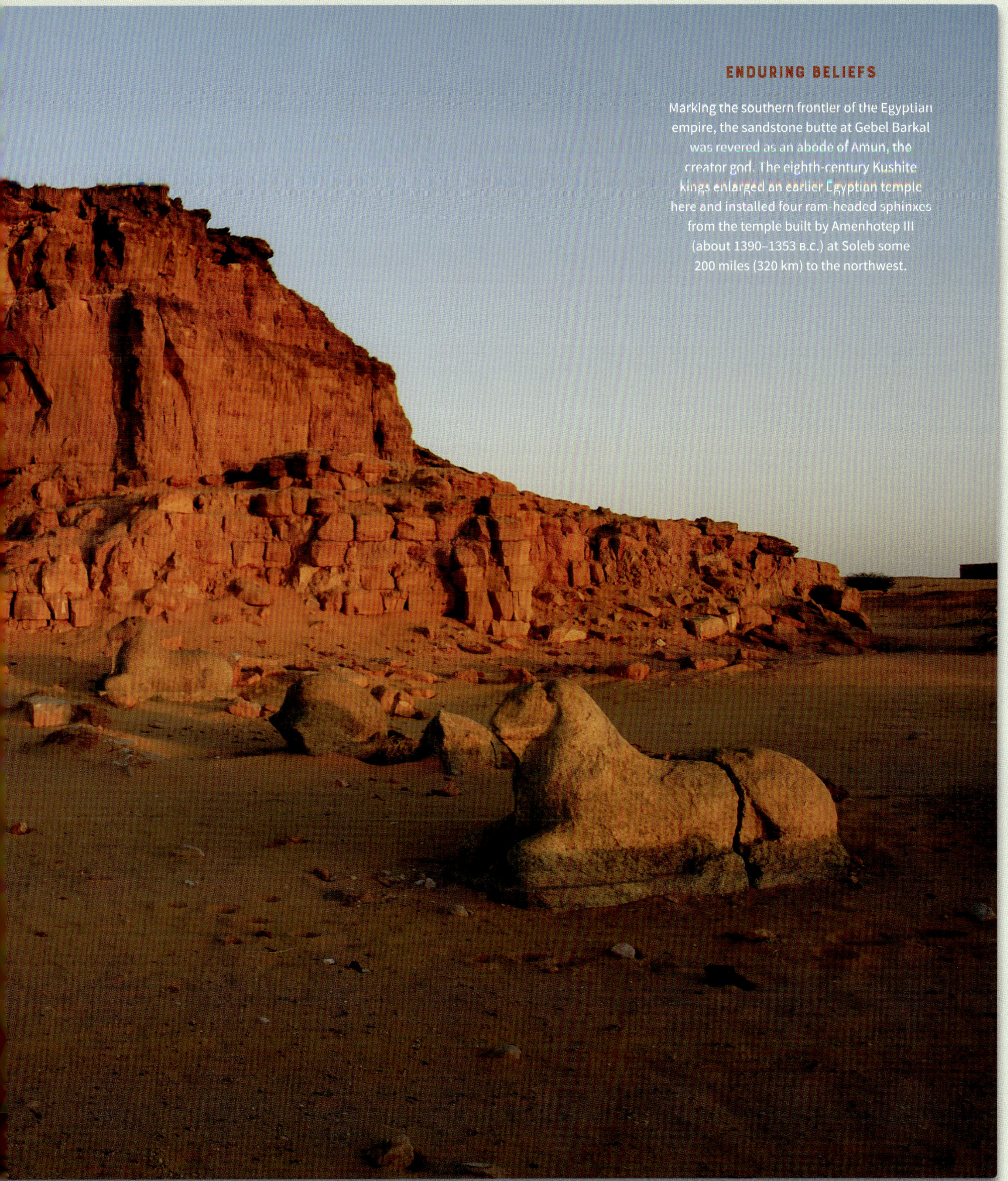

ENDURING BELIEFS

Marking the southern frontier of the Egyptian empire, the sandstone butte at Gebel Barkal was revered as an abode of Amun, the creator god. The eighth-century Kushite kings enlarged an earlier Egyptian temple here and installed four ram-headed sphinxes from the temple built by Amenhotep III (about 1390–1353 B.C.) at Soleb some 200 miles (320 km) to the northwest.

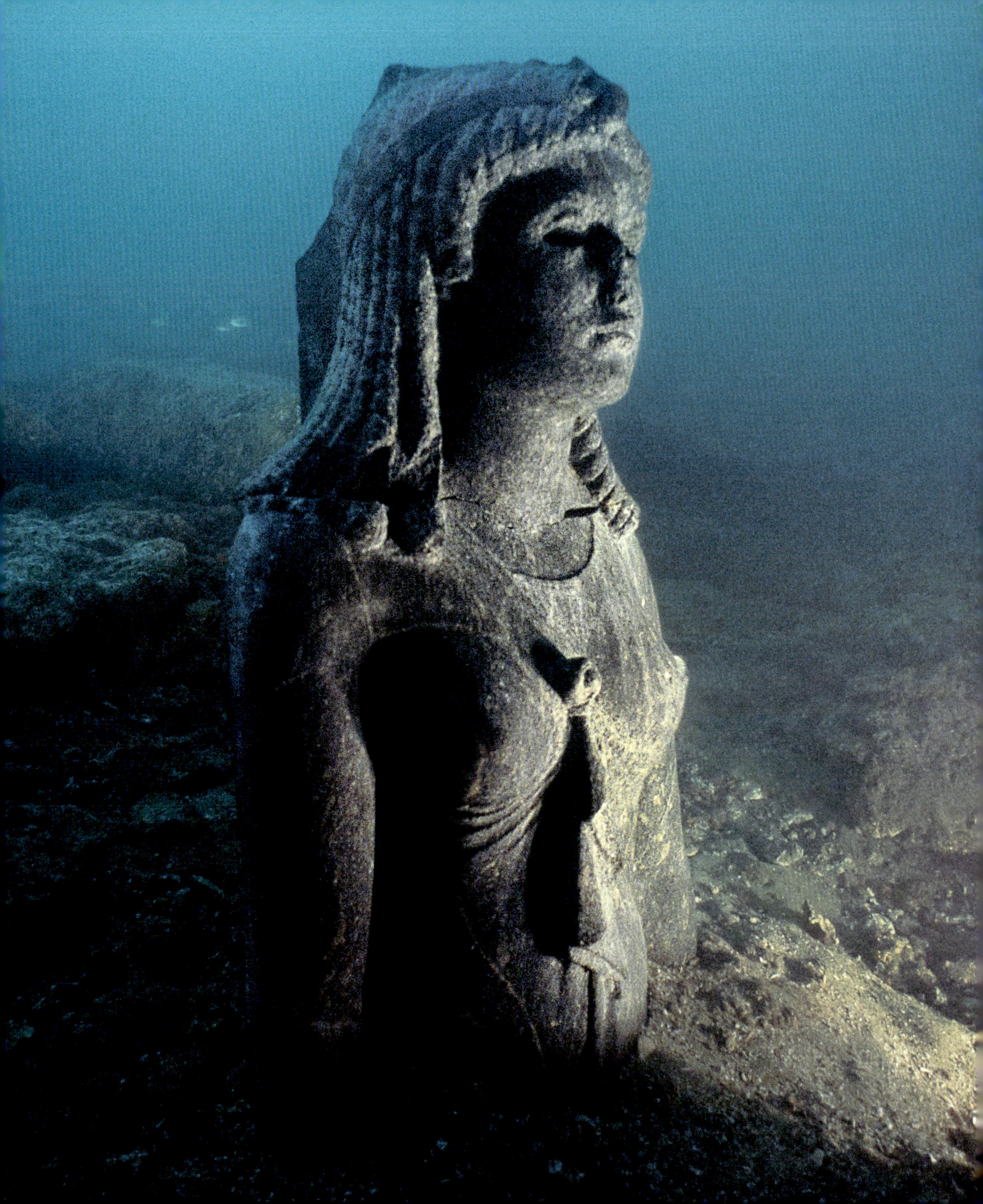

CHAPTER EIGHT

ALEXANDRIA AND THE DELTA

Gateway to the World

FANNING NORTHWARD from Memphis and Giza, the Nile Delta opens Egypt to the Mediterranean and all the lands around it. In the days of the pharaohs, five tributaries meandered to the sea through this fertile area; this made it very different geologically from the rest of the country, which was defined by one narrow river valley. The contrast may have led to the ancient Egyptians' idea that the first king had created a single country by uniting two lands: Upper Egypt (upriver) and Lower Egypt (downriver).

Until recently, archaeologists hadn't focused much attention on the delta, preferring to work on the grand temples and tombs farther south. But modern excavations are slowly revealing more of the region's tumultuous history.

As political fortunes shifted at the national level through the centuries, the delta's circumstances changed dramatically. Especially in transitional periods when dynasties collapsed and Egypt had no strong central authority, foreigners often invaded the region, and one city after another briefly became a center of power.

This scenario was exemplified during a troubled, chaotic time at the end of the Old Kingdom, between about 2125 and 1975 B.C. Egypt was split between rival factions: Warlords based in Herakleopolis, south of the former royal capital in Memphis, controlled much of Lower Egypt, while strongmen based in Waset, modern Luxor, controlled Upper Egypt. Frequent border clashes occupied their attention, allowing people from lands northeast of Egypt to take over the delta.

King Mentuhotep I managed to reunify the country in about 1948 B.C., ushering in the Middle Kingdom and a new era of royal art and architecture. But when this period ended, in about 1630 B.C., foreigners again gained control of the delta. The group, known as the Hyksos, were Semitic peoples who had been migrating to Egypt for some time. Now, they began to rule the north from the city of Avaris.

Beginning in about 1539 B.C., Egypt overthrew the Hyksos, and the great warrior pharaohs of the New Kingdom took the country to a peak of wealth, power, and influence. Seti I founded a new city, Piramesse, in the eastern delta. His son, Ramses II, made this his residence and seat of government (likely because he was often fighting the enemy Hittite army as it marched southward from Anatolia along the eastern Mediterranean coast). Archaeologists have identified the remains of enormous horse stables, workshops for building and repairing chariots, and the remains of a palace with a gilded floor bearing the cartouche of Ramses.

By the 21st dynasty, about 1075 B.C., Egypt was again divided, with the high priests of Amun in charge of Waset and kings ruling from Tanis in the delta. Royal tombs at Tanis, discovered in 1939, held treasures of gold and silver—coffins, funerary masks, elegant vessels, jewelry inset with semiprecious stones—that rival the best pieces from King Tutankhamun's tomb.

From its earliest dynasties, Egypt had traded with countries around the Mediterranean, as well as with islands in the Aegean. Around the first millennium B.C., a busy port arose on Egypt's north coast, called Thonis in Egyptian and

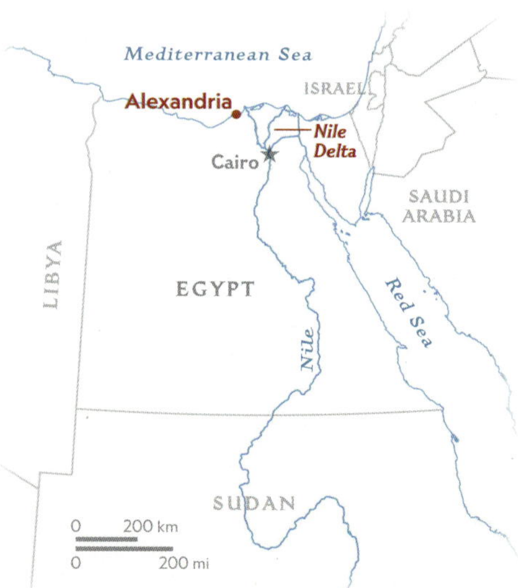

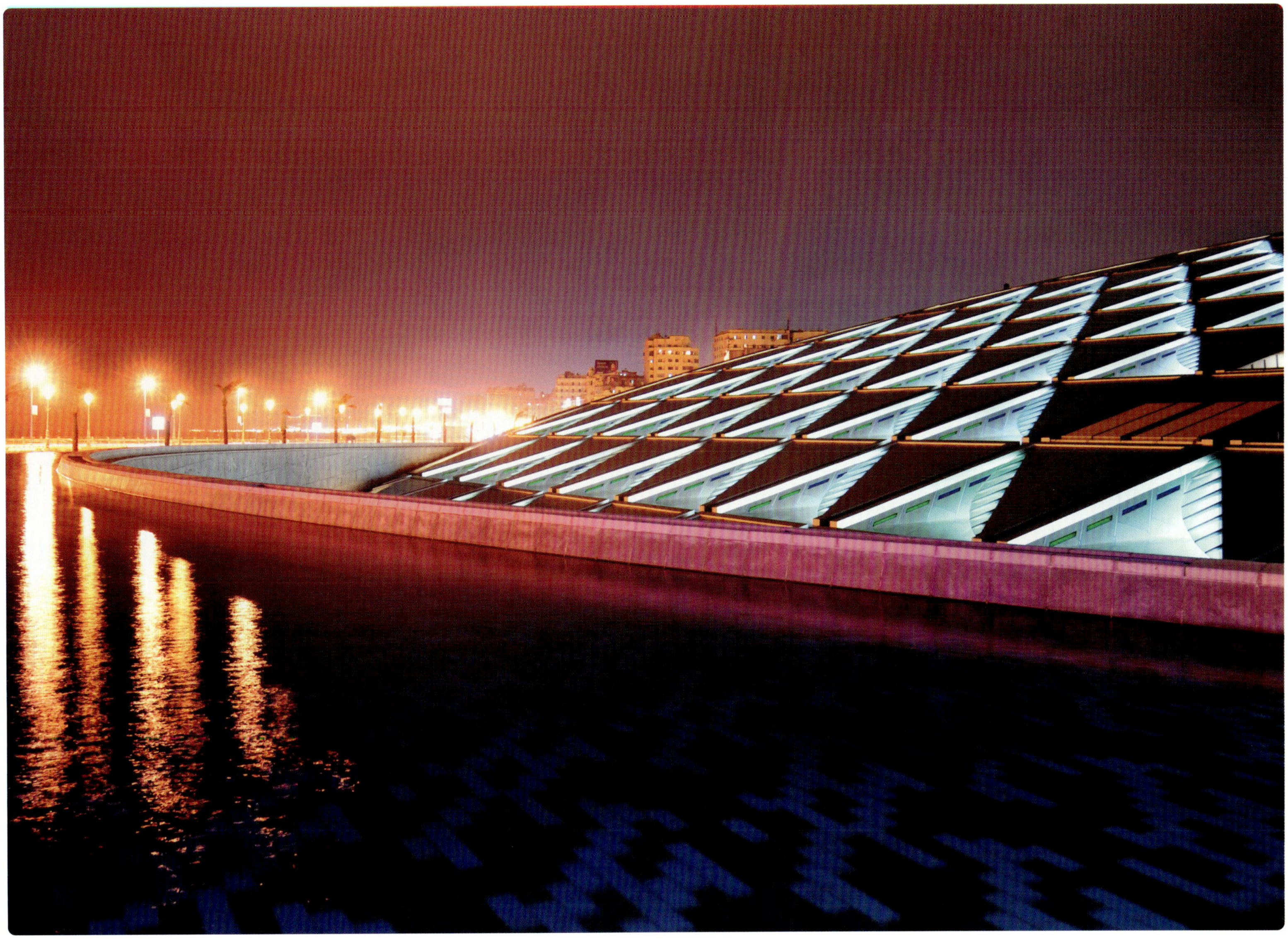

Alexandria's ultramodern library (above) was inspired by one of the ancient city's most famous buildings, a great repository of writing that burned down in the third century A.D.

PREVIOUS PAGES: Underwater archaeologists discovered this statue of a queen from the Ptolemaic era (332–30 B.C.) amid the ruins of Thonis-Heracleion, which sank into the sea off the Mediterranean coast.

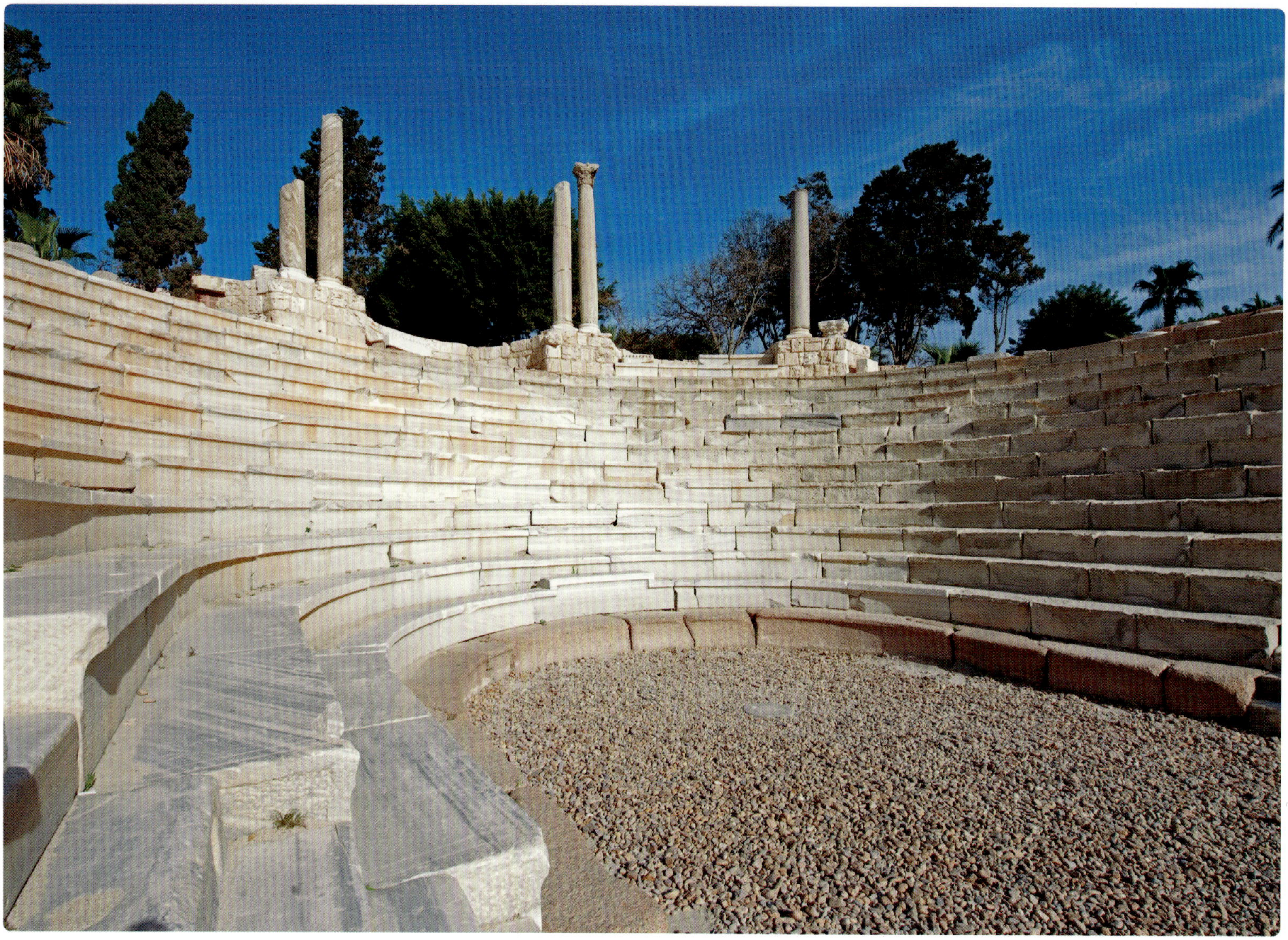

During the first centuries A.D., Romans living in Alexandria attended performances at this theater. Built of white marble imported from Europe, its 13 tiers would have seated some 800 people.

Heracleion in Greek. Several anchorages serviced ships laden with merchandise. And, like Venice, the city was distinguished by its canals and lagoons, bridges and ferries.

Two miles (3.2 km) to the west, Canopus was a religious center connected to Thonis-Heracleion by a network of waterways. It was also, apparently, quite a party town—"remarkable above everything else is the multitude of persons who resort to the public festivals," wrote Strabo, a first-century B.C. Greek geographer. "For day and night there are crowds of men and women in boats, singing and dancing, without restraint, and with the utmost licentiousness."

In 332 B.C. Macedonian king Alexander the Great invaded Egypt, upending everything, everywhere. The dynasty founded by one of his generals, Ptolemy, would rule the country until the Roman conquest in 30 B.C. Alexandria, the city named for its founder, would replace Memphis as Egypt's capital and main port, soon turning Thonis-Heracleion and Canopus into backwaters.

The new city was a cosmopolitan center of trade, culture, and learning. It boasted a grand avenue 100 feet (30 m) wide, gleaming colonnades, harborside palaces and temples, and a towering lighthouse—one of the Seven Wonders of the Ancient World—possibly standing more than 300 feet (90 m) tall. Its famous library held priceless manuscripts from Greece, Assyria, India, and other countries.

But Egypt's coastal cities were built on soft, wet ground. Over time, a combination of earthquakes, floods, tidal surges, and a rising sea caused the earth to liquefy, sending temples, houses, and all their contents tumbling into the ocean. Thonis-Heracleion may have started to go as early as the first century A.D. The low-lying eastern part of Canopus was in trouble, but sections held on until sometime in the eighth century. Around that time Alexandria lost land around its harbor, including buildings in the royal quarter.

"Until recently, archaeologists hadn't focused much attention on the delta, preferring to work on the grand temples and tombs farther south. But modern excavations are slowly revealing more of the region's tumultuous history."

For the last three decades, French archaeologist Franck Goddio has been exploring the underwater ruins of the sunken cities. Working off the coast northeast of Alexandria, in Abu Qir Bay, he has found the remains of Thonis-Heracleion and Canopus, including parts of temples, colossal statues, inscribed stelae, jewelry and coins, ritual offerings, high-end Greek ceramics, and wicker baskets filled with seeds from the grapes they once held.

Thanks to the work of Goddio and other intrepid underwater archaeologists, experts are now able to map the drowned portions of Alexandria. In fact, the barnacled discoveries brought to the sea's surface—massive stone sphinxes, giant limestone paving blocks, granite columns and capitals—reveal a city that was surprisingly different from what ancient texts describe, and whose royal, religious, and maritime structures reflect more of a Greco-Roman character than traditional Egyptian.

The rest of the glory that was Alexandria is now mostly buried under the modern city of shoulder-to-shoulder bayside buildings and crowded streets. But recent excavations in a public park have uncovered a section of the ancient royal quarter, creating the tantalizing possibility that the long-lost tomb of Alexander himself could come to light when archaeologists remove the next shovel of dirt. ▲

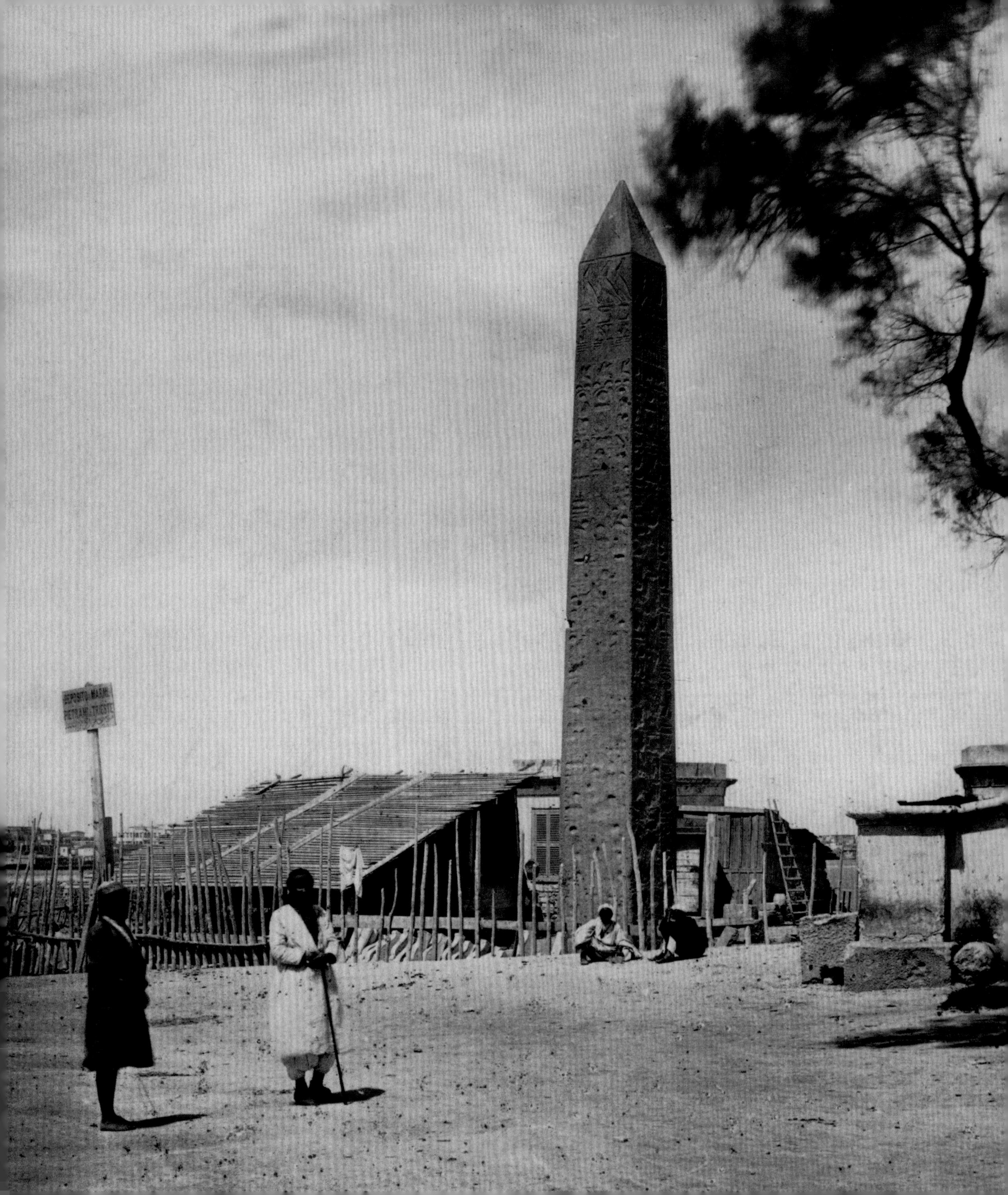

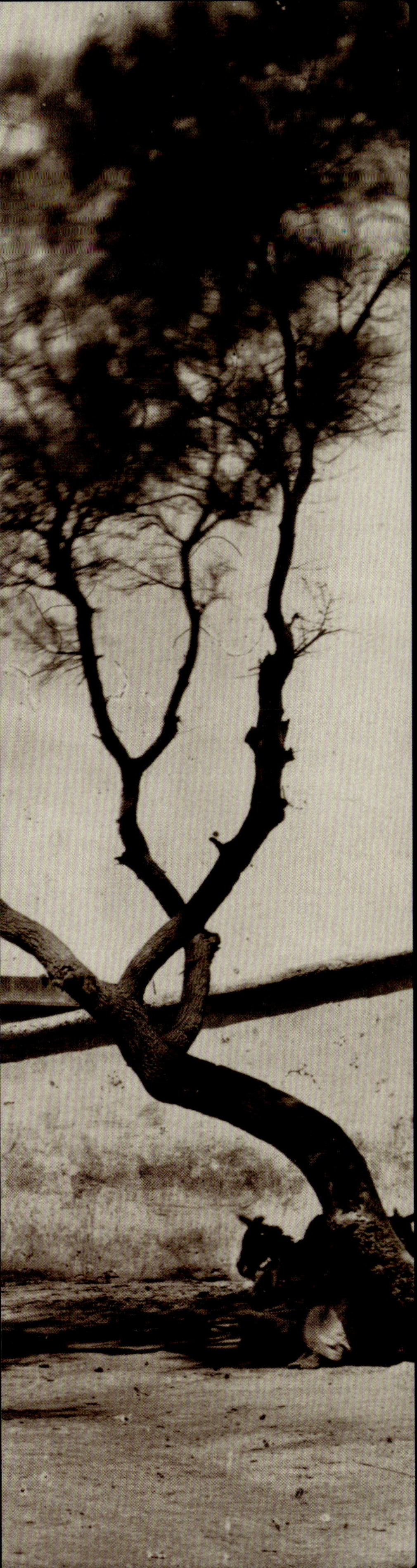

FIRST PHOTOS

King Thutmose III (about 1479–1425 B.C.) erected two obelisks at a temple in Heliopolis, now a Cairo suburb. The monuments had fallen over by 12 B.C., when the Romans moved them to Alexandria. One was photographed there in the mid-1800s (left).

Shortly thereafter, Egypt gave one of the obelisks to the United States. Nicknamed Cleopatra's Needle, it was installed in New York's Central Park, where it remains today (below).

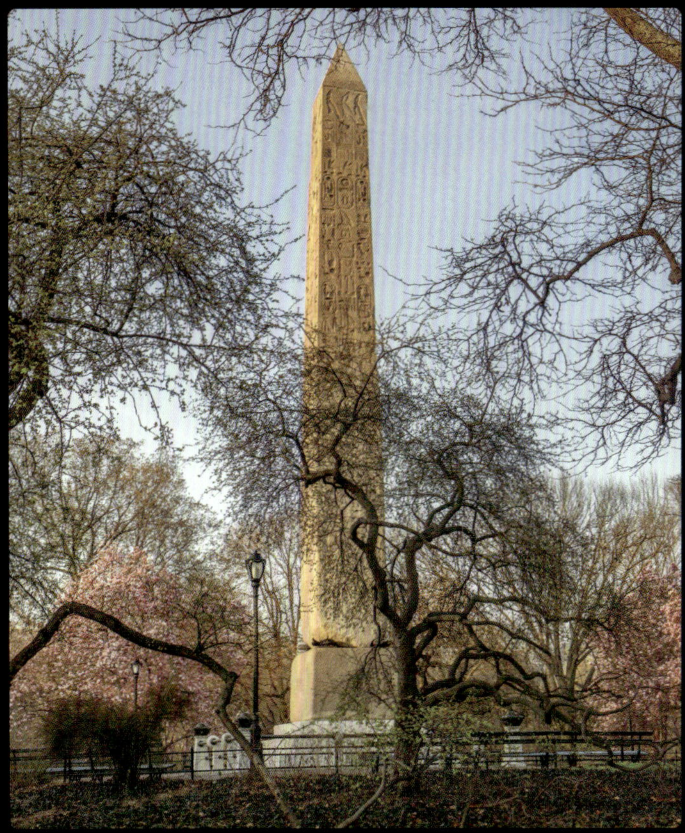

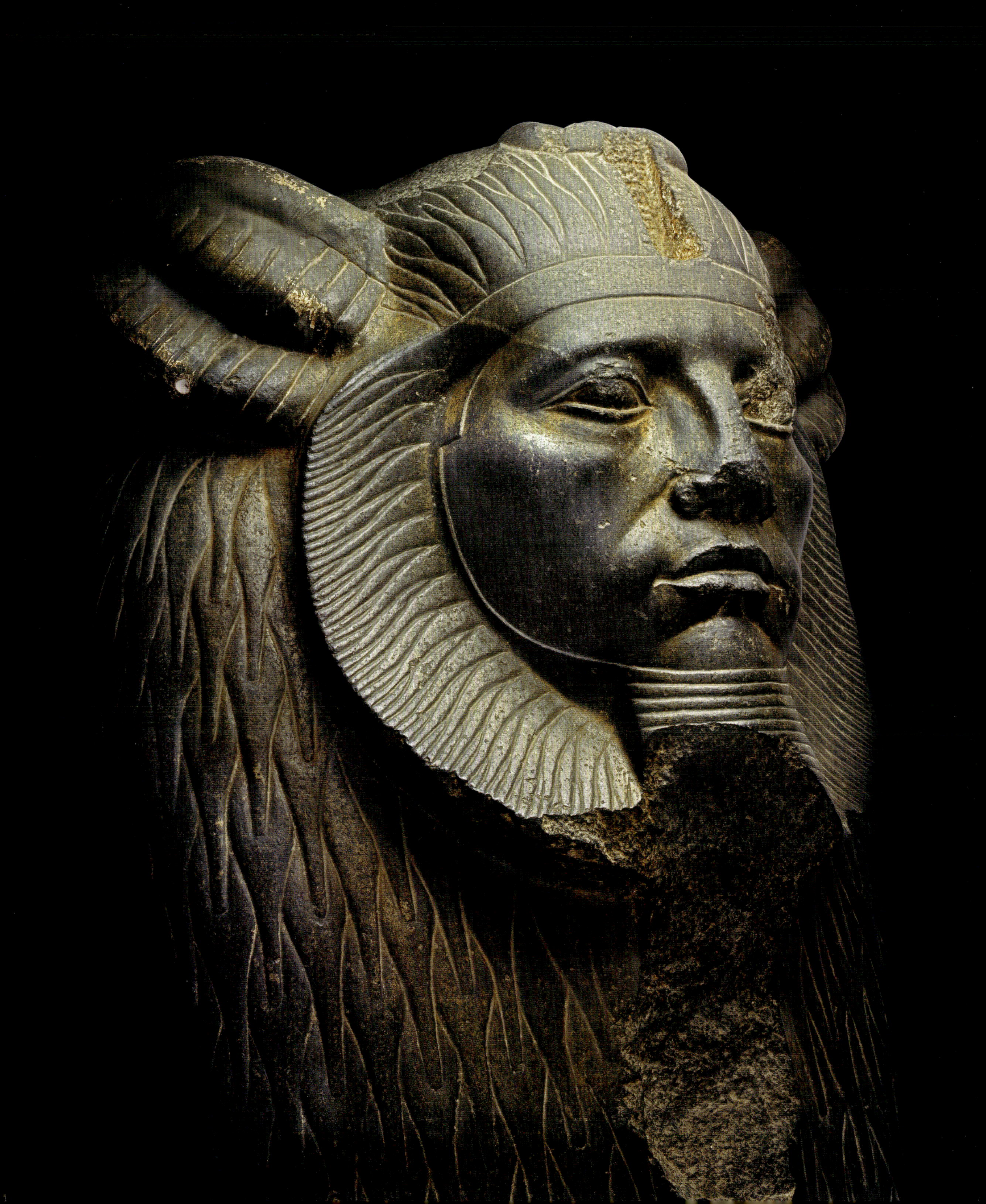

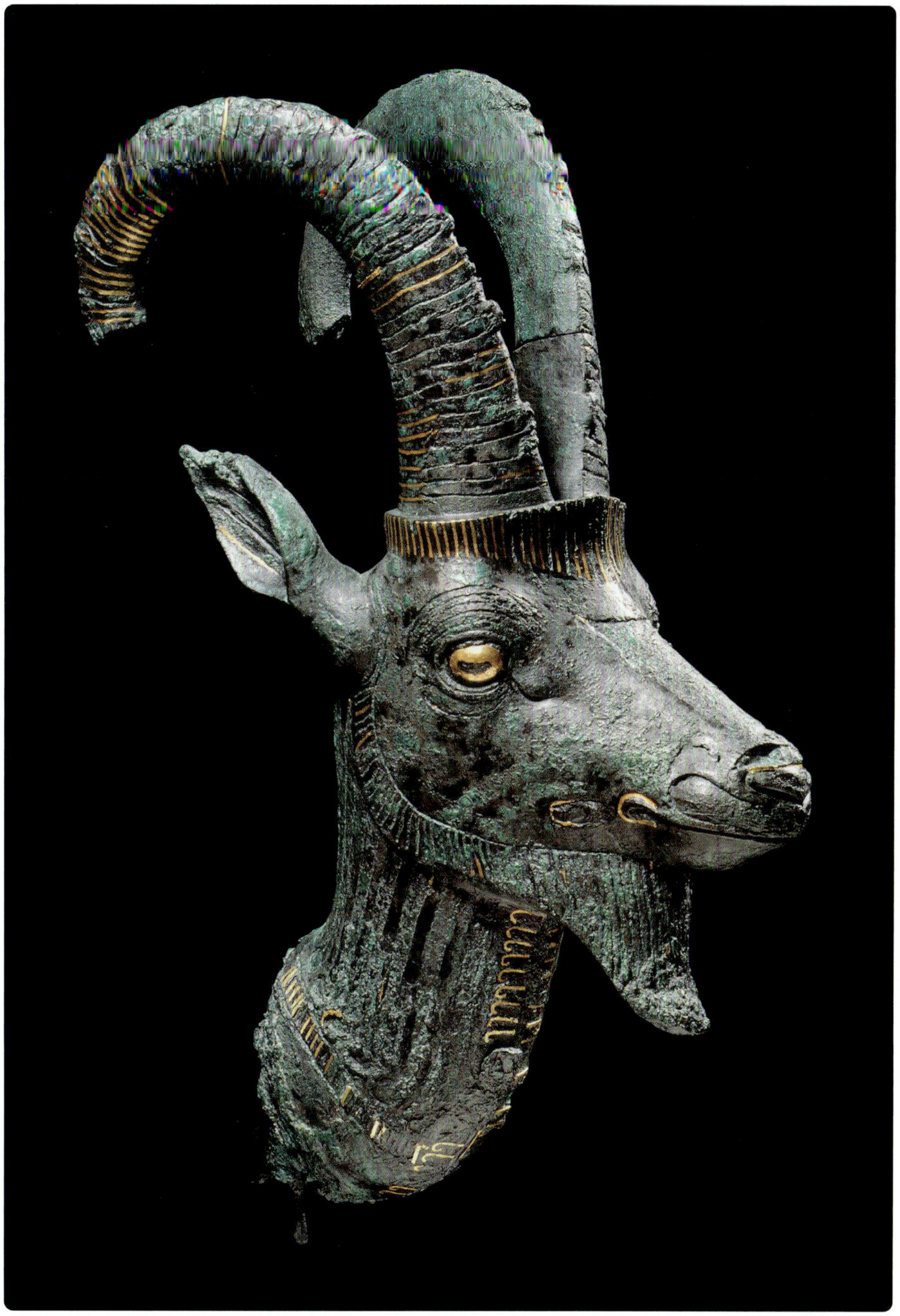

Like many of Egypt's kings, Amenemhet III (about 1818–1770 B.C.) had himself portrayed as a sphinx, a mythical creature associated with the sun god. This example (opposite) probably stood in the temple to the cat goddess Bastet at Bubastis.

A bronze head of an ibex with gold highlights (above) likely graced the bow of a ceremonial boat at the same site in about 1000 B.C.

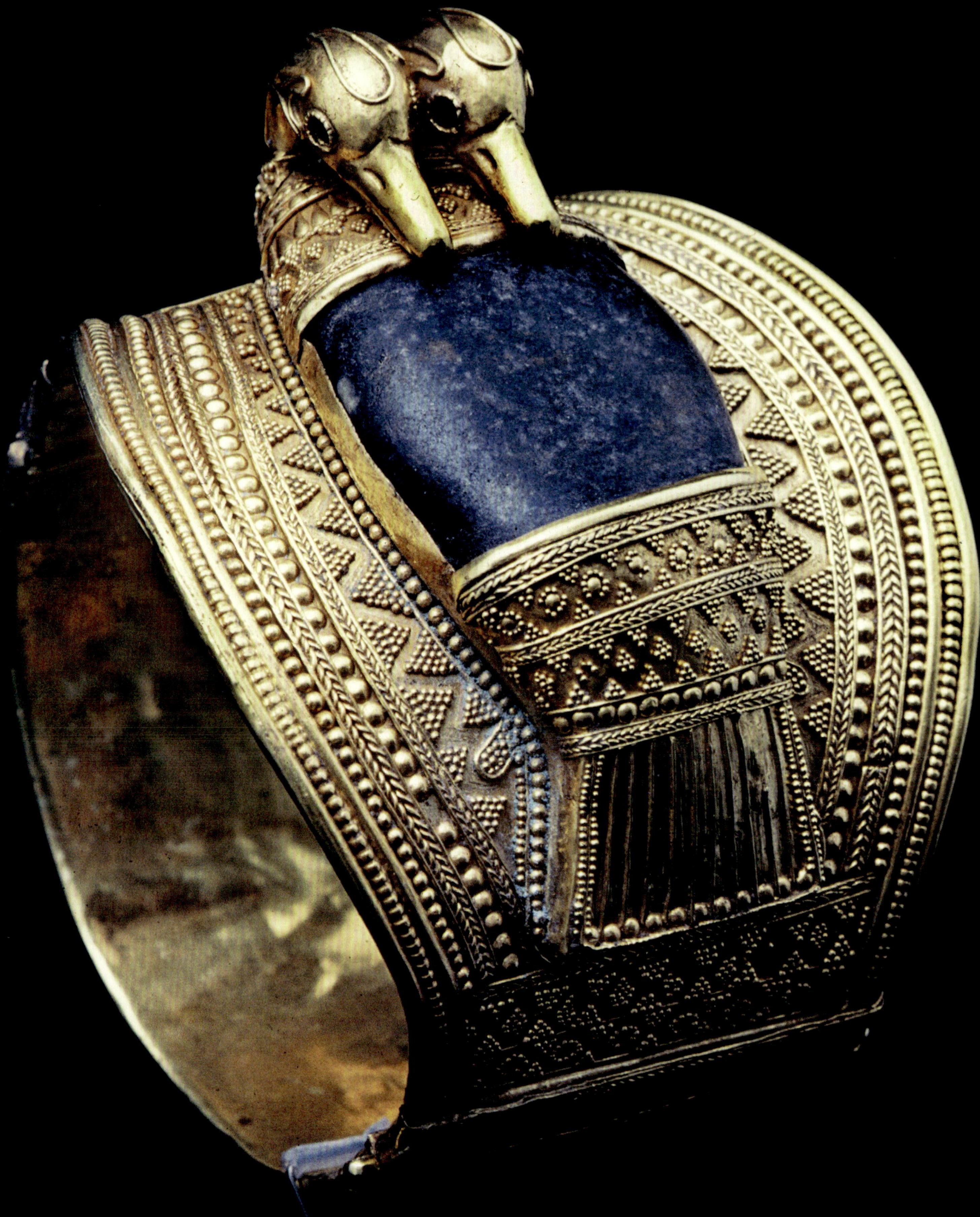

While building a railway at the site of Bubastis in 1906, workmen uncovered a cache of gold and silver artifacts that once likely belonged to a temple. The bracelet seen here (opposite) is one of a pair engraved with the name of Ramses II (about 1279–1213 B.C.), who may have offered them to the goddess Bastet.

A small cup (right) bears the cartouche of Queen Tausert, a wife of Seti II (about 1204–1198 B.C.), as well as a lotus flower motif often associated with eternal life.

A wine strainer (below) from about 1200 B.C. may have been used in temple festivals.

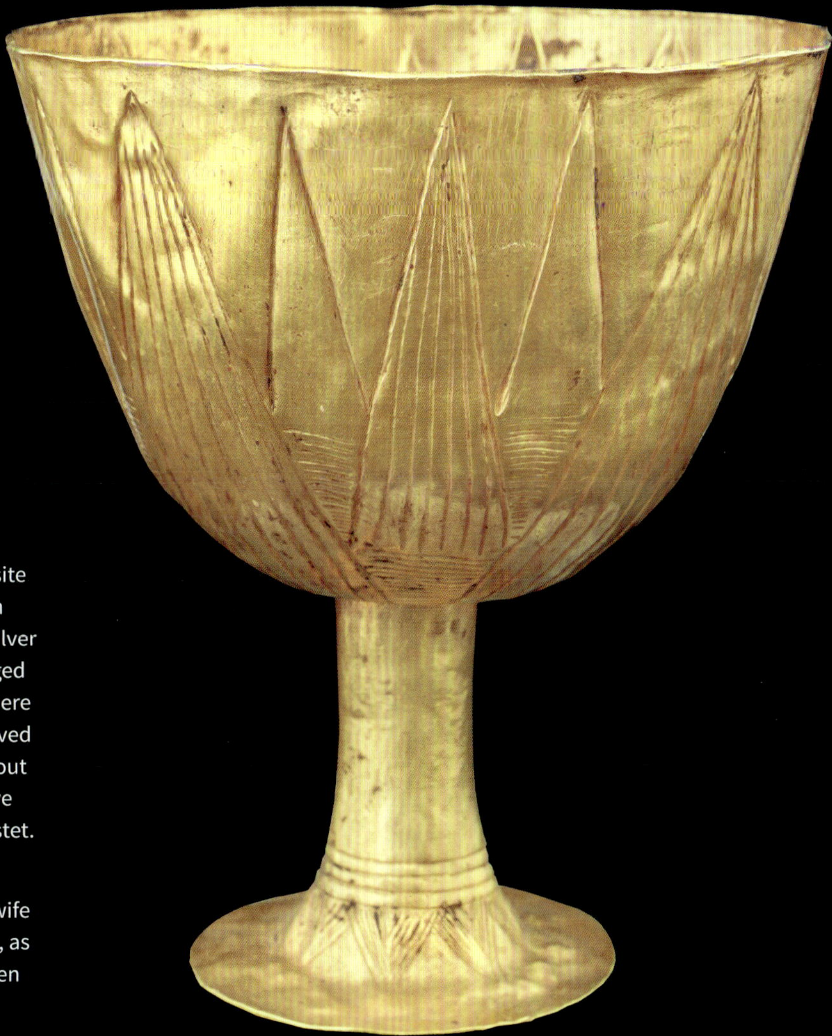

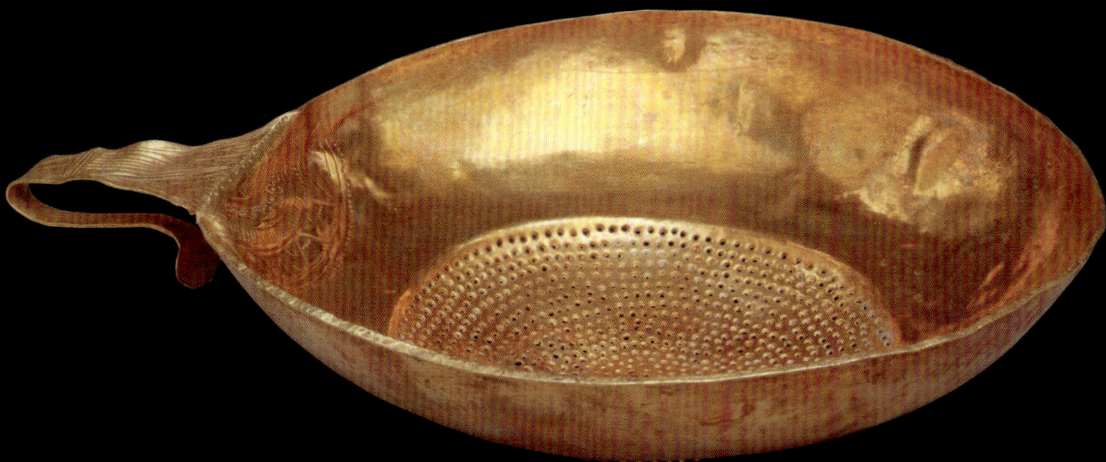

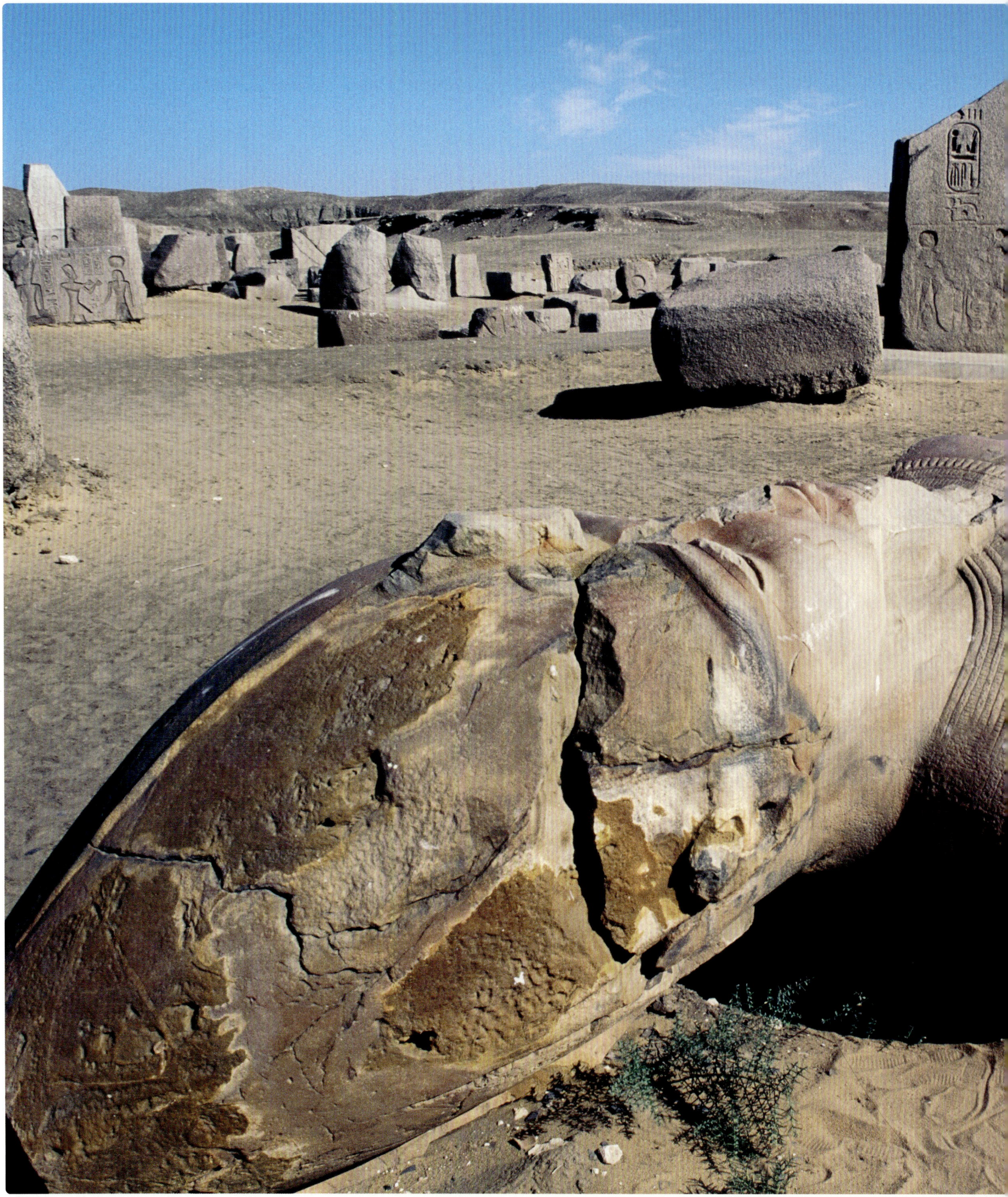

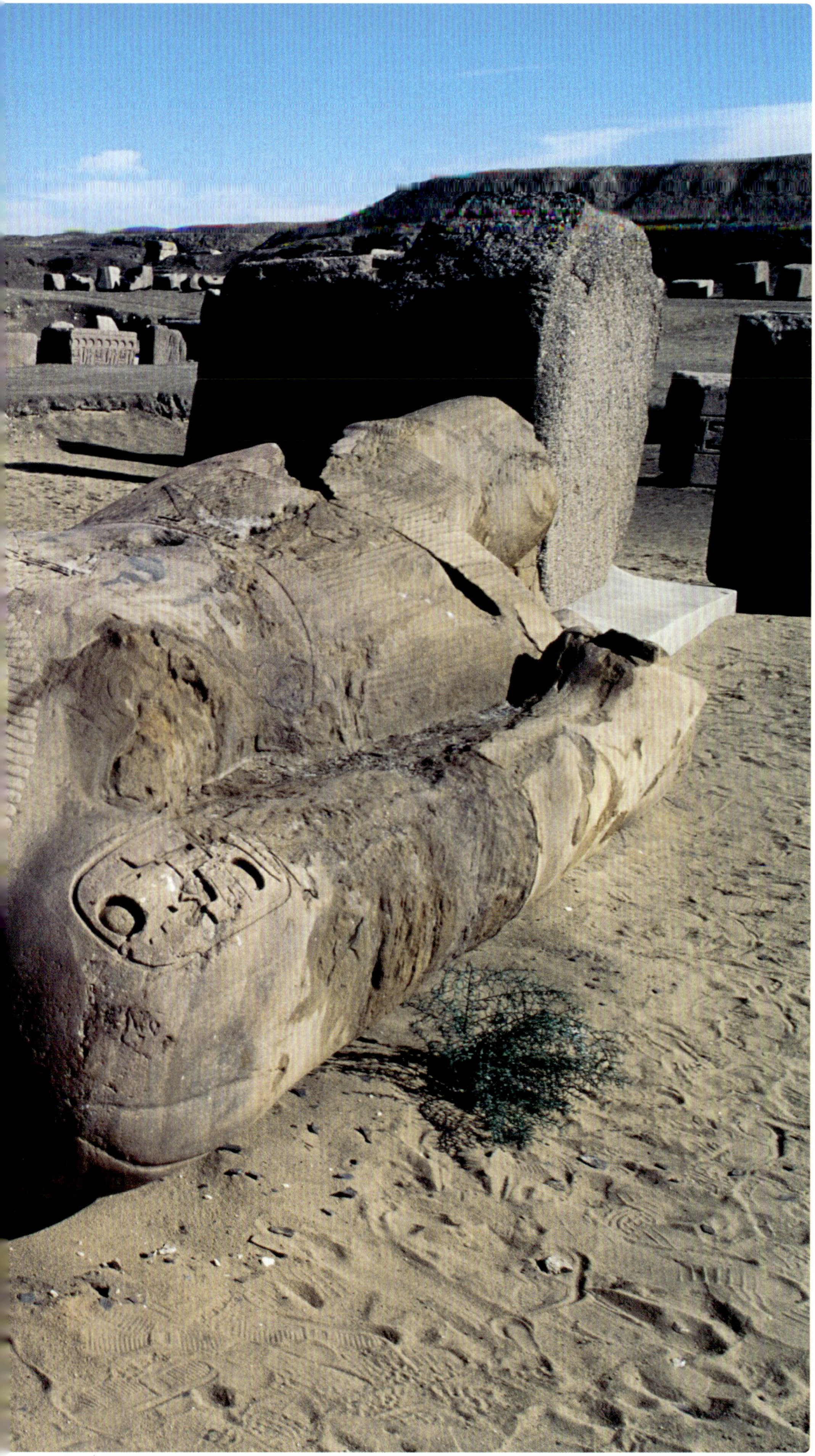

The fallen statue of a pharaoh marks the site of ancient Tanis, the northern capital of Egypt from about 1075 to 715 B.C. Much of the statuary here probably came from Ramses II's city Piramesse, about 14 miles (23 km) away.

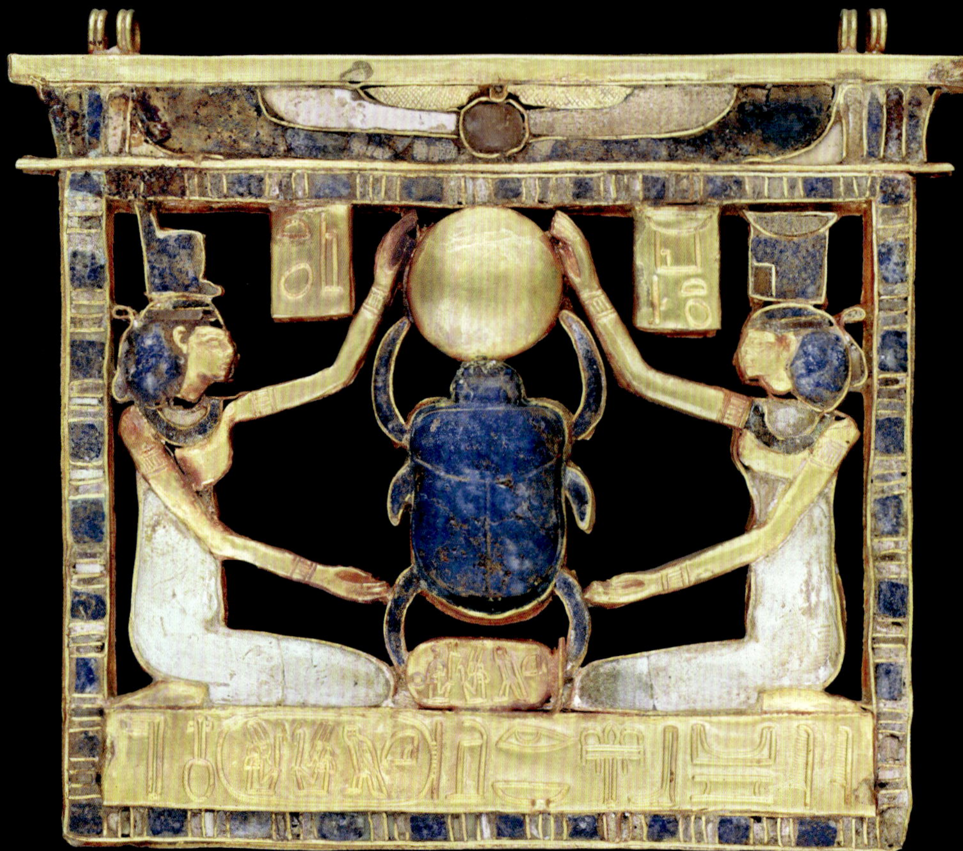

Archaeologists digging at the site of Tanis in 1939 uncovered a royal cemetery that included tombs untouched by looters. This pendant (above), displaying protective goddesses Isis and Nephthys, once belonged to King Amenemope (about 994–985 B.C.).

These bracelets (below) adorned the arms of Shoshenq II (about 885 B.C.) along with five others. The decorations were meant to secure eternal protection for the king.

The mummy of Undjebauendjed, an army general in about 1000 B.C., wore this gold mask inlaid with glass paste (opposite).

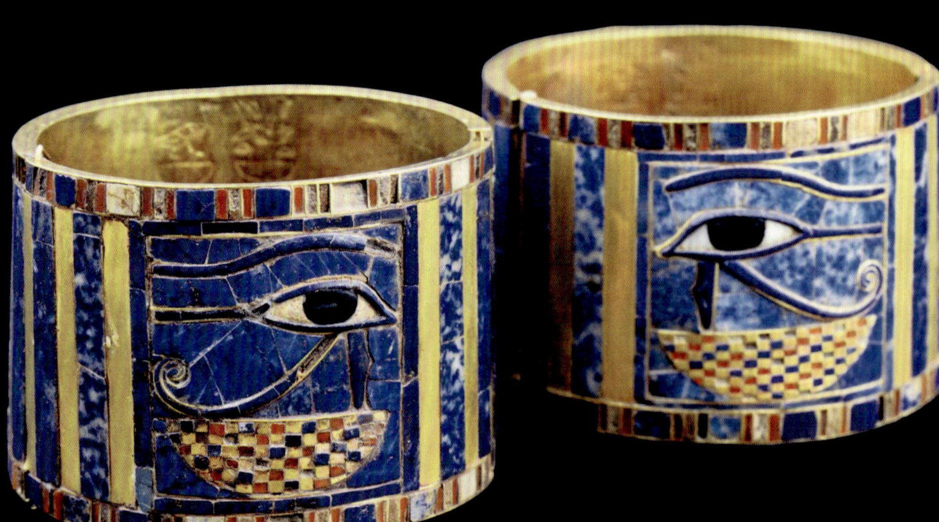

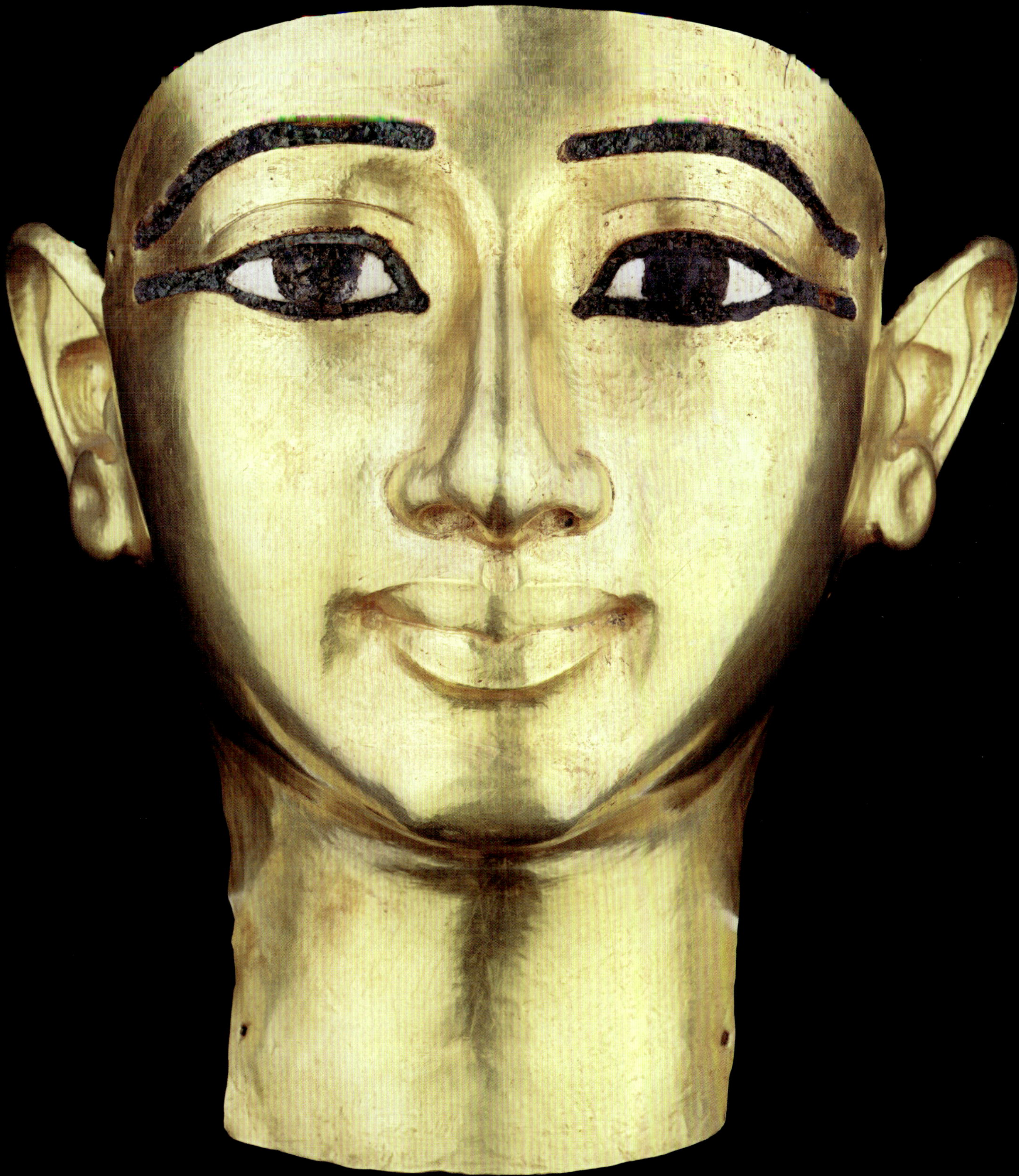

DIGGING DEEPER

A Treasure Overlooked

IN EARLY 1939, French archaeologist Pierre Montet made one of the greatest discoveries in Egyptology: a royal burial complex that included the intact tombs of three ancient kings.

Montet was working at the site of Tanis, the home base of kings in the 21st and 22nd dynasties (about 1075 to 715 B.C.). By then, the country's power had diminished greatly, and the country was divided, with kings controlling the north and religious officials holding court in the south in Waset (modern Luxor).

Judging from what Montet found, though, the royals were still fabulously wealthy. In the tomb of King Psusennes I, for example, a gold-trimmed coffin of silver (below) held the king's remains. A mask of gold (opposite) covered his head and shoulders, and gold sandals enveloped his feet. In death a king became a deity, so it was fitting for his mummy to wear gold, believed to be the skin of the gods.

Sadly, Montet's discovery never got the recognition it deserved. World War II soon dominated the news, and people had little interest in archaeology, no matter how big a treasure it might have unearthed.

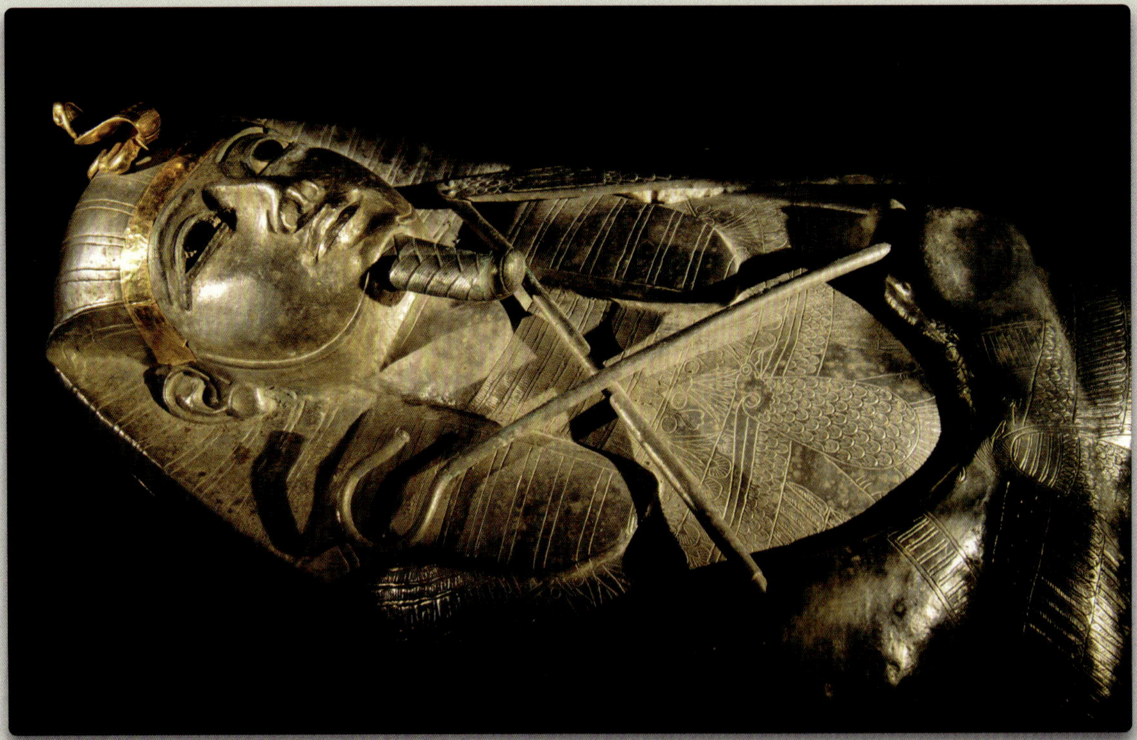

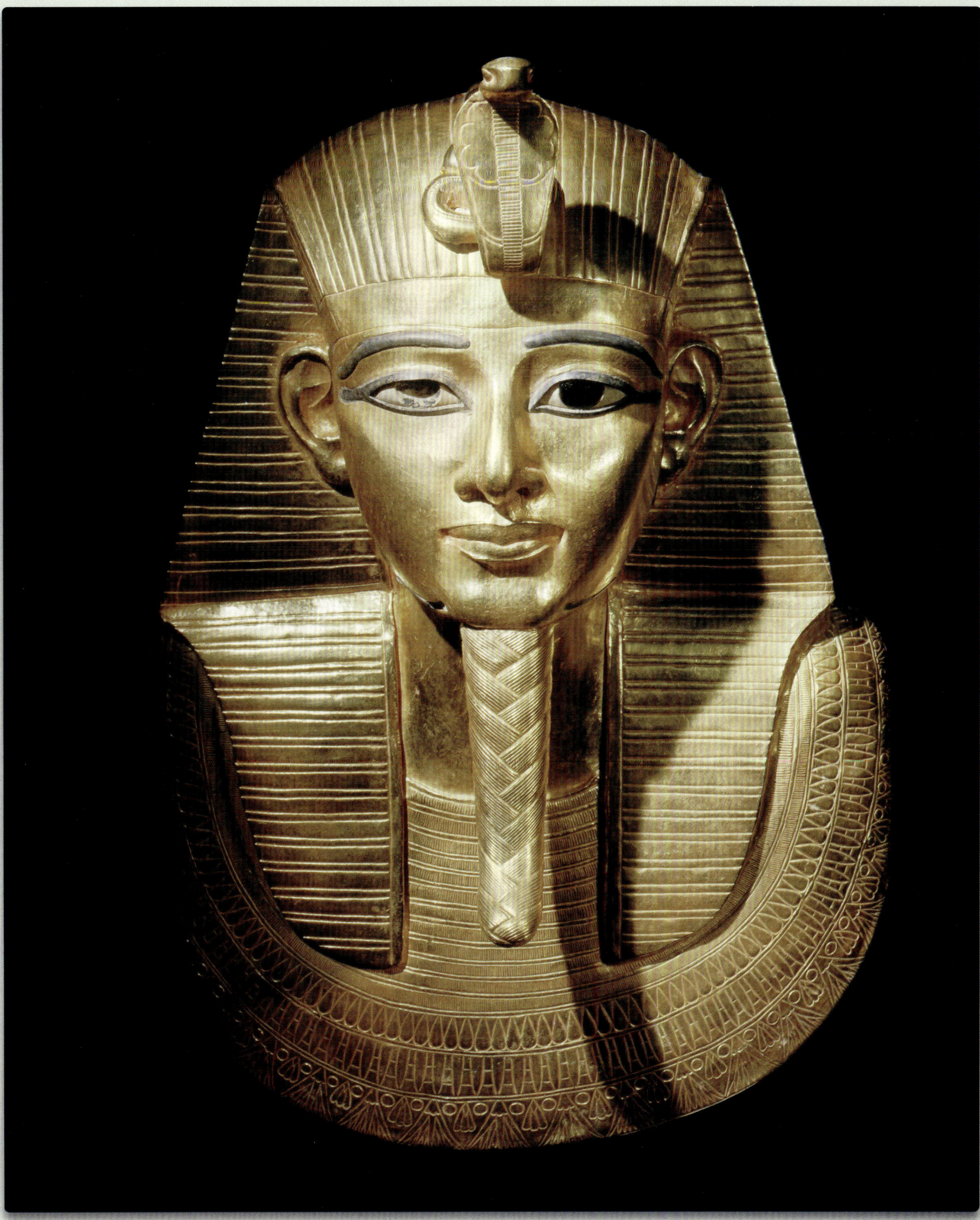

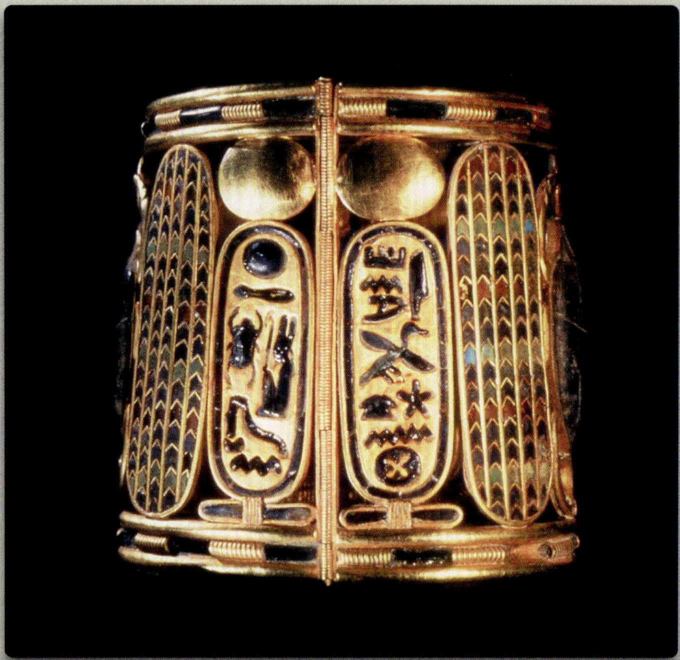

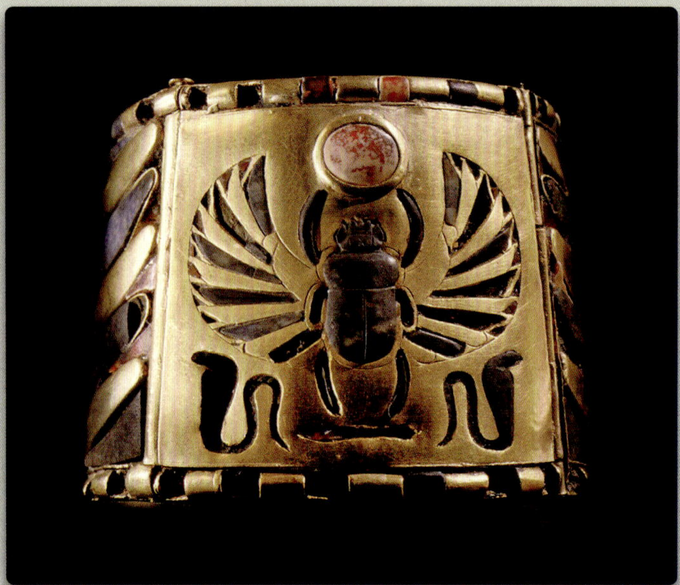

TREASURE FROM TANIS

A bracelet of gold and semiprecious stones (top) bears the cartouches of King Psusennes I (about 1040–995 B.C.).

The decoration of this anklet (above) spells out Aakheperre, the throne name of Psusennes I.

The king's mummy wore this elaborate collar (right) made of more than 5,000 gold disks and some 100 fluted flowers.

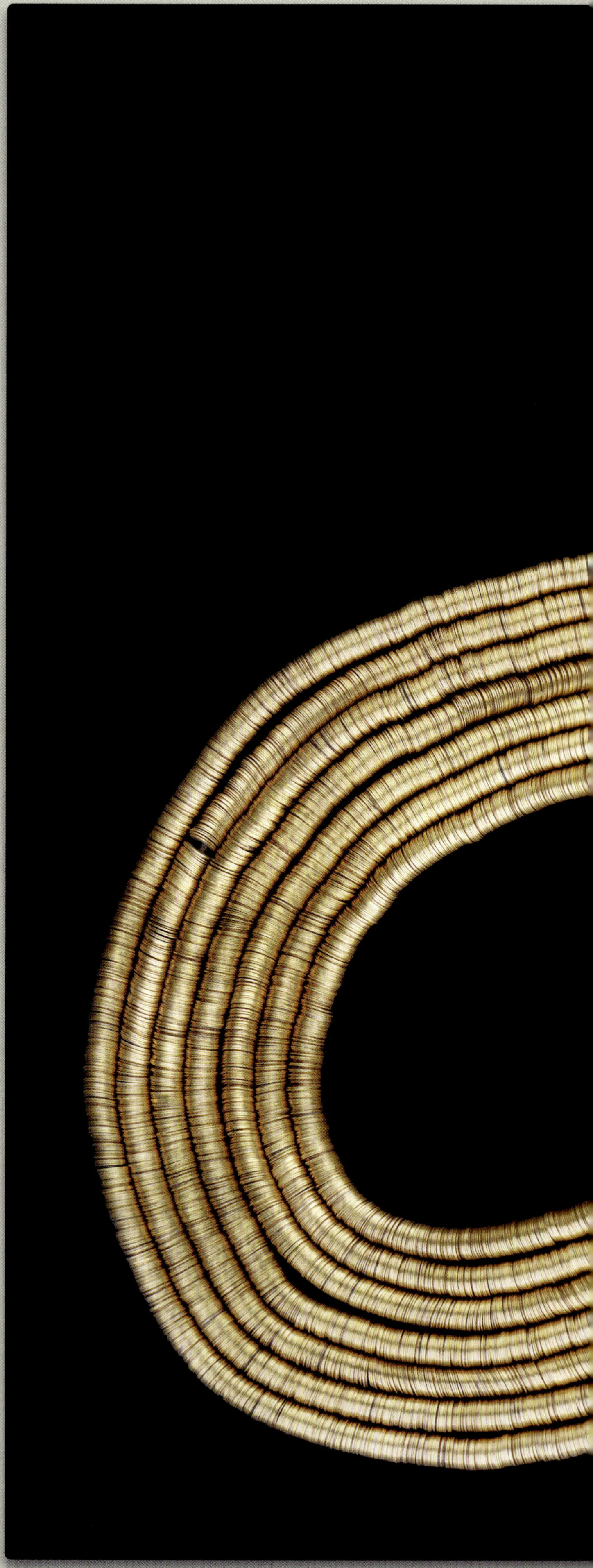

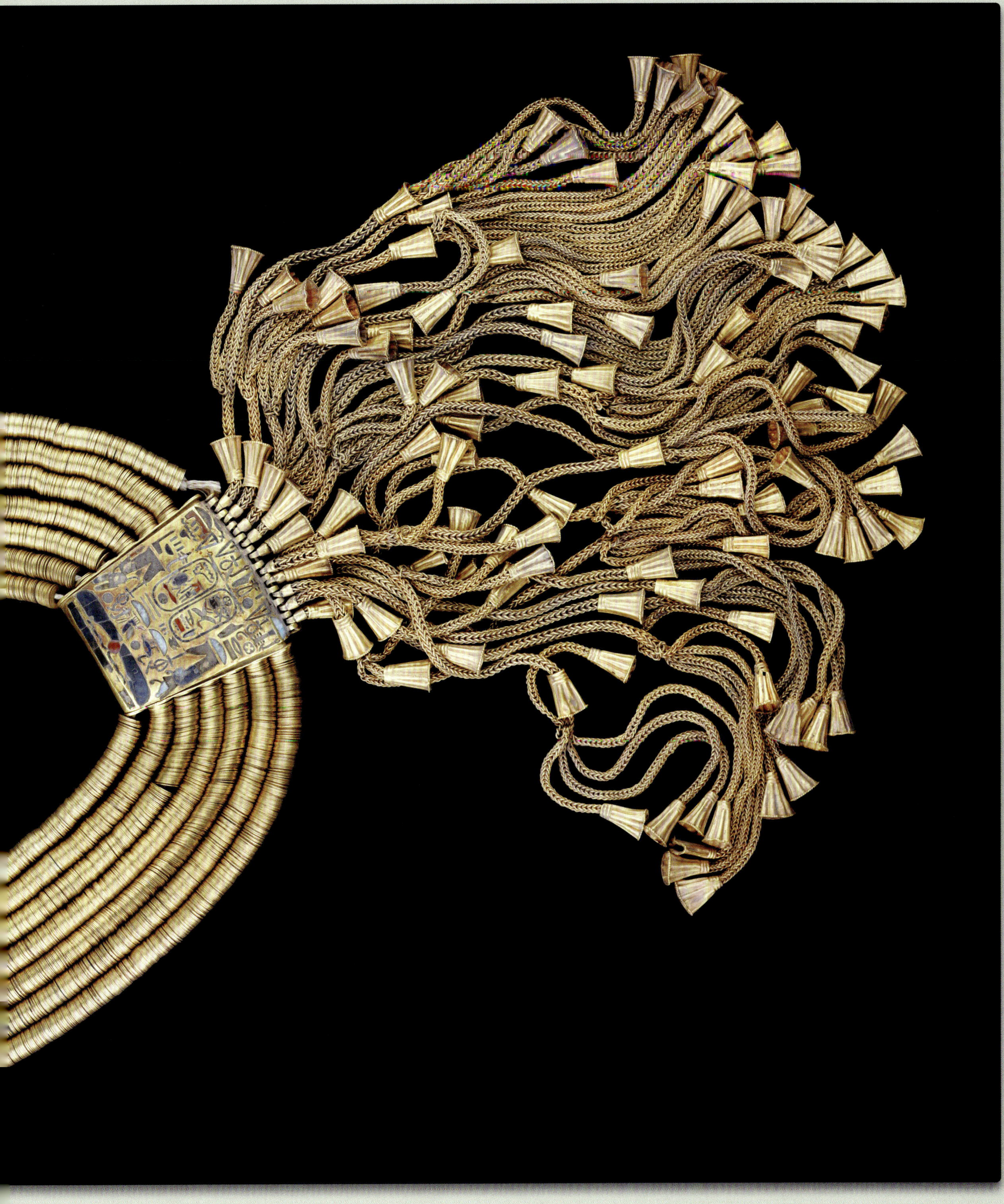

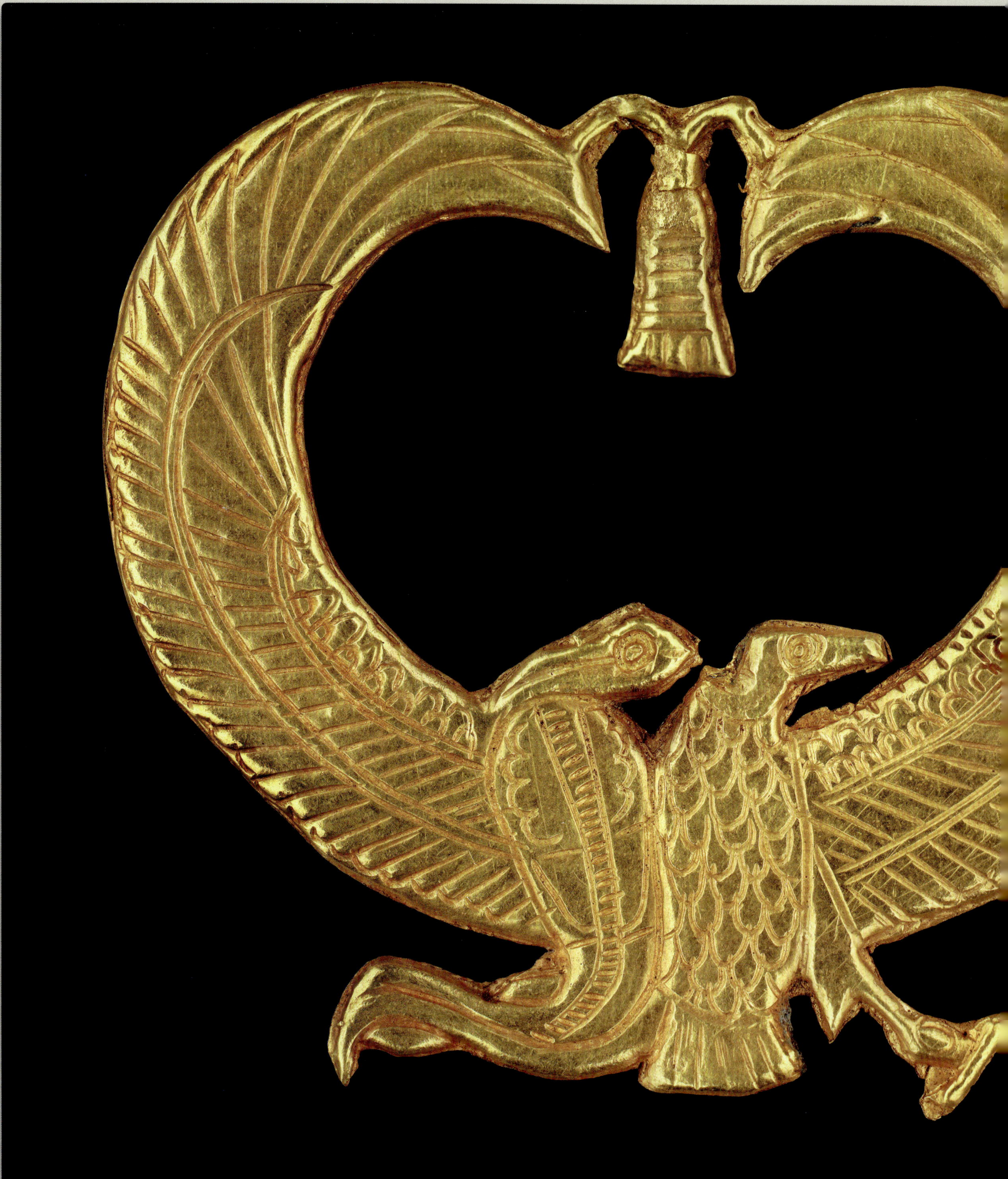

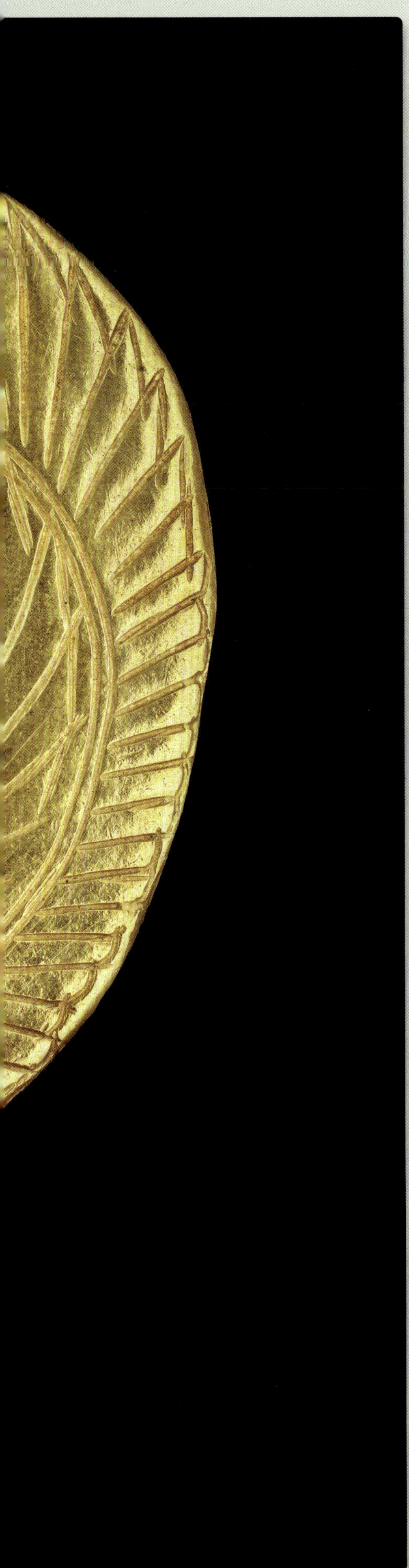

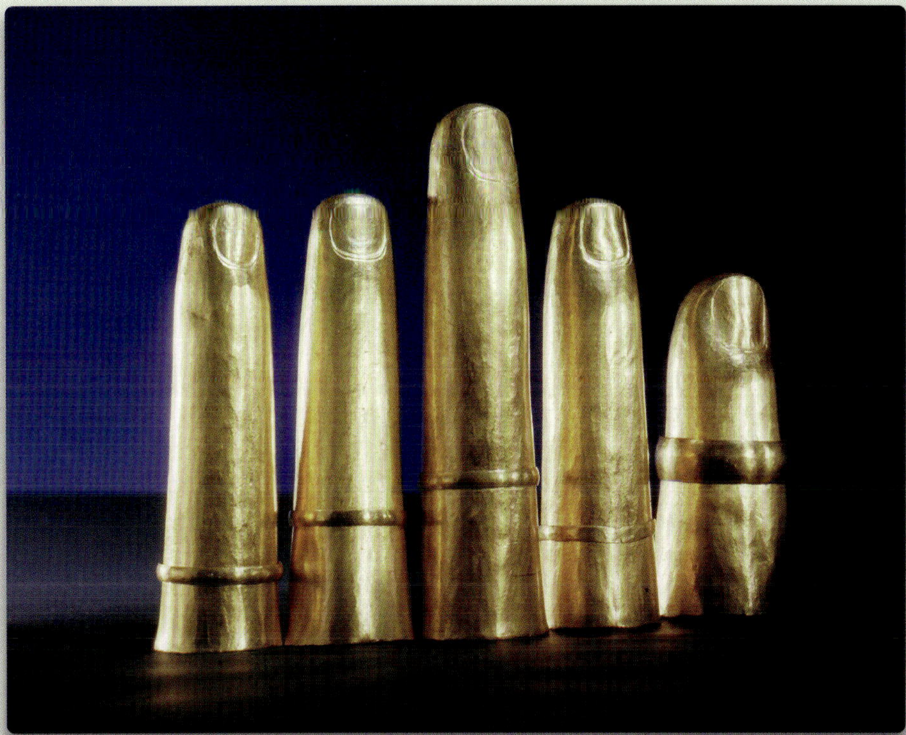

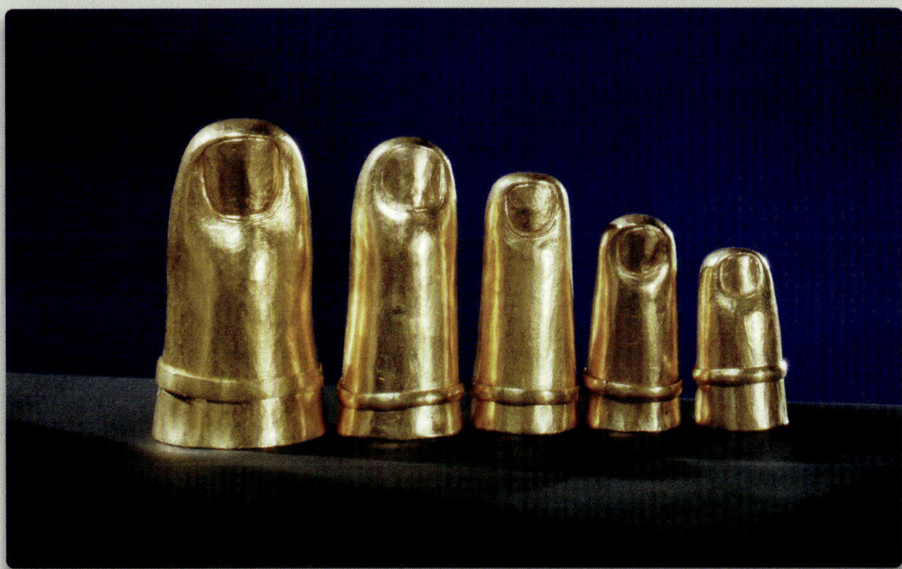

ROYAL PROTECTION

Two powerful deities adorn an amulet (left) found with the mummy of Psusennes I: the vulture goddess Nekhbet and the cobra goddess Wadjet.

Gold caps on the king's fingers (top) and toes (above) were meant to preserve the appendages and revitalize them in the afterlife. The king also wore a pair of gold sandals.

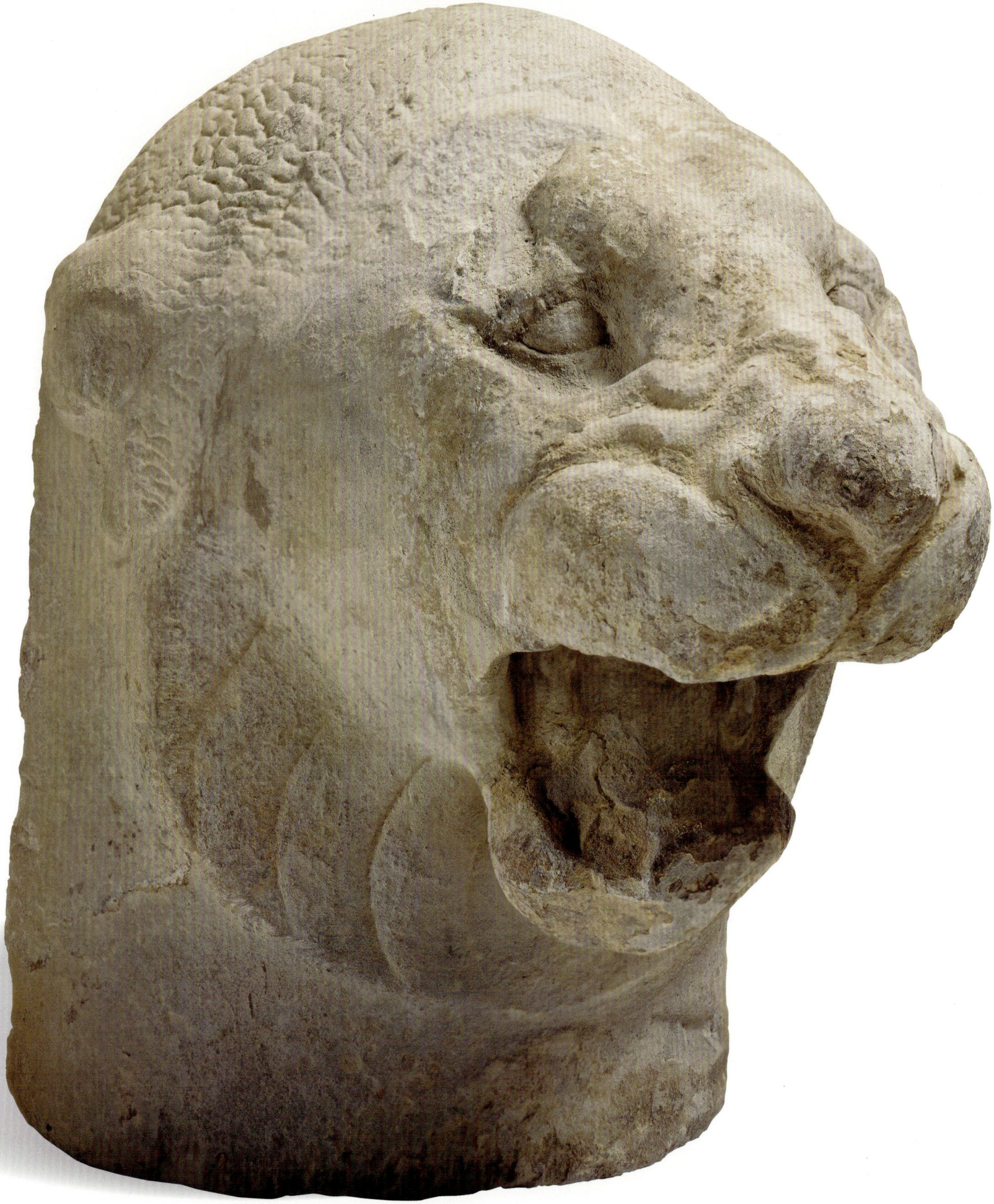

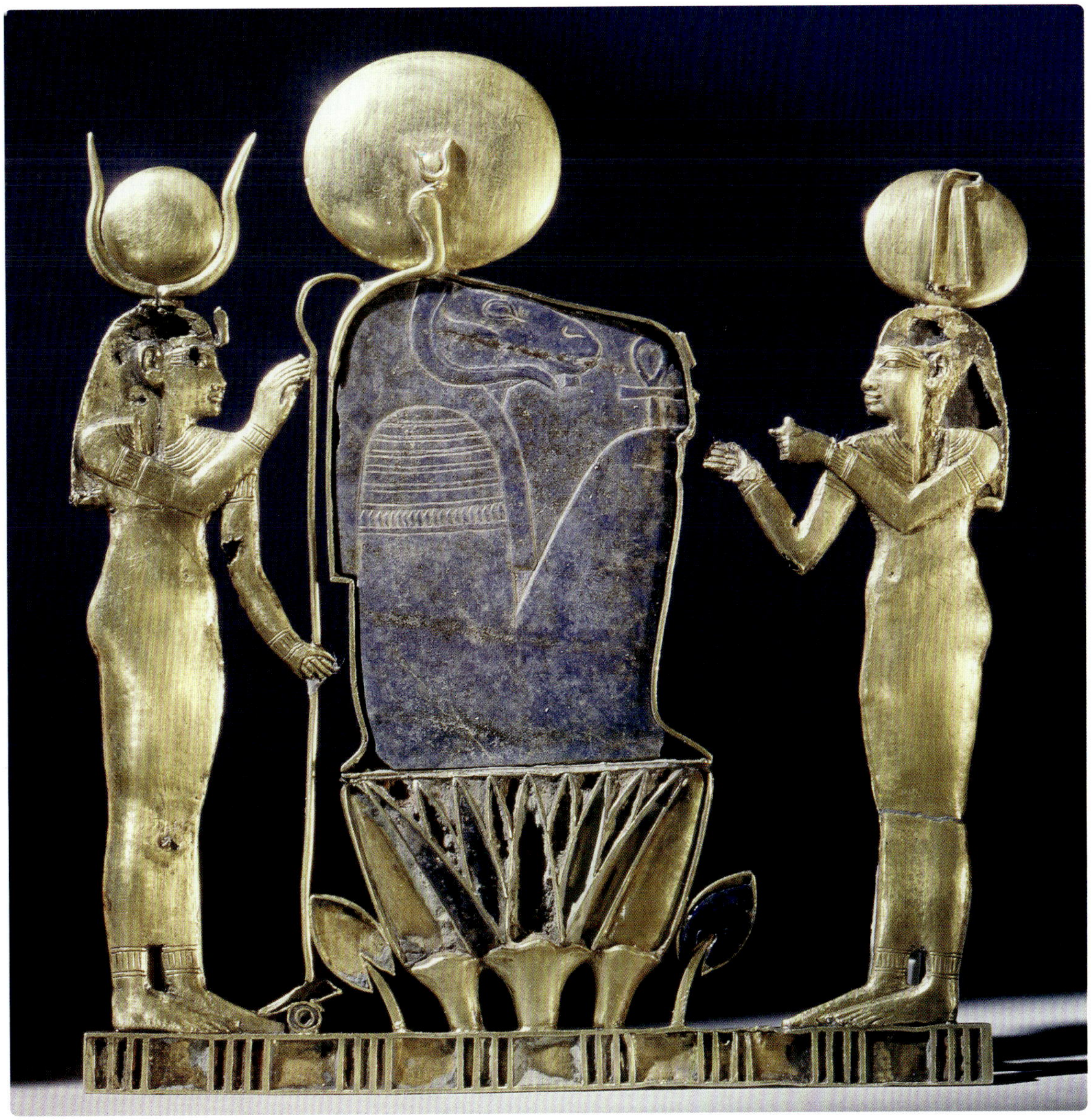

The tomb of ninth-century B.C. queen Kama at Tell el-Muqdam included a pendant (above) that shows the goddesses Hathor and Maat flanking the ram-headed god Khnum.

When Persians ruled Egypt in the fifth century B.C., this limestone head of a lion (opposite) may have served as a sculptor's model or a votive offering at Taremu, the ancient name of el-Muqdam.

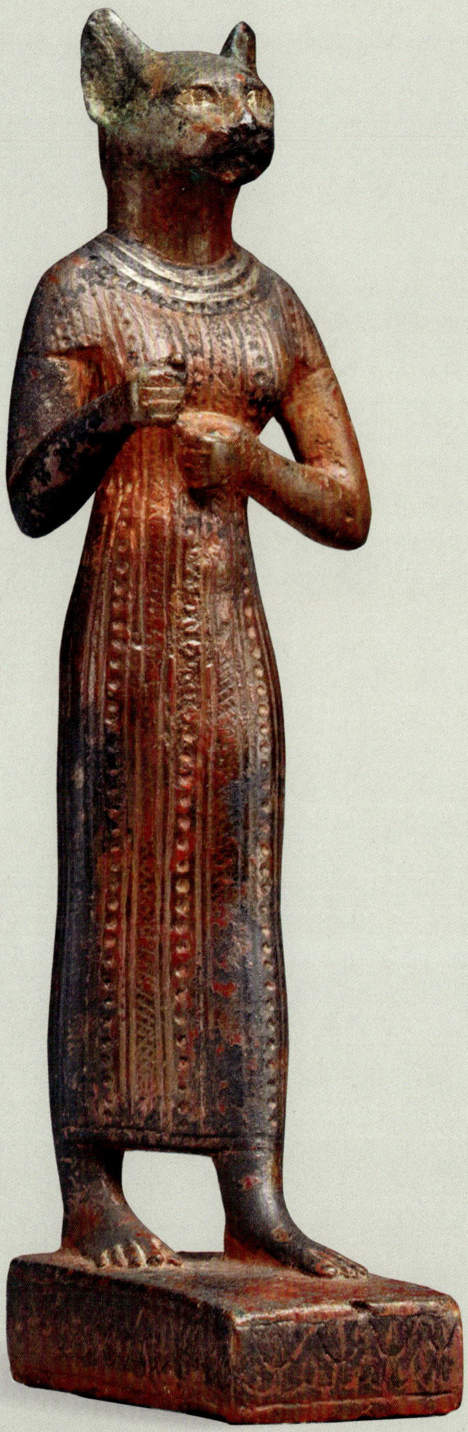

Cult of the Cat Goddess

THE EARLIEST KNOWN images of Bastet were sculpted onto stone vessels in the second dynasty, around 2775 B.C. The goddess was shown then with the head of a lioness on the body of a woman, likely signaling her protective role. But her form changed over time as her character was considered less ferocious. In some depictions, she's a cat-headed woman, as seen in this ornate seventh-century B.C. bronze statuette (left). In others, she's entirely feline, like this elegant, simply adorned bronze (opposite) from Bubastis.

The city of Bubastis, about 50 miles (80 km) northeast of Cairo, was the main cult center of Bastet. In the first millennium B.C., thousands of cat mummies were buried there as votive offerings to the goddess.

Greek historian Herodotus visited Bubastis in the fifth century B.C. He described the goddesses' red-granite temple as "a pleasure to the eyes," surrounded by water and shaded by trees. He also wrote of the city's year-end revelry, which included singing, dancing, and drinking—"more wine of grapes is consumed upon that festival than during the whole of the rest of the year."

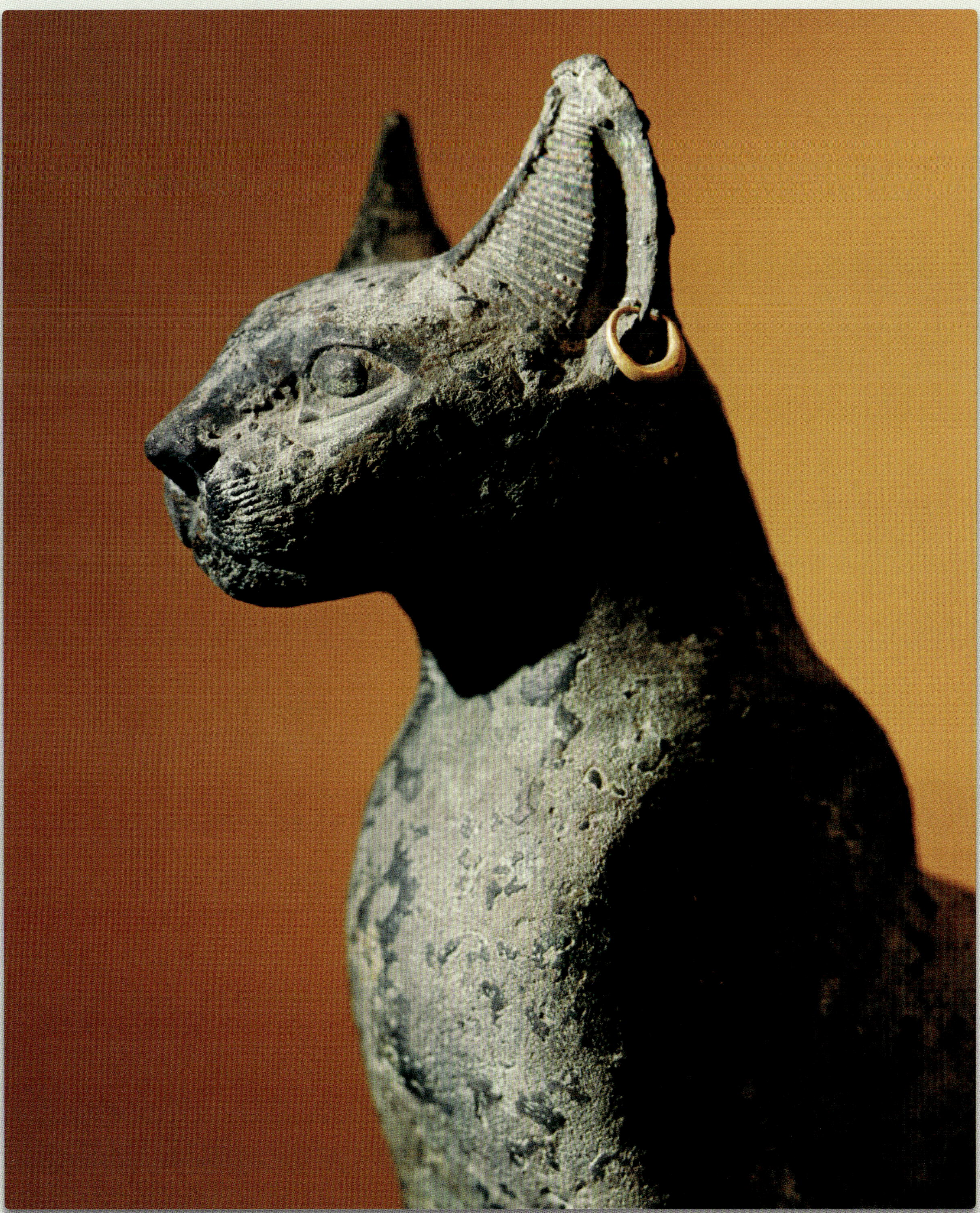

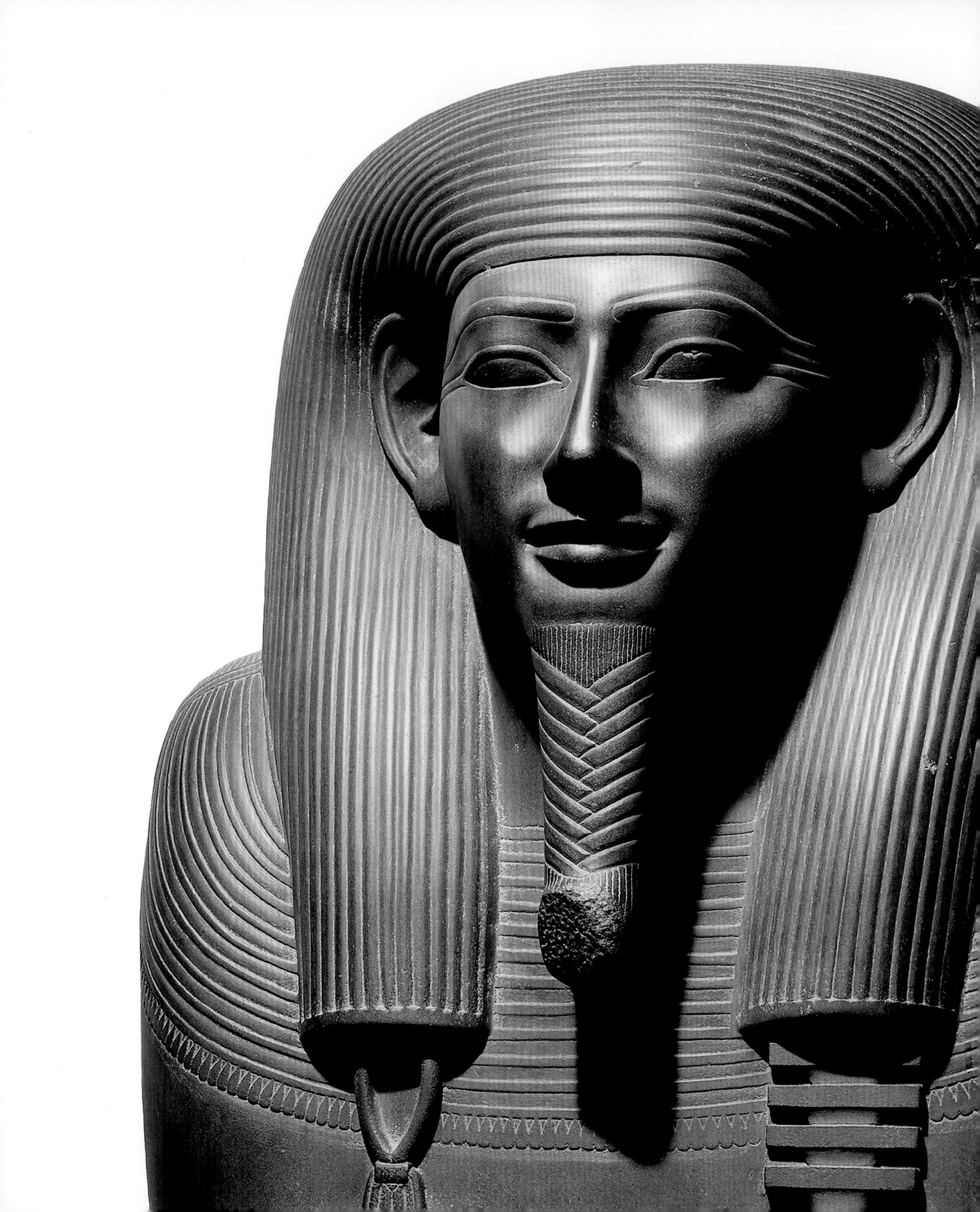

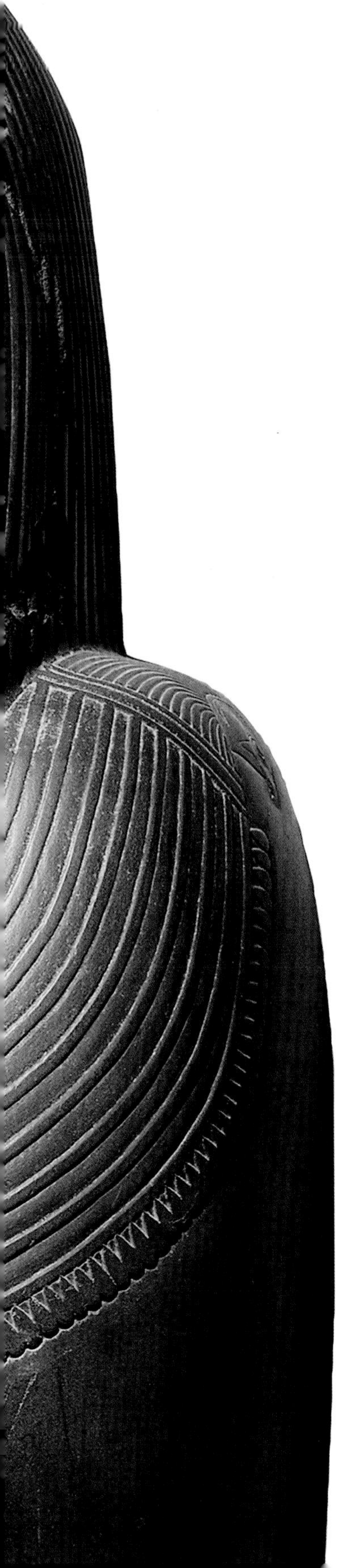

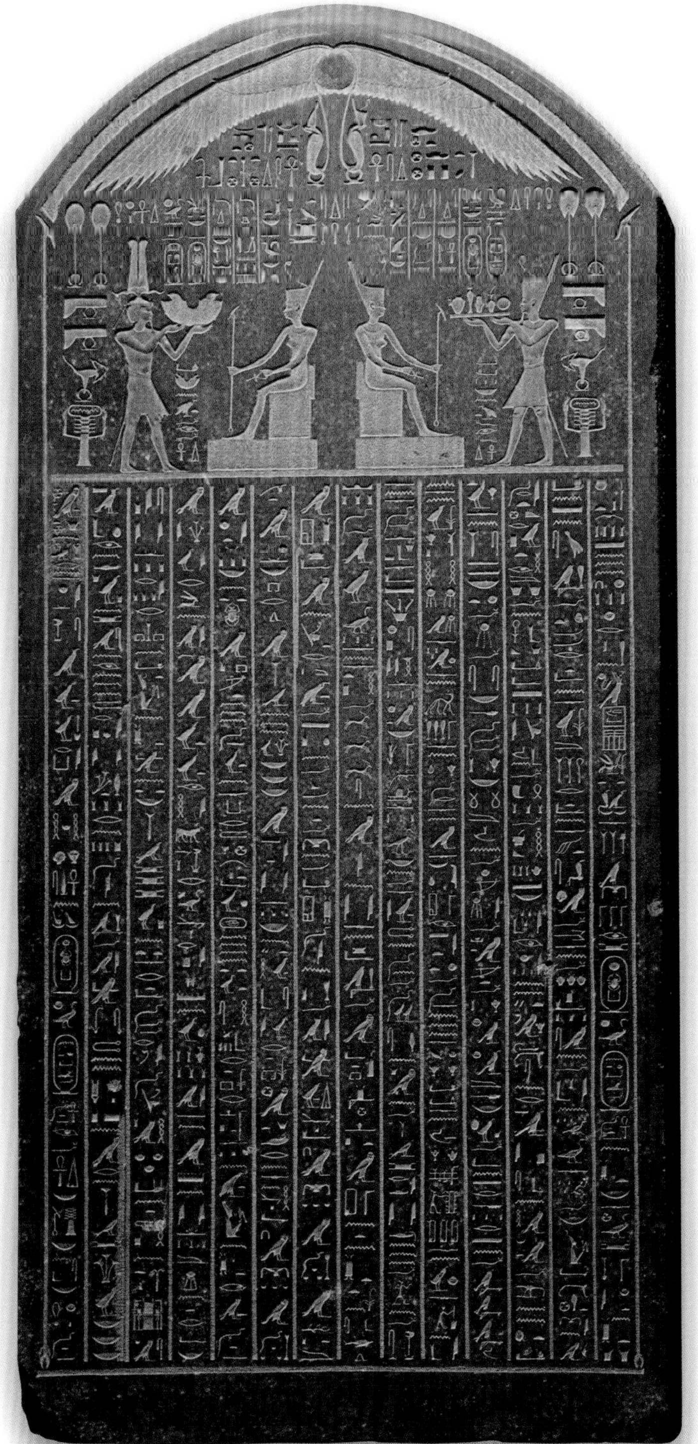

The serene face of Sasobek, a seventh-century B.C. vizier, adorns his siltstone sarcophagus (left). The location of his burial is unknown, but it may have been Sais, his ancestral home.

A fourth-century B.C. stela (above) records a decree about donating taxes to a temple in Sais. It was probably recycled as a building stone at Thonis-Heracleion, where it was found.

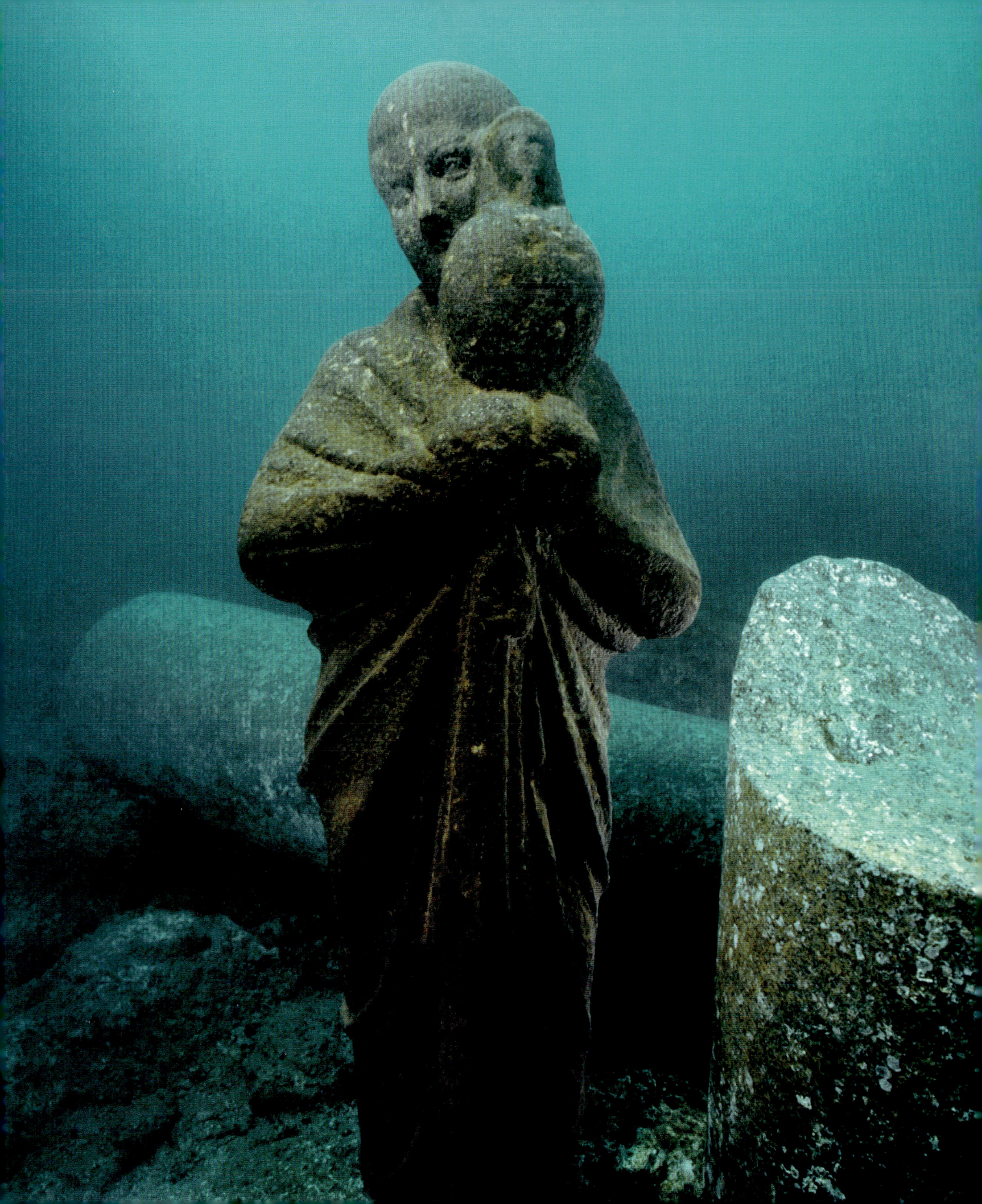

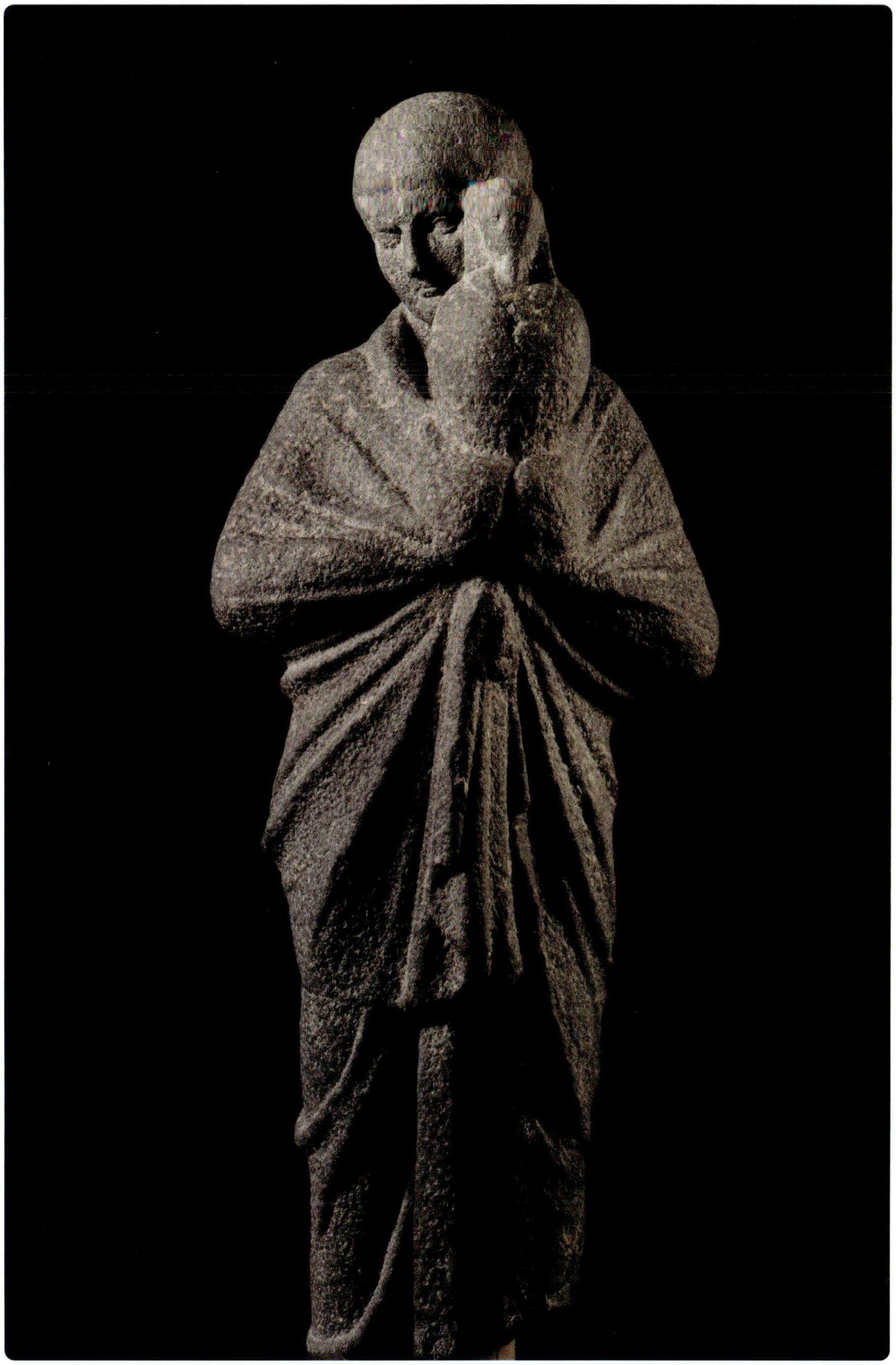

A life-size stone priest holding a sacred jar (opposite) once stood on Antirhodos, an island in the eastern port of ancient Alexandria. An earthquake in about the second century A.D. toppled it and led to the island's sinking.

After the classically inspired sculpture was retrieved from the sea, experts soaked out the salt and removed centuries of accretions to preserve it (above).

Cracking the Hieroglyphic Code

FRENCH SCHOLAR Jean-François Champollion was a whiz kid. In 1807, before he turned 17, he penned an academic paper on ancient Egypt. By the time he began to concentrate his studies on the country's largely undeciphered hieroglyphic writing, in his early 20s, he already knew Hebrew, Arabic, and Coptic, among other languages.

Champollion worked with texts copied from various sources, including the Rosetta Stone (opposite). Discovered in 1799 during Napoleon Bonaparte's invasion of Egypt, the stone displays three scripts: Greek at the bottom, which Classicists were able to translate quickly; a cursive writing called Demotic in the middle; and hieroglyphs at the top. All convey the same message: a decree from 196 B.C.

Until the discovery of this artifact, progress in understanding hieroglyphics had been slow. Now, linguists could match the stone's hieroglyphic signs with Greek words, a key to cracking the code. Egyptologists, including Thomas Young in England, Johan Åkerblad in Sweden, and Silvestre de Saçy in France, were working on the puzzle. But it was Champollion, de Saçy's student, who made the first big breakthrough in reading the ideas represented by the signs. He published his findings on September 27, 1822, just before he turned 32.

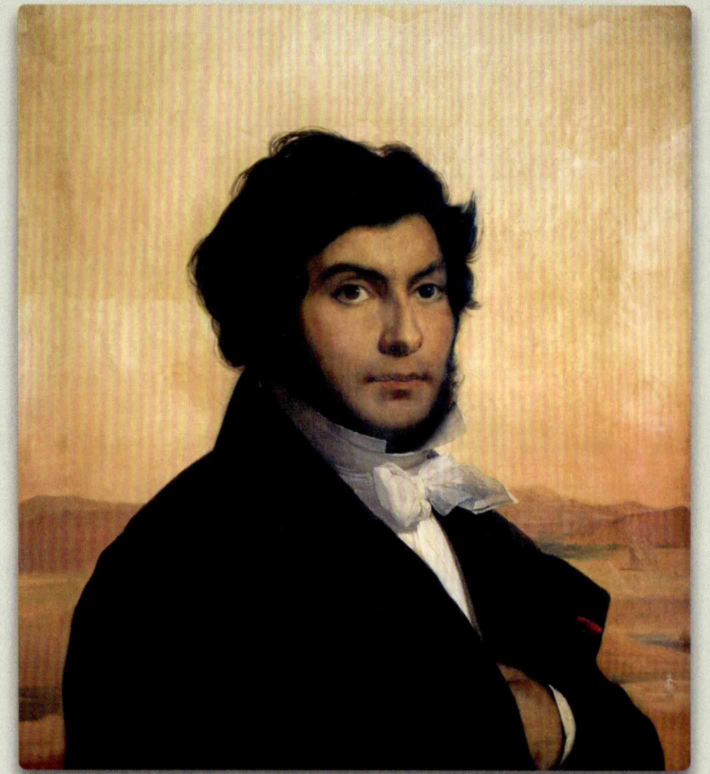

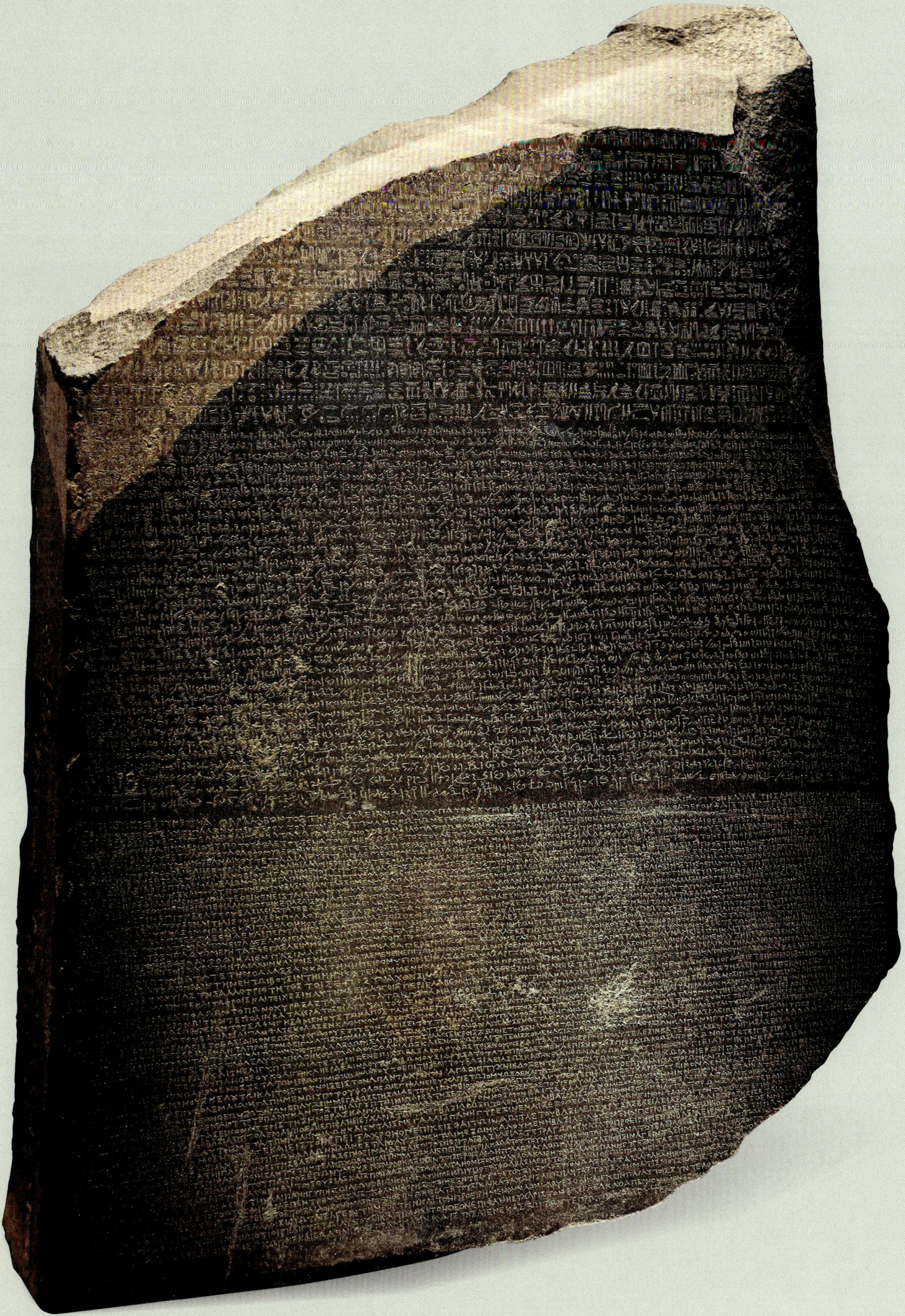

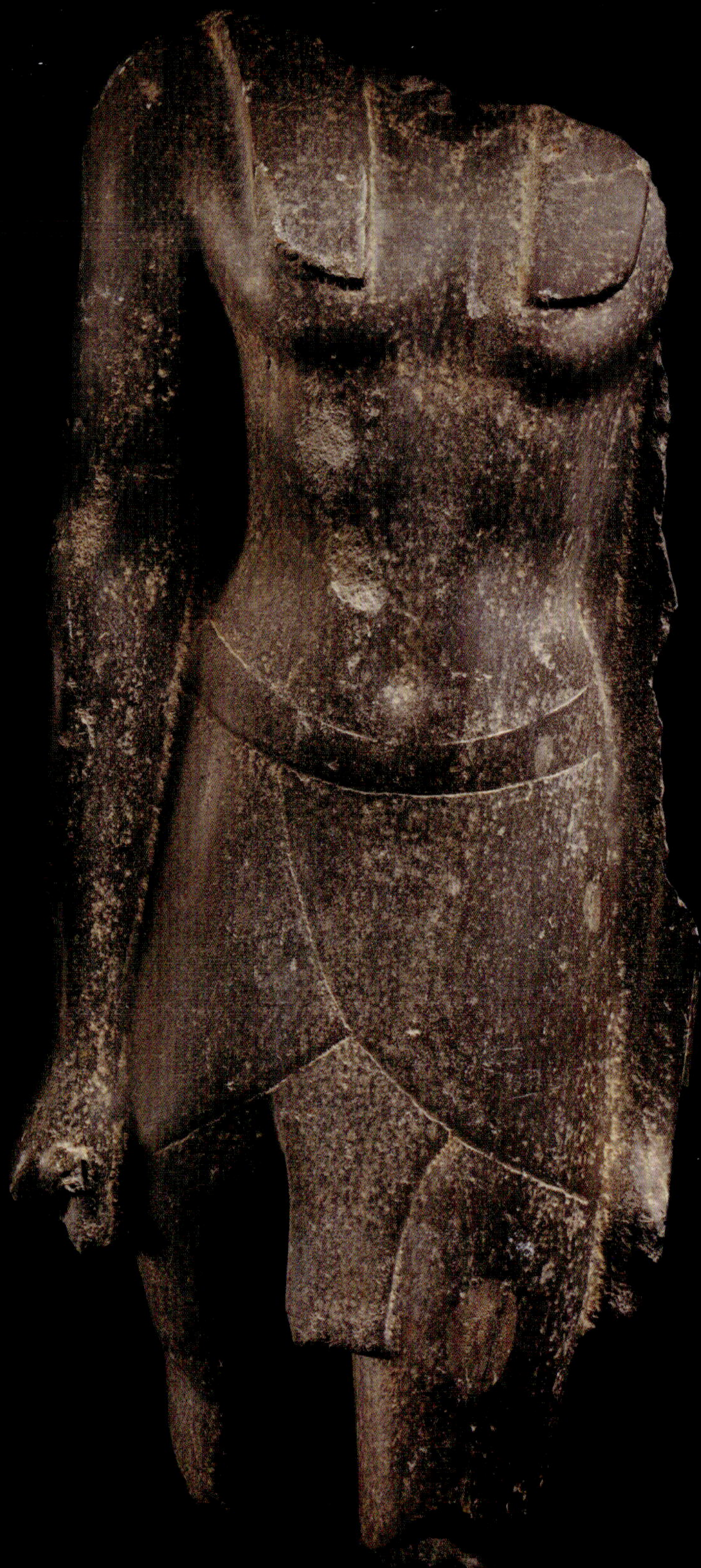

Archaeologists working at Taposiris Magna, a city founded in the third century B.C. some 30 miles (50 km) west of Alexandria, are hoping to uncover clues about the lives of famed Roman general Mark Antony and his paramour Queen Cleopatra. This fragment of a face (opposite) could indeed portray Antony.

A granite torso (left) may represent one of the Macedonian kings of Egypt, the dynasty that ended with Cleopatra's suicide in 30 B.C.

A bronze coin (below) bears the image of Roman emperor Augustus (30 B.C.–A.D. 14).

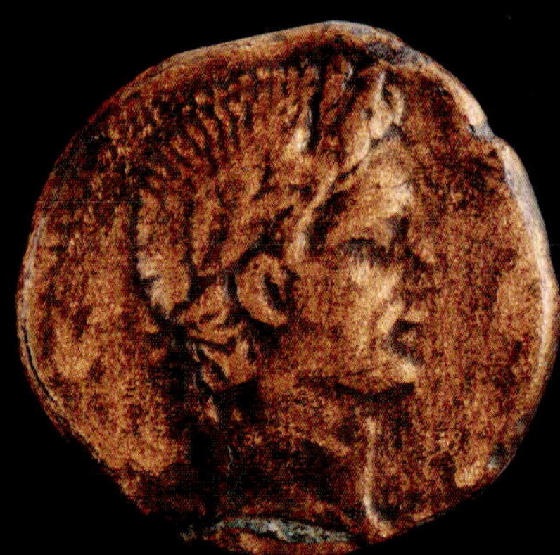

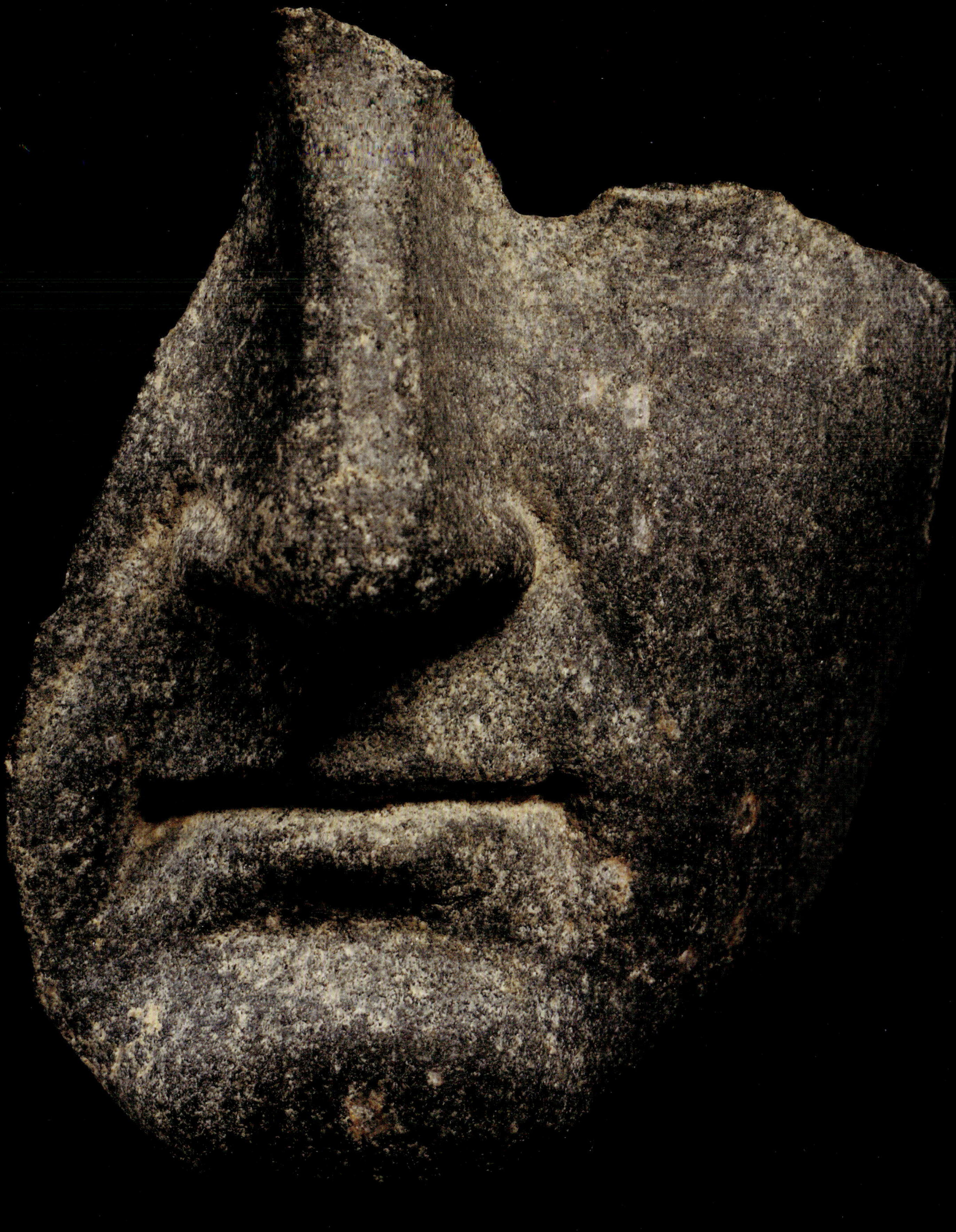

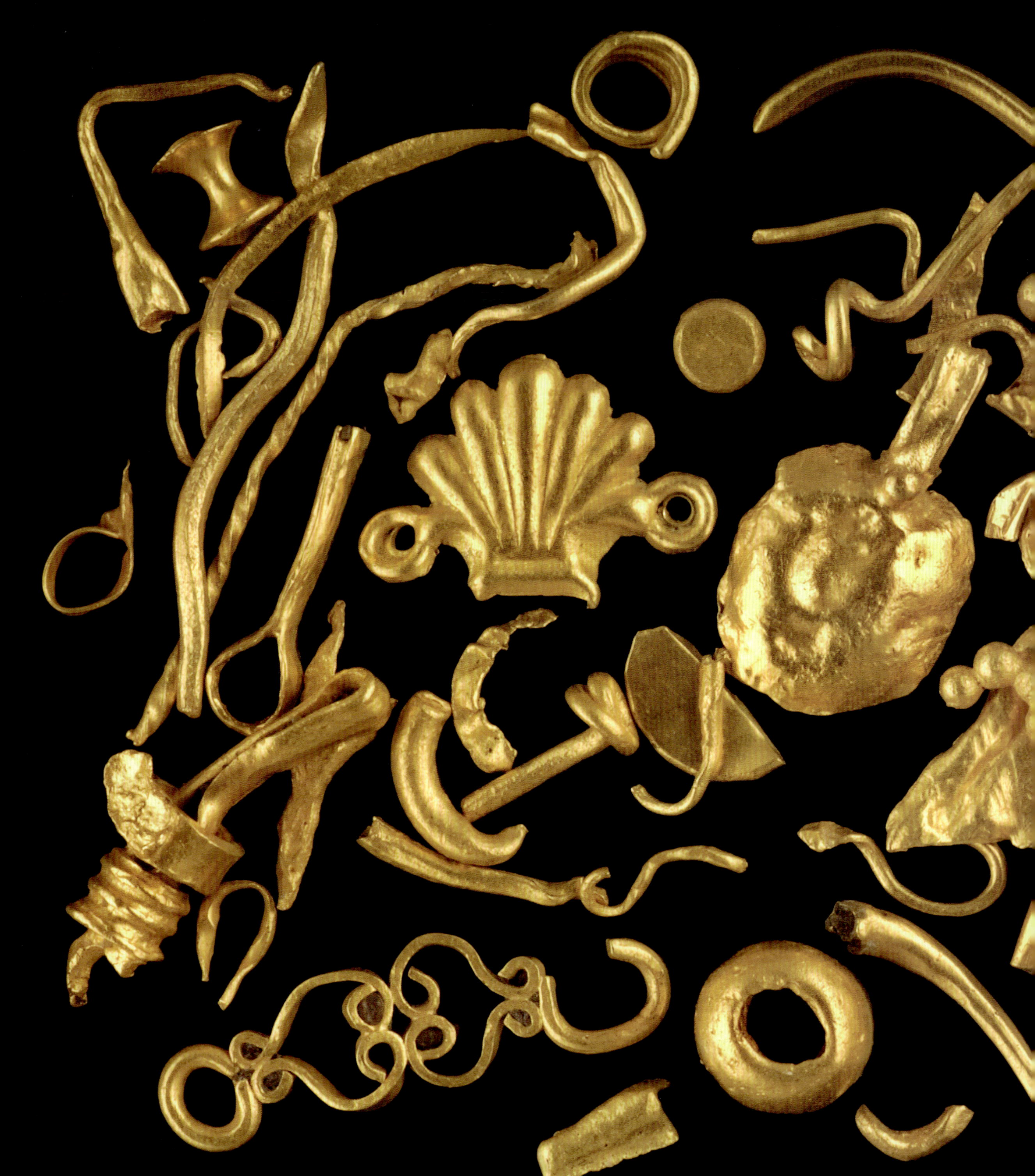

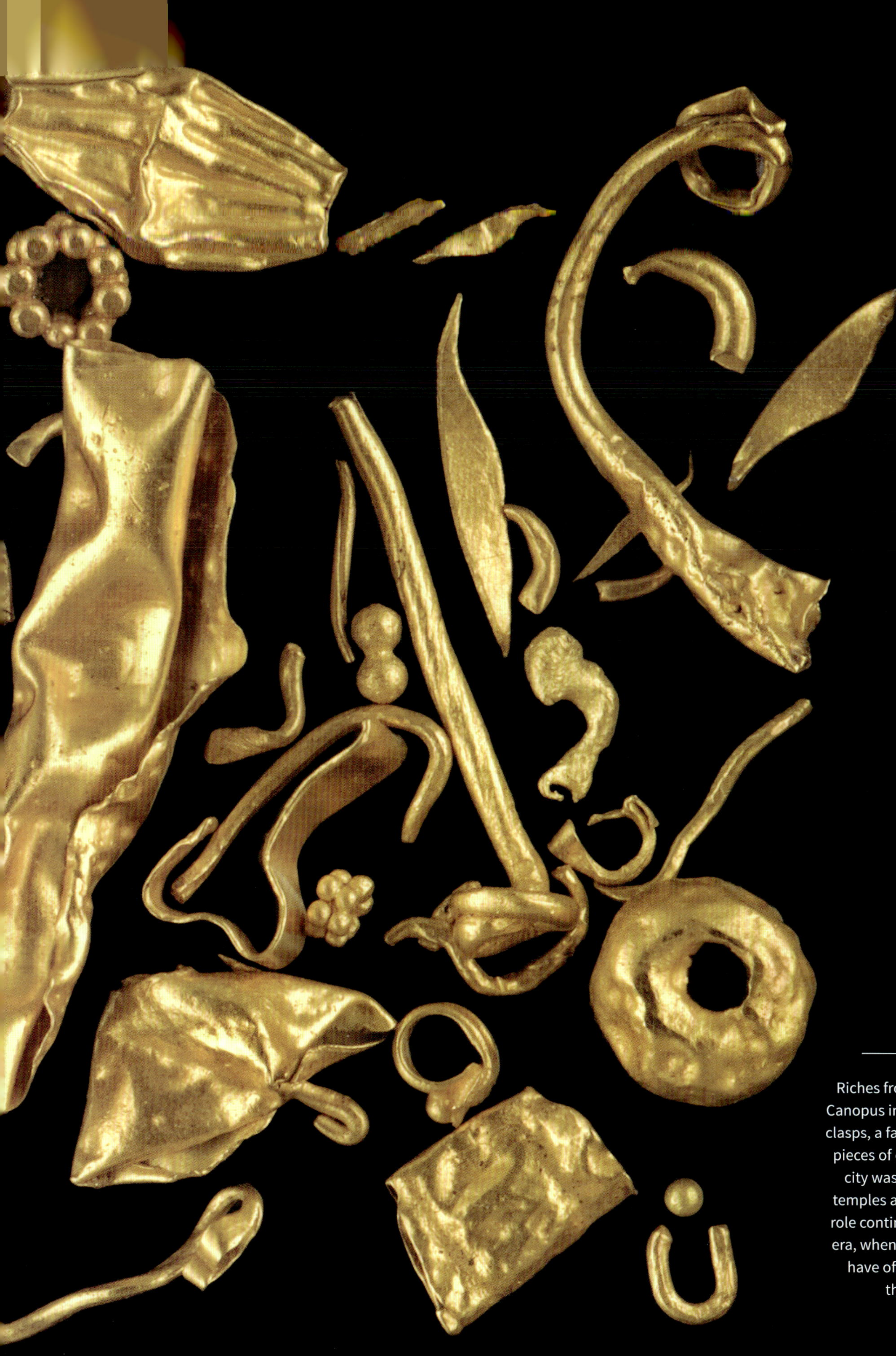

Riches from the sunken ruins of Canopus include pendants, beads, clasps, a fan-shaped appliqué, and pieces of other adornments. The city was the site of pharaonic temples and shrines. Its spiritual role continued into the Byzantine era, when Christian pilgrims may have offered up valuables in thanks for cures.

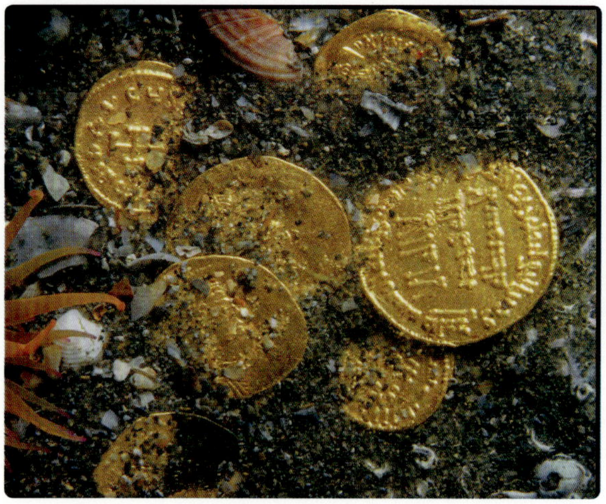

The head of a pharaoh from the seventh or sixth century B.C. keeps fish company amid the toppled buildings and monuments of Canopus (right).

Testifying to the long history of the city, a collection of gold coins (above) that came to light on the seabed dates to the end of the Byzantine era (seventh century A.D.) and into the Islamic period (eighth century A.D.).

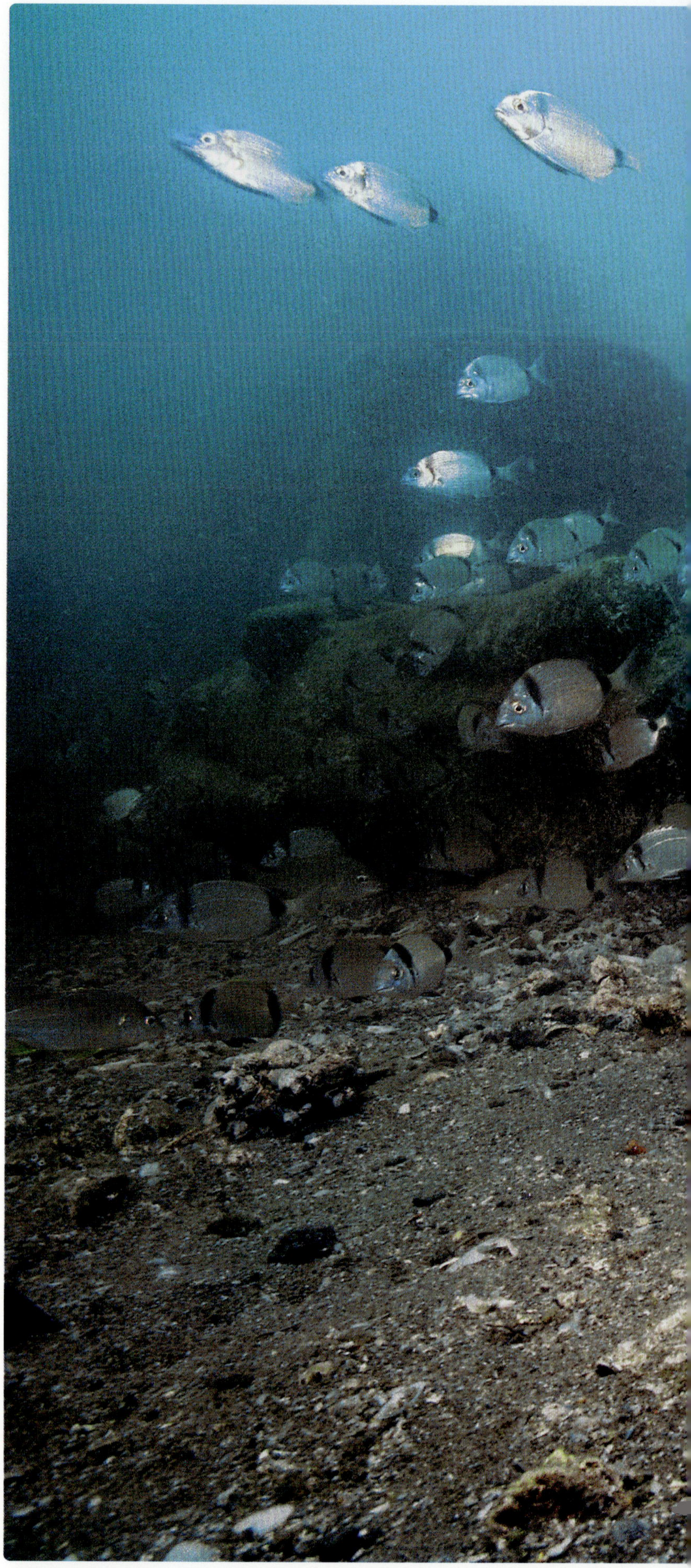

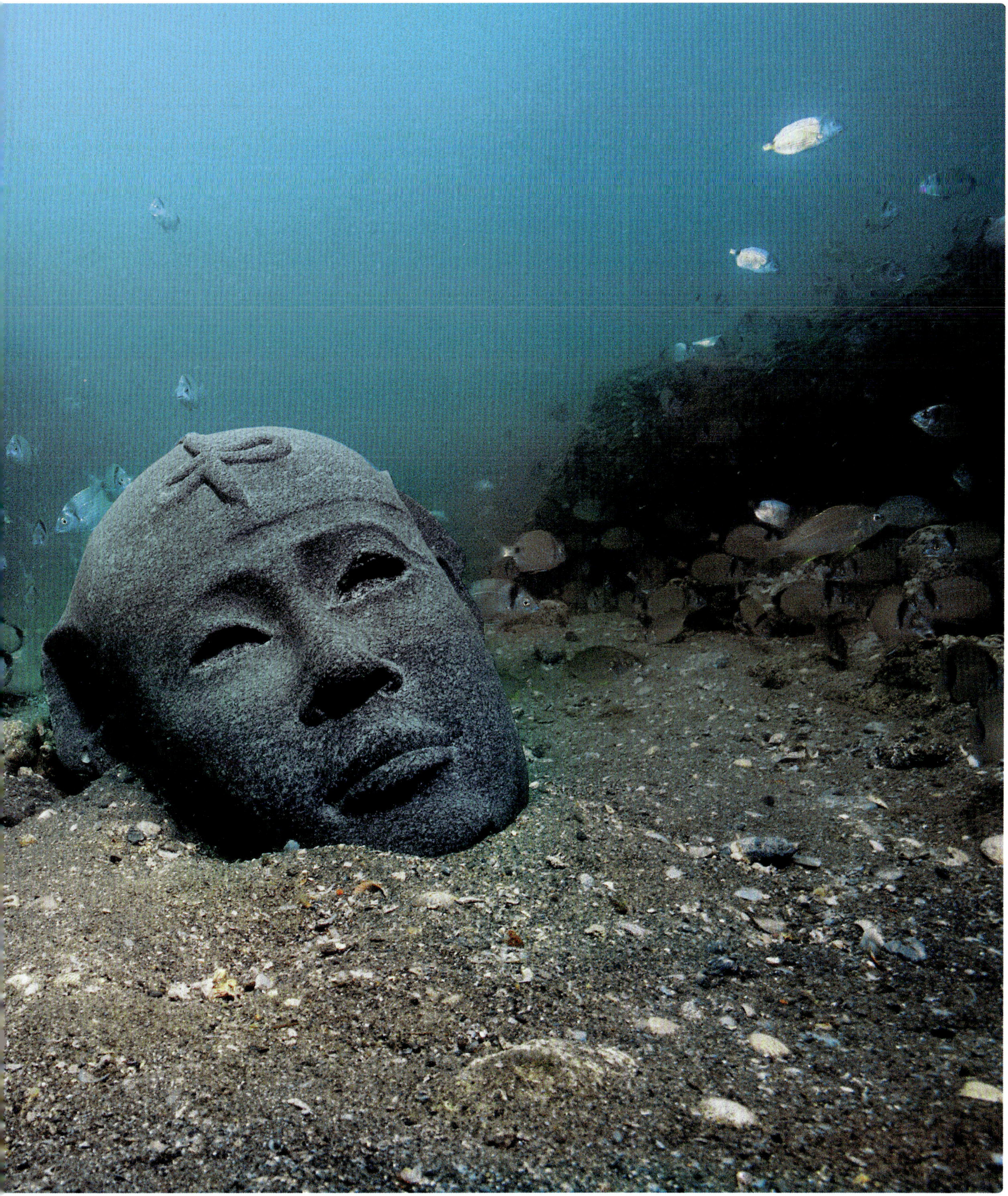

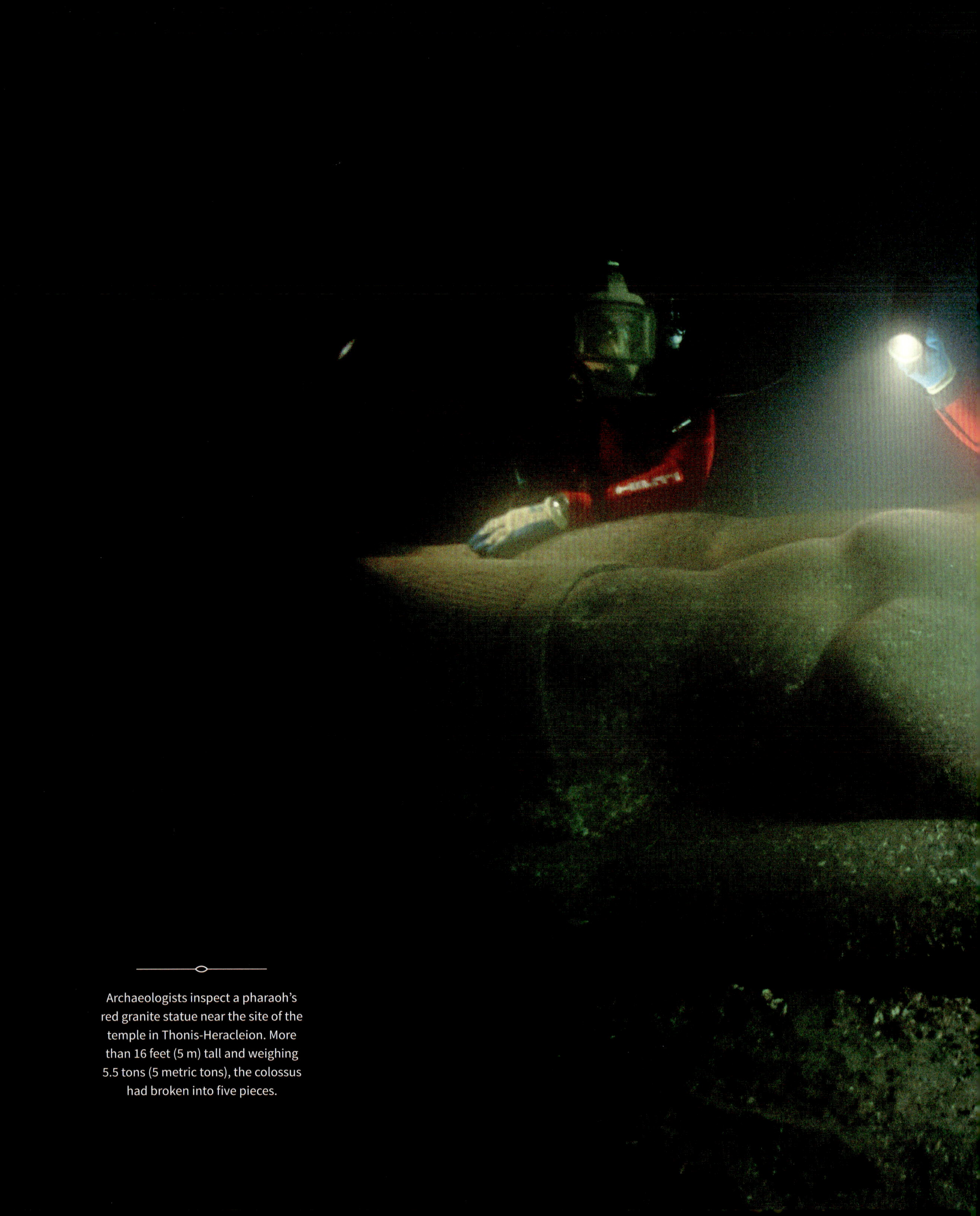

Archaeologists inspect a pharaoh's red granite statue near the site of the temple in Thonis-Heracleion. More than 16 feet (5 m) tall and weighing 5.5 tons (5 metric tons), the colossus had broken into five pieces.

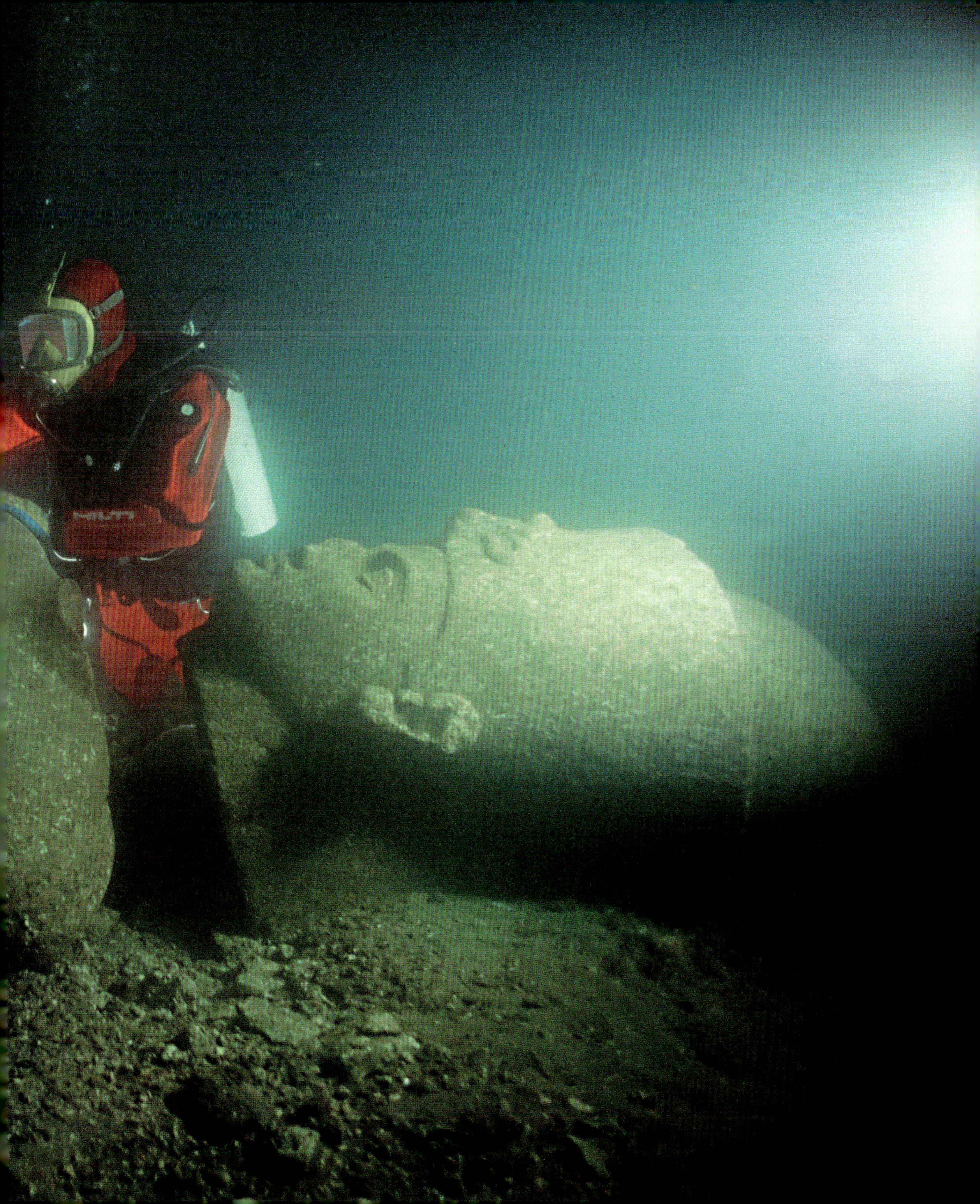

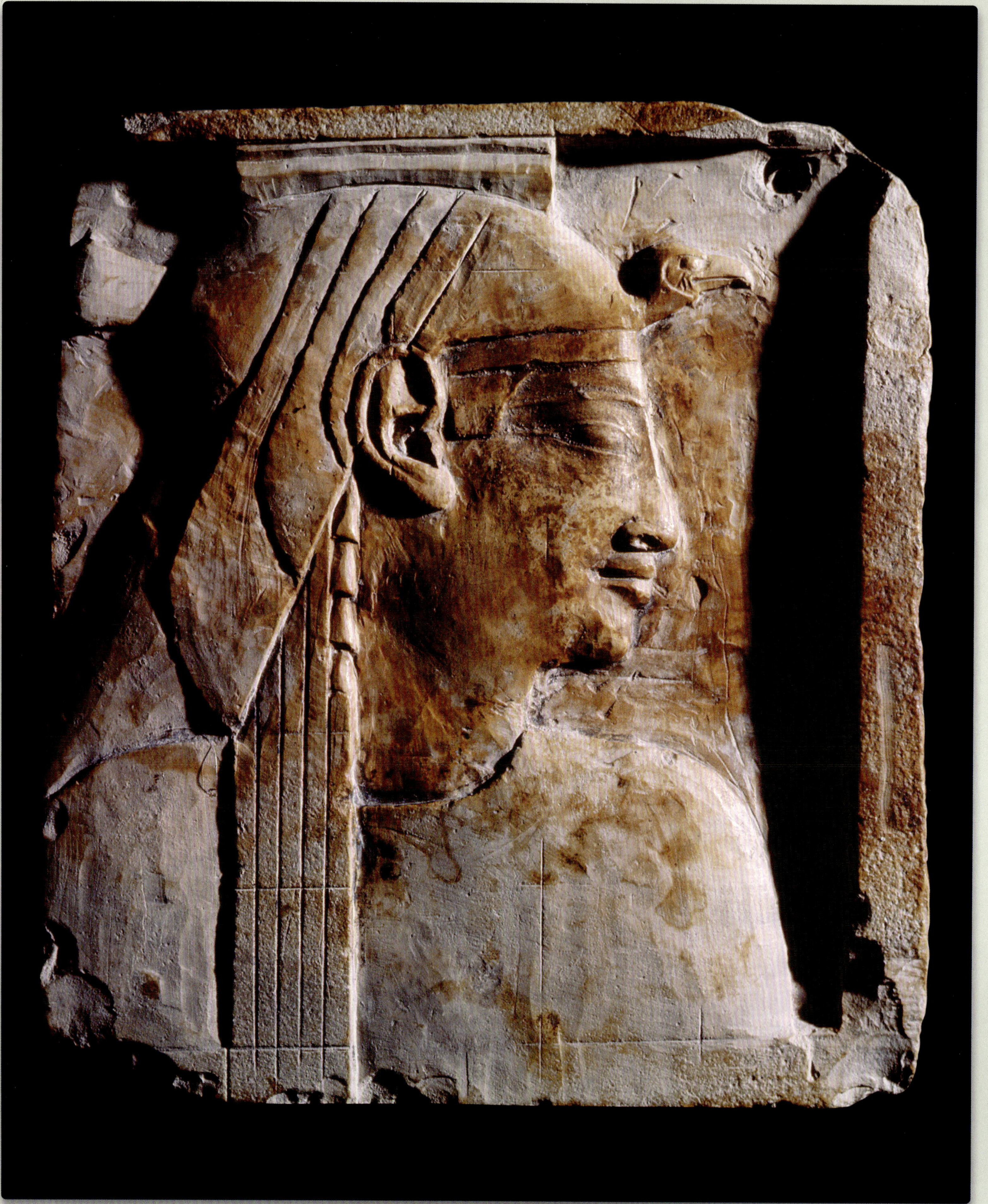

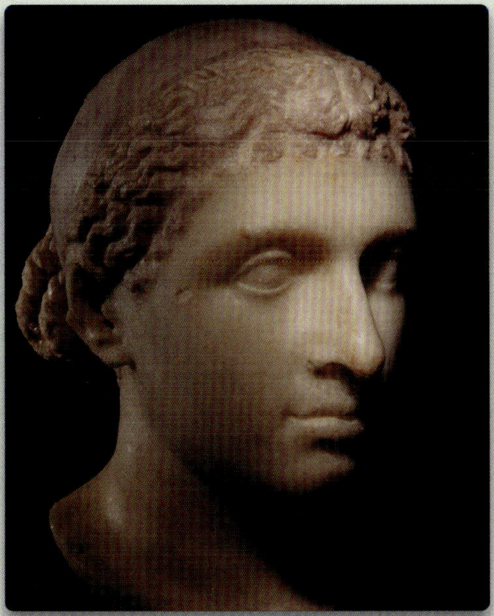

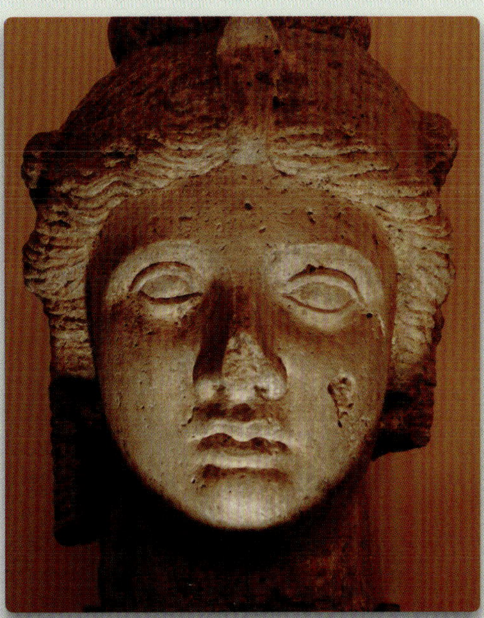

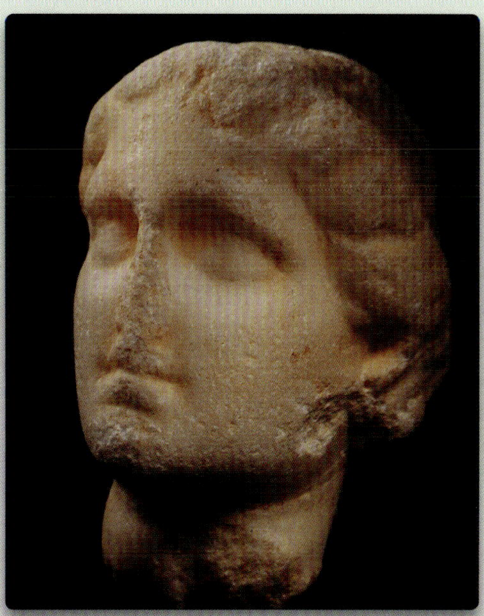

A Tragic End

LIKE A ROCK STAR, Cleopatra is known the world over by a single name that evokes a life of both personal and public turmoil. A descendant of Ptolemy I, one of Alexander the Great's generals, she was Cleopatra VII—Q-li-u-pa-d-r-a in hieroglyphics. She inherited the throne upon the death of her father, Ptolemy XII, who held power only with Roman support. Her 10-year-old brother, Ptolemy XIII, became her co-regent and husband. After Ptolemy XIII drowned in a battle against the Romans, Cleopatra married another brother, Ptolemy XIV. She also became Roman consul Julius Caesar's mistress and bore him a son.

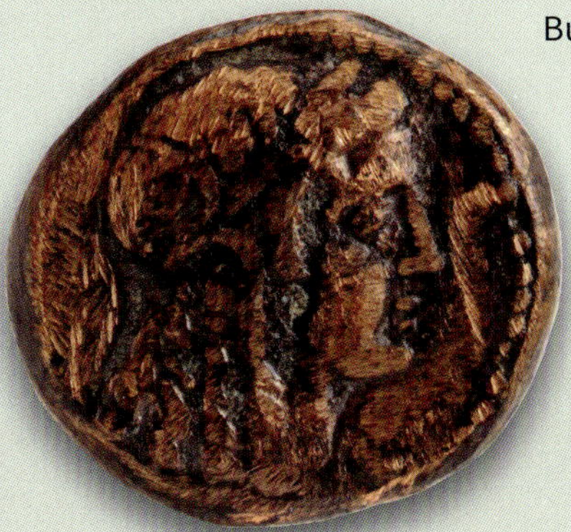

Caesar was likely attracted to Cleopatra's intelligence and wit, rather than her looks. Artists have depicted her in different ways, as seen in the examples on these pages, but her profile on a coin (below) may be closest to the truth.

Whatever Cleopatra's allure, Roman general Mark Antony was smitten with the glamorous queen after Caesar's assassination. But as a rival faction in Rome pressed in to claim Egypt as its prize, Cleo and her man famously committed suicide, bringing the curtain down on Egypt's millennia-long history of royal dynasties in 30 B.C.

INDEX

Bold page numbers indicate illustrations.

ILLUSTRATIONS CREDITS

KENNETH GARRETT/NATIONAL GEOGRAPHIC IMAGE COLLECTION: Cover, endpapers, 10-11, 14-15, 16, 22 (LO CT), 23 (LO LE), 31, 39, 41, 44, 45, 50 (UP), 54-5, 56, 61, 66, 68-73, 78, 81, 101, 104, 112-3, 114, 117, 119 (LE), 124-5, 126, 127 (LE), 128, 130-1, 135, 136 (RT), 137, 142, 146, 146-7, 153, 156, 160, 167, 171, 176-7, 182, 185, 186-7, 187 (LO), 192-3, 195, 197, 199, 204-5, 207, 214, 215, 222, 224-5, 230-1, 238-241, 243-9, 254, 260-1, 269, 270, 274-7, 282-3, 286, 290-1, 294-6, 327, 328-9, 342-3, 350-1, 355, 368, 377, 381, 384-5 (ALL), 393 (UP CT, UP RT, and LO), 400

NATIONAL GEOGRAPHIC IMAGE COLLECTION: 2, Nathan Benn; 6-7, Paolo Verzone; 12-13, Taylor Kennedy; 27, Paolo Verzone; 84-5, Farrell Grehan; 94-5, Victor Boswell; 108-9, O. Louis Mazzatenta; 111, John G. Ross; 118 (RT), Deddeda/Design Pics; 120, Publishers Photo Service; 121, NG Archives; 129, Victor Boswell; 139, Jules Gervais-Courtellemont; 140-1, Alex Saberi; 144-5, O. Louis Mazzatenta; 148, Richard Barnes; 150-1 (ALL), Richard Barnes; 152-3, Richard Barnes; 154, Richard Barnes; 155, Richard Barnes; 162-3, Underwood & Underwood; 164-5, Taylor Kennedy; 168-9, Richard Barnes; 178-9, George Steinmetz; 183, Richard Barnes; 194, Sean White/Design Pics; 196-7, Martin Gray; 198, O. Louis Mazzatenta; 208, 1922/3 photo courtesy New York Times Company; 210, A.W. Cutler; 220-1, Alex Saberi; 242 (UP), 1922/3 photo courtesy New York Times Company; 250-1, Cary Wolinsky; 255, Michael Melford; 266, Victor Boswell; 292, Rena Effendi; 293, Rena Effendi, Excavation by Amarna Project; 298-9, Rena Effendi; 302-3, Emory Kristof; 322-5, Georg Gerster; 346-7, Robbie Shone; 363, O. Louis Mazzatenta

KENNETH GARRETT: 4-5, 38, 46-7, 105 (by permission of British Museum), 134, 136 (LE), 149, 159, 169, 184, 187 (UP), 191, 218, 223, 252, 288-9, 304, 318-9, 379

NICOLAS REYNARD: 8-9

SCIENCE SOURCE: 18, MMA/Gilman Collection; 42, Petrie Museum of Egyptian Archaeology, UCL/SPL; 92-3, Brian Brake

RICHARD T. NOWITZ: 21

ALAMY STOCK PHOTO: 22 (UP LE), Mike P Shepherd; 23 (UP LE), Peter Horree; 23 (UP RT), Eddie Gerald; 23 (LO CT), Dallet-Alba; 40-1, Ivan Sebborn; 60, Mike P Shepherd; 77, Angus McComiskey; 98-9, Juergen Ritterbach; 100-1, Werner Forman Archive/Egyptian Museum, Cairo/Heritage Images; 118 (LE), Dordo Brnobic; 119 (CT), Jose Lucas; 119 (RT), Peter Langer/Design Pics; 123, mauritius images/Frank Nesslage; 237, David Cole/Press Portrait Service; 272-3, Cola Images; 278, The History Collection; 280, Werner Forman Archive/Egyptian Museum, Cairo/Heritage Images; 303, Mike P Shepherd; 349, Marcin Jamkowski/Adventure Pictures; 356, Hackenberg-Photo-Cologne; 383, Bertrand Rieger/hemis.fr

METROPOLITAN MUSEUM OF ART: 22 (UP RT), (13.182.3), Rogers Fund, 1913; 22 (LO LE), (12.182.14), Rogers Fund, 1912; 22 (LO RT), (20.3.8), Rogers Fund and Edward S. Harkness Gift, 1920; 57 (UP), (26.7.982a-c), Purchase, Edward S. Harkness Gift, 1926; 57 (LO), (01.4.1a), Gift of Egypt Exploration Fund, 1901; 62-3, (00.4.7a, b), Gift of Egypt Exploration Fund, 1900; 64 (UP), (03.4.13), Gift of Egypt Exploration Fund, 1903; 64 (LO), (03.4.1), Gift of Egypt Exploration Fund, 1903; 86, (30.8.239), Davis Collection, Bequest of Theodore M. Davis, 1915; 89, (06.1231.1), Gift of Egypt Exploration Fund, 1906; 102 (UP), (17.9.1), Gift of Edward S. Harkness, 1917; 102 (LO), (13.182.53), Rogers Fund, 1913; 102-3 (LO), (22.3.73), Rogers Fund and Edward S. Harkness Gift, 1922; 110 (UP), (20.3.6), Rogers Fund and Edward S. Harkness Gift, 1920; 110 (LO), (20.3.5), Rogers Fund and Edward S. Harkness Gift, 1920; 127 (RT), (1976.63.2), The Adelaide Milton de Groot Fund, in memory of the de Groot and Hawley families, 1976; 172-3, (16.1.8), Purchase, Rogers Fund and Henry Walters Gift, 1916; 173 (UP), (16.1.24), Purchase, Rogers Fund and Henry Walters Gift, 1916; 173 (LO), (09.180.1182), Rogers Fund, 1909; 174, (26.7.1452), Purchase, Edward S. Harkness Gift, 1926; 175 (UP LE), (27.3.167), Rogers Fund, 1927; 175 (UP RT), (27.3.208), Rogers Fund, 1927; 175 (LO), (27.3.164), Rogers Fund, 1927; 188, (25.10.20.357), Rogers Fund, 1925; 189 (UP), (25.10.20.354), Rogers Fund, 1925; 189 (LO), (25.10.17), Rogers Fund, 1910; 190-1, (10.177.2), Rogers Fund, 1910; 200, (00.4.33), Gift of Egypt Exploration Fund, 1900; 201 (RT), (23.6.54), Gift of Lily S. Place, 1923; 227 (RT), (30.8.56), Davis Collection, Bequest of Theodore M. Davis, 1915; 229, (86.1.1a, b), Funds from various donors, 1886; 232, (26.8.97), Fletcher Fund, 1919, 1920; 232-3, (26.8.121a), Fletcher Fund, 1919-1922, Rogers Fund, 1922; 233, (26.8.99), Purchase, George F. Baker and Mr. and Mrs. V. Everit Macy Gifts, 1920; 234 (UP), (11.215.240), Rogers Fund, 1911; 234 (LO LE), (11.215.300), Rogers Fund, 1911; 234 (LO CT), (11.215.306), Rogers Fund, 1911; 234 (LO RT), (11.215.346), Rogers Fund, 1911; 235 (UP), (11.215.246), Rogers Fund, 1911; 235 (CT LE), (11.215.362), Rogers Fund, 1911; 235 (CT), (11.215.263), Rogers Fund, 1911; 235 (CT RT), (11.215.222), Rogers Fund, 1911; 235 (LO), (11.215.253), Rogers Fund, 1911; 252-3, (30.8.67), Davis Collection, Bequest of Theodore M. Davis, 1915; 256, (31.3.35a, b), Rogers Fund, 1931; 257 (UP), (26.7.1335), Purchase, Edward S. Harkness Gift, 1926; 257 (LO), (26.7.1287a-k), Purchase, Edward S. Harkness Gift, 1926; 258-9, (40.3.2), Rogers Fund and Edward S. Harkness Gift, 1940; 259 (UP), (35.3.63b), Rogers Fund, 1935; 259 (LO), (35.3.79), Rogers Fund, 1935; 262, (20.3.8), Rogers Fund and Edward S. Harkness Gift, 1920; 264, (20.3.13), Rogers Fund and Edward S. Harkness Gift, 1920; 281 (UP), (21.9.8), Gift of Edward S. Harkness, 1921; 300 (UP), (1985.328.22), Gift of Norbert Schimmel, 1985; 300 (LO), (1985.328.9), Gift of Norbert Schimmel, 1985; 301 (UP), (1985.328.16), Gift of Norbert Schimmel, 1985; 326 (BOTH), (43.2.1), Rogers Fund, 1943; 363 (LO), (30.8.369), Davis Collection, Bequest of Theodore M. Davis, 1915; 376, (34.6.1), Gift of Florence Blumenthal, 1934

ART RESOURCE, NY: 23 (UP CT), © The Trustees of the British Museum; 28, © The Trustees of the British Museum; 64-5, Bucranium. From Egypt. Second Intermediate Period, Dynasty 14–17, ca. 1640–1550 B.C. Horn, bone, paint, overall h. 41.5 cm (16 5/16 in); w. of antlers 75 cm (29 1/2 in). © The Metropolitan Museum of Art, Rogers Fund, 1916, (16.2.23); 67, © The Trustees of the British Museum; 74-5, © The Trustees of the British Museum; 86-7, National Archaeological Museum, Palestrina, Italy/Nimatallah; 170, Erich Lessing; 177, © The Trustees of the British Museum; 227 (LE), Egyptian Museum, Cairo/Scala; 263, © The Trustees of the British Museum; 264-5, © The Trustees of the British Museum; 308 (BOTH), © Musée du Louvre, Dist. RMN-Grand Palais/Christian Décamps; 316 (LO), Musée du Louvre, Paris/Erich Lessing; 330, Musée du Louvre, Paris/Erich Lessing; 331, RMN – Louvre; 361, bpk Bildagentur/Ägyptisches Museum und Papyrussammlung/Staatliche Museen zu Berlin/Juergen Liepe; 378-9, © The Trustees of the British Museum; 392, Private Collection/Werner Forman; 393 (UP LE), bpk Bildagentur/Antikensammlung/Staatliche Museen, Berlin/Christoph Gerigk

GETTY IMAGES: 23 (LO RT), Fine Art Images/Heritage Images; 43, Hulton-Deutsch Collection/Corbis; 48, DEA/G. Dagli Orti; 50 (LO), Cris Bouroncle/AFP; 50-1, Universal History Archive/UIG; 90-1, MyLoupe/UIG; 92, DEA/G. Dagli Orti; 118 (CT), Cris Bouroncle/AFP; 132, adoc-photos/Corbis; 133, adoc-photos/Corbis; 143 (LO), DEA/A. Dagli Orti; 166, Joël Ducange/Gamma-Rapho; 216-7, Laurent Sauvel; 219, Nick Brundle Photography; 279, DEA/Chomon-Perino/De Agostini; 284-5, DEA/A. Dagli Orti; 296-7, Werner Forman/UIG; 299, Werner Forman/UIG; 301 (LO), Heritage Arts/Heritage Images; 359, johnandersonphoto; 369, Werner Forman/UIG

BROOKLYN MUSEUM: 32, *Ibis Mummy*, 30 B.C.-100 A.D. Animal remains, resin, linen, Ibis mummy with headdress: 30 5/16 x 5 1/2 x 8 1/4 in. (77 x 14 x 21 cm). Gift of the Egypt Exploration Fund, 14.655a-b. Photo by Gavin Ashworth; 374, *Sculptor's Model Head of a Lion Roaring*, ca. 525-404 B.C. Limestone, 5 9/16 x 3 3/8 x 5 1/16 in. (14.1 x 8.5 x 12.8 cm). Charles Edwin Wilbour Fund, 34.1190

LIBRARY OF CONGRESS: 34, LC-DIG-matpc-01519; 36-7, LC-DIG-ppmsca-04550; 80-1, LC-DIG-ppmsca-03657; 82-3, LC-DIG-stereo-1s01881; 122-3, LC-DIG-ppmsca-03953; 210-1, LC-DIG-ppmsca-04521; 212-3, LC-DIG-ppmsca-04544; 310-1, LC-DIG-stereo-1s21754; 312-3, LC-DIG-ppmsca-04475; 358-9, LC-DIG-ppmsca-0446

ROBERTHARDING: 35, Michael Snell; 226, Richard Ashworth; 307, Andrew McConnell

BRIDGEMAN IMAGES: 49, British Museum, London; 58-9 (ALL), Egyptian National Museum, Cairo/© Sandro Vannini; 88, © Ashmolean Museum, University of Oxford; 97, Temple of Hathor, Denderah, Egypt/Luisa Ricciarini; 106-7 (BOTH), Private Collection/© Christie's Images; 138 and 138-9, Egyptian National Museum, Cairo/© Sandro Vannini; 143 (UP), Egyptian National Museum, Cairo; 201 (LE), © Museum of Fine Arts, Houston, Texas/Gift of The Merrin Gallery, Inc; 202, Private Collection/© Heini Schneebeli; 203, © Museum of Fine Arts, Houston, Texas/funds provided by the Brown Foundation and Isabel B. Wilson; 228, Egyptian National Museum, Cairo/© Sandro Vannini; 281 (LO), British Museum, London/© Zev Radovan; 282, © Ashmolean Museum, University of Oxford; 287, Egyptian National Museum, Cairo/© Sandro Vannini; 316 (UP), Luxor Museum of Ancient Art, Egypt/© NPL - DeA Picture Library/S. Vannini; 317, © Israel Museum, Jerusalem/Gift of Wilma and Laurence Tisch, New York, to American Friends of the Israel Museum; 332-3, © A. Dagli Orti/© NPL - DeA Picture Library; 360, Egyptian National Museum, Cairo/© Sandro Vannini; 363 (UP), Egyptian National Museum, Cairo/© Sandro Vannini; 366-7 (ALL), Egyptian National Museum, Cairo/© Sandro Vannini; 370 (UP), Egyptian National Museum, Cairo; 370 (LO), Egyptian National Museum, Cairo/Werner Forman Archive; 370-1, Egyptian National Museum, Cairo/© Sandro Vannini; 372-3, Egyptian National Museum, Cairo/© Sandro Vannini; 373 (BOTH), Egyptian Museum, Cairo/Werner Forman Archive; 375, Egyptian Museum, Cairo/Werner Forman Archive; 382, Louvre, Paris/© Photo Josse

PENN MUSEUM: 52, Image #151106, Object #E9217; 53, Image #250888, Object #69-29-1

AGE FOTOSTOCK: 88-9, DEA/G. Dagli Orti; 364-5, De Agostini/W. Buss

CHRISTOPH GERIGK © FRANCK GODDIO/HILTI FOUNDATION: 96, 352, 380, 386-391

EXCAVATIONS AT AMHEIDA, NEW YORK UNIVERSITY: 180, 181

HARRY BURTON © GRIFFITH INSTITUTE, UNIVERSITY OF OXFORD: 236, 242 (LO)

REDUX PICTURES: 273, Serge Sibert/REA

STAATLICHE MUSEEN ZU BERLIN, ÄGYPTISCHES MUSEUM UND PAPYRUSSAMMLUNG: 288, Sandra Steiß; and for kind permission to include the Nat Geo photo on 266 and the Kenneth Garrett photo on 288-9

GEORGE STEINMETZ: 311

AKG-IMAGES: 314-5, Rainer Hackenberg

© ENRICO MARTINO: 320-1

SHUTTERSTOCK: 332, Werner Forman Archive

MUSEUM OF FINE ARTS, BOSTON. Harvard University-Boston Museum of Fine Arts Expedition. Photographs © 2022: 334, *String of gold and carnelian beads*. Nubian, Early Napatan period, 860-840 B.C. Findspot: el-Kurru, Nubia, Sudan. Gold, carnelian. Length: 98.5 cm (38 3/4 in.) 21.309; 334-5, *Cartouche beads from horse trappings*. Nubian, Napatan period, reign of Shebitka, 712-698 B.C. Object place: Nubia, Sudan. Faience. Legacy dimension: Length: of string 0.556 m. 21.10565; 335, *Pendant with ram-headed sphinx on a column*. Nubian, Napatan period, reign of Piankhy (Piye), 743-712 B.C. Findspot: el-Kurru, Nubia, Sudan. Gilded silver, lapis lazuli, and glass. Height x width: 10.3 x 3 cm (4 1/16 x 1 3/16 in.) 24.972; 336, *Hathor-headed crystal pendant*. Nubian, Napatan period, reign of Piankhy (Piye), 743-712 B.C. Findspot: el-Kurru, Sudan (Nubia). Gold, rock crystal. Overall: 5.3 x 3.3 cm (2 1/16 x 1 1/4 in.) 21.321; 337 (UP), *Collar*. Nubian, Napatan period, reign of Shebitka, 712-698 B.C. Findspot: el-Kurru, Nubia, Sudan. Electrum. Diameter and length: 17 cm (6 11/16 in.) 21.307; 337 (LO), *Plume holder for a horse's bridle*. Nubian, Napatan period, reign of Piankhy, 743-712 B.C. Findspot: el-Kurru, Nubia (Sudan). Gilded silver. Height x width: 13.8 x 3.2 cm (5 7/16 x 1 1/4 in.) 23.877; 338-9, *Eye of Horus (wedjat) amulets* (detail). Nubian, Napatan period, reign of Shabaka, 698-690 B.C. Object place: el-Kurru, Nubia, Sudan. Lapis, green stone, jasper. 21.354; 340 (LE), *Amulet of Ra-Horakhty*. Nubian, Napatan period, reign of Piankhy (Piye), 743-712 B.C. Findspot: el-Kurru, Nubia (Sudan). Faience. Height x width: 9.2 x 5.3 cm (3 5/8 x 2 1/16 in.) 24.675; 340 (RT), *Pectoral with the god of eternity, Heh*. Nubian, Napatan period, reign of Piankhy (Piye), 743-712 B.C. Findspot: el-Kurru, Nubia, Sudan. Faience. Height x width: 7 x 5 cm (2 3/4 x 1 15/16 in.) 24.626; 341, *Winged goddess pectoral*. Nubian, Napatan period, reign of Piankhy (Piye), 743–712 B.C. Findspot: El-Kurru, Sudan. Faience. Length x width: 8.5 × 6.2 cm (3 3/8 × 2 7/16 in.) 24.616; 344-5, *Shawabty of King Taharqa*. Nubian, Napatan period, reign of Taharqa, 690-664 B.C. Findspot: Nuri, Nubia (Sudan). Gray serpentinite. Overall: 26.4 x 10.2 cm (10 3/8 x 4 in.) 21.3015; 348, *Shrine*. Nubian, Meroitic period, 100-200. Findspot: Gebel Barkal, Sudan. Stuccoed and painted sandstone. Height x diameter: 62.5 x 59.2 cm (24 5/8 x 23 5/16 in.) 21.3234

Since 1888, the National Geographic Society has funded more than 14,000 research, conservation, education, and storytelling projects around the world. National Geographic Partners distributes a portion of the funds it receives from your purchase to National Geographic Society to support programs including the conservation of animals and their habitats.

Get closer to National Geographic Explorers and photographers, and connect with our global community. Join us today at nationalgeographic.org/joinus

For rights or permissions inquiries, please contact National Geographic Books Subsidiary Rights: bookrights@natgeo.com

Library of Congress Cataloging-in-Publication Data

Names: Hiebert, Fredrik T. (Fredrik Talmage), writer of foreword. Williams, Ann R., editor.
Title: Treasures of Egypt : a legacy in photographs from the pyramids to Cleopatra / foreword by Fredrik Hiebert, Ph.D. ; general editor, Ann R. Williams.
Description: Washington, D.C. : National Geographic, [2022] | Includes index. | Summary: "The images in this breathtaking volume celebrate the vibrant beauty and rich cultural heritage of Egypt on the 100th anniversary of the discovery of King Tut's tomb"-- Provided by publisher.
Identifiers: LCCN 2021061162 | ISBN 9781426222634 (hardcover)
Subjects: LCSH: Egypt--Antiquities--Pictorial works. | Egypt--Pictorial works.
Classification: LCC DT60 .T735 2022 | DDC 932.0022/2--dc23/eng/20220119
LC record available at https://lccn.loc.gov/2021061162

ISBN: 978-1-4262-2263-4

Printed in China

22/RRDH/1

FOLLOWING PAGE: An Egyptian gold bracelet from around the time of Cleopatra takes the shape of two coiled snakes, symbols of protection and regeneration.

ENDPAPERS: Magical spells and ritual texts meant to help the deceased cover a wall inside the pyramid of King Pepi I (about 2275 B.C.) at Saqqara.

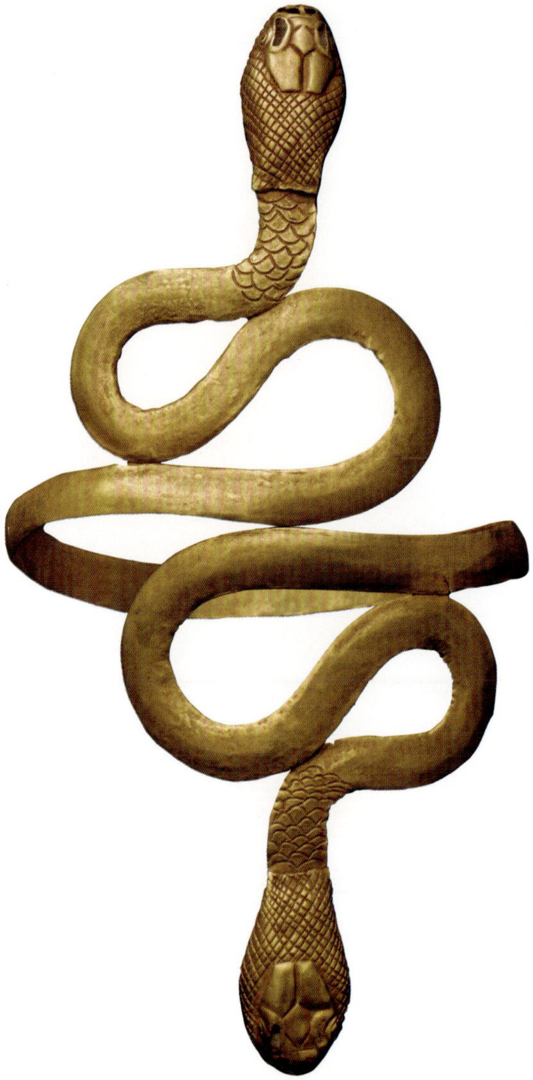

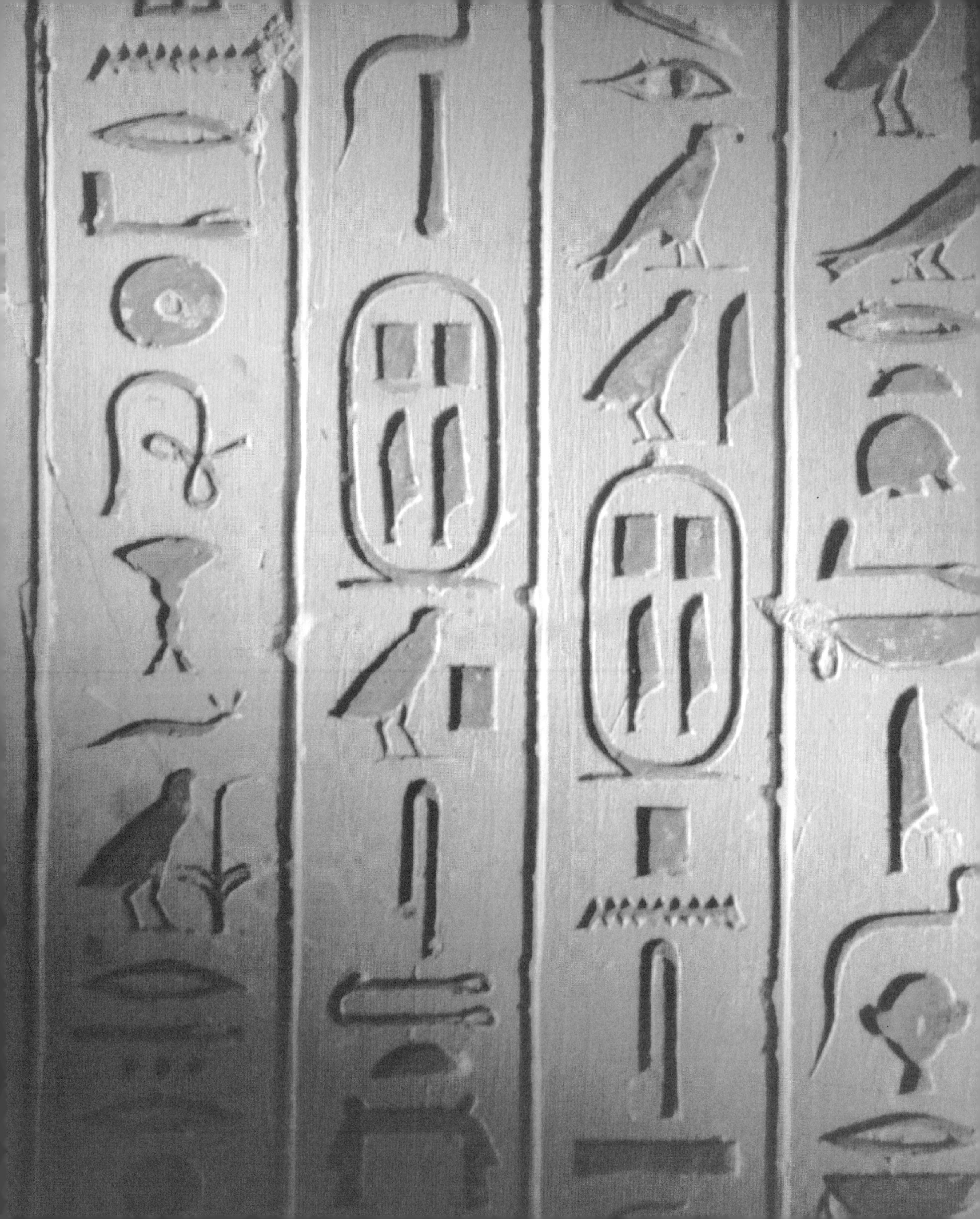